Princeton Theological M

C000225374

Dikran Y. Hadidian

General Editor

28

GLADSTONE
THE MAKING OF A CHRISTIAN POLITICIAN

The Personal Religious Life and Development
of William Ewart Gladstone, 1809-1832

GLADSTONE
W. BRADLEY (1839)

To Nigel McCulloch

W.d. the author's
Best Wishes for the future

GLADSTONE

THE MAKING OF A CHRISTIAN POLITICIAN

The Personal Religious Life And Development Of
William Ewart Gladstone
1809-1832

By

Peter J. Jagger

PICKWICK PUBLICATIONS
Allison Park, Pennsylvania

Copyright © 1991 by Peter J. Jagger

Published by
Pickwick Publications
4137 Timberlane Drive
Allison Park, PA 15101-2932
USA

Printed on Acid Free Paper in the United States of America

Library of Congress Cataloging-in-Publication Data

Jagger, Peter John.
  Gladstone : the making of a Christian politician : the personal
religious life and development of William Ewart Gladstone. 1809-
1832 / by Peter J. Jagger.
      p.   cm. -- (Princeton theological monograph series ; 28)
  Includes bibliographical references and index.
  ISBN 1-55635-012-0
  1. Gladstone, W. E. (William Ewart), 1800-1898--Religion.
2. Prime ministers--Great Britain--Biography. 3. Christianity and
politics. I. Title. II. Series.
DA563.5.J34 1991
941.081'092--dc20
[B]   91-22928
                                                         CIP

To

MARGARET, CATHERINE AND MARK

CONTENTS

FOREWORD

William Ewart Gladstone is widely recognised as one of the most thoughtful and influential of lay Anglicans of the nineteenth century. Anyone with a smattering of Victorian history knows that the future prime minister almost became a clergyman; that he committed to paper in his diary his most intimate daily reflections on his Christian life—with powerful emphasis on his sinful nature; that, taking a catholic view of the Anglican church, he remained a steadfast member of the Church of England when many of similar leanings went over to Rome; and finally that he devoted much time and energy to sincere and scholarly but rather unorthodox theological writings.

Equally well recognised are Gladstone's extraordinary stamina, longevity and distinction on the political stage. A member of the last unreformed parliament in 1832, a cabinet minister under Sir Robert Peel in 1846, Chancellor of the Exchequer under Palmerston during the high tide of Victorian prosperity, and prime minister of four governments between 1868 and 1895, he was indeed a Colossus upon a colossal stage. His statesmanship was characterised by a historic respect for Christendom. It is not too much to say that he created the political concept of international Human Rights as we know it today, ranting in the 1850s against political imprisonments in Italy, in the 1870s against racial discrimination and massacre in Bulgaria and in 1896-97 on behalf of Armenia and Greece; accepting the adverse judgment of the International Court in Geneva on the Alabama case after the Civil War, and finally sacrificing his whole political capital on the altar of Irish peasant rights in the face of English landlords.

Not only do we find the seed of modern Human Rights campaigns in Gladstone: we also find in him a pioneer of twentieth century ecumenism: the son of intensely evangelical Scottish presbyterian parents who had become a high church Anglican, he later did much to fuse the thinking of Anglicans and liberal Roman Catholics. Dr Döllinger, the great German liberal catholic, whose portrait hangs in St Deiniol's Library here at Hawarden, was indeed a kindred spirit.

Gladstone's personal religious development is an interesting study in itself: we see the transition from the narrow evangelical to the broadly catholic churchman in his teenage years, in the face of extraordinary emotional and intellectual pressures. In the context of his forthcoming influence on the political and intellectual life of his country, this transition perhaps deserves the epithet "significant." Be that as it may, what makes this current study by Dr Peter Jagger exceptional is the unique documentation of a young man's pilgrimage. There is no comparable example, whether of a layman or of a clergyman, of written sources of the religious development of any young human being. In this respect, the Gladstone family is unusual if not unique. Collections of family letters have been preserved—and here under Dr Jagger's spotlight we share the pressures of a close-knit, ambitious, self-made, emotional, critical, argumentative family, immigrants from an economically struggling and still predominantly agricultural Scotland to Liverpool, the second-richest city in Britain and thereby the second-richest city in the world.

Peter Jagger allows the original and hitherto unpublished sources to unfold the childhood of this exceptionally gifted boy under the influence of an almost maniacally religious invalid older sister and an overbearing money-mad but sanctimonious father—his mother was an invalid. William is sent to Eton, the leading establishment secondary school, in 1821, and there he experiences liberation from this appalling family regime. Eton is earthy, protestant and utterly unreformed, but there the child finds, amongst the aristocratic philistines of their day, not only a remarkable group of friends—gentle, sensitive and intelligent—but also intellectual stimulation from a study of the Classics in the widest sense. The most celebrated and intimate of his friends at Eton was Arthur Hallam, later to go to Cambridge where Alfred Tennyson took over Gladstone's role; but the majority went on, with Gladstone, to Oxford.

Gladstone's liberation, spiritual and intellectual, began at Eton. There, too, he was a founding member of the debating society ("Pop") at which learned topics were fodder for the budding orators of anglican pulpits and of the House of Commons. Eton remained his lifelong love. Oxford, where he became a member of the most aristocratic college,

Christ Church, never held quite the same central place in his affections. But it was at Christ Church that the child became a man. It was during his Oxford years that he was weaned from the narrow vision of his early christian upbringing to a sophisticated understanding of the Church. It was also at Oxford that—under the intense if self-imposed pressure of academic examinations—he had to decide whether to seek ordination.

This question, which has been the subject of investigation from Morley to Foot, Shannon and Perry Butler, is dealt with exhaustively in the present work; and one can say with some confidence, since he has relied upon and quoted extensively from original sources, that Dr Jagger has had the last word upon it.

This book takes us to the point where, after apparently unending soul-searching hesitations, the young man finally decides to become not a clergyman but a politician. Any reader who finds the work interesting will hope that there is more to come. We see in the final chapters how Gladstone, without specifically identifying the pregnancy of the Oxford Movement, came independently to much the same position as its founders. Gladstone's personal development, interesting though it is from several points of view, is revealed as being also a part of something much wider and more important. Long and detailed though the present work may be, it whets our appetite for the sequel.

Hawarden Castle,   William Gladstone
1990.

INTRODUCTION

For Willlam Ewart Gladstone the Christian faith was the foundation of every word and daily action in both private and public life. His politics were always subordinate to his Christian convictions and thus it is impossible to understand his political career without understanding his position as a churchman.

His family felt that John Morley, Gladstone's official biographer, was not a suitable person to write about his inner and personal religious life, and this restriction was placed upon him, although Morley contrived to bring out the centrality of his subject's faith, and to do so movingly. They hoped that the gap would be filled by D. C. Lathbury's *Correspondence on Church and Religion of William Ewart Gladstone*, but his sons regarded this as a failure. The late Professor S. G. Checklands's seminal work, *The Gladstones*, was the first major study in this area and has placed this writer and others in his debt. With the progressive publication of *The Gladstone Diaries*, and their excellent introduction by the editors, M. R. D. Foot and H. C. G. Mattthew, the way has been eased for a fuller study of this aspect of his life. Previous works have been mainly concerned with Gladstone the politician; this present study is the first exploration in depth of Gladstone's spirituality. Even so, it has its necessary limitations. Because of his profundity and complexity Gladstone is not always easy to understand. There is also the fact that in a study of spiritual growth the written record is only part of the story and the hidden depths are not always, and sometimes never, recorded and in view of this one can occasionally do no more than speculate.

This volume examines Gladstone's religious background and pilgrimage, tracing the Christian heritage passed on by his grandparents to their children and the influence of his own parents, brothers and sisters upon his personal religious development. Gladstone's spiritual formation at Eton is investigated, followed by a full analysis of his religious life at Oxford, with a critical examination of his "evolution" to the position of a "Catholic-Evangelical." His inner search to know God's will for his life, whether as a priest in the Church of England or as a politician, is crucial for an accurate understanding of Gladstone. The book ends with his election as the Member of Parliament for Newark. With that appointment he set out on what he came to believe was a career as a Christian politician called by God to serve both Church and State.

Many factors which influenced Gladstone's spiritual development have been examined by the author who, as Warden and Chief Librarian of the Gladstone Memorial Library, has been in a privileged position with free access for over twelve years to the manuscript collection and Gladstone's personal library. All the Gladstone manuscripts in the St. Deiniol's Glynne-Gladstone Collection and at the British Library, up to 1833, numbering many thousands, have been examined. Additional family papers, until recently housed at the Gladstone estate at Fasque, have thrown new light on the subject. Fragmentary and often meaningless diary entries have been drawn together, offering further insight into his religious life, growth and ideas. What Gladstone read had a profound effect upon his development as a churchman and a Christian politician unique in Victorian and world history. Because of this his diaries and the correspondence and other material in the British Library and at St. Deiniol's Library have been cross-referenced against his books and pamphlets, to note their contents and his annotations, scorings and other marginalia. The nature of the subject and the available material make it clear that a study of this aspect of his life requires the discipline of both history and theology. While a number of previously held views have been clarified or corrected, this work lays bare the formation of the Christian faith and call of a tremendous personality.

Peter J. Jagger

ACKNOWLEDGEMENTS

This book is the result of many years of research and writing during the course of which numerous people have been involved in discussions on its contents. Others have had to live almost daily with Mr Gladstone including colleagues, students and above all my family. Many people have been consulted, a number of whom have offered valuable suggestions. Publication of this book provides an opportunity to acknowledge my debts and to offer thanks, for without these various contributions this work might never have been completed; it certainly would not have been published in its present and much improved form. Despite all the help received, the author alone must bear responsibility for any errors or omissions in what has been published.

My wife Margaret and my two children, Catherine and Mark, were captive listeners as new discoveries were made and the themes and controversies worked out. Unfortunately they sometimes suffered neglect as Mr Gladstone demanded every spare moment. They must be thanked for their tolerance and support. Present and former colleagues were supportive and encouraging and for this I am grateful, especially to my former colleagues, the Revd Dr John Turner and not least to Jean Turner who read the entire manuscript detecting and correcting many mistakes, and to David Anscombe and Geoffrey Lewis. Gordon Connell, my Assistant Librarian is to be thanked for his help with the Name Index. Rene Mycock, my colleague and friend is to be thanked for typing up the two Indexes. Special thanks are due to the Revd Michael Burgess who read the whole manuscript, and some parts more than once, discussing crucial points and throughout offering wise and valuable observations. Former students often had to listen and, albeit unknown to themselves, made their contributions during the evolution of the manuscript. Yet again my friend Lucy Donkin, who gave so freely of her time to type the manuscript and whose keen eye detected many small mistakes missed by others, has placed me deeply in her debt. Sincere thanks are offered to Dikran Y. Hadidian, General Editor and Jean W. Hadidian for all their help in seeing the manuscript through the press to publication.

Some of the ideas, statements and conclusions in this work are controversial, some contradict or reject the views of other Mr Gladstone students. Among those with whom I sometimes differ are friends and acquaintances. During my years of research I have met many of them and corresponded with others. Their scholarship, insights and opinions on Mr Gladstone which have been shared with me have prompted a reconsideration, and sometimes a revision, of previous ideas. In some instances I am indebted for what they have written about Gladstone. While not always agreeing with them, I wish to acknowledge my debt to Dr Perry Butler, Professor Owen Chadwick, Professor Travis Crosby, Professor G. Donaldson, Mr M.R.D. Foot, Dr Agatha Ramm, and Professor Richard Shannon. In a different way I am indebted to Mr E.G.W. Bill, the Lambeth Palace Librarian, and to two Keepers of Manuscripts at the British Library, Dr D.P. Waley and Dr C.J. Wright and to their staff for their assistance over many years.

Sincere thanks are due to Sir William Gladstone, who from the outset, and through our regular contact, has always been helpful and encouraging, placing me further in his debt through his excellent Foreword. Christopher Williams, Deputy County Archivist at the Clwyd Record Office, an authority on Gladstone in his own right, has kindly helped and assisted me in connection with the many thousands of manuscripts consulted over the past twelve years. Geoffrey Vesey the County Archivist has also offered help and encouragement throughout.

Dr Leslie Barnard, the Revd Canon Michael Hennell, Professor Vincent McClelland and Dr David Steele, four notable scholars, were of considerable help at the final stage reading the penultimate draft of the manuscript and offering a host of valuable observations from their own academic areas and thereby making a significant contribution and improvement to the accuracy and quality of the final draft. To these I express my gratitude and acknowledge my debt. To David Steele I am further indebted for his advice, help and encouragement throughout the whole period of my research on this book.

Thanks are offered to the following for granting their permission to reproduce material used in this book:

Sir William Gladstone for extensive quotations from the Glynne-Gladstone manuscripts housed at St Deiniol's Library, Hawarden and the property of Sir William Gladstone. Also for his permission to reproduce, as a Frontispiece, William Bradley's portrait of *The young Gladstone*. The picture of *W. E. Gladstone reading the Lesson in Church* is reproduced by the kind permission of the Board of Trustees of the National Museums and Galleries on Merseyside. The British Library Board, for unlimited use of the Gladstone Papers, Additional Manuscripts 44086-44835. The Lambeth Palace Library for use of the Gladstone Papers.

A final tribute must be paid to three outstanding scholars, who recently died, all of whom had an indirect but significant influence upon this book, and also upon some of my previous publications. The encouragement over many years from Archbishop Michael Ramsey, Bishop John Moorman and the Very Revd Ronald Jasper to give time to research and writing will never be forgotten and will be a lasting stimulus to do just this.

ABBREVIATIONS

1. *Names*

A.M.G	Anne Mackenzie Gladstone – sister
H.J.G.	Helen Jane Gladstone - sister
J.G.	John Gladstone – father
J.N.G.	John Neilson Gladstone - brother
Mrs. G.	Mrs. Anne Gladstone - mother
R.G.	Robertson Gladstone - brother
T.G.	Thomas Gladstone - brother
Thos. G.	Thomas Gladstones of Leith - grandfather
W.E.G.	William Ewart Gladstone

2. *General*

Add. MS — British Library, The Gladstone Papers - Additional Manuscripts 44086-44835

Autobiographica. W.E. Gladstone I: Autobiographica, eds. John Brooke and Mary Sorensen

Autobiographical Memoranda. W.E.Gladstone II: Autobiographical Memoranda 1832-1845, eds. John Brooke and Mary So rensen

BL — British Library

Diary — *The Gladstone Diaries*: 1825-1880, Vols 1-9 OUP

G-G — The Glynne-Gladstone Collection of Manuscripts housed at St. Deiniol's Li brary, Hawarden

CHAPTER ONE

A CHRISTIAN HERITAGE

On 29 April 1800, in St Peter's Church, Liverpool, John Glad-stones, the son of a Leith corn-dealer, married Anne Mackenzie Robert-son, the daughter of Andrew Robertson, a lawyer and provost of Ding-wall. John was conscious of his social inadequacy in his early relationship with the Robertson family,[1] his father having risen from humble origins and he himself having become a leading shipowner and Liverpool businessman through his own powerful drive and business acumen.

John's outlook was more worldly and Calvinistic than his wife's, of whom nothing except that her parents were Episcopalians of Jacobite ancestry, is known about her religious upbringing.[2] However, many letters to John Gladstone, formerly "Gladstones," from his father Thomas, have survived, which tell us about John and the religious envi-ronment in which he was nurtured. Thomas, born in 1732, was ten years old when the "Cambuslang Wark," an evangelical revival, took place in his locality. He was brought up in strict religious surroundings where belief in an all-seeing and knowing God touched every part of life, and sin, accountability, judgment and punishment loomed large. In addition to prayer, bible reading, Sunday worship and sabbath obser-vance, Thomas nurtured his spirituality through the reading of the print-ed sermons of Scottish divines, while a chapter of scripture was read to his family each evening.

On 31 March 1787, the year that the 23 year old John moved to Liverpool, he received a long letter from his father setting out the life to be lived by a godly merchant.[3] Aware of John's obsession with mak-ing money, Thomas seeks to impress on him that "this is not our place of abode and that the fashion of this world soon passeth away." He ends his letter of wise godly counsel, "I devoutly commend you to the protection of the Almighty, that He may direct you in all your difficulties, support you effectually under all your trials, and keep you always in the paths of religion and virtue;" earlier in the letter John is advised to read the bible and books on divinity, morality and history, but not novels or romances which his father thought "pernicious." Gambling is to be avoided, the sabbath strictly observed, prayer and worship practised. The moral duties of his business life must include the strictest honesty, avoiding covetousness; he is to be chaste, temperate, sober, active, diligent and persevering. Divine Providence will guide his business activities, his choice of friends and even the choosing of a wife.

Through other letters he commended caution and prudence in business,[4] a reliance upon God in all things,[5] a recognition of providence in the events of life,[6] the keeping of a short account of his daily conduct,[7] and a careful watching over his every word and action.[8] "Providence has been kind indeed"[9] and "I hope you will bear your prosperity with becoming moderation and that your endeavours will still be blessed so as to set you in comfortable circumstances;"[10] "such providential care should not be overlooked."[11] Thomas found his son's increasing success somewhat daunting[12] and was apprehensive about an enterprising and adventurous trip to America:[13] "I have my fears," he wrote, "about this business of yours, it is of such extreme magnitude."[14] John's responsibility was indeed such as must have made him glad of the assured support of his family's prayers,[15] for the wheat he had gone to purchase was in short supply and the ships to transport it back to England were already on their way to America. Aware of the confidence placed in him by his syndicate he decided to purchase a wide range of merchandise to fill all the ships, so diverting what could have been a complete financial disaster into a total loss of only £1,500.[16]

John did not always welcome his father's advice, however, and he resented it when a misunderstanding between himself and his senior partner prompted Thomas to advise "prudence and discretion."[17] Later, when his father was in his seventies, John took exception to something he had written[18] and the old man replied, "I rejoice at seeing my children prosper in this world, but not at making it their chief concern; it grieves me to find you still retain a grudge . . . Our duty is plain, to forgive errors, as we hope for forgiveness."[19] His final letter to his son declared, "the world gives no substantial happiness further than we make it a state of preparation for another and better . . . keep your affairs in such bounds as makes them subservient to what is more important."[20]

Thomas Gladstones of Leith died in 1809. By the standards of his day he was a reasonably wealthy man, leaving an estate estimated at £18,000. But this paled into insignificance when compared with the wealth of his eldest son who by 1812 had amassed a fortune of £145,000. When John joined his relatives to pay his last respects perhaps he called to mind his father's counsel, "I entreat you will not let the affairs of this life so occupy your attention as to shut out a serious concern for the more important interests of life ... For we know neither the day nor the hour we may stand before the awful tribunal."[21]

To the end of his life John Gladstone remained domineering and assertive, in business, politics, family life, and in his church and charitable activities. Ever mindful of the certainty of death, he did not share his father's intense feeling of accountability and the awesome fear concerning the future judgment before an omniscient God. John's Christianity was more earthly based than his father's. Even so the environment of a Christian home at Leith, during those formative years, with family prayer, sabbath worship and observance, bible and devotional reading and the strict outworking of a moral code, not to mention the Calvinistic ideas of the nature of God and his relations with his accountable creatures, all these and the over-riding conviction of divine Providence played their part in John's early life. Through twenty years of correspondence, Thomas offered him the spiritual counsel which he believed God required of every Christian father. Unfortunately, this correspondence is one-sided, only Thomas' letters having survived.

The underlying theme in these letters of spiritual guidance is that of providence in matters both spiritual and material. John Gladstone's business success was recognised by his father as a mark of God's blessing, but John was never quite so emphatic about providence. For him success was due to good business acumen and the blessing of God. The correspondence shows how the dour Presbyterian Thomas could freely mix godly counsel with business advice: he could both offer and receive correction and rebuke without animosity, something which John could never do. Religious convictions, innate business acumen, a desire to succeed and a grim determination, all helped John to face the pressures of life. The early separation from home and the country of his birth, business difficulties and successes, the uncertainty of safety while travelling abroad, the sadness caused by the death of his first wife, all these things were taken into his marriage with Anne Mackenzie Robertson. However much he had rejected, compromised or re-adjusted the faith of his father, that faith was his Christian heritage and was to be fused with the evangelical faith of Anne and thus provided a powerful Christian heritage for their own children.

CHAPTER TWO

THE FORMATIVE YEARS

On 29 December 1809 William Ewart Gladstone was born as the fourth and last son of John and Anne, and he was baptised in St Peter's Parish Church in Liverpool.

i. *A Pious Evangelical Mother*

Despite constant ill-health, Mrs Anne Gladstone was to set the religious tone of the family. Her evangelical fervour and piety must have profoundly influenced all her children, not least her youngest son. William wrote in his autobiographica in 1894, "My environment was strictly Evangelical. My dear and noble mother was a woman of warm piety but broken health and I was not directly instructed by her."[1]

Strictly speaking he may not have been "formally instructed" by her, but this does not mean that she did not exercise a profound influence upon his religious development, both directly and indirectly. On 8 July 1892 he wrote in his "Beginnings or Incunabula"[2] that he had not received any Christian heritage from his grandparents, including Thomas Gladstones: "My father's father seems from his letters to have been an excellent son and a wise parent: his wife a woman of energy." Had he read all the letters referred to above with their constant reference to providence and living out the Christian life? In these autobiographical fragments of his early religious development William attributes nothing to his father apart from a little political influence.[3] Life in the family home at Seaforth House undoubtedly influenced and fashioned William's Christian belief, conduct, practice and piety. If he was not oblivious to such environmental influences, did he simply overlook them, or fail to acknowledge how much had come to him from that environment? Alternatively, did the idolizing of his sister Anne, who played a major part in his early Christian development, blind him to the religious influence of others?

Evangelicalism embraced certain theological convictions, a number of essential Christian practices and a particular "temper" or way of life. In what follows we shall examine the main aspects of the religious beliefs and practices and way of life of William's parents and siblings, all of which must have had some impact upon him. Surviving manuscript material relating to Mrs Anne Gladstone is in two categories: correspondence with a number of different people including notable evangelical figures such as Hannah More; these letters provide insights into the "public side" of her evangelical faith, and some offer brief glimpses into the more private side. The second category of material is devotional in character, largely composed of a collection of her private prayers and meditations. These tell us much about her "theology," especially her belief in the nature and purpose of God, his relationship with his children and the fallen nature of man. Her understanding of Christian spirituality, as well as the nature of the Christian life, and what God expects of those who are called by his name, are all woven into prayer, meditations, a devotional journal and religious verse. Together they give much new insight into Mrs Gladstone and her probable influence upon William.

As an Evangelical Mrs Gladstone believed that suffering and ill-health, as trials of life, were instruments used by God to offer strength and consolation and through which he spoke to his children. In Hannah More Mrs Gladstone found a kindred spirit who practiced and encouraged a fervent evangelical piety with its emphasis upon the struggle and pilgrimage of the individual seeking to fulfill the will of God and to be free from the temptations and sins of this naughty world. Following a visit from Mrs Gladstone Hannah More wrote to her "Let me congratulate you that . . . you find in religion support and consolation under the trials of life, . . . we shall one day find that our sickness and sorrow were among our mercies, provided they are turned to the purposes for which they were sent."[4] A few weeks later she wrote "Let us not . . . covet too heavily our want of health, if it is graciously made the means of drawing us nearer to *Him* in whose hands are the issues of life and death."[5] Concern for one's own soul must not blind the sinner to the duty to help and educate others. Mrs Gladstone encouraged her children's involvement in pious and charitable work, and to be God's instruments in making His will known to others. Hannah More encouraged her in such activities "there is no praise worth having, except that of having been, in one's small measure and degree, made the instrument of a little use or a little comfort."[6]

Acknowledging God as the source of anything that is good in one's life or actions, with an overt sense of unworthiness and humility was something taught by Hannah More and practised by Mrs Gladstone. Mrs More also wrote to her "May it please God to give you the satisfaction of seeing your children educated upon Christian principles."[7] Mrs More had in fact recommended the governess employed by the Gladstones: "I trust that under her forming hand they will become all your heart can wish for I know you will agree with me in the notion that those are not accomplished characters who are not also genuine Christians."[8] Above all things Mrs Gladstone wanted her children to embrace the Christian faith; they were to realise that the eye of God was ever upon them and his hand of providence upholding and guiding them. While her delicate constitution seems to have limited her involvement in their Christian education, nevertheless she could offer them the greatest of all gifts, a share in her evangelical faith and piety and the support of her godly guidance, concern and prayer. But that intense piety, the negative side of her evangelical faith, her constant preoccupation with sickness, death and the preparation for the life to come, may have had an inhibiting effect upon them.

In later life Gladstone was to recall his own meeting with Hannah More: "My mother took me in 181 (sic) to Barley Wood Cottage, near Bristol. Here lived Mrs Hannah More . . . . during that afternoon visit . . . [she] took me aside, and presented to me a little book. It was a copy of her *Sacred Dramas* and it now remains in my possession with my name written in it by her."[9] The year was 1815 when she wrote to Mrs Gladstone, "My affectionate regards to the amiable little fellow I had the pleasure to see here."[10]

Evangelical tracts were both written and distributed by Mrs More in an attempt to propagate the Christian faith. Through Mrs Gladstone she tried to elicit Mr Gladstone's support. Rivingtons had published several of her tracts in a cheap book form, a copy of which was sent to Mr Gladstone and a suggestion to Mrs Gladstone, that after seeing the specimen he might be willing to recommend its circulation among his friends and the booksellers of Liverpool, adding "I know how much he has the good of his country at heart."[11] On 23 August 1817 Mrs More wrote to Mrs Gladstone, telling her of the increased circulation of the scriptures in America and the establishment of Religious Societies. "My friends assure me that my feeble attempts to stem the torrent of sedition were not altogether in vain."[12] Years later when confined to her sickroom, Hannah wrote of her hope of seeing her , "if not I humbly hope we may meet in a world where there will be neither sin, sinner nor separation." Hannah More, who died in 1833, was later described by William Gladstone as a "person of some note."

Various items of correspondence to and from Mrs Gladstone tell us about the evangelical circles in which she moved and of her evangelical faith, in which she brought up her children. Two letters forming part of a correspondence between Mrs Gladstone and her cousin Divie Bethune, living in New York, are examples of the kind of pious correspondence which went on between Evangelicals. Divie wrote, "It gratified me much to learn . . . that your heart appeared so affected with love to the Redeemer's cause . . . May you and I my dear friend, and all that are dear to us, be found at last amongst the Redeemed of the Lord."[13] Her next letter observes "I know full well that God in his providence had bestowed on you many temporal blessings . . . but how often do abounding mercies lead us to take satisfaction in present enjoyments to a degree of excess which shuts out a proper valuation of that spiritual good which is divine and eternal."[14] Here indeed Anne had a friend who realised the fleeting nature of this world's goods. The gifts of the Spirit and ultimate hope of eternal life were what really mattered. These convictions and her confidence in the Redeemer's Cause, and the mercies she had received, encouraged her to keep all these things before her children and her beloved husband. She wrote to John on the occasion of King George III's death, "May you . . . be guided by those motives that are the best accompaniments for either private or public life, and which, however despised by men of the world, were to the dear departed King, through his Saviour, the way to that Thornless Crown he now wears."[15] This comment reflects the kind of tension which the Gladstones and other wealthy Evangelical families had to face up to. They had to reconcile their evangelical faith with their wealth and life-style, their worldly careers and advancement, their aspirations for their children, and their future social advantages. A strict sabbatarian, Anne told John, "I wish you could avoid your Sunday engagements."

From time to time letters to and from Mrs Gladstone made reference to clergymen and the preaching of the Gospel. To Anne she wrote of "the gratification to hear from Mr W Jones such a sermon as gives the clearest evidence of his being a Gospel Preacher . . . and especially as your father is so highly satisfied."[16] Thomas wrote to his father from Eton "Tell my mother that Mr Sumner preached today, and a better sermon, without exception I have never heard. His sermons are particularly impressive, and full of strong and conclusive argument. He attracted the attention of *all*, which is here. I assure you, a very uncommon thing."[17] His mother supported any able preachers of the Gospel of salvation, a correspondent stated, 'The account you sent me . . . (of) your faithful and diligent labourers in their Master's Vineyard are indeed a treasure, . . . may the glad tidings of salvation be proclaimed all around you, . . . there are I believe two or three really pious and excellent Ministers among the Dissenters."[18] On another occasion she received a letter commending to her the Revd I. W. Douglass "his preaching has been followed by revivals of religion, his whole soul is enlisted in his holy calling." Another Evangelical correspondent wrote "I feel confident that the Lord whom you both serve will order everything in mercy." Anne and John Gladstone both sought to serve their Saviour but each in their own way. She was a typical Evangelical of the period, using the language and vocabulary of the party and practising daily prayer, bible reading, sabbath keeping, soul-searching, discerning the hand of God at work in this life and preparing for that to come. These were the essential issues of life with which she was always much preoccupied. John acknowledged their importance, but he had neither the inclination, zeal or time which his dearest wife devoted to them. In some ways Anne continued the role of her father-in-law, constantly reminding John not to become so much immersed in the things of this world that they overshadowed the necessity to consider the things of the world to come.

Manuscripts recently transferred to Hawarden from the Gladstone estate at Fasque, initially wrongly attributed to Miss Anne Mackenzie Gladstone, have now been recognised as belonging to her mother.[19] These provide new information about Mrs Gladstone's spirituality and theological convictions. They also help us to understand more about William and the influences which fashioned his religious growth. This collection of private papers was intended only for God's eye: here she reveals her deep sense of sin and unworthiness, her entire dependence upon the goodness and mercy of God, her understanding of God's grace and strengthening aid, especially when suffering pain. Such self-examination and devotional practices were typical of fervent and excessive nineteenth century evangelical piety. In a book of jottings and prayers begun in 1812 she touches on two themes often in her thoughts and prayers: sin and suffering. She asks God to support her suffering relatives and prays "dispose my sinful heart to this season of visitation." A prayer of 29 April 1813 asks God to enable her and her husband to carry out their sacred duties in the Christian upbringing of their children "grant that he to whom thou hast been pleased to join me be found thy faithful servant—Have mercy upon us as well as the offspring with whom thou hast blessed us, and may the aweful responsibility that rests upon us of leading them in the way that they should go strike deep into our hearts." Strength to fulfil her Christian duties in the upbringing of her children was to be found through prayer. The content of her prayers and heart-searching were unknown to her husband and children, but not so the discipline of her devotional life, including her daily prayer and bible reading. Her dependence upon God is expressed in prayer, "Author of my being, God over all: I adore thy name for encouraging me thus to approach thee in prayer." Many of her prayers contain biblical texts in which she found both guidance and consolation, "Almighty Father, may Thy word come to all who call themselves Christians: and may we in our different degrees act as becometh thy Creatures." Divine grace is sought through prayer to check every sinful propensity and cheer and comfort her in all her suffering: "Raise, Almighty Father, my feeble voice that I may with my best powers offer adoration to thy Sacred name." The words which follow could have been those of William many years later "O let me then, with divine aid apply, with increased diligence, to the fountain of living waters. In mercy, O Holy Father, strengthen my reason and enlighten my understanding, that I may be enabled with spiritual mindedness to seek after the works of 'the Man of God' . . . O, may I, by thy grace, be enabled to bear testimony to the benefits I have derived from the works of the 'Just made perfect'."

Regular bible reading was essential for Evangelicals who believed the scriptures to be the very word of God, offering guidance in life and setting before the believer the truth about God and His will for those seeking salvation and immortality. Mrs Gladstone's devotion to scripture, and her deep penitence for its neglect, was typical of Evangelicals of her time. She can pray "Encouraged by thy precious word I prostrate myself at thy cross O Saviour." Later she writes "Glory to Thy name . . . for encouraging me . . . to resume a regular perusal of thy word." Three years later she is offering the same sentiments that God has encouraged her to return to a regular reading of scriptures "O Almighty Father prepare my heart to seek thee in this sacred search, precious Saviour let me see that they testify of thee." The sabbath day was God's gift, providing His children with the opportunity to fulfil some of the obligations which He had laid upon them. Evangelicals looked upon it as a day which must be devoted to spiritual things, public worship, prayer, self-examination, the reading of scripture and devotional works, listening to sermons preached in the church, and read by the head of the household. Such Evangelicals felt accountable to God for their use of this holy day and Mrs Gladstone was no exception. William, as the diary shows, was obviously influenced by and came to accept his mother's convictions concerning the use of the sabbath. On Monday evening, the 28 November 1814, she wrote "Yesterday the Sabbath of the Lord our God passed unprofitably to me." Even so it was not lost, "In the evening I had the comfort of hearing my dearest husband read one of Cowper's Sermons, whilst our beloved children, with the exception of our youngest, attentively listened." The absent child must have been Helen, born 5 months before, and if so William was introduced to listening to sermons read by his father at a very early age.

        Almost endless references are made to her utter sinfulness and unworthiness before God and in this her prayers and spiritual reflections border on obsession. Was it she who gave William what was to become an extreme sense of his vileness, sin, corruption and unworthiness before God? She can write of sorrow for sin, "indwelling corruption," and of conduct "unworthy of the name of Christian." A written account of Mrs Gladstone's soul-searching reveals that she spent part of the morning of Saturday 26 November 1814 engaged in such self-examination, her prayer and soul-searching being interwoven. "Through the merits of my Redeemer accept my sorrow for sin—and in compassion to my indwelling corruption give me holy Father . . . spiritual aid . . . encouraged by thy precious Word, I prostrate myself at thy cross O Saviour: wash me thoroughly by thy blessed intercession." She beseeches God to bless all her actions and in his wisdom to direct all her intentions. "It is now night and would to God I could give a better

account of the hours that have passed since I last took up my pen—
Father of heaven pardon me . . . look with pity upon me and all under
this roof and prepare our hearts to seek thee in the approaching blessed
day."

Fragmented daily accounts of her spiritual pilgrimage were
not quite the same as the diary entries written by William from 16 July
1825 until the end of his life. Nevertheless, the object of the exercise
was the same—putting pen to paper to produce a written account of the
daily use of God's gift of time during our earthly pilgrimage, an account meant only for God. Mrs Gladstone's account concentrates on
spiritual matters, William was to record, albeit often in brief and "short-
hand" terms, the chief events of each day, recognising his accountability to God for the use or misuse of that day. Although his spiritual ac-
count-keeping was fuller and more systematic than his mother's, it is
quite possible that it was she who suggested it to him in the first place.
In fact most Evangelicals of the period kept such a diary (Wilberforce
being a good example), which was an evangelical alternative to the
"confessional."

On another occasion thanks are offered for a faithful and dear
husband "all that man can possibly be." God is asked to draw him and
their children closer to Himself and to give them an increasing desire to
"study thy word." She implores God "give to my afflicted fellow creatures a part of that abundance which thou hast so mercifully bestowed
upon me and my beloved husband." For herself she prays "Holy Saviour . . . by thy compassionate offering 'once offered' wash me in the
blood of the cross and so strengthen my trust of acceptance with my
heavenly Father." Prayer moves into self-analysis: "I find it difficult if
not impossible to number myself amongst the loved of the Lord and
this because of my sinfulness." Half a century later, when William had
moved away from his inherited evangelical piety, that same sense of utter sinfulness before God remained. In both Mrs Gladstone and William
there was that same theological paradox of being accepted by the Father through the sacrifice of the Saviour and yet, because of an acute
sense of personal sin, an unwillingness to number oneself among the
beloved of God. One may ask whether Gladstone or his mother, at this
stage, really fully understood the evangelical doctrine of assurance that
though the believer remains a sinner he is accepted by God who sees
him "in Christ." Both Evangelical and Catholic piety find expression in
the prayer which emerges out of this self-examination.

Pleading her sin and utter unworthiness she acknowledges how much worse she would be without the help of the great Physician. "Physician of Souls in this hour of comparative ease teach me to consider that but for the wholesome Medicine administered . . . my soul might have been in a still worse state." But the God who is offended, who offers his grace, also reveals man's unworthiness, it is "by grace that I have had this experience of my own unworthiness in mercy look upon my diseased frame—withdraw not the light of thy countenance that I may be enabled to touch thy divine hand in all my sufferings." As she experienced ill-health for most of her life it is understandable that suffering finds such a prominent place in her prayers. She moves from reference to her ill-health to her sin and unworthiness, as though the two were connected. But there is no suggestion that she saw her suffering as a punishment for sin. In one prayer she acknowledges God the Creator as omnipotent and omnipresent and prays "O holy Father, holy Saviour, and holy Spirit, look upon me and if it still be thy will that I should suffer, grant me heavenly armour, that all my desires may be humbly to endeavour after the example of my gracious Redeemer." She offers complete submission to the will of God "strengthen my confidence that through the merits of my blessed Saviour thou wilt afford me the comforting trust that all will work together for my good." While her prayers express an attitude which is both resigned and respectful at the same time there is an openness and informality as she shares with her Creator her feelings and experiences.

For fourteen months she abandoned her practice of expressing her inner feelings and prayers on paper, but on 7 March 1816 she wrote: "I resume a desire of committing to paper part of that experience which is mine . . . Holy Father . . . Thou hast done great and precious things for the salvation of my soul—Lord if it be thy will grant unto me such a teachableness as will enable me to trace thy providential hand as well in the small things as in the great." On Thursday 28 March 1816 she wrote, I "acknowledge thy gracious providence in making a beloved child (thy gift) serviceable to me at breakfast . . . William just six years old . . . asked his father if *he* did not like 'Pilgrim's Progress'—his father replied in the affirmative but added 'do you like it better than the Arabian Nights?'—dear child answered 'Yes father much better.' he then entered into such details as convinced me the Lord brought him there to speak (in my afflicted state a word in season)." Having seen God's providence at work in this simple incident and through her infant son William, she slips into prayer "O compassionate Jesus . . . look in mercy upon me." She rejoices that while she receives drugs and medicine He is her Physician and can make her whole. It is possible that the six year old William caught a glimpse at this early age of her entire and unreserved commitment to God in Christ.

Among Mrs Gladstone's literary remains are a few examples of religious verse; an undated manuscript probably from about 1825/26 gives an example of the type of things she wrote:

> Oh: is there a heart that has known
> The Bliss which the Bible can give,
> The Blood that for sin can atone,
> The Breath by which dead bones may live . . .
> And pray with devotion intense
> That the Kingdom of Sin be destroyed.

She ends with a reference to this world and the folly of pursuing its pleasures.

Through the hard work of John Gladstone and his business acumen she enjoyed all the benefits which came with wealth. At the same time her religious convictions, expressed in her private papers and in the Christian upbringing of her children, overshadowed by her ill-health, reveal how, for her, the things of this world must be set in their proper perspective. Because of their fleeting and transient nature they can never compare with those spiritual treasures which give lasting bliss and happiness; the redeeming work of Christ in the believer, the lasting comfort and treasures given through God's holy word. The experiences and pleasures of this life were nothing to her compared with the promised reward of the life to come. Like many Evangelicals she was often preoccupied with her personal salvation and so blind to the corporate implications of the Christian life, faith and Church, a point mentioned by William in later life. But preoccupation with her own salvation did not blind her to the responsibility of nurturing her children in the way of salvation. An undated letter, among the Glynne-Gladstone manuscripts, from Dr Thomas Chalmers states "It gives me pleasure to be informed of your earnest desire after that which is right—and more particularly of your own high sense of the necessity of religiously training your young family."

Mrs Anne Gladstone died on 23 September 1835. William's

diary entries during her final days and his "Recollections of the last hours of my mother" tell of her Christian Faith and influence upon her children, and of his own feelings about her. The funeral took place a week later—he reflected "We laid a body in the grave: but, from whatever cause, I do not feel separated from the spirit which possessed it: and which I rejoice to think is now very near us," thus expressing his experience of the "Communion of Saints."

During the evening and night of Wednesday 23 September William wrote the "Recollections of the last hours of my mother;"[20] "we wept for her who perhaps at that very moment was employing her young immortality in bringing truths and consolations to our minds from Him who is the source of both. Tender, affectionate, unwearied in love and devotion as she was, she is perhaps nearer to us than ever." Although during the course of her last illness she did not receive the Sacrament, "we cannot feel it a cause for permanent regret while we know that in her daily life she had realised that communion with her Lord, which the ordinance is intended to convey and assure." Sorrow for sin which had dominated her life received the largest coverage in this personal recollection; "Sin was the object of her hatred . . . Sin is the cause of all the sorrow in the world: she can now no more add to the sin nor to the sorrow which is its fruit alone. She departed in seraphic peace . . . She was eminent in the discharge of every duty: she sorrowed for sin: she trusted in the atonement of Christ. But this was not all: these elementary sentiments of religion were matured in her by the power of God, and she was made partaker of the nature and very life of her Redeemer, and her will conformed to his." Letters reached William following her death which spoke of her "simple unaffected piety which overflowed in Christian feelings towards every fellow creature," she was a "mother of prayer," "one of those who with views fixed on another world make themselves eminently useful and beloved in this." It is impossible to believe that she did not have a notable influence on his religious development.

ii. *A Devout But Worldly Father*

Exactly why and when John Gladstone left the Presbyterianism of his father and turned from the Scots Kirk, perhaps by 1804, is uncertain. It is possible that like many successful businessmen with

Free Church backgrounds John Gladstone moved into the Church of England because this was socially acceptable and an indication of his new status in society. The Test Act, which remained in force until 1829, proved a difficult obstacle for any non-Anglican with political aspirations.

John Gladstone was becoming increasingly successful and influential as a business man. Shipping and associated interests, including marine insurance, provided capital to invest in property where large profits were to be made. By 1807 he acquired interests in the *Liverpool Courier*. Along with many successful nineteenth century businessmen his thoughts turned to politics and he was elected to Parliament in 1818. The building of Seaforth House was the outward mark that he had joined "the landed gentry." Increased wealth and political and social prestige demanded a "Seaforth House" to reflect the dignity of its owner and provide a suitable setting for his wife to bring up their family, a house where his influential friends could be entertained. George Canning and William Wilberforce were among their guests and those with whom he corresponded between 1817-30. Wilberforce occasionally mentioned in his letters their friendship and his desire to maintain this.[21]

During his election campaign for Lancaster in 1818 John wrote to his wife of his conviction that God's hand was at work in his new political career, "the blessing of God seems to be permitted to be with us . . . often have I felt overpowered whilst reflecting on what is passing."[22] Imminent success prompted him to write to her,"the universal and almost unanimous support I have received is too gratifying, but it will, I trust, fill our hearts . . . with gratitude to God for making us in such a manner the instruments of his will; may we be enabled by his aid to discharge faithfully the additional duties and responsibilities thus laid upon us."[23] He tells her "the seat may be considered as secured for life and . . . there is not a more reputable or independent one in the House of Commons."[24] John felt justly proud of his victory having received 1728 votes, his two opponents receiving 991 and 990.

Much of John Gladstone's wealth and success came from his extensive investments in West Indian plantations, i.e. slavery.[25] His first plantation, aptly called "Success," involved an investment of £80,000 producing an annual income of well over £10,000.[26] The increasing opposition to slavery, and even the uprising of slaves, which began on Gladstone's estate in 1823,[27] did not deter him from further investments, calculated in 1829 to be in the region of £160,000.[28]

Abolitionists were gaining strength and there was a very active Anti-Slavery Society in Liverpool. As one of the leading investors in West Indian plantations and the owner of many slaves he was attacked by the abolitionists. Mrs Gladstone and Anne found their situation as slave owners, and Mr Gladstone's conflict with the London Missionary Society, both painful and embarrassing.[29] Claiming complete independence from her husband's business enterprises Mrs Gladstone was able to absolve herself but John's outspokenness towards some of the leading Evangelicals must have caused further embarrassment. He described their friend William Wilberforce as "that well-meaning but mistaken man."

No man so deeply involved in slavery could be objective towards the views of the abolitionists. He attempted to justify himself and his position against every opponent. The female side of the Gladstone family were subservient, the three elder sons supported both plantation ownership and slavery, or at least their father's position. With such a strong willed father, their sense of filial obedience and their financial dependence upon slavery, were they, and even William, as objective as they thought themselves? Robertson visited his father's West Indian plantations in 1828, producing an extremely critical report[30] on Frederick Cort, his father's attorney in Demerara who had mismanaged estates belonging to Gladstone and others. While it substantiated what his opponents had said, Mr Gladstone would not retract either his private or public pronouncements. Despite his philanthropic activities to improve the condition of the slaves, and his concern for their spiritual welfare, he claimed that negroes when not enslaved were "idle, insolent, slothful and averse to outdoor work." Robertson eulogised the happy lot of the slaves who ought to be "allowed to live undisturbed." On 7 April 1831 Mr Gladstone wrote a long letter on slavery to Sir Robert Peel. He referred to his earlier communication to him on the subject which had been printed and circulated as a pamphlet, with the title *A Statement of Facts connected with the present state of slavery in the British sugar and coffee colonies . . . contained in a Letter addressed to . . . the Right Hon. Sir Robert Peel. Bart.*[31] Here he outlined what could be expected to follow an early emancipation.[32]

Even if he had agreed with the religious and humanitarian

grounds in support of emancipation, would not the accompanying social and economic effects upon Great Britain be sufficient cause for
compromise, or at least some delay in abolition? John Gladstone, believing himself objective as both a businessman and a politician, provided a host of facts and figures to support his claims.

Mr Gladstone's ambitions were not satisfied with his own success in business and politics. His sons must continue the upward climb
and for this he decided that an Eton and University education were essential, not so much for the education as for the social advantages to be
had by mixing with sons of the nobility. He can have been under no il-
lusions regarding the irreligious atmosphere of Eton. Mrs Gladstone's
letters to Tom show how she was aware of "the very awful state of the
Church at Eton"[33] and the "general indifference to religion"[34] there was
well-known, but both were confident in the Divine Providence to whom
they committed their charges, as they were sent to face that alien environment.

Just as Thomas Gladstones had written to John when he left
home to face the godless and tempting world of London and Liverpool,
so now John wrote to his eldest son. Thus on 21 April 1821 he wrote
concerning the decision to send him to Eton and reflecting on how he
had been denied such a privilege; he observed "a greater proportion of
eminent and distinguished men have been sent forth into the world
from Eton than any other [school] . . . we therefore did not hesitate in
selecting for you this School, tho' the most expensive. It is our anxious
wish to give you a right direction to your mind."[35] John's letter, unlike
his father's, expresses more of a temporal and worldly concern, than the
eternal and spiritual counsel which he had received many years before;
"your Mother's earnest wish and mine [is] to promote . . . your temporal
and eternal interests . . . If you have the laudable ambition of being distinguished through life amongst your fellows, of possessing the power
of being eminently useful to yourself and others, now is the time for
the foundation being laid." Two opportunities will be open to him when
his education is complete: "Public Life as a Profession, or the business
of a merchant. The first is the road to honour and usefulness . . . great
respectability is to be gained. . . the great object of mercantile men is
to accumulate or acquire property." A gentleman is expected to speak
modern languages, to have some knowledge of science and the fine arts
"with a well-cultivated mind and a deep sense of the duties he owes to
his Creator and his fellow creatures." When surrounded by the cares

and anxiety of life, his religious duties will bring him comfort, "his devotion to truth will hold him up, when all other resources prove of no avail . . . God has placed much in our own hands, and therefore on our individual responsibility."[36]

God's providential activity is linked to worldly achievement and effort, "Providence has given you powers of mind . . . but . . . the Almighty has wisely determined that it is only by great exertion and the application of talent and acquirements with a sound judgment (that) prominence can be attained."[37] Amusement and relaxation, while necessary and desirable, must be carefully controlled and made subordinate to higher objects, his time at Eton must not be wasted. "When you have leisure for general reading, I would recommend history." He is to take advantage of all that is placed before him "such as will qualify you to fill any situation in which it may be the will of the Almighty to place you . . . Always remember that no good, no distinction, or attainment worth possessing in this world, is to (be) gained without labour and exertion." No letter survives giving similar advice to William, but it is to be expected that he would have written in the same vein if occasion arose.

Religious direction to Tom is summed up in these words: "Let me not omit to place before you the primary and still more important subject of our religious obligations, for unless your sense of duty to our fellow creatures is founded on a growing out of and up with, a love to God, and a right sense of all his goodness and our own unworthiness, our exertions must ultimately be vain and found fruitless."[38] Much of what Thomas Gladstones believed to be essential went unmentioned— prayer, bible reading, sabbath observance, control of the tongue, and temperance in eating and drinking. What is included and what is omitted, reveal a different understanding of God and the Christian life. But some of the omissions may have been remedied for Thomas by his devout and somewhat unworldly mother. From all this it can be seen that John Gladstone's approach to life was largely pragmatic with religious overtones. But in many Evangelicals of his time there was this dichotomy between worldly ambition and spiritual humility. Talents, the gifts of God, must be used.

The worldly and the spiritual sides to John Gladstone's nature and work were noted in a testimonial acknowledging his public service to Liverpool.[39] The newspaper reporting the event stated that "John

Gladstone, Esq., M.P., had rendered important service to Liverpool by his zeal and ability in promoting and increasing its trade, and by his support of all establishments having for their object the advancement of its prosperity and refinement." His formation of commercial associations was praised "in the different public institutions, whether formed for the purpose of relieving distress, promoting happiness, diffusing knowledge, improving morals, or refining taste, his name is found amongst their most liberal and zealous patrons and friends." This is the testimonial's nearest approach to what one of Mrs. Gladstone's correspondents refers to as "the Mr. Gladstone . . . who has so much influence in Church Interests." Perhaps this complementary understanding of worldly life and the Christian faith, found in Anne and John Gladstone, was required to fashion a son as deeply religious and politically able as William Ewart Gladstone, who would undoubtedly have preferred the letters of counsel written by his grandfather to the more worldly-wise letters of his father.[40]

iii. *The Evangelical Environment*

"My environment was strictly Evangelical."[41] Such was William Gladstone's later assessment. Lathbury wrote in his book *Mr. Gladstone*, "As regards religion, however, he was very much left to himself. Home teaching of any direct kind there was very little. His father was too busy, his mother too ill, to give it."[42] Mrs. Gladstone wrote that she "believed William to have been truly converted to God."[43] But William wrote "Of. . . any true conversion of the heart to God I do not dare and indeed I am not competent to speak."[44] The necessity of a conversion experience was a tenet of the evangelical faith. Other essentials are, the belief that the bible is authoritative in matters of faith and conduct and as such is to be read individually in the home as well as in church, the doctrine of justification by faith, good works and a way of life which is recognised as holy and a proof of true faith, a personal relationship with God through Christ, which is the result of a conversion experience, the chief task of the church is mission or evangelism which involves the preaching of the Gospel or Cross of Christ.[45] Sabbath keeping, family and private prayers, and sermon reading were also essential; while evangelical terminology and language often found expression in prayers, correspondence and other written material. Of this early evangelical background William wrote towards the end of his life "Childhood and boyhood placed me in very close connection with the evangelicalism of those days, and very notable it was . . . It had large religious philanthropy—e.g. in missions—but little political philanthrophy. The great case of Wilberforce was *almost* purely an individual case, nor was he more against slavery than Dr Johnson. Speaking generally, I am sorry to say, the Evangelicals of that day were not abolitionists."[46] He was both to learn and imbibe much about the evangelical world view and philanthropy from his parents.

In an autobiographical reflection on his childhood he wrote, "Drawing a clear distinction between religious opinions and religious character, . . . I proceed to give some account of the formation of my opinions in the matter of religion. In childhood I accepted those current in the domestic atmosphere without question and without interest."[47]

Gladstone's autobiographical reflections, written in old age, have prompted a number of his biographers to propound the theory that his mother gave him no direct religious instruction. This issue needs careful clarification. Checkland is nearer the truth when he sums up the evangelical home atmosphere in which the Gladstone children were brought up. "Willy's parents, especially his mother, could convey to him a compelling sense of religious responsibility through piety, family prayers, talk, sermon attendance, and a preoccupation with sickness, death and after-life."[48] But even this conclusion needs to be qualified; Checkland's theory supports the view that "religion is caught and not taught." But Willy was also taught, especially by Anne, who was obviously influenced and taught by her mother. We must seriously question any suggestion that his mother did not have any direct influence upon him nor teach him anything about the Christian faith. That the evangelicalism of his childhood "had large religious philanthropy" was certainly true in the case of his own family. Mrs Anne Gladstone may have been frail, but her wide-ranging charitable works and the support and energy expended upon them, suggests that Lathbury's description that she was "too ill to give home religious teaching" needs qualifying. Thomas, writing to his father from Eton, suggests her ill-health was in part due to her active involvement in charitable works, rather than that she was always too ill for teaching and works of piety. Tom wrote "I suppose she has caught cold by being too negligent of herself while she attends to others."[49] A later letter throws a different light on her ill-health "I

was much concerned to hear . . . that my mother has again been un-
well, indeed it appears to me that she never was intended to be *gay*, as
an evening party generally knocks her up."[50] Her ill-health was often
touched upon in letters from the boys at Eton, indeed at some periods in
every letter home. Such a concern was something of a "Victorian phe-
nomenon" and in Mrs Gladstone's case one is led to wonder whether it
was partly psychosomatic.

        Mrs Gladstone's support of various forms of religious instruc-
tion make it difficult to believe that she did not directly involve herself
in the religious teaching of her children. The author of a little book of
religious instruction wrote to her "As I know the lively interest which
you take in what relates to Religious Instruction I beg your acceptance
of a copy of a little book I have been able to publish."[51] Her support of
religious instruction through Sunday Schools went back at least to the
early days of her married life. Alex Simpson wrote to her from Ding-
wall in 1804 about her support of their Sunday Evening School enclosing a receipt for £16.

        Another correspondent in connection with her charitable
works was Miss Margaret Buchan. This correspondence was sustained
over a number of years touching upon a range of religious topics, especially Sunday School work and the religious teaching of both the young
and adults.[52] In 1823 she describes how young persons, and indeed
adults, in North Wales were learning to read Welsh through the Sunday
Schools, but no Welsh tracts could be obtained in the different Welsh
towns. A plan to remedy this deficiency was presented to Mr and Mrs
Gladstone.

        Mrs Gladstone offered financial support to a wide range of
charitable organisations including the London Hibernian Society, the
Society for the support of Gaelic Schools, Ladies Aid to the Moravian
Missions, Aged Pilgrims' Friends Society, Society for the Improvement
of Prison Discipline and the Reformation of Juvenile Offenders, London Female Penitentiary, Society for Bettering the Condition of the
Poor, the Bristol Clerical Society and the Church Missionary Society.

        Of the Liverpool charitable societies supported she was most
actively committed to the Ladies Auxiliary Bible Society, which provided a link between the Gladstones and Zachary Macaulay and other
Evangelical leaders who were members of the Clapham Sect. She was a
founder member and the first Treasurer of this Society which supported

the British and Foreign Bible Society, but its chief objective was the local distribution of the Holy Scriptures. A copy of the Society's inaugu-
ral address, preserved in the Glynne-Gladstone collection, outlines its
strategy and work in the city. The Secretary, Miss Maria Hope, wrote to
her, "I sincerely hope that all your efforts for the spread of our Redeemer's Kingdom may be crowned with . . . success and that, as an unwearied labourer, you may hereafter receive a full reward, . . . We are all as
busy as bees . . . we shall be very glad dear Madam to see our Queen
Bee amongst us again." Mr and Mrs Gladstone believed that through
the bible "the Gospel of Salvation is made known to depraved sinful
humanity" and so they sought to make it available to the poor of Liverpool, that they might hear the "glad tidings of salvation." This "high
view" of scripture and her husband's reverence for the same must have
influenced their son William's understanding of the bible.

Practical charitable organisations in Liverpool also gained Mrs
Gladstone's active support. These included the Dorcas Society,[53] the Indigent Clothing Society, [54] the Liverpool Female School of Industry[55]
and the Liverpool Ladies Repository.

Mrs Gladstone did not, and was not expected to, play any part
in her husband's business affairs, but she did elicit his support in religious philanthropy and in some charitable causes acted as his adviser.
When Dr Thomas Chalmers published his book *On the Christian and
Economics Policy of a Nation, more especially with reference to its
Large Towns,* he presented John Gladstone to the wealthy men of Britain as a "patriotic and enlightened gentleman" and one who provided a
fine example of Christian philanthropy.[56] Mr Gladstone's charitable
work also extended to his homeland; the pastor at Leith, Dr David
Johnson, wrote "I often admire the beauty of Providence in conferring
wealth upon individuals and at the same time giving a heart to use it for
the benefit of their fellow creatures."[57]

An ambitious and forward looking project in Liverpool was
the building of a Charitable Institution in Slater Street. In 1818 Gladstone and two other philanthropists, James Cropper and Samuel Hope,
established this new venture, to house in the one building various charitable committees and activities. The Institution was to be made "as useful as possible in the furtherance of all charitable Institutions calculated
to promote either the religious or moral improvement of their fellow
creatures without regard to any distinction of sect or denomination."

The salaries of the two staff and other costs were to be borne by the Societies having permanent offices in the building. Little wonder Dr Chalmers congratulated John Gladstone that his philanthropy was self-financing. Nevertheless, such a central, ecumenical and all-embracing Institution illustrates the vision of John Gladstone and his two friends, for it was well in advance of the thinking of many in his day.

The Merchant Seamen's Bible Society elicited John Gladstone's active support and resulted in correspondence over a number of years with Zachary Macaulay, who wrote in May 1818 about the progress of this Society.[58] Work in Liverpool continued to expand and Macaulay commended to Gladstone Lieutenant Smith of the Royal Navy as a possible agent for the Liverpool Society.[59] Smith was willing to go to any port to "circulate the *Holy volume* among the seamen that are still destitute of this invaluable treasure." This devotion to his task must have impressed the Gladstones who believed the bible would cause the people "to be awakened to a deep sense of their present sinful state . . . [and] . . . lead to inquire how they could be saved."[60]

John Gladstone kept an "Account Book"[61] where he recorded his charitable giving. Between January and October 1818 he lists ten gifts to public charities amounting to £331 and six private donations amounting to £133, a total of £464. The floating chapel for seamen, the Mechanics' and Apprentices' Library, the Mechanics Institute and the Liverpool Society for Bettering the Condition of the Poor, all owed much to Gladstone who was active both in their creation and their ongoing work.

As the Gladstone wealth increased so their charitable work became more ambitious, wider in scope and more financially beneficial to the recipients, and their name more widely known. Submissive to God and ever mindful of the transient nature of this world Mrs Gladstone saw the increasing charitable activity as the required working out of her Christian faith. John, while supportive and respectful of his wife's piety, and in some ways sharing her views, albeit with less conviction, saw such charitable work largely as an obligation. For Mr Gladstone the affairs of this world in business and politics were the dominating themes of his life. Believing himself accountable to God in these spheres he did not see this accountability in quite the same way as his wife; for him charitable work, i.e. his stewardship, was largely the public expression of what society expected of a successful Christian businessman. Letters reached the Gladstones reminding them that wealth is a gift of God and that Christians must be good stewards of His gifts.[62] The Revd William Patterson informed Mrs Gladstone of his poverty with a wife and eight children to maintain, reminding her that the intention of God in making a person rich is to make him charitable.[63]

Houses and property owned by John Gladstone in 1846 are listed in a manuscript which indicates his increasing wealth in just one area which produced an annual income of £6,900.[64] His fortune grew from £333,600 in 1820 to £745,679 in 1848. In all he invested £40,000 in charitable ventures,[65] including the building of churches and schools. Evangelicals believed that the building and endowing of churches was a duty owed to God, man and society and essential for the furtherance of the Gospel. For Mr Gladstone such activities were not entirely un-motivated. In his non-Anglican days, when there was no Scots Kirk in Liverpool, he formed a syndicate with six others to build a Kirk in Old-ham Street, and later the Caledonian School opposite. When he became an Anglican he and his pious wife were not impressed by the unin-spired preaching they heard and so, occasionally, attended Evangelical chapels. Dissatisfaction with the services and sermons of the Estab-lished Church in Liverpool led him to the conclusion that the only way to resolve the situation was to build his own church and place a preach-er of his own choosing in the pulpit. St Andrew's Episcopal Church in Renshaw Street and St Thomas's at Litherland were both built by Glad-stone and were consecrated in 1815. Events leading up to and connect-ed with these two churches offer an insight into Gladstone's personali-ty, business acumen and his evangelicalism, and that of his day.

An interesting letter of 27 September 1814 from Charles Sime-on to the Revd. P. Charrier of Liverpool was sent to Mrs Gladstone. Simeon wanted to offer the Revd John Blackburn "the most important situation in India", but Mr Charrier was after his services for Liverpool. "I want," wrote Simeon, "genuine piety, good learning, considerable industry, great quality of manners and no little elegance of address and above all a single eye to the glory of God. In him I find it all; and you want to rob me of him."[66] Always on the look-out for situations where the right kind of man could be appointed, and the true gospel preached, Simeon mentioned a chapel in Liverpool: "Had I bought it, it would only be to plant the gospel there, and send such a young man as Mr Blackburn." He suggests that his correspondent might purchase it. Simeon was impressed by the building activities of Gladstone as a pa-

tron of the Evangelical cause in Liverpool. In due course he approached
Simeon to find the right man to occupy his pulpits. Zachary Macaulay,
who was acquainted with Simeon, told Gladstone he could receive
Simeon's recommendation with the utmost confidence.

Nineteenth-century bishops encouraged the building and en-
dowment of churches by wealthy churchmen but such benefactors did
not always have a free hand, as John Gladstone was to realise in his
correspondence with the bishop of Chester. Free pews for the poor
were the main issue raised by the bishop in his letter to Mr Gladstone
on 4 July 1814 and in subsequent correspondence. On a visit to inspect
the new chapel the bishop reminded Gladstone of his rule that he would
not consecrate a chapel where there was insufficient accommodation
for the poor, as in this case. Another point of controversy was the stipend paid by Gladstone. £80 per annum was too low, £100 was the
minimum. The Rector of Liverpool suggested £200 per annum. Gladstone quickly accepted the bishop's recommendation, offering £100. On
29 September 1815 the bishop wrote that he could not accept or even
ordain Gladstone's first nomination, Mr John Blackburn, because of his
unacceptable position on grace. But when Blackburn re-stated his belief
on grace the bishop agreed to ordain him priest and allow him to work
in the diocese.[67]

St Andrew's Church and the attached school, the object of
which was the charitable education of the children of poor but deserv-
ing parents, were built at a cost of £10,600. St Thomas', named after
John Gladstone's father, also had its own school for the sons of gentlemen, including the Gladstone children. Built to further the evangelical
cause it was imperative that the right men were appointed to conduct
the services and preach the Gospel in a way acceptable to Evangelicals
and, in particular, Mr Gladstone, to this end he sought the advice and
recommendations of Charles Simeon.

William later wrote: "My father had built . . . St Thomas' . . .
and he wanted a clergyman for it. Guided in these matters very much
by the deeply religious temper of my mother he went with her to Cambridge to obtain a recommendation of a suitable person from Mr Simeon, whom I saw at the time. I remember his appearance distinctly. He
was a venerable man, and . . . was more ecclesiastically got up than
many a Dean or . . . a bishop of the present less costumed if more ritu-
alistic period. Mr Simeon (I believe) recommended Mr Jones, an excel-

lent specimen of the excellent Evangelical school of those days."[68] In the same account he wrote "the Rev Mr Rawson of Cambridge who had I suppose been passed by Mr Simeon . . . was to be incumbent of the church [i.e. St Thomas'] . . . [he] was a good man, of high No Popery opinions. He never showed violence in the school and he preached twice and performed the services creditably on Sundays; he had also prayers on some or all days in the church during Passion Week. His school afterwards rose into considerable repute, . . . Everything was unobjectionable. I suppose I learnt something there. But I have no recollection of being under any moral or personal influence whatsoever."

John Gladstone visited Bristol in October 1815 to see and hear William Rawson. Three large pages were written to his wife, "His sermon was scriptural . . . his views those of a practical Christian . . . there is much to please you, collected, and rather dignified . . . easy and at home in the pulpit." He felt him suitable for the education of their "boys" and concluded, "I really think we shall be fortunate."[69]

William Wilberforce wrote to John Gladstone describing Rawson as "my worthy friend." A short time later the Revd Dr Thomas Chalmers wrote thanking Mr Gladstone for his recent hospitality and commending him on his commitment to build and provide churches in Liverpool. Chalmers wished to encourage others to do the same and asked for Gladstone's advice on the subject.[70] In the ensuing correspondence he informed Gladstone that his example and advice had helped the great cause of church building in Glasgow.[71] A letter from Hannah More to Mrs Gladstone touched on the same subject, "I extremely honour the zeal of Mr Gladstone . . . in . . . building churches. It is to little purpose that we exclaim against the growth of Methodism while we do not take every precaution to prevent it. Among the best methods of opposition . . . is the building of churches and . . . the placing in them pious and enlightened Ministers. I hope Mr Simeon will be fortunate in procuring such as will meet Mr Gladstone's wishes."[72]

Christian conviction, philanthropic intention and business enterprise were all interwoven in many of John Gladstone's good works. He looked upon the building of these two churches and their adjoining schools as an investment on which he calculated a 5 per cent return per annum.[73] Stipends and pew rents were to cause considerable dispute between Gladstone and his highly recommended and initially highly regarded incumbent, William Rawson. The strictly confidential correspondence on these subjects provides further insight into John Gladstone's personality and Christian convictions.

On 4 September 1821 John Gladstone rendered a personal account for pew rents to William Rawson; two days later Rawson replied.[74] He reminded Mr Gladstone that for six years he had sought to live at peace with all men and wished to continue his ministry in the parish. However, circumstances too often occurred which frustrated his ministerial duties. He objected to the account he had received and then accused Mr Gladstone of being more interested in making money than in people being able to worship God. "Last Sunday," commented Rawson, several strangers were "informed that you insisted upon their taking sittings for a month, or they could not be allowed to come in," and so they went away. "Ought we not to . . . make the admission as easy as possible? I find it no easy matter to convince those who see, or fancy they see you so anxious to make money by their admission, that you have any desire to promote the glory of God in what you have done." Gladstone's reply suggested Rawson consider whether his "language and tenor are consistent with the doctrines of the Religion of which you are a Teacher, or of the example of that Master, whose . . . Servant you are." On the admission of strangers he comments "I endeavour to do what is right to the best of my judgment, and . . . I care not for the opinions of others."[75]

Mr Gladstone insists that Rawson's attitude to his own pew rent and "your conduct" "is the real problem . . . unless a sense of error is felt and expressed by you, and some apology made for the rude and offensive manner in which you thought proper to conduct yourself, future intercourse between us must necessarily cease with this correspondence." A brief letter from Rawson and £4.4/– for the pew rent provoked a six page reply. Rawson is told "an incumbent has at all times the power of retiring, if he *becomes* dissatisfied;" his manner and conduct were thought dictatorial and dogmatic, failing in the common courtesies of life, and he must remember that his stipend is paid out of pew rents. Again Gladstone demands a full apology, threatening the withdrawal of his son Robertson and others from Rawson's school. William Rawson's reply to Gladstone's threatening letter contains nothing to cause offence "I shall leave the whole matter in the hands of Him who cannot err." Gladstone was not appeased. Copies of the correspondence were sent by Mr Gladstone to the Reverends Buddicom, Jones and Bowstead. After discussion with Jones, Rawson wrote to Mr Gladstone, acknowledging that his first letter was calculated to give offence, "I do not hesitate in apologising for it . . . I trust you will not hesitate to meet it in an amicable manner, and that henceforth every unpleasant feeling may terminate on both sides."[76] The apology was accepted and Gladstone agreed that what had passed between them should be forgotten. If the matter had ended there John Gladstone, in spite of his arrogance and threats to his incumbent, would have emerged in a better light. Two days later Bowstead sent his observations to Mr Gladstone stating that some expressions contained in his answers to Rawson's letters "are equally calculated to give offence. Therefore, whatever is requisite on one part on Christian principles is requisite on the other." Gladstone could not accept such criticism, nor offer an apology, "I consider your conduct to me to be such as becomes neither a Christian nor a Gentleman. I therefore take leave of you." Mr Gladstone then received the Revd R.R. Buddicom's reply, commenting that some of Mr Gladstone's statements were as offensive as Rawson's and some expression of regret ought to be offered to Rawson. Gladstone wrote, "I find it impossible to admit to your conclusion."[77]

This well-documented but unpleasant incident helps us to understand much about John Gladstone and his approach to Christian virtues. It also tells us a lot about a father who had a powerful influence on his children and the environment in which they were brought up. Was John Gladstone blind to his faults in this affair, to the tone of his letters to Rawson, his incessant demands for an apology, his threats and his arrogance towards Bowstead and Buddicom and his unwillingness to accept their criticism, and his own dictatorial attitude, and ungentlemanly conduct? This incident presents John Gladstone as an outright autocrat with an unbending and dogmatic attitude towards anything which he found unacceptable; it presents the picture of a man whose Christian faith did not touch the whole of his life.

Evidence suggests that in a number of areas in his Christian life and practice John Gladstone's attitude and actions reflected more of the self-made businessman than the redeemed sinner. There is nothing to suggest that he saw any incompatibility between his Christian profession and some of the things he said and did. His wife Anne may have rationalised such inconsistencies, as she did with their slave ownership; perhaps she had learnt, as did their children, that it was no easy thing to disagree with John Gladstone.

Mr Gladstone was never willing to admit to any fault on his part and whenever reconciliation was required it was on his terms and usually in an attempt to vindicate himself. Later evidence will show that Thomas was akin to his father in certain aspects of his personality. William may have inherited some of his father's traits, but having from an early age recognised his own utter unworthiness before God, who alone can offer forgiveness, William sought to be a mediator of reconciliation, especially in the case of family disagreement. Years later William wrote to his Aunt Johanna, who had resolved never again to enter their house, "for the sake of that God before whose judgment seat we must one day stand, for the sake of that Saviour who endured for us infinitely more than we can ever endure from others, and who as he loved us bade us love *one another*, I entreat you to reconsider the resolution to which you have come."[78] In the light of the correspondence with William Rawson one would not expect such words from John Gladstone, and yet it was he and his fragile wife who had considerable influence upon William's religious development in many hidden ways during his formative years.

CHAPTER THREE

THE SIBLINGS

i. *The Elder Brothers*

Willy's three older brothers Tom, Robertson and John Neilson were all born between July 1804 and January 1807. The family papers housed at St Deiniol's Library and the autobiographical manuscripts at the British Library offer little insight regarding their influence on William's religious development.[1] The only relevant autobiographical reference was to "My brother John, three years older than myself, and of a moral character more manly and on a higher level, had chosen the Navy and went off to the preparatory college at Portsmouth. He was a lad of popular as well as upright character. But he evidently underwent persecution for righteousness' sake at the college ... Of this ... his letters bore the traces: and I cannot but think they must have exercised upon me some kind of influence for good."[2]

While there was a notable influence between Tom and William, nevertheless their relationship was never easy. Letters written to William by Tom, while at Christ Church, indicate how tensions and differences of opinion could emerge between them. Tom expressed his disappointment that William had failed to mention taking a scholarship, prompting William to record on 1 April 1829 "Letter from TG and HJG—much misunderstanding: God grant it may be set to right—wrote a long letter to him." This misunderstanding about the Ireland Scholarship was soon forgotten but not so with religious differences which arose, from time to time, causing a breach in their relationship. On May 22 1829 Thomas wrote to the nineteen year old William, "One word on the subject you allude to, . . . that of communication on religious topics."[3] William's religious sentiments were, felt Thomas, "imbibed evidently much more thoroughly than mine: I hope the difference is in the quantity rather than quality." He suggested "if differences do exist, let them not be "painful"— let them rather offer the hand of conciliation, and emerge in liberality and good feeling." Breaches in family relationships were always painful to William, but he would never compromise on important religious issues in order to keep the peace. Later that year Tom told him he ought to take greater care in expressing his views in his letters, "better taste would have led you to omit certain expressions that cannot be necessary, and that cast a gloom over letters that have so much excellence in them."[4] While an excellent letter writer, William's style could be tortuous and confusing to the recipient, and his letters were sometimes so long as to become wearisome. Many among the thousands preserved illustrate how occasionally William could have been more careful and diplomatic in expressing his strong opinions on certain issues.[5]

A letter from William to his mother and another to Helen in 1831 touched upon miraculous healing, speaking with tongues and God's providential activity. Their contents prompted a stiff rebuke from Tom, "I am desired and feel bound by my own feelings" and no doubt the feelings of his father, "to beg that you will not allow enquiries which are at best but speculative to direct your attention from those pursuits which can hardly be compatible with such subjects . . . I shrink from saying anything that might give you pain."[6] Such candid and brotherly advice was readily accepted as a message, prompting self-examination and personal reproach. William's diary on 29 October 1831 records his reaction, "had a letter from Tom, which gave me a caution concerning abstinence from religious speculations, kindly meant and kindly expressed. God knows it ought to be a reproach to me . . . my thoughts have been much on the means and too little on what is I trust the end: too little on Him who died for us all and in whom we ought to live." Unfortunately, Tom never really understood his brother's fervent religious convictions.

One can only speculate on Tom's reactions if William's letters to their mother and Helen had mentioned the eschatological speculations recorded in his diary on 22 October 1831. "Surely the actual signs of the times are such as should make us ready for the coming of our Lord." Tom's rebuke prompted William to write "a letter to his father giving an explanation."[7] Extreme sorrow is expressed for making his father think that he was neglecting his studies. He was not neglecting his academic work as he had written to Helen on Sunday, which was not a study day. Neither Tom nor his father were to think that his religious convictions and interests were distracting his thoughts, wasting his time or contributing towards possible future academic failure.

Of William's three brothers Tom was the most regular correspondent, often acting as his father's advocate. Letters preserved at St Deiniol's indicate that during the period from Eton in 1822 until the end of 1832 Thomas wrote at least 134 letters to William, but only 65 letters from William to Tom have been preserved over the same period. During that time, of the letters written by Robertson to William, 49 have survived and 47 of William's to him; but only 13 of William's to John which is unfortunate in view of their close relationship and William's affection for him. But William kept 58 of John's letters.

Despite nearly four hundred letters between William and his brothers up to 1832 this correspondence, apart from Tom's letters already quoted, tells us nothing of William's religious development or of any influence his brothers had upon his spiritual growth or his understanding of the Christian faith. They may have avoided religious topics in their letters because of William's earnestness and intensity in religious matters as seen in a letter from the thirteen year old William to John on the death of their grandmother, "but where . . . did that soul go? It went to Heaven, it made itself a path through the trackless air and ascended far above the clouds, to the realms of endless day—O what felicity does she now enjoy: she hath washed white her Garments in the blood of the Lamb, and her mouth utters the praise of her Redeemer. It has always been my prayer to God that she might so depart this life, and God has heard that prayer—Death has not snatched her but life has left her body, praise be to God."[8] While his brothers seem to have played little part in his religious development the situation with his two sisters was just the opposite. In their regular and frank correspondence religious topics were the rule rather than the exception.

ii. *A Sainted Sister: Anne Mackenzie*

The influence of Anne upon William's religious ideas and development has been touched upon by a number of recent writers, especially Checkland, followed by Foot, Matthew, Butler and Shannon. But a systematic examination of all the available evidence is still required.

What follows is an attempt to provide a fuller insight into an intimate
relationship which more than anything else fashioned Gladstone's early
religious growth.

His autobiographical accounts record recollections of her profound influence upon him. Numerous diary entries tell of their relationship and their long and intimate conversations and the value he placed
upon these. Unfortunately there are no detailed records of what was discussed at these memorable meetings. Surviving correspondence is a
major source of information, but has its limitation. Of Anne's letters to
William 144 have survived covering the period 1820-1828, but it must
be remembered that because of her ill-health he often tried to dissuade
her from writing. It is regrettable that of William's letters to Anne only
29 have been preserved over the period 1822-29. The reason for this
discrepancy, which also occurs in the correspondence with his brothers
and Helen, is uncertain but may be entirely due to the fact that William
was a born "hoarder" and preserved more of what he received than they
did. Various correspondence with other members of the family, a note
book containing devotional writings, 1818-26, and a collection of miscellaneous papers, 1820-26, make up the remaining manuscripts belonging to Anne.

The following draws upon all these sources and tells us something about Anne's character and her relationship with William as well
as providing insight into her religious ideas and convictions. However,
because of her considerable influence upon William's "theological ideas" and religious practices and convictions, references to her influence
in the documentation mentioned appears in many sections of this work.

Morley's index makes only two references to Anne, and one of
these is in a footnote. Magnus' one reference suggests that he was unaware of how much William owed to his elder sister in his religious development, and thus to his later understanding of his life as a Christian
politician. Shannon's biographical contribution to Gladstone scholarship indicates the new awareness of Anne Mackenzie's religious influence. But he is prone to psychological analysis: thus, when referring to
Gladstone's later consideration of ordination and Anne's influence, he
writes "Almost certainly this was part of his response to the psychic
shock of Anne's death." But William's inner searching regarding ordination began long before Anne's death and was more complex than has
hitherto been realised. "What could be a more fitting tribute to her
memory," wrote Shannon, "than to dedicate himself to the profession of

Holy Orders?"[9] While her death had a powerful impact upon Gladstone, Professor Shannon's conclusion is questionable in view of Gladstone's intellectual ability and his theological understanding of the nature and purpose of God.

In his autobiographica he wrote "My god-mother was my elder sister Anne, then just seven years old, who died a perfect saint in the beginning of the year 1829."[10] Two years later Gladstone wrote in an unfinished account of his early religious opinions,[11] "During 1828 I had much of the society of my elder sister, deeply beloved by all. Her mental gifts were considerable, her character most devout and fervent; her religious rearing had been in the evangelical tenets but her mind was too pure for prejudice. She must have infused into me some little warmth, and I think she started me on some not very devious bypaths of opinion." Elsewhere he wrote "Intercourse with my saintly elder sister Anne had increased my mental interest in religion" and comments that she was "generally of Evangelical sentiments."[12] Apart from scattered references in William's diary our knowledge of Anne and their relationship emerges from the autobiographica and their correspondence, some of which has only recently come to light.[13] But the "public nature" of these letters must always be remembered. Anne occasionally expressed her desire to exchange letters on "private matters" but this was impossible because of the "public nature of their correspondence", in that the whole family read her letters to him and his to her. Therefore personal and "private matters," especially religious, were often left until they had the opportunity to meet and thus much of her influence and the topics discussed have not been recorded but at the same time the diary and autobiographica leave us in no doubt about her influence upon him. Occasionally some letters must have been written or received without being made public. One marked "Private and Confidential" commanded "Burn this and don't let anybody read it." William did not burn the letter; perhaps it was too precious for such radical treatment. Here she wrote "I sit down to plague you and play the part of 'Godmother', by giving you a lesson in patience." Later she wrote "This day month is your birthday when I hope that you may be so near me that I shall be able to lecture you at my ease."[14] Years later she was stressing both the importance and mutual benefit of their meetings, "May God grant us to build up one another in the most holy faith for without His blessing, we cannot really enjoy even this long desired meeting."[15] This letter, as many others, contained numerous scriptural quotations.

Separation from William was difficult to bear. "We have greatly regretted your absence but that pain is mitigated by the recollection that the cause is for your good, and we trust that the Lord God Omnipotent, Omnipresent and Omniscient, will preserve and bless you."[16] Her relationship with William was sometimes threatened; in an incomplete and undated fragment we read "I feel that I am going further from you."

Like many Evangelicals of her time she expressed in "Private" notebooks some of her inner religious aspirations, occasionally in prose, often in verse, or hymns and also in prayers. Sometimes these were copies of what others had composed, on other occasions they were of Anne's creating. One such notebook preserved in the Glynne-Gladstone Collection, containing hymns, poems, ballads, literary extracts and private composition, provides penetrating insights into the religious ideas and practice of William's mentor. On page 98 she wrote "have now copied all my hymns in my possession—some *hymns* written when quite a child . . . some scriptural verses have either been lost or destroyed . . . perhaps it were better had these *done so* likewise, yet it will be in my power, to destroy them should I think it right at any time to do so: they have been threatened more than once. This book however can never excite my *vanity* while it contains such humiliating proof that my best efforts were so *unworthy* . . . My endeavours for the future to improve myself when I feel the . . . impulse and dedicate at least some part of my talents to Him who gave them 30 January 1823." The manuscript was reprieved and further entries, while not inspiring, tell us something of the writer. Suffering was to be her lot for many years; during a night of pain on 22 December 1824 she composed the following prayer—

> Lord: if it be thy Holy Will
> That I should suffer still,
> I pray thee, sanctify my pain
> And send Thy peace again:
> If tis thy purpose to restore
> The health I had before
> Oh! let me live to Thee alone
> And make Thy Will my own.

Their mother's attitude towards ill-health and her acceptance of suffering as being the will of God undoubtedly influenced Anne and William's position towards such visitations. A typical example is Anne's comment "I regret to tell you that our beloved mother has been very ill . . . I trust in God, that with care, she may soon recover." A few months later Mrs Gladstone wrote to William "Anne . . . is taking a course of powerful medicines very faithfully and you my dearest William will unite in praying to God that they prove effective."[17] In such an environment of suffering and Christian piety it was natural for William to refer to these things in his letters and in his diary. On Anne's birthday in 1827 he records "Thank God for her passing it in better health than the last. May it please Him to grant a further amendment. Above all, let us thank Him for the good gift which He has bestowed upon her of a true and fervent Christian spirit and heart."

On 25 February 1825 Anne wrote to William, "Should our Almighty Physician see fit to continue my indisposition . . . may [He] . . . bless the new means to be used . . . But above all may we be enabled to say in thought, word and deed . . . Thy will be done." Just over three years later,[18] as she faced declining health, she can still write "that merciful, long suffering God, who has before bestowed my strength, can do so again if He sees meet."

Amid such suffering she writes in her private prayers of her utter unworthiness before the One upon whom she is entirely dependent. She cries out

> When shall I keep the strait path
> That leads to Eternal delight . . .
> Alas! of myself, I am weak:
> Unable to think a good thought;
> Thy strength then, Oh! Lord, let me seek
> That grace, which Thine Own blood hath bought . . .
> Renew by thy Spirit; I pray,
> This heart that is froward and cold;
> And wash all these guilt-stains away.

In the midst of suffering she can write "May we and all dear to us, be enabled indeed to love and pray earnestly for our Enemies." To William she expressed the view "we ought to be thankful that we are all well," encouraging him to drink "port wine" for his health.[19] A few months later she writes, "could we but realise to ourselves the truth that we are his and ought to do all things to his glory,"[20] and then turns to the subject which was to be an intolerable burden to Gladstone throughout his life, "Secret faults." "Yet how well . . . to know at least some of our "Secret faults." She apologises for sharing these observations with him but "such are the taxes friendship must pay patiently, and I have reason to thank God that he has given me my best *friends* in my dearest and nearest relations."

William was the one with whom she shared all her inner feelings, longings and aspirations, which often tumbled out in her rambling letters. On 14 February 1826 she wrote a spiritual epistle, covering various religious topics. For some time she had been "desirous to have a chat with him." This being impossible she put pen to paper, "our Merciful Lord has not only given you talents, but directed you to use them to His Glory. . . May it please Him . . . to sanctify you wholly to Himself —to strengthen you to serve Him faithfully." Other topics included eternal salvation and how a distinguishing mark of love to the souls of man must extend to the whole human race, friends and enemies alike. Regeneration and new birth were theological issues discussed on a number of occasions. "One should think that the Lord's Prayer were enough to convince us of the necessity of being born again; . . . Oh that we may be indeed regenerated, that we may forgive freely all who trespass against us."

A personal relationship with Christ is seen by Anne as essential to the Christian life. She reminds William of "the infinite mercy of that God, who loved us when we did not even know him, and sent his Son to be a propitiation for us." In February 1827 she appeals to Willy "May He [God] be your Shepherd and may you be the blessed instrument whatever your profession may be, of leading sheep into his fold." For some years she had believed that God was fashioning the life of her talented brother, and wrote to him at Eton, "We have greater reason to be thankful that you are taught by a hand Divine."[21]

From time to time she mentions the evangelical paper *The Record*;[22] articles which she found interesting were brought to his attention, suggesting that after reading it he send the copy to anyone he thought would benefit by reading the same articles.[23] They were both avid sermon readers and listeners. Sermons were topics of both conversation and correspondence. Preachers were commented upon, their eloquence, their zeal, or the acceptability of what they had said or written. Of the Sumner brothers Anne informs William "John Bird is decidedly my favourite." She recommends him to read a visitation sermon on baptismal regeneration, a subject on which he had corresponded with Helen. Here, she observes, the question of whether to preach "Regeneration" or "Repentance" and faith is clearly presented. The same theological topic received her attention in a letter the following month.[24] "I read again your letter to H [Helen] on Regeneration where I think you have been led to a most clear view and I long for your seeing Jeune's Sermons, because like you he thinks *not* Regeneration, but Repentance and Faith should be preached to baptised Christians."

Sunday observance played an important part in his life and religious discipline from childhood. Correspondence with Anne shows that it was a central issue while at Eton. "I know my dear William," wrote Anne, "how little opportunity there is at Eton, to keep Sunday, in the manner you would wish, for I believe that in all things you endeavour to act as you think: which were half the thinking world to do what a different world this would be." Theatre-going was anathema to Anne and the subject of a four page letter to her "Beloved William" on 15 August 1827.[25] While believing this to be inconsistent with his Christian faith he had gone to please his brother Robertson. Anne reminded him of an agreement they had made long ago, "Never to go anywhere where we could not seek the presence of God (where we could not remember his omnipresence with pleasure) never to undertake or do anything on which we could not seek his Blessing. If you think of theatres as I suppose you must, can you do this there?" Acknowledging how much they all gave up for her, she felt it wrong to interfere with his pleasures; nevertheless "I am too well convinced that the end of these things is Remorse." She told of how, in spite of her disapproval of theatre-going, she had once been persuaded to go, "what I suffered there and afterwards, I would that others should avoid. I hope that Robertson will yet see he should not go."

Death and the world to come were subjects which occupied much of their thoughts and on which she had much to teach her younger brother which, partly, accounts for his later attitude to death and particularly to her own premature death. Six months before he left for Eton Anne told him of a boy who, as a result of wet feet, had contracted rheumatic fever and died a few days later. "His death ought to be a warning to all of us." Of their grandmother's death she commented "may this death be blessed to all of us—Death, which closes our eyes for ever on terrestrial objects opens them on Celestial ones . . . which God hath prepared for them that *love* him. Do we *love* him?"[26] Towards the end of William's time at Eton she wrote of Christian death and the Heavenly State "I never felt so much that I have an idea of the Happiness of Heaven—that it will consist in joyfully loving the will of God . . . and Deliverance from sin—its Power, Guilt and Pollution—a continually increased degree of such a blessed State." "May we and ours while on earth, seek another country, and have our conversation in Heaven."[27] He wrote to her of a recent death "We ought indeed to be thankful that we have the happy and sure hope of his having been released from the troubles of this world and to enjoy eternal life and eternal peace in a far better."

Fourteen pages of news and information from Anne reached William on 10 February 1828, "I have written of the things of this world, I wish we could have an hour's conversation on the things of another." Death and the heavenly state were topics of ongoing conversation and correspondence between these two earnest Christians. But the following year it was to come to an end. His father wrote from Seaforth House on Thursday 19 February 1829 to convey the devastating news "your dearest sister is now with our heavenly father . . . but we praise God that she was allowed to depart without pain or suffering; we mourn our loss but we rejoice in her eternal happiness, you know well how firm was her faith, and humble her hope, among her last words was the expression of her reliance on her precious God and Redeemer." On the anniversary of Anne's death the following year his mother wrote, "with our Angel 'time is no more,' it ought to be an unspeakable blessing that she has been so long robed in white . . . But my beloved son, I ask you not to touch on these matters but I entreat your prayers."[28]

To the secret pages of his diary he committed his innermost thoughts about his sister's death. Of the funeral on Thursday 26 February 1829 he wrote, "Surely never could mourners receive the glorious consolation which that sublime service is intended to impart, with better or surer confidence." A week after the funeral he was back in Oxford "arranging all my letters from dear Anne & other papers . . . . Labelled the letters and read a good many: it was delightful to dwell on what Tom beautifully calls "the sweetening recollections of that spirit which was but too pure for an impure world."

Christmas Eve, Anne's birthday, 1829, naturally turned his thoughts to "the birthday of dearest Anne who will never count birthdays more but rejoices in the boundless expanse of eternity." The sad death of his sainted sister and his reflections upon her life, death and the heavenly state undoubtedly influenced his annual self-examination five days later and what he records there about his belief and practice during the past year, as well as his aspirations and good intentions for the future.To understand these things it is necessary to quote extensively from the diary. Having touched upon his "one besetting sin" he goes on to write: "I have become persuaded of several things during the last year more strongly, as

1. That I must look for salvation from God.
2. That I am the chief of sinners.
3. That my wants are:
   a. Pardon through the blood of Christ
   b. Sanctification through his Spirit
4. That the main matter is, to eradicate the love of self, & substitute the love of God. . .
5. That I cannot think a good thought, speak a good word, do a good deed.
6. That we are regenerate by Baptism and Baptism alone.
7. That we ought to love all men as ourselves.
8. That pleasure is identified with virtue . . . and virtue is an abused & corrupted name for holiness. . .
9. And I am not to seek salvation for my own interests, but for the glory of God, for he may be glorified in the redemption of the meanest & worst of creatures.

And 10. Of all I think I am most certain of my own utter sinfulness—and yet this certainty is not a pervading nor a living belief.

And may God be merciful to me a sinner & an hypocrite. Well it is good to think that a day will come when all my hypocrisy will be detected. My mind has continued strongly inclined to the Church throughout."

The content of these ten points had been examined in detail during his correspondence and conversations with Anne, including the essential element of baptismal regeneration to which his beloved sister had turned his attention. With her he had shared many of his inner thoughts, his supposed sinfulness as "the chief of sinners," his spiritual anguish as he grappled with his sense of vocation to the ordained ministry, "My mind has continued inclined to the Church throughout." His ordination was a possibility in which Anne found much satisfaction and on which she offered encouragement.

Gladstone made strenuous efforts to support, deepen and inform the faith he professed through a disciplined spiritual life and wide systematic and careful reading; nevertheless, his diary reveals him as a young man in inner torment, grappling with what he felt were the ultimate issues of man's very being and the purpose of his existence. These searchings were influenced by the thoughts and ideas of one who had previously shared in those searchings and whose personal convictions and sanctity he had admired and now perhaps over-emphasized and idolized. On 19 February 1830, prompted by the anniversary of Anne's death, he analyses the cause of the supposed decline in his Christian life and the areas of weakness, with the inevitable depravity which such spiritual death brings.

"I consider myself to have been leading a more unchristian life lately . . . I attribute it to . . . the indulgence of bodily intemperance, and a grossly careless & sinful habit of saying my prayers when half asleep at night and half awake in the morning . . . O may God deliver me from *my* pride, *my* sloth, *my* lust, *my* covetousness, *my* envy, *my* greediness; for *mine* they are, & made mine by resistance to the Holy Spirit. . . . May I feel what I am, & what I ought to be, and may the love of God destroy utterly the love of self in me". But if these strictly private accounts of his rigorous self-examination have any objectivity then, in spite of private prayer, bible reading, hearing and reading sermons, worship, Holy Communion, charitable giving and works and his striving for sanctification, the entry in his diary on the anniversary of Anne's birth in 1830 reveals a man in spiritual torment. Was he experiencing something of the "dark night of the soul"? An experience of which there are many records in the history of Christian spirituality, and certainly not confined to Victorian piety, Evangelical soul-searching, or even post-bereavement depression.

Once again we need to quote extensively Gladstone's own words if we are to understand this outstanding young man, the depth of his Christian faith and the influence of his elder sister and the effect of her memory upon his soul-searching and spiritual pilgrimage. Mindful of his utter sinfulness before God, the evil within him, the power of Satan and the hypocrisy of his life, he is fully convinced of God's unchanging love, a love fully demonstrated in the sacrifice of the Cross. There is no doubting the depth of God's infinite love and redeeming power, and yet, in the darkness through which his soul was passing he writes: "I, who might by God's power have escaped sin, I, the sinner, the two-fold sinner, the sinner within & without, sinner within my rankling passions, (passions which I dare not name—shame forbids it & duty does not seem to require it) and sinner without in the veil of godliness and of moderation . . . I, the hypocrite, and the essence of sin, am indeed deceitful above all things and desperately wicked . . . I half believe what I write, half scorn it . . . another & perhaps more powerful voice rises from within assuring me that I am less sinful than my neighbour. *If* I were, what then? but am I? I *know* how I ought to answer the question . . . I will leave the question then to the day of judgment: but O Lord God grant that ere that time arrive I may have grown far deeper & far more practically into the knowledge of those high & engrossing truths, the intensity & inveteracy of my sinfulness, the measure and stability of the love of God as shown forth in the sacrifice of God upon the Cross, of God upon the Cross, true & very God.

Perhaps even at this moment, I, the evil I, am encouraging myself, under Satan's guidance, in the use of these violent epithets . . . in the war of words . . . *I* cannot believe: *I* cannot pray: *I* cannot repent: *I* cannot desire to believe or pray or repent."

Gladstone's objectivity about his sister Anne, especially after her death, is open to question. The least objective time is the period immediately following bereavement; four days after this event we find Gladstone attempting to analyse the situation, "I felt a wonderful apathy, considering how many opportunities I had enjoyed of conversation & intercourse with my dear deceased sister: of knowing her character; of estimating her powers of mind and her tenderness of heart and numberless Christian graces; how unworthy I had been of the love, and the attention, with which the departed saint had honoured me, as well as others more worthy."

If this comparative apathy was the result of a *just* view of the case, it was well: if it arose from that estimate which Christianity teaches us to form of time and eternity, life and death, earth and heaven; and from—not a careless belief—but a deep rooted conviction that *she* was happy, and that *our* first and highest duty, after suffering the tribute of tears to be paid, was to seek what she had sought, and to honour her memory in following (by God's grace) her footsteps. But it was not so. It was from a torpor of mind & habitual selfishness, which she [who] is gone was freed from & from which 'Good Lord deliver us'."

Mrs. Gladstone wrote to William at Oxford on the first anniversary of Anne's death that "the nineteenth would not be a day of sorrow." In a letter later that year she describes Anne as William's "sainted sister".[29] William wrote,[30] "I trust indeed . . . it will be a day never marked by any feeling except one of calm joy and thankfulness to God for the many and great mercies of this time . . . The only causes of sorrow which I feel laying on my mind are firstly that so much has been practically lost to us all by the removal of a burning (and) a shining light, by the want of her example, her advice, and her consolation. And there is another consideration which painfully suggests itself, in the reflections how little has been done towards attaining that eminence . . . which dearest Anne had reached . . . But it is well to remember that . . . He who had led her thither can raise up others like her." Theologically Gladstone may have believed in the sufficiency of God's grace to transform and redeem even the most sinful, but he was often slow to apply his theological convictions of God's activity in the sanctification of his own life.

Two years after her death he is still reflecting on his own utter sinfulness when compared with her saintliness. "Read some of dearest Anne's letters . . . is it possible that such a saint can have held communion with such a devil? Alas, I deceived her and many another. O merciful God, open unto me the fullest and largest views of mine own utter sinfulness . . . May I know thee and in knowing love thee, and from loving serve thee. Here more especially enable me to glorify thee and raise up many other worthier instruments through Jesus the Mediator of the New Covenant and his precious blood." What Gladstone clearly lacked was the "evangelical" experience of "Assurance," although he did seem to have an experience of the "Communion of

Saints."[31]

Prayers for the departed and the annual memorial of the dead is a primitive Christian practice and a part of Catholic tradition. For many Christians it is a right and healthy practice for which they can find theological justification. Gladstone accepted this facet of Catholic teaching and practice, remembering the anniversaries of Anne's birth and death in the spirit of thankful prayer, based upon his understanding of the nature of the Church triumphant and the Communion of Saints. But this was by no means the practice of mainline Evangelicals. At the same time, comments in his diary about his own "depravity" when compared with Anne's "saintliness" which accompany these occasions are sometimes questionable and unhealthy.

However, what can be said, with little qualification, is that Anne Gladstone had a profound effect upon the spiritual life of William, both in life and in death. But her influence was not limited to what might be called his spirituality; for Gladstone his Christian faith was the foundation of his whole life and influenced every facet of his day-to-day living, including his political activities, until the end of his life. In view of this he would have said that his sainted sister Anne had influenced the whole of his life. Whether, if she had lived a few years longer, she would have radically influenced the spiritual crisis he had to face concerning what at one time he believed was a clear call from God to the ordained ministry of the Church can be no more than a point for speculation.

iii. *The Devoted Helen*

Helen's influence upon William was meagre compared with that of Anne, which is understandable because he looked upon Anne as his "spiritual director," while Helen accepted him as her "mentor." This section tells us something about Helen, but especially about William's religious influence upon her.

Helen Jane Gladstone was born on 28 June 1814; the first evidence of the relationship between her and William is a letter written from Eton where he tells her "Always making it a rule to keep promises, I now . . . begin a correspondence which I hope may be carried on without interruption"[32.] Whether the adamant Eton schoolboy kept his promise, or whether the young Helen failed to treasure his letters, we do not know, but the next letter preserved in the Glynne-Gladstone Collection is dated 20 May 1823, and the next 3 March 1825. Indeed only nine letters to Helen during the Eton period have survived, suggesting that she did not preserve all his letters.

An undated letter from Helen to Anne has been attributed to 1820 but its maturity suggests that it comes from a later period. Whatever the date it helps illustrate the relationship between the two sisters, providing insight into Helen's early religious development, "Thus far my beloved sister I have endeavoured to satisfy your wishes. The employment has proved both instructive and interesting for 'All Scripture is given by inspiration of God'." Anne felt a spiritual responsibility for Helen, encouraging her to undertake the private study of scripture. Helen quotes the passage "Preach the word", and goes on to write, "Surely my beloved sister we may apply to ourselves most of this and even though females cannot according to the excellent laws of our Church preach, yet . . . enabling others to do so they can assist in propagating the Word of God among their less enlightened fellow sinners." Their letters were often accompanied by religious verse, exchanged as a means of spiritual enrichment and a mark of piety. Referring to some unhappy news, the seven year old Helen wrote offering comfort to her mother through the words of scripture, "I write this to console you 'Trust ye in the Lord for ever, for in the Lord Jehovah is everlasting strength'."

In considering the correspondence between Helen and William, the difference in their ages and the deepening relationship between William and Anne, which was profoundly different from that between William and Helen, need to be remembered. A handful of surviving letters from William and a few brief entries in his diary provide some useful insights. Telling her of the unexpected death of a boy he adds, "I trust it may be a lesson to all of us and not restricted to those alone in whose immediate vicinity the scene lay." He freely moves from such awesome spiritual observations to practical advice about her methods of letter writing, "let me advise you to write on lines." The pencil lines drawn across her future notepaper indicate her willingness to accept his guidance. On 21 September 1825 he wrote, "Dearest Helen, *pray* do not let writing to me engross time which you could better employ—pray never let it either interrupt your studies, nor curtail your hours of leisure."

Having recently established the practice of keeping a daily

diary he commends it to Helen "I think you would find it a good plan to put down in a kind of diary what you do on every day." Entries were to be a record of the use of one's time, based upon a belief in the sanctity of time and accountability to God—rather than a diary of events.[33] For a ten year old her reply is quite extraordinary, "we are arrived at the beginning of another month under the conscious responsibility of knowing that it's never to return, and that it is given to us by God for the purpose of improving it, too many perhaps caring not for the soul . . . not knowing where to find their Saviour. *We* do know where to find him and it is our own fault if we do not."[34] Her letter suggests she had accepted his belief in the sanctity of time, and that even at such a tender age she had imbibed the evangelical concern for the salvation of one's own soul and the need for a personal relationship with Christ, while concerned for the sinner still in darkness and unbelief.

Was her "Darling Willy" being astute, or a prig, when writing to her about the study of languages in November 1826, "I do not see why learning them is at all necessary for women: nay more, I think that they are a great deal too exclusively attended to in the education of men." Such was the observation of a seventeen year old after spending five years at Eton grappling with the mastery of "dead languages." In later life he not only commended the importance and use of languages, but also exercised considerable linguistic ability, enabling him to read literature in several languages, including French, German and Italian, in addition to Latin and Greek.

Much of his vacation time while at Eton was spent with his two sisters. The diary tells of some of their devotional activities, for instance, on Monday 23 June 1828 "Read bible &c. with AMG and HJG and alone" adding "which I shall not make particular mention of for the future—as it is brief and ordinary." Saturday 28 June, "Festivities for H.J.G's birthday . . . may God bless my dear Sister, & make her to grow in every grace." Sunday that week includes in the entry "Church morning & Evg. Bible with A.M.G. & alone. Conversation with her." That day he also notes "Began a book of 'Opinions of Eminent divines'." This was to be a collection of extracts on the subjects of baptism and fasting.[35] The following day "Read part of Quarterly Review on Baptismal Regeneration—wrote down Jewel & Hammond's opinion." The same subject comes up on Wednesday 2 July, "Finished Quarterly on Baptismal Regeneration. Wrote more opinions . . .Got tracts &c. on Confirmation for H.J.G. Read Hale's Method of Prepara-

tion for Confirmation." That Sunday he wrote, "Read Pott's Discourses
for people after Confirmation."

These brief diary extracts tell us something of the spiritual relationship between these three members of the Gladstone family, with
their natural and open attitude towards religion, regarded as a normal
and essential part of life. They offered one another mutual support and
encouragement. William initiated and shared in their religious conversations. We find him praying for God's grace in the life of his younger
sister. Preparation for her confirmation in January 1829 prompts him to
study the subject so that he can offer her spiritual counsel both before
and afterwards. Baptism and baptismal regeneration were topics for
correspondence and discussion; Helen wrote on 2 August 1828 that she
was longing to speak to him on the subject of baptism, "The more I
think of it, the more I feel disposed to believe that we are necessarily
regenerate in Baptism." Regeneration, the state of grace of those baptized and infant baptism are all touched upon. "In Oxford I wish you
would consult Jerome, Cyprian and Chrysostom," an ambitious request
for a fourteen year old girl. "And not only on this subject, but every
other, I would ask your advice." That same month Helen turned her
hand to sermon writing and part of such a sermon has been preserved.[36]

Her letter of 2 August 1828 appealing for William's help on
the subject of baptism prompted a fourteen page reply[37] and provides a
mine of information about Gladstone's early views on the subject and
an example of his method of presenting complex and controversial material. It also provides glimpses into William's personality; "May it
please God to give us wisdom and a right understanding on this and on
all other things which it is fitting for us to know . . . I am not aware
that any man ever held that an adult, coming unworthily to the Sacrament of Baptism, neglecting its conditions, and despising its obligations, received the spiritual grace in receiving the outward sign." Such a
person would, to all intents and purposes, remain a heathen. Anglican
Divines and the early Fathers are then quoted on various aspects of baptismal theology, the implication being they that he now held the doctrines they expressed. In support of baptismal regeneration he refers to
the teaching of Latimer, Tillotson, Cranmer, Ridley, Hooker, Nowell,
Jewel and Chrysostom. Let us "examine the peculiar nature of regeneration. It is neither conversion nor renewal. Conversion is not a *change*
(strictly speaking) but a turning . . . Renewal we know to be distinct
from Regeneration."

Having quoted John 15:2 and 2 Peter 1:9 Gladstone states, "With these two verses before our eyes how can we doubt that there are a class of men, . . . who have been baptised into the Church of Christ, yet who have not received the power of his word, nor fulfilled the conditions of the Covenant." "May God keep me from . . . supposing that a regenerate man has no need of further change . . . the life of the Christian should be one of continual change: of unwearied exertion: of unceasing progress." He affirms his acceptance of what he believes to be the teaching of scripture and the position of Cranmer, Hooker and Nowell, that in the case of adults faith and baptism are necessary for salvation and new birth; in the case of infant baptism the promise of others is enough. He ends his long letter, "Delighted shall I be if what I have written appears to my sister, [Anne] and to you, to be sound."

An autobiographical statement follows: "I remember the time when I had a horror of anything that upheld the doctrine of Baptismal Regeneration. Fool that I was: every Sunday repeating a belief in 'One Baptism for the remission of sins' and yet neither knowing nor caring for its spiritual grace, . . . how can I, dare I, refuse assent to a doctrine I cannot deny, and a reason I cannot refute?" He refers to this letter as a "public communication," but felt that Helen and Anne were the only members of the family who could "possibly have patience to read my nonsense. I do not like boring my mother with these things." If William saw the letter as a "public communication," perhaps he was taking this opportunity to declare his acceptance of a "high view" of the sacrament, including baptismal regeneration. This was five years before John Keble's Assize Sermon on 14 July 1833, recognised by Newman as the beginning of the Oxford Movement, which was to see an acceptance of baptismal regeneration as the touchstone of the High Church Movement, linked with high views of the eucharist, church and ministry. While Helen may have thought the doctrine of baptism important, was this really the type of letter to address to an unconfirmed fourteen year old girl, however devout? On Wednesday 14 January 1829 William went to her confirmation and "after some waiting and difficulty got in and just managed to see H.J.G. confirmed. The scene was very interesting but order destroyed by the immense number . . . conv. with H.J.G. at night."

Just over two weeks later he wrote "had a most affectionate letter from H.J.G. but a sad account of Anne." The sad news turned to tragedy—Anne died the following week. Twelve days before Anne's death Helen wrote "My earliest recollections of you are as loving you almost more than any other, and now, I cannot avoid looking to you as my principal friend, and one day perhaps my stay."[38] Anne's unexpected death resulted in a change in this brother-sister relationship. William became Helen's spiritual mentor, the one to whom she was to turn for guidance. To some extent Helen took Anne's place in William's life.

Only a few hours before Anne's death William was writing to Helen of Mr. Bulteel, the evangelical at St Ebbe's, I "liked him, for the most part, very much." While of John M. Turner, who had just accepted the appointment of the bishopric of Calcutta he wrote, "I can well imagine that he looks upon himself as one in great measure separated from all worldly ties, and entirely justified in endangering health and perhaps life in the service of that religion to which he is devoted."[39]

Less than three weeks after Anne's death Helen wrote a "Private" letter to William, "Indeed my beloved brother my earnest prayer is that looking unto Jesus I may be enabled to supply the place of her who is not lost but gone before . . . that I may be made the instrument of some consolation." But then adds "as you lead, I follow. If my dear Wm., I may ever seem reserved to you believe me it is a feeling which I endeavour completely to banish." Not always able to communicate in person or by letter, "we may meet at the same Throne, and there thank One who is ready to hear and ready to forgive. That we have been called to sustain a peculiar loss, you feel it and I know that he who had made so painful a void alone can fill it."[40] Helen now became William's link with home and through her letters provided him with details of their family life. Her letter to him on 20 March 1829 suggests that the death of Anne may have prompted their father to return to bible reading: "Dear Papa has lately begun to read the Scriptures with Mama and me. . . this reading will not interfere with ours." Their use of Mant is mentioned, which is interesting in view of William's later reflection "I was brought up to believe that D'Oyly and Mant's Bible was heretical."

Religious topics played an increasingly important part in their correspondence and conversations. William kept her informed of religious activities in Oxford. "Mr Turner, soon to be bishop of Calcutta, preached a very excellent sermon . . . He called on me on Monday and asked me to breakfast with him every day till his departure."[41] One month later Helen wrote to him "I owe a great deal to your *example* and *counsel* and this debt I am most anxious to increase."[42] Neglect in her correspondence prompted Helen to apologise to William "to whom of all others I love best to write to." In an undated note she says "How shall I thank you for tonight's conversation. I should rather say that Gracious God who has given me such a brother. May I be enabled to be to you but half what you are to me." The note probably refers to their conversation mentioned in William's diary on Sunday 11 October 1829 "out with HJG, sat with her at night wrote a long letter to her."

The eleven page letter, marked "Private" and addressed to "Miss Gladstone" was delivered by hand[43] and tells us mainly about some of William's religious convictions. He declares "in conformity with a covenant long tacitly held by us . . . we have agreed to perform for our mutual benefit one of the most painful, one of the most profitable, and one of the most sacred offices of friendship—we have agreed to tell one another's faults, small and great, without fear or favour." As the elder he felt it his duty "to act *first* upon the provision of this agreement." Professor Richard Shannon considers that William "attempted to forge a replacement by making a solemn pact with his younger sister Helen that they should henceforth collaborate and monitor one another's religious and spiritual development in memory of their sister. This proved more troublesome than edifying. Helen, now a rather 'difficult' fifteen year old, was in no mood to submit to William's rather officious direction."[44] Unfortunately Shannon gives no reference to support his speculations, but if based on William's letter of 11 October 1829 it is an inaccurate account of the relationship. It certainly does not take into account Helen's previous correspondence with William, or the undated note referring to the conversation from which this letter emerged, nor the covenant long held between them, indeed prior to Anne's death. Nor does it take into consideration Helen's later correspondence with William or his diary entries on this point. Shannon tries to sum up in six lines a growing spiritual relationship between two deeply religious young people. William's relationship with Anne, his position and supposed duty as the elder, and his intense religious convictions, might have made him somewhat overbearing to his younger sister. But all this must be considered in the light of her exalted view of William. He tells her that acting the part of "monitor" is a humbling experience. Offensive and dictatorial expressions must be avoided at all costs and so he implores the aid of the Holy Spirit, adding, "I wish to say a few words on three topics, my dearest Helen, your dress, your use of time and of money."

"On dress" he did not want to bring her to the level of his own ideas on the subject, but observes that all should be done to the glory of God. "I believe . . . you are a good deal beyond those of your own age generally in your manner of dressing . . . There is a happy medium to be observed . . . let us remember that thousands and ten thousands have been grieviously injured by conformity to the world." He sums up his "spiritual counsel" on this subject "Only leave the matter in childlike simplicity between your conscience and your love of our blessed Redeemer—on no other ground than that of love would I ask you to ground the adoption or relinquishment of any practice whatsoever and all will be well. Be a Christian and a lady." Was William unaware of the natural desires of a teenage girl, confusing the inner longings of growing up and establishing a personal identity with "sin"? Was he overbearing and puritanical towards his younger sister? One can answer these questions in the affirmative and yet recognise that he was simply applying the strictures of scripture as understood by the evangelicals of his day.

"On the subject of money it does give me the most heartfelt delight to see you free, I believe completely free, from that most debasing passion, the love of it—a passion by which I have suffered much." He reminds her of Wesley's admonition "Give all you can" but tells her she must not forget "Save all you can . . . Lucre is an instrument . . . a gift of God for which we shall render account: a means of relieving the afflicted and oppressed." Here he sets out the basic tenets of his own all-embracing concept of Christian stewardship, which includes his next topic, the Christian use of time and accountability to God for its use or misuse. "Of your time, I trust you will always be very jealous." He then proceeds to develop the subject in a somewhat diffuse and complicated manner which must have confused his fifteen year old sister.

"I leave you with fearless confidence in far better hands: first in the hands of those who are under God 'set above you': to parental wisdom and tenderness: and all other aids from other quarters: . . . as long as you lay hold upon the blood-stained Cross with the energetic grasp of a humble, a contrite and self-devoting spirit, you are safe . . . May your faith never fail, your consecration of body and soul to God never be annulled, your rejection of self be rendered day by day more efficacious and more complete." He ends by expressing the hope that "we may live and die one in heart and affections, our thoughts, words and deeds flowing in the same course—and that course our beloved sister's—our desires and designs entwined together." A note at the end states, "I have put 'Private' merely to prevent the letter being read by anyone into whose hands it might fall from accident."

Helen's four page[45] reply does not reflect Shannon's conclusions that she "was in no mood to submit to William's rather officious directions." She tells him that on first reading his letter "my natural pride and self-love were awakened fully, yet I trust I even then felt thankful that I was not left alone, and suffered to stray further without being warned . . . I know that it has been painful to you to see my faults and to reprove them, and therefore I feel your kindness the more." She assures him, "Your letter has, I would trust, been blessed to me in awakening and teaching me . . . May I be enabled to earnestly seek and find that Grace by which only I can even mortify these unholy affections." Acknowledging her need for a more responsible and mature attitude towards money, she expresses the hope "you will assist me." "My distribution of time has lately been much upon my mind. I feel *now* just what you say that I have not been careful enough of this talent, like many others committed to my care."

Her closing paragraph expresses her profound gratitude, "and now, my darling brother, my support, my comfort, my guide . . . accept my earnest thanks for all you have done for me and especially for this last act of kindness . . . Pray for me, that I may have a heart purified from the love of the world." Her writing drastically reduced in size, she notes "I find I have left little room for the last part of your letter—I can never express how precious it is to me. I can only pray that we may be daily drawn closer together in the holy bonds of Christian love, without any reserve . . . May the mantle of our beloved Sister be upon us." In an attempt to express her final wish her writing becomes even smaller, "do not let me in future think that you feel my faults, but from kindness do not *tell* them." Having filled every scrap of space on the last page she returned to the first, using every inch of space, "I will not call myself grateful . . . but I must ever be so . . . May the God of all grace perfect in you the work of His Spirit . . . till he take you to himself purified by His blood . . . Forgive everything proud and presumptuous in this letter—tell me every fault, for next to my parents you are surely my best friend."

The spiritual direction and practical guidance offered by this

twenty year old Oxford undergraduate may appear, to a later generation, over-pious and priggish, but it was the kind of Christian counsel
which an older person would have given without any reservation and
without the criticism of others. This examination of all the available evidence seriously questions the view that following Anne's death William deliberately and emotionally sought to forge a replacement for her
in Helen. She undoubtedly played a more prominent part in his life after Anne's death, but partly because she was actively seeking, and increasingly pressing him, to establish such a relationship with her and,
as that relationship deepened, they draw closer. The full implications of
this relationship must be realised if Gladstone's later feelings towards
Helen are to be understood, especially when she left the church of her
birth to become a Roman Catholic.

    In 1829 William was absent from home on the occasion of his
birthday. A "birthday letter" from Helen referred to "our sainted Sister,"
whom she then described as "our best earthly counsellor."[46] She expresses the hope that he will increase in holiness, faith and happiness
and that in the ensuing year they would be bound together in love and
would extend the warmth of charity to each other being led by the Spirit of God in their prayers. Mutual support and encouragement in their
Christian life was expressed in a variety of ways, including the recommendation of Christian literature. On 13 November 1829 Helen wrote,
"I am trying to collect *verses* on Holiness"; as this had been suggested
by William she hoped he would approve of her venture. The following
January he commented, "You will be glad to hear that a number of
Hannah More's Tracts have been put on the Christian Knowledge Society's supplemental catalogue."[47] A month later he is telling her about
the religious duties involved in his appointment as a "Prickbill"; these
included Chapel attendance twice daily instead of once, saying grace in
Latin before and after dinner in Hall and finding lessons in Chapel. Occasionally he mentions his fellow students and thus provides interesting
insights on some of his contemporaries. Of F. D. Maurice he wrote "I
thought him a very modest, clever and well-informed person—he has a
great deal of his sister's quietness and kindness of manner." Of Arthur
Hallam he commented "All his efforts, and all his emotions, were as I
believe, to fix and concentrate the longings of his soul upon that which
constitutes our true and only happiness, the true and only fulfilment of
our being, the love and likeness of God."[48] With such an exalted view

of Hallam is it any wonder that the young Gladstone found in him a kindred spirit—whom, like Anne, he tended to idolize.

Helen wrote to William, "You know Mama never likes anyone's departure to be talked of"; nevertheless Helen felt that death was an issue to which she did not give sufficient thought: "I fear it is too much that I do not enough look forward to the end of all earthly years . . . which we must learn to look on with hope."[49] William's diary entry on 23 October 1831 states, "Wrote a letter to Helen on miracles, etc."[50] Here he attempts an objective examination of miracles: recent miracles had all involved young females, such he believed were liable to strong nervous affection and powerful action of the physical frame through the medium of imagination. These supposed miracles had brought peace of mind and a cessation of pain but none of them, he observes, had the decisive character of the New Testament miracles, like opening the eyes of the blind or the restoring of limbs. Miracles are normally used by God as a means of convincing those who do not believe, but both recipients and witnesses of the modern miracles were "religious persons." He saw no reason why miracles should not occur "today, tomorrow or any day." But they must be accepted or rejected on the strength and merits of the testimony which supports them. In dealing with such a controversial subject, the twenty-two year old William was demonstrating a great deal of common sense and in so doing trying to help Helen to adopt a realistic attitude to the subject.

At this stage Helen's "churchmanship" was an inherited evangelicalism, including a little Anglican bigotry towards non-Anglicans and perhaps a touch of the "high church position" which William, her guide and mentor, had now come to accept. She informs him in February 1831 "Do you know I am returning to the Higher Church feelings," while a few months later she writes to him "Here there are women preaching, or rather ranting . . . in the Wesleyan Chapel. Better it should be so, for an act so out of place, should have nothing to grace it." Her evangelical faith was expressed in a letter to the children she had taught at the Seaforth Sunday School "but dear children, all the instruction you have ever received, will do you no good, unless you seek *His* blessing upon it who is the *One Great Teacher* of the way to Heaven . . . the very Gospel of Life and Light, which the King of Glory *died* to bring you."[51]

During his Newark election campaign William shared with

Helen some of his innermost thoughts about the political activities in
which he was engaged.[52] A speech soon to be delivered weighed heavily upon him "the only thing I really dread is, the fierceness of internal
excitement." But with firm and unwavering conviction he wrote "May
God pour upon it his tranquilizing influence. It is very painful to feel
one's self mastered by turbulent emotions, which one can condemn but
not control." While in many things Helen depended on William as her
guide, a role he gladly accepted, he was, at the same time, willing to
share with her his own inner turmoil and dread, perhaps an indication
that he did not want to stand aloof from those spiritually or intellectually less able than himself. His correspondence with Helen reveals something of the early development of his all-embracing faith which was to
be the foundation and inspiration of his future political life.

     When, years before, William moved from Seaforth House to
the new world of Eton College he was to experience many things which
were far removed from his home surroundings and the protective religious environment provided by his evangelical parents. The personal
contact with his sisters was replaced by a relationship dependent upon
the written word which, because of its "public nature", restricted the
sharing of intimate feelings, especially religious. What he encountered
at Eton came, at first, as a tremendous shock. How he adapted and grew
in this new environment, and how his religious convictions and practices survived and developed, and how the foundation of his future life
and work was laid will be considered in the next chapter. The six years
at Eton resulted in long periods of separation from home, but both the
Eton and Oxford years must be considered in the light of his family
background and the views and religious convictions of his parents,
brothers and sisters.

CHAPTER FOUR

ETON 1821 - 1827

Childhood for Gladstone terminated "in September 1821 when I was first sent to Eton." Later he reflected upon the "features of innocence and beauty" which he had seen within his own home and indeed elsewhere. Admitting that he had not led a vicious childhood he felt the plank between him and all sins was very thin and that he was occasionally drawn into falsehood, meanness and indecency. He went to Eton "wholly without any knowledge or other enthusiasm, unless it were a priggish love of argument which I had begun to develop."

When the eleven year old William arrived at Eton his brother Robertson had left after only two years, but Tom, after four years, was well-established. Tom's presence was regarded by the family and by William as a blessing. Eton's reputation for greatness did not ease Mrs Gladstone's uncertainties about sending her sons to a place of which she wrote to Tom of, "The very awful state of the Church at Eton."[1] Thomas and William certainly found life there very different from the somewhat sheltered and controlled school environment which they had experienced under William Rawson. When Tom wrote home about the lack of attention and respect shown by the boys in chapel it may have been indicative of both the restrictive nature of his previous church experience and the appalling state of religion at Eton. The Gladstone children had been taught a deep respect for worship, prayer, the bible and preaching. Tom's father wrote that he must behave in the religious manner in which he had been brought up. Remember "you are in the immediate presence of your Creator . . . who seeth the heart and searcheth the motives." In view of Mr and Mrs Gladstone's apprehension concerning the religious state of Eton it is surprising that they allowed their children to be educated there. But both parents were conscious of the social advantages of an Eton education and the possible future benefits

of this privilege. Although Mrs Gladstone had serious reservations
about the threat to their religious life, the risk had to be taken. Mr Gladstone certainly felt that the future rewards outweighed the risk. On the
other hand their friend William Wilberforce seemed to feel that public
school was inadmissible "from its probable effects on (the) eternal
state," while Hannah More saw such schools as "nurseries of vice" with
an almost complete absence of religious education. Simeon regretted
"that the atmosphere of Eton is so unfavourable for the health of the
soul."[2] For his first year William not only acted as Tom's fag but also
shared his bedroom; this protective contact helped him to settle gradually into what were alien and hostile surroundings. When independence
came in his second year he had to face the struggle and continual ad-
justment to school discipline and the whims of masters and senior boys.
He had both to adjust and compromise his religious ideals in an ethos
very different from that in which he had been brought up. Excessive
swearing, gambling, smoking and sexual talk, as well as bullying and
brutality were all to be found. Altogether a situation which Magnus describes in William's time as "virtually pagan."

Of the three Gladstone boys only William really enjoyed life
at Eton and, in spite of his mother's forebodings and his father's uncertainties concerning the school's spiritual ethos, his religious life grew
and blossomed there. Nevertheless, many years later Gladstone wrote,
"At Eton, the greatest public school of the country. . . the actual teaching of Christianity was all but dead, though happily none of its forms
had been surrendered."[3] A few weeks after his arrival William wrote "I
do not think I ever saw anything so really shameful as the whole system
of going to church; for it is really not possible to derive the least good
from it, and I regard it only as an invention of the masters to cheat the
fellows out of their time."[4]

Unfortunately, Gladstone did not start keeping his daily diary
until four years after going to Eton; however, the 151 pages of the
printed diary from July 1825 until his final day at Eton on Monday 3
December 1827 enable us to examine in greater detail the last two and a
half years of this exceedingly important stage in his spiritual growth.
Whatever the reservations of his parents Gladstone's reflections in his
diary on his penultimate day there record what Eton meant to him."I sit
down with a heavy heart, to write an account of my last Eton day . . .
May God make my feelings on leaving Eton—my feeling, that the hap-

piest period of my life is now past—produce the salutary effect of teaching me to aim at joys of a more permanent as well as a more exquisite nature—and to seek humbly, penitently, constantly, eagerly, after an eternal happiness which never fades or vanishes. But Oh! if anything mortal is sweet, my Eton years, excepting anxieties at home, have been so! God make me thankful for all I have enjoyed here . . . received Sacrament . . . read Bible." The following day he wrote in his diary "my last at Eton . . . Left my kind and excellent friends, my long known and long loved abode at three." Gladstone's final assessment of his Eton years provides a valuable starting point for a systematic examination of his spiritual pilgrimage during those notable years.[5]

i. *The Foundation of William's Spirituality*

The essential elements of evangelical spirituality were already established as part of the young William's daily and weekly religious discipline; these included nightly prayer, bible reading, self-examination, charitable giving and sabbath observance. Regular worship, at least on Sundays, and hearing of God's word through sermons, as well as the reading of sermons and devotional literature, the writing of religious verse and poetry, all played some part in his spiritual life. In this new environment he found that some of the essentials of life, which he had been taught to practice and respect, were not so regarded by many of his fellow pupils. There is ample evidence to illustrate how, in public school life which is often hostile or indifferent to religious belief and practice, a young boy will yield to the temptation to neglect the things he has been taught to believe, cherish and practice, but not so with William Gladstone. What he had inherited from his parents and Anne was not to be allowed to wither and die; instead it gradually developed into something much richer and broader, but this cannot have been easy in such a difficult and strained environment. To sustain any spiritual growth while dealing with the temptations, problems, corruptions and brutality of Eton life demanded a very strong character.

Private prayer is not by its very nature a topic touched upon in correspondence, although it is something which occasionally finds a place in a personal diary. Thus it is not surprising that we can glean little of William's prayer life in his pre-diary period. Even so, one can reasonably assume that he continued the practice of daily private prayer.

Such an assumption finds support in a manuscript in the British Library and items in the Glynne-Gladstone manuscripts.[6] In the Hawarden Collection, among items originally wrongly attributed to Sir John Gladstone, there is a small *Book of Common Prayer* bearing the name "William Ewart Gladstone, January 1821." With this book have been preserved the "fragments" of a number of Prayer Books. The manuscript preserved at the British Library ADD MS 44832 entitled "Prayer for Home Use" Eton 1822, is made up of cuttings from the books preserved at Hawarden, put together by William on a scissors and paste method. Many of the items are Collects and extracts from the Psalter. The book bears the inscription "WEG 1822—W. E. Gladstone, Eton College, Bucks." This "Eton Prayer Book" is divided into two parts. The first provides a system of prayers for every day of the week, for both morning and evening. The second part is a section from the Book of Common Prayer containing Sunday Collects from the B.C.P., while "Occasional Prayers for Special Events in the Family" come from another source. Part 1, with Gladstone's hand-numbered pages, one to fifty-five, is the most interesting and valuable part of this "scissors and paste" "Prayer Book". There are a few hand-written benedictions and final graces. The printed prayers stuck in the first section, taken from the fragmented Prayer Books preserved at Hawarden, are cut from a number of books printed in different type styles and sizes. Prayers from the various sections of the *Book of Common Prayer* are mixed together to form Gladstone's personal collection of prayers for daily morning and evening use. The Prayer Book services from which he has extracted material include the Sunday Collects, Form of ordaining or consecrating of an Archbishop, Morning and Evening Prayer, Order for Holy Communion, Commination Office, Occasional Collects and the Litany. The last item was, significantly, used to make up the prayers for Wednesday and Friday, the traditional days on which the Litany is said. Examining and cross-referencing these rather unusual items at Hawarden and the British Library provides, for the first time, insight into Gladstone's practice of private prayer during his early days at Eton.

There is no evidence to indicate whether the "Eton Prayer Book" was produced at Eton or at Seaforth House, nor that it was completed in 1822, but it is possible that it was compiled and used within months of his going to Eton, or at home during an early vacation, suggesting that even at this early stage in his religious growth he may have

already established the discipline of morning and evening prayer. The
sources used in compiling this "Prayer Book" and its form suggest that
he was attempting to follow an ordered pattern of daily prayer which
was "liturgical" in its structure and *Prayer Book* and catholic in its content. The layout of the contents and the care with which the book has
been produced tell us something of the young Gladstone who was willing to spend his spare time on such a religious activity. Throughout the
whole period 16 July to 31 December 1825 the diary makes only one
passing reference to any form of prayer; "Sun 20 November . . . read
Prayers &c . . . Bible". Lack of conclusive evidence prevents a clear
statement about the regularity or the form of his prayers. However, his
diary entry on Friday 11 November concerning his practice of bible
reading ought to be borne in mind in connection with prayer: "reading
Bible a regular thing which however I do not put down every day."
Was this also the situation with regard to his private prayers? Gladstone's diary provides an invaluable record of the books he read; here
we are told that on Sunday 1 October 1826 he read Samuel Johnson,
Prayers and Meditation (1785). Whether he had read or used any significant book on prayer and meditation previous to this, or used a collection of printed prayers, we may never know.

    Temptation, sin and self-examination are, in ascetical theolo-
gy, all closely related to the practice and understanding of prayer. They
were all subjects concerning which Gladstone was eventually to give
considerable thought and undergo much heart-searching. A letter from
the fifteen year old Gladstone to his mother states "Today we had a sermon from Pope . . . he left his congregation in a lamentable state having
set before them the temptations, inward and outward, to which Christians were exposed, he concluded (without one word of comfort or the
means by which those temptations were to be avoided) by saying that
the ruins of Babylon did not present so sad a spectacle as man, once the
noble heir of immortality, in his fallen state . . . I think you will agree
with me in thinking the termination rather abrupt."[7] Sin was the subject
of another sermon referred to in his diary, "Wright preached well on sin
against God, direct, as opposed to sin against man, indirect."

    John Gladstone as a man of the world must have known all
about human nature and sin and how easy it is, even for the committed
Christian, to yield to temptation and in so doing to sin against God or
man. Sin should lead to repentance and it was on this subject, in rela-

tion to the Swedenborgian Resolutions, that Mr Gladstone wrote to
William, provoking a twelve page reply.[8] Repentance was a central issue for evangelicals, and so one can understand the enthusiasm with
which he sought to enlighten his enquiring father. In his diary he
records "wrote home", rather than his usual "I wrote to Mr G", perhaps
an indication that the letter was addressed to the whole family.

The importance and duty of repentance, declares William, is
something no one will dispute. It is individual Christians and not the
"Christian Church . . . not the church collectively" who are neglectful
of repentance. "The desire to repent (the first drawings of Grace in the
heart) must precede the act of repentance itself." Even as a teenager
William believed that the power to root out sin in man depended, not
upon man's own efforts, but upon the divine initiative. Surely it is not
safe to give man, "seeing how naturally vain his heart is, the belief that
it rests with *him* to root out his sins and repent." To say that a man can
come to a "pitch of wickedness of which he may not repent would be,"
he argues, "to set bounds to the boundless love of God." The man who
taught us such a position would "assume to himself the power of con-
trolling the omnipotence of Christ's blood." Swedenborgian Resolutions are wrong, says William, when they ascribe the power of consciousness of sin—confession thereof to God—and repentance for it, to
man, because we ascribe to God every good thought and gift. When we
give ourselves the glory we are, he says, "receding from" rather than
approaching to regeneration and salvation. For a youth of fifteen he
handles the subject well, even though a number of his views need more
careful clarification. On some occasions Gladstone showed great mastery in presenting his case succinctly and with clarity, while at other
times he was verbose and complex.

"My birthday—aged seventeen—retrospect does not give me
much reason to congratulate myself on great industry in any branch of
improvement." Gladstone, even at that age, was not only acutely aware
of the fallen state of the world which rejected its Redeemer, but also of
his own sinful nature despite the redeeming blood of the Saviour whom
he loved and sought to serve. I "trust that another year, if granted, may
afford a somewhat fairer prospect." Anticipated improvements in his
life and progress in sanctification during the coming year did not mate-
rialise. Perhaps he never expected any significant change. Introspection
often made him forget his own dictum that every good thought and gift

comes from God. He was so self-condemning that he could not see, or admit, a good thought or gift in his life. And so on his eighteenth birthday he wrote, "My birthday: & accompanying retrospect—a retrospect of time misapplied or lost, advantages neglected—I am sorry to say, that I cannot perceive any great improvement . . . in any respect as regards my disposition & conduct—my temporal or spiritual duties . . . May God give the time and the grace for a better life." Hopefully but not convincingly, he wrote in his diary on New Year's Day "May this year or any part of it which God may give, be better spent than the last: as regards God, man, & myself." His exalted view of Anne did not help for he saw in her a degree of sanctity which he could not reach—"had a long and most excellent & pious letter from my beloved sister— unworthy am I of such a one." While Anne could write about "secret faults" and in theory he could share everything with her, there was one notable exception, his inner and endless conflict in connection with his strong sexuality, which weighed heavy upon him during adolescence. There seems little doubt that in emphasising her "saintliness" and purity he exacerbated his profound feeling of guilt and sin. Sexual temptations were to him odious and vile but to give way to them was unforgivable, a denial of his Saviour and his Christian faith. Such an act was so devastating that in his self-examinations his self-condemnation is excessive; branding himself as a hypocrite he experiences a feeling of utter unworthiness and unfit for any kind of relationship with the saintly Anne.

While we have no conclusive evidence that he practised daily bible reading during his early years at Eton, his diary in 1825 and subsequent years reveals the important part which the bible played in his life and spiritual formation. Regular bible reading was not part of a "hidden discipline," but something which could be discussed without any inhibitions, at least with the family. Thus it was natural for the fifteen year old William to write to his mother about the bible[9] as he was aware of her convictions concerning the authority of scripture and the part which regular reading of God's word ought to play in the life of the Christian.

William's practice of personal bible reading is first mentioned in his diary on Sunday 25 September 1825 "reading Bible," the same entry ends "Read a little Greek Testament." On the last Sunday of October he wrote "read . . . Bible in Old and New Testaments as usual," later adding "got into 2 Samuel." Up to this point all his references to bible reading were recorded on Sundays but it was not confined to that day for on 10 September 1826, "Read Bible. I do not put down in my diary my nightly reading of Bible during the week." Daily bible reading, while usually an evening activity, also took place during the day, at least when he was at home. Regularity in such reading was not sufficient, it had also to be systematic and informed, and embraced the whole of God's word. Accepting scripture reading as providing essential food for his spiritual life, and the daily channel through which God speaks, in no way detracted from the need to undertake an academic study of the bible in order to understand its true meaning. Numerous diary entries throw light on this subject. On 14 January 1827 he "Read Bible—with Mant's Compilation of Notes" referring to G. D'Oyly and R. Mant, *The Holy Bible . . . with Notes, explanatory and practical: for the Use of Families*, in three volumes. A few weeks later we have an illuminating entry "Mant's Bible for about 1 hour and a half." This was his first introduction to Mant, the following Sunday he wrote "read Bible, O & N Testaments: began Mant, reading the Introductions, Notes &c: therefore slow work, . . . they are bulky, but excellent."

Reflecting on his childhood evangelical environment in later life he wrote "I was brought up to believe that D'Oyly and Mant's Bible (then a standard book of the colour ruling in the church) was heretical."[10] Mant's supposed heretical position, so far as the Evangelicals were concerned, arose largely from his *Tracts on Regeneration and Conversion* where he argued that infants are regenerated in baptism and if brought up in a Christian environment will not need to undergo a later conversion experience. Such ideas were unacceptable to most evangelicals, but probably sympathetically received by Gladstone. His acceptance of baptismal regeneration marked his move away from the evangelical school. The fact that Mant's work on the subject was published in 1815 by SPCK gave many the impression that his views were the "official" teaching of the church on such controversial matters.[11] However "heretical" Mant's views, he was appointed a bishop in 1820. Using Mant extensively when he returned to Eton after the Christmas vacation suggests he had his own copies, which came to play an important part in his bible study. Throughout 1827 Mant was in constant use; indeed, between April and October 1827 William undertook a systematic study of Matthew, Mark, Luke and John all with the aid of Mant. Overlapping his study of the Gospels he undertook a study of other sections of scripture including Jeremiah, and the Acts, which he began on 4 April. On 22 July he wrote "Finished Acts in my daily reading and St Luke in Mant." The suggestion is that he had a daily scheme of devotional bible reading in addition to his study with the use of Mant. He wrote on 28 October "Remarks on the Gospels &c in Mant, and 2 Chapters Acts with Notes &c."[12] Having established a daily pattern of bible reading, sometimes of considerable length, he had pangs of conscience when he fell below his norm: "I must make up in allowing more time to the Bible thro' the week."

The exposition of the scriptures through sermons was recognised as an important vehicle used by God to convey his word to others. As a boy at Eton he was not only an eager hearer of sermons, but also an avid reader of printed sermons. Belief that God spoke through the sermon did not, however, exempt it, whether spoken or printed, from being criticised. Half truths are sometimes expressed in order to prove a point; this certainly seems the case with what others have written about sermons Gladstone heard while at Eton. Magnus wrote "sermons in Chapel had been mumbled by toothless fellows," while Checkland states "The sermons . . . contained none of the earnest exhortation to which he was accustomed from his father's Evangelical ministers."[13]

John Francis Plumptre, a Fellow at Eton from 1822, whose sermons have been described as "a perpetual source of amusement to his hearers" does not invoke such "irreverent" remarks from the young William, who wrote of his sermons as "fairish," "middling," "preached well." A sermon on swearing "from Wright" was described as good while on other occasions he preached "extremely well"; George Bethell, later to be Vice-Provost, preached a "fairish sermon" yet on another occasion he is said to have "preached well." These quotations are representative of many from the Eton period. A careful examination of every Sunday diary entry at Eton does not support the extreme criticism of the preachers there in Gladstone's time. In the majority of cases he quotes the title, subject or text, with no other comment. John Lonsdale who was elected a Fellow in February 1827 and later consecrated bishop of Lichfield, was a preacher whom Gladstone highly regarded. Of his sermon on 29 July 1827 he wrote "An excellent sermon . . . much pleased"; a later sermon provoked the comment "another *good* sermon he may I hope do good here." It is true that few Eton preachers elicited such praise from this self-appointed sermon critic. Some preachers were poor, others inaudible, many fair, some good, a few were excellent. Strong criticism could be offered on one occasion and praise on another. But was the position at Eton very different from other parts of Anglican church life at that time, or since?

Sermon reading was inherited from his father, which he in turn inherited from his father. But William was unquestionably the most avid sermon reader of the Gladstone line. Sunday diary entries throughout his life refer to his reading of the printed sermon, but the practice was not confined to Sunday. Such readings in 1825 included a Collection written by J. B. Sumner; five volumes by Hugh Blair were described as "more flowery than solid." Charles Simeon's *The Excellency of the Liturgy, in four discourses* (1812) were "excellent." Four collections of sermons are mentioned as Sunday reading in 1827, Gladstone's final year at Eton. Sermons were read both for personal devotion and to others. He read to Anne from R. P. Buddicom, *The Christian Exodus*. That same day he read, privately, G. S. Faber *Sermons on Various Subjects and Occasions.* For the next three Sundays he read to Anne from Buddicom's sermons and privately from Faber. George S Faber, a controversial evangelical, who wrote on Justification, Prophecy and other subjects, so impressed William that on Sunday 9 September he limited his bible study in order to get through a good deal of Faber, reading about 140 pages. Three weeks later he finished the first volume and wrote "he is very able, but his subjects above me, in general at least." Two more volumes of sermons were begun on 9 December, they were *Sermons on Various Subjects* (1815) by John Eyton, read aloud to his mother and Anne. But the following Sunday Mr John Gladstone read Buddicom's sermons aloud in the evening. William also read T. J. St John, *Fifty-two Original Sermons* (1790). Mr Jones who preached at the reopening, after its enlargement, of St Andrew's, received his greatest praise, "A most excellent and appropriate sermon. He is a good servant of his Heavenly Master." For William the preacher was to be just that—"a good servant of his heavenly Master," who, in seeking to make God's word known would preach a good sermon. From the regular diary references to sermons preached and read, the importance of the sermon and the value which Gladstone placed upon the awesome task of preaching the word of God clearly emerges.

Returning to Eton Chapel in later life Gladstone recorded "much interest in the sight of that living mass of hope & promise."[14]

Fifty years earlier his forced attendance at Chapel invoked the observation "I do not think I ever saw anything so really shameful as the whole system of going to church."[15] Was it the behaviour of the boys and the system which provoked this reaction, or his views concerning the right attitude and behaviour of those who worship in the "house of God"? Four years later he wrote "Disgusting to see the theatrical airs of Hobbes & another singer while singing the anthem—laughing and talking after it," and a short time later "Beautiful anthem (but) . . . conduct of the singers in church disgusting from levity."

Gladstone could be priggish, judgmental and condemnatory, but this may have been the intolerance of youth, coupled with the attitudes imbibed from his pious background. His diary entries on many Sundays reflect his strict sabbath observance, almost to a point of excess. Hilarity, sliding and skating on the sabbath are condemned as a breach of common decency, but were acceptable on other occasions. Descriptive sabbath diary entries began on 25 September 1825 and from then increased in detail. "Wrote to T. G. & to Dear Anne; middling sermon from Plumptre—employed at theme writing[16]—saying Juvenal—reading Bible—Sumner[17]—Young[18]—scribbled a little. Read a little Greek Testament" all this during one Sunday. On Sunday 29 January 1826 "Sermon from Grover[19] on obedience—almost inaudible. Said some Juvenal. Wrote long letter to Dear Anne & John. Read Bible O & N Testaments— two of Blair's sermons—two of Sumner's—learnt and copied into scrapbook part of a hymn of Kirke White's & read part of Montgomery's Greenland."[20] A few months later he writes, "Champnes preached on . . . Joseph . . . Long Talk With Hallam on subjects of Trinity, Predestination, &c. Read Bible . . . Made analysis of 4 First Chapters of Genesis. Read 8th book of Paradise Lost—Sermon of Blair on Candour, & some of Corneille's Polyeucte—a fine piece." His diary entry on 11 March 1827 reflects a changing pattern in his midweek reading of Christian literature. "Bethell preached; Briggs read Lectures in Evg, after Catechism, read Secker's; said private business; sat & talked with Hallam & Hamilton[21] after four; construed Play; in Pros—finished Table of Authors[22]—read Mant's Bible—read fewer things now & more of them on Sundays." These quotations, drawn from a period of over two years, show that for Gladstone Sunday worship was normally both morning and evening. Sometimes there is no reference to his church going, but this does not imply that on those days he neglected this sacred duty. The few occasions when he was unable to attend, normally due to ill-health, are recorded in his diary. Surprisingly the study of Latin and other items of academic work were undertaken on Sundays, but this was not to continue. Bible reading was an essential activity, with the additional reading of sermons and Christian literature. Poetry on religious topics could be either read or written. Discussions on religious subjects with friends were not only acceptable but regarded as an essential part of evangelical witness.

At home sabbath restrictions were not carried over into Christian festivals. Christmas was free from all such abstentions; Christmas Day 1827 provides an example of the evangelical mixture of pious activity and leisure pursuits: "Read Paley's Life. Church in morning, & Sacrament—Drew Anne in Chair, & Walk. Chess with H. J. G. Draughts with Aunt J. Read Sure Methods." Ash Wednesday, Good Friday and Easter Day were all occasions for churchgoing and in some cases for private devotional activities but, on the whole, the major festivals of the Christian Year were not celebrated in any special way, as they were to be after the Oxford Movement. The diary at this period makes no reference to Lenten discipline or fasting which in due course did find a place in his spiritual discipline. Gladstone did practice some abstinence at Eton, 19 January 1827 "socked at Leightone—mem. not to sock this half, unless really hungry, and then the plainest."[23] There was, however, some observance of Lent at Eton for he wrote to Anne on 25 March 1827 that she would be pleased to know that during Lent a lecture is given on the Catechism every Sunday afternoon.

Time was regarded by Gladstone as one of God's gifts to man which carried grave responsibilities. With this conviction came an increasing sense of human accountability to Almighty God for the personal use or misuse of the time God had given. The doctrine was nothing new, but for Gladstone it became acute. He began to keep his diary as a daily account of his use of this gift. It was initially a kind of "account book" the contents of which were written down "in the presence of God" to whom alone they were known. Full and casual entries in the diary, even while at Eton, reveal something of William's understanding of this stewardship of time. "Today," he wrote on 27 September 1825, "as every day, I have wasted much of the time committed to me. May God enable me to make a better use for the future." Four days later we read "3 quarters of this year gone —how little of what is good done by me hitherto! with how much opportunity." A few days later he wrote of *"a good deal of time wasted."*

Late rising is seen as a misuse of time and at the age of thirteen was a cause of genuine concern. He wrote to Anne about his forthcoming holiday "I assure you I intend really to get up at six or at the latest half past every morning."[24] Early rising did not come easily and failures resulted in penitence and self-recrimination. During the Christmas vacation of 1825 he wrote on 9 December "rise abominably late in the morning," the next day, "resolutions to amend in getting up" and three days later "new regulations about getting up—rose at eight." But the following day he confesses "Resolutions about getting up broken"; the next day he considers amending the new regulations, "Great need of new getting up regulations." A little consolation is found the following day "Up somewhat earlier this morning."

Idleness was often confessed by this exemplary schoolboy; needless to say that his self-condemnation was often unjust. He writes of being "very idle—shamefully so." A sermon on "Redeeming the time" in January 1826 cannot have helped this sensitive youth. Six months later he is grieved and pained by his continued failure, "prepared for carrying resolutions into effect." A year later he is still troubled "Day wretchedly dribbled away, I do not get up as I ought." His entry a few days later suggests he was setting his standards too high "An eventful day. Up soon after five." Inevitably he slipped back; on 14 December 1827 he notes "I am vilely idle; and short of matter for my diary." The shortage of material for his "account book of time" was seen as proof of his bad stewardship, but a full and active day did not necessarily indicate a day well spent. As with the sabbath, so on other days, it was possible to engage in activities which were not pleasing to God and therefore a misuse of time. Travel, especially by coach, had to be avoided at all costs on the sabbath, but safe arrival without harm to body, mind or soul was a cause for thanksgiving to God. Letter-writing to one's family was a solemn duty which could be carried out on Sundays, but other factors could dispense with this obligation. William wrote to his father "With regard to (Anne) writing to me, I only wish you could dissuade her from doing it . . . I am sure it must be fatiguing to her."[25] Another letter to his father touched upon a very different topic, "I hope your caution about newspapers was only a caution, viz, I am not aware of having been guilty of writing in them." Academic achievement was seen by William not as a personal success, but the result of a proper use of God-given intellectual ability. Thanksgiving to God and even greater endeavour in future were the right responses which prompted him to write to his mother that his tutor had told him that he was to be "sent up," I "trust it may urge me, by God's grace to make further exertions."[26]

Charitable activities were accepted as the practical expression of stewardship. Time could be properly used in the pursuit of good works as talents and wealth ought to be. Such things were always to play a major part in Gladstone's life. During this period we can trace the development of his early ideas in this area. The charitable activities of his parents both influenced him and provided a firm foundation upon which he built, gradually establishing and extending his "good works." Unfortunately only a few examples are available in this period; on 4 August 1825 "Told William I wd pay for W. D(igges)'s schooling. Bought him a 'Bib.' " This was a reference to a poor Merseyside child who received Gladstone's charitable support from an early day. The giving of a bible was a typical act of evangelical charity. The following year he bought a watch for William Digges whom he described as "the Poor Man."

The stewardship of money implied accountability and so it was natural for William to follow a pattern inherited from his parents, keeping an account of all he spent. This early practice prepared the way for the much greater stewardship he would exercise in future years in a wide range of activities. On 12 July 1826, he wrote "Made up accounts for last quarter, and found a deficiency of three pence."

Illness and death were often on Gladstone's mind during this period and throughout his life, and brought a further sense of accountability. Preparing to return home for Christmas he wrote to his mother "I trust we may spend (Christmas) in happiness whether God be pleased to restore my dear sister to health, or to delay his mercies."[27] Anne and his mother suffered almost constant ill-health and so it was inevitable that illness is frequently mentioned in his diary and letters. When Dr Baron was to operate on Anne, William wrote "May God bless his attempts—may we cry God's will be done." The following day he wrote to his father "It is painful to me to recollect that my beloved Mother and Sister have been suffering pain—while I have been well and happy."[28]

William believed that as suffering and ill-health were the will of God all he could do was to commit his loved ones to God's providential keeping. The same was true of death, which was meted out or held back by the hand of God. The inevitability and the message of death, especially in tragic circumstances, were facts of life with which he was expected to come to terms at an early age. From childhood his home background taught him to believe that such events were the outworking of God's will. Thomas wrote to his eleven year old brother telling him of the sudden death of a boy at Eton, who received a scratch on the wrist from a dog "without having even felt anything of it, he was suddenly taken. I am sure so sudden a death ought to make a deep and lasting impression upon all of us."[29] Writing from Eton to his father about a boy named Johnny Larkin, William comments "I should be exceedingly grieved if he were to die, though the change would be infinitely better for him."[30] By the age of thirteen William is writing verse on the melancholy subject of death –

> What sadly sounding bell
> They mourn their mother's death
> Unheard her parting breath
> By them to know 'twas not allowed
> Her illness for a breath
> Before they knew her death.
> So suddenly she sought her shroud
> Praise be to God above
> To the great God of love
> Who's pleased to take her to his breast!
> To share her sorrows cease
> To where she lives in peace
> And where her troubles are at rest.[31]

These mournful verses were written about 1823, and must have been inspired by the shadows hanging over his mother and sister. They express the pious understanding of how the last enemy takes a loved one. For the Christian death should prompt praise because the loved one has passed to the Redeemer's breast, there to inherit immortality, freedom from pain, sorrow and trouble and to live in peace. With so many children and young people dying in Gladstone's day it was inevitable that the subject of death was much talked about, even among the young. Even so was it not rather morbid for one so young to be writing about death? Alternatively it may have been his mother's constant suffering, and his own confident hope of immortality for the faithful, which enabled him to think and write on the subject.

"The Dying Christian" was the theme of religious verse composed in 1825, which may reflect his own thoughts and uncertain situation:[32]

> The mighty God, whom he adored,
> Heard his imploring call;
> His Lord assuaged his grief, his Lord
> Was Parent, Brother, All
> Yes, All, and more, in Life his guide
> Jehovah cheered him as he died

In these simple verses Gladstone is expressing his ultimate faith in God, in the One he adored, the One who answers prayer. He is more important than parents, brothers, sisters, than all else in life. For the Christian he is "his guide" in trials and tribulations. Even in death He offers consolation, indeed he cheers the dying.

Writing to his father from Eton William recalls the funeral of "poor Ashley,"[33] he sees this untimely and unexpected death as an instrument of God through which he speaks to others, he hopes with beneficial effect. The diary entries of mid-October to early December 1826 contain almost day by day accounts of illness and death. On November 6 Tom wrote that there was no hope for his cousin Eliza, nor for Aunt Fanny and Mr Ogilvy. Gladstone's reactions and comments during these days reveal a somewhat detached attitude towards death. For some it is to be expected because of old age, for others it is the will of God. At the same time he remembers to pray for Eliza's father and family. In many ways William's reactions and convictions were typical of a nineteenth century evangelical, but perhaps not normal in one so young.

Arthur Hallam, like William Gladstone, held Mr. Canning in high esteem, and wrote to William about Canning's illness and the threat of death. "What an awful thing, to come to sober sadness, Canning's illness is. Good God! That he should die now, in the very zenith of his powers and the very fervency of England's hope. Death is a fearful thing . . . but, when the destinies of Europe are staked on the life of one man, how momentously terrible an aspect the agonies of dissolution assume."[34] When Canning died Gladstone wrote, "It has pleased God to remove him and I trust to a better place," a view very different from Hallam's. Although William added "the recollection of the past, and the anticipation of the future involve us in sorrow, and in uncertainty [35] . . . all is for the best, and I trust in God this has been to him a happy release."[36] Some saw Canning's death as untimely and politically inconvenient. Gladstone saw it as included in God's will. During a visit to London on 22 September 1827 he went to Westminster Abbey "to see poor Mr Canning's burial place." His admiration for Canning was to remain and to remind him of his influence he obtained a framed picture of his departed hero.

Throughout his time at Eton he was consistent in his descriptions of death and the life hereafter. His theology of the last things was in the evangelical tradition. Death is not an arbitrary event—it is always the result of God's will, whether it be the death of a loved one, a child or a supposedly irreplaceable statesman. It is not an event to be feared, but a cause for thanksgiving, for the life lived and for the influence upon others. Gladstone's doctrine of death was in some respects world-denying, he speaks of a "release from this world." Passing to a better life is neither world denying nor specifically evangelical but biblical, referring to the "fuller life" which death alone can bring. One thing which is laid upon the Christian at such times is the duty to pray for the bereaved.

ii. *Christian Literature*

Reflecting upon his childhood as an old man, Mr Gladstone observed that while he had no early love for the House of God, he did have an early love for literature. Autobiographical fragments refer to books he read, or which were read to him, at an early age including T*he Pilgrim's Progress, Arabian Nights, Tales of the Genii, Scottish Chiefs, Life and Death of Wallace*.[37] Another childhood memory connected with Christian literature was his meeting with the evangelical writer Hannah More who presented him with a copy of her book, *Sacred Dramas*.[38] Towards the end of his life he proudly declared that this book was still in his possession, probably the copy he used at Eton.[39]

The diary during his Eton period, and throughout his life, indicates both the breadth and quantity of his reading. Concentration in this work on so-called Christian literature is not to be seen as a failure to acknowledge how other forms of literature helped to fashion his development. While recognising that good literature, including novels, poetry, books on travel, art, education and agriculture, and a variety of other subjects were all instructive to the Christian, nevertheless, without confining theology, or Christian literature, to "religious books," for Gladstone specifically Christian literature formed a particularly important category for Christian formation and "divine learning." A casual reference in the diary of 11 March 1827 suggests that the young Gladstone was already making such a distinction. In future religious books are to be confined more to Sundays, perhaps because of his increasing reading in connection with his studies and his hope of obtaining a place at Oxford. The extensive range of "religious" books read between 1825 and 1827 reveal a growing independence in his choice and the increasing catholicity in taste, influencing and deepening his understanding of the Christian faith and church during his formative years. Among the religious books read in 1826 were a number of anti-Roman publications, and a few substantial theological works. On 31 December 1826 he began to read the first of Dr George Tomline's two-volumed work *Elements of Christian Theology*. Volume Two was started on 6 May 1827 and completed 8 July, when he observed "as far as I can judge a very good and useful work." These volumes were designed principally for the use of young students in divinity; their contents are wide-ranging and include proofs of the authenticity and inspiration of the Holy Scriptures, an examination of several books of the Old and New Testaments and a short section on the Liturgy of the Church of England. The exposition of the Thirty-nine Articles in the second volume covers over 450 pages.

Tomline's *Memoir of William Pitt*, Edward Young *Night Thoughts*, Hugh Blair *Lectures on Rhetoric*, Thomas Chalmers *A Series of Discourses on the Christian Revelation. viewed in connection with the Modern Astronomy* and his book *A Doctrine of Christian Charity Applied in the Case of Religious Difficulties* were all read in 1826. The year 1827 witnessed a substantial increase in the number of religious books read. The time spent on such reading was largely prompted by his inner searching concerning his future profession, the possibility that God was calling him to ordination.

The Athanasian Creed had occupied his attention in 1826 and

in 1827. He read *A Critical History of the Athanasian Creed. Representing the Opinions of Ancients and Moderns concerning it* (1724), W. Dodwell *The Athanasian Creed Vindicated and Explained*, John Locke *Reasonableness of Christianity* (1695) and Archdeacon William Paley's influential work *A View of the Evidence of Christianity* (1794). Many of the books read by Gladstone had some implication for his Christian faith. He turned his attention to Edward Gibbon's twelve volumes of *History of the Decline and Fall of the Roman Empire* on Wednesday 26 October and completed volume two ten days later, recording in his diary "Gibbon (finished 2 vol containing the obnoxious chapters)." He was referring to the ironical account of the early growth of Christianity in chapters xv and xvi. Hannah More also found Gibbon wanting. Less than three weeks passed before his completion of volume five, when he commented "The style of his history beautiful, but much sneering at Christian religion, partially disguised"; the sneering however did not deter him from continuing to read this monumental work. He read novels like Amelia Bristow's *Sophie de Lissau; or A Portraiture of the Jews in the Nineteenth Century*, a Christian account of Jewish domestic arrangements, written in the form of a novel. Deism occupied his attention in 1826, the following year it was the Dissenters. Articles were read in the *Spectator*, the *Christian Guardian*, the *Westminster Review*, the *Edinburgh Review*, and also the *Quarterly Review*. Interest in other branches of the church prompted him to read *A Sketch of the Denominations of the Christian World* (1795). Robert Southey's narrative poem, *A Tale of Paraguay*, was felt to express a "dangerous doctrine of human innocence," while of Blair's *Lectures* he says "he has or seems to have formed too high an estimate of our character as 'men'," which may be more a comment on Gladstone's doctrine of human nature than Blair's. During August 1826 he read what might well have been his first book on sex, *Aristotle's Master Piece.* recently purchased in Liverpool—"It seems to me not bad; whether useful or not I do not know."

Slavery, a sensitive issue for evangelicals, was a subject with which William grappled in his mid-teens. On 25 September 1825 he wrote to Robertson "I left . . . Father . . . engaged in a correspondence about the purchase of some W. India Estates; (to which dear Anne seems very averse) . . . these particulars & others I was let into by copying the letters." As in all things, especially those connected with the Christian faith, Gladstone tried to reach an informed opinion. The following April he "read a good & very just article in 'Quarterly' on W. India Slavery" and "Mr. Wilberforce's admirable speech & several more on the Slave Trade in 1791." Biographies always played an important part in his reading, some being read in haste, others over a long period. Among the many read at Eton were John Sargent's evangelical classic *Memoir of the Rev. Henry Martyn, Some Account of the Personal Religion of Margaret Gray* and George Herbert's Anglican Classic *The Country Parson.* On 10 August 1826 he recorded "My father said to me—you shall be my biographer, Wm."

Walter Scott was one of his favourite authors and he read many of his novels while at Eton, some of them twice. *Don Quixote* was read in April 1827 and that same month Joseph Forsyth's *Remarks on Antiquities, Arts and Letters . . . in Italy,* 2 vols. (1813). In connection with his school studies works were read in Greek, Latin and French. On one occasion he wrote in his diary that he took a book in his pocket so as not to waste time and yet, the following month, with his usual self-condemnation, he wrote "Reviewed my past employments, reading &c which has not been very great."

Poetry was read including James Montgomery *Greenland and other Poems* (1819), C. A. Elton T*he Brothers, a Monody: and other Poems* (1820), Mary Collyer *Messias* (1749), on which he commented "very heavy— bears no comparison with Paradise Lost or Regained." *Paradise Lost* was begun on 26 February 1826. William not only read poetry, but also tried his hand at writing it, especially religious verse. The thoughts he expressed in these jottings were influenced by a number of sources, especially his reading of Christian literature, including the bible, theological works and poetry. It is not always possible to know whether he is copying verse written by others or composing his own, or if what is written is a mixture of both. Such verses expressed his theological insights as well as his personal devotion and religious convictions. In May 1824, at the age of fourteen, he wrote:

> Bless Him, my soul, for mercies past,
> And spend this day as if thy last
> Store up, my soul, His Holy Word,
> Trust in the mercies of thy Lord,
> Thro' Christ, for him is pardon given
> Thro' Christ, thou hast thy hopes in Heaven,

> And whether life or death he give
> O in Him die, O in Him live.[40]

What follows probably dates from 1824, thus expressing the religious sentiments of an Eton schoolboy after about three years in that environment and separated from the direct influence of his evangelical parents apart from vacations.

> And let a poor and humble youth
> Sing loud thy praises and thy truth . . .
> A faith in that unseen defence
> Which guides us on our weary road,
> Which made, which keeps us, Providence
> Tis that reliance on our Rock
> That keeps us safe from every shock
> Tis trust in that Almighty Power
> That soothes us in the doleful hour.[41]

On the subject of a mother and suffering daughter and expressive of deep and personal feelings, he wrote:

> My Mother! Hope shall bring relief
> And calm the stormy sea of grief . . .
> Then shall our Sister bloom again
> Free from all sickness, grief and pain.

He ends in confident hope

> So sure shall prove our High Defence,
> Our Friend and Father, Providence!
> So, through the mercies of our Lord,
> May we be taught his Holy Word.

He added "With the exception of from thirty to forty lines, these rhymes . . . were written on the night of 28 December 1824, to the stress of the time I may attribute some of them."

On the front sheet of a collection of religious verses Gladstone wrote at a later stage in his life "Scraps of Boyish verses English 1825 onwards to (1829)."[42] These verses offer examples of his religious thoughts and evangelical piety at this period. For example –

> The fount that flows from Calvary
> My Brother, flows for thee and me:
> Come, let us wash and cleanse us there
> In meekness, penitence and prayer.

Another contains the words

> Blood that flows from Jesu's side
> Tells how the Lord for sinners died.[43]

Further examples of his religious poems including Death and Hope, with some sent to his mother and sisters, have been preserved in the Glynne-Gladstone manuscripts.[44]

Serious books on Roman Catholicism as well as anti-Roman Catholic novels were read at Eton and must have influenced his opinions on Catholic Emancipation which was a hotly debated and controversial subject among members of the Eton Society and one on which members were divided, as were adherents of the evangelical party. Writing to his father to congratulate him on being returned as member of Parliament for Berwick, William turned to the Catholic question.[45] "Our Society men are great politicians . . . On the Catholic question we are of course split; (I am happy to say, however, that I believe those for the Catholics form the majority) . . . we are anxious about the members who get in & the questions asked now are, instead of whether they are Whigs or Tories . . . whether they are for or against the Catholics." Parliamentary supporters of catholic emancipation had some warm partisans among his schoolfellows, including Gaskell. In a later letter he expressed the hope that Canning would adopt the line of conduct favoured by his father on the Catholic question.[46] Gladstone presented his position on the subject in two letters to William Farr.[47]

Disagreeing with Farr he comments "I rejoice at what you fear, namely that the Catholics would now gain the day in the Society. I hope to see the time when we shall win the day in Parliament, believing as I do that justice and expediency united their powers to demand at our hands reparation to an injured people . . . Then shall our Church give a noble instance of the first and greatest Christian virtue, charity." Lamenting the opposition of the English clergy to the Catholic claims, he admits that many Catholic priests are bigoted and superstitious, many violently adverse to "our Church." He concludes "God grant that emancipation may be given, before it be extorted: and that English injustice may be removed and forgotten that we may not expiate it by the blood of poor England. Three things appear to me to require Catholic emancipation: justice, eternal justice, expediency, a strong and cogent collateral argument; and consistency. Do then as quickly as possible this action, expedient, as politicians; consistent, as wise men; and just as brothers and Christians."

Catholic Emancipation was opposed by Eton's bigoted Vice-Provost; William noted "Catechism—after some reading the Vice-Provost brought in, as usual, his prejudice against the Roman Catholics." Three weeks later he wrote, "Vice Provost lugged in Ch of Rome for 3rd time in the Evening lecture." Gladstone was expressing increasing sympathy towards the Catholic cause and wrote on 7 March 1827, "Received the horrible news of the defeat of the Catholics."

The Society continued to discuss the controversial topic and Gladstone wrote of their meeting on 29 April 1825 "Question at Society—Was Queen Eliz. justified in her persecution of the Roman Catholics? voted for 'not justified'—in a majority of one." On Saturday 16 June he wrote "Finished reading for question—spoke for Catholics—majority for them."

Newspapers, parliamentary debates and other literature were read by Gladstone to enable him to reach an informed position on this complex and divisive issue, in preparation for the Society debates. As an evangelical he had been brought up in an atmosphere which, on the whole, was intolerant of and opposed to the Roman Catholic Church. Indeed the evangelicals had a deep-seated horror of the Roman Catholics and of the papacy, which was seen as a "dark power" seeking to undermine society, a fear in the minds of many opponents of the Reform Bill. While William was anti-papal he was sympathetic towards the Roman Catholic Church. Even in his schoolboy political pronouncements he could argue for justice, expediency and consistency towards Catholics, while mindful of the superstitions and bigotry of that Church and its hostility towards the Church of England. Aware that much of what the Roman Catholic Church believed, taught and practiced was heretical to evangelicals, nevertheless, he held fast to his convictions on this point.

Gladstone's first interest in Roman Catholicism seems to have arisen from reading anti-Roman Catholic books. His life-long practice of reading publications or literature about the Roman Catholic Church was firmly established during this period. Circumstances which prompted such reading varied, but his intention was always to obtain greater insight. The practice goes back to at least Sunday 18 December 1825, "Read a little of *Father Clement*"; this was an anti-Roman Catholic novel written in 1823 by Grace Kennedy. On 14 March 1826 he "began The Crisis" and on Saturday 18th "Finished Crisis." Four of the five days between these entries were spent reading this visionary anti-Romanist work by Edward Cooper, *The Crisis: or, an attempt to show from Prophecy, the Prospects and Duties of the Church of Christ* (1825). The day he finished that book he began an anti-Roman historical novel by Miss Grierson, *Pierre and his family: or, a Story of the Waldenses.*

More serious reading on the subject was undertaken, usually in response to a particular interest, as in the case of the Catholic Liturgy which prompted him to read the Roman Catholic Mass on Sunday, 3 September 1826, on which day Rawson preached "well save a piece of bigotry and I grieve to say untruth, that Roman Catholics ask pardon of their saints and angels." Some weeks later he "read little of the Roman Catholic Prayer Book," and the following Sunday "read. . . more of Catholic Prayer Book." A 51 page pamphlet by C. H. Wharton entitled *A Letter to the Roman Catholics of the City of Worcester from the late Chaplain of that Society. Stating the Motives which induced him to Relinquish their Communion and become a Member of the Protestant Church* was read in October. Interest in Roman Catholicism stimulated some rather unusual reading for a teenage boy, including G F(ox) *Iconoclastes: or a Hammer to break down all invented issues* (1671) which he judged to be "abominable." He read two articles in the *Edinburgh Review*, both of which were strongly in favour of Catholic emancipation.[48] "Vindication of the English Catholics under Queen Elizabeth," in a collection of eight letters in the Reverend John Milner's book *Letters to a Prebendary : Being an Answer to Reflections on Popery by the Revd. J Sturges. LL.D. Prebendary and Chancellor of Winchester, and Chaplain to his Majesty* was read in preparation for a Society debate. Some of the other topics must have attracted his attention: they included a discussion on the Pope's supremacy, the present universal dread of superstition and the groundless prejudice against Catholics. Pitt's letters to George III on the Catholic Question, reprinted in the *Quarterly* were also read. On the whole, Gladstone's approach to catholicism was sympathetic, in spite of his evangelical upbringing.

iii. *Confirmation*

In 1823 William told his father "There was a confirmation here today at which I, though present, was not of course confirmed."[49] Strictly speaking his own preparation for confirmation began before he went to Eton, for while at Seaforth he was already being catechised. This was the most widely used method of confirmation preparation at that period.[50] Tom wrote to the eleven year old William "I would advise you to speak to my mother again . . . on the subject of your standing up to be catechised: if she consents . . . you will of course mention it to Mr Rawson when the time arrives.[51] Were William's parents thinking about his confirmation at that time? The majority of Anglicans in the nineteenth century, especially evangelicals, would consider him far too young. Nevertheless the subject of confirmation and preparation for the Sacrament were already on his mind at least six years before he received the laying-on of hands. "I must," he wrote to his mother, "do Eton the justice to say that the Masters take a good deal of pains in preparing fellows for confirmation."[52] By July 1826 Gladstone was giving serious thought to the possibility of immediate confirmation as he wrote to his father "A confirmation takes place here on Thursday next—I believe I am to be confirmed, as my Tutor sent me a kind of invitation to that effect, and as no answer was returned to my queries sent home on that subject."[53.]

When the seventeen year old William wrote in his diary on 25 January 1827 "Tutor tells me there is to be a confirmation here next week—notice just received," he began to consolidate his previous private preparation by personal and intensive spiritual preparation. Meagre instruction was offered by his tutor the Revd H. H. Knapp, in two preparatory sessions, the first on Sunday 28 January "Tutor read to all his pupils to be confirmed a most excellent sermon in a most impressive manner," two days later, "Tutor read us another very good sermon on Confirmation." His personal preparation was much more thorough and searching. Having read his Sunday quota of the bible with Mant and some of "Buchanan's Psalms" and one printed sermon as well as some of Tomline's *Elements of Christian Theology*, he added "also endeavoured to prepare myself for the sacred aweful rite of Confirmation." On 28 January he rightly links the rite he is to receive with his previous baptism. He reflects upon his unworthiness, the sufficiency of Christ and the goodness and mercy of God. Concern about his own salvation does not blind him to the needs of his fellow Etonians about to receive the sacred rite; "May it please the Giver of all good things, for the sake of his Dear Son, our Adorable Redeemer, to give unto me and my fellows the grace of His Holy Spirit, and to grant efficacy to the means which have been ordained for our assistance, in working out our salvation. May He have compassion on our weakness, and remove our corruption; may He give us both the power to promise, and the strength to perform; and when we take upon us our Baptismal Vows, may we do it with a steadfast resolution to fulfil them." The following day he read Robert Nelson's *The great duty of frequenting the Christian Sacrifice* prefixed by *Instruction for Confirmation* (1707). Additional reading included the Catechism, biblical passages relating to confirmation and part of the Sermon on the Mount.

On 1 February 1827, with about two hundred other Etonians, Gladstone was, in his own words, "confirmed according to the apostolical rite preserved in the Church of England." From that day forward he was a "Church of England" man and always faithful to her and confident that she had retained those apostolic rites so essential as means of grace. That day God's redeeming love and his own sinfulness were very much in his mind. "Purify my thoughts, my words, and my deeds . . . enable me to *govern myself* . . . not seeking after vain things . . . And not unto me alone, O Most Merciful God, but unto all thy people, especially unto those who have this day gone through the solemn rite of Confirmation . . . guard us from temptation; support us under what seems to us evil; excite us unto Virtue, strengthen us in Faith . . . lead us to the mansions which are prepared for those who are washed in the blood of the Lamb." William's prayer was that "these ordinances of thy Church may not be to me unmeaning ceremonies and formal rites." He asks for the strength of the Holy Spirit, for the inward and spiritual strength and the refreshing of the soul that he may love God and serve his neighbour.

Confirmation that day was administered by George Pelham, 1766-1827, consecrated bishop of Lincoln in 1820. Gladstone records that although he was not dignified in appearance he administered the rite with great feeling and piety, giving an exhortation after the Blessing. Benson tells us something of the content of that exhortation where he listed the things that the newly confirmed ought to avoid, adding "and let me urge you to maintain the practice of piety, without lukewarmness, and above all, without enthusiasm."[54] This confirmation was one of Pelham's final public acts, as a week later he collapsed and died after catching a cold at the Duke of York's funeral. William believed the bishop had made his cold worse by his visit to Eton for the confirmation.[55]

The day following the confirmation Gladstone wrote "May it please God to render me more worthy of the blessing I received, & more able to keep the vows I have taken upon me." A week later Anne expressed the hope that he would be "enabled to renounce all that he had promised" and receive a spiritual mind, and that he, as well as her other brothers and sister, would be transformed by the renewing of their minds. Her one regret was that her "darling brother" had not been confirmed by another bishop, as Pelham, when bishop of Exeter, had "a card playing reputation"; however, observed Anne, "he may have changed since then, and after all as our Articles say the instrument does not affect an ordinance."[56]

Within the Church of England the culmination of the initiatory process is the reception of the Holy Communion following confirmation.[57] Gladstone naturally took his first communion very seriously. Notice of the administration of the Holy Communion on the first Sunday in Lent was given on 25 February. To prepare himself to receive the Holy Sacrament he read the day before two sermons on the Holy Communion from T. J. St John's *Fifty-two Original Sermons*. On the day he received his Communion for the first time he read Secker's Lectures on the sacraments which are contained in his second volume and include three lectures on the Lord's Supper, with a concluding lecture and sermon on confirmation. That day he wrote "It is a blessed institution indeed; a work worthy of the Divine Grace." His letter to his mother, written later that day, throws further light on his feelings, "Today we had a sermon on the Sacrament . . . and afterwards I received it: with the whole of the sixth form . . . Champnes did not seem to me to have any real sense of the importance, holiness and dignity of the office in which he was acting. I trust that it may not be lost upon me,"[58] his next communion was on Good Friday. If the diary records everything, which is doubtful, then it was almost two months before he received the Sacrament again. On Sunday 18 June, "Received the Sacrament . . . would that I had a fit and deep sense of the immense importance and inestimable value of the Holy Supper. But may God give it me: and all the requisites: repentance - faith - gratitude - resolution - charity." Six weeks later he received the Sacrament, "Late, too late in getting up: read &c in preparation—received the Sacrament." A new practice emerged in connection with the Holy Sacrament viz. suitable preparatory reading on the Saturday evening before he receives his communion. On 1 September 1827, "Read in Evg for Sacrament," the next day "Received the Sacrament." On Saturday 29 September he noted "To receive the Sacrament tomorrow. Read &c." His next communion was received on his last Sunday at Eton. From his first communion to leaving Eton, a period of eleven months, he received the Sacrament seven times. Both before his confirmation and first communion and afterwards Gladstone read, thought and prayed about the Holy Communion.

A small undated notebook, part of a collection of notebooks from his Eton days, ascribed 1826-1827, records some of his thoughts on the Holy Communion during his final months there and most probably after his Confirmation as he became a regular communicant in the Church of England.[59] Page one of this notebook contains four texts—Matthew 26:26-29, Mark 14:22-25, Luke 22:14-20 and 1 Corinthians 11:23-26, followed by twelve and a half pages of notes on the subject of "The Supper of the Lord, or Holy Communion." Here he analyses the rite through which the Sacrament comes to us. "As the *dying* command of Him who died for us shall we not obey it? It is the *last* command before his agony and death shall we not esteem it? Thus we must seek to *understand* it." Part two of his study is entitled: "Necessity of inquiry upon this subject." We are to judge how far the Holy Communion suits our condition. "We are miserable sinners , yet His absolutely and entirely by Creation and Providence. . . He . . . *redeemed* us, Adam sold his soul to sin but Jesus Christ came down from Heaven and paid the price required to recover it."

"Do we love . . . to speak of Him?" William did speak to others about his Christian faith, but perhaps he felt that he was not doing so as often as required. He then raises the following questions, possibly reflecting his own inner struggle, both sexual and spiritual. "Do we for his sake resist our evil passions? Do we for his sake hate our sins? . . .

Do we deny ourselves in all things which are not good for our souls? Do we live in strictest purity?. . . Do we desire to live in communion with God here?" He observes that what man wants is a "new, a spiritual inclination." What has God done to help man in such things? He has provided the sacrament of baptism, through which we have been made his children. But "will it save us? No, but it covers us with tenfold shame and condemnation." Does he by this mean that although the baptized should live in holiness and purity they constantly fall short of their baptized status and remain in sin? We have promised at confirmation "to obey God, and we have not obeyed him. Now that His Table is spread before our eyes and we are invited to come—now his Word is in our hands able to make the praying soul wise unto salvation either we must go on and be blessed as servants of Christ, or we must hold back." To hold back means to reject the benefits of the Atonement. With true evangelical piety he put forward the only sure way, to "acknowledge our wretchedness" and to look to Jesus crucified for us and to fly to him for refuge. Christ the all-sufficient Mediator gives his "sanctifying Spirit" to deliver us from the power of sin which tyrannizes over our souls and bodies.

Two things are required of those who wish to enter fully into the baptismal covenant, the blood of Christ to wash us from the guilt of sin and the Spirit of God to abide within us to purge our hearts from the power of sin. The change need not be sudden but it is a great one. Conscience helps those who respond to know if they are living according to the will of God. The new life is seen in the love and service of Christ. The spirit of God works in the soul nourishing it and gradually forming it after the image of Christ. He ends with an ecclesial statement: "this new life is the very life which was in Christ. And it is derived to us only in as much as we are members of Christ, members of his Church which is his body." Did Gladstone intend to end at this point or had he anticipated writing more about the subject on which he began, viz. the Holy Communion? Whatever his original intention, what we have here is an account of the Christian life which, while written in evangelical language, puts forward convictions about the Sacrament of the Lord's Supper, Baptism and the Church which were not the ideas of many mainline members of the evangelical party, most of whom had little to say on these three subjects, but a great deal about salvation from sin through the blood of Christ. This does not imply that there was a complete absence of books or interest among evangelicals on the Sacra-

ments. Edward Bickersteth (1786-1850) who after ordination became
one of the secretaries of the Church Missionary Society, and perhaps
the leading evangelical theologian after Simeon, wrote a *Treatise on the
Lord's Supper* and on *Baptism* which influenced the ideas of many evangelicals of that period and later.[60] But many of the party had a somewhat unhealthy preoccupation with sin, as did Gladstone.

iv. *Social and Academic Life*

Gladstone's religious observance and commitment were somewhat tense and tinged with the evangelical world-denying attitude. In
some areas of his social life the young William did have pangs of conscience and pressure from Anne. On Friday 4 May 1827 he went to the
theatre with Tom; a few weeks later he was there again and wrote in his
diary "went to theatre after six—wretched." A short time later Anne,
hearing of his theatre-going, wrote urging him to give up such an activity for "the end of these things is remorse."[61] His experience of wretchedness and Anne's pleas failed to deter him; he wrote to his father on 23
August 1827 that Robertson and he were thinking of going to the theatre the following evening to see Shakespeare. Theatre-going continued,
but was not always a pleasing experience; on 25 October he wrote "At
theatre–*disgusting*. . . Heard from home—several letters." Among these
was one from his beloved Anne. Fortunately nothing is said about the
theatre although she expressed both approval and disapproval of some
of the items in numbers six and seven of the *Eton Miscellany*.[62]

Diary entries for the second to sixth January 1826 record that
his brothers "went to meet the hounds," and Tom and John went hunting; they also went to a ball. None of these activities aroused his disapproval. But did he question the propriety of his own attendance at a
ball? His first, with his brothers, on 13 January 1826 prompted three
exclamation marks in his diary. He occasionally went to musical concerts and also attended and took part in school plays—these were not in
the same category as the soul-destroying theatre. William was no prig
so far as most leisure activities were concerned. The diary tells of his
playing billiards and bowls, rowing was a regular activity, he certainly
enjoyed bathing throughout his life and occasionally he went horse riding. In his early days at Eton his first pursuits were football, and cricket, at which he was mediocre. Table games included draughts, chess

and backgammon. Card playing was acceptable and, while opposed to heavy betting, he would from time to time play cards for money. He wrote to Tom "Betting goes on here to a terrible extent; I mean terrible for a school."[63]

Wine drinking was an acceptable social practice for the Gladstone family and the majority of evangelicals. At Eton William was a regular drinker of wine and received a constant supply from home. The fourteen year old schoolboy had no inhibitions about writing to his father "The only remnant of the wine I had here was rather flat . . . I hope you will send me a bottle or two as soon as you can."[64] He drank wine with his school friends and with his brothers; the many diary entries like those of 13 and 15 February 1827 indicate that this was a normal activity. Supplies were received from different sources; on 20 March 1827 "received some wine, &c sent to me by T. G. from London." Evangelical attitudes concerning dancing, balls, cards, opera and theatre varied; for many there was a distrust of all "worldly amusements." While in some cases such activities were not denounced, they were regarded as inappropriate for those who professed the Christian faith. Wine drinking, however, was acceptable to most evangelicals, but "total abstinence" was sometimes looked upon with suspicion.[65] William was elected to the Eton Debating Society on 15 October 1825 which was far from being stuffy and could be noisy and also much fun.[66]

On the whole William's social life at Eton was what one would expect of a reasonably wealthy growing adolescent in the early part of the nineteenth century. He was willing to try most things so long as they were not incompatible with his religious convictions. Theatre-going is one example of how he was not beyond compromise and was willing at least to try something to which others objected. There is no evidence to suggest that he participated in the more extreme forms of behaviour which he felt would be unacceptable to the all-seeing eye of God.

Henry H. Knapp was Gladstone's tutor and like most at that time was a clergyman; he was a kind-tempered man, with "a sense of scholarship," but Gladstone could only recall one piece of advice from Knapp: "that I should form my poetical taste upon Darwin, whose poems (*The Botanic Garden* and *Loves of the Plants*) I obediently read." Knapp was a fanatical theatre-goer and may have encouraged

Gladstone's early flirtation in that area. A master who had a little more influence upon him was Henry Joy, who sought to inspire in him a love of books "if not of knowledge." "Joy had a taste for classics and made visions for me of honours at Oxford," but "I remained stagnant, without heart, or hope." This feeling was short lived. In 1822 he was under Edward Hawtrey who "for the first time inspired me with a desire to learn and to do, which I never wholly lost." He described Hawtrey as by far the best of the Eton tutors, while Thackeray in his biography of Hawtrey described him as "a man to foster and stimulate the spirit of learning." Dr John Keate, the Headmaster, was the only other to impress Gladstone.

Among his schoolfellows[67] were a number of boys who later became leading churchmen; they included Gerald Wellesley, later Dean of Windsor; Lord Arthur Hervey, later bishop of Bath and Wells; George Selwyn, successively bishop of New Zealand and of Lichfield; Walter Hamilton, later bishop of Salisbury; James Milnes-Gaskell, later a member of Parliament; Francis Doyle and Arthur Hallam.

Most of William's friendships were established and nurtured through the Eton Debating Society. From October 1825 there were endless references in his diary to the Society, its activities and the *Eton Miscellany*. Among the most active supporters of the Society were Arthur Hallam, Arthur Hervey, James Milnes-Gaskell, George Selwyn, Francis Doyle, William Farr, Edward Pickering, Charles Canning, William Wentworth-Fitzwilliam and Gerald Wellesley. Gladstone's diary records his regular contact with all of these, not only in connection with the Society but socially. Most of them, along with H. H. Hamilton, P. Handley, W. E. Jelf, F. Rogers were his companions from time to time for breakfast, wine drinking, walking and talking. His most frequent contact was with Hallam and Gaskell; these two along with William Farr[68] were the only Eton friends with whom he corresponded during the vacation. While such letters were few in number they were important to him.

Gladstone helped to launch the *Eton Miscellany* in 1827, although Selwyn was the "prime mover." Indeed Hallam wrote to Farr "Selwyn is our prime man." The first issue appeared on 4 June 1827 and the publication continued to flourish until the following December, Gladstone and Selwyn acting as joint editors. In the course of its short life Gladstone made the largest contribution to the varied items published. But, apart from religious verse, religious themes were fragmentary and often vague, and not from William's pen. The many collections of verse where the word "death" finds a place in the title came from other pens, as did the items which expressed moralistic themes on lying, stealing and ambition. William's most religious contribution was *Reflections in Westminster Abbey*[69] written in October 1827, after his visit "to see poor Mr Canning's burial place."

> Canning died.
> Death aim'd the stroke at him, at him alone,
> Claimed him, the first, the noblest, for his own:
> Knew that, in him by one unerring dart,
> He gain'd the fatal goal, and pierce'd proud Britain's
>   heart ...
> Yet times the bellow'd anthem's notes arise,
> And waft the Christian's worship to the skies.

But nowhere in Gladstone's contributions are there any signs of "Methodist Hymns," or expressions of evangelical piety or convictions, a subject touched upon in correspondence between Hallam and Farr.

During the period of his joint editorship of the *Miscellany* Gladstone had almost daily contact with George Selwyn. Of the first issues he wrote in his diary on Sunday 3 June 1827 the *Eton Miscellany* occupied "too much of my mind which I hope and pray will not be the case again." This may imply that it took too much of his attention on that particular day, a Sunday, which ought to have been devoted to "higher" and more spiritual occupations. However, his numerous references to the work involved in producing the *Miscellany* illustrates the considerable amount of time spent on this venture.

Typical of many diary entries between May and July 1827 is that of June 30, "worked at corrections with Selwyn at night till a quarter to twelve," or two weeks later, "Hard at work till between twelve and one with Selwyn—got the fifth number ready to go up in the morning." Most of the references are to their correcting of manuscripts for publication; a few mention talking and wine drinking. But there is not a single reference to any religious discussion. It is difficult to believe that religion was never a topic of conversation in view of the important part the Christian faith played in both of their lives. Perhaps it was to such topics that Gladstone referred when he wrote on Monday 21 May 1827,

"Selwyn sat with me in Eg, and we reviewed ourselves & others."

Friendships were sacred to Gladstone and a cause for thanksgiving to God. Deep and personal relationships were not easily formed and to the end of his life he had few intimate friends. Those at Eton can be divided into three categories: the inner group included only three, Hallam, Gaskell and Doyle. The second group embraced Farr, Pickering, Hervey, Selwyn, Rogers and Canning. The third group which played little part in his life included Jelf, Handley and others. In varying degrees of regularity these and others are mentioned in his diary. It is impossible to say what influence, if any, they had on, William, or he upon them, in religious matters. They felt at ease debating historical and political issues but religious topics were rarely discussed.

William's supposed silence on religious matters might have been the result of an adolescent compromise, in that he would freely discuss those subjects which interested his friends and were seen to be important, especially historical and political issues, even when their political affiliations differed. Did he only speak on religious topics with his closest friends, and then only when it seemed appropriate or when they raised such issues? Gladstone seems to have influenced at least some of his contemporaries. Walter Hamilton, later bishop of Salisbury, whose saintly life impressed many, stated that while at Eton he was a "thoroughly idle boy," but that he "was saved from worse things by getting to know Gladstone." The view of many of his contemporaries, in spite of his supposed reluctance to talk about his religious convictions, was that he was "pre-eminently God-fearing, orderly and conscientious."[70] But even if he had not been a Christian whose quality of life could not fail to impress others, there is little doubt that he would still have been recognised as a person of remarkable ability. The diary and other available documentation tell us something of Gladstone's relationship with his two closest Eton friends, James Milnes-Gaskell and Arthur Hallam.

From his earliest days at Eton in 1824 James Milnes-Gaskell wrote regularly to his mother. These letters provide an interesting insight into the life at Eton at that time. Gaskell suffered his fair share of bullying and cruelty at the hands of the older boys.[71] His father, Benjamin, became the member of Parliament for Maldon in the West Riding in 1812, holding the seat until 1826.Thus from his birth Gaskell grew up in a political environment and had first-hand knowledge of politics and Parliament which stood him in good stead at Eton and Oxford. The letters to his mother help us to understand why he and Gladstone got on so well. His unwillingness to compromise resulted on occasion in his being beaten by other boys because of his refusal to participate in their excessive swearing. The behaviour of many of the boys in chapel, their profaning of the sabbath and excessive drinking, all appalled him. Requesting his mother's advice on how to face up to the bullying and abuse of others, he tells her how after church his prayer book was taken from him and kicked about in the mud.[72]

Gaskell first appears in Gladstone's diary on 26 June 1826, "After 4 and after 6, with Gaskell, . . . He is a great politician . . . (and) . . . a very pleasant fellow." Three days later they are together again and a friendship was already developing "he seems to me to be a very good youth." The next day, June 30, Gaskell wrote to his mother, "I was out all yesterday evening with Gladstone, who is one of the cleverest and most sensible people I ever met with." Their political and religious convictions were very different. Gaskell was a Whig and from a Unitarian background, William a Tory and an evangelical and yet a firm and lasting friendship was established, and one of the closest ever experienced by Gladstone. It is possible that in this relationship with Gaskell we have the genesis of Gladstone the Christian politician working out the occasional need for compromise and at the same time holding fast to deeply held beliefs in a largely hostile and unsympathetic environment.

From June 1826 until July 1827, the duration of the close Eton friendship between Gladstone and Gaskell, there are countless references in the diary to Gaskell. They tell of the things done together, including sharing breakfast, drinking tea or wine, boating, walking and talking. Their time together at the Eton Society, subjects debated, the time and place of meetings, even the voting figures, are all in the diary. But we are told little of the topics discussed during their intimate meetings and while walking, or when taking refreshments together. At the end of that term Gladstone wrote "last term . . . by far the happiest I ever spent at Eton." This happiness was probably largely due to his intimate friendship with Gaskell and Hallam. The Eton Society, the *Miscellany* and interest in political and historical issues seem to have been the ground upon which these friendships were established and sustained, but this does not mean that religion played no part in these relationships.

Gladstone's new friendship with Gaskell and his admiration of his political acumen were brought to his father's attention. "He applauds you as one of the most independent, enlightened, and able members of the House of Commons, he says there are not more than three or four more such in the House, Sir Thomas Acland one of them. He is a clever fellow and has by far the most extensive political knowledge and intimate acquaintance with English History of any boy I ever saw. He is altogether a very desirable fellow both as a scholar and as a friend. We are getting very deep into politics, I am afraid too much so."[73] The following year Gaskell wrote to his mother "Gladstone is no ordinary individual and perhaps were I called on to select the individual I am intimate with to whom I should first turn in an emergency, and whom I thought in every way pre-eminently distinguished for high principle, I think I should turn to Gladstone.[74] Later he wrote "The idea of being separated from Gladstone is really distressing to me, in fact, writing upon the subject is enough to make me melancholy."[75] The anticipated painful separation was because his mother wanted him to go to Cambridge, while Gladstone was going to Oxford. In the end Gaskell went to Oxford and their friendship continued.

Recalling his early friendship with Arthur Hallam[76] Gladstone records that this began about 1824. It is therefore interesting that there is no reference to Hallam in the diary until 4 February 1826. Writing about his friendship in 1898,[77] Gladstone described that boyhood friendship as "surpassing every other" that he ever enjoyed in his life. Truly an outstanding tribute to a 9 year friendship established 60 years before. In the article he describes Hallam as standing "supreme among all his fellows." Sir Francis Doyle believed him to be "the most brilliant and charming Etonian of his time."

From February 1826 until Hallam's departure from Eton in July 1827 there are regular, sometimes daily, references to him in William's diary. This intimate friendship, later described by Gladstone as "without any doubt the zenith of my boyhood," terminated in 1827, after which their contact was infrequent.

Subjects debated at the Society had to be of a strictly historical nature and not concerning events within the last fifty years. Hallam did admit that politics were discussed, a point which he brought to the attention of Dr Keate about which Keate was displeased.[78] In addition to many diary references to Society activities, others record the things they did together, but without giving personal details. Breakfasting, tea and wine drinking were regular activities often shared with other friends, time was spent sculling and walking, accompanied by the inevitable talking, was a regular pastime. Frequently they met simply to talk—although the subjects of these conversations, if not Society matters, are rarely mentioned. What Gladstone wrote of this friendship in his diary on Sunday 24 September 1826, and reiterated in 1898, suggests that behind such terse references to Hallam there lay a close friendship with one whom Gladstone never forgot and whom he described as "the greatest living Englishman." The boyhood description of September 1826 observes "I esteem as well as admire him. Perhaps I am declaring too explicitly & too positively for the period of our *intimacy*—which has not yet lasted a year—but such is my present feeling." Professor R. Shannon sees the relationship as having an "unconscious homosexual aspect."[79] He also states "There were no arguments about religion."[80] This statement seems to be based on Gladstone's autobiographical recollections of 1893[81] but on this issue, as on other occasions, Gladstone's memory was either inaccurate or, as is sometimes the case with autobiographies, he was consciously or unconsciously adjusting the facts to suit his purpose. Shannon is not alone in relying too much on these statements. Dr Perry Butler, using the same source, states "Though he tended to keep his religious convictions to himself, in all other respects Gladstone surrounded himself with like-minded boys who were more likely to arouse hostility for being self-consciously highbrow than by being sanctimonious."[82] The general view is that in spite of the intimacy of his friendship with Arthur Hallam they did not talk much about religion.

Gladstone had been brought up in the evangelical faith which he had been taught to regard as another name for Christianity.[83] Adherents of the evangelical party were expected to witness to their faith and to speak out and to speak often for Christ. The argument of reluctance due to adolescent embarrassment or sensitivity concerning his social origins are put forward as possible reasons why Gladstone failed to speak about his faith to his school friends.[84] Such a conclusion is open to serious question.

James Milnes-Gaskell was one who refused to compromise his principles and some of his schoolfellows tried to beat him into submission.[85] Did Gladstone compromise and fail to witness to his Saviour? This question is important and requires objective consideration. The main sources of information on this subject are first the diary, second correspondence with his family, third correspondence with his Eton friends and lastly, his autobiographical writings.

The autobiographical writings, while extremely important for Gladstonian studies, like all documentation written long after the event are sometimes inaccurate and need to be checked against the contemporary documentation. Gladstone's excessive self-criticism must always be borne in mind when examining this material, for however much or well he spoke out for and witnessed to his Saviour, and his religious convictions, it is unlikely that this would have been sufficient to satisfy him. The only remotely connected autobiographical statement belonging to the Eton period is "I had been educated in an extremely narrow churchmanship, that of the evangelical party," and he goes on to write that his emancipation from this position began through Oxford and bishop Butler.[86] References in the autobiographical reflections to his evangelical position not only confirm that he should have been witnessing to that faith as an important duty expected of those who held such a theological position, but he also recognises that evangelicalism, which he equated with Christianity, was "bigoted." Such a position is often judgmental of others and intolerant towards those who do not share the same convictions. This attitude is often repellent to others, not least the young.

Hallam and Gladstone corresponded during vacations but, says Gladstone, it was "a practice not known to me by any other example." Gladstone was mistaken; other Eton boys did correspond. He wrote to Gaskell and Farr, and Gaskell and Hallam corresponded, as did Hallam and Farr. But Gladstone's own correspondence with Farr, Gaskell and Hallam did not touch upon religious topics. Hallam's comments in a letter to Farr in the summer vacation of 1826 about letters he had received from Gaskell and Gladstone are, on the whole, an apt description of many of the vacation letters to friends. He described them as "breathing politics at every pore."[87] Regular letters passed between Eton and Seaforth in which William's touch upon religion and related subjects. At home he could freely, at least with his mother and sisters, speak about and practice his religion without any embarrassment.

The diary is the most informative source concerning Gladstone's religion while at Eton. But even if evidence of his attempts to talk to others about his faith is limited, or if explicit evidence is practically non-existent, this does not prove that he did not seek to propagate his faith in this way. On the other hand the contents of the diary might be rather like those of the New Testaments: Infant baptism is not explicit in New Testament teaching, but this does not prove that it was not practiced in those times. Many reputable scholars have found evidence of various kinds, although not explicit, to support the belief that infants were baptized at that period.[88] It would be possible to argue that as Gladstone does not record in his diary that he said his prayers and read his bible daily, that he did not use these means of grace regularly and was thus neglectful of things the church believes are essential to the Christian life and sanctification. References in the diary show the danger of drawing such conclusions; on 7 August 1826 he wrote "there are some things which happen every day which I leave out. Family prayers and reading Bible—walking which I do much in the garden." Was Gladstone reminding himself, informing God, or noting for posterity, that regular or essential parts of his daily life are not recorded in his diary? For the young Gladstone daily prayer and bible reading were an inviolable part of his daily Christian practice and therefore did not need mentioning. It must also be realized that Gladstone did not always complete his diary on a daily basis; indeed from time to time he admits his irregularity in this particular duty. While at home on vacation in August 1825 he wrote "Journal now very defective: somewhat irregularly kept." What we can say is that regular activities were not normally recorded and that while his activities on a particular day were usually recorded daily, this was not an unalterable rule.

When Gladstone stated, in connection with his friendship with Hallam that "In religion we had no disputes: I think we were agreed," he did not mean that they did not discuss religious issues. In making this statement he may have been extremely careful in his use of the English language. "We had no disputes on religious issues" may have meant "We had no difference of opinion." On some other issues they were in dispute—on duelling,[89] on political issues and on various historical subjects. But on religious matters they had no fundamental differences, they were not in dispute.

Gladstone did have discussions with Hallam on religious matters; on Sunday 23 April 1826 he noted "Long talk with Hallam on sub-

jects of Trinity, Predestination, &c." We do not know whether this was
their first talk on religious subjects, but it is the first record of such a
discussion in the diary. Exactly two weeks later he wrote "Read Leslie
on Deism; also his letter to a convert; & began his conversation between a Deist & a Christian." He ends, "Hallam lent me the book," possibly an indication of a practice of a mutual loaning of books on religious topics or it could have been an isolated occurrence. Three days
later he writes, "Finished. . . Leslie's Conversation on truth of Christianity—Excellent." While there is no record of Gladstone discussing
this particular book with Hallam, on Sunday 14 May 1826 we do have
a statement of considerable importance "Stiff argument with Hallam, as
usual on Sunday, about Articles, Creeds, &c"; not a dispute, but an argument. The point of crucial importance is the statement "*as usual on
Sundays.*" This shows that he and Hallam had regular arguments or
talks on Sundays about religious or theological topics. Having made
such a categorical statement, does Gladstone need to record that every
Sunday he usually had such a discussion with Hallam? Or, if he records
a talk with Hallam, does he have to state that they discussed a religious
topic? Lack of such a statement does not prove that religion was not included in their discussions.

  The fact that there are no references to his meeting or walking
with Hallam for some weeks after these theological discussions does
not prove that what he had declared to be a regular practice had been
abandoned and they did not meet on Sundays. References to Hallam occur regularly on other days in various connections, so clearly there was
no breach in their friendship and it seems rather unlikely that they had
dropped their regular Sunday meetings. "Hallam breakfasted with me.
We generally mess together now." This reference to one of the most intimate of Eton activities is mentioned in William's diary on Sunday 19
November 1826. It is doubtful if these two close friend could have eat-
en together on a day which Gladstone regarded as sacred and set aside
for religious activities, and yet not discussed at least some aspects of
the Christian faith. He certainly felt it was right to spend the sabbath
talking about religious subjects, but he was not convinced it was right
to discuss politics or the many other topics debated at the Society the
day before. The sabbath was reserved for religious activities and discussion, and in this, as in all else, Gladstone sought God's guidance to do
what was right.

The first issue of the *Eton Miscellany* was published on 4 June 1827. Referring to that time Hallam later wrote to William Farr, "remember, when we used to talk over the issue of a new Etonian, little dreaming one would be started in our lifetime, we used to set poor William Ewart down for nothing but Methodist hymns. Let me tell you however . . . Gladstone has shown a great deal of sound sense, and a great deal of powerful talent in this publication." Was this a humorous or a derogatory remark about Gladstone's evangelical position or his social origins, from one whom Gladstone regarded as his closest and most intimate friend?[90] Or was it an uncritical remark to Farr, who was Gladstone's closest friend during his early days at Eton?[91] Perhaps it indicates that both Farr and Hallam were aware of Gladstone's evangelical convictions, with which Methodism was often associated, and that they were probably aware of his religious upbringing because he discussed this with them. As religion was so important to Gladstone, he might want to write in the new magazine on some religious topic. If such a hypothesis is feasible this could imply that while in his early days Gladstone might have been reticent to speak about his religious convictions, he no longer had any such inhibitions. The suggestion that he did speak about these with his friends, especially Hallam, is supported by a statement made in his 1898 article on Hallam. Writing of their meals, walks, talks and arguments while together at Eton, the aged Gladstone observed "It is difficult for me now to conceive how during these years he bore with me; since not only was I inferior to him in knowledge and dialectic ability, but my mind was "cabined, cribbed, confined" by an intolerance which I ascribe to my having been brought up in what were then termed Evangelical ideas—ideas I must add, that in other respects were frequently productive of great and vital good."[92]

Internal evidence indicates that the diary does not record every talk discussion and debate with acquaintances, masters or friends but it does record some and imply others. A long argument with his French tutor S. Berthomier on the subject of religion is noted on 2 February 1826. Only a few days before he had had a long talk with John Carruthers, when they discussed the prophecies in the bible concerning the Millennium. The Eton Society was not immune from topics which could provoke religious discussion, and elicit personal "prejudice" or convictions. Such a topic was introduced on Saturday 4 February, when William acted as President, and the subject under consideration was

Archbishop Cranmer's character.

The evangelical school required adherents not only to witness through deeds but also to speak about their faith. It is impossible to believe that a person of Gladstone's religious calibre and zeal did not constantly seek to witness to his faith in and through everyday activities. Gladstone described Hallam as "one of those to whom it was more given . . . to *be* than to *do*." The same could have been said of him; he was in no doubt that he had to *be* a Christian and all that this implied; not just talking about his faith, but living it out. Sabbath observance was an important part of his Christian life and witness, as was regular worship. Both could prompt ridicule, but on neither could there be any compromise. Bible reading and prayer, including intercessory prayer, were an essential part of his daily life and are means through which God's grace is given to the Christian. The evangelical emphasis was pietistic and individualistic, but personal faith and salvation required witnessing to the Adorable Redeemer through word and deed. This the young Gladstone believed and sought to practice. If Hallam could write to William Farr of "the more serious business of preparing for a Confirmation which is to take place the day after tomorrow," then surely it would be right to assume that Gladstone would endeavour to discuss the implications of that sacred rite and other religious matters with his friends.

His discussions on religious topics and on the religious books he had read are unlikely to have been confined to Hallam. Reference to talks, conversations and arguments are scattered throughout his diary during this period but rarely, apart from Society debates, does he give any indication of the topics discussed. It is unrealistic to believe that, when Gladstone had a long conversation with Handley on Sunday 13 November 1825, and in the many conversations with others, that Christian belief and practice were never discussed. Those religious "themes" which occasionally occupied his time and pen on a Sunday, such as that on "principles of a holy life" on Sunday 19 February 1826, must have occasionally been topics of conversation. Were the scrapbooks in which he recorded his sacred poetry, on which he often worked on Sundays, put away when his friends arrived and never discussed? No definite answers can be given to such questions and speculations, but a negative answer is open to objection. When he noted in his diary that he would pay for the schooling of W. Digges, a poor Merseyside child,[93] he was simply referring to one part of his Christian life, namely his charitable work, regarded as a fundamental part of evangelical witness.

Offering a subscription for the relief of distressed weavers in manufac-
turing districts, as proposed at the Society in May 1826, which received
unanimous support, was a corporate charitable activity.

Visiting the aged, the infirm, the poor and the lonely were essential elements of evangelical piety. While there is little evidence to
show that at this stage Gladstone sought to fulfill his Saviour's teaching
on this point it was not altogether unheeded, for he records that on 7
January 1826 he visited old Jimie Wood.

Practicing hospitality was part of his Christian life, but entertaining school friends could hardly be looked upon as offering Christian hospitality. However, on the morning of 25 January 1827 Gladstone had Edward Robertson and William McKay, a new boy, to
breakfast. A few days later Hallam wrote to Farr "Our friend Gladstone
seems to find a congenial atmosphere in the 6th Form, & is dignified
towards lower boys; a species of rigour which is nowadays most rare,
as the inferiors are more presuming, & the superiors more lax than I
ever remember."[94] These are examples of his Christian friendship and
hospitality towards the young and supposedly inferior boys, regarded
by most older Etonians merely as fags or objects of derision and bullying. He wrote of his first fag James H. Trevelyan "my fags began on
Monday; answered very well indeed." Aware of the ill-treatment and
bullying often meted out to Eton fags Gladstone would base the treatment of his fag on Christian principles. Perhaps his treatment in this
area was partly due to the wise counselling of others. "Keate put me
into the sixth form, told me to take pains &c. be careful in using my authority." Checkland states, it was at Eton he came to believe that those
in authority over him were not always right, nor always to be followed,
or even to be obeyed. But for Gladstone, believing that parents had a
God-given authority over their children, such liberated views would not
extend to parents, especially his father. It was, says Checkland here that
he learned that in contrast to the moral absolutes of his home, boys and
men lived not as individuals in direct converse with God, but as members of sub-cultures each with its own rules and conventions that were
implicit, subtle and cruel.[95]

The will of God, providence, divine and parental authority, a
right use of the gifts of time, and man's final accountability to God for
the use of his life and his obedience to the divine will all had to be considered at this time, and in the future, as William pondered on God's

will for his own life and his future profession.

v. *God's Will—A Call to Ordination*

Most previous writers on Gladstone suggest that he first gave serious thought to the possibility of entering the Church or, more correctly, ordination in August 1830; a few have pushed the date back to 1828.[96] Does the date and evolution of his belief that God was calling him to the ordained ministry really matter? His feeling that God might be calling him to serve as a clergyman, rather than in law or politics, began to occupy his mind, thoughts and prayers long before 1828. This earlier preoccupation with ordination helps us to appreciate and understand the content and quantity of his "theological" reading while at Eton and later.

Prime source material now available on the subject of Gladstone's heart-searching and careful consideration of "going into the Church," or taking Orders, i.e. especially from 1828 onwards and even after he was elected the member for Newark, proves that the issue was far more important to Gladstone than has been recognised or acknowledged by many scholars and students of Gladstone. His concept of a call from God to the ordained ministry must be carefully examined in the light of what he actually believed about God and providence. Did he later come to believe that he had given way to the pressure and expectations of his father and Thomas, who anticipated a distinguished career in law or politics, and thereby denied God's call to ordination? If he realized that he had rationalised his decision to enter politics how did he come to look upon his subsequent relationship with God and his personal life, not least as the head of a Christian family? But above all, if he had failed to fulfill God's will, how did he really look upon his political career and future activities, exercised under the providence of an omnipotent and omnipresent God whose only Son, Gladstone's Blessed Redeemer, had died for the salvation of the world? Gladstone's call to ordination was much more than the aspiration of a very religious and sensitive adolescent, who was the product of a "bigoted" evangelical environment. The conquest was far more complex than a youthful searching for a satisfying and rewarding profession, or the decision faced by many wealthy Victorians whether to enter politics, the army or the church. James Hope considered the possibility of entering the church while at Eton. Later he even thought of abandoning law but eventually dropped the idea of Orders and came to believe that he was destined by providence to follow law as his profession.[97] One can only speculate on how the careers of both Gladstone and Hope might have been altered if they had known each other at Eton and been able to share such intimate thoughts, especially when Hope was being encouraged by his father to give serious thought to ordination, while Gladstone was being discouraged by his.

Ultimately the issue was about obedience to the will of God and God's purpose for the life of William Ewart Gladstone. For the Christian it is only when God's will is accepted that the believer finds the peace of which St Augustine wrote "Our hearts are restless until they rest in thee."

Gladstone fully accepted the traditional church teaching that failure to respond to God's call could jeopardize a man's salvation and lead to a life of perpetual turmoil and uncertainty. Therefore he recognised the vital importance of seeking to know God's purpose for his life and future profession, and his thoughts turned to the subject of the possibility of ordination at an early age. The seed was sown long before 1828 and was to affect the whole of his life and his commitment to serve God and His Church.

On 3 November 1824 he acknowledged receipt of a letter from his father and one from Tom.[98] Tom's letter was about William's future entrance into Christ Church. William explained that the delay in his replying was "because I knew that in case any objection should occur to me, you would kindly take it into consideration . . . From the faint idea which I am enabled to form of my future profession, I should suppose (am I right?) that it was of consequence to me to begin the study of the law as early as possible." The "faint idea" of a possible future profession is an understatement; his father had great expectations for his gifted son and those expectations always laid heavy on William. He wanted him to pursue law as a profession and believed that he ought to begin his study as soon as possible. If Gladstone had raised any objections with his father about studying law, would he have "kindly taken it into consideration?" William raised no objections, not because he had none to offer, but possibly because he was unwilling to face the consequences of so doing. Perhaps he ought to have been honest and told his father of the uncertainties which seem to have been in his mind and which found expression in religious verse written on 22 October 1824, twelve days before his father's letter:

> My Father calls, and shall I stay?
> And shall I doubt, to choose
> Twixt Virtue's path and Vice's way?
> Or man, or God to lose?

He goes on to write of the Christian's fight against vice and concludes:

> He fights not, save in Jesus' fight,
> He fights and conquers too.
> My Father calls: I hear, I hear it,
> He calls, how should I stay?
> I'll come, and aided by thy Spirit
> I'll seek thy Holy Way.[99]

Whether the young Gladstone had an inner feeling at this stage that God was calling him to be a clergyman is uncertain, although this may have been the case. What can be said without any qualification is that he had a sense of God's call, that God had a definite purpose for his life and that he must seek to discover and fulfill that purpose. Similar sentiments were expressed, but in a much more complex way, in his later letters to his father about choosing a profession. There he speaks of the task of those called to the ordained ministry as entering into the fight against the powers of evil, sin and vice at work in the world and in man. In these verses he expresses the idea of the choice which exists of answering God's call, in the power of Christ and aided by the Holy Spirit, or giving way to the persuasive powers and the appeal of vice, or of the world, or perhaps the pressures and expectations of others.

At Eton and throughout his life he was convinced that in the day-to-day issues of life he, and all Christians, stood in constant need of God's help and guidance. He writes "prepared to start in the old routine on Monday, please God—who I trust will be my guide and my defender."[100]

Gladstone left Eton on Sunday 2 December 1827 with a heavy heart and full of melancholy, but determined to fulfill God's will for his life and "to seek humbly, penitently, constantly, eagerly, after an eternal happiness which never fades or vanishes."[101]During the months of preparation between Eton and Oxford his thoughts often turned to the question of ordination. Would this alone offer the way to eternal happiness which never fades or vanishes?

While engaged in his detailed study of baptismal regeneration the question of ordination never seemed far from his mind. He wrote "Every man, it appears to me, whose mind has been in any way accustomed to contemplate the prospect of labouring as a Minister in the vineyard of Christ, must feel the immense importance of using every means which may conduce to settle his opinions on the question of Baptismal Regeneration."[102] Perhaps this reflection in 1828 was autobiographical, in that he felt the need to clarify his position regarding baptismal regeneration before going further with the possibility of Orders. Having clarified his doctrinal position on the subject of baptism he was left in a position of doubt, indeed a dilemma, in that he was still uncertain about God's will and the question of ordination.

CHAPTER FIVE

A PERIOD OF PREPARATION AND SEARCHING

Ten months were to elapse between Eton and Oxford, covering the period 3 December 1827 to 10 October 1828. Events during this time were to influence some of William's religious ideas. His inner searching to know God's will concerning his future continued and remained with him. December was spent at Seaforth, providing him with many opportunities for long conversations with Anne, of whom he wrote, "The more one sees the more one *must* admire." Her birthday was celebrated on Monday 24 December, "Let us thank God for the good gift which he has bestowed upon her of a true & fervent Christian spirit & heart." Five days later, on his own birthday, he mourns his misused time, neglected opportunities, no great improvement in his life, idleness in temporal responsibilities and neglect in spiritual duties. His earnest prayer was that God would give both the time and the grace to live a better life. His diary entries this month reflect an endless round of activities. He introduced a new approach to his daily bible study, including making notes and marginal references in his new interleaved bible, resolving that this would be his future practice, "May God guide and enlighten me in studying it."

Wide reading occupied most of his time during this brief respite. It began after his return to Liverpool with Sir Walter Scott's *Chronicles of Canongate,* two days later he started a life of Paley, on that same Sunday he read a pamphlet defending the Bible Society, and a sermon aloud from John Eyton's two volumes of *Sermons on various Subjects* (1815). Both volumes of Scott's *Chronicles of Canongate* were completed after five days, when he turned to *Don Quixote,* having obtained the fourth volume. Further reading included Samuel Hay, *Some accounts of the Personal Religion of Margaret Gray,* T. J. Graham,

Sure Methods of Improving Health and Prolonging Life, Walter Scott., *Tales of a Grandfather,* S. Lowell, *Reasons for Dissent* (1825) Homer, Euclid, Cicero and the Greek Testament. Periodicals included the *Edinburgh Review,* the *Guardian,* the *Christian Observer,* the *Quarterly* and the *British Review.* At his father's request he wrote to Oxford seeking advice on the subject of his "Oxford reading." A letter from Samuel Smith, the Dean of Christ Church, prompted him to write "I am I believe to matriculate next term." Ten days later he packed his books. The reading achieved in just over forty days, among the festivities of Christmas and a host of other activities, hardly indicates the idleness of which he accused himself.

Travelling through the night of 21 January he arrived at Oxford at 2 p.m. the following day, where he matriculated and subscribed to the Thirty-nine Articles. Eton had provided him with a good educational and social grounding; there he had held his own with his peers and through hard work demonstrated that he was a young man with notable academic ability and a bright future. Reflecting on his life fifty years later Mr Gladstone wrote, "The desire of my youth was to be a clergyman. My mental life (ill represented in the moral being) was concentrated in the Church: in the Church understood after the narrowest fashion, that of the Evangelical school, whose bigotry I shared but whose fervour if it possessed me at all possessed me only by fits and starts."[1]

Before, during and after the cramming period for Oxford William was earnestly seeking an answer to the question was it God's will that he enter the Church and serve his Redeemer as a clergyman, following in the footsteps of such men as George Herbert? Did his inner peace and eternal destiny depend upon his acceptance of ordination? Within his family there were two factions: his mother and sisters encouraged his aspirations for ordination, his father and brothers, especially Tom, had other plans and ambitions for him which did not include the church. These radical differences of opinion within the family did not help. During the period January to October 1828 people and events beyond his family began to influence his thinking about his future profession.

Now a mature young man, of considerable intelligence and outstanding ability, and a little ambition, he sought through prayer, bible study, thinking and extensive reading, to inform himself on what he regarded as the major issues of life and topics of fundamental impor-

tance, especially in the fields of theology and politics. Periods of prolonged separation from his parents, while at Eton, made him increasingly independent and forced him to formulate his own opinions on
many issues. As a dutiful son he was mindful of the deference he must
pay to those in authority over him, notably parental authority, and their
intentions for his life and future profession. But what should he do
when the house was divided against itself? This short but important period leading up to Oxford can be divided into three parts, each of which
brought new pressures to bear concerning the future and the purpose of
providence for his life.

On the evening of Thursday 24 January Gladstone arrived at
Wilmslow Rectory, the home of the Reverend and Mrs John M. Turner,
to begin his cramming. The next day he unpacked his books and met
Mr Turner who decided upon his future reading and set out the daily
timetable— breakfast at 9, lunch at 1, dinner at 5, tea at 8, supper at 10.
William noted , "Plenty of food, at any rate." That night he got down to
reading his Greek Testament with bible "endeavouring to work at it
with my interleaved copy." His diary entry the next day was to be typical of the cramming procedure in the coming months, "Read Testament— Homer, beginning (Il(iad) 1—Cicero—beginning de Officiis—
& Euclid's Definitions c. & 15 propositions & did them with Mr Turner . . . Began Prior's Burke, putting down some chief facts. Read
paper—made an inventory &c. Long walk." This entry supports the
conclusion that William did not record every normal or regular event.

For the following day, Sunday 27, he noted "We have family
prayers & reading every morning (save Sunday) & every evening."
This corporate act of prayer and bible reading constituted an essential
and invariable part of the Turners' daily discipline, but was not previously or subsequently recorded in the diary. The following day he did
nothing but Testament with Mr. Turner and that evening he "learned
Greek Testament." During the day he managed to visit the parish priest
of Macclesfield and also some local factories. Two others were cramming at Wilmslow Rectory, Charles Alexander Wood, an Etonian, and
Horatio Powys, later bishop of Sodor and Man. Powys, four years older than Gladstone, had already obtained his degree at St. John's College, Cambridge and was preparing for ordination later that year.[2] The
three young men had time to spare and, among other things, resorted to
gymnastics as a time-killing and body-strengthening exercise. One

might wonder if during this free time William shared his inner feelings about possible ordination with the twenty-two year old Horatio Powys. Horatio taught William how to turn wood which was something to enjoy and became, at this period, almost a daily activity. They walked and talked together regularly, including Sundays. Charles Wood was often their companion, but there is never a word in the diary about discussions on religious topics with Powys, possibly because they became a regular and normal event. The Rector had given him a copy of his *Six discourses on the Evils of Unbelief*, read on his first Sunday when he also began T. Gisborne, *Familiar Survey of the Christian Religion* (1799). A week later he received the Sacrament, there were about 20 communicants and this was his only attendance at church that day.

Gladstone took with him his "Private Account Book" dated 1826—1830,[3] which provides valuable insight into the nature and extent of his charitable activities as a teenager and young man. That day he noted in his book "Sacrament 2/6." In 1888 he wrote "N.B. at about thirty years old I gave up keeping my accounts in detail, thinking that the advantage of the practice lies in the mental habit, which shall by that time have been attained." The first charitable entry in this book is dated 12 October 1827. "Poor man 6d; a man in distress 1/-, gave a poor black 6d." On Saturday 1 December we have "poor woman 1/-" on another occasion a "poor woman ld." None of these charitable activities is recorded in the diary, nor are the entries for November 24 and 27, which were hardly charitable, "A bet to Lydle 2/6" and "A bet to Nichols 1/-." We are not told what the bets were about, but his diary on 24 November does record that that night he played both chess and cards. His giving at the Sacrament finds a regular entry throughout, although the amounts vary—6d., 1/-, 2/-, 2/6. Giving to various societies is recorded, including the Christian Knowledge Society, Society for the Propagation of the Gospel, Church Missionary Society, Jewish Society and the Bible Society, which all received £1.1/-. Books purchased are listed, including Mant's Tracts at 6d and the same amount was given to a poor box.

Contact with the rector and with parish life must have had some influence upon Gladstone. He worked under Mr. Turner almost daily on New Testament Greek, classical studies and mathematics. On Sunday 2 March he noted that there were few communicants, but Mr. Turner "preached well on the Lord's Supper"; the forenoon service was "dismal." "May God make it otherwise." Perhaps he thought his prayers had been answered when the following Sunday "Mr T preached very well . . . congregation better than I have yet seen it." A week later "Mr Turner preached well and boldly in afternoon on the state of religion in the parish." A prospective curate from Liverpool visited the parish and William observed "he seems a good & agreeable man." Good Friday "scantily observed in this country, it appears & by myself too." Easter Day was his last Sunday in the parish, when there were upwards of 40 communicants, "an improvement." Pastoral work was only mentioned once when he walked with the rector on his visits to the poor. At the rectory and socially he met a variety of clergymen. From Wilmslow he continued correspondence with his family, but his future career was never mentioned.

Among the books and other literature read during this period were religious periodicals, Parliamentary debates, poems, plays and pamphlets, including an anonymous one *Plain and Short Instructions on the Sacrament* and a published letter by Mr. Turner on the Catholic Question. Books included Robert Hall's sermons on *Modern Infidelity Considered*, the 524 pages of which constituted his sermon reading for five Sundays. Sermons by this Baptist divine included "The Advantages of Knowledge to the Lower Classes," "On the Discouragement and Supports of the Christian Minister" and letters to Baptists on the "Work of the Holy Spirit" and "On Hearing the Word." Hall undoubtedly impressed Gladstone, who later obtained all six volumes of *The Works of Robert Hall A M*. He read John Warton, *Death-bed Scenes and Pastoral Conversations*, edited by his sons and published in two volumes. In bringing out a new edition in 1828 it was felt not to be unacceptable to parish clergy, and the public in general, to bring out a third volume. The object of the first two volumes was to provide a practical manual of pastoralia for the active parish priest. Rather unusual reading for one who was thought to have laid aside the idea of being a clergyman and was supposedly preparing for a career in law or politics. On Sunday 23 March he managed to read half of the 498 pages which made up the first volume, covering Infidelity, Atheism, Despair, Parental Anger and Baptism. The book was read during three days of the following week and occupied him "pretty fully" the following Sunday and on Good Friday. On Easter Day he wrote "finished Warton." Only three topics are covered in the 534 pages of the second volume— Impatience, Religious Melancholy and Scepticism; unfortunately the books have no scorings or annotations. Gladstone's reactions to volume three, which he must have read later, and where "The Eucharist" takes up nearly 200 pages, would have provided a valuable insight into his thoughts on this sacrament which became central to his Christian life.

Halfway through his time at Wilmslow he wrote to William Farr "We have not much to do." He certainly did not feel that his cramming was stretching him. One wonders if these three young men were failing to take full advantage of the opportunity offered. A letter from Charles Wood to William on 27 August 1828 suggests that this might have been the case, certainly with Powys, to whom Turner had written, "expostulating a little on his conduct, and advising him to set to work seriously and prepare himself for entering the Church." William's time there was unexpectedly shortened as a result of Mrs. Turner's illness. For nearly three months he had lived in the rectory of a very able and devoted Anglican priest whom he could not fail to admire. Gladstone's reading and spiritual discipline during this period, coupled with first-hand observations of the life of an Anglican clergyman, must have kept the inner fire burning and left the question of God's will for his life unresolved.

On Friday 11 April he left Wilmslow by coach for Edinburgh, travelling through the night and arriving there the following day. The purpose of his visit was to spend the Easter vacation with his family. The afternoon of Low Sunday found him at the Episcopal Chapel where he had gone to hear the Reverend Edward Craig preach. His diary records that he called upon Mr. Craig daily for the next three days, but on each occasion Craig was out. Finally he was successful; on Thursday 17 April "found Mr. Craig at home—sat long with him." Persistence in trying to see Craig was the result of an introduction given to him by Mr. Turner.

Edward Craig had gone to St. James' Chapel, Broughton Place, from St. Edmund Hall, Oxford, regarded as an evangelical stronghold which encountered many difficulties and controversies from the mid-eighteenth century.[4] Craig's ministry in the Episcopal Church of Scotland was not without its problems. He attacked the Scottish Liturgy and was vehement in his rejection of baptismal regeneration, but his argument was to have the reverse effect upon Gladstone and contributed towards his move away from his inherited evangelicalism. Craig was an opponent of the British and Foreign Bible Society and actively involved in the anti-Apocryphal movement and the presentation of a resolution in 1825 to the Edinburgh Committee of the Bible Society in connection with the inclusion of the Apocrypha in bibles to be sent to the continent. An eloquent and earnest man he introduced into Edinburgh the doctrines of the English evangelical party. His views created something of a sensation and succeeded in securing a following among the episcopalians. Bishop Jolly helped to still the unrest by the publication of his learned treatise on baptismal regeneration.

Dr. Perry Butler insists that Craig had a profound influence upon Gladstone's theological development during this brief visit to Edinburgh and his conclusions have been mistakenly accepted by Richard Shannon and Colin Matthew.[5] Unfortunately this thesis has been compounded on a myth. Butler states that Gladstone "visited Craig almost daily during his six week stay at Edinburgh and attend his chapel regularly."[6] The inference is that during this time, which was in fact nearer eight weeks, William had regular discussions with Craig on theological issues. According to his diary, during his fifty-five days in Edinburgh he visited and met Craig only twelve times, on the last occasion simply to bid him farewell. This can hardly be described as a daily visit, but there were nearly as many abortive visits when Craig was out. A careful examination of the diary reveals that he undertook a wide range of social visits, and some nearly as frequent as those to Mr. Craig. There is no distinct evidence to suggest that the purpose of his visits to Craig was to engage in theological debate. Craig, who is supposed to have had such a profound effect upon Gladstone at this time, receives only a passing mention in the Autobiographica. "There was a Mr. Craig, Minister of St James' Episcopal Chapel in Edinburgh to whom I think I was introduced by Dr. Turner. He showed me active kindness and gave me a letter to Dr. Macbride at Oxford. But he shocked me much as a youth of eighteen by coolly asking me one day 'Is your father a Christian?'."[7] True the account was written sixty-six years after the event but, as the aged Gladstone remembered the comment about his father, it is rather strange that in an autobiographical account of the development of his religious opinions Craig's supposed influence is not even mentioned. A reference to "active kindness" hardly merits the suggestion of "profound theological influence."

What, if any, was Craig's influence upon the young Gladstone? His successful visits to Craig, when one assumes they talked together, amounted to three during the eighteen days of April. Of their

first meeting Gladstone says that he "sat long with him" after which
Craig gave him a tour of the city. There is no indication of the subjects
discussed. Gladstone had heard him preach four days before— but does
not record the subject of the sermon. If it had been profound or controversial, so as to warrant a long conversation, it is surprising that it is not
recorded. A visit the following day prompted the comment "sat some
time with" Craig. The next morning he went to hear Craig preach, but
again his sermon elicited no comment in the diary. There was no attempt to meet Craig until Saturday of that week, although on the Monday Gladstone had written "lazy & doing little since I came to Edinburgh." On the Thursday of that week he began to read Craig's
Respectful Remonstrance. It was two weeks before he finished this
pamphlet, although he read numerous other things in the intervening
period. Normally when Gladstone was gripped by a book or pamphlet it
was read regularly until completed. One can only speculate on why he
took so long to read this particular pamphlet. Two days after his introduction to Craig's pamphlet he "called on Mr. Craig & sat with him,"
but there is no reference to the pamphlet nor to the British and Foreign
Bible Society. The next day he heard Craig preach for the third time, recording the subject "the temple of Christ's body & resurrection." The
following Wednesday he heard the bishop of Edinburgh preach and
commented "a very good sermon." William's attempt to see Craig on
Monday 25 April was frustrated by Craig's absence. The following
Sunday morning he went to Craig's church. "Mr. Golding preached
very well on the Lord's Supper—of which I partook. God bless it to me
for Christ's sake." That afternoon he attended Dr. Robert Gordon's
church at Hope Park and noted "he is a very able preacher—on Christ
as suffering Redeemer."

   That day, ten days after reading part of Craig's *Respectful Remonstrance*, Gladstone read the section on the Sacraments in Isaac Barrow's *A Brief Exposition of the Lord's Prayer and the Decalogue: to
which is added The Doctrine of the Sacraments*. What this former Master of Trinity College Cambridge had to say on the subject of baptism
must have made Gladstone think again about Craig's views on this sacrament. Barrow clearly expounds the benefits of baptism, the purgation
from guilt and cleansing from sin, including children, thus applicable to
the baptism of infants. The gift of the Holy Spirit is conferred and with
this gift comes regeneration, "implying our entrance into a new state
and course of life: being endowed with new facilities, disposition, and

capacities of soul, becoming new men, as it were, *renewed after the likeness* of God." He concludes that with these benefits "is conjoined that of being inserted into God's Church, his family . . . there is with Baptism conferred a capacity of, a title unto, an assurance. . . of eternal life and salvation," adding that with the benefits come important duties including conforming our lives to His will. Barrow's views on baptism were very different from Craig's.

Gladstone then read part two on the Eucharist which, writes Barrow, is intended to Commemorate our Saviour's Passion, participators are fed with holy food and united with Christ. Those who approach the Lord's Table must examine themselves and consider what they are about to do, that through this sacrament they may grow in grace.

On Sunday 11 May William went to St. Paul's in the morning and St. George's in the afternoon, on both occasions noting the subject of the sermon. His worship in the Church of Scotland during this brief visit to Edinburgh may have been prompted by notable preachers, rather than the belief that it was the established church. Episcopalian churches attended were those characteristic of English churches; none were of the non-juring tradition with a "high" eucharistic doctrine and certainly did not represent the native Scottish Episcopacy. Over two weeks elapsed and Gladstone noted in his diary "Called on Jas Moncrieff & Mr.. Craig." He heard Craig preach the following Sunday and in the afternoon went to St. George's.

During his last 18 days in Edinburgh William heard Craig preach twice, recording the subject, but refrains from any comments. Eight meetings took place in the remaining busy days. Three occasions are simply noted "called on Mr. Craig." He dined with him three times, once recording "sat with him some time. He has treated me with great kindness," but adds "as have the Hagarts & others." After dining one evening they went to a prayer meeting of communicants, then spending the evening together. Tea and a walk made up another meeting and the final one was to bid him goodbye. This is the sum total of Gladstone's recorded contact with Edward Craig and there is nothing here to suggest that this controversial and extreme "Calvinistic evangelical" had any profound influence on Gladstone. True he heard him preach more often than anyone else, but is very reserved in his comments on his sermons, though not about others. Thus it is difficult to say that William was influenced by his preaching.

On his last Sunday he noted "Read . . . Mr. Craig's *Christian Circumspection.*" Had this been given to him the previous week, when he dined with Craig, noting his kindness? Three weeks before he finished, after two weeks, Craig's 41 page pamphlet *A Respectful Remonstrance, addressed to the Rev. James Walker. M.A. senior minister of St. Peter's Chapel; on the subject of a Sermon preached before the Bishop and Clergy of the united diocese of Edinburgh. Fife, and Glasgow in St. John's on the 22nd June. 1825.* This copy has been preserved in Gladstone's bound pamphlet collection under "Theological Tracts— Controversy." It has a few scorings, question marks, signs and notes on the back sheet. The full title shows that the editor of volume one of the Gladstone *Diaries* is incorrect when in a footnote on this pamphlet he notes "A pamphlet on his dispute with the local bible society." It was a dispute with a fellow clergyman described as "our newly appointed Theological Professor." Craig's sole object in the pamphlet is "to deal with . . . a fearfully, unsound and delusive statement . . . respecting Baptism." Walker was no mean opponent, the following year he received his D.D. and in 1830 became bishop of Edinburgh and professor in the Scottish Episcopalian College, in 1837 Primus of Scotland. Craig's controversy with Walker was a fight in the "cause of true religion." Walker, he claims, states that Christ has conferred upon the Apostles and their successors the power to administer the means of grace, Baptism and the Supper of the Lord "that by these two sacraments, to the exclusion of preaching, the Christian life is conferred, formed, fed, and brought to maturity." He attacks Walker's classical Anglican belief that "Baptism confers spiritual life, so a baptized infant is a spiritual child of God." We are to believe, without any proof, that "Baptism lays the foundation of the Christian life in repentance, faith and obedience." He rejects the belief that "in every case in which Christian baptism is applied by an Episcopal minister, it is regeneration, or a change of the individual by spiritual conversion . . . a man may always look back and believe . . . that then because he was baptized he was regenerated." What Craig is rejecting is the doctrine of baptismal regeneration, seeking to establish his objections that such a doctrine "is not the doctrine of the Bible," nor "the doctrine of the Church of England." To prove his first objection he marshals a mass of biblical evidence.

Turning to the doctrines of the Church of England, Craig declares the church never asserts that "baptism is regeneration"; neither

the Articles nor the baptismal service state such a doctrine. Scripture
and the church, he argues, separate baptism and regeneration. The offices of the church, including the baptismal office, were written for believing members, but the situation has changed and "a deluge of unfit
partakers of these sacraments" have poured into the church. "I still
maintain the propriety of our baptismal office, for all those who come
to it in sincerity and faith; that is, for the individual for whom it was
written, and to whom, by the appointed discipline, it was limited. The
believing church is still a separate body, though indiscriminately mixed
up externally with the world of formalists and unbelievers." Gladstone
at some stage scored this passage and placed a question mark in the
margin. Craig may have vehemently denied the doctrine of baptismal
regeneration, but not all members of the evangelical party did, although
since the publication of Richard Mant's *Appeal to the Gospel* in 1812 a
denial of baptismal regeneration had become for many in that party a
sign of their orthodoxy. At this stage Gladstone had no informed opinion on this doctrine. Contact with Craig offers no evidence to suggest
that he discussed his pamphlet with him, although he may have done
so. What we do know is that later Gladstone raised this topic with
Anne, both in conversations and in correspondence. Two days after
starting *Respectful Remonstrance* he went to see Craig and sat with
him, but the following day he "sat a good many hours in conversation
with Anne" and probably discussed with her Craig's extreme Calvinism
and baptismal regeneration, a subject which was to be crucial in his
spiritual pilgrimage.

Dr. Butler notes that Gladstone re-read Craig's pamphlet on
his return to Liverpool and the reply to it by Dr. Walker and that this
stimulated him to undertake a thorough investigation on the question
and that he began assembling the opinions of Anglican authors on the
subject in order to reach a definite conclusion.[8] The diary entry for 29
June records "began a book of Opinions of Eminent Divines." But it
does not state that he re-read Craig, but simply, "looked over again Mr.
Craig's *Respectful Remonstrance*." When Gladstone began his work of
drawing together the "Opinions of Eminent Divines" on baptism and
fasting, was it to confirm and substantiate a position which he now
held, or was moving towards, rather than to disprove Craig's position?
What Butler fails to mention is that five days after returning to Liverpool Gladstone read in full the sermon preached by James Walker

which had first prompted Craig's pamphlet. The full title of Dr. Walker's sermon is interesting: *The Gospel Commission—its Import —its Obligation and its Influence in the Commencement and Conduct of the Christian Life: Considered in a Sermon preached in St. John's Episcopal Chapel . . . Wednesday. June 22, 1825.*"[9] The following Sunday he wrote "read the Notes on Dr. Walker's Sermon." Published in Edinburgh in 1826, the 31 pages of this sermon are followed by 28 pages of notes. It was the following Sunday that he looked over Craig again and then read Dr. Walker's *Serious Expostulation*, a 35 paged reply to Craig's sermon. Gladstone then began Craig's reply to Dr. Walker covering 68 pages of small type. That day he had a conversation with Anne. And so he began to draw together a collection of Opinions of Eminent Divines. But was it his conversations with Craig, and Craig's supposed influence upon him while at Edinburgh, or his reading of all four pamphlets and other literature, or the encouragement of Anne which moved him to pursue a course of searching and reading on the subject of baptismal regeneration, which was to influence both his churchmanship and also his consideration of Ordination?[10]

His later record of his early religious opinions[11] states that a breach was made in his inherited ideas in 1828 when he spent much time with Anne, who started him on some devious bypaths of opinion, not Edward Craig. He then wrote "Whereas baptismal regeneration had of course been registered as a heresy in my mind, I fell upon an article in the *Quarterly Review* which appeared to deduce all manner of patristic testimonies in its favour. I was not at all prepared to stand fire of this description: in the question what was true Christianity I could not but suppose that these Fathers must have known something about it. But what struck me most was that St. Augustine was included among the witnesses: for I had always heard of him as a truly Evangelical Christian." In another autobiographical fragment Gladstone reflected on how Anne had increased his mental interest in religion through their contact in 1828. She was, he noted, generally of evangelical sentiments and was of the opinion that the standard divines of the English Church were of great value. He also refers to his study of Hooker's *Ecclesiastical Polity* read at that period "But I think that I found the doctrines of baptismal regeneration, theretofore abhorred, impossible to reject and the way was thus opened for further changes."[12]

Gladstone read the article on baptismal regeneration in the

Quarterly Review during the course of the three days following his start on collecting together the opinions of various eminent divines on the subject.[13] On the first day he copied out the opinions of Jewel and Hammond, the next day Bradford and Hooker. This work continued until at least the 24 August, and was added to later. During the same period he read a number of related publications including S. Bradford, *Discourse concerning Baptismal and Spiritual Regeneration* (1709) Richard Mant's two tracts on Regeneration and Conversion, Bishop Thomas Wilson *The Lord's Supper,* and S. C. Wilks *On the Signs of Conversion and Unconversion in Ministers of the Church* (1814).

Whatever first prompted Gladstone's analytical study of baptismal regeneration, at this crucial stage of his spiritual pilgrimage, his acceptance of the doctrine and all it involved led to a rejection of the evangelical position held by his parents.

On 24 August 1828 he wrote to Helen informing her of his acceptance of baptismal regeneration. Thirty-five years later, in 1864, Gladstone wrote a note "This was a mark of my boyhood as I wrought my way towards sound belief in which the Divine Mercy has kept me. Trained in the idea that the Sacraments of Christ were no more than signs of that which they truly signify, I was utterly shaken out of it by the perusal of the Holy Scriptures and then fearful lest I should be erring I sought to prop myself with testimony. This is my distant but I think substantially accurate recollection. I may add that at the time of making these extracts (i.e. on baptismal regeneration) I had no conception whatsoever of the Church as a divine polity, the Kingdom of God upon earth."[14] General reading at this time included P. A.Valpy, *Greek New Testament with English Notes, Critical, Philological and Explanatory,* S. Knight, *Forms of Prayer, for the Use of Christian Families,* and Isaac Barrow, *Brief Exposition of the Lord's Prayer and Decalogue, A Discourse on the Objects, Advantages and Pleasures of Science,* a life of Wolsey, an anti-Romanist novel and Parliamentary debates on the Catholic Question and a pamphlet on Catholic Relief, a work on Natural Philosophy and a number of periodicals. His cramming was very limited apart from work on his Algebra. On 23 June he wrote "made up my list of books read for three months—very unsatisfactory."

He declined invitations to the theatre and a concert, perhaps due to Anne's presence and influence. His daily contact with her during this period, their long conversations, sometimes after his meeting with Craig, their joint devotional exercises were all treasured moments to her greatest admirer. But despite this and his regular readings and wide-ranging social and other visits, and the fact that he was on vacation with his family, William cannot help condemning himself once again for the misuse of his time.

Was this period at Edinburgh, which came to an end on Friday 6 June, quite as important as Dr. Butler states when he wrote concerning Gladstone's contact with Edward Craig, that he "was to have an important influence on the course his religious development would take at Oxford, which made this short period between school and university more significant than might have been expected." Butler also claims that Craig's attack on the British and Foreign Bible Society's policy of including the Apocrypha in bibles to be sent to the continent led to Gladstone's resignation from the Bible Society. The evidence for this conclusion is not found in the diary. On Tuesday 20 May Gladstone began to read "part of a 'Statement' in favour of Bible Society by Editor Corresponding Board" and finished it the following day. But this is the only reference to the Bible Society. Over two months later, while at Seaforth, he wrote to William Rawson who replied thanking him for his present of a copy of Dr. Sumner's Sermons and adding "I shall dispose of your subscription as you desire, but not without considerable regrets that you withdraw from the Bible Society,[15] especially as the Society had ceased to circulate the Apocrypha. Whether Craig's strong opposition to the Society on this point contributed towards Gladstone's decision seems to be a matter of speculation. On the basis of the available evidence it is impossible to be dogmatic regarding the extent of Craig's influence on the eighteen year old William as he grappled with what he felt was the most important issue of his life "What was God's will for his life?"

Before his final period of cramming Gladstone spent nearly two months with his family at Seaforth and at Leamington. His immediate task on reaching home was to unpack and move his books to the "large upper wing room . . . now to be my domicile." With Edinburgh behind him he felt he must exercise a more careful stewardship of his time. For a short period he records daily his time of rising, but it lasted only ten days and was normally between 6:30 and 7:30 a.m. He noted "John's being here affords some palliation to idleness, wh wd probably have existed without, had he been absent." Academic reading did not absorb all his time. During six days he managed to read volumes two and three of Scott's *Fair Maid of Perth*. Religious literature of various kinds was always at hand. On the journey from Edinburgh he read two pamphlets by Hannah More and Craig's *Foundation of Christian Hope*; the 319 paged *Life of the Right Reverend Beilby Porteous, D.D.. Late Bishop of London* (1811) was read in one week, while Bishop Porteous, *Review of the Life and Character of the Right Rev. Dr. Thomas Secker, Late Lord Archbishop of Canterbury* (1797) was completed a few weeks later.

In spite of his commitment to study appropriate works in preparation for Oxford, reading Christian literature was not confined to Sunday. He read Josiah Thomas *An Address . . . with a Protest*, Daniel Wilson *Defence of the Church Missionary Society*, Reginald Heber *Journey through India* (1828) 2 vols. Throughout this period he was actively working on his collection of "Opinions on Baptismal Regeneration," reading Richard Mant, *Two Tracts Intended to convey Correct Notions of Regeneration and Conversion According to the Sense of Holy Scripture and of the Church of England*. A copy of these tracts, which belonged to Gladstone and which consisted of extracts from Mant's Bampton Lecture of 1812 bound with George Bugg's *Spiritual Regeneration, not necessarily connected with Baptism. In Answer to a Tract on Regeneration published by the Reverend Dr. Mant . . .* (1816) has been preserved, but unfortunately contains no annotations. It played a significant part in Gladstone's thoughts on this subject and in aligning himself with Mant he took up a position opposite to many evangelicals of his day.

All too soon Oxford dominated his thoughts, "It is now I believe nearly settled that I am to go to Oxford." He arrived there on 4 August and met the Rev. Augustus Page Saunders (1801-1878) under whom he was to cram at Cuddesdon. He wrote in his diary the following night "out at night—met a woman & had a long conversation with her. Up late Bible as usual." The next night he records "met the poor creature again, who is determined to go home." This is probably his first encounter with "fallen women" and his introduction to what he later called "rescue work."[16] On Thursday 7 August he left the Angel Inn and travelled to Cuddesdon. Saunders, who was to be one of Gladstone's tutors at Christ Church, and four years later Headmaster of Charterhouse, was acting as "vicar" in the village, or curate to the bishop of Oxford.

Once again the young and searching Gladstone found himself living in a parsonage. This was to be his final bout of cramming and the uncertainty about his future profession still remained. No doubt it had been one of the major topics discussed with Anne during their recent numerous and often long conversations. Events in the coming weeks must have kept this burning issue uppermost in his thoughts.

A fellow lodger at the vicarage was Christopher William Puller, an old Etonian. Gladstone's main occupation was to work at his mathematics and so Algebra and Trigonometry are often referred to in his diary. Classical studies were not neglected and included Homer, the Odyssey, Herodotus, Horace. Settling into his new environment was not easy; he was impatient. On his second day he wrote "As yet unsettled and fidgetty." Perhaps he regarded his fishing with Puller that day and with a large party the following afternoon as a misuse of his time. Sunday he is "still unsettled" and wrote "Altogether a Sunday but little employed, and that little but ill."

He tried to discipline himself and decided on early rising on the first day "Up 1/2 past 6. Read an Ode of Horace." "Past seven the next morning and on the third day 1/4 past 7. Bad," but the next morning it was to be 6.20. The day following, Sunday, he wrote "Redeem thy misspent moments past. Not up to near 8." As usual he criticises himself for late rising and never commends himself for early rising. It was a battle he could not win.

Teaching at Sunday School was undertaken on his first Sunday and became a regular Sunday activity at Cuddesdon, both morning and afternoon; otherwise his Sundays were spent according to his now established pattern. Reading included Reginald Heber *Hymns written and adapted to the Weekly Church Service of the Year* (1827), Bishop Thomas Burgess, *First Principles of Christian Knowledge* (1804), Robert Gray *A Serious Address to Seceders and Sectarists* (1812). A few tracts, at least two biographies, the *Record*, *The Letters* of Thomas Gray, Edward Craig's *Reply* and Sermons and other publications formed a part of his regular Sunday reading until his last Sunday at Cuddesdon. William Paley's *Natural Theology* (1802) was started on 10 September and finished on 21st having been read almost daily during the intervening period, Gladstone's only comment being "Finished Natural Theology."

In spite of his systematic cramming Gladstone did not neglect his religious reading, though he did less than previously. Cuddesdon was not all work, he had regular meetings with a wide range of people, some of whom received a passing mention in the diary—Saturday 23 August "Mr. Newman of Oriel, dined here." "An excellent sermon from Mr. Pusey." Charles Lloyd, the bishop of Oxford, "preached a powerful sermon." Numerous clergy called to see Saunders and William met many of them. The "giraffe" or piano was a regular pastime, walking another, including a walk beyond Nuneham which was a nostalgic event "It is a pleasure to me even to walk on the road which leads to Eton, as renewing associations of memory & connection in imagination."

Newspapers from home were read regularly, but on learning that twopence was being charged to deliver newspapers to him at Cuddesdon he wrote to his father "I beg you to limit your bounty in the supply of newspapers a little, & not to send them unless there happens to be something particular in them."[17] To Anne he wrote about the *Record* "as being in new hands. I suppose we have yet to learn its principles" and then informs her "the name of the author of Xn Year is Keble."[18]

The day after Saunders left Cuddesdon in haste to see his ailing mother William wrote to Anne, "It is impossible not to feel much for one who is so kind, liberal & warm hearted to all around him."[19] He obviously had a great admiration for this scholar-priest.

Cramming came to an end, but not his friendship with Saunders. The diary entry for Friday 10 October 1828 records "went to Oxford . . . got put into my rooms . . . Slept in Ch Ch."

CHAPTER SIX

THE EVOLUTION OF A CHURCHMAN

The ideal position at which to consider the question of "God's Will: Church or Politics?" is immediately after the Oxford period, but where is it best to evaluate the evolution of Gladstone's churchmanship? A number of factors suggest that this is the most appropriate place, for while his churchmanahip influenced his understanding of God's will for his life and his consideration of ordination, these are, in many ways, two separate issues.

From leaving his home to go to Eton in 1821 to taking up residence at Oxford in 1828 William had undergone considerable spiritual growth and changes in some of his theological ideas. With his acceptance of baptismal regeneration there was a notable shift in his churchmanship and a quickening in the evolutionary process. Placed at this point this chapter acts as a bridge between the formative years of spiritual growth at Eton and what is to evolve at Oxford, helping to determine, in the analysis of his religious life at Oxford, those issues which contributed towards his evolution as a churchman. On his first morning at Oxford he attended Chapel, going there twice on his first Sunday and to St. Mary's in the afternoon. That day he wrote "At Staniforth's rooms at lunch and in Evening to wine and dine him—but did not suit me." Such social activities were not acceptable on the sabbath, a day to be devoted to pursuits conducive to spiritual growth. William soon found that there were many things at Oxford which were unacceptable, and a cause for sorrow and spiritual concern.

i.. *The State of Religion in Oxford*

While very few undergraduates in Gladstone's time can have felt as he did about the deplorable state of religion at Oxford, some must have recognised the need for improvement. A few months after his arrival he wrote eight pages on the state of religion in Oxford.[1] Gladstone believed it to be an objective account of the situation in which he found himself, and in which he was to be engaged in spiritual combat. What he saw and felt about the state of religion in this ancient university city undoubtedly influenced his desire to serve God and in so doing save others.

He received distressing and melancholy reports about Anne's condition. The news of her death on 19 February reached him on Saturday 21st; he left for Seaforth immediately. The next day he wrote "Blessed and praised be God's Holy name for thus calling to Himself first from among us one who was so well prepared, so thoroughly refined, so weaned from earth, so ripe for Heaven." His phrase "so ripe for Heaven" suggests he still retained his evangelical belief in assurance, at least for others.

Gladstone's recurring desire to offer himself for ordination was not, as Shannon postulates,[2] a post-bereavement reaction at the death of his sainted sister. He had long felt such a call and it was a possibility he had discussed with Anne. But the call to ordination, if it was genuine, was from God and of this Gladstone had little doubt; it was certainly not something implanted by his older sister and a promise he felt he ought to fulfill in honour of her sacred name. Gladstone's understanding of God's will and providence, even at this early stage, was too profound to make such a mistake. At the same time the advice and encouragement of his spiritual mentor profoundly influenced him, and was certainly in his mind when he wrote about the spiritual state of Oxford a month after Anne's death.

"A paper on Oxford &," is how his diary describes this account which begins "The state of religion in Oxford is the most painful spectacle it ever fell to my lot to behold." The paper is about the godlessness of the University, but at the same time it is an account of Gladstone's religious introspection as he tries to live out his own Christian life in this alien and hostile environment. Behind much of what he writes is his unanswered question whether or not he should be preparing himself for the service of God through ordination. Here he is reflecting on his first six months at Oxford. What was Gladstone's assessment of the religious state of this university at that time? It was a place well suited for the preparation of clergymen. "Here is a seminary for furnishing with ministers a reformed and Apostolic Church." Dedicated to the honour and service of God "there are no spiritual, no intellectual, no physical advantages, which Oxford does not seem to possess"; nevertheless "Here, irreligion is the rule: religion is the exception."

He mourns the lack of unity among the Christians at Oxford, "between supporters of what are called High and Low Church principles." There are a few with a warm attachment to the Church of England who have "a piety, wide, fervent and consistent: but oh! how few." More numerous is a second class, whose zeal appears to outstrip discretion." These are full of predestination and regeneration "understood in a sense believed by others to be erroneous." But the others are considered as outcasts and so discord and suspicion ensue and those seeking to serve God are divided. Nevertheless, he sees those whose doctrines are erroneous as having utterly renounced "earthly ambition and pleasure, swearing, lusts, drunkenness, idleness, envy, slandering, malice, disobedience, vainglory, and *self-dependence*." Gladstone asks, "Who . . . shall dare to say of such men—even granting that they do hold erroneous doctrines . . . (and) do lay too great a stress on these doctrines . . . and do betray uncharitableness *occasionally* towards their brethren, that they are not within the fold of Christ." Here we see the development of a Gladstone who was tolerant even towards those whose views were unacceptable.

Another group existed in Oxford, "the younger members" some "who have a sincere but not a consistent respect for religion." "There may be some who like the poor worm that writes are made up of a compound of this and every other absurdity." What follows is obviously autobiographical: "Such feel at times as though they could really bear the cross of Christ before the face of men, they wish, or persuade themselves they wish, to spend and be spent in His service, to maintain His honour, to bear His reproach, to adhere manfully to the truth of God." Reflecting upon his own experience he wrote, "Then comes the deadening and debasing influence of everyday pursuits and pleasures. Learning, power, distinction . . . how often have I my interest . . . in my heart, but the door barred against God." Christianity in many cases, has not produced much practical effect on the heart and life; *favourite* lusts are not abandoned." Fault finding, hypocrisy and lukewarmness, serving God out of fear rather than love are all found in such professors of Christianity, along which he numbers himself. Perhaps he was pondering on a call to ordination when he cried out "God take away . . .

my own waverings and vacillating resolutions, and place in their stead a permanent and habitual sense of thy presence; a lively . . . faith and may I walk in the footsteps of my beloved sister: my once suffering, but now glorified sister." But he must also do his duty to his parents, brothers and remaining sister; he prays that they may each fulfill their calling.

While the life of the University left much to be desired, those who professed the name of Christ were not without blame. Gladstone believed that God was calling men in Oxford to serve him in redeeming others both there and within his church. The implication is that he was among that number but needed to commit himself without reserve, abandoning the glory and success of this world that he might serve God. This was the situation in which Gladstone was to continue his search for his own identity and clarification concerning his future. These also were the aspirations and the inner longing which were inter- woven with that search.

Two years later the state of religion in Oxford was once again on Gladstone's mind, as was God's use of him in bringing His word to others. "Had an interesting conversation with Mr. Cunningham, about the state of religion here, and his son. I like him very much. Gaskell had tea with me: had a good deal of conversation with him on religion . . . O that God in his mercy may grant that the words which proceeded from my polluted lips may be purified and enlarged and so made instru- ments of good to him."[3]

ii. *A Catholic Evangelical*

In his Autobiographica Gladstone recalled how through intro- ductions provided by the rector of Wilmslow he was thrown "into par- tial relations with the small Evangelical group at Oxford, which was for the most part Calvinistic." These Oxford evangelicals had two meeting points, St. Edmund Hall and St. Ebbe's Church; contact with this group partly held and partly repelled him, "Amidst these diverse surround- ings, and undoubtedly with a large increase of religious interest testi- fied by observances and otherwise, I continued to hold in the main mildly Evangelical opinions, without any real ideas of the Church."[4]

Saturday 15 November 1828 provided his first contact with St. Ebbe's. He was introduced to Alfred Hanbury by Henry Moncrieff, whose brother James he had met several times during his summer vacation in Edinburgh. Hanbury invited William to have wine with him at St. Mary Hall, where he met "A new party—hearers apparently of Mr. Bulteel at St. Ebbe's." The diary records what is perhaps a fictitious dialogue between "a Mr. Q" and W. E. G. Gladstone is asked if he has heard Mr. Bulteel to which he answers in the negative. He is then invited to hear Bulteel preach and judge for himself. Mr. Q. comments, "Unless I am disappointed in your name, I think you would like him." W. E. G. "In my name! Sir," to which he received the answer "Yes, Sir, in the name of your family and principles." After further inquiry he finds that Bulteel's Sunday services clash with the University Sermon and his divinity lecture and Gladstone is unwilling to miss either of these. When, after some time, he did go to St. Ebbe's it marked the beginning of an interesting period in his religious development. Devotees of this party were those whom Gladstone describes as "full of predestination and regeneration." He found their position unacceptable and had already embraced a very different stance on baptismal regeneration. Nevertheless, he was still classed by his friends as an evangelical. Gaskell wrote to his mother[5] about him, with neither malice nor conceit,[6] as an evangelical, but he was a little concerned about Gladstone's zealous preoccupation with religion. This concern was shared by Tom Gladstone.[7] In what way did William Gladstone's belief and practice differ from those of other evangelicals of the period?

Dr. Peter Toon offers the following statement of evangelical faith in the 1830's:

> An Evangelical Anglican has a strong attachment to the Protestantism of the national Church with its Articles of Religion and Prayer Book. He believes that the Bible is authoritative in matters of faith and conduct and is to be read individually and in the home as well as in church. He emphasises the doctrine of Justification by faith but with good works and a specific (holy) life-style as the proof of true faith. He claims to enjoy a personal relationship with God through Christ, the origins of which are usually traced not to sacramental grace but to a conversion experience. And he sees the primary task of the Church in terms of evangelism or missions and so emphasises preaching at home and abroad.

Dr. Toon goes on to state that under this umbrella many people, clerical and lay, male and female, Arminian and Calvinist, millenarian and non-millenarian, sheltered from, and more often than not, challenged the storms of life.[8]

Where did Gladstone fit into such a definition? He had a strong attachment to the protestantism of the national church, he claimed to have been fed upon Burnet's *Thirty-nine Articles* and accepted the *Book of Common Prayer*. The bible was his supreme authority in matters of faith and conduct. He accepted the doctrine of justification by faith and good work, and a holy life was regarded as the outward expression of faith. But while he lived in union with Christ he claimed no conversion experience. He would not accept that grace and a deepening relationship with God in Christ were not the outcome of participation in the dominical sacraments. He was strongly committed to the view that the church's task was mission and evangelism through the preaching of the gospel. Gladstone's position was thus reasonably compatible with the evangelical faith of the period, but there were certain facets he did not accept and others which he was now questioning.

Predestination, a doctrine held by many evangelicals of a more Calvinistic persuasion, including Bulteel, he found unacceptable, but he could not reject it until he had undertaken a systematic study of the subject. During the period 1829-1831 Gladstone wrote, at Oxford, a collection of "Papers . . . Chiefly Theological" which include a paper on Calvinism.[9] He argues that there are two objections against the Calvinistic hypothesis, first that it seems to make God the direct author of evil, second that if "I myself had a firm hope of salvation by the Lord Jesus Christ, looking into my own soul I should discern there such an infirmity of pollution, and depravity so much more deep and pervading, considering my opportunities than that of others . . . But beholding what the boundless mercy of God has done in Christ, you Calvinists . . . circumscribe the power of God. If he be omnipotent, can he not do what he will with his own creatures? But according to you we are to be saved not by his will but by our own."

Three pages of undated notes have been preserved on the subject of predestination, undoubtedly those which he began on 20 June 1830.[10] "Rest . . . satisfied that as the foreknowledge and the decree are simultaneous in Him so are the predestination and the faith in us—and to inquire no further—for now thou seest that it is . . . *absolutely im-*

possible that the question should be answered . . . since it goes to make *two* of things which are *essentially and therefore indivisibly one.*" Recognising the limitations of his argument Gladstone adds: "it is not pretended that the question is *solved*—no, far from it—by this reasoning—but something is done if it be shown that (it) is necessarily *insoluble*" and thus is removed into the realm of "mystery." It must be deposited in the bosom of God who has perfect knowledge, "there let it rest, and let us implore the grace of God to keep us from troubling ourselves, or from being troubled by others upon it." Gladstone had obviously been pressurized by the Bulteel party, and wanted to be free of the conflict and doubts raised by this doctrine.

The evangelical emphasis upon the need for a conversion experience, as an assurance of salvation, was something which troubled Gladstone and which he did not altogether understand. Considering the subject he quotes Matthew 18:3 "Except ye be converted . . . here something called by the name of conversion is laid down as absolutely necessary for salvation."[11] He interprets conversion to mean "neither more nor less than turning," but what did this imply? He referred to this study on 10 January 1830 "At night, wrote on conversion," perhaps it was partly stimulated by his reading of *Sermons on some of the fundamental truths of Christianity* by T. V. Short, and his long religious discussion that day with his friends Tancred and Anstice, as well as Tancred's brand of evangelicalism.

If it was necessary for salvation, where did he stand? Mrs. Gladstone believed him to have been "truly converted to God" when about ten years old[12] but he never acknowledged this experience. Perhaps it was his lack of such a conversion, coupled with the conviction that salvation, "in all cases," did not depend upon such an event, which prompted his systematic study of both conversion and baptismal regeneration. The study of conversion seems very autobiographical[13] even if objective. Baptism is the church's sacramental assurance of salvation, he had been baptized, he had turned to Christ, he had faith in the redemptive power of the blood of Christ, he used the means of grace, he continued to grow in grace, he therefore believed he was saved. To reject the necessity of conversion and to place the emphasis upon baptism was heretical to many evangelicals, but if Gladstone had had a wider knowledge of evangelicals he might not have been so concerned about his lack of a conversion experience. John Venn of C.M.S. had no such experience. Evangelicals growing up in Christian homes like Gladstone realized as they grew up that they were Christians.

The year 1830 was for Gladstone a time of theological searching and consolidation. His incessant theological reading was motivated by the desire for true knowledge, "divine learning," the conviction that on all essential issues he ought to be well-informed, the need to understand the Faith of the church in which he hoped to be ordained, and his spiritual growth. One wonders if he was also motivated by his religious insecurity and his inner need for theological stability now that he was moving away from his inherited evangelical position. Perhaps he is simply using conventional evangelical language and also expressing his own conviction when in June 1830 he wrote "Tell me not of any *cause* of salvation save the free mercy of God in the precious blood of Christ: of any instrument, save the faith that clings to his cross: of any test, save the meek and yet abiding glories of a Christian life—of purity and self-denial—of energy and zeal—of love and of peace . . . (not) forgetting that from the pierced side of Jesus together with the blood to atone, flowed forth the water of purity." He had been grappling with the insistence of some evangelicals about the instrument and test of salvation, namely predestination and conversion. These he declares are not necessary, for faith in the atoning work of Christ achieves salvation. However regularly he confessed his sinfulness, he must have recognised his own attempts to live a life of holiness, purity and self-denial. He was full of zeal, striving to live a life of love, to know that peace which God alone can give. His faith was grounded in the redemptive work of Christ. The reference to the water of purity may be an attempt to link baptism, the sacrament of salvation, with the atoning work of Christ.[14]

Like many evangelicals he was concerned not only about his own salvation, but about making the gospel known to others. A manuscript headed "What? Why? and Whither" expresses some of his feelings on this subject. "It is intended to put for the consideration of those into whose hands these lines may fall, three . . . questions on the answers to which . . . may depend our immortal soul. They are

1. What am I?
2. Why am I?
3. Whither go I?"

May God . . . send his Spirit to aid this humble attempt, to guide the
pen of the writer and to fit the heart of the reader."[15] Christ's centrality
in the salvation event is the foundation upon which Gladstone always
builds. In these simple lines he was trying to get others to consider
three crucial questions which every man must ask and answer. But such
a written challenge was not a sufficient witness to Christ; Gladstone
had to speak out for his Saviour. This he often did "Oh that the Father
of light would so order my conversation and footsteps, that others
might be led."[16]

Towards the end of his life Gladstone tried to reflect objective-
ly on the evangelicalism of his youth and on the evangelical party of
that time. Observations have been recorded in at least five sources, first
in 1843 and then over the period 1879-1896 and although fragmentary
they provide mature reflections.

The *British Quarterly Review* for July 1879 published an article by Gladstone "The Evangelical Movement; its parentage, progress
and issue" and it was later reproduced in the *Gleanings of Past Years*.[17]
He argues that the points where the evangelical school permanently differed from traditional Anglicanism, "were those of the Church, the Sacraments, and the forensic idea of justification." Evangelicals were
strong and outspoken against the "prevailing standards both of life and
preaching," their aim was to bring back the preaching of the Cross, sadly neglected in the majority of Anglican pulpits.

According to Gladstone's assessment the "Evangelical movement never became . . . dominant in England"; in both town and country its adherents were "thinly scattered." In Liverpool there had been
only one evangelical clergyman in his youth until his father introduced
two more. Neither at Eton nor at any other principal public school was
there "any trace of the religious influence of the Evangelical party." In
Cambridge the movement grew under the energy and influence of Mr.
Simeon.

At Oxford in the 1830s evangelicals hardly existed; there were
four or five individuals of the teaching or officiating body, the parish of
St, Ebbe's, and "a score or two of young men," at St. Edmund Hall.
"Morality" was taught "without . . . reference to the Person of Christ"
while salvation from sin and its penalties was dealt with as a sort of
joint-stock transaction. Evangelicals had moved away from the question of Justification, and there was a need to represent the "Justifier,"

the setting forth of the Person, life and work of Christ which is the per-petual office of the church. The Person of Christ, the Justifier, was in fact central to Gladstone's understanding of the Gospel of salvation even before he went to Oxford, although at this period he does not elab-orate on what he believed about Christ the "Justifier."

Thirteen years after the publication of the article he wrote an account of his "Earlier Political Opinions"; "I was not in sympathy with the high and dry Toryism of contemporary Oxford . . . what estranged me from it was . . . its hostility to Evangelicalism which my early train-ing had taught me to regard as another name for Christianity."[18] Writ-ing to the Rev. Dr. Fairbairn in 1893 he admitted "Childhood and boy-hood placed me in very close connection with the Evangelicalism of those days, and very notable it was."[19] At Oxford Gladstone no longer regarded himself as a boy, so was he implying that at that stage he did not have "very close connection with the Evangelicalism of those days?" If so, he was not denying his contacts with the Oxford evangeli-cals but indicating that by that time he was in a different position. He was no longer the boy who imbibed evangelicalism without question, but a young man who through thought, reading and prayer, was seeking to clarify his theological position and establishing his own identity and ultimately his own informed churchmanship.

"I had," he wrote in 1894, "been educated in an extremely nar-row Churchmanship, that of the Evangelical party, and though Oxford and Bishop Butler had begun my emancipation it had as yet made but a limited progress."[20] But his emancipation began before his reading and accepting of Butler. Two years before his death Gladstone wrote "My opinions, though they had been to some extent qualified, and rather se-riously shaken, by the study of Butler at Oxford, were still when I en-tered Parliament the rigidly narrow opinions of the Evangelical school in which I had been bred."[21] While in 1832 he still held some narrow opinions and the basic tenets of the evangelical faith, the accuracy of his description is open to question. He does not seem fully aware of the extent of his gradual and sometimes undiscernible move away from his inherited evangelical faith. Two years earlier he stated that while at Ox-ford he "continued to hold in the main mildly Evangelical opinions, without any real idea of the Church." His idea of the church changed at Oxford following his acceptance of baptismal regeneration, which re-sulted in other fundamental changes.

Lathbury suggests that an unidentified fragment dated 15 January 1894[22] "may be taken as his final judgment on the religious tradition in which he had been brought up" as it puts forward a view of the evangelical party very different from that in the *Gleanings*. "The Evangelical clergy were the heralds of a real and profound revival, the revival of spiritual life. Every Christian under their scheme had personal dealings with his God and Saviour. The inner life was again acknowledged as a reality . . . . " While the service of this party was inestimable, it was incomplete, it had a high view of scripture but a low, almost non-existent view of the church, "of the perpetual indestructible existence of the Church of God." There is always the danger when someone changes their theological position, party or church, of disparaging what they have rejected. Was Gladstone guilty of this?

Reynolds writes "Gladstone seems to have been curiously unaware of the strength of the evangelicals at Oxford at this time."[23] What was Gladstone's involvement with the Oxford evangelicals? He recognised St. Ebbe's as a center of the evangelical party "where the flame was at white heat." The diary shows that he had regular contact with a number of young men who were supporters of Bulteel. These included Henry Moncrieff, Alfred Hanbury, Owen and Francis Cole, Charles Childer, Thomas Tancred, Henry Seymer and Benjamin Harrison, who later introduced Gladstone to the *Tracts for the Times*. When he returned to Oxford after Anne's death he had regular contact with most of these extreme evangelicals. But wine drinking, walks and long conversations were not confined to this group. Among other friends with whom he had regular contact were Doyle, Hope, Anstice, Gaskell, Rogers and Acland. Surviving correspondence with these and some of the St. Ebbe's group shows how all these developed into friendships which continued long after Oxford. Countless diary entries record his social contact with all of these, and many others who made up Gladstone's increasing circle of friends and acquaintances.

There are many references to conversations with Doyle and others, often on religious subjects: "Doyle here in Evg. . . talked about religion. More satisfactory than usual thank God." A few days later he notes "Sat up till one and wrote a very long letter to Doyle on religion." Meetings, religious conversations and correspondence with Doyle continued. The implication is that Doyle's religious position and commitment were not all that Gladstone desired. Was Gladstone fulfilling his evangelical responsibility by trying to bring his friend to a "true and consistent religion"? Group discussions on religion also took place, for example, between Gladstone, Doyle, Hope and Gaskell

Contact with James Hope was less frequent than with many others, although he had much in common with Gladstone, not only in his desire for ordination, but in his spiritual discipline, self-examination on his birthday and the keeping of a "spiritual diary."[24] Countless references to religious conversations in the diary prove that he did not neglect this aspect of his evangelical responsibility, although he usually regarded them as unsatisfactory, "the weapon is weak in such hands as mine."

Let it not be thought that the only things which bound many of these young men together was religious commitment, albeit at different levels and of different persuasions. The "Oxford Essay Club" which drew a small group of them together intellectually and socially was instituted and its rules passed at a meeting held in Gaskell's rooms on Friday 23 October 1829; the two Aclands, Anstice, Doyle, Gaskell, Harrison, Leader, Moncrieff, Rogers, Seymer and Gladstone were present. Twenty-eight rules were passed, number nine being "That no class of subject be excluded from discussion except those relating to religion." The young Oxford evangelicals were earnest and demanding with regard to their religious convictions, but the "Essay Society," to which a small number of the St. Ebbe's group belonged, was equally demanding. The Society rules show that mediocrity was not tolerated. Gladstone wrote of their first meeting "I trust it may work well, and that nothing in it may be displeasing to our Heavenly Father, but all in strict subordination to His will." What Gladstone actually means is not clear. Surely he did not think that the formation of the Society might be displeasing to God? Perhaps it was the embargo on the discussion of religious topics. The "Minute Book" records the meetings and subjects discussed, including a few religious topics.[25] Gladstone became Secretary and eventually "plucked up enough courage to speak."[26]

In view of the membership of the Essay Society, including some of Bulteel's supporters, the comments made by Gaskell in a letter to his mother are rather surprising "I much regret that Gladstone has mixed himself up as he has done with the St. Mary Hall and Oriel set, who are really, for the most part, only fit, as Robinson said, to live with maiden aunts and keep tame rabbits."[27] Gaskell was certainly not op-

posed to Gladstone's deep religious commitment and so the implication
seems to be that he saw a notable difference between Gladstone's evangelicalism and calibre and that of the young extreme evangelicals who
lodged at St. Mary Hall, but it could have been their politics to which
he objected. The Noetics of the Oriel Common Room, who were Whigs
in politics, freely criticised traditional religious orthodoxy, seeking to
increase the comprehensiveness of the Church of England.

Gladstone continued to have regular contact with many whom
he had described as "a new party—hearers apparently of Mr. Bulteel."
There is no indication whether or not those with whom he kept contact
continued to worship at St. Ebbe's or retained their original evangelical
position. The diary indicates that during his time at Oxford he went to
St. Ebbe's only four times. Eventually Bulteel's extreme Calvinism was
to prove his undoing, when on 6 February 1831 he thundered defiance
from the university pulpit, resulting in the charge of antinomianism.[28]
When Bulteel left the Church of England[29] Gladstone observed "pity
that it should be found necessary to make such an example of a man of
God." The diary gives no suggestion that these extreme evangelicals influenced his beliefs, nevertheless they must have had some effect upon
his religious development during those years, if only by prompting him
to study in detail those doctrines which he found unacceptable including Calvinism, predestination and conversion. His thirst for an ever
deepening relationship with Christ and an increasing desire for new
knowledge, especially theological, in order to establish a tenable and
coherent faith directed him on a course which eventually led him away
from a traditional evangelical position.

Gladstone claimed "The upshot is that I am unable to trace,
down to this date, any appreciable influence of any individual or individuals whatsoever upon the formation of my religious opinions."[30]
William Rawson may have been near the truth when he wrote "May
you my dear friend always draw from the fountain of living waters, and
find it sweet for your taste—let the plain truths of God have the first
place, and then others may have that share of your attention which their
importance demands."[31] His whole life was to be a search for truth, to
know and do the will of God.

Many and divers influences fashioned Gladstone's religious
development and what may be called his "evolving churchmanship."
On a personal level the study of God's word, on an intelligent, system-

atic and daily basis, was central to this development and the touchstone of his doctrine and religious practice. Coupled with this was his voracious reading of Christian literature, including biblical commentaries, theological works, devotional classics, church history, religious novels, controversial tracts, religious newspapers and periodicals. Such a catholicity of reading helped to fashion his thinking and the evolution of his "evangelical catholicity." Religious discussion with a host of different people, parent, brothers, sisters, especially Anne, Etonians and fellow undergraduates, clergy and academics, all contributed towards his theological evolution. He can never be accused of only entering into discussion with like-minded people.

His aim was to seek the truth, to establish his own position and to change that position when it was found wanting. Some individuals did contribute towards the formation of his religious opinions; Anne had the most profound effect. Edward Craig's influence is impossible to ascertain. Such clergymen as William Rawson, John Turner and Augustus Saunders, as well as George Herbert through his *Country Parson*, provided him with many insights, as he observed them at work in their parishes, thereby helping to sharpen his own thoughts. Sermons heard and read were means through which God spoke, making His will known. Holy Communion and prayer were used by God to this end, as well as for the spiritual sustenance of the faithful. Against such a background is it any wonder that Gladstone was unable to pin-point any particular individual who influenced his religious formation?

What is clear and indisputable is that by the time he had completed his studies at Oxford, many changes had taken place in his religious life, and in his understanding of the nature of God and the Christian church. The move from being "mildly evangelical" to what can best be described as "a Catholic Evangelical" was consolidated during his time there.

Does Gladstone's assessment of his theological position at Oxford provide us with an accurate picture? "I continued to hold in the main mildly Evangelical opinions, without any real ideas of the Church." The use of the word "main" implies that some of his opinions could not be labelled "mildly evangelical," and what evangelcals did not accept was a "mild" or mediocre view of the faith. In his *Gleanings* he admitted "it was a strong systematic, outspoken and determined reaction against the prevailing standards both of life and preaching." Ev-

angelicals demanded religious zeal, whole-hearted commitment, dogmatic theological views. To describe an evangelical as holding "mild
opinions" was, perhaps, a contradiction in terms. One wonders if Gladstone's use of this phrase was prompted by his uncertain position at that
time. Because he was involved in a process of "theological evolution" it
was impossible to give a clear definition of his exact position. He had
started out an evangelical, but had abandoned some of their beliefs and
practices and found others questionable. His article in *Gleanings* shows
that he had begun to investigate some doctrines which the evangelical
school did not embrace in accordance with "traditional Anglicanism";
these included the church and the sacraments. It is in connection with
these doctrines that Gladstone's theological change is most obvious,
and can be seen as a move from the evangelicalism of his birth to that
of "traditional Anglicanism." In this study the extent of that move is
confined to his development up to his election as member of Parliament
for Newark. In connection with the sacraments and the church, as in
other aspects of doctrine and faith, Gladstone's spiritual pilgrimage was
one of theological evolution, although the basic framework was to be
established in the period covered in this volume. While coming to accept a more "catholic" view of the sacraments, church and ministry,
there were other facets of his faith which remained evangelical, including his attachment to the Prayer Book, Thirty-nine Articles, the authority and study of the bible, a "holy life-style," a personal relationship
with Christ, Christian service and witness and an emphasis upon the
church's function of preaching and mission. The complexity of his
churchmanship, and the fact that he was never a "party man," made it
difficult for others to understand him. For one earnestly seeking to establish his own spiritual identity and to be clear about God's intention
for his life, his unusual position must have been somewhat confusing.

    Gladstone's dissatisfaction with certain aspects of the evangel-
ical school, expressed in an article in the *Foreign and Colonial Quarterly Review*,[32] while published some years after his departure from Oxford, can be taken to represent his position and feeling in those earlier
days when, perhaps albeit unconsciously, he was searching for a new
type of churchmanship. He refers to the period of amendment in the
church before 1833, the year in which John Keble delivered the Assize
sermon on "National Apostasy," marking the beginning of the Oxford
Movement, one of the main subjects examined by Gladstone in this ar-

ticle.

Many of the clergy had fallen below the level of their calling. A few continued to exhibit it in their teaching as well as in their life, and to "embody the true spirit of the Church." "The sum and substance of our charge against the Evangelical system . . . is that it was a partial and defective system, and required the admission of new and potent elements." Then follows a profound statement, indicative of what can best be described as Gladstone's search for a "Catholic Evangelical" position. "The secret, so to speak, of a close relationship between what is Catholic, and what is, in the best popular, sense, evangelical, had not been discovered."

Even when writing this article in 1843 Gladstone had to admit "We do not say that the elements of which the best theological teaching ought to be composed, have as yet, in any school, or in any large proportion of writers or teachers among us, adjusted themselves, by their reciprocal action, in a perfect equilibrium." Such was the unconscious aim of Gladstone in those Oxford years, the drawing together of the best of each "school." A number of kindred spirits were involved in such a search, although perhaps unknown at that time to themselves, or to Gladstone. Some would identify many of these as the eventual supporters of the early Oxford Movement.

Gladstone's search was for a new understanding of the faith where the best of his evangelical inheritance could be preserved, along with an acceptance of the corporate nature of the church, the sacraments as means of grace and the divine function of the ordained ministry. The search was for a synthesis, the fusing of the essential elements of the evangelical and catholic schools into something much fuller and in keeping with the truth of scripture and "traditional Anglicanism."

He felt that the evangelical teaching concerning the church and sacraments fell below the standard of the Prayer Book and Articles of Religion. Much later he believed that he reached a new stage of development about 1841[33] but the statement implies gradual growth, which reached a more consolidated position at that time. "In the year 1841 or 2, under a variety of combined influences my mind had attained a certain fixity of state in a new development. I had been gradually carried away from the moorings of an education evangelical in the party sense to what I believe history would warrant me in calling a Catholic position in the acceptance of the visible historical Church and the commission it received from our Saviour to take charge in a visible form of His work upon earth. I do not mean here to touch upon the varied stages of this long journey . . . the Oxford Tracts had little to do with it: nothing to do with it at all I should be inclined to say, except in so far as it was partly and very considerably due to them that Catholicism so to speak was in the air, and was exercising an influence on the religious frame of men without their knowing it." Gladstone accepts that his spiritual pilgrimage to "Catholic Evangelicalism" had been a long journey with varied stages. He also acknowledges that men's religious ideas and development can be influenced without their knowing it.

iii. *Baptismal Regeneration*

As an evangelical Gladstone had been taught to regard baptismal regeneration as a heresy. Edward Craig strongly opposed the doctrine and represented the position of many evangelicals of his time. His views helped to fan the unquenchable flame which had been kindled within William, who felt impelled to clarify this doctrine once and for all. Anne encouraged his systematic study which took in wide ranging reading and which left no stone unturned. The 1894 account of his religious development tells how during 1828 when he spent much time with Anne, he read an article on baptismal regeneration in the *Quarterly Review* where patristic testimony, including that of Augustine, whose teaching the evangelicals accepted,was used to support the doctrine. "I was thus lifted up to the level of baptismal regeneration and so I think must have been my dear sister. This probably set me upon reading Hooker's works which I found in my father's library."

In another manuscript written in old age and covering his religious development from 1828-41 he states "In the spring and summer of 1828 I set to work on Hooker's *Ecclesiastical Polity* and read it straight through . . . Anne had . . . an opinion that the standard divines of the English Church were of great value. Hooker's exposition of the claims of the Church of England came to me as a mere abstraction but I think that I found the doctrine of baptismal regeneration, theretofore abhorred, impossible to reject and the way was thus open for further changes." Unfortunately Gladstone confused the date and perhaps even the ultimate contribution which Hooker made to his acceptance of baptismal regeneration, at that stage. His mistake has been accepted and compounded by others.[34]

Gladstone was not at Seaforth for the spring and summer of 1828; he was there from 11–21 January when there is no mention of reading Hooker. The first reference to Hooker was on 1 July 1828 when he copied Hooker's opinions on baptismal regeneration into his "Opinions of Eminent Divines" begun on 29 June. Gladstone remained at Seaforth until 29 July but there was no further reference to Hooker, and certainly not to his reading the whole of *Ecclesiastical Polity*. His wide reading on other subjects and his family and social activities during the four weeks after his first mention of Hooker would not give even Gladstone time to read this monumental work.

Did Hooker's *Ecclesiastical Polity* therefore play the part that Gladstone claims it did in leading him to accept the doctrine of baptismal regeneration? Or did the reading of the entire work (covering three volumes and about 1,500 pages in John Keble's edition), later confirm his new position on baptismal regeneration and contribute towards his wider understanding of the "traditional Anglican" position on both the church and the sacraments? There is no denying that in the summer of 1828 Gladstone did read part of Hooker's *Ecclesiastical Polity* viz. his opinions on baptism, which undoubtedly influenced his views, but that year he did not read the whole of Hooker.

On 24 August 1828 William wrote to inform Helen of his acceptance of this doctrine in the light of his study of the Fathers and the Anglican divines: "Regeneration is a birth; the principle of life only is imparted therein: it is an admission into the covenant . . . I remember the time when I had a horror of anything that upheld the doctrine of Baptismal Regeneration. Fool that I was: every Sunday repeating a belief in one baptism for the remission of sins . . . I do not see how the argument from the Apostles' preaching can be answered and how can I, dare I, refuse to assent to a doctrine I cannot deny and a reason I cannot refute."

Between 6-10 January 1829 while on his Christmas vacation he was engaged in this pursuit on all but one day. Back at Oxford he continued his study and on Sunday 8 February wrote "Began compiling opinions on Baptism in another form & on a fresh plan. Wrote also concerning it... May God vouchsafe to sanctify and direct all my few and poor studies." Baptism continued to occupy him even during his unexpected return to Seaforth following Anne's death. Sundays and occasional week days on his return to Oxford saw him pursuing it further. Indeed on Monday 6 April he began to examine the Public Formularies of Baptism in the Prayer Book[35] and on Tuesday 28th he was taking extracts from the Adult Baptismal Service and so his study of what had become an essential and acceptable doctrine continued. Number seven of the ten issues listed at his annual self-examination that year was "That we are regenerate by Baptism and Baptism alone."

Hooker and many other Anglican divines, the Fathers and the Prayer Book formularies, all made their contribution towards his intellectual and emotional acceptance of a doctrine which had previously filled him with horror. On 7 December 1828 he began and on 26 January 1829 "finished Walton's beautiful Life of Hooker." It was possibly this biography which stimulated Gladstone to begin to read the whole of *Ecclesiastical Polity* on Sunday 12 July 1829. Never can Hooker have had a more assiduous student —he read some part of this theological classic every day from 18 July until Sunday 8 September, when he finished book seven starting book eight on 25 September. For some reason he laid it aside for two days to read Hooker's *Learned Discourse on Justification*; on 29 September he noted "Finished Hooker's Eccl. Polity: began Analysis." Work on his analysis of Hooker took some of his time during five days of the following week. He produced ten sides of notes covering Books 1-3,[36] but nothing more is recorded about this study which demanded more time than anything else he had ever read.

His systematic study of baptismal regeneration had far reaching consequences on his future religious development. He had moved away from the position of a bigoted evangelical prejudice to a catholic approach to doctrine where he was willing to consider not only the authoritative works of Scripture but also the Fathers of the Church whom he now believed "must have known something about" the fundamental doctrines of the Church. He was also willing to give serious consideration to statements by eminent English divines. Even writers whose views were initially different from his own had to be examined in order to reach a balanced position. Prejudice was not to stifle the search for truth, and truth had to be followed wherever it led. Anne was to be thanked for encouraging him to take a much wider approach to studying the faith. At first he felt she was leading him down some "devious bypaths of opinion," but he was never to look back. It marked the birth of his "theological liberation."

Acceptance of baptismal regeneration was his first conscious step away from the evangelical school. Far more than an intellectual decision it was a fundamental change concerning a doctrine that constituted part of the very foundation of the Christian faith. It was an acceptance that God can and does convey grace through the sacraments and that regeneration and salvation depend upon a sacramental act, baptism, not upon justification by faith in isolation from the church and her sacraments, nor upon a conversion experience. If through baptism, why not through the eucharist? If through the sacraments of the church, why not through the church—the body of Christ? And if through the church, what about her ministers, successors to the Apostles of Christ? For Gladstone "the way was thus opened for further changes." Lathbury was incorrect when he stated Gladstone "read Hooker's *Ecclesiastical Polity* and accepted the "hitherto abhorred" doctrine of Baptismal Regeneration—a very important addition to his stock of belief, but not one that at the time carried him much further on the road to churchmanship."[37] On the contrary, from that moment onward his whole approach was different.

iv. *The Holy Communion*

What is written here must be seen in relation to what is written in the chapters on Eton and Oxford. For the majority of evangelicals the Holy Communion, or the Lord's Supper, was not accepted as an essential part of the evangelical faith, or acknowledged as a sacramental means of grace. While they did not disregard the sacraments their piety and understanding of the Christian faith was not centered upon these ordinances. Their spirituality was based on early rising, prayer and bible study;[38] baptism and the Lord's Supper were seen as no more than symbolic and commemorative acts, enjoined by scripture. Their approach to the sacraments, especially the Lord's Supper, largely explains the meagreness of the information available for they certainly did not accept them as central to the Christian life.[39] Although some like J. B. Sumner and E. Bickersteth encouraged evangelicals to receive Holy Communion as regularly as available.

Over a number of years Gladstone drew together a collection of prayers and devotional material. An undated compilation "Devotions for intervals of the Eucharistic Service"[40] was revised many times dur-

ing his life. Lathbury speculated correctly in commenting on this collection of eucharistic devotions "There is nothing to show at what time
the *Devotions* . . . were put together, but upon this, as upon Baptism,
his convictions seem to date from a very early stage of his religious
progress.[41] A small notebook dated 1826-27 preserved from his Eton
days, which has already been examined, records some of his early
thoughts on the Holy Communion. Here he writes of the sacrament as
both "a Command" and a "Blessing" and relates the Lord's Supper to
baptism. Strictly speaking he says very little about Holy Communion;
what he writes is largely a pious statement about God's love and man's
redemption through the Blood of Christ. Nevertheless it is the attempt
of an evangelical schoolboy to discover the importance of the Sacrament and to put his thoughts on paper.

"Secreta Eucharistica" is the title written inside a Gladstone
manuscript at the British Library. It is the fourth of six small volumes
with uniform binding marked "A" to "C," the first three are marked in
Gladstone's handwriting "Ch Ch 1831", i.e. Christ Church, and although the fourth volume is not dated it probably belongs to the same
date, 1831, and is the embryo of that reproduced by Lathbury. The
three pages of notes contain prayers in both English and Latin to be
said privately at the Eucharist.[42] Here we have some of Gladstone's
thoughts concerning eucharistic devotions, although it is meagre compared with his work on baptism. Nevertheless it shows the importance
he placed upon Holy Communion and preparation for it, thus setting
him apart from those evangelicals who valued it less highly.

After his first communion Gladstone seems to have availed
himself of every opportunity to receive the Sacrament. This was usually
monthly as was customary in many churches at that period.[43] He was
certainly not averse to a more frequent reception for there were occasions when he received the Sacrament two weeks in succession and
sometimes on Good Friday and Easter Day. On the day before his first
communion he prayed "May God hallow it to me." Good Friday provided the next opportunity when he pleaded "May God make me a worthy partaker in so solemn and healthful a feast." From late 1827 there is
often only a brief note "received sacrament"; there is no reference to
preparation on the Saturday evening or the Sunday morning. Was this
because he had dropped the practice? In many ways he was a creature
of habit and so like his daily prayers and bible reading, preparation for

receiving the Holy Communion as an essential part of his spirituality was not recorded in the Journal. A passing reference suggests that this was the case—31 January 1829 he "read Barrow on the Sacrament" in the evening before receiving his communion the following morning. Such preparation may have come from family tradition and [been] influenced by Presbyterian practice, but for frequent communicants was expressive of a "high view" of the Sacrament, as well as a recognition of the unworthiness of the recipient. Terms used in connection with the Lord's Supper also express a high doctrine; it is a means of Divine Grace, a healthful feast, of inestimable value, a Holy Supper, the Blessed Sacrament, the Holy Sacrament .

Numbers of communicants at Oxford celebrations are often noted in the diary sometimes with such comments as "few, too few Communicants" reflecting the importance he placed upon this Sacrament for those committed to Christ and seeing absence as a sad neglect of this means of grace. His high view of the Holy Communion seen in the part it played in his spirituality, his preparation before and during the service, his regularity of receiving, the titles used, the books read in preparing himself to receive the sacred ordinance and to help him to understand its nature and purpose, all indicate that Gladstone was certainly not a typical evangelical. Not only evangelicals but others would have regarded him as a sacramentalist, who believed the Holy Communion was essential to Christian spirituality and a real means of grace. After his Oxford days his life became increasingly centered upon the Eucharist which he regarded as fundamental to Christian sanctification and man's approach to God in Christ. Eucharistic doctrine and practice were firmly based upon wide and careful reading. From leaving Oxford until 1874 he read at least 52 books on various aspects of the Eucharist, including preparation for the Sacrament, the regularity of reception, devotional manuals, sermons on the Holy Communion and general works on eucharistic doctrine. His increasing understanding of and devotion to the Eucharist eventually led to an almost daily reception at certain periods in his life.

v. *The Nature of the Church*

Evangelicals, according to Gladstone, had no doctrine of the church, "I had been brought up with no notion of the Church as the

Church or body of Christ. Not only was there no visibility, but there was not even any collectivity in my conception of outward religion and religious observance."[44] Was he accurate in that statement or did his views change while at Eton? In his commentary on the Lord's Supper, written possibly in 1827, he wrote of how the Spirit of God works in the soul nourishing it and gradually forming it anew after the image of Christ. He ends his commentary "this new life is the very life which was in Christ, that is to say, members of his Church which is his body." This brief statement stresses the corporate nature of the church as the body of Christ in which the Christian is nurtured. On a coach journey to Eton a passenger asked "Come now, what is the Church of England?" to which another passenger replied 'It is a d ... d large building with an organ in it." "I think," wrote Gladstone, "this expressed the ideas of my childhood." In view of his note about the church as the body of Christ this must reflect his views during his early years at Eton.

Oxford, Richard Hooker, Bishop Butler and Augustine were only some of the influences upon his changing doctrine of the church. "Of the greatest of historical facts, the fact that we had among us a divine society, I had no conception."[45] This was his understanding of the church as a result of his evangelical upbringing; that view radically changed with his theological liberation.

His claim to have been fed on Bishop Burnet's *Exposition of the XXXIX Articles of the Church of England* may not be altogether accurate. Gladstone began to read this book on 24 January 1830, reading it almost daily until he finished it on 28 February. An analysis of Burnet was started on 4 April but referred to only once more on 11 April; the notes are brief suggesting Gladstone had little interest.[46] Annotations made by him appear on many pages of his copy preserved with the rest of his library. A scoring appears on the Article "Of Baptism" where Burnet comments that "Our Lord has ... made Baptism one of the *precepts* though not one of the *means,* necessary for salvation." Baptism is not necessary for salvation, "Faith is the means of salvation." The purpose of baptism is to admit "to the society of Christians, and all the rights and privileges of that body ... which is the Church." Baptism "makes us the visible members of that one body ... but that which *saves* us in it ... must be a thing of another nature." Of the church Burnet wrote "A true Church is, in one sense, a society that preserves the essential and fundamentals of Christianity; in another sense it stands for a society, all whose doctrines are true." Gladstone scores Burnet's conclusion "So when we acknowledge that any society is a true Church, we ought to be supposed to mean no other than that the covenant of grace in its essential constituent parts is preserved entire in that body." Of the visibility of the church Burnet states "A visible society of Christians is a true Church," such a church is "founded upon Christ and upon his doctrines." There is no concept of the church as necessarily visible and the body of Christ, certainly no doctrine of a "divine creation" or a "divine society." It is a congregational view "a society made up of true believers," rather than an existing divine society which those who have faith enter through baptism.

Burnet, a staunch Whig, whose *Exposition of the Thirty-nine Articles* had been famous for more than a century, was latitudinarian in theology. Such a position did not appeal to Gladstone as he began to move increasingly to a more "catholic" understanding. He did not return to Burnet but within a few days of completion joined the sons of Oxford for whom Butler became a mentor. But he admitted that his emancipation was slow in spite of Oxford and Butler.[47] The study and influence of Bishop Butler was to be lifelong. Later he placed him among his "four doctors," the teacher to whom he owed the most. Statues of these four, Butler, Aristotle, Augustine and Dante adorn the niches on the outer walls of St. Deiniol's Library, a perpetual reminder at a place dedicated to "Divine Learning" of those who fashioned the thinking of its founder.

Gladstone's introduction to Bishop Butler came through reading on 31 March 1829 his *Charge delivered to the Clergy at the Primary Visitation of the diocese of Durham in the year 1751*. No comment is made about the merits of the *Charge* but the zealous Gladstone must have been impressed for here Butler was emphasising to his clergy many of the things which Gladstone held dear. Religious decay was a sign of the times—the clergy must defend their religious convictions. Their sermons should be affirmative. More regard must be given to the services of the church. In country places people can often only attend church once each week, but this was not sufficient for their spiritual well-being. Butler advises prayer "(a) family, (b) secret, (c) morning and evening, (d) at set hours, (e) grace at meals." A holy life must be sought. He exhorts his clergy to give themselves wholly to all these things, "this, my brethren, is the business of our lives. . . as according to

our Lord's *appointment we live the gospel.*" These were the things
Gladstone longed to hear, and this was the calling he felt God had set
before him both as an undergraduate and potentially as a priest, "to live
the gospel." Butler gave William much food for thought that Lent as he
occupied himself in writing "Lent verses."

"Ecclesiastically I was fed upon Bishop Burnet's ... Thirty-
nine Articles, not then superseded by higher teaching ... The religious
atmosphere of Oxford generally was calm, and indeed stagnant. Happily for her sons the study of Butler had come into vogue. In due time I
read him as closely and intensely as Aristotle ... I became an interested
reader of St. Augustine ... and found him in accordance with Butler so
that I was profoundly satisfied."[48]

Admiration for Butler following his impressive *Charge* did
not, however, immediately prompt him to read further. Indeed a year
was to pass before he turned to *The Analogy of Religion. Natural and
Revealed, to the Constitution and Course of Nature.* His extensive
study of Butler began on 27 April 1830 and he then continued to read
him spasmodically over the next three months. July 17 marked his completion of the *Analogy;* he simply recorded "finished Butler." After that
he continued his "marginal analysis of Butler" over the next few days.

A master of calm exposition, Butler was inspired with a supreme belief and a triumphant faith. Both heart and head were in what
he wrote. In the *Analogy* he seeks, with all his power and ability, to
commend the Christian faith to his readers. He argues that the revelation of God contains a "particular" dispensation of providence, carried
on by his Son and Spirit, for the recovery and salvation of mankind. We
are commanded, as part of that revelation, to be baptized. Baptism is a
positive duty. Worship of God is a moral duty. Scripture represents
Christ as the mediator between God and man. "He is the light of the
world; the revealer of the will of God." Christ "has a kingdom which is
not of this world. He founded a Church, to be to mankind a standing
memorial of religion and an invitation to it; which he promised to be
with always even to the end. He exercises an invisible government over
it ... a government of discipline, for the perfecting of the saints, for the
edifying of his body ... Of this Church, all persons scattered over all
the world, who live in obedience to his laws, are members."[49] Here the
church is presented as a "divine society" the creation of God, not a
man-made institution. All who live in obedience to Christ throughout

the world are through baptism members of that church which is both visible and catholic. Amid the complexity and logic of Butler's argument Gladstone no doubt took special note of this brief statement of the church as a "divine society" and all that this implies. The doctrine of the church as a "divine society," which in the purpose of God's revelation is an essential instrument for the salvation of mankind, was now implanted in Gladstone's mind or perhaps confirmed previous thoughts on this subject.

On 19 July 1831 he read "Butler's Preface and third sermon on Human Nature." We cannot be sure if he read any of the other sermons where much was said about the doctrine of the church. This may well be the implication when he later made references to the influence of Butler's sermons, "I do not doubt that in 1830 and 1831 the study of Bishop Butler laid the ground for new modes of thought in religion."[50] Part of the new ground now open to consideration was the visible nature of the church as a divine society, "the living and perpetual stewardess of the ordinances of grace."[51] Among his "papers written at Oxford" are some notes about man and the church. Reflecting on man's sinful nature and plight Gladstone declares "God gave us one ark of refuge, He built his Church in the midst upon the Rock of Redemption." There is no reference to conversion, faith or justification, his stress is upon refuge and salvation in the Ark, the church created by God, built upon Christ the Rock of our Redemption; men enter that Ark, they do not create it.[52]

Wide reading and associated thinking influenced his growing understanding of the nature of the church which had reached a formative, although not the final, stage of development by May 1832. At that stage the contents of the Book of Common Prayer, the formularies of which had influenced his changed position on baptism, came to play an unexpected and yet fundamental part in his new understanding of the church.

New light dawned upon the mind of Gladstone at Naples on Sunday 13 May 1832: "I have been employed in examining some of the details of the system of the English Church, as set forth in the Prayer-book, with which I was before less acquainted." His study gave him insights "which now seem to be afforded me of the nature of a Church, and of our duties as members of it, which involve an idea very much higher and more important than I had previously had any conception

of." Before this he had taken a great deal of teaching in connection with
the church and other doctrines direct from the bible "as best I could."
But he observed "now the figure of the Church arose before me as a
teacher too, and I gradually found in how incomplete and fragmentary a
manner I had drawn down truth from that sacred volume, as I had
missed in the Thirty-Nine Articles some things which ought to have
taught me better." This he felt was his first introduction to "the august
conception of the Church of Christ." What he had discovered presented
"Christianity under an aspect in which I had not yet known it: its ministry of symbols, its channels of grace, its unending line of teachers joining from the Head: a sublime construction, based throughout upon historic fact, uplifting the idea of the community in which we live, and of
the access which it enjoys through the new and living way, to the presence of the most High." From that moment, "I began to feel my way by
degrees into or towards a true notion of the Church."[53]   On that day in
Naples "I felt that an event had happened in my life." A blow was
struck by the Prayer Book which "set my mind in motion and that motion was never arrested. I found food for new ideas and tendencies in
various quarters." His theological position concerning the true nature of
the church was thus changed before the Oxford Movement, which
"properly so-called began in the next year, but it had no direct effect
upon me."[54] Without any influence from the Oxford Movement Gladstone had moved a long way from his inherited notions of the church.
Gradually and imperceptibly and over a number of years he had moved
towards a "catholic concept of the church." No longer could he claim to
belong to the evangelical school so far as his doctrines of the church
and sacraments were concerned.

William Palmer's *Treatise on the Church of Christ* (1838), was
recommended to Gladstone by James Hope.[55] He later wrote of it "a
great book" which "took hold upon me; and gave me at once the clear,
definite and strong conception of the Church which through all the
storm and strain of a most critical period has proved for me entirely adequate to every emergency and saved me from all vacillation . . . I conceive that in the main Palmer completed for me the work which inspection of the Prayer Book had begun."[56] Whatever Mr. Gladstone's later
recollections, the evidence considered shows that "the work" i.e. the
change in his churchmanship, especially his doctrine of the church, began before May 1832. New ideas began to fashion his evolving church-

manship as far back as 1828, indeed in some areas even before that.

vi. *The Church's Ministry*

By 1832 baptism, the eucharist and the church, all of which
played little part in evangelical theology, were essential to Gladstone's
churchmanship. His doctrinal position on the church's threefold ministry is not easy to define and a precise statement is impossible. In November of 1832 Benjamin Harrison wrote to Gladstone "I send you two
Oxford tracts to show you how exactly you have arrived at the line
which they draw respecting the Apostolical Succession and Episcopacy
as related to each other."[57] At this stage Gladstone does not seem to
have reached any clear position regarding the historic episcopate. But
in May 1832 in connection with his new conception of the church he
wrote of "its unending line of teachers joining from the head." Possibly
a recognition of the church's historic ministry, the historic episcopate
going back through the Apostles to Christ the Head of the church. The
new insights "imparted to the framework of my Evangelical ideas a
shock from which they never thoroughly recovered." I found "that in
regard to the priesthood and to sacramental doctrine in its highest essence we remained upon the ground of the pre-Reformation period, and
stood wholly apart from the general mass of Protestantism. And I think
that the discovery was to me a matter of satisfaction."[58] It may have
given him satisfaction but it was anathema to evangelical protestants
who, at heart, were post-Reformation in their theology and believed
that the Book of Common Prayer and the Articles of Religion pro-
pounded this position.

If his study of the Prayer Book had brought him to a new understanding of the priesthood and the "unending line of teachers," the
episcopate, was this a completely new insight as he suggested?

What we know about Gladstone makes it difficult to believe
that what he read did not fashion his thinking. His reading on the doctrine of the ministry before 1832 especially the episcopate and priesthood, and the quality of life expected of the clergy, undoubtedly contributed towards his new position, which he recognised as catholic
rather than evangelical. His Prayer Book studies simply consolidate and
crystallize his ideas on the doctrine of the ministry as on the church and
sacraments. Thus his reading on the ministry over a number of years

must have contributed towards his move to a new doctrinal position. Was not such a ministry founded upon God's call and had this not been the case from the beginning? If so, then the ordained ministry must also be of divine creation, in which case only the highest and the best was acceptable. And so, concluding that God was calling him to Orders, Gladstone filled his mind with ideas about the way the clergy were to give of their best in their parish ministry.

His later *Gleanings* offer some insight into his ideas of the ordained ministry. Many clergy had "fallen from their lofty calling" and those considering such a "calling" and who were pious and earnest "had for the most part to frame standards of character, of discipline, and of action for themselves; (because) . . . the priestly type in its sanctity and elevation, was almost obliterated. A faithful few, indeed, ever continued to exhibit it, and in their teaching as well as in their life, to embody the true spirit of the Church, but they were lights rather each to his own sphere, than to the country as a whole."[59] Fortunately he had been influenced by a faithful few through their teaching and life and thus impressed by the opportunities and awesome responsibility of serving God in the salvation of mankind. Through reading, discipline and religious practice he had sought to frame his "standards of character, of discipline and of action, on the highest and best."

Gladstone's thought about ordination can only be understood when considered against his total background between his days at Eton, when such thoughts began to germinate, and the completion of his time at Oxford. Clergy he felt ought to be learned men, men who read widely in order to inform their opinions. Gladstone seems to have been attempting just this in considering this "lofty calling" and at the same time trying to establish a doctrine of the ministry which was compatible with his new doctrine of the church and sacraments.

The "lofty calling," holiness of life, parish clergy, commitment to learning, had all been firmly fixed in his mind when he read George Herbert's *Country Parson* while in his final year at Eton. Herbert's thoughts on the subject prompted him to write immediately and with great enthusiasm to Anne, to whom he recommended the book. He later read *On the signs of Conversion and Unconversion in Ministers of the Church*. Sermons and episcopal Charges constituted an important part of his reading throughout his life, and also at this period, a number being on the subject of the quality of life and the high calling of the cler-

gy. Butler's *Charge* of 1751 had touched upon the high calling of those
serving God in the parishes. John Bird Sumner's works were highly esteemed in evangelical circles; Gladstone read a number of his Charges
and sermons touching upon clerical duties, but there is no record that he
read Sumner's *Four Sermons on subjects relating to the Christian Ministry*, preached between 1820 and 1828. He did read a number of Paley's *Sermons* but we have no evidence to suggest that he read those
which were addressed to the clergy regarding their office and administration, although he did read his *Parochial Letter from a Beneficed
Clergyman to his Curate* (1829) on parochial duties. Two volumes of
sermons by Reginald Heber were read from 18 June 1829 until 5 October.   Heber's sermon on "The duties of the Ministry" presented what
many evangelicals regarded as a "high view" of the ministry. The rule
of episcopal ordination is supported, the presbyterial ministry of Geneva rejected. Clergy are to be preachers and teachers of the gospel and to
"dispense those graces which are necessary for the feeding of his
flock," they are to be servants of the people, called and commissioned
by God they are offered His Holy Spirit to fulfill their divine calling,
and to Him they will have to give an account of their ministry.

The devotional literature which Gladstone used to feed his
spiritual life brought before him the ideals of holiness expected of clergy in the fulfillment of their divine office. Among such books read during this period were William Law, *A Serious Call to a Devout and Holy
Life*, and Jeremy Taylor *The Rule and Exercise of Holy Living*. In 1829
he also read John Keble's *Christian Year* which was eventually to play
a decisive part in the Oxford Movement. His verses on St. Matthias'
Day must have been particularly moving and challenging, offering
Gladstone new insights on the sacred ministry.

> Who is God's chosen priest?
> He, who on Christ stands waiting day and night . . .
> In witness of his Lord,
> In humble following of his Saviour dear:
> This is the man to wield th'unearthly sword.
> Warring unharm'd with sin and fear . . .
> But Thou hast made it sure
> By Thy dear promise to Thy Church and Bride,
> That Thou, on earth, would'st aye with her endure,
> Till earth to Heaven be purified.

Keble goes on to speak of the presence of Christ with his Church,

> Who then, uncall'd by Thee,
> Dare touch thy spouse, thy very self below?. . .
> Where can thy seal be found,
> But on the chosen seed, from age to age,
> By thine anointed heralds duly crown'd
> As kings and priests thy war to wage?

Here Gladstone is presented with a high view of the clerical life and calling within the church, the Bride of Christ, God's creation. St. John the Baptist's Day inspired Keble to write

> So glorious let thy Pastors shine,
> That by their speaking lives the world may learn
> First filial duty, then divine,
> That sons to parents, all to Thee may turn;
> And ready prove
> In fires of love,
> At sight of Thee, for aye to burn.

Biographies also gave Gladstone new insights into the implications of the ordained ministry. Grimshawe's *Memoirs of Legh Richmond* and Robert Southey, *Life of John Wesley: and the Rise and Progress of Methodism* offered accounts of leading figures in the evangelical revival. Reading Heber, Taylor, Law, Wesley and Keble and many others in 1829 must have influenced what he wrote in his birthday self-examination "My mind has continued strongly inclined to the Church throughout the year."

It took Gladstone five days to read the 400 pages of Richard Mant's valuable book on pastoralia, *The Clergyman's Obligations considered: as to the Celebration of Divine Worship. Ministration of the Sacraments, Instruction of the poor, preaching, and other official duties and as to his Personal Character and Conduct, his occupations, amusements, and intercourse with others; with particular reference to the Ordination Vow.* Such reading undertaken in connection with the clerical life to help clarify Gladstone's understanding of the sacred office certainly produced in him a "high view" of the office and work of the ministry. His doctrine of the historic episcopate at this period can-

not be given, but in Burnet's *Exposition of the XXXIX Articles* he read
that a succession of bishops is no certain note of a true church, although
Heber's *Sermons* had stressed the importance of the episcopal office in
the Church of England. In 1829 Gladstone read *Lay-Baptism Invalid.
An Essay to Prove that Such Baptism is Null and Void, when administered in Opposition to the Divine Right of the Apostolical Succession,*
by Roger Laurence. The introduction to volume one presented Gladstone with a catholic understanding of the Apostolic succession, soon to
be the clarion call of the Oxford Movement. Laurence states that the authority of the bishop comes from Christ and the authority of the priest
from Christ through the bishop, on the basis of Apostolic succession.
He makes no comment on what he read, but it was far removed from
the position of the evangelical school. Returning from Naples and his
continental tours with eyes now set upon the House of Commons, Gladstone still made time for theological reading including Robert Meek
Reasons for Attachment and Conformity to the Church of England
(1831). Meek's arguments must have consolidated Gladstone's position
reached at Naples three months before. The chapter on episcopacy was
particularly apposite with regard to his idea of the church's ministry as
"an unending line of teachers joining from the head" and the priesthood
and sacramental doctrine. Episcopacy, argued Meek, can be traced back
to the New Testament and apostolic days as its source. Full details for
episcopacy are not to be sought in the writings of the apostles, but the
"decided opinions and usages of the primitive age of the church—will
furnish us with the most decisive proof in favour of episcopacy, and
justify us in claiming for the mode of church polity which characterizes
the Church of England, the high sanction of apostolic times."

Such a line of argument supported Gladstone's new approach
that both scripture and the church are teachers of the faith. The writings
and practice of the apostles appeared to Meek as decisive support of
episcopacy and of the threefold ministry. Gladstone scored, in his copy,
Meek's first conclusion "there were at least two orders of ministers both
inferior to the apostles, and receiving ordination and ministerial authority from them." Following his examination of the New Testament evidence and considering the growth of the church, Meek wrote "What has
been thus gathered from the writings and practice of the apostles as
proving episcopal government to be of apostolic origin, will derive
confirmation from the universal practice of the church immediately af-

ter the apostles." Meek thus establishes the apostolic authority of the
episcopate and the threefold ministry, and its necessity for the church.

Gladstone's scorings throughout this chapter show that he read
it carefully. His observations regarding his doctrinal position reached at
Naples would suggest that by 1832 he had possibly come to accept a
"catholic" view of the threefold ministry and the apostolic origin of the
episcopate. Such a doctrinal position was to be worked out in detail and
consolidated in the years ahead, when he was to read at least twelve
works on the episcopate, as well as numerous other books on the
church's ministry in general. By 1832 Gladstone had reached what
could be regarded as a "catholic position" so far as four central doctrines of Christianity were concerned, doctrines which he believed were
neglected by the evangelical school—baptism, the Holy Communion,
the church and the ministry. Fortunately William had an enquiring
faith, an approach encouraged by Anne. During these years his faith
was in process of evolution as he searched for the truth, and in that
search refused to be associated with a particular party, or theological
position, either evangelical or catholic.

"I can," he wrote in his final year, "give a tolerably clear account of the steps by which I was theoretically by a gradual process
built up into a Churchman." It was indeed a gradual process, but when
he made that statement he seems to have overlooked many factors
which contributed towards his new theological position, a position
which can best be described as a "Catholic Evangelical" embracing the
best and the essentials of both parties. A careful analysis of the various
parts of his spiritual life, his ascetical theology, during his years at Oxford and up to his election as member of Parliament for Newark, will
help to confirm the thesis that by 1832 he had sufficiently moved away
from the evangelical school as to warrant the description that he was a
"Catholic Evangelical."

CHAPTER SEVEN

AN ANALYSIS OF GLADSTONE'S RELIGIOUS LIFE AT OXFORD 1828-1831

i. *Gladstone's Maturing Spirituality*

Gladstone's diary records details of the numerous individuals with whom he had contact and at the same time provides a unique insight into his religious development during these formative years. But the diary does not offer a full or accurate account. It is not always written up daily and so things are forgotten. Towards the end of January 1830 he even lost it, "I could not lay my hand on my Journal book, so I fear it will not be very accurate since Jan. 12." The many people noted in the diary during this period must have had a cumulative effect on his life, Anne having the profoundest influence upon him. On 18 February 1830 he "dined with Pusey with whom I had a great deal of conversation . . .Tomorrow if it please Almighty God I purpose to remember the removal of my beloved sister—but I cannot promise; for my body has the mastery over my mind." Both Anne's life and death had considerable impact upon his spirituality. Whenever he recalled the life of his sainted sister he wallowed in his own sinfulness.

Her death resulted in a much closer relationship between William and Helen. They made a pact to watch over each other's conduct as William had done with his dearest Anne. Correction was to be offered whenever necessary.[1] The diary tells of this new relationship, his concern for her health and spiritual well-being and their ongoing correspondence.

The correct use of time lay heavy upon Gladstone at Oxford and throughout his life. Endless references are made to the subject. Early rising was an essential part of evangelical piety and a practice which

Gladstone strove to establish. Vows were often made to be much stricter with himself because of his acute sense of accountability to God. On the last day of 1828 he wrote "Thus ends the old year. Praise be to Him who gave it, and pardon to us who have abused it." He can write of idleness, of villainously spent days, lethargy and laziness. Coupled with the records of his supposed mis-spent time are occasional ejaculatory prayers, asking for God's deliverance and forgiveness. Self-condemnation is prompted by professed neglect of his spiritual life, or study, or too much time spent at wine parties, talking or in pursuing leisure activities. Others were conscious of Gladstone's diligence in all things, but he acknowledged none of this. Sir Francis Doyle wrote to the young Gladstone asking him to persuade his son, Gladstone's friend, to do some work. William felt himself unfit to advise others and suffered remorse having tried to respond to this request.[2]

Thankfulness to God was a genuine part of his spirituality; "It would be impossible," he wrote to his father, "to look back over the last three months, without at once seeing what abundant and peculiar obligations to thankfulness towards Almighty God they impose upon me. How can I ever be sufficiently thankful to my parents and all around them, and above all to God." It would be unnatural not to feel gratitude to the "Source of all goodness" for all that he bestows upon his children.[3] His father replied expressing the hope that to the end of his life he too would be thankful to his "Almighty and most Merciful Father." He assures William "you have done *your duty*, the rest is with God . . . you justly say that you cannot be too grateful to your heavenly Father."[4] These sentiments suggest that William had been taught to live in thankfulness to God.

Appreciation for William's letters did not deter his father from mentioning his illegible writing: "your writing is so very small and close, tho I admit surprizingly distinct," nevertheless, "I was frequently at a loss to make out particular words" which make it difficult to follow the "chain of your reasoning."[5] John Gladstone may have found William's writing difficult to read, others sometimes found his reasoning, logic and language difficult to understand. His evangelical terminology is certainly not always clear in its meaning.[6] At Oxford he made at least one attempt to set out the essential marks of evangelical religion, in a letter to the Editor of the *Liverpool Mercury* on 22 December 1828, which was not published.

Typical of evangelicals William was convinced that God uses both the ordinary and the dramatic events of life to speak to his children. On Wednesday 16 February 1831 he reflects on "poor Osborne's appalling death . . . If this hath not a voice, all things are dumb to us." It prompted him to write to his father "What will you say when you learn . . . that he was called to meet God from the very midst of intoxication and profaneness . . . it was talked of a good deal yesterday—less today—less tomorrow. In a few days its warning . . . will be heard no more. God in his mercy grant that it may touch some thoughtless and reckless hearts."[7] When beaten up by fellow students he believed that through this event God had spoken to him and he hoped would speak to his assailants.

Verse was used to express some of his religious convictions, while a commonplace book, described as "Selections" begun in August 1829[8] contains quotations from a variety of writers. Letters written during his Oxford years also provide insight into his religious development. One to his Aunt Elizabeth covers a number of religious topics, including how God can use many things as instruments to do His will, the image of God, lost in Adam but regained in Jesus Christ, and the sanctification of the soul.[9] Not a few felt that William was too religious. Theoretically religion should make a person happy rather than gloomy and William expressed such convictions in a manuscript entitled "The alleged gloominess of religion."[10] "Is religion gloomy or is it not? It creates no cause for gloom, for the Christian religion aims at holiness, and entails happiness as its result . . . But irreligion . . . causes . . . gloom." He argues gloominess is not a part of Christianity, but sorrow for sin may be.

Producing written accounts of religious themes became an important part of his life from his Oxford days. He wrote of "Christian Privileges," "Christian Obligations" and "Christian Convictions." "Convictions are sometimes imparted by a process which our intellectual faculties are unable to analyse or explain . . . the grounds of belief cannot always be verbally stated in such a way as to wear that aspect of certainty under which they appeared to the mind originally receiving them."[11] Answering the question "What is faith?" he wrote "The deep and settled conviction of the soul that Christ Jesus the Son of God . . . took upon him our human nature and died upon the cross to save sinners . . . What sinners? All sinners? No: sinners in whom repentance and belief are wrought by the operation of the Spirit of God." This implies that we are "guilty . . . infinitely guilty," our choice lies between "the atonement and perdition,"[12] a very Calvinistic remark.

Serious doubts were expressed on Sunday 25 April 1830 "I wish I were duly convinced of the extreme importance of residence at Oxford, both as regards individual progress in religion and influence exercised directly or indirectly on others." His earnest desire is to seek "a sense of sin," "the faith and love of Christ" and "deliverance from the punishment of sin by his precious blood—from its power by the energy of His Spirit." God's will and spiritual growth are to be sought in "1. the spirit of love; 2. of self-sacrifice; 3. of purity; 4. of energy. Amen Lord Jesus." So he prayed and so he tried to live.

Intense religious convictions produced an acute feeling of sin. Not just because of sexual difficulties, as a number of modern Gladstone biographers have felt. This extreme sense of sin came from his daily reflection on the love of God as revealed in Christ, and the cost of sinful man's redemption. He experienced what all who draw near to God feel, namely an increasing sense of unworthiness in the presence of a Holy God, from whom no secrets are hidden. Added to this was his anxiety about God's will for his life. Could his hesitation be disobedience to God's will? His final year came and what he felt to be the most important decision of his life was still to be made. He grappled with the inner question about whether or not he should devote his life to being an instrument in the hand of God for the salvation of his fellow men by becoming a clergyman in the Church of England. His mother and sisters shared this hope.[13] Politics, the subject of a letter from his father in February 1831[14] was regarded by his father and brothers as his true vocation; their expectations for him ran high, impressing upon him a feeling of obligation. The following month, the Reform Bill and the accompanying political debates demanded much of William's attention;[15] on 22 April he wrote "The excitement in politics is now too much for my reading."

Two months later it was the life of a parochial clergyman which attracted his attention and probably threw him into further confusion about which path he should choose. He stayed with Charles Thomas Baring, later bishop of Durham, "delighted with him and all about him—sat up till one with him talking on interesting, very interesting, questions." One wonders why Gladstone does not give any details of

the very interesting questions which they discussed until the early hours
of the morning. They may have included the life of a clergyman in the
Church of England and Gladstone's desire to serve God in this way.
William observed in his diary "They have prayers night and morning,
grace before and after breakfast, the form of godliness and the power
too." A letter to his mother stated "I was fully as much delighted with
him and all about him as I had expected. He seemed to be full of zeal
and as full of prudence in the performance of his duties."[16] Baring invited him to return to his parish whenever he wished.

      Augustus Saunders was another clergyman who evoked great
admiration from Gladstone and seems to have stirred in him the desire
to serve God as a clergyman. He went to stay with Saunders on 30 August, "Saunders received me most kindly—I trust this little break will
show me my helplessness and make me think of Him who was the giver of all my health and strength." His diary the next day states "Much
conversation with Saunders, returned to Oxford in evening." Did the
long conversation with Saunders only touch on his overwork and his
eye problem and perhaps anxiety about his studies? Surely Gladstone's
future profession must have been raised. Writing to Tom that day he
makes no attempt to hide his admiration for Saunders,[17] "kind and
friendly beyond anything . . . he begs me to come and live with him as
a friend from this moment . . . in short, there is no one thing in his power I am confident which he would not do for me with the utmost pleasure. Were he my own father he could do no more."

      When Gladstone started a new volume of his diary on Sunday
11 September 1831 he wrote "This little book may carry me through
very eventful time! God send the best." While the next twelve months
determined the rest of his eventful life at that moment the way ahead
was clouded with uncertainty. His spiritual development during three
years at Oxford suggests that the only possible way forward, if he was
to be obedient to God's will, was to accept the call to ordination and to
serve God in and through the church.

ii. *Prayer*

      Of his private journal William wrote "There are some things
which happen every day which I leave out," these omissions included
his private prayers. The omission of such essential parts of his life

makes it impossible to give a completely accurate account of his spirituality.

The prayer life of others often impressed Gladstone. After a family party with the high church bishop of Oxford, Charles Lloyd, he noted that there were prayers that night in the bishop's chapel. Prayers were offered morning and night, and grace at meals when he stayed at the home of Charles Baring. As family prayers were part of Gladstone's own life perhaps these diary references to the prayers of others was because in his experience the practice was not widespread. When unable to attend Sunday worship he "read prayers" at home, by this he probably meant Morning or Evening Prayer. At Oxford when he occasionally missed chapel he would read "prayers" alone in his room.

Concern about the propriety of informal prayer meetings prompted him to seek the advice of Edward Craig "Was it right for young men during their college course to meet together for extempore prayer?" Craig felt that there could be no objection to such professed Christians meeting together in this way, or to the use of extempore prayer and encouraged him to continue the practice.[18] The contents of the reply and other "interesting religious topics" were discussed with his friend Harrison. "I seem to be more bold in theory, but am more cowardly in practice." By this William may have meant that while persuaded about the value of prayer meetings and extempore prayer, neither came to him easily. There is no record of attendance at such meetings. Harrison's spirituality impressed William "Oh for his godly meekness and remarkable candour and simplicity." For Gladstone every act of public worship was an occasion when prayer was offered to the throne of grace. Of an ordination he wrote "It was a solemn service, and good to think that probably much prayer was ascending."

Prayer is the means through which man speaks to God, and God to man, therefore it is practised rather than read about. Nevertheless an informed view of prayer and ascetical theology requires appropriate reading. Gladstone's included Barrow's *Exposition of the Lord's Prayer*, Knight's *Forms of Prayer for the Use of Christian Families*, Head's *Observations on Early Rising and on Early Prayer*, and Stanhope's *Prayers and Meditations*. On 9 July 1830 he wrote something on meditation, but this does not seem to have survived; because of lack of evidence nothing can be said about his understanding of this type of prayer or whether he practised it. *The Rise and Progress of Religion in the Soul: . . . with a Devout Meditation or Prayer added to each chapter* (first published 1745, Gladstone's edt. 1817) by P. Doddridge was given to him by Helen. He began reading this on Sunday 26 June but there is no further mention of it, possibly because he used it as part of his daily prayers and devotions, although the volume shows little sign of use and contains no scorings or annotations! Another book read, but on which no comments are made, was Hannah More's *Spirit of Prayer*. A new edition of Charles J. Blomfield's *Manual of Family Prayers*, published in 1832 certainly used by Gladstone in the months after leaving Oxford, may have been used before that time in its first edition. It consists of a collection of prayers for the morning and evening of every day of the week. Scorings and annotations in both pencil and ink suggest it was used more than once. In two places Gladstone makes his own additions, both of which are significant and reflect his churchmanship. In a general intercession for the church he adds the words underlined "our intercessions, *as for the church established in this realm, so likewise*, for the universal Church . . ." Was he already an "establishment" man? In a prayer to be said on days when the Lord's Supper is administered, he added "*make us seek the table of the Lord, there* to discern the Lord's body." The diary contains occasional references to learning Sunday Collects by heart. An important part of his prayer life was the offering of ejaculatory prayers, in almost every circumstance of life, his studies, his shortcomings, sermons preached, sickness, friends with whom he discussed the Christian faith, and those who neglected the faith. Perilous coach journeys prompted prayer, as did his continental journey. "Let me pause for a moment on the eve of departure to offer my unworthy prayer." He asks God to be their guide that His purpose may be fulfilled in them. The sentiment of that prayer was applicable to the whole of Gladstone's life. He never seemed to doubt that God answered the prayers of the faithful and that such prayer could achieve miracles. A letter to his mother told of a young woman who had been an invalid for two years. Bulteel accompanied her and her mother in a whole night of prayer, which was followed by a miraculous recovery; William could not deny that it was a striking answer to prayer.[19]

In February 1830 he believed himself to be "leading a more unchristian life lately" largely because of failure in his prayer life, including "a grossly careless and sinful habit of saying my prayers when half asleep at night and half awake in the mornings." While self-critical, it is a sound theological observation, that when Christians neglect prayer there is a decline in the spiritual quality of their lives. But it is doubtful if Gladstone was really so neglectful.

Returning to Oxford in January 1831 he was determined to give himself without reserve to his studies. A reading plan was established requiring ten to eleven hours daily, but he acknowledges that success even in such temporal duties can be achieved only through prayer and the help of Christ. "Through Him and Him alone can I hope for any benefit or blessing." But prayer which touched every aspect of his life was only one of the means of grace used as part of his spiritual discipline and through which he sought to know God's will and to receive His help and strength. Scripture was another means available to achieve the same ends.

iii. *Holy Scripture*

Bible reading, another daily practice, was also generally omitted in the diary, but is referred to far more often than prayer. For Gladstone the bible was the word of God. Spiritual growth depended upon its daily reading, while an informed faith requires its systematic study. Diary references indicate how there is not always a clear distinction between the devotional and academic reading of scripture. Some of his views about the divine authority of scripture are mentioned in the unpublished letter to the Editor of the *Liverpool Mercury*. The *Mercury* had previously published some of his views on the usage of scripture texts. In this unpublished letter problems concerning the various interpretations of the bible are examined. He declares that there are many clear biblical exhortations to prayer, to earnest prayer, to continued prayer, to habitual prayers, to prayer for the light and guidance of God's Holy Spirit.[20]

With absolute confidence he states "that no man . . . having striven to humble his soul in prayer for light and understanding of the Scriptures and use of all other 'means of grace,' eventually remains in ignorance." The meaning of God's word is made known through faithful preaching. "Have we attended constantly those places where God's word is expounded by men whom we believed ordained to the Ministry? Have we used every means which long and deep consideration would suggest, for arriving at a right apprehension of the Word of God?" Throughout his life Gladstone sought to use every means available to arrive at a right understanding of scripture and its message of salvation. These convictions were the motivating force of his ceaseless reading and systematic study of God's word which in later life prompted him to write his book *The Impregnable Rock of Holy Scripture.*

Daily bible study could be private or corporate, sometimes it was both. Within weeks of going to Oxford he had begun reading a few verses of the Greek Testament "first thing" each morning. At home during his first vacation he "Began reading St. John's Gospel with A.M.G. and H.J.G. to which an hour a day is to be allotted & from which I hope to receive benefit." Neglect of daily bible reading was a rare occurrence, demanding special mention! "forgot to read the bible at night," an almost unforgivable sin. The Easter vacation finds him, with Helen, reading daily between 10-11 a.m. Paul's Epistle to the Romans, sometimes using Mant's commentary. Such bible study was in fact often assisted by suitable commentaries. On the return home from his continental tour he wrote "Resumed old practice—reading the Bible with Helen. May God grant it be not without its fruits."

Corporate bible study was not confined to his sisters; he and Anstice joined in such study during their time together with Saunders in July 1830. It may have been a regular practice until leaving Cuddesdon for, on Sunday 3 October, we have the brief comment "finished Genesis with Anstice."

In March 1831 William added a new item to his spiritual discipline. He resolved "From this time forth I purpose, please God, to commit to memory a passage of Scripture, say from four to eight verses, every Sunday." Such an exercise would bring spiritual benefit, for surely though "God has hidden much of his truth from our eyes, yet he has accorded to us in his word all the stirring motives, and all the cheering encouragements which could be derived from its full manifestation."[21]

Francis Doyle wrote to Gladstone in 1829 with a codicil added by Gaskell,[22] "I cannot disguise from you . . . that I entertain doubts" about the Christian religion. He asks if Gladstone can resolve these difficulties or direct him to books which would "restore me to a better state of mind." He hoped that William through his "advice and instruction may become in a great measure the means of fixing (his) wavering opinions." Issues raised included the inspiration of scripture. Unfortunately the diary makes no reference to either the letter or his answer. But what Doyle requested Gladstone had always practised, the reading of appropriate books and committing to paper his observations and sometimes his conclusions. Many of the points raised by Doyle and Gaskell were of a doctrinal nature. Perhaps it was the uncertainty and probings of his friends that prompted William to write in a "Private Notebook"[23] "let us prepare to accept a system from the Bible instead of bringing one to it: and by the efficacy of humble prayer, through Christ our Lord, we shall perchance be brought if not to reconcile the conflicting doctrines, yet to realize the practical use which appears to flow from each respectively."

The New Testament occupied his attention throughout 1829 and his reading included Hannah More *Essay on the Character and Practical Writings of St. Paul* (1815), Richard Whateley *Essays on Some of the Difficulties in the Writings of St. Paul, and in other parts of the New Testament*, and Richard Mant's nine sermons, covering 540 pages, which constituted the Bampton Lectures of 1812. Gladstone's scored and annotated copy of Mant has been preserved and has a note at the end "In these lectures there are very many passages which would offend those whose cause he seems to advocate." He also read *The Unconditional Freeness of the Gospel: in Three Essays* (1829) by Thomas Erskine and Erskine's *Remarks on the Internal Evidence for the Truth of Revealed Religion* (1820), which was very much in line with some of the questions raised by Gaskell and Doyle.

Notes on his daily bible reading of St. Matthew and St. John were recorded in a notebook.[24] Forty-one pages of small handwriting, including a verse by verse examination of Matthew's Gospel, are followed by twenty-one pages devoted to St. John, both containing quotations from the Greek text. Another manuscript was produced at this period; the first part, in three columns is a "Harmony of Matthew and John." The second part is a "Harmony and Chronology of St. Matthew and St. John" covering the whole of both Gospels, which is carefully and systematically laid out.[25]

Whether Gladstone completed Isaac Newton's two part book *Observations upon the Prophecies of Daniel and the Apocalypse of St. John* (1733) is uncertain, but what he read may have influenced his manuscript "Scripture Oppositions." Nine small pages of "Scripture

Oppositions" in parallel columns are followed by notes on Prophecy and various quotations on prophecies relating to Christ. Gladstone makes no reference to the pre-millennial, post-millennial debate which had once again become popular in the early part of the nineteenth century. Among those who contributed towards the revived interest was Iscac Newton. The French Revolution convinced many that the return of Christ must be imminent.[26] In addition to notes on prophecy topics on which quotations are given include unction, fasting, ordination, participation in Christ's death and intercessory prayer. Among other biblical works read were T.W. Lancaster *The Harmony of the Law and the Gospel* (1825) and W. Selwyn *The Doctrine of Types, and Its Influence on the Interpretation of the New Testament* (1829).

A "Collection of Psalms" produced during this period marks the beginning of Gladstone's lifelong devotion to the Psalter, which played an increasing part in his spiritual life. This interesting compilation is a "scissors and paste" collection of psalms cut from several books.[27] Unfortunately we are told nothing about its purpose, although pencil annotations in Gladstone's hand suggest that it might have been used as "appointed psalms" for special seasons; the headings include Advent, Christmas, Epiphany, Lent, Good Friday, Easter, Whitsunday, Trinity and Harvest. Such compilations as this, his various written studies, his systematic reading on the subject, his regular biblical study and his daily devotional bible reading together demonstrate the importance Gladstone placed upon holy scripture, God's word to man. He was convinced that whether the bible was read devotionally or academically the Holy Spirit assists the reader: "Surely at each and every occasion on which we sit down to read the Scriptures we ought to remember to seek, and as far as possible to realise to ourselves the presence and aid of the Holy Spirit."[28]

Gladstone believed that through bible reading, guided by the Holy Spirit and the illumination of Christ, the word of God is made known to the believer. This word reveals man as he really is, a sinner before God standing in need of salvation. "It contains all that is necessary for salvation . . . The writings of the Apostles must be to us especially precious since in them only it is that we see the perfect form of Christianity revealed."[29] His own systematic study of scripture, especially the New Testament, kept before him the true nature of God and the cost of man's redemption. Reflecting on these things he became in-

creasingly conscious of his utter unworthiness. He stood before God as
a condemned sinner and yet redeemed in Christ. Unfortunately,
throughout his life, Gladstone had a tendency to dwell upon his depravity, his fallen and unredeemed nature, rather than the redemption already secured for him in and through Christ's death, in which he participated through baptism, faith and the eucharist.

iv. *Sin and Self-examination*

Gladstone's acute sense of sin prompted constant self-
accusation and self-examination, particularly on his birthday, the last
day of the year and the anniversary of Anne's birthday or death. Even
by evangelical standards his self-abasement seems excessive. What he
saw as human weakness in connection with his emerging sexuality and
the opposite sex caused him to bewail his sinful and fallen nature.
Some Gladstonian writers have over-emphasised this point because of
their failure to understand the finer points of ascetical theology. Gladstone himself was often confused; he fails to be objective about his sin
and weakness, recording everything which tells against him and belit-
tling his triumphs. Occasionally he confuses temptation and a propensity to sin with actual sin, failing to acknowledge that a sense of sin and
guilt leading to true repentance results in forgiveness and renewal. Obsession with his sin thus often blinds him to a sound doctrine of forgiveness and redemption. In many areas of theology Gladstone read
round the subject but there is no record of his having read between
1828 and 1832 a single work on systematic, dogmatic or ascetical theology specifically relating to sin, repentance and forgiveness. At the
same time, some of the books he read did deal with the subject. *The
Rise and Progress of Religion in the Soul* is typical of such books; here
the word "sinner" appears in the title of the first nine chapters.

A number of sources contributed towards William's obsession
with sin: his evangelical upbringing, his reading of scripture, his personal prayer, the church's liturgical rites, his growing understanding of
doctrine and ascetical theology, his sexuality and his own very sensitive
nature. The interrelatedness of doctrinal and ascetical concepts and the
complexity of Gladstone's nature and his language make it impossible
to determine exactly what made him so sensitive on this issue. Failure
to measure up to Anne's sanctity, failure to accept God's will and a call

to ordination, academic pride and ambition, sexual temptations, the neglect of some aspects of his spiritual discipline, all contributed towards
his sense of sin, sometimes verging upon Calvinistic "total depravity."

So far as his understanding of sin was concerned, scripture, especially the Psalter and New Testament, was his schoolmaster. A study
of the Psalms in 1830[30] moved him to reflect on the Psalmist's invitation that men should commune within their heart and be still before
God. Such servants of the Lamb withdraw themselves for a while to
dwell on the doctrine of the Cross, contrasting their sinfulness with the
boundless love of God. For others the face of Jesus, the mighty and the
merciful, is veiled in clouds, his voice gives chastisement, to show
"how sinful is his heart." Was this a spiritually objective examination?
Perhaps not, for he continues "My conscience, the mirror of my soul,
exhibits nought but deformity . . . much pride, much pretension: but of
the profession of godliness little." Pondering on his own sinfulness he
writes what can only be described as the prayer of a penitent sinner:
"Chasten me O my God . . . Give me pain O Lord, if by pain I may best
be refined into Godliness." But he does not go on to ask for forgiveness, but "a perception of the depth of my sinfulness and my condemnation . . . the wretchedness of my lost estate . . . the utter foulness of
mine own soul." Even when he moves to a more positive note there is
no clear cry for forgiveness, or an acceptance of what the Gospel offers; "let me thank thee through Jesus Christ our Lord, let me pant and
long earnestly for deliverance by his blood."

On another occasion he writes of man's fallen nature "Does
not the Bible expressly declare that we are fallen from the image of
God? If so . . . Is it the deep and fond desire of our souls, the earnest
and continual prayer of our life, to be renewed."[31] This is undoubtedly
autobiographical, why then cannot Gladstone accept for himself the
Gospel he believes and preaches to others? Perhaps he was blind to his
obsession with sin and his failure to apply the message of forgiveness
to himself, that in Christ God accepts and forgives the penitent sinner.

In a letter to Robertson he touched upon a weakness in their
sister Helen, a temptation to magnify things beyond reality including
illness and her own weaknesses.[32] Aware of the human temptation to
magnify things beyond reality, why did he not see this as one of his
own weaknesses? And why did he not always see the profound difference between temptation to sin and actual sin? Past sin often invokes

the feeling of guilt moving the sinner to repentance and then to receive
forgiveness. But Gladstone's understanding of "guilt" is not always
clear. It is not clear exactly what he meant when he wrote "In estimating our guilt as to the past, we cannot look too much to ourselves: in
framing our resolution for future conduct, we cannot work too little."[33]
Perhaps he was suggesting that man needs to reform himself rather than
to rely upon the grace of God and His unmerited love and free forgiveness. "Repentance," he wrote, "in the sense in which it is . . . necessary
to faith and justification, is indeed a determined movement of the soul
from sin towards God."[34] But he does not go on to say that it is in that
act of true repentance and the determined move from sin towards God
that the sinner is offered and must accept God's free forgiveness.

It is against this theological background and aware of Gladstone's blind spots concerning his "supposed" sinfulness and his need
for a clearer understanding of God's free forgiveness to the penitent sinner that the written accounts of his self-examination and declared "depravity" must be examined. To do this on a chronological basis will
help to reveal whether, with the passing of time, there were any significant changes in his understanding of this part of his spiritual life.

"May this year, or any part of it which God may give, be better spent than the last: as regards God, man and myself." Such was
Gladstone's earnest prayer on 1 January 1828. That year he hoped the
Liverpool Mercury would publish his article on the Christian faith, including the nature of human sin. "Man," he wrote "enters the world
with the taint of sin upon him, God's infinite justice required a satisfaction for sin which was found in Christ. "There is *one* Mediator between
God and man . . . there is *one* full, true, perfect and sufficient sacrifice
of expiation . . . there is one price paid for our ransom." It is very much
the doctrine of penal substitution. With such a view of sin and forgiveness one can begin to understand why he failed to be amicable towards
himself.

Looking back on his nineteenth year on 29 December 1828 he
can discern no marks of improvement, but can see "many grievous
crimes, many unlawful fears and defections." At this stage in his life his
self-condemnation and introspection about his sinful nature are comparatively mild. A sense of sin and humiliation would, he felt in May
1829, prove to be a happy state, but in November he wrote of his "deep,
inveterate, pervading depravity." Is he inferring that he was depraved

and yet had no genuine sense of sin? That can hardly be true.

Self-examination on his twentieth birthday was more rigorous than ever before. The central thought is his own sin. A besetting sin is acknowledged but not named, and is a matter for speculation—"there has been black sin on my part," but "The blood of Christ cleaneth from *all sin*." His list of ten points is an account of how a Christian seeking above all else to live in Christ sees his life; as he draws nearer to God he becomes increasingly conscious of his own sin and utter unworthiness. Seen in this light, were Gladstone's self-examinations unhealthy, self-condemnatory exercises, or the sincere exercises of one seeking sanctification? The tenth point returns to sin "I am most certain of my own sinfulness yet this certainty is not a pervading nor a living belief." Possibly a vague confession that secretly he believed himself holy and well on the way to sanctification, and was inwardly proud of his Christian life. If such were his hidden thoughts he would be right to declare that while recognising himself as "the chief of sinners" this was not really a "living belief," in which case he was confessing an hypocrisy known only to God.

A number of events in 1830 motivate even more introspection and self-effacement: these included the anniversaries of Anne's birthday and death, events in Oxford, including violence from his fellow students, his birthday and the New Year. In a notebook marked "Private" he wrote out a self-analysis and an account of his own sinfulness. Such accounts were not meant for any human eye. Passing references in the diary touch upon hidden feelings concerning his failure to live out his Christian life and calling. An unchristian life, sinfulness, pride, sloth, greed, lust, envy, covetousness, debasement, self-disgust and hypocrisy are all listed.

An objective study of "self-examination" was attempted in June 1830.[35] "We speak of self-examination: if we practice it in addition, so much the better: but who can understand it? Who can investigate and analyse that mysterious process, in which *the understanding* sits in judgment on *the heart*: which itself so powerfully affects the source from whence the verdict is to proceed. And while the accused influences that which acts as judge and accuses and almost forms the decisions of that tribunal before which it is arraigned, who is that third party, that mysterious 'I' who watches the process, scrutinises it in all and each of its steps, and registers and records the result? O mystery of mysteries, all is mystery." Introspective he may have been, but at least he tried to understand the process and the hidden influences which are brought to bear in such an exercise. Dangers involved were not sufficient reason to abandon the practice. Self-analysis was applied to his own life that November.[36] "I having the name of religion inseparably attached to me am destitute of its power, and have neither love, service, sorrow, nor alarm to offer to my God." Gladstone desired, above all else, that the love of God should be the governing principle of his life. Yet other things monopolise his attention and hamper his spiritual progress. Out of such inner conflict he prayed "But still there is hope in the crucified one. May he teach me to live and die for him, transformed from my present dark chilly habitual indifference."

This same "private" notebook contains an account of his battle with pride. 'In the constitution of my own pride there is something peculiarly subtle and intangible," making his pride a "formidable enemy." Victory over such pride can come only through a "heaven provided instrument" or by "assiduous and fervent prayer to the throne of grace." Searching his soul he asks himself whether he really believed himself the "chief of sinners," or was it a term he used without meaning and without believing what he was saying?[37] Another study in this same book, but possibly written earlier that year, reflects on his sloth, greed, pride and selfishness. "O sinner, vile and depraved as thou art, learn a lesson . . . for if thou dost know some of the greatness of the love of Christ—if thou hast tasted some of those pleasures which belong to the sanctified only beware how thou continuest to grieve the Spirit of God."[38] Was this a heart-felt cry prompted by his continued uncertainty regarding God's will for his life, or because many other influences were now monopolising his attention and squeezing out his desire to serve God in the church?

Utter despair came upon him at the remembrance of Anne on 24 December 1830. Reading some of her letters to John, where she mentioned William with approval, he is overcome with sorrow and shame by what he reads and accuses himself of being a sinner veiled in godliness, desperately wicked and a hypocrite. He goes on to confess that he only half believes what he writes about himself, adding that there are some things which guilt and shame prevent him from committing to paper, the "sinner within my rankling passions (passions which I dare not name—shame forbids it and duty does not seem to require it)."

In his diary Gladstone tries to be honest with himself and God and his highly sensitive conscience spurs on his incessant struggle for the inward truth about himself. The quotation given is the nearest the diary gets to an explicit reference to the inner and hidden battle with his sexuality. Unfortunately, lack of any other explicit references have encouraged some to undertake a "witch hunt," finding sexual connotations in what they regard as implicit references, emotional events and close relationships. Examples of this are found in connection with his confirmation, his friendship with Hallam, his social contact with girls, and the normal temptations of healthy adolescence. No one would deny that Gladstone was a person of strong sexuality and this caused him many inner tensions at Eton, Oxford and throughout his life.

There can be little doubt that many of his acts of self-examination and his sincere self-accusations, coupled with the recognition of his sin, his utter unworthiness and many other strong descriptions of himself as the "chief of sinners" were influenced by his feeling of guilt in connection with sex and his own sexuality. But there is a great danger in over-emphasising his sexual problems and associated guilt in such a way that the genuineness of his deep Christian faith and love of God are overshadowed or distorted. The aim of his life was to love Christ, to love God. God's holiness and the depth of His love revealed in Christ were a constant reminder to the young Gladstone of his own unworthiness. Drawing near to God each day through prayer and bible reading also stirred in him a deep and genuine sense of personal sin and of his lack of true Christian love. His devotional reading, his regular reception of Communion, his periodic acts of self-examination, all made him acutely aware of his "vileness" and shortcomings. The influence of his sexual turmoil, however strong, can hardly have been a daily influence on his profession of sin as he drew near to God through these appointed means of grace. Obviously they sometimes did and the diary shows that there were particular circumstances and occasions of heart-searching, or sexual temptation, which profoundly affected the wording of his confessions of sin and "depravity."

The holiness and purity seen in his mother and his sainted sister Anne did not help, and occasionally made him bewail the "blackness" of his own character, making him feel that his own spirituality was false; that he was surrounded with the "veil of godliness," when in fact he was "deceitful above all things," a "hypocrite, and the essence of sins" and "desperately wicked." And so, his so-called "besetting sin," his guilt about sex, aggravated by adolescent sexual temptations, to which he may from time to time have yielded (although there is not the slightest indication of how often he gave way) may have resulted in masturbation, schoolboy sexual talk and flirtations with erotic or pornographic literature. But at best this is no more than speculation for there are no explicit references and even those seen to be "implicit" may be open to serious question.

Reflecting on the life of his saintly sister, while aware of his sexual tendencies, made him feel "unworthy of her love" and a "devil" in disguise. Much of this was exaggerated through sexual ignorance, made worse because of veiled references by preachers, schoolmasters and others to "degrading temptations." William cannot have been very different from many other boys of his time, or indeed since. He found it difficult to deal with his own sexuality, and his ruthless and unsuccessful attempts to suppress the natural experiences and urges of adolescence, which he saw as appalling temptations, produced an intense feeling of guilt. Intimate schoolboy friendships, not only a problem in public schools, while not an actual problem to William, may have caused him a little concern. Gladstone was unprepared for close encounters with the opposite sex—a fact seen in his diary account on 12 January 1831 of a party when he met some young ladies and reflected on this obviously enjoyable experience. "But it seems to me that female society, whatever the disadvantages may be, has just and manifold uses attendant upon it in turning the mind away from some of its most dangerous and degrading temptations." His dislike of balls may have been caused by the fear of close physical contact with females and the possible thoughts and temptations which might accompany such an activity. A number of writers feel that his rescue work, which began at Oxford, was an attempt to sublimate his strong sexuality and its accompanying temptations. His birthday self-examination in 1831, having left Oxford, tells something of this inner warfare referred to as "the blackness of my natural (& vigorous) tendencies," which he says "might well strike despair in my soul." While they make him feel a sense of "shame and humiliation" he is mindful of God's love and abiding presence and prays that he "might grow into the image of the Redeemer." However strong the tensions and temptations of his sexuality, the love and service of God in Christ were for him always stronger and uppermost. Four days after that heart-searching experience when he mourned his "rankling passions," he undertakes his annual self-examination, which was much briefer than the previous year. A new interest is listed "Politics are fascinating to me, perhaps too fascinating."

Entering 1831 and still uncertain about his future profession he prays "May God keep me during the coming year and from day to day may I approach more a practical belief that *he* is my friend. I mine enemy." As a result of the objective studies of certain aspects of his spirituality he now had clearer notions on a few subjects. On 17 January he accuses himself of being a "hypocrite," "inconsistent," "wavering," "uncertain." Anne's letters prompt new accusations of deception and move him to pray "'May I know thee and in knowing love thee and from loving serve thee." The love and service of God must be supreme in his life, but how was he to serve God?

His waning interest in the church might be an indication that the love and service of God were no longer uppermost in his life. Politics and the Reform Bill had become major occupations. His skill as a debater was increasingly recognised and reached a new height during the three days debate, "a debate such as was never known in the Society before" was his comment to his brother Robertson.[39] Gladstone had spoken for three-quarters of an hour on an amendment. The vote was decisive, ninety-four votes *to* thirty-eight. Dr. Perry Butler concludes "It was from this speech that Gladstone's political career derived."[40] Following his outstanding success in this Union debate he wrote in his diary on Monday 30 May 1831 "It has happened to me of late since my speech to receive more compliments than usual. It has also happened that I have never had cause to feel my own utter and abandoned sinfulness before God more deeply. Oh who can look at these bitterly instructive contrasts and yet deny that there is a Providence wonderfully framing out of a seeming series of accidents the most appropriate and aptest discipline for each of our souls." What actually does Gladstone mean? Is he saying that through the recent events, the political activities in which he had been involved, the Reform Bill and other happenings in his life "a seeming series of accidents" that God's will for his life was now becoming clear, that he was to serve God and bring the nation to the foot of the Cross? Or was it his adoption of politics and the abandonment of the idea of "entering the Church," which he saw as an abandonment of God? The day before he commented "how can one so lost as myself be fit to advise or in any way benefit friends." If he was now more uncertain than ever about his love of God and his obedience to God's will, how could he on that sabbath day of 29 May 1831 offer any real spiritual advice to his friends?

Within the seclusion of Seaforth House, with Oxford and academic success behind him, and his future still uncertain Gladstone must have spent considerable time on Thursday 29 December producing his longest ever self-examination. Reference is made to the "melancholy tale of my own inward life"; there had been no improvement in his moral conduct, but he was convinced of the necessity and benefit of prayer.

At this crucial stage in his life it was natural that his thoughts should be dominated by the future. He asks God to use him "as a vessel for his own purpose." May he ever be mindful of God's love and "abiding presence." He then records what he now believed was God's will for his life and writes of "a desire of higher aim than I could ever have imagined, a fervent and a buoyant hope that I might work an energetic work in this world, and by that work . . . I might grow into the image of the Redeemer. Would that I could feel in the particularity and clearness of detail all that these words imply." What matters is "that the Will of God concerning me is to be found, and all the purposes of God through me are to be wrought." But if a career in politics was now believed to be God's will and the way forward, there were possible dangers, threats to his relationship with God upon which all else depended. Thus he prays "May those faint and languishing embers be kindled by the breath of the everlasting Spirit into a living and life-giving flame, and with a heart and mind struggling continually upward, may I never, O never, leave the cross of Jesus Christ, nor forget its simplicity and power."

At last Gladstone seemed confident about God's will for his life. Politics offered a sphere in which he could serve both God and his fellow men. The shadows and uncertainty had passed, but unfortunately doubt returned with future events and further reflections. Nevertheless, it was now clear that Gladstone was a deeply committed churchman who believed that God's will and purpose for his life, and the part that he must play in the salvation of his fellow men, was of ultimate importance.

v. The *Dominical Sacraments*

(a) Baptism

Gladstone's pilgrimage towards a high doctrine of baptism reached its zenith with his acceptance of baptismal regeneration and has been partly examined already.

For an evangelical, acceptance of baptismal regeneration had several implications. It was contrary to the Calvinistic doctrine of predestination which reserved God's redemption for the elect, those whose salvation is predetermined. Thus it offered a new understanding of God and the means He uses for the salvation of mankind. With Anne, William came to believe that true believers who received this sacrament could and did enjoy the full benefits of God's grace. They were regenerated, born anew, received into the church, the ark of redemption, assuring them of salvation and the forgiveness of sins. Denial of baptismal regeneration had become the touchstone of evangelical orthodoxy and so Gladstone's acceptance of the doctrine not only made it impossible for him to hold, if he ever did, certain Calvinistic doctrines concerning man's salvation, but it also marked his move away from the evangelical school. Insistence upon a conversion experience being necessary for true believers and salvation was also rejected by implication.

Many books were read and eminent divines consulted before he embraced this doctrine. Such a systematic examination illustrates how he could not accept a radical doctrinal change until he was convinced that the doctrine was sound, scriptural and the teaching of the church. On the day William arrived in Liverpool for Anne's funeral he began to read John Bird Sumner's *Apostolic Preaching considered in: An Examination of St. Paul's Epistles*, in which Sumner examined predestination, grace, justification, sanctification and intercourse with the world. Eight days later the book was finished. It is heavily scored throughout. Sumner stated that the church is the authorised interpreter of scripture; this statement is not scored, but Gladstone was soon to hold that the church, as well as scripture, is a teacher of the Faith. A few pages later he scored the statement that "infants by baptism, are regenerate." Only a matter of days before he began compiling "Opinions on Baptism in another form and on a fresh plan." That day he wrote some notes on baptism and read a *Brief Discourse about Baptism* by Thomas Moore.

Further reading took place during the year, including the public formularies on baptism. The following month he read *Conversations on Infant Baptism* (1819) by the evangelical divine Charles Jerram. Gradually his new collections of opinions began to take shape and were laid out in three parts, under the title "A Collection of Testimonies concerning Baptismal Regeneration."[41] Part 1 was given the title "From Public Formularies and Other Authorised Documents"; here he examines the evidence from scripture, the testimonies of the Fathers, the language of the authorised formularies, including the baptismal services, the Catechism, Articles and Homilies. Part 2. "From Church Divines Since the Reformation down to . . .," includes quotations from Archbishops Parker, Leighton and Secker and Bishops Hooper, Jewel, Andrewes, Ridley and many others. Part 3. "From Church Divines since and of the present day." Among those quoted are Archbishop Richard Laurence, whose book *The Doctrine of the Church of England upon the Efficacy of Baptism vindicated from Misrepresentation* (1816) he read in October 1829. He also quoted from *Essays on St. Paul* by Dr. Whately, Sumner's *Apostolic Preaching*, Heber's Bampton Lectures, *The Personality and Office of the Christian Comforter*, Herbert's *Country Parson* and Hooker's *Ecclesiastical Polity*. Gladstone expressed the conviction that "believing parents who have their children baptized will have every reason to believe their own children regenerate."[42]

Over thirty years later he added a note to this "Collection": "This was the work of my boyhood";[43] there is no evidence that in the intervening period he read *Treatise on Baptism* published in 1840 by the leading evangelical Edward Bickersteth. This "boyhood" pursuit made a fundamental contribution to his development as a churchman, his acceptance of the doctrine of baptismal regeneration and his ability to hold an informed view of that doctrine. His appended note continues "Trained in the idea that the Sacraments of Christ were no more than signs of that which they truly signify, I was utterly shaken out of it by perusal of the Holy Scriptures: and then fearful lest I should be erring I sought to prop myself with testimony. This is my distant but I think substantially accurate recollection."

The 1829 "Collection" was not his last word on the subject, for on Sunday 16 September 1832 he wrote "began to write on the subject of Baptism—God prosper it." The next day he recorded "interesting conversation with my Mother, mainly on the nature of Baptism." Had she been won over to the doctrine of baptismal regeneration? Not only did his views on baptism change while at Oxford, but his position on the eucharist, the second of the "Sacraments of Christ," also underwent a change, but not quite so radical at this stage, as his acceptance of baptismal regeneration.

(b) The Eucharist

Unfortunately during this period Gladstone neither read nor wrote very much on the eucharist and this makes it impossible to say much about the writers who influenced his thoughts or his own doctrine. Gladstone's understanding of the eucharist from his Eton days and in connection with his evolving churchmanship has already been examined. There is therefore little to add to what has already been written. During his student days he received Holy Communion on average monthly, occasionally recording the number of communicants and rejoicing when there was an increase; when there were twelve he noted "Sacrament—a great increase thank God!" It was a rare occurrence for him to miss the Sacrament. Despite his preparation before receiving Communion he often felt ill-prepared "Sacrament: as cold and unprepared as usual"; "went to Sacrament at St. James's—but never went to it less as a feast, more as a medicine God mend me."

A long letter to his recently confirmed sister Helen provides some insight into his beliefs about the eucharist.[44] His use of the words "you all" suggest that this was a "public" letter, thus the whole family would be informed of his views. "I have thought of you at the Sacrament today." Did this imply that he offered special intentions at the altar, perhaps on this occasion for Helen receiving her first communion? "I take it for granted from what you say you have been there." What follows suggests that he was moving away from an individualistic and pietistic understanding of the Sacrament:" may we all find its pleasures and privileges with its responsibilities." Turning to the situation at Oxford he wrote "Here, there is a great deal that is painful immediately preceding the celebration of it: but it would appear there is great cause for thankfulness . . . since I am told that about five or six years ago a very clever and excellent man named Trower (of Eton) was hissed publicly for attending that solemn rite here." A marked improvement is seen in the fact that "Now there seems to be always five or six undergraduates."

Christmas Day 1829 was spent at Cuddesdon with Saunders. That day he not only received the Sacrament but also read Archbishop Edward Synge's tract *An Answer to all the Excuses and Pretences which Men ordinarily make for their not coming to Holy Communion. To which is added a Brief Account of the End and Design of the Holy Communion, the Obligation to receive it, the Way to prepare for it. and the behaviour at and after it.* The title page bears an additional note *Fitted for the meanest Capacities, and very proper to be given away by such as are charitably inclined,* to which end copies were available at 20s per hundred. Never can a pamphlet have had a more sympathetic reader, not least of the prayer printed at the end for use before, at and after the Communion. Two days later be began to read Jeremy Taylor *The Rule and Exercise of Holy Living*; his preserved copy is full of scorings and annotations. While the copy is an 1828 edition we cannot be certain that the annotations belong to this period, as Gladstone reread this devotional classic twice in 1836. That year he also read *Holy Dying*, returning to *Holy Living* again in 1841. Like Archbishop Synge's work this also contains guidelines "Of Preparation to, and the manner how to receive the Holy Sacrament of the Lord's Supper." It also contains a collection of prayers for preparation, during and after Holy Communion.

Publications such as Synge's and Taylor's might have prompted William to compile his own collection of prayers for the eucharist. Somewhere about or before 1831 he began to produce his own manual for Holy Communion, "Secreta Eucharistica."[45] Much later he drew together a carefully prepared collection of prayers which became his regular companion at the eucharist. After his death his family gave serious thought to the publication of the final collection used by their father to the end of his life.[46] His first attempt at such a manual was extremely limited, but marked a decisive step for one nurtured in the evangelical tradition. It is also a further indication of his "high doctrine" of the eucharist even in these early days. The first part of "Secreta Eucharistica" has the heading "Before the Office, or the part of it peculiar to Celebration," and begins "Ps. 116,vv.11 12" the verses are then given in full. Part two "At the Oblation of Bread and Wine or of alms." This is followed by a prayer from the Scottish Office and a prayer in Latin. Part three "At the close of the prayers for the Church Militant, if there be time." This is followed by the beginning of a prayer in English and Latin, but it is incomplete.

While at Oxford the Holy Communion became an essential part in Gladstone's spiritual life, requiring careful preparation. In receiving the Sacrament the recipient not only received grace, pleasures and privileges, but also the responsibility to live out the Christian life in all its fullness.

The importance of the eucharist in Gladstone's later life was undoubtedly built upon the firm foundation in practice, devotion and understanding laid during these years at Oxford.

vi. *Christian Living*

While for the young and maturing Gladstone prayer, bible reading and the eucharist were all essential parts of his religious life, they were regarded as but parts of a total spirituality finding both private and public expression.

The sabbath was a subject on which Gladstone had very definite ideas. Typical of many Sunday diary entries is that of 13 December 1829. "Ch & Sermon morning & aftn—out with Harrison & Moncrieff, & evg alone. read Mant—Shuttleworth's Serm. at Festival of Sons of the Clergy, very able and good—Barrow on the Crucifixion (admirable)—Heber's J. Taylor—Bible—writing &c." Essential elements included churchgoing, the Sacrament when available, hearing and reading sermons, prayer, bible reading, and reading any subject which it was felt would benefit Christian growth. Other acceptable occupations were walking, talking, ideally on religious topics, and writing family letters. Entertaining friends to wine or tea was acceptable but not wine parties. Academic study and writing, pleasure pursuits and travel were all unacceptable.

His understanding of the sabbath had been influenced by his family but he felt it essential to read round the subject, which was touched upon in many printed sermons, episcopal Charges and devotional works. In Taylor's *Holy Living* the section on the keeping of the Lord's Day bears Gladstone's scoring, highlighting what he felt essential. Worship is a sabbath activity and Gladstone indicates his approval of Taylor's observations "God's rest is to be understood to be a behold-ing and rejoicing in his work finished: and therefore we truly represent God's rest, when we confess and rejoice in God's works and God's glo-ry." There is no confusion between keeping the sabbath and the Lord's Day, a point covered in Holy Living and again scored by William. "The observation of the Lord's Day differs nothing from the observation of the sabbath, in the matter of religion, but in the manner." What is for-bidden gains his approval "Upon the Lord's Day we must abstain from all servile and laborious works, except such, which are matters of ne-cessity, of common life, or of great charity: for these are permitted by that authority, which hath separated the day for holy use." Finally, Gladstone places an NB in the margin against the words "Those, who labour hard in the week, must be eased upon the Lord's Day; such ease being a great charity and alms but, at no hand, must they be permitted to use any unlawful games, including games prompting to wantonness, drunkenness, quarrelling and superstitious customs." His final words re-ceived Gladstone's wholehearted support "let Lord's Day refreshments be innocent, and charitable, and of good report, and not exclusive to the duties of religion." Gladstone occasionally had reservations on the last point, for some of his "non religious" sabbath activities did cause him a little heart-searching.

Sabbath reading over a period of four months included *The Di-vine Authority and Perpetual Obligation of the Lord's Day, asserted in Seven Sermons*. This 206 paged volume was written by the evangelical Daniel Wilson, Vice-Principal of St. Edmund Hall, Oxford. The diary and the scorings in both pencil and ink indicate that the work was read gradually and possibly more than once. Unfortunately Gladstone had the book re-bound, when it was obviously "cut" affecting some of his annotations. Three statements scored in the sermon on "The Practical Duties of the Christian Sabbath" supported his convictions: "We must rise to the standard of the Sabbath as set forth in the Bible, not sink the Bible to the level of our wayward passions." A double scoring high-lights the observation "To rise up to the dignity of the Sabbath, and to perform any of its duties aright, we must understand what sanctification is, who the great God is to whose service we are to be devoted, what that Creator and Redeemer claims of us who on this day rose from the dead." Wilson's comments on the responsibility of the head of the Christian family also receive double scoring "The head of every family has a charge of souls, as it were, committed to him; he is a priest in his own house. He has to promote the sanctification of all under his roof. His order, his piety, his appearance, in public, church and in his house, surrounded with his children and dependents, is an acknowledgment and badge of the God whom he worships." Gladstone, ever critical of his supposed laziness, recognised that the harder a man worked the more he needed the God-given sabbath rest. Occasional comments express his conviction that the correct keeping of the sabbath was essential for sanctification and preparation for eventual death. His "double approval" marked "The more lawful business any Christian has, the more is the necessity of a thorough religious interval on the Sabbath increased. Every man must find time to die, and ought to find time for devoting to God that day which prepares for death." Gladstone read "Whately on Sabbath," making no comment, but he was critical of a sermon preached by him when made Archbishop of Dublin, "his anti-sabbatical doctrine is I fear as mischievous as it is unsound." Respect for the dignity of the office did not place Whately beyond criticism.

The Portraiture of a Christian Gentleman, 1831 written by the barrister William Roberts, occupied part of Gladstone's sabbath reading on 3 July 1831. Three weeks later he wrote "Finished Christian Gentleman, which I like extremely." He probably used later sections of the book, devoted to "The Sabbath of the Christian Gentleman" when he wrote in his diary "Christian Gentleman—wrote out some arguments on the Sabbath." The author's observations on the sabbath bear William's scorings. Unfortunately we do not have a copy of his "arguments" but we do have letters and diary entries. A letter to Helen on 1 February 1829 expresses his feelings concerning the abuse of the sabbath, touched upon again a few days later.[47] "We were *all* shocked with the abuse of Sunday at Christ Church: Is it not in the Dean's . . . power to stop anything so scandalous?" Thomas complains that letters written by William on Saturday were two days old when received and comments "I cannot think that you *seriously object* to putting on paper, to *your own family*, on Sunday, what you would if with them, verbally, though you may to the habit of common letter writing." Letters to his father imply that William did not object to family or charitable correspondence on Sunday.[48] The diary refers to mis-spent Sundays described as "poor," "useless" and "unprofitable" when an observer of his activities and spiritual industry would acknowledge them as exemplary.

Such rigorous sabbath keeping was the approach of all main line evangelicals of that period.[49] Religious conversation was a part of evangelical witness; numerous explicit references to Sabbath "religious conversations" are recorded in the journal, in addition to countless references to meetings, talks, discussions and conversations on Sundays with a host of different people, with no explicit reference to religion but the people involved and other activities of the day make it impossible to believe that religious topics were not sometimes discussed. Conversations also took place on weekdays, sometimes until midnight, but they were certainly not confined to religion; politics, poetry and ghost stories were among the things discussed.

Churchgoing was obligatory on Sunday and assisting at Sunday School was a commendable activity. Mid-week chapel attendance is not a frequent diary entry, but occasional references such as "in chapel as usual" suggest that he was a regular, if not daily, attender. In January 1830 he "began prickbillship" a duty which fell upon junior students who had to keep the roll of undergraduates attending chapel. He also had the duty of "Surplice prayers." "I now read responses in chapel at Veysie's request and it helps to fix one's waywardness or at least to check it." Wandering thoughts during worship were obviously a problem to Gladstone. Sunday worship was shared between the Cathedral, which served as college chapel, and other churches in Oxford. Chapel was however sometimes missed through over-sleeping: "Wrote an imposition, for skipping chapel—3rd time in five days—of which I am really ashamed. It was however owing to a long and interesting conversation I had with Egerton which kept me up till late." The discipline of regular college chapel services played an important part in his spirituality at Oxford and was something he appreciated. But was it right for Sunday worship? On Sunday 24 July 1831 he wrote "Chapel mg & aftn. Heard Buckley and Newman. The former better than ever, the latter good too. I do not quite know what to do about evening church. There is little satisfaction in our chapel, the service is scarcely performed with common decency: and the time prevents my going to hear Buckley whom I regularly attend in the morning. I can however come in for part of the sermon at St. Mary's, but it is not altogether an agreeable arrangement."

Lack of dignity and decency was not the only thing which deterred him from worship for he confessed on Good Friday 1831 "At Ch & Sacrament . . . Too late for aftn Ch from seeing John off—But I should have gone had I expected a good sermon—was I right in keeping away? I wish I could see the rule on this subject." This confession touched upon what Gladstone regarded as an important part of his religious observances, listening to sermons.

"An *excellent* sermon" was the extent of Gladstone's comment when he first heard Edward Bouverie Pusey. Much more was said about him a few weeks later in a letter to Anne;[50] later he informed his mother that he dined with Pusey "who is an exceedingly nice and modest man. It seems odd that an undergraduate should be the eulogist of a Regius Professor's modesty, but certainly his air and manner are less assuming than those of many guests at his table."[51]

When William heard Newman preach for the first time his only comment was "heard parts of Mr. Newman's sermon." "Much singular not to say objectionable matter if one may so speak of so good a man" was Gladstone's assessment of a sermon preached by Newman in March 1831. Later Newman, whose preaching at St. Mary's profoundly affected the lives of many Oxford undergraduates, received more favourable comments from the young Gladstone. "A good sermon," was the sum total of his description on more than one occasion. "A most able discourse of a very philosophical character: more apt for reading than hearing," was his response to a sermon in December 1831. The most that Newman's sermons evoked from Gladstone was "very able indeed."

John Keble did not fare any better: "earnest on love and recollection of our Lord" was his comment on first hearing Keble. Later his preaching is "good," but on the same day the evangelical preacher Richard Sibthorp's sermon is described as "beautiful." Some of Keble's sermons evoked no comment, but one in June 1831 raised the question "Are all of his opinions those of Scripture and the Church? Of his life and heart and practice none could doubt, all would admire." A sermon by Frederick Oakeley received no comment. These outstanding figures of the Oxford Movement, whose teaching and preaching influenced so many and transformed the life of the Church of England did not over-impress Gladstone. There were however other preachers in Oxford whose sermons were highly regarded by this self-appointed sermon critic. He wrote to Helen on 1 February 1829 "Today I heard a remarkably able and practical sermon from a Mr. Girdlestone, rather celebrated here." William was obviously impressed by this evangelical preacher's exhortation to "do away the false and destructive system of judging ourselves by the standard of those around us instead of the laws laid down in Scripture." Sermons preached by Frederick Blackstone and Charles Clerke were described as "excellent." William J. Palmer preached "an able and excellent sermon." Philip Shuttleworth preached a "powerful and admirable sermon," the following Sunday his sermon was "very able and philosophical, but I fear not calculated to be of general use like the last." Philosophical sermons did not gain Gladstone's approval. The Rector of Headington, George J. Majendie, preached "admirably" at St. Mary's on "confessing our Lord before men," while his next sermon received unqualified praise "may God raise up many more such preachers." Many sermons provoked no comment. Preachers could be "impressive" in their manner, or display "extraordinary eloquence." Perhaps Gladstone's greatest compliment was that given on 14 August 1831 when the sermon at St. Peter's was said to be "an admirable sermon; simple, earnest, scriptural. Many other things I might say— but his praise is of God."

Preachers may be servants of God and sermons a means of speaking to His children, but neither preacher nor sermon were beyond criticism. Charles Ogilvie received comment as he was so inaudible that Gladstone fell asleep in St. Mary's. A sermon on the Atonement preached by Dr. Edward Burton, Regius Professor of Divinity was "I trust . . . misunderstood in the idea formed." Another sermon was "not so exclusively a sermon." "A most painful sermon" caused him to sit up late on 9 January 1831 to write to Mr. Crowther earnestly expostulating with him on the character and doctrine of the sermon he had delivered and another to Mr. Downes begging him to "read and pronounce an opinion upon it."[52]

Walking back from Marsden, just outside Oxford, William stood at the door of a Dissenting Chapel and heard a prayer. Remaining at the door does not necessarily imply reservations about dissenting worship. In June 1830 he went with F.D. Maurice to hear John Porter, a Methodist preacher, whom he describes as "a wild but splendid preacher." He wrote to his father "Dr. Chalmers has been passing through Oxford, and I went to hear him preach on Sunday evening, though he was at the Baptist Chapel . . . his sermon was admirable and quite as remarkable for the judicious and sober manner in which he enforced his views."[53] Edward Bulteel's sermons both impressed and repelled Gladstone, who questioned whether some of them were "strictly Scriptural."[54] Bulteel's controversial university sermon on Sunday 6 February 1831 prompted a long letter home and an enlightening entry in his diary. The sermon "must rouse many and various feelings. God grant it may all work for good. May my proud heart never lose one jot of the truth of God through its prejudices and passions." Gladstone believed that prejudice and passion must always be laid aside and the heart and mind opened to hear God's word. The word heard and accepted must be the truth, the truth which sets men free and unites them with God through Christ. This same approach was applied when practically every Sunday, in addition to sermons heard, he read printed sermons. His taste for published sermons was extremely "catholic."

An analysis of Gladstone's reading at this period reveals that he read more books of sermons than on any other subject. In addition to those already referred to by Heber, Hall, Barrow and Wilson he also read in 1829 collections by Robert Morehead, Robert Burrows and Samuel Walker. Volume two of a collection by Charles W. Le Bas, Principal of the East India College, gripped Gladstone for he read it daily from 14 June to 5 July. From 18 March 1830 he read almost daily *Nine Sermons on the Liturgy* by Dr. Francis Close the evangelical divine and later Dean of Carlisle. Three days after starting Close he read a sermon by W. Tiptaft and on the same day turned his attention to the four volumes of sermons by John Hewlett. Thirty sermons by Dr. Thomas Arnold of Rugby were read almost daily between 1 May and 10 June when he noted "an admirable book." He returned to Arnold's *Sermons* in December when they were "read aloud." George Townsend's *Sermons on Some of the Most Interesting Subjects in Theology* were read after Arnold's. Sermons by Daniel Wilson, Joseph Butler and Samuel Horsley, the bishop of St. Asaph, were read in 1831. Horsley's two volumes covering over 700 pages, were started in early December, but after four sermons he seems to have lost interest and returned to Arnold.

The festivals of the Christian year did not interest the majority of contemporary churchmen. Gladstone, however, read J.B. Sumner's *Sermons on the Principal Festivals of the Christian Church to which are added Three Sermons on Good Friday*. Started on Palm Sunday 1829, three Sermons were read on Good Friday; on Easter Day William wrote "read nothing else but Sumner's Sermons on Festivals which I wish to finish." That week he read twenty-one sermons and 415 pages, covering the festivals of Christmas, Good Friday, Easter Day, Ascension Day, Whit Sunday and Trinity Sunday. Sumner, in the preface, states that the annual recalling of the successive festivals display "the Redeemer in the various stages of that great work which he undertook for our salvation. They enable Christians to follow Christ from the cradle to the cross and to the triumph of his resurrection and ascension, to the giving of the Holy Spirit and the institution of his spiritual Kingdom." Such objectives from a revered evangelical must have impressed Gladstone.

On the whole he seems to have observed the major Christian festivals and whenever possible received the Holy Communion. Occasionally the name of the festival is mentioned in his diary, but he is not consistent in this practice. Christmas Day, Good Friday and Easter Day are normally noted; Ash Wednesday is noted in 1830, but is not referred to the previous year. However, in 1829 he records "did a kind of copy of Lent verses," perhaps a secret discipline for Lenten observance. We know that as early as 1828 Gladstone gave some thought to the subject of fasting, whether it was an "academic interest," or a serious consideration for its spiritual value, with a view to its implementation, if not already used, or whether he was considering fasting as a Lenten discipline, are all matters of speculation.

In some of the books he read the subject of fasting was encouraged as a valuable form of spiritual discipline. Richard Hooker's *Ecclesiastical Polity* offers a careful study on fasting and commends its practice. While Gladstone's original abridged copy of William Law's *Serious Call to a Devout and Holy Life* has not survived, a personal copy, published in 1824, has. Here a cross and scoring mark the words "If religion requires us sometimes to *fast* and *deny* our natural appetite, it is to lessen that struggle and war that is in our nature, it is to render our bodies fitter instruments of purity, and more obedient to the good motions of divine grace; it is to dry up the springs of our passions that war against the soul, to cool the flame of our blood, and render the mind more capable of divine meditation." Gladstone needed no reminding of the struggle and inner warfare which Christians have to face. What he desired was a means to triumph, to be a fitter instrument of purity, to be open to receive divine grace. Here was one solution— fasting. Could he fail to accept such spiritual counsel?

Christmas 1830 was spent with the family, until his return to Oxford on 14 January. On Monday 3 January he wrote in his diary "Conversation on Fasting &c at night. Awkward." No indication is given or even the slightest suggestion made regarding the person or persons with whom he discussed fasting, nor in what way it was "awkward." He may have been commending the practice, but having it rejected; or being accused, once again, of taking his religion too far. Fasting occupied his attention again during the summer months when he "Read . . . Taylor and others on fasting." He was already indebted spiritually to Taylor's *Holy Living*, first read in 1829. Scorings indicate the importance placed by Gladstone on three parts of the section "Of Fasting." Taylor writes of how in imitation of the apostolic practice of fasting "the Christian Church hath religiously observed fasting, before the holy communion; and the more devout persons . . . refused to eat and drink, till they had finished their morning devotions," double scoring marks these words. William also marked the following: "All fasting, for whatsoever end it be undertaken, must be done without any opinion of the necessity of the thing itself without censoring others, with all humility, in order to the proper end; and just as man takes physic, of which no man hath reason to be proud, and no man think it necessary, but because he is in sickness, or in danger and disposition to it." If fasting was accepted and practised by Gladstone at this time it was part of a hidden discipline. William Law stressed the need for fasting if the Christian is to triumph in his inner and spiritual combat. Fasting is undertaken to help purify the body. Taylor takes the subject a step further saying it is like medicine taken to cure sickness and is undertaken in humility and in secret. Later evidence reveals Gladstone's increasing interest in this subject and the fact that he did practice self-denial and some fasting, but we cannot be sure, because of the hidden nature of fasting, whether at this early stage he had put into practice what Hooker, Law and Taylor so earnestly commended.

Somewhere about 1829 Gladstone wrote "a check-list for Christian Living," which helps us to understand some of his brief diary entries. Indeed this list explains a great deal about many aspects of his life. Strictly speaking it is no more than a collection of headings: "The Christian—in his family: at public worship: in the university: at school: in General Society: upon public amusements: upon conformity to customs: on the Sabbath: in his closet: in his studies: in the working of his

calling: in recreation: in alms-giving: in visiting: in reproof: in conversation 1, with infidels: 2, with wicked Christians: 3, with holy Christians: in Obedience to the Church: in Obedience to the State: in conversation: in contemplation: in teaching: in learning: in his household: at
Sacrament: at meals: in the government of his body."[55] To which he
adds "The Christian's privileges, obligations, connection of faith and
practice, on his death bed, in his humiliation, in his temptation, in estimating self, in concern for the souls of others, comparative."

A brief note offers the only information we have about this
fascinating list "If he that writes should say, he seeks to fashion his
work after the model of George Herbert, and if he that reads should reply, who art thou that boastest thyself to tread in the footsteps of that
most humble, most exalted man? . . . We reply not, save that we are to
follow him as he followed Christ." George Herbert's *Country Parson*
had a profound effect upon the young Gladstone, and the list quoted is
indebted to him. The *Country Parson* obviously consolidated much of
William's reading about the Christian life and marked a move forward
to a more mature and all-embracing Christian faith which he attempted
to establish at Oxford.

Always an omnivorous reader he was fed from divers sources.
Books read during this period suggest links with some of the points listed. Was such reading undertaken at random, or did he have a "master
plan" aiming to be informed about all the essentials of Christian living?
Did he therefore read, *The Fable of the Bees: or Private Vices. Publick
Benefits . . . And a Search into the Nature of Society* written by Bernard
de Mandeville with a view to understanding society? These two volumes are preserved with a fragment of paper bearing notes in Gladstone's handwriting among the pages of the first volume, perhaps having been used as a bookmark. Hume's seminal work *Essays. Literary,
Moral and Political*, read in 1829 for academic reasons, must have influenced his understanding of society and man.

The salvation of mankind was more than a theological issue, it
fed the flames of Gladstone's desire to serve God in the church. At Eton
he realised that the Christian faith did not engender an enthusiastic response in everyone and that many who professed Christianity did not
live accordingly. Perhaps these insights prompted him to read William
Wilberforce, *A Practical View of the Prevailing Religious System of
Professed Christians, in the Higher and Middle Classes in this Coun-*

try, contrasted with Real Christianity, given to him by Anne in 1828.
Here Wilberforce contrasts the unhappy consequences of nominal
Christianity with the effects of true Christianity; the book remained a
best seller for forty years.

Evangelicalism was repellant to some; was this why he read
John Foster *On Some of the Causes by which Evangelical Religion has
been rendered Unacceptable to Persons of Cultivated Taste*? Gladstone's outline for Christian living refers to controversy "with infidels,"
and so he read *Mahometanism Unveiled: An Inquiry. in which the
Arch-Heresy, its Diffusion and Continuance, are examined on a new
principle, tending to confirm the evidence and aid the propagation, of
the Christian Faith* (1829) by Charles Forster. *Social Duties on Christian Principles* by H. Drummond, read in October 1830, must have enlightened him on the subject of Family and Social Duties.

He became increasingly aware of the need to work out and
practice his Christian convictions within his social life. This was not
easy for a young man living in a university setting where many sought
enjoyment rather than academic excellence, moral goodness or Christian virtues. The diary reveals Gladstone the Christian, seeking to know
and do the will of God; Gladstone the student, engrossed in his academic work, determined to fulfil his father's ambitions; and Gladstone the
young man enjoying a social life within his self-imposed restrictions.

If his journal had been meant to record the important events in
his life, then wine drinking would appear fundamental to his time at
Oxford. Apart from religion there are more specific references to wine
drinking than anything else. He records regular social wine drinking
with a host of people. Invitations were received to many wine parties;
on Saturday 22 May 1830 he went to two. Was it these which prompted
him to write that evening "My lethargy grows deeper. O that I could
say God deliver me"? Perhaps it was lethargy that encouraged him to
find relief and escape in his wine drinking. His increased consumption
the following month certainly raises some questions. On 8 June he gave
a "large wine party," the next day "Gave another wine party," while the
next day he is drinking wine with Tancred. Four days later "gave a
large wine party," the following day "another wine party," "out at wine"
the next day and so also the next two days. At this period he was reading Thomas à Kempis *Imitation of Christ*! Wine drinking was approved
by his parents and was part of their normal way of life and the society

in which they moved; it was also acceptable to the majority of evangelicals who had no convictions about abstinence. Whether William always exercised moderation in his wine drinking may be open to question.

On the second Sunday in November 1831, under the pressures of cramming and examinations, he wrote "wine with Hamilton; more a party than I quite liked, or expected." Was this because it was Sunday? The remainder of the entry provides some insight into Gladstone's inner life at that period. "I am cold, timid, and worldly, and not in a healthy state of mind for the great trial tomorrow: to which . . . I am utterly and miserably unequal . . . God grant that he who gave himself even for me may support me through it, if it be his will: but if I am covered with humiliation, O may I kiss the rod." The next day he was to face examinations in divinity, science and history.[56] He tells Thomas that he felt "somewhat debilitated, owing as I think to my working too hard for my bodily state, which was not sustained by a sufficiently nutritious diet: in particular, I had neglected wine."[57] Thomas and Robertson helped to keep him supplied with wine, William thanked Tom for the cask containing candlesticks and twenty-seven bottles of wine.[58] Three weeks before he had written to Robertson asking him to send "First, a dozen of claret—concerning which be it remembered that I can do without it altogether. Secondly, a dozen Madeira which I can do without for some time."[59] Further correspondence shows how his brothers provided large quantities of wine glasses and decanters[60] as well as replenishing his wine stock.[61]

Re-reading Anne's letters in April 1831 may have prompted him to write "on the principles of social intercourse,"[62] a cause for concern ever since he went to a party on 12 January, where he met a number of young ladies and also played cards. "All this time I ought to be asking myself, do I mix in society (wretchedly capacitated for it as I am) for the gratification of self? My opinion of it has been in some measure changed or rather I have had little opportunity previously of forming one. But it seems to me that female society, whatever the disadvantages may be, has just and manifold uses attendant upon it in turning the mind away from some of its most dangerous and degrading temptations." This latter comment has been taken by some to mean masturbation.

A letter from Benjamin Harrison, later archdeacon of Maidstone, refers to Gladstone's "high principles of morality which you

helped in your generation to instil into the Society."[63] While a reference to the Debating Society, it probably expressed what a number of
his friends felt about his contribution to their general society at that period. But Gladstone's "high principles" were never reached without
much heart-searching and prayer, and sometimes written reflections
and guidelines.

Leisure activities now included the playing of chess, draughts,
backgammon and whist, much walking, some fishing and a little cricket, as well as occasional shooting and riding. He received singing lessons and seems to have enjoyed both singing and listening to music.
Card playing, sometimes associated with gambling, was an occasional
activity in 1830 and, in spite of reservations, continued on into 1831.
The diary on 27 August 1830 records "Commerce at night: lost: indeed:
never won a farthing at cards. Saunders has a good rule of giving all to
charities." A month later he wrote "Cards at night. I like them not for
they excite me and keep me awake." The following month his conscience was troubled because he had been playing cards at the actual
time of Huskisson's tragic death,[64] "he poor man was in his last agonies
when I was playing cards on Wednesday night. When shall we learn
wisdom? Not that I see folly in the fact of playing cards: but it is too often accompanied with a dissipated spirit." Card playing was acceptable
at Seaforth; he noted on 21, 22, 23 December "Card," but not on Christmas eve when he recalled "dearest Anne's death." Christmas Day found
him playing again, he wrote "cards-q right?" Did this entry mean that
he questioned the rightness of playing cards in general or on Christmas
day? Two days later he had a conversation with his mother "What a
hypocrite I am. Cards." Even after his birthday act of self-examination
he engaged in "cards," as he did on the next three days and later wrote
"Cards every night—papers every day—pretty ingredients of employment with a view to an Oxford degree."

Stewardship of time and possessions, especially money, was
seen by William as an important aspect of Christian living. His stewardship of time has already been covered. One of his monthly "obligations" was the balancing of his financial account, rarely mentioned in
his journal. His private account book at Oxford offers a detailed record
of his charitable giving, which constituted a divine obligation, illustrat-
ing not only the breadth of his Christian concern and commitment, but
also some insights into his theological convictions. Religious organisa-

tions in the nineteenth century were usually supported by those committed to a particular theological position. Among those to which William gave financial support were the Christian Knowledge Society, Gospel Propagation Society, Church Missionary Society and the Jewish Conversion Society. While these societies represented a spread of churchmanship they all existed to spread the Gospel, thus being in line with the evangelical commitment to mission. Other societies supported included the Church Building Society, Oxford Benevolent Society and Liverpool Mariners, each receiving a guinea a year.

Personal charities were wide-ranging and included "blind man and his wife 5d, a poor printer's family 5/-, a poor sailor "once in my father's employ" 1/6, an out-of-work bookbinder and his family 2/4, a poor man from the infirmary 1/-, poor woman (wet night) 1/-." Travelling provided opportunities for helping the needy "a distressed coachman 2/6, or a poor person on the road 2/7 1/2d, turnpikes and beggars 6d, a family about to emigrate 10/-." Sometimes the recipient received both a gift and money, like the poor Roman Catholic Irishman who received an English Testament and 2/-; a shirt for Harris 3/6; coals for the poor 2/6d. Devotional works for charitable distribution were purchased: Mant's Tracts 6d., Prayer Books and Testaments £1.0.2d, six Prayer Books 3/9, "a Testament for R. Jones 2/-." His friend Saunders was given £3 for the education of children, Grove Church (Pusey) £2, Church Poor Box £2.5/- and Cholera Collection 2/6.

He kept a regular account of what he gave as alms at the "Sacrament" and sometimes the church; in 1829 this was usually 1/-, but from 1830 2/6d. He also accounts for personal expenditure—Almonds £1 and Oranges and Apples £1, and extravagances like "silk and velvet waistcoat £1.5/-, walking stick £2" or a payment to Gaskell for four bottles of Claret. The cost of books is recorded and of book binding "Ward for binding about 130 vols £19.12/6'." He even records that 4d was stolen from his room, a necessary entry if his accounts were to balance. There are also entries which relate to hidden aspects of his life, not mentioned in the diary. Wilberforce a bet (to be applied to building Lane End Church) 10/-, a bet Anstice 6d, "lost at cards." In a letter to Robertson he states that £6.6/- had been paid for subscriptions for him "which I had no idea would be paid without my hearing of the application for them." His objection was because £3.3/- ought never to have been paid and the other £3.3/- he had sent himself. The payment of these subscriptions, without informing him, had created confusion and also left him six guineas out of pocket.[65]

Gladstone was not unique in his student charitable activities. Gaskell wrote to him "'My mother desires me to express to you her best thanks for your kind subscription to the Church. Shall I pay the money for you? . . . What excellent persons we are. You intend to beautify a church, and I to send to the Tong Islanders some dozen of enlightening tracts.'"[66]

Practical charitable work was also an expression of Christian living. For Gladstone at this time this included: visiting the needy, the poor, the aged, the sick and the dying. He went to "see poor T. Parr, dying of consumption." Tragic deaths were recorded in the diary such as that of the surgeon William Wadd of Liverpool who died in a carriage accident in Ireland. On 23 August 1829 Gladstone wrote "Received the awful account of poor Mr. Wadd's death. O may God comfort the widow and the fatherless, and turn even this to their unspeakable and everlasting benefit and may we hence learn how great is the mercy of God and towards ourselves, and how wonderful his tenderness." But prayer was not sufficient—he visited the Wadds three times the following week.

He visited old people; William Harris, a cottager in St. Ebbe's, is called on and on at least two occasions they had a long conversation. On at least one occasion he went visiting with his brother John to see a poor blind invalid; they both read a sermon to her. He went to a poorhouse to examine the two little children of Rachel Jones "in Testament" After seeing a Lunatic Asylum, near Wakefield, with Gaskell, he noted "very interesting indeed," a rather detached comment after such an experience. However, when his friend Canning was sick with fever Gladstone exercised great care and vigilance in watching over him and even then found time to go out "to get a subscription or two in aid of those who are endeavouring to provide relief in the severe weather for the poor." Servants were also considered, like the discharged servant he met and to whom he gave a 1/-, or those for whom he managed to procure servants' sittings in St. James' Church, while being unable to obtain one for himself[67] or the servants at home for whom he established a library.

As already mentioned "Rescue work," or his attempts to save prostitutes, may well have begun on his very first night in Oxford. He may have been referring to another rescue incident on Saturday 24 October 1829 when he wrote "some conversation and business with two persons both really, I believe, in great distress."[68] The evidence is not explicit.

vii. *Theological Reading*

Books, notably theological, were inseparable from Gladstone and a fundamental part of his life. A study of what he read is essential to our understanding of his theological development and spiritual growth.

The "catholicity" of his reading from his latter days at Eton fashioned new theological convictions. As alternatives emerged he began to question his previous evangelical position. Many of these imperceptible changes and much of his theological reading have already been examined, but the scope and effects of this up to 1832 require further elaboration in order to establish the part books, chiefly theological, played in his life and towards the making of this Christian politician.

From time to time, as he completed a volume of his journal, he listed at the end of the book the reading accomplished during the period covered.[69] There are also lists produced for reading during a particular period, such as that on 27 July 1830 for the coming vacation which contains nineteen items, half of them theological, including Bishop Butler. Shortly before that vacation he wrote in a small notebook seventeen pages of tightly packed notes on Butler's *Analogy*.[70] Obviously some of this reading was for his divinity examinations.

Devotional reading was both evangelical and "catholic," including sermons and books often by leading evangelicals, but Jeremy Taylor's *The Rule and Exercise of Holy Living* and William Law's *A Serious Call to a Devout and Holy Life* played a profound and lasting part in his spiritual formation. While the diary suggests that his first introduction to the writings of Thomas à Kempis', *Imitation of Christ* was 1 June 1830, this is not strictly correct for a "Prose Selection" dated 1829 contains quotations from à Kempis.[71] However, after regular reading throughout June 1830 he wrote on the last day of that month "finished T. à Kempis," with no further comment. One would have expected Gladstone to say more about what is perhaps the most famous manual of spiritual direction. Here the writer aims to instruct the Christian on how to achieve perfection by following Christ as his model. What he had to write about the Holy Communion must have had some influence upon William's understanding of this Sacrament. In time the *Imitation* became the book which during his long life he read more than any other, returning to it especially in times of stress. Other devotional works included John Keble's *Christian Year* and Blaise Paacal's *Pensées. The Brazen Serpent; or Life Coming through Death* by Thomas Erskine bears heavy scoring and underlining. Like many other books this one may not have been read as a strictly devotional work, but it must have fed his spiritual life. He underlines the statement that the Christian is called upon to both live and work by the Gospel and that "we are called on to do this work in the strength of the provision which God has committed to our care."

Doctrinal issues, which often fascinated him, absorbed a great deal of his time, some have thought too much. Episcopal and archidiaconal Charges were part of his regular diet of reading. Bishop John Pearson's Anglican classic *An Exposition of the Creed* read in 1831, was re-read in 1841 and Gladstone's copy shows the marks of careful reading. *An inquiry into the Origin and Intent of Primitive Sacrifice* by John Davison, covering 199 pages, was almost completed in a day, being scored and annotated; the following Sunday he began *An Answer to . . . Primitive Sacrifice* by John Molesworth. Gladstone could never be satisfied by considering only one side of an argument. Complex doctrines had to be returned to from time to time and demanded wide reading. In September 1829 he read *A Letter to the Common People, in Answer to Some Popular Arguments against the Trinity* by William Jones. Two years later he carried out what he called a "superficial" reading of Jones' original and much fuller work on the subject, entitled *The Catholic Doctrine of the Trinity proved by above an hundred short and clear arguments expressed in the terms of the Holy Scriptures.* Butler, Hooker and Paley were among those whose works were a regular source of reference. Church history was sometimes read as an introduction to doctrine, including John Kaye *Ecclesiastical History of the second and third Centuries* (1826), J. Ballantyne *Comparison of English and Dissenting Churches* (1830), J.J. Gurney *Observations on the . . . Society of Friends* (1824), T. Belshaw *Letter to the Bishop of London, in Vindication of the Unitarians* (1815), and Isaac Taylor *The Natural History of Enthusiasm* (1829). Marginal works included W. Huntington, *The Arminian Skeleton*, a violent anti-Calvinistic book, and R.M. Beverley *Letter . . . on the present corrupt state of the Church of England* (1831), which was an attack on rich bishops and foxhunting parsons. Biographies, a regular part of his reading, covered a host of subjects, historical, doctrinal and liturgical, such as Sargeant's *Life of Cranmer*.

Ceaseless reading made Gladstone bubble over with ideas, many of which were committed to paper; anticipated projects, selections, collections, commonplace books, theological themes and even a book. One projected study was to convey "i. A Collection of Testimonies concerning Baptism and Regeneration: ii. A Collection of Arguments &c. on the same subject: iii. The Christian in sundry respects and conditions: iv. Dialogues."; this latter included Arminian and Calvinist, Death-beds, Schism, Conduct to Schismatics, Baptism and Lord's Supper.[72]

The diary for 12 August 1829 notes "Began my Selections," which resulted in a commonplace book, on the cover of which is "Prose Selection."[73] Part one contains quotations from a wide range of authors including à Kempis, Arnold, Augustine, Cyprian, Jewel, Laud, Mant, Hannah More, Pascal, Pearson, Sumner, Tertullian, Taylor, Wesley and Daniel Wilson, not to mention Butler and Hooker, his most often quoted authors. Subject headings under which quotations are listed include: Repentance, Death, Humility, Duty of the Clergy, The Preacher's Office, Conversion and Doubting. Part two is very different, with quotations from Palmerston, Canning, Coleridge and Hooker, subjects including Civil War, Public Opinion and Tyranny. Towards the end of the work is a quotation from à Kempis: "He is truly great, who hath great charity, he is truly great, who is little in his own estimation, and rates at nothing the summit of worldly honour: he is truly wise, who counts all earthly things but as dross, that he may win Christ, and he is truly learned, who hath learned to abandon his own will and to do the will of God." This advice became Gladstone's guide to Christian living, reading and writing.

Another project, conceived the following year, was "A Summary of the Evidence of Religion in general and Christianity in particular." This three-part work was never completed, but covers eight pages of notes.[74] Had the young Gladstone a future book in mind, or merely autobiographical notes when he wrote on 3 October 1831, "Yesterday an idea, a chimera entered my head—of gathering during the progress of my life, notes and materials for a work embracing three divisions—Morals—Politics—Education . . . if it shall perish while in embryo, (it will) serve to teach me the folly of presumptuous schemes conceived during the buoyancy of youth, and relinquished on a discovery of incompetency in later years."

Among other theological subjects, including some already examined, were Predestination, the Fulness of Time, Saints, the Book of Common Prayer, Conversion, Death, the Second Coming, Heaven, Hell, the Lord's Supper and, of course, Baptism.

Some subjects, such as slavery, had both religious and political implications and demanded continuous thought and reading. Breakfast with Acland in October 1830 gave him the opportunity to spend "a good deal of time in discussing a paper about slavery with him and told him my position." The subject was discussed until half-past one in the morning with Cunningham and Gaskell in May 1831. Gladstone became preoccupied with slavery on which he was to speak at the Oxford Union on 2 June, when he wrote in his diary "At debate—made a quiet and dull speech about W. India Slavery." His notes for this speech have been preserved.[75] He objected to the motion on the abolition of slaves as "vague and unintelligible" and because "emancipation is not I conceive the legitimate, or at least the immediate object which ought to be sought." There were two major issues, first to secure the personal rights and comforts of the slave, and second to raise him to the dignity of a moral agent which he has not yet attained, to the great disgrace of the whites; to which he added the advantages for education afforded by the system of slavery.

A commonplace book marked "Christ Church 1831" may have been produced in connection with his Oxford Union speech or his speeches on slavery during the Newark election.[76] It reflects some of his thoughts after further reading: "As fitness progresses so let emancipation . . . In the meantime provide efficient religious instruction." Abolitionists are inconsistent; Gladstone wanted "effectual emancipation" and wrote it is "all a question of degree—as to their being less fit for freedom than ourselves." Associated matter is gathered under the headings of "fear of bloodshed," "factory children," "Irish poor" and "rights of property." For Gladstone the subject of slavery had political, financial, commercial and social implications, but it was also a religious issue on which, through reading and thought, he attempted to reach an objective and balanced position.

viii. *Gladstone's Academic Work and Success*

The diary reveals how, in spite of his extensive religious reading and activities, his regular confession of neglected study and his very full social life, it certainly cannot be said that as an undergraduate he neglected his academic work. The Scholarships for which he worked tell us something of his ambitious nature. October 1829 saw him working for the Bishop Fell Exhibition, about which Tom wrote "although you estimate your new honours so humbly, we are happy to congratulate you."[77] A few days later William wrote to his father "Now that I have gained this accession of wealth by worthy Bishop Fell's Exhibition, I think of purchasing a share in King's College . . . unless you object to this disposal of money which it is hardly fit for me to put into my own pocket, while I am abundantly supplied by you."[78]

"Dean told me I should have a Studentship. May I be grateful to him and thankful to the giver of every good and perfect gift," so wrote Gladstone in his diary on 11 December 1829. To his father, he wrote of it as "an undeserved blessing." On Christmas eve he was "made a Student after Chapel" and asked "For this may God make me thankful, and sensible too of the duties and obligations it involves." A letter arrived from home "our hearty congratulations on your well earned honours—I hope they may only be the commencement of many." Mrs. Gladstone expressed her conviction that all his studies were "under God's governance and he was safely in God's keeping," observing that this was "the only means of making a university education safe." William also believed that God was watching over and inspiring his academic work and so he could take no credit for academic success, or receive for his own use any accompanying financial benefits. Of the Fell Exhibition he wrote "declared first of the Fell candidates—little credit, so not much food for vanity, thank God." While after his Studentship he wrote to his Aunt Elizabeth "It is agreed that I have been much more favoured than I deserved."

Success was partly due to the rigorous discipline of reading which he imposed upon himself. He told his father of his time-table during the summer vacation: he would rise between five and six and carry out systematic reading until 10.00 p.m.[79] To Tom he wrote "the only part of the arrangement not fairly fulfilled by me is the getting up: I generally do not get to my reading before half-past six."[80] Whatever his claims about doing "wretchedly little," his parents advised him to guard against overwork and to recognise that "health is the first of blessings."[81] Thomas suggests that in his letters home he should not mention minor ailments which cause great concern to their mother.[82] Overwork affected his eyes the following August when he wrote "compelled to debar myself from books," later adding "I trust this little break will show me my helplessness and make me think of him who was the giver of all my health and strength."

His father wrote in 1831 "in your reading for the university prize, I hope you will go straight forward with your work . . . you can only do your *best* and the *best* can do no more, make up your mind with determination to win if you can and *work* with that before you."[83] Thursday 10 March saw him working on the examinations for the Ireland Scholarship which he failed, as he did the Craven Scholarship. It may have been his over-concern with academic success and the effects of this upon his spirituality which prompted him to write in his journal "O that I may remember throughout this matter what shall it profit a man if he shall gain the whole world and lose his own soul? . . . Would God I may follow these objects solely and singly as means for a dear and high purpose." Failing to win the scholarship he considered postponing his degree "as I thought I could see, particularly from the singular form of the examination, the Divine purpose pointing to the path I have chosen, though this is perhaps not a thing to be noised abroad." The following day he wrote to Robertson "I have no right to be otherwise than pleased as well as thankful, which I ought to be in all cases as knowing that all these things *are ordered for the best*."[84]

As the year progressed, increasing thought and time were given to systematic study for his degree. Oral examinations began on Monday 14 November 1831, "Examined by Stocker in divinity: I did not answer as I could have wished: Hampden in science—a beautiful examination and with every circumstance in my favour." After this "followed a very clever examination in history from Garbett" with an "agreeable and short one in my poets from Cramer. I could not help . . . giving thanks inwardly to Him without whom not even such moderate performances would have been in my power." Later that week he was hard at work on written papers. At 4.30 p.m. on 24 November he found that he was one of two candidates in the first division. Phillimore, who was in the second, congratulated Gladstone who commented "could I have done the same, if our circumstances had been reversed? How much he is my superior, even in his adverse circumstances. God help me." While working at his mathematics he had many misgivings about his success in this area. His fears were unfounded for on 14 December his name appeared in the first class; "How much thankfulness was due, and how little paid! It was an hour of thrilling happiness, between the past and the future. For the future was I hope not excluded." He read the Articles and took his Bachelor's degree on 26 January 1832. Oxford now lay behind him. God had blessed all his endeavours and crowned him with academic success. In the immediate future lay the continental tour, but what then? He believed Divine providence had set out the path he must take, but what was that path, what was God's will for his life? On the eve of his departure for Europe he prayed that God "may be our guide, and may direct our path so as shall most effectually conduce to the fulfilment of his purposes for us." It was also his prayer for the ultimate issue—to find and follow God's will for his life.

CHAPTER EIGHT

GOD'S WILL—CHURCH OR POLITICS?

From childhood to old age Gladstone believed that God was personally active in his life. At the age of eight he wrote of a "miraculous and providential escape from being killed by a madman with a hatchet."[1] After giving a brief account of the incident he wrote:

> O Lord how good thou wert in saving
> A frail creature like me,
> When over me death was waving,
> Then in the grave I should be,
> Now I am devoted to thy service . . .

He believed unreservedly in divine providence, that God rules over his creation and is active within it. His understanding of this doctrine was based upon scripture, where God is seen as actively at work in the realm of history and more especially in the lives of men, which are inseparable from history. God governs the heart of man and is at work within the soul, He determines all things and to Him man is ultimately responsible. All this Gladstone applied to his own life. As a child of God he believed He was at work in his life and had a purpose for him to fulfil. William's responsibility was to discover and fulfil that purpose. Only then could his restless life be lived to the full. Correspondence, chiefly with his family, his personal diary, religious verse, written accounts on theological themes, all make reference to the subject of "providence" in relation to his life. God's will, for the young Gladstone, was in part related to the issue of filial obedience. This acute sense of divine providence and the need to be sure of knowing and actually doing God's will weighed heavily upon him during his later years at Eton and throughout his time at Oxford.

God's providential activity and influence touched every part of his life. When he failed to achieve the anticipated success in the scholarship examination at Oxford, he wrote to his father of his failure "I trust I may be enabled to remember that it was God's will."[2]

While both failure and success could be attributed to God he was never able to give due recognition to his success. Towards the end of his life he wrote "I am by no means sure, upon a calm review, that Providence has endowed me with anything which can be called a striking gift."[3]

Obedience to parents was taught by scripture and accepted by William as a Christian responsibility. This conviction was shared by other members of his family. At Anne's request Tom wrote out a list of biblical texts on the subject of "obedience to parents."[4] William was both devoted to his parents and obedient to the biblical command to honour his father and mother. A parental wish was sometimes equivalent to a divine command, but this requires clarification. During the Newark election campaign he told his father "I am truly delighted. . . that the sentiments I have expressed meet with your approbation . . . for next to the law of God, I know of no higher sanction than a parent."[5] Parental authority was God-given, but second to that of God himself, a point on which William was not always clear. A few years later he wrote "if my father desires me to do anything, it becomes my duty. . . so I am to recognize the will of God in that which is apparently of slight utility and might be done as well nay better by others."[6]

An Oxford contemporary, Charles Childers, wrote to Gladstone after his academic success "you have my most sincere congratulations, and my poor prayers that God may enable you to turn your success to the best account for His glory and yourself. Pray let me hear whether your future prospects have become more definite."[7] Some now believed his future prospects were definitely to be in the sphere of politics rather than the church. Others were not convinced that this was God's will. William continued to be tortured by doubt and uncertainty. On the day that Childers wrote to him William wrote "Had a good deal of conversation with dear Helen: and found she felt a good deal the change in my plans." The next day, 20 January 1832, he noted "had much conversation with my dear mother on future matters." That day he set off to Oxford to receive his degree. On Sunday he "talked with Saunders: on matters on which I knew I ought not." Can there be any doubt that his conversations with Helen, his mother and Saunders touched upon his future profession, the decision to enter politics rather than the church, resulting in the guilty feeling that he might have deserted "the most High God"?

Despite the strong convictions of his father, brothers and some Oxford friends that his future lay in politics, which he publicly accepted, William was denied such unequivocal assurance. Was it really God's will that this should be his profession, or was this self-delusion and a denial of God's purpose for his life? That God could and did use politics and politicians to further His work he was in no doubt. He also acknowledged politics as a function of religion, but was not sure that this was the sphere in which he was called to serve. Writing on the subject of the Nation and Religion he asked "Does God deal with nations as well as individuals? Then nations must have a religion—for why have individuals need of a religion, but because God has dealings with them."[8] In a commonplace book he wrote of a "Church sanctifying a State" and that the State "is charged in our own country with the solemn duties of spreading its religion."[9] Political excitement in 1831 may have captured and stimulated Gladstone's interest in politics, but this was nothing new—his correspondence with Doyle, Gaskell, Farr, Hallam and others, dating back to his Eton days, shows that he had been deeply interested in politics and had had political "temptations" for many years. Some of his Eton contemporaries already recognised his great ability and his future potential as a politician. On 24 February 1831 he recorded "a long letter from my father on politics etc."[10] On his twenty-first birthday he wrote in his diary "Politics are fascinating to me, perhaps too fascinating." But such a private "confession" did not dampen his increasing enthusiasm for politics over the next two years. The conclusions of some political historians regarding Gladstone's "abandoning" ordination for a career in politics need to be qualified. Michael Foot states "Gladstone was only thrown into politics by filial obedience and by chance: this was the profession in which he passed his life, but not where his heart lay. His father would not let him follow his vocation and take orders."[11] Richard Shannon states that John Gladstone allowed William to argue himself to a psychological standstill on the question of ordination and concludes "Gladstone manoeuvred himself into a political career."[12] Philip Magnus, quoting from the important letter written by William to his father on 17 January 1832, wrote "Although he considered it likely that the entire social order would shortly be overturned, he was willing to make the law his profession, and to seek to enter politics."[13] Did his father really forbid him? Did

John Gladstone have such a profound psychological insight into his
son's psyche? Was William willing to abandon the service of God in
the church and seek to enter politics?

Gladstone's complex nature and personality, his academic ability and informed position, and his deep Christian commitment and spiritual development up to 1832 suggest that it is a failure to do justice to
all the evidence to postulate a simple answer to the question, Why did
he abandon the long-standing desire for ordination and accept a career
in politics as God's will for his life? For Gladstone the discovery and
acceptance of God's will was paramount. Disobedience here would
leave him answerable to God on the last day. When in 1894 Gladstone
reflected "the desire of my youth was to be a clergyman" this was no
self-created "myth." Such aspirations can be traced back to his Eton
days and may have been in his mind when he wrote on 21 January 1826
"I trust (God) will be my guide and my defender." Gladstone's happy
days at Eton came to an end in December 1827. When he arrived home
the unanswered question about God's will for his life continued to lie
heavily upon him. Diary entries in December 1827 and January 1828
refer to long and interesting conversations with Anne; undoubtedly
these touched upon the possibility of ordination. Was it through ordination that he would receive the "joys of a more permanent" nature, that
"eternal happiness which never fades?"

Anne was his spiritual mentor and it was to her that he wrote
from Eton on 25 March 1827 about the impression made upon him on
reading George Herbert's *Country Parson*. Was that letter written with
the intention of making his aspirations and spiritual longings known to
the whole family, particularly his father and Tom? Of Herbert's work
Gladstone observed "The prose work is very curious, he must certainly
have been a most able, and what is more, a most excellent man: his mu-
nificence seems to have been unbounded: but his race was very short;
he was not quite three years actively engaged in clerical duties . . . The
book represents him to you as a man of the most perfect simplicity, the
most extensive charity, and the most indefatigable diligence. I hope it
may please you, and I think it will." Herbert's book was unlike anything
ever written before and at that time was unique as a work on pastoralia,
outlining the true quality of life and service expected of the parish
priest. This life was to include the orderly conduct of divine worship,
the pastoral and spiritual care of souls, the gradual sanctification of the
priest's own life, and the careful study of the Fathers and the School-

men. It was hardly the kind of book that one would expect a seventeen year old schoolboy to read, unless he had good reason for doing so. It cannot have escaped Gladstone's attention that Herbert had fought against the idea of ordination, but eventually had been prevailed upon to recognise that this was God's will for his life. The following week he was at home with his dear Anne for the Easter vacation. His Autobiographica recalls that he spent much time with her during that period, when they had many discussions on religious subjects, perhaps on Herbert; some of these discussions had a profound and lasting effect upon him.[14]

Intense cramming and undivided academic commitment in preparation for Oxford was seen by the family as the purpose of the period 3 December 1827 to 19 October 1828, but Gladstone could not get the question of his future vocation out of his mind. The division in the family did not help. His father and Tom were pressing him to abandon any thought of the church; his mother and sisters were sympathetic and encouraging about his becoming a clergyman. But the tensions were also within himself—and perhaps partly of his own creation. Had he no aspirations for a career in politics? We may wonder whether he had dreams about his future contribution to the House of Commons. Perhaps he was never really convinced at this period, or indeed at any time, that God's will was ordination and all that was required was his total surrender. Were not such dreams and uncertainties expressed just before leaving Eton when, in copper-plate handwriting, he wrote on a number of envelopes, which he carefully preserved "THE RIGHT HONOURABLE W. E. GLADSTONE, M.P.?"

The political debates of the Eton Society and the intellectual discussions with his intimate friends, who were infatuated by politics, influenced his development and thoughts in the years leading up to Oxford. While his intense religious convictions and the desire to serve God may have been paramount, lurking in the back of his mind was the tantalizing allurement of a political career. Ultimately only he could resolve the inner conflict. Pressure from his father and Tom may have been more helpful than he was willing to admit, eventually enabling him to justify politics as a profession and to rationalise the decision he made. And yet Gladstone had no theological doubts about God's omniscience. Indeed, it was his growing understanding of the nature of God and about the cost of man's redemption in Christ and a recognition, even if not always objective, of his own sin, and the supreme cost of his personal salvation which fostered his sense of vocation to the priest-hood and his desire to be a faithful instrument in the hands of God in the redemption of his fellow men. Many factors contributed towards this sense of vocation; by their very nature most secret soul-searchings and longings are known only to God and so it was with Gladstone. However, we do know that he had an intense conviction that divine providence was ordering his path in the direction of ordination and that his life was to be given to God's service.

It is the thesis of this volume that William Ewart Gladstone, the greatest statesman and politician of the nineteenth century, and an outstanding churchman, can never be understood if his life and work are divorced from his Christian commitment and convictions. Indeed, the spiritual development of Gladstone and the inner conflict concern-ing his vocation in church or politics, and the possibility that he made a mistake and had wrongly chosen politics rather than the church must never be overlooked. A man of Gladstone's theological stature had little doubt about the consequence of such disobedience. He knew that only as God's will is accepted, at whatever cost, can there be inner peace. His spiritual pilgrimage can be seen as a continual striving for that in-ner peace and assurance that God's will had been, and was being, ful-filled in his life. When uncertainty reappeared did Gladstone try to jus-tify himself before God through his service to his nation and others and through means not always understood by himself or even his family and friends, let alone his opponents and the countless observers of his life and work? The question for Gladstone was whether he should serve God and his fellow men as a priest in the Church of England or as a politician in the House of Commons. The many issues and pressures which eventually led him to accept that it was God's will that he should enter politics must now be examined in an attempt to understand why he "abandoned" the idea of entering the church in the belief that he was called by God to serve state and church as a politician.

Confidentiality was not easy to maintain in the Gladstone family when letters were regarded as common property. Mr. John Glad-stone's letter to William on 2 November 1829 makes this quite clear: "All your welcome letters are duly received, the last to me, but the whole are always considered common property whoever they may be addressed to." The "common property" of his letters had an inhibiting effect upon his correspondence, preventing him from raising confiden-tial matters with particular members of the family. "Private" letters do not, therefore, provide a full or accurate picture regarding his feelings about his future profession, or indeed other personal matters. Even letters to him were not confidential because two or three members of the family sometimes wrote on one sheet of paper and would refer to what the others had written. On some occasions they read the letters of others before their posting. Mindful of the "public nature" of Gladstone correspondence, nevertheless family letters and the diary provide the greatest insight into this controversial subject. Sometimes it is clear from the contents of what at first seems a personal communication that it has been written as a "public communication," in order to convey information "indirectly" to other members of the family as well as the recipient.

The fourteen year old Helen wrote to William on 25 October 1828 reproducing a conversation with Tom in dialogue form. Tom said to her "Suppose we shall hear from Wm tomorrow. Yes I suppose so." Tom "Do you think Wm wishes to be a clergyman? 'H,' I will answer you candidly, I think he does wish it, but he has not decided. 'T,' Do you think so, but have you heard him say so? I replied in the affirmative—When? The last night I saw him. Ah! I was sure it would be so—you have told me nothing new; I knew it though William is always reserved with me on these subjects." Tom commented that it did not matter what tutor William had "since yr attention wd naturally be directed to Divinity, and that he was hurt and vexed."

On 16 November 1828 Tom wrote to William about his imminent visit to Oxford, but makes no mention of ordination. Tom arrived on the evening of Wednesday 19 November, leaving the following day. The diary makes no mention of anything discussed, but two days later William wrote a long letter to Tom. It was to be an important "public communication" placing the subject of his future before the whole family. "I must take this opportunity to . . . speak . . . of my future profession."[15] This he does not because he had reached any conclusion, but because Tom was hurt by his silence. He refers to Helen's conversations: "It appears that the impression you received from that conversation was in the first place that my mind was made up and had been for some time: and secondly that, my own resolution being formed, I had spoken of it to others, but concealed it from you." His mind was not made up, "excepting this, that my conduct ought not to be swayed by my own inclinations, without deference and attention to those of others." There were two reasons for his silence: "1st. That my mind was not made up . . . 2nd. That my ideas were so little matured, and particularly, that I found them so liable to variation, and that I did not wish formally to make a declaration, especially in opposition to the inclinations of some whom I ought most to love and to respect."

Perhaps to avoid further misunderstanding he adds "When I say my resolution is not formed, I do not mean that I have no inclination either way. There appears to me to be a decided preponderance of reasons, which make the Church appear preferable." As a "public letter" did he deliberately push his argument a stage further in order to clarify his position? There were other reasons for his silence; "one is that I believe (the word *your* is crossed out) my father's inclination is, that I should enter the law. This may change: so may that of my brothers on the same subject, which I believe is the same; and you will easily believe that it would be much more satisfactory to me to state my own inclinations when *in accordance* with those of *all*, than when opposed to those of some. Were it not for this I should soon come to a conclusion on the subject." The implication is that if his father agreed to his entering the church then he would do so. But "I could not dare to hope we should agree . . . That our opinions should not coincide, I lament but it would be most undutiful towards my father if I wished to act upon my own in opposition to his." His deepest longings were now made known to the family.

William must have hoped that the letter would evoke some response from his father. The way was now open for all to join in the correspondence either encouraging or dissuading him from entering the church. Tom was the first to reply, possibly acting as his father's spokesman: "While I feel sure your relinquishing the first intention of going to the Law will be a source of regret to my father . . . and the *male* part of the family, I am also sure that *he* would be the last to thwart you in what you considered best for your happiness—on the contrary he would object to your making a selection only in accordance with the wishes of others—You are the party most interested in your future profession, and yours the choice should be, but take time to consider the pros and cons—and above all, lose no time in consulting my father on the subject so interesting to both, when you have finally ascertained the balance of your own wishes and impressions."[16] While not specifically mentioning his mother, Tom states that he considers her "as necessarily a party to whatever concerns his or your interests." He also recognises that William had already discussed the subject with her.

His plan was to visit William in Oxford for "a quiet chat." William records "T.G. came, had tea and wine with me and sat till 12, talking on several things, at last on profession." A few days after Tom's letter and visit William began a letter to his mother, completed three days later, altering the date to December 4 1828. It is rather strange that he tells her he has nothing to write about; there is not even the slightest reference to his future profession.

Tom raised the subject of their recent meeting and correspondence with their father and wrote to William[17] assuring him that their father is "quite satisfied" concerning his reasons for silence. Their father had reacted as he had anticipated, "he would be the last to *thwart* your wishes or *constrain* your choice so long and so anxiously has he looked forward to you entering the Law," which, writes Tom, their father sees as a desirable introduction to public life and possible distinction. Their father's only wish is that William should take ample time to weigh the matter before coming to a decision. He was all kindness in considering William's position and in whatever he says or does he had only William's good in view. Having disclosed his father's feelings he tells William that what he had written was *strictly confidential* and should not be mentioned to any of the family. Possibly an attempt to prevent correspondence between William and the female members of the family. William replied to Tom on 6 December, but the letter has not survived. What Tom writes about his father's sympathetic response, and his primary concern for William's happiness, and that in spite of his own ambitions about William's future profession, that the final decision would be left entirely with William is a somewhat different picture from what William would later have us believe.

In view of this correspondence William must have wanted to discuss his future with his father and family during the Christmas vacation, but the diary makes no mention of any conversation with his father or any member of the family. This does not mean that it was not discussed, but we have no evidence of any further developments. It is possible that silence was regarded by all as the simplest solution to what had become a controversial issue between the male and female members of the family. However, in a letter to William Helen comments "I often think of you and what you are doing—and it is my most earnest prayer that you may be enabled to serve God as He commands."[18] Whatever the pressures put upon William by his father and

Tom, the young Helen felt that he must obey God's will.

Two letters left Leamington on 1 April 1829, one from Tom and one from Helen, Helen's being added to Tom's. Tom wrote about the scholarship William had taken. The diary notes "Letters from T.G. and H.J.G.—much misunderstanding: God grant it may be set to rights --wrote a long letter to him."[19] And all because Tom felt that his younger brother had not kept him fully informed about the Ireland scholarship which he had attempted in March, and failed. After further correspondence with Tom William enquired whether in future letters they were to touch upon "religious matters." "For if not, that is certainly a restriction, and in a most important branch: if it is, I trust those painful differences of sentiment which seem to prevail among us may be diminished . . . I believe little has passed between us on it, since the time when, at Eton, you asked me whether I read the Bible, and strongly recommended my doing so."[20]

William found this an intolerable restriction, in view of his religious convictions and growing interest in the church. In November that year he wrote in his diary "After lecture, my Tutor asked me whether I was going into the Church," but William adds no comment. While family correspondence and diary entries in 1829 reveal no development concerning his future profession, in spite of such silence, in his annual self-examination he wrote "My mind has continued strongly inclined to the Church throughout." Tom and his father were wrong if they thought that he had dropped the idea of ordination. They may have tried to discourage him, but his mother took a very different line and actively encouraged him. It was a subject upon which she frequently thought and she was mindful of how in this matter he no longer had Anne's advice.[21]

Tom's paternalistic attitude and hostility toward William did not encourage him to share his inner feelings, especially about entering the church. And so Tom accused him of being cold, reserved, secretive and far too religious. In spite of her good intentions William found Helen a poor substitute for Anne. What he needed at that time was a "spiritual director." The "common property" of letters had restricted his correspondence with Anne, but he had valued her advice and their long conversations. Support from his mother and Helen was no match for his father and Tom's opposition and did not fill the gap left by Anne's death and so he stood alone.

John Morley's four pages given to the theme of Gladstone's

"Thoughts on future Profession" and the two letters reproduced in the appendix of Volume one, can give a simplistic picture of an issue which for Gladstone was paramount in his life for a number of years. For many subsequent writers on Gladstone, down to the present day, the two letters in Morley's appendix have been regarded as the heart of the issue. This is far from the truth. Those letters were the "tip of the iceberg." There were at least fifteen letters between William, his parents and brothers in 1830 alone, where "his future profession" was a major issue, if not *the* major issue. There are also nearly as many intimate diary entries on the subject. The thought of ordination had evolved over a number of years. William's spiritual growth and wide theological reading all pointed in the direction of the church as the sphere of his future life and work, if he was to be obedient to the will of God. Believing in the God-given authority exercised by parents over their children, and that God could make his will known through parents made the decision more agonising.

The early days of January 1830 found him feeding his spiritual life on Taylor's *Holy Living*, while consolidating his theological position with other reading. Religious conversation occupied many hours of the second Sunday of January; two weeks later these talks with his friend Anstice continued and that same day he had conversations with Doyle and Gaskell, described as "painful" and "exceedingly distressing, which continued until two o'clock the next morning." Did these touch upon his future profession or were they part of his apostolic zeal to bring his friends to a deeper Christian commitment? On the anniversary of Anne's death he bewailed his "unchristian life," praying "May I feel what I am, and what I ought to be, and may the love of God destroy utterly the love of self in me." True to orthodox and ascetical theology he knew that if he was to obey the will of God he must die to self and live to God alone. Religious conversations, sometimes of great intensity, continued from time to time with his closest friends.

His inner searching finds expression in his diary on Sunday 25 April, when he prays to be renewed in the image of God and asks that the "love of God may become the *habit* of my soul." He longed to die to self and to serve God and his fellow men. A month later he wrote "My lethargy grows deeper. O that I could say God deliver me." During the summer vacation, while staying with Saunders, he spent much time with Anstice of whom he had written "would I were worthy to be his

companion." Together they engaged in bible study and spent much time
in religious conversation; perhaps unknowingly for Gladstone, he was
taking Anne's place. There was a growing spiritual affinity and Gladstone found that he was able, as never before, to discuss with Anstice
those secret longings of ordination. On 24 July he recorded "conversation with Anstice on Rel(igion) at night—He talked much with Saunders on the motive of actions, contending for the love of God . . . well, I
trust God will teach me to bow to him."

On Monday 2 August 1830 he wrote in his diary of a meeting
with Anstice: "Conversed with him from ten to twelve on subjects of
the highest importance. Thoughts then sprang up in my soul (obvious
as they may appear to many) which may powerfully influence my destiny. O for light from on high: I have *no* power, *none* to discern the right
path for myself." The next day he spent two hours walking alone in the
garden at Cuddesdon and feeling very uncomfortable. He felt a fearful
weight on his mind and that he was "trifling over matters . . . while
souls throughout the world are sinking daily into death." He lists his excuses for failing to respond to God's call: "I am not old enough well
God knows: shall I be able to urge this as a plea in the last day?" He expresses the conviction that God will answer these inner and ultimate
questions "and gently lead my mind to the right conclusion. And O that,
whithersoever he calls, I may follow! Strange thoughts of my future life
and of giving up home, friends, University, passed through my mind:
that I can do little is no reason against it—no reason why that little (by
God's grace) should not be done."

This account of his inner pilgrimage makes it clear that he had
reached a point of decision. He recalled that the fearful day of judgment
would reveal all things. Providence had brought him to this point. His
utter unworthiness, his limitations, the fact that he could do little towards the salvation of mankind, fast sinking into sin were no excuse. If
he really believed in God and in the sufficiency of His grace he must
respond to what he now believed was God's call. But even when he had
reached the point of decision, the next day he still felt uncomfortable
and much distracted "with doubts as to my future line of conduct. God
direct me. I am utterly blind." Were these doubts prompted by the uncertainty about how his father and Tom would react when he raised
again a subject which they found so unacceptable? He recorded in his
journal "wrote a very long letter to my dear father on the subject of my

future profession, wishing if possible to bring that question to an immediate and final settlement."

And so he penned that now famous letter of 4 August 1830.
The final letter covered nearly seven large pages of small neat handwriting; the draft copy which has been preserved is a little longer and
contains many careful corrections and alterations. The next day he
wrote in his diary "Less distracted, but I fear rather from smothering
my inquiries than satisfying myself. Wrote over and slightly corrected
my letter." The following day . . . "Read my letter over again and sent
it." For the first time William laid everything before his father, fully ex-
plaining his wish to enter the church. The length, style and complexity
of the letter do not make it easy reading.

In the opening sentence William set what he has to say within
a "divine context." He writes of his "future destiny," what God wills for
his life rather than what he wants to do. Eighteen months had passed
since his father's request that he should take time to consider the question of his future and if he remained uncertain then to go into law. William felt that sufficient time had elapsed and adequate thought had been
given for him to come to a final decision. His mind is inclined to the
ministerial office, to the ordained ministry. This conviction has grown
day by day in a "gradual and imperceptible manner," to the best of his
ability he had sifted and resifted the factors which had influenced his
thinking and development along these lines. There had been times of
uncertainty and doubt, but these had been temporary. It was not a decision of "blind impulse or transitory whims," he had now been moved
"with an irresistible accumulation of moral force to this conclusion and
this alone." Nothing could compare with the dignity of the ministerial
office, the end of which is "the glory of God, and the means, the restoration of man to that image of his Maker." True, there were other fields
of service for the use and improvement of all, but God had not called
him to other fields of service. He is convinced that God has called him
to ordination "the conviction flashes on my soul with a moral force I
cannot resist, and should not if I could, that the vineyard still wants labourers . . . there can be no claim so solemn and imperative as that
which even now seems to call to us with the voice of God from heaven,
and to say . . . why will you not bear to fellow-creatures sitting in darkness and the shadow of death the tidings of this universal and incomprehensible love?" Can he disobey God's voice and such a heavenly vision? His own impotence and incompetence can no longer be seen as

arguments against his seeking to serve God in this way. He would have to answer for his obedience or disobedience "before the judgment seat of God, and there give the decisive account of his actions at the tribunal whose awards admit of no evasion and no appeal."

Having considered all these things "I can come to no other conclusion, at least unaided, than that the work of spreading religion has a claim infinitely transcending all others in dignity, in solemnity and in usefulness." He had an overwhelming obligation to respond to God's call to fulfil his destiny and seek ordination. Despite such overwhelming convictions he has, nevertheless, to admit that these were his personal convictions and views "because I do not now see that my own view can, or ought to stand for a moment in the way of your desires. In the hands of my parents, therefore, I am left." He has "consulted with none in this matter" and has now laid everything before his father without even the smallest reservation. Little has passed between him and his mother on this subject and certainly nothing since he last spoke with his father on the matter "yet I have long been well aware of the tendency of her desires, long indeed before my own in any degree coincided with them." He now waited with deference his father's answer; if he was mistaken in his reasoning or conclusions then he prays that he "may, by His mercy and through your instrumentality or that of others, be brought back to my right mind, and taught to hold the truth of God.".22

A further section, not produced by Morley, is added to the letter. Here he reflects on the degree for which he was working and the irrelevance and self-indulgent nature of such academic work, which he fears unprofitable when seen against his future profession.

While awaiting his father's reply he wrote in his diary on Sunday 8 August "Out—alone and with Anstice: spoke to him about that awful subject which has lately almost engrossed my mind." He records how the previous Monday he had witnessed a parade in Oxford with flags and bands of music and was moved to reflect upon how "men had missed the purpose of their being."As he pondered on the implications of that scene was he already expressing reservations, even doubts, concerning what he had written to his father?—"At present I am come to a somewhat different state of mind . . . the idea which then threw me into doubt and perplexity with reference to the duty of acting upon them, is much modified. For I must not I think consider myself as a man exercising the unfettered judgment of a man: but as a being not yet competent for self-direction nor fitted to act upon his own uncorrected impressions, but under the guidance of others for his present course."

Were these genuine expressions of doubt about his objectivity and ability to discern God's will for his life? They were more likely the anxiety experienced while awaiting his father's uncertain reply. The delay was intolerable. A letter from home, but not from his father, provided him with the opportunity to write to Tom.[23] "I wrote a letter to my dear father last week on the subject of a future profession and since sending it I have been very uneasy from apprehension lest my dwelling at such length on reasons which influenced me might appear presumptuous . . . I do not put much confidence in sentiments which have been the result of my own solitary reflections without communicating with others upon them because I know that the appearance which things present depends so much upon the particular state of the individual at the time he is viewing them . . . having acted without any advice from those who are wiser than myself . . . makes me fearful lest I may have stated anything in an exaggerated and unbecoming manner. I can only trust to his kindness and indulgence, should such have been the case."

Knowing that this letter would be "common property" he may have been expressing doubts about the decision he had reached, or perhaps he was trying to pre-empt any suggestions of either exaggeration, or that before writing such a letter he should have discussed the matter with his father. When he wrote to his father that he had "consulted with none in this matter," was he implying no member of the family or no person whatsoever? It is difficult to believe that he had not discussed his possible ordination on this and on previous occasions during some of those long discussions with his Oxford friends.

At last the anxiously awaited letter arrived, six days after he had sent his own. The letter is about a sixth of the length of William's. Mr. Gladstone had hoped that William would have delayed his decision until he "had completed those studies connected with the attainment of the honours or distinctions of which you were so justly ambitious." John Gladstone's own ambitious nature, not only for himself and his own success, made him ambitious for his children, especially William. Here there is no mention of William seeking to fulfil God's will. While William is praying for the death of self his father counsels him that when his mind is finally made up to seek that which is "eventually for your good. Let nothing be done rashly . . . avail yourself of all the advantages placed within your reach." These were very much the directions of the self-made businessman. William's belief that a clergyman's work can have a wide-ranging, even a world effect, are rejected, his influence is confined to the parish and thus his ideas about saving mankind are groundless. Other professions, including law, would provide him with a more general intercourse with mankind, such work is "eminently useful to others, with credit and satisfaction to yourself." He requests William to devote his attention to his degree, adding "You are young and have ample time before you." But, says his father, once his degree has been completed should "you continue to think as you now do, I shall not oppose your *then* preparing yourself for the church, but I do hope that your final determination will not until then be taken."[24]

There is no mention of William exaggerating the situation in order to prove his point, nor of his acting without first seeking the advice of others. It was possible that John Gladstone believed that by advising delay, first to obtain his degree and then to give serious consideration to anything else which occurred, that eventually William would drop the idea of the church. The reservation expressed by William in his diary on Sunday 8 August and in his letter to Tom on 9th and the agreeable terms in which he records receipt of his father's letter all seem to suggest that he was not altogether convinced that God was calling him to ordination, or at least that there were not other professions, including politics, which did not fascinate him as alternative means of service and satisfaction. His father's reply did not rule out ordination, it simply advised him to wait. William accepted this without question, perhaps leaving open the possibility of a future compromise and a chance to delay his ultimate decision because of his own uncertainty. He replied to his father on the same day that he received the letter.[25] Now that he had shared his aspirations and pent up feelings with his family, especially his father, the pressure had been removed. Thanks were expressed for the kindness and consideration of his father's reply. Apologies were offered, he had not expected an immediate decision in favour of the view he had adopted, nor did he mean to give the impression that he himself had reached a decision about his future. The aim was to lay all that was on his mind before him. This he had now done and his father had treated the whole matter sympathetically. He could now give his entire attention to his degree.

Next came another letter from Tom on 14th, in reply to William's of 9th. Their father felt "much disappointment and thinks your decision made unnecessarily soon." He expressed regret "because you appear to have made up your mind deliberately." Brotherly concern prompts Tom to warn William against "the extravagance of religious effervescence" and not to believe that human nature is so utterly worthless. He had an unfeigned respect for the sincerity of William's zeal, his only regret was its present direction. Having "disappointed my father's fond hopes" he calls upon him to "strain every nerve'" to obtain his degree and in so doing "gratify his, and I will add, *our* ambitions."[26] A joint answer arrived from his mother and father.[27] His mother made only a passing reference to "the development of your future life," perhaps because the joint letter prohibited her from writing what she really felt. His father wrote that he was gratified by William's determination to meet "our wishes as regard your future studies."

In a letter to Robertson informing him of the recent correspondence and their father's reactions William once again raises the issue of parental authority and admits that in due course his father might well oppose his choice "and I ought to be ready to acknowledge the justice and kindness too of such a course on his part and immediately accommodate my own to it."[28] The next day four pages of small script were dispatched to Tom,[29] who William felt had now broken the vow not to discuss religious issues with him. While William's letter to Tom on 9 August may have reflected a loss of confidence, even a shift in his position, here he expresses no compromise or watering down of his earlier strong convictions. He rejoices that Tom has broken his principle not to write about religious matters. He maintains that it is impossible for a man to refrain from religious inquiry. Love of truth must prevail above all else. Tom had accused him of believing human nature to be utterly worthless; this he denies, "but I believe it alienated from God." He moves the argument to another level: Man must above all else be obedient to the will of God, a position he had argued in connection with his own life when he wrote to his father on 4 August. "As creatures we are bound to do this will; and our own only in as far as it coincides with His . . . our will must be subordinate and obedient to His." All that a man does is sin unless done in obedience to the will of God. Having established his theological position he applies it to his own life, "I have ever striven to invent reasons or if not reasons yet seeming reasons against it." Let love of God "be the mainspring of our actions: let that be the pervading and sustaining tie which links them . . . If we do not love to hear of Christ and speak of Christ on earth how shall we love to hear of him and sing of him in heaven?" He writes of God's redemptive work through the precious blood of Christ and reaffirms what he had said to his father, that he could see "no employment so noble as that which makes us the messengers of this wondrous love to others." Here indeed was renewed confidence and a renewed attempt to make his position clear to his family.

It is possible that William deliberately misunderstood Tom regarding his ban on religious discussion. Tom felt that he had both misunderstood him and taken advantage of the situation. "I hoped that I had made myself clear as to my situation not to enter into the discussion of the religious theory in which your mind appears to be wrapped up—but as I have been misunderstood allow me now to say that I was tempted to touch upon the subject in the hope—not of altering your opinions—but of moderating what I conceived and still conceive to be the enthusiasm of your views." William had achieved his objective, for Tom admitted he ought to have realized that William would have steered his arguments in the direction of his future profession and so prompted further discussion among members of the family. He must not be allowed to feel that he had won the day, or that his religious convictions should go unchallenged. But Tom was no match for William in such controversies. Sarcastically he comments if all "think as you think" we shall all "become Clergymen." William is told of Tom's hope that "time will moderate the present fervour of your zeal and induce you to think that we are placed on earth with worldly as well as heavenly duties to perform; that those who best . . . perform the former will not be the worse fitted for the latter; and that the enjoyments of this life are not so incompatible with those of a life to come as you seem to consider them."[30]

The strong terms used by Tom in this letter reflect the delicate nature of their relationship and help to explain the conflicts which emerged from time to time throughout their lives. William's religious convictions, enthusiasm and zeal were all too much for him. A reply to Tom contains profuse apologies for any misunderstandings and then answers carefully all his comments and criticisms.[31] Concerning the duties of the clergyman, these bring him more directly into contact with the things of another world than of this world, and those things are of a *higher* order than temporal objects. Even Tom's quip that everyone should become clergymen is not allowed to pass: "I do not see that it is a matter of right or wrong to become a clergyman or not: therefore I do not see that it is a point of duty not to press my inclinations should they continue unaltered, against those of a parent." Every Christian is to "serve God in that state of life to which it pleases him to call us." All can discover God's will for themselves through the bible and when they seek to know his will in prayer and humility.

William believed that God was calling him to communicate the gospel to his fellow creatures. He objected to Tom's comment "those who think as I think"; there is "nothing I dread more, in my present state, than being identified with any supposed or real party." Exception is taken to Tom's expression "the way in which I adopt my intended profession." "It is hardly fair that I should be spoken of by others as having adopted it, while I am precluded from myself viewing it as chosen . . . I would remind you of the position in which I now stand: that my father has enjoined me to withhold my conclusion but not to check my thoughts . . . I . . . . therefore continue in suspense, stating my present view and the reasons for it as occasion seems to offer, but not presuming to think it beyond the reach of further modification."

Continuing clashes with Tom on religious matters gave William the opportunity to keep his convictions before the family. If he now regarded the restriction imposed upon him by his father as unacceptable this would explain his comment "I am precluded from myself viewing it as chosen." He had agreed to devote all his attention to obtaining a good degree, but was it just, after eighteen months of waiting for his father to request that he delay, once again, any decision about entering the church?

Robertson now joined the attack on William, his letter[32] arriving a few days after William had written defending himself against Tom. Their father had sent Robertson all the correspondence relating to William's future profession on the ground that there should be no secrets among members of the family. Robertson observed that if he kept silent he would not be acting "with that degree of candour, towards you, that I ought both to show and to feel." He expressed strong objections concerning some of William's views in the letter to their father. What follows suggests that their father's request that William should delay any decision about the church was indeed in the hope that he would forget ordination. "My father with his usual kindness towards all of us, (never) endeavoured to dissuade or interrupt a choice of pursuits; but he has . . . considered from the first, that the Law was a profession likely to be consonant with your feelings, and a proper field for the exercise of your powers rendered more so than any other profession."

John Gladstone might have been willing to let his other sons have some freedom in the choice of their professions, but not without his direction. His plans for his most able son certainly did not include ordination. Robertson was not trying to persuade William to abandon his inclinations, but that the subject might be allowed to "lie quietly."

Much of William's reply to Robertson[33] repeated what had already been written to other members of the family, but he adds that his case was presented without the benefit of wise counsel and when he had little time to give to the matter. "Then why write at such a time?" William's answer throws new light on the subject "because my mother had repeatedly told me of late that I should hardly be behaving with that dutiful and unreserved freedom which I ought certainly to maintain, if I suffered a much longer period to elapse without informing my father how the bent of my inclinations lay." His first reason, concerning the fallen state of humanity and its need for redemption, was based not on his own reasoning but the rock of scripture. The second "That the noblest employment for one human creature is to save . . . his fellow men" was of his own deduction and he did not "wish to act upon it in opposition to those whom (he) ought to love and to obey." And he could not prepare himself for such duties if he commenced his preparation for this sacred task "by the desertion of earthly ones: when both alike rest on one and the same foundation." He wished to serve God in the church but could "not pretend to have arrived at the truth;" because of this he valued the advice which other members of the family were able to offer and believed that if such advice be "dictated by the Spirit" it would be of the highest value to him and help him eventually to reach the right conclusion "whatever it may be."

A letter from the family estate at Fasque, Fettercairn, was dispatched by Tom in answer to William's of 1 September.[34] Assurance is given that there would be no opposition from their father "when the proper time comes, that no alternative was likely to take place." He was pleased to hear that William would take the opportunity of maturing his thoughts on the subject of his future profession by considering the advice of others. Their father had made his position clear to William in his letter of 10 August;[35] "His first wish for you, as for all of us, is your happiness, whatever be the profession." If eventually William felt unable to enter law and persisted in entering the church then he was quite sure that this was what their father would want.

For a while the subject was allowed to rest, but not for long.

William became frustrated and impatient; on Tuesday 2 November he noted in his diary "wrote letters to Mr. G. & T.G. about my degree." To his father he wrote "Now supposing I go up at Easter, by the time this period has elapsed I shall have passed my three and twentieth year and that is no small proportion of life to devote to education only and that not to education for a specific profession . . . Whether my profession is to be law or not . . . I think that age is quite late enough for turning my attention in a more immediate manner to it."[36] His letter to Tom was more specific: "Supposing I go up next Easter, I cannot be ready to enter on my profession whether studying for the law or Church before I am twenty-three. I should be very sorry that it should be later, particularly if it should be the latter but scarcely less so if the former."[37] Once again he takes advantage of the opportunity of expressing his opinion that the ordained ministry was superior in dignity and usefulness to every other profession.

Mr. Gladstone replied to both communications[38] stating that he had discussed William's future plans with Tom and approved of his proposal to leave undetermined the decision about law or the church until he returned from the continent. After the completion of his education, and the tour, he will have seen more of the world and at the same time "have greater confidence in the choice you may make, for it will then rest wholly with yourself to do so, having our advice whenever you may wish for it." Thus the final decision between law or the church would, in due course, rest with William.

On 29 August 1830 William wrote a long letter to John. Earlier that year he had written a letter covering most of the points found in correspondence with other members of the family. The clerical office "seems to transcend all other in dignity and usefulness, not because a man may not serve God in other professions . . . but because here *I think* he is admitted to the high honour of serving Him in that mode which is, of all others, the most efficacious and direct." He was torn between responding to what he believed to be God's will for his life and the will of his father. Parental authority may be God-given but William never seems to recognise that his dilemma on this point was a conflict between his ultimate duty to God and his duty to his parents. Could he not see that parental authority is tinged by the fallen sinful nature and thus prone to its own selfish ends? "It tortures me," he tells John, "to think of an inclination opposed to that of my beloved father—and more of carrying that inclination into effect."[39] Four months later he wrote to

John that he was becoming increasingly convinced that the choice of his future profession would in fact be made known by God through his parents.[40] Admitting that although his father insisted he followed his own inclinations, his father was "also anxious that those inclinations should coincide with his own . . . I feel exceedingly solicitous to come to no decision which shall in any way interfere with his wishes." Still claiming that God's will was that he should enter the church, he tells John "I have neither the right nor the desire to act upon it in opposition to a parent's wishes." What were his parents' wishes? His father wished him to pursue law, his mother that he enter the church. Why then did he not respond more positively to his mother's encouragement, who also exercised God-given authority? Was the truth of the situation that deep down Gladstone thought he ought to be a priest, but was secretly more attracted to politics and thus unable to accept that God was calling him to ordination, and therefore he shifted the responsibility from himself to his parents, more correctly his father? He tells John "People say, indeed that you are to follow the will of God in these things, but that will must have channels of conveyance and what more natural one than the wishes of a parent." Did he really believe this or was he, even unknowingly, using this "theological conviction" to resolve his own inner conflict?

Tom and William spent some time out together on 11 and 12 January 1831. William returned to Oxford two days later "full of good resolutions but no stamen for performing them." Writing a few days later "I am sick of all my prospects and doings," he accuses himself of hypocrisy "deceiving myself as well as others: so inconsistent, so wavering, so uncertain." But his uncertainty was not so extreme as suggested by Dr. Perry Butler, as to prompt such an early change in his choice of a profession. Tom, according to Butler,[41] had been informed that at last William had decided upon law. Unfortunately Dr. Butler's conclusion is based upon a mistake in the date of Tom's letter; he wrote 1831 on his letter of 24 January, but this is incorrect—the post-mark is 1832. However inconsistent, wavering and uncertain he was, no decision about his future had been made at this stage. "Work, work, work occupied me throughout 1831" was how he later described a momentous year begun with good intentions, but with grave reservations. He had promised that his undivided attention would be given to his academic work. Family hopes ran high with the expectation of a first class and a scholarship. While the ultimate decision about his future profession could not be forgotten it was rarely mentioned in family correspondence that year.

The diary entry of 17 January shows that William could not drive it out
of his mind, nor prevent the occurrence of events and contacts which
turned his thoughts towards the church.

The fallen state of the human race and its need of salvation
had throughout the family correspondence of 1830, been put forward as
an important reason for William's desire to enter the church and to be
used by God in His redemptive work. Towards the end of February he
wrote to his mother[42] of the appalling death at Christ Church of G. T.
W. Osborne, son of the Duke of Leeds, who while in a state of drunkenness, died during a scuffle with some of his equally drunken companions. He describes the event as a "visible and palpable judgment of
God." His words may be thought uncharitable but, he declares,"I for
one am sick of the world's charity; alas how often does it consist merely in permitting reckless and thoughtless men to rush headlong into ruin
when a word of sober warning might have purchased for them everlasting safety." Around him he witnesses "horrible barbarity" beastly
drunkenness, scores of men with the "name of sin upon their fore-
heads." And this, he reminds his mother and the family, "is in a Christian and a protestant country—in a university, the seat of religion and
the nursery of the Church of England . . . This is the place where youth
is trained up to godliness instead of being left as at the London University." Recent events had been sent by God to the university authorities
as "a most powerful medicine but they will not administer it." Those
who speak out and call for change are "denounced as enthusiasts." He
must call upon his fellow students, and tutors where necessary, to accept the message of salvation "that God must reign in the heart; that
they can never be happy but by being holy . . . clinging to the cross of
Christ . . . seeking deliverance by his precious blood, and renewed after
his own divine image."

Perhaps there was in all this a message even for William, for
he wrote "If we reject the admonitions of God what can we look for but
his wrath?" Ordination was not mentioned but many associated ideas
had again been brought before the family. At this stage he had written
ten pages of small script with six more still to go. He may have been
thinking of a future divine mission to institutions in addition to individuals when he wrote of "a radical taint which must be burnt from out of
these institutions if they are to live in that conflict of opposing principles in politics, morals and religion." But what could he do? He ought
to speak, but was aware of his shortcomings: "I am too young and act

too much upon impulse." Such reservations had been fostered by the male members of his family when he had tried to establish his grounds for entering the church.

John, away at sea, received two letters from William on the subject of his future profession. His reply touches upon the "forbidden" subject and expresses the hope of seeing William in the near future.[43] They met a few days later, but William records nothing of their conversations. However he does record that he had much talk about his future and the way ahead with Saunders and Biscoe, mentioning the possibility of postponing his degree in the event of his missing the university scholarship. He felt that he could see "the Divine purpose pointing to the path I have now chosen, though this is perhaps not a thing to be noised abroad." Unfortunately he says nothing about his chosen path.

During the final days of March his mind was much occupied with the Reform Bill: "heard with mixed feelings of the passing of the Reform Bill (2nd reading);" two days later "finished Article on Reform, and read Southey's on State of England. After thinking and talking about Reform—since I came home, I trust in God the Bill will not be carried." The Reform Bill and associated Parliamentary debates are noted in his diary; at the end of March the Bill reached a crucial stage. From then on Gladstone was actively engaged in opposing it. In April Arthur Hallam wrote: "I have had a long letter from Gladstone; he is very bitter against the Reform Bill." His opposition was seen in his joint formation, with his tutor Charles Wordsworth, of the Oxford Anti-Reform League. Placards were displayed throughout Oxford and a petition organised. On Tuesday 17 May he "spoke at the adjourned debate for 3/4 of an hour." His indignation against the Bill raised him to an unusual pitch of eloquence, denouncing it as destined to change our form of Government and ultimately to break up the very foundation of social order. One of those present noted "Most of the speakers rose . . . above their usual level, but when Mr. Gladstone sat down we all of us felt that an epoch in our lives had occurred. It certainly was the finest speech of his that I ever heard."[44] Charles Wordsworth later commented that his experience of Gladstone at that time "made me (and I doubt not, others also) feel no less sure than of my own existence that Gladstone, our then Christ Church undergraduate, would one day rise to be Prime Minister of England."[45]

Dr. Perry Butler sums up this important event and its consequences for Gladstone: "It was from this speech that Gladstone's political career derived. Unless its intensity and extremism are understood, his change of mind, the forsaking of a clerical career for a life of politics is incomprehensible. Only in the light of his violent opposition to the Reform Bill can the sentiments expressed in the letter to his father in January 1832 be appreciated."[46] Butler sees William's letter to his father as the working out of the implications of his new position. It was not merely individual souls that must be brought to the foot of the cross, the whole political and social order had lost its bearings and stood in urgent need of redemption. The implication, according to Dr. Butler, was that Gladstone thus abandoned his idea of ordination, the aim of which was to be an instrument in the hand of God to bring individual souls to the foot of the Cross. But did this important event, and Gladstone's increased interest in politics, mark such a radical and clearcut change in his thinking and commitment about his future profession, and how he could serve God and his fellow men?" His father, arguing against ordination in his letter to William on 10 August 1830, had already pointed out that there were other professions which would offer greater opportunities of service and a "more general intercourse with mankind."

There is no doubt about the importance of this event, but it need not have been as decisive as Butler and others suggest. Could there be such a simple and straightforward solution to such a major issue in Gladstone's life? Two weeks later he wrote in his diary "I have never had cause to feel my own utter and abandoned sinfulness before God more deeply." Was this feeling of divine abandonment because he was now seriously considering politics as an alternative to the church? He ends this entry on 30 May "there is a Providence wonderfully framing out of a seeming series of accidents the most appropriate and aptest discipline for each of our souls." Perhaps he honestly believed that in recent events God was redirecting the course of his life, or at least making it plain.

Helen was excited about William's Union speech, chiefly because of the religious implications.[47] Mr. Gladstone felt that William had gone astray when he connected religion with political controversy. "I think (it) should, on this occasion have been left out for the reasoning founded upon it, and the conclusions you draw from it, do appear to me even if they were called for, much over-strained."[48] That Sunday, 17 July, he wrote in his journal "Denison and Phillimore had tea in my room. Oh that the Father of light would so order my conversation and footsteps, that his truth might be shown forth in my paths, if perchance others might be led."

If a political career was the path of service ordered by divine providence as the area where he could do battle for God, working for the salvation of both individuals and society, then what he wrote to Tom in response to his father's long letter of 12 July suggests that not everyone, including his father, saw things in the same light. Had William, in the enthusiasm of oratorical success, responded too quickly and without sober thought? Was he once again praying to the Father of light to show forth the path he must take? He wrote to Tom "I am, I confess, a good deal disappointed at my father's having formed so strong an opinion about what I wrote as to preclude all idea of its publication." What worried William was the reason for his father's objection, that he had connected religion with political controversy. "Now I cannot deny it is highly probable that many of those conclusions in the details may be much strained, and therefore if this had been made the main ground of objection, it would have been quite another thing." William's fear was that his father's fundamental objection was to his attempt to "directly connect the question with religion at all."

Because of his father's objections he was now apprehensive whether he could ever give full satisfaction to his father whether in politics or in the church. Was his enthusiastic move towards politics no more than a compromise in order to satisfy his father and to avoid any conflict with God-given parental authority and guidance? Had he reasoned himself into believing that politics would offer a wider sphere of religious service? "For if there is one thing which seems to me more clear than another as a general proposition, it is this, that extensive questions of this kind, evidently and immediately involving the whole scope of national welfare, ought to be viewed in reference to their principles as well as their details." He is against what he sees as the popular and growing movement to overthrow all political power. Such a system would seek to deny and, if possible, "to abrogate the Providential government of God in seeking the national concerns, as well as the individual ones, of mankind." Had he misunderstood his father's real objections and, if so, would it be possible to satisfy both God and his father by serving in the field of politics? He ends "I still hope however that it has not been to the principles of viewing great national questions in their religious bearing that my dear father's objection has been made, but to strained application of it and to a too decided and authoritative tone, and too little exception made in favour of the persons and opinions of our adversaries."[49]

Tom replied to William on 21 July. He did not think their father objected to William's considering the religious tendency of the Bill, but to his decided tone. He was of the opinion that his "*political*" view of it would have been more effective without the combination." In other words he ought not to have linked it with religion. On the subject of giving their father satisfaction whether in politics or the church Tom was anxious to set William's mind at rest. While William's views differed from his father's, their father had too high an estimation of William's ruling motives to permit him to feel dissatisfaction on account of such differing views. He may regret such differences and may wish to give the best direction in his power "and with that gentle prerogative he is content."

As Gladstone continued to revise for his final examinations he was still not sure what path he would take on completion of his degree. On Sunday 11 September 1831 he wrote in his new journal "This little book may carry me through very eventful times! God send the best." It was indeed to carry him through momentous times, for this volume of the diary was not completed until 20 July 1833! He obtained his double first in Classics and Mathematics, left Oxford and returned home to Seaforth on 21 December 1831. Eight days later he wrote out his spiritual reflections on the past year and his aspirations for the future.

With Oxford and his degree behind him and completing the twenty second year of his life William felt the occasion provided an opportunity "to examine the course of my life," including the "melancholy tale of my own inward life." Reflecting on the Reform Bill he was moved to write "Fearful things have passed in the world around me, and no small impression have they wrought within—may it issue for good." Prayer is accepted as essential for a life of obedience and dependence and self-sacrifice. He prays that God will "use him as a vessel for His own purposes," but he makes no mention of what they may be. Perhaps he could not bring himself to write down the change in the direction of his life, that he now saw his service of God not in the church, but in the field of politics? He writes of "a desire of higher aim than I could ever have imagined, a fervent and buoyant hope that I might work an energetic work in this world, and by that work (whereof the worker is only God) I might grow into the image of the Redeemer. Would that I could feel in the particularity and clearness of detail all that these words imply . . . It matters not whether the sphere of duty be large or small—but may it be duly filled." What lay behind these words—service in the church or in politics? Whatever that duty and wherever the path was to lead, his earnest prayer was "may I never, O never, leave the cross of Jesus Christ, nor forget its simplicity and power." Was he totally convinced that politics was not a rejection of that call which began at Eton?[50] He prays "that the will of God concerning me is to be found, and all the purposes of God through me are to be wrought or prepared for completion, by the patient and faithful resistance of ungodly will and appetite in the round of daily duty. Amen, Blessed Lord! Amen."

A further eighteen months had passed since William last communicated with his father concerning his desire to be ordained. He had devoted himself to obtaining a good degree and he and John were about to embark on the planned continental tour. When William sat up late at Seaforth House on Saturday 7 January 1832 writing a letter to his father about his future profession, he realized that as it was only a matter of weeks before he left the country; the important communication could not be delayed. The next night he sat up "very late to complete my letter: finished it, but did by no means complete it." Nearly a week passed before he returned to the letter. Perhaps yet another sign of his uncertainty. "I reconsidered what I wrote a week ago" and the following night "again reperused and began to re-write my letter." The next day, Tuesday 17 January was decisive: "Finished my letter: gave it to my dear father: and had the gratification, high indeed, of hearing from him, that it met his wishes and my dear mother's. God be praised."

The letter covered twenty-two pages. Unfortunately only the corrected draft seems to have survived.[51] William informed his father it was "high time" to reconsider "once and for all"what he now described as his "future destination." He explained why he had used the form of a letter when they were under the same roof. Three reasons were given: 1) in order to give clear expression to his thoughts; 2) so that it can be considered by his mother; 3) so it was available to his brothers and sister.

Since his last letter, the subject of his future had caused him much anxiety. His mind remained the same concerning the fallen nature of the world and man's need of redemption. But his conclusion that he could best serve God as a clergyman had been shaken by the events of the previous July. Aware of the "tendencies of every human heart, which make us forget the true aim of our being—to do the will of God —and erect in its place another and an alien purpose—to do our own will." He had to answer the question "how shall I best be enabled to do in my sphere and calling the will of Him whose property I absolutely am, that will bring the extirpation of sin and misery from the world?" From this it is clear that what he believed to be the object, the outworking of God's call remained the same, "Now it seems to me true beyond all question that in every calling, and in every station , this will, or in other words, out duty, may be performed." The difficulty was to know which was the sphere in which this can best be done. "I formerly entertained, that duty might be most extensively and effectually performed in the clerical profession." This he states had been his *former* belief, so the transition has been made and he now felt able to tell his family that he no longer believed himself called to the ordained ministry. That he had a call from God, and a sacred duty to perform, he was in no doubt, but this was to be exercised not as an ordained priest, although as a committed Christian layman it would, in the correct theological sense, be exercised in the church and in the sphere of his work.

The human race, the civilised world, was rapidly approaching a crisis, by which he seems to be implying the "final Coming" of Christ, a conviction he had expressed in his diary the previous October "Surely the actual signs of the times are such as should make us ready for the coming of our Lord." Such signs he saw in the "measures now pending in Parliament and indeed elsewhere too, to the confiscation of the property of the church: hence to its destruction as an establishment: through the destruction of the church establishment to the overthrow of our own kingly government . . . through the overthrow of kingly government in this country to the degradation of its national character and through the degradation of the British nation to wide and irredeemable ruin through the world." These were the issues on which he now believed the battle was to be fought. A major cause of concern within society was the erosion of "filial relations" which no longer demanded the obligation and obedience of the past. For him filial obedience, the acceptance of parental authority, constituted a divine element in society, a means through which God makes His will known to successive generations. Latitudinarianism which placed so little emphasis upon dogmatic truth and ecclesiastical organisation was also seen as a growing national threat.

With society, the world, being under such a threat Gladstone tells his father "I am compelled to give up all peaceful anticipations of the comparative calm and ease of a professional life in any department whatsoever." He admits, as previously, "that there is no station in life without its obligations, its honours and its rewards." The implication of this belief, particularly in the field of politics, is now stated; "In public and in private alike, by the performance of all individual duties, both public and private, and by the unhesitating avowal and defence of sound though now comparatively despised principles in religion, in politics, in education—every man may perform his work under the Providence of God." If he believed and accepted such a theory for himself—then, under the providence of God and if, in fulfilment of God's known will, God could be served with equal dignity and at an equally exalted level as that of the clergyman in other areas of service. Ordination was, therefore, not the highest form of serving God, but one of many forms. What matters above all else is the fulfilment of God's will or call. He informs his father "I am free and happy to own, that my own desires as to my future destination are exactly coincident with yours insofar as I am acquainted with them—believing them to be a profession of the law" eventually leading on to "what is called public life." To be a public man requires, says William, zeal, consistency, a soleness of religious principles, together with intellectual powers and, with his usual modesty, he disclaims possession of such requirements. But if this was indeed his father's wish and plan then "so far as I individually am concerned, such an arrangement would meet all my wishes." If future circumstances indicated that he was unsuitable for such work the steps taken were easily revocable.

And so William of his own volition placed his case before his parents for their consideration and decision; adding a codicil to his own copy, "May I not pray for the direction of God in devising and his blessing in executing, feeling as I am sure I ought to do from the evidence of facts, my own utter blindness and total incompetency either to discern or to pursue the line of duty in such a case—and being firmly persuaded, that under that supreme guidance, the question if lodged as above will be lodged in the best hands."

Mrs. Gladstone, according to William, accepted his change of course and the fact that he no longer believed himself called to be a clergyman. The day after reading his letter, in spite of being very ill, she had further conversations with William concerning it. Helen was a ready listener the next day, but was not happy with the change in his

plans. William also began to have second thoughts. Only two days after
handing the letter to his father, he notes in his journal on 19 January,
"My thoughts being thus turned upon the subject, soon showed themselves not to be at rest." Had he made the right decision or was he trying to escape from God's call to ordination? "There is a weight of responsibility which I cannot support: a dread of self-deception which I
cannot escape from; a fear lest under specious names I should have
veiled to myself a desertion of the most High God. May he by his Spirit
help me: may he build me up in his faith and truth : and so dispose of
this worthless vessel, that it may show forth his glory." He was concerned at these emerging doubts. "What a confession is mine! that after
all my anxiety (perhaps because it was carnal) I have come to a decision, and am utterly ignorant not only of the goodness of the decision,
but of the purity of the motive." Further conversation took place with
his mother before he left for Oxford to take his degree.

From Oxford he wrote to Tom, receiving his reply two days
later.[52] "I cannot tell you how I rejoice at your having determined upon
the Law." So far as the male members of the Gladstone family were
concerned, the decision about William's future was settled and he and
John left London for Belgium on Wednesday 1 February 1832.

Professor Richard Shannon is not the only writer on Gladstone
who has failed fully to understand Gladstone's genuine conviction that
it was God's will that he should seek ordination and thereafter as a clergyman in the Church of England serve Christ and His church. At least
two main factors are responsible for such misunderstanding on an issue
which Gladstone believed to be of paramount importance. First, the
lack of theological knowledge, not least in the fields of ecclesial and ascetical theology, and secondly in a failure to consult the mass of manuscript material now available in connection with this subject.

Shannon says it was impossible for Gladstone "to admit that,
in a free choice of careers, he deliberately chose secularity and political
ambition. It was later to be a great feature of Gladstone's own mythology about himself that it was the "desire of my youth" to "be a clergyman" . . . "the change in the professional direction of my life". . . "took
place in deference to my father's wishes" . . . . "Apart from one intense
phase of yearning for ordination in the summer of 1830, evidence as to
what course of professional life Gladstone desired in youth tends decidedly in the secular direction."[53]

Evidence given in previous chapters of this work proves that from his days at Eton Gladstone gave serious consideration to the possibility of ordination. His thoughts on the subject gradually matured into the conviction that he really had such a vocation. Some of Shannon's observations are reasonable, but on the whole they are half-truths. If Gladstone had a genuine call to the ordained ministry of the church, but accepted a career in politics then this was an act of disobedience to the divine will, rather than an indication of a fabrication of a "mythology" established by Gladstone. Such a suggestion is a grave injustice to Gladstone, to his concept of religious truths to his understanding of the all-seeing and all-knowing nature of God and to his insight into the nature of the Christian church and ministry. All these things would prevent Gladstone from establishing a myth, that the "desire of my youth" was to be a "clergyman." If it had been a youthful myth then in later life he would have been more careful and accurate in his language. Deliberate and known disobedience to the divine will was not something which a churchman of his stature would have made so public, but rather something he would have confined to the pages of his private diary, his annual act of self-examination and his prayers.

In August 1835 he wrote in "a paper on my position," "I saw a great paradox before me in relinquishing the Church for Parliament: but I followed what seemed to be a star in heaven, and thus far I am satisfied with my opportunities though not with my performance."[54] On 8 June 1839 he told Catherine Glynne of what he believed was "my original destination and desire in life, in what sense and manner I remained in connection with politics."

That Gladstone's original destination and the desire of his life was ordination was no myth. He either came to the conviction that he had made a mistake and this was indeed the dream and desire of youthful religious enthusiasm, and that later God had truly called him to serve in politics; or alternatively, Gladstone had a genuine call which he disobeyed when he entered politics and for the rest of his life he was haunted by this act of disobedience and attempted to make amends by serving God as a layman in both state and church. If this alternative is correct, or if Gladstone was never absolutely sure, then his ceaseless activities as a churchman may be seen as an attempt to justify himself before God for his earlier disobedience.

William Gladstone knew that a call to ordination was no whim or passing fancy, but something implanted by God which could not be escaped. For many years he wrestled with this inner call. Even before

going to Oxford he sought, both spiritually and theologically, to prepare himself for such a calling. On many issues in life Gladstone had to
grapple with inner doubts and uncertainties; he was a man who needed
to be convinced before committing himself. Such assurance and unequivocal certainty regarding ordination were denied him, but he saw, or
convinced himself he saw, divine guidance in the wishes and advice of
his father, on the basis that parental authority is God-given and stands
next to the authority of God, and cannot be in contradiction with God's
will. With such a high view of filial obedience he believed that parents
were instruments used by God to make His will known to successive
generations. In addition to the carefully worded and persuasive letters
from his father, Tom, who acted as their father's spokesman, appealed
to him to abandon the idea of a career in the church or at least to delay
his decision and to study law, with a view to entering public life. Success in political debate and oratory at Oxford at the time of the Reform
Bill and his increasing interest in politics which began while at Eton
suggested an alternative sphere of service. Politics were acceptable if
they could be seen as a means of actively forwarding God's work of redemption among men, and in society, and in the corridors of power and
decision making. All these things brought pressure on the young Gladstone who, in the end, in an attempt to satisfy all parties, including God,
accepted politics as an area of service seen to be agreeable with the will
of God. Having accepted this he then sought to rationalise and theologically justify this alternative form of service so that he was not culpable.

Dilemma, paradox and uncertainty did not help Gladstone when
the decision about his future could be delayed no longer. Whether his
father really meant that in due course William would be free to enter
the church is questionable. He was capable of putting pressure upon his
children, while giving the impression that they were free agents, Ultimately they were expected to respond to their father's wishes and predetermined plans. For William that situation never arose and on the
face of it the choice and the decision were his. Was the true situation
that he was unable to admit either deliberate disobedience to God, or
that he had chosen a secular profession in place of the church and so he
continued to shift the pressure of that decision on to his father, who had
the authority of God and was His instrument and therefore whose wishes he had to obey?

When he left for the continent on 1 February the intention was
that on his return he would begin his study of law, but doubts about

whether or not he had made the right decision were to remain with him until entering Parliament and indeed afterwards.

CHAPTER NINE

THE CONTINENTAL JOURNEY: 1832

John and William Gladstone's first activity on arriving in
Ghent, Belgium, on Thursday 2 February 1832 was to witness a procession through the streets taking "the Host" to a sick person's house. They
visited the Cathedral where they saw images of the Blessed Virgin
Mary, which prompted an extremely lengthy entry in his travel diary,
mainly about the Virgin, images and the Roman Catholic Church. It
was William's first contact with the Roman Church in Europe and so
wherever they went he tried to see and explore as much as he could of a
system he had been taught to look upon with suspicion and distrust, in
the belief that it was heretical. During this tour he wrote more about
that church than any other subject. What he saw and heard had an important effect upon his own religious development. He was to be surprised by what he experienced of what was good about Roman Catholicism on the continent, compared with the inherited horror and loathing
of the Catholic Church and papacy in England.

Of the Blessed Virgin Mary he wrote "If I enter a temple decorated with images, and behold one image more prominent than all the
rest, in magnitude, in position, in the attention directed towards it: I naturally conceive it to represent the deity of the place: and other images
less conspicuous, I readily take it for granted, belong to his or her satel-
lites. What conclusion then are we to form, when we enter the temple
of Jesus Christ, and . . . find that the Virgin is the prominent figure of
the place and the Saviour represented as an infant *in her hands*?" Reflecting on the theology of the Virgin and Child he states that the
Atonement and the spotless righteousness of life are the most important
points and these are not demonstrated in the infant Jesus. Such a use of
images is pronounced as wrong for while they may be regarded as a

step between earth and heaven they are, by their very nature, preparatory.

Visiting Savoy he saw many crucifixes, but felt that there was nothing superstitious in the act of erecting these at different places in the country, but he pondered on whether or not a crucifix could move the believer "to contemplation of high and heavenly things."

The use of Holy Water was a questionable practice, especially when he read a list, accompanying such water, which outlined ten spiritual and four temporal benefits procurable by its right use. To him the whole thing seemed unreasonable. Another unacceptable notice, fixed to a church door, advertised plenary indulgences connected with particular seasons or purchased by auction—this, he declared was "exceedingly bad taste." Roman Catholic services of various kinds, and in almost every place visited, were attended with interest and commented upon, and they certainly saw nothing wrong in attending such services.

Whenever possible they attended Protestant services to receive Holy Communion or to hear sermons. Sometimes several churches and services were attended in one day. On their first Sunday they went to Low Mass: "I confess it was an unmeaning and sorrowful ceremony." Visiting Chiavari they found High Mass in progress, the people were all on their knees and chanting "a more imposing scene I never beheld," but it was spoilt by the prostrations of the priests before bringing out the Host. At Florence they attended a baptism "dissatisfied with the matter, disgusted (I cannot use a weaker term) with the *manner* of the service. Much irreverent ministering of holy things have I seen in England: but never any to equal this." Attending St. Joseph's Church two days later he found it painful to speak disrespectfully of any religious service, but had to state "certainly these seemed no better than mummery." After nearly two months on the continent and having visited many Roman Catholic churches he observed "As yet, I have not heard any one mass, I believe, read with common decency."

English places of worship and Protestant churches were found to be reasonably numerous. On Sunday 20 May they heard three sermons: "a good sermon" at the English church in the morning. In the afternoon a sermon on the resurrection, "the groundwork was excellent and the spirit good—but the manner humourous even, sometimes, to buffoonery." Part of a Catholic sermon was heard, which he describes as "whining, ceremonial, and dull," nevertheless he had to admit that the people were attentive. The following Sunday they heard another sermon on the resurrection "very vapid and Popish: terms I would not use without thinking seriously that the occasion warranted them."

William recorded his feeling on first entering St. Peter's, Rome: "In entering such a Church as this most deeply does one feel the pain and shame of the schism which separates us from Rome." He believed that guilt for this schism rested upon Rome and not on the "English Reformed Church." Of the worshippers at St. Peter's he acknowledged "those who are here it may be worshipping the same Redeemer in precisely the same inward form of faith and dependence as yourself." His experience and sympathetic understanding of his divided brethren prompted him to pray "May God bind up the wounds of his bleeding Church." Obviously he had moved a long way from the anti-Romanism of his evangelical upbringing. Roman Catholics might have been regarded by members of the "English Reformed Church" as heretical, but their worship had to be respected as the worship of God in Christ. The chanting of nuns is described as "exquisitely touching and beautiful." He admits "surely we are as much too remiss, yet not the Church of England, but her members, in commemorations of saints, as the Romanish Church is *officious and audacious*." After hearing Benediction at St. Peter's, described as an "innocent ceremony," what followed was felt to be both ludicrous and blasphemous "the dropping down indulgence from the Gallery to be caught by . . . the people . . . They must have an odd notion of sin to believe the penalties of sin could be mitigated by procuring a piece of paper."

On Palm Sunday they visited the Sistine Chapel from nine until after twelve noon; William "Thought the Pope's appearance ordinary and undignified, but the expression of his countenance is benign, simple and devout." What he witnessed did not come up to his expectations of solemn splendour "but rather *down* to the idea one naturally forms of the present condition of popery." Maundy Thursday was a full day and included witnessing the washing of feet at St. Peter's. "The Pope's manner was at once kind, easy and *dignified*." On Good Friday they attended the English church where they received Holy Communion and from there went to St. Peter's. Holy Saturday provided an opportunity to attend both a Roman Catholic baptism and an ordination. Easter Day found them at St. Peter's, where they spent three hours at the Mass, followed at 12 noon by Benediction, when William estimated there must have been 20,000 people present. He describes the scene in rather poetic language, the Pope "authoritatively declares the blessing of the Eternal Father upon the multitudes gathered from all quarters of the world . . . essentially one fold, and visibly marshalled under one Shepherd." Undaunted by hours of worship they went to the English church to receive the Sacrament.

Sermons were usually commented upon; one heard in Venice was preached by "a young and zealous Irishman, of more decidedly Calvinistic views (I thought) than are strictly warranted by the tenets of the Church whose orders he bears." Of a Catholic priest and sermon in the same city he wrote, "I respected him. In his sermon there was scarcely anything that savoured of Popery." Nearly three months before while in Florence he had declared "There seems to be little to hope from the Romanish Church." This first insight into the Roman Catholic church was, however, to make him realize that it contained a wide variety of services and devotional practices, and that genuine piety was to be found as well as abuses of many kinds. Some sermons were full of "popery," others were accepted as God's word. Some services lacked dignity and order, others were devout and reverent. Commemorations of the Virgin and saints may have been extravagant, but served to indicate Anglican neglect of the saints. He found that not all Anglicans were opposed to the practices of the Roman church and wrote to his mother of an old acquaintance "a Cambridge man who uses holy water and kneels before the altars here, and passes with some for a Catholic."[1.]

Ignorance about protestantism, even among the Roman Catholic clergy, shocked Gladstone. An Irish friar in Rome did not know that Protestants were baptized or that they used the New Testament. A church box appealing for alms for the souls in purgatory evoked no indignation. At least two libraries were visited. The Vatican Library was found to contain many protestant books and even a presentation copy of Henry VIII's Book on the Sacraments. They saw Dr. Wiseman, head of the English College and in the college library William noted a copy of John Foxe's *Book of Martyrs* and also a book containing a list of martyrs to the catholic faith in England.

Gladstone observed the Roman Catholic church on the continent as one which had been nurtured in a spiritual and political environment which was prejudiced towards anything connected with that church. From time to time his travel diary reveals such prejudice and sometimes misunderstandings. While he witnessed much which reinforced his anti-Roman prejudice, many other things excited him and made a favourable impression.

His eagerly awaited visit to the Valley of the Vaudois, an idealised Protestant sect who "have perhaps suffered more at the hands of Popery than any other men" was a disappointment. They did not portray that purity of faith and zeal which he had expected. His most enthusiastic comments were "May He who hath preserved to himself this remnant, yet continue to preserve it . . . as far as *we* had experience of them, their honesty fully bore out the purity of their principles."

Continued exposure to the Roman Catholic church and a limited supply of books to read, helped to prompt his examination of the Prayer Book in Naples on 13 May. Later he declared this event to have had a lasting effect upon his understanding of the nature of the Church of England. His new insight is duly recorded in the diary. This examination had provided glimpses "of the nature of a Church, and of our duties as members of it, which involved an idea very much higher and more important than I had previously had any conception of."

A few books were taken with him, including Keble's *Christian Year* and Henry Blunt's *The Lord's Day*. He wrote of the general uneasiness he was experiencing about the manner in which he had been spending his Sundays and "their grievous incongruity with that tenor of occupation and of thought which ought to mark this holy season." He was appalled to hear that the English in Paris give dinners on Sundays. "I believe there is no more exact criticism of the moral advancement of a people, than the sanctity which they accord to the Christian sabbath." Of a sabbath day in Paris he wrote with sadness, "This city, on this day, is indeed a melancholy sight."

At the outset of their tour William had decided that while the ordinary transactions of the journey were to be committed to this journal "it may still be desirable to keep in this private record some occasional notices of that inner life which shall always be our first care to tend." Was this a justification for what was to follow when he wrote on 5 February about the inner doubts and troubled spirit which he was experiencing concerning the decision he had made and conveyed to his family concerning his future profession? "Another thought lay very heavy on my heart: it was the harrowing fear lest, in the steps which have lately been determined on in reference to myself, I should have betrayed the cause of God to my worldly ambition, and sold even the cross of Christ for the love of earth and the things of earth. My conscience is indeed unsatisfied." Was he wrong to give way to the will of his parents, his family, or were they the instruments of God's message? "And I pray that those who are near and dear to me . . . may be enabled to open before mine eyes the path of duty, by shedding upon it the beacon-light of the will of God."

Three weeks passed and the clouds of uncertainty still hung over him. "My waking thoughts . . . were of my future prospects and they brought with them as usual their own bitterness. God forbid . . . that if it be sent as a warning, I should fail of attaining to its meaning." Reflecting on the life of his Blessed Saviour he sees the purpose of human life, in particular of his own life, as "the renewal of the image of God in the soul of man, and that all things, be they sweet or be they bitter, are truly valuable and of good to us only in proportion to the efficacy with which they act in prompting this single end: in forwarding and fitting that system of discipline which God has ordained to be the instrument for completing his designs of mercy to mankind."[2] It was Gladstone's old argument that God's will for him was that he should be actively engaged in the battle for the redemption of mankind. As February passed the clouds of uncertainty disappeared, but they were to return.

Perhaps it was this continued uncertainty about whether or not he had disobeyed God's call, that made him impatient to know more about his future. A letter from Rome requested Tom to ask his father what he ought to look forward to on his return home.[3] From Verona he wrote to his father, on the same subject, but couched in religious sentiments about the salvation of mankind "Naturally enough one's mind is turned with concentrated interest, to that class of question which seem most to be agitated in one's own time, and with most effect on the peace and happiness of mankind." Undoubtedly he was referring to the Reform Bill which was on his mind even though he was far from home. Indeed a few days before he had recorded in his journal "Papers— containing the disastrous but expected news, that the Reform Bill had passed the Lords."[4]

He wished to direct his reading to the principles which bind society together and influence the mutual conduct of governor and governed. There were, he felt, two kinds of reading to undertake, "the one, legal and historical, as law and history bear upon this question: the other, the works of those authors who have investigated the same subject in a more general and abstract form."[5] These topics "are intimately blended with the happiness of mankind—and, in the realization of instruments to an end, with the final triumph of that religion in the world, whose propagation I trust will ever be the dearest desire of my heart, and the ultimate end of all my actions . . . I trust this will appear to you in conformity with what is right, and with the sentiments formerly expressed, which you were good enough to approve." If there had been any compromise in his ideals concerning the means of serving God there was to be no compromise regarding the ends. Whatever profession he pursued would be directed to the propagation of the Christian faith to which God had called him.

News from home and papers from England not only informed him of the passage of the disastrous Reform Bill, but of another grave disaster, the outbreak of cholera. As the epidemic had spread a Day of Fasting was called in England. The fast had not been "wholly forgotten by me at Florence, however imperfectly kept." He believed that the appointing of a Fast day was reasonable in itself and supported by scripture and the practice of older days and was "a sign for good in the history of our country at one of its most critical seasons."

Despite shadows of uncertainty, political disaster and changes which he believed heralded the disruption of his beloved England, and rampant disease, nevertheless he and John continued their tour undaunted. Page after page of his travel journal records their varied travels and activities, visits to the theatre, the opera, philharmonic concerts, art galleries, fortifications, scenic spots, endless churches and even "balls." "The subject of balls and evening parties has been a good deal on my mind, and was one of conversation between John and me." The issue was weighing heavily upon William whose experience in such areas, and in connection with the opposite sex, were extremely limited. "As Christians I think we are at least bound to strive to preserve in our amusements, something better than amusement: and still to be busied more or less directly, in improving the moral, the spiritual, the intellectual, or the social man." Personally he did not want to go to a ball to dance "and why go to do nothing?" His decision was to avoid them in the future.[6] He later added the note "A record of inconsistency which ought not to be erased." The next night his high-minded principles were shattered, for he went to a ball. Soon all such pursuits and concern about their propriety for the Christian and himself were to be overshadowed by far more important matters conveyed in a letter from England.

Unknown to him moves were afoot which were to determine his future profession. During early May Lord Lincoln had returned to Oxford to continue his studies for while he wished to enter politics it was not the right time for him to be considered for Newark, one of his father's parliamentary constituencies. He suggested to his father his friend William Gladstone for nomination. He wrote, "I have now known him for several years and feel convinced that his honest unflinching integrity of character combined with talents far above the common stamp even of those who are called clever men, will be at once an ornament to, I fear, a most unornamental House, and an honour to the patron who shall introduce him." Gladstone's religious convictions were mentioned: "He always was both here and at Eton so strict with regard to religion &c as to incur from some a charge of sanctity; but as this term implies to my mind in its usual acceptation *hypocrisy*, I never could perceive anything of the sort in him. I believe him to be most perfectly orthodox, and in short think that when you stated what he should be you only drew a picture of what he is."[7] That letter set in motion an unexpected train of events.

The Duke of Newcastle wrote to Mr. John Gladstone on 21 June, informing him that he was looking for a candidate to nominate for Newark. He had heard his son "speak greatly in favour of Mr. Gladstone as a young man of great abilities, I wrote to him to inquire if his high principles and attachment to Church and State were likely to be as distinguished as his ability, and also whether he possessed that courage which would enable him to take such a line in the approaching Parliament as might make him really useful to his Country." Lord Lincoln had answered all his questions in the affirmative; could Mr. Gladstone "answer for his (William's) accepting my offer."[8]

John Gladstone wrote two letters on 26 June, one in answer to the Duke's letter and one to William in Milan, enclosing a copy of the Duke's letter and his reply. To the Duke he expressed the opinion that William had a mature mind "beyond his years" but he doubted if his experience was sufficient for the proposed position. He was a man of integrity and others at Eton and Oxford had informed him of his ability as a public speaker and that his "powers afford much promise." Unfortunately he was unable to speak on behalf of his son without first communicating with him.[9] His letter to William advised him to accept the offer. It would have been much better if William had been a year or two older; indeed he personally felt him too young to enter Parliament. William might think that this would interfere with his Law studies, but these, suggested his father, could be followed up in his general reading. "Going now *may* open new fields to you of great importance . . . besides such an opportunity of going into Parliament to support your own principles . . . may not soon again occur."[10]

Before William received these letters, which arrived 9 July, he had one from Lord Lincoln informing him of the Duke's offer. That evening he wrote to thank Lincoln, and to his father to tell him the news, but their letters crossed in the post. In his letter to his father of 6 July William told him of the Duke's offer and added "For the present I will only say that independent of all direct obligation it is my great comfort to think that the decision even on the propriety of accepting a contingent offer will at once be placed in the hands of those from alone under *God*, I could receive the sanction which would justify me at all in entering on the consideration of the question. But of course it is desirable that the answer to this preliminary and general question should be sent as soon as it conveniently can."[11]

His diary refers to the day as "the most remarkable of my life." William saw it as "one which may be fraught with the weightiest consequences, to me at least if not to others." Pondering on how "insuperable my difficulties would have been" if he had had to send an immediate reply he noted "Happily, God, who established the order of nature, and who seals parental wisdom and experience by parental authority, did by this order relieve me. To learn his will, the first human means is to refer to my parents—and this was done." Having sought parental guidance he was not neglectful of the need for divine guidance. "It remained to add earnest supplications to the throne of grace for defence and guidance on this arduous and delicate occasion, defence most of all from my own personal ambition, rashness or vanity, or all."

He reflects "decidedly more than mere permission would be necessary to authorize him entering on such a course," but if his father urged him forward he must be prepared to respond. "What then am I to ask myself?" "Simply . . . whether my acceptance or the contrary will most contribute to forward those merciful purposes, with which God sent me and every other being into the world—and for the effectuation of which in us all Jesus Christ shed his precious blood upon the Cross."

If politics were to be his sphere of public service then above all it must be a means of serving God's purpose for the salvation of the world for which Christ died upon the Cross. He wrote three letters on Saturday 7 July. One was a short note to his mother in which he mentions his brief letter to his father of the previous evening and the "extraordinary communication" he had received from Lord Lincoln, to whom he had replied, and to whom he had just written a second letter of which he enclosed a copy. He tells his father of the contents of this letter to Lord Lincoln the previous evening, of which he encloses a copy.[12] It was, he told Lincoln, his obvious duty to refer the matter to his father for his authority and opinion. "Without higher sanction than my own judgment I dare not act. Without more sufficient and legitimate aid, I dare not even think on such a matter."[13]

To Lincoln he wrote a long and carefully worded second letter[14] written in "a moment of more collectedness" than that of the previous evening. Here appreciation is expressed for Lincoln's kindness in influencing his father's decision to consider him as a suitable candidate for Newark. He had referred the matter to his own father without whose authority and opinion he felt unable to act, for he looked upon his parents as "next to God in such a matter." But he would also seek God's guidance in reaching a final decision. He was committed to "the great cause of Truth," and in view of the Reform Bill to the maintenance of the foundations of society which he believed "essentially necessary for the support and propagation of the religion of Christ."

On 9 July his father's letter of 26 June with its enclosures arrived and were noted in the diary "Letters from home of great importance, in consequence a resolution taken—God help us—a part of which is to return home immediately." Eight hours were spent that day in writing. He wrote to his father, the Duke of Newcastle, Lord Lincoln and Milnes Gaskell. To his father he wrote concerning his future prospects in politics as a result of the Duke's offer of support at Newark in the coming elections. Those prospects would be based upon a good many years of silent reading and inquiry. He hoped that God would prosper the change for good.[15] A copy of his letter to the Duke was enclosed. Would he be justified in availing himself of the Duke's offer in view of his slender years, defective preparation and inadequacy?[16] However, he had received a communication from home in which his father and family strongly recommended his acceptance of the offer. To

Lord Lincoln he made his admiration of Canning known "in view of the Duke's opinion of the same. His father had had much to do with and admiration for Mr. Canning which he had inherited and held on to."[17]

His letter to his old friend Milnes Gaskell was probably in answer to Gaskell's of 30 June, in which he had expressed his earnest hope that Gladstone would accept the Duke of Newcastle's offer. For "with the strong opinions you now hold, I do not think you would find yourself much hampered in the free expression of your opinions in Parliament. Every man whose heart is in the right place, much more those whose power of doing the State good service is great," is "not to shrink back upon any doubtful or personal grounds."[18]

On 15 July he wrote in his diary "I have committed myself." Success at Newark was, he believed, far from certain. "But, be that as it may, I stand pledged to this bold and terrible experiment." The resolution had been taken in prayer to Him "who is the Author of all good counsels, all holy desires, and all just works." In addition to divine assistance and assurance he had received the strongest human warranty in the "unanimous advice of the members of our family, particularly of my father." This support could not be overrated. Naturally he felt the awesomeness of what had suddenly and unexpectedly fallen upon him and so he casts himself wholly upon "the merciful God of my redemption and the redemption of the world. O holy, blessed and most glorious Trinity, hold me up in the arms of everlasting strength . . . conform my soul to thine image, my thoughts, words and deeds to thy purpose of love: through the Crucified Redeemer, Amen and Amen."

He arrived back in London at 7 a.m. on the morning of Sunday 29 July; that afternoon he went to St. James' Church "It is no small matter to have regained the stated ordinances of our beloved church."

CHAPTER TEN

THE CHRISTIAN POLITICIAN

Gladstone stood poised ready to do battle to secure Newark and a place in Parliament, there to be God's instrument in the redemption of his nation and fellow men. Reservations about whether or not he had taken the right path still remained, but the responsibility for his changed direction was laid upon his father, whose authority was next to God's. Over sixty years later he still held to the conviction "The change in the professional direction of my life which took place in deference to my father's wish did not imply a transfer of my governing interest to the field of politics."[1]

From London Gladstone wrote to the Duke of Newcastle informing him of his arrival. The Duke's reply was accompanied by a letter from Edward S. Godfrey, the Chairman of Gladstone's election committee and the President of the Red Club. Godfrey recommended Gladstone to prepare his election address. Three drafts were made and eventually a final copy produced which, after "some trifling alterations" was published. It appeared in the *Nottingham Journal* on 11 August. Three days later an advertisement was published in the *Guardian* by the Anti-Slavery Committee denouncing Gladstone "as a person who they were persuaded would not co-operate in the promotion of their objects." Their opinions were rejected by Gladstone, who wrote in his diary "In my soul and conscience, as I shall answer at the day of judgment, I do not feel that I have any bias on that question." The battle had begun. Ought he to go immediately to Newark? The answer came— "not yet." And so he decided to have a holiday with the family at Torquay.

Endless reading, largely theological, churchgoing, charitable work, private bible study, note taking, the Greek Testament, the old practice of daily bible study with Helen, letter writing and the composition of a long account of his views on slavery for Mr. Godfrey filled his days at Torquay. He had a number of long conversations with his mother "on the subject of the religious state of the family," a "topic full of anxiety." Prayer for a settlement to the family problem was offered at the altar on Sunday 2 September: "we all knelt together at the Altar. May the Father of Mercies bless his own ordained mysteries and may we attain to more than outward unity. At present I dare not rely much here. I do not feel that (we) are on a sound footing as a Christian family." William tried to turn his thoughts to other things and began to write, yet again, on the subject of baptism. Most of the following morning was taken up with an "interesting conversation" with his mother "on the nature of Baptism" and "embracing family concerns." He records the confession "it is painful, but I feel when speaking on any religious questions that I am always at bottom seeking to glorify myself."

Cholera hit Torquay and William records on 13 September that it was not far removed from their own dwelling and that already one or two had died "said to be bad livers." He saw this outbreak as "the awful instrument" of God's will, sent for the "softening of our obstinacy and the salvation of many souls."

On the morning of Sunday 23 September as he lay contemplating a "tranquil day" his father burst into his room at 7:45 a.m., telling him he must leave immediately as the "canvass was going on and my presence necessary." Leaving without delay he later reflected on that journey "It was painful to sacrifice the Sunday to the purpose of travelling but under the circumstances it appeared to be called for. I very soon afterwards however found reason to apprehend, that among the many dangers and temptations attaching to anything like political life, not the least would probably be, the preserving inviolate that rest which God's mercy has ordained for his self-wearing and self-afflicted creatures."[2] Occasionally when emotionally or spiritually moved Gladstone wrote verse as a means of relieving his feelings. This act of sabbath breaking, through travel, stimulated eighteen verses under the title "A Sunday Journey. September 1832."[3]

Temptations of many kinds came from God himself. Writing on this subject in his book of theological themes, Gladstone stated "Temptation from God, is merely *trial*, i.e. the presenting to the mind circumstances of pain or pleasure essentially dynamical and neither good nor evil." On the other hand he noted that "Temptation from Satan

. . . is the presentation of objects positively *evil*."[4] Gladstone did not apply this understanding of temptation to the sabbath, but if the sabbath was a divine institution and sabbath observance a divine obligation then the temptation to break the sabbath must originate from Satan and giving way to it be "positively evil" and certainly sinful. Having broken the sabbath his conscience continued to trouble him; everything had been "hurry and bustle" giving him no "chance of judging impartially." "Was I right?" he asked himself. He reached Newark at midnight the following day where he found Robertson and John and "affairs in prosperous condition." The next day, Tuesday 25 September, the canvass began in earnest, led by the favoured candidate.

From the outset Gladstone's high Christian principles and moral attitude were fundamental in all his political decisions and behaviour. In the "Private" account of those momentous days in Newark entitled "A Visit to Newark"[5] William wrote "I was immediately launched upon our canvass: well supplied with directions to shake hands with everybody . . . and to kiss all the daughters." For Gladstone even the shaking of hands involved moral principles. His rule was always to be ready to shake hands and "distinctly seek it whenever *anything* favourable was said" but to do so without this was unacceptable. For him the handshake was "a sort of sign accompanying and signifying thanks"; wrongly used it would "convey a suspicion of insincerity." Nevertheless he wrote to his father "My practice in shaking hands has been most extensive," adding "the kissing has been done chiefly by proxy." The need for such kissing created a moral problem: he had "doubts of its desirableness" believing that it could cause distress or embarrassment to others." He resolved it on the basis that the kissing was expected and that when he was engaged in the act he was doing it in a "sort of public capacity." In his private reflections on this subject he admitted, "I fancy however that my performances were considered rather sparing for a report was circulated that I was a married man." He observed "On this and other subjects I am sure it is a sacred and solemn duty to be cautious, and to manifest a marked coolness of manner where there is anything like forwardness exhibited in a female."

Political parties at that time did not go by names, but colours; Gladstone was a "Red." Red wives and widows, who did not have the vote, were boundless in their enthusiasm and he was in fact well supported by most of the women in Newark who were actively canvassed, because they often influenced their husbands' votes. "One poor old creature seized me by the hand . . . Are *you* Mr.— I forget his name, the 'Red'?" To which he retorted "Yes I am, my good woman." Her response must have moved Gladstone: "God Almighty bless your eyes and limbs and every bit of you." Visiting the homes of people he was gratified to see that in many cases they were "well supplied with Bibles and religious books" and often had pictures representing the Crucifixion and scenes in the life of our blessed Lord. When one man said some disparaging things about the bible "I was disgusted at this avowal of the unfortunate man—for the tendency to infidelity is surely very rare among our peasantry."

Few voters, Gladstone believed, were able to form an opinion for themselves and so it was natural and proper that they should look to those from whom they received kindness and in whom they had confidence. The Duke of Newcastle had shown, and continued to show, kindness and favour to many of the people of Newark and so it was natural that they would want to vote for his candidate. However he had heard of people being ejected from their homes for not offering their vote, and he knew this was a common threat and practice. This was an important moral issue which Gladstone had to tackle. The question was whether a landlord in any case may eject a tenant—not whether he may in every case. He wrote "Here was perhaps the *flaw* in the argument of the Duke of Newcastle's expression 'May I not do what I will with my own?' A man may not always do, morally, that which he may do legally. The Duke's argument *seemed* to be that the legal right in itself conferred the moral right." The Duke offered his tenants houses at a low rent and thus the relation between tenant and Duke was "one of favour on his part, of gratitude on theirs." In this situation the tenants, not acting by compulsion but from spontaneous gratitude would be acting fairly by making a "free will offering of their political influence to support . . . their benefactor." In withdrawing a tenancy the Duke was. therefore, "simply withdrawing a favour. Has he not a right to confer favours on whom he pleases?" Gladstone postulates the question, for the "happiness of this country, may he not use his influence for their promotion, provided it be without either corruption or cruelty?" Fortunately for Gladstone many of the people of Newark, including the Duke's tenants, had an attachment to the Duke and his family and willingly and freely supported his candidate.

A common inducement to win votes was the provision of ale. Two days after starting the canvass William wrote to his father on a number of "moral issues" including the provision of ale, in the light of his views about drunkenness.[6] Strict limitations regarding the quantity of ale given by Clubs to members in order to influence their votes had to be determined. Many of his supporters did not share those convictions and felt him unrealistic and far too strict. "Unhappily," he wrote to his father, "without the smallest authority direct or indirect, some of the publicans did give liquor away upon the Canvass. The amount of their bills altogether . . . will not I believe be considerable—perhaps £20-£30. If it should be greater it will not be paid."[7] Restriction would prevent a recurrence, voters in future would be given tickets, and in order to avoid noise and drunkenness the quantity of ale would be strictly limited. His father counselled wisdom, a little toleration and more freedom. William replied that "as regards open houses" he had seen enough to judge what the effects of this would be and he felt it necessary to avoid this.[8] Rewards of such a nature to helpers and voters were not a priority for Gladstone and so easily overlooked. He received a letter stating "Our friends are becoming somewhat impatient for the treat which usually follows a canvass." Later he wrote to Helen that he lamented the practice of the other parties in "treating in public houses . . . while for us not a drop of ale is drawn," on the morning of the Poll a "very limited" amount would be given to each person "when they had their treat"; on 5 November the people were most orderly and "no man, as I understand, was intoxicated."[9]

Correspondence with Mr. Godfrey after the election concerning the payment of election accounts gave Gladstone the opportunity to vent his feelings on the provision of ale to win votes. Open houses, which allowed publicans to supply unlimited quantities of ale and charge it to the candidate is "a practice which I detest."[10] His continued refusal to pay the outstanding account for election expenses, because of the unauthorised amount charged for ale, led to an official declaration from the Newark Election Committee, who felt "greatly disappointed" to find that bills incurred at the election had not been paid. A compromise was eventually reached and the accounts of the Public and Beer Houses, twenty-nine in all, were reduced from the original total of £1,002 to £499.[11]

Through systematic daily canvassing, numerous speeches in a

variety of situations and "wild" meetings, Gladstone formed some firm opinions about the political interests and ability of the people of Newark. Of the 1,500 voters in the constituency he felt that about 1,100 had no "notion of politics." Even the remainder did not have the competence to form opinions. This political ignorance did not worry Gladstone who felt that it was not "highly desirable . . . that the people should learn to take an interest in general politics, except in so far as such is necessary to secure their good government." There were more important things to occupy their mind, "the demands of their spiritual being and their physical necessities." People in poverty or distress recognised as "visited" by the hand of providence moved him to write, "God knows . . . they bring home to the inmost heart a living consciousness of the unreal character of all the immediate objects of pursuit, and teach him who covets a blessing, to look through them and beyond them for his motive and his reward."

The experience of the canvass brought home "to my mind a deeper and more sincere hatred of the Reform Bill, on this account, than I had before entertained." Friends wrote offering him their support and prayers. "I trust," wrote Benjamin Harrison, "you may have the means there of doing all the good which I know you have the will as well as the ability to do in this crisis of our country."[12] A few weeks later he wrote again, " I believe there is a merciful adoption to the circumstances in which we are severally placed, if we are placed in those circumstances by the appointment of Providence and seek for guidance under them from a power and wisdom superior to our own."[13] Charles Childers assured him of his prayers and his best wishes for success in politics, adding "your success if God sees fit."[14] Anxious, and yet confident in God, William wrote to his father "You know how entirely I depend on your writing to me—Anxiety does exist but it is at least checked *if not* regulated by the belief that we shall be guided aright."[15]

The canvass led him to the conclusion that the tendency of the newspaper system at such times is to "pervert the minds of the people." He informed his father of how an article in the *Chronicle* on 4 October had falsified the report of recent events.[16] Even before his arrival at Newark the Press misinformed the people about his position on slavery. During the canvass he was asked about sixty questions about this, eight on the Ballot and on six other subjects no more than three questions. One heated discussion on slavery proved too much for Gladstone, who

lost his temper "completely, and very foolishly." The man who had provoked his downfall commented "I'll tell you what, Mr. Gladstone, I
hope you'll keep your temper a little better than that when you're on the
hustings." Gladstone wrote "Sour was his charity." But his opponent
was right, he could not afford such an outburst in private discussions or
in public debates. Opponents at Newark believed Gladstone was vulnerable on the issue of slavery, and Sergeant Wilde, whom Gladstone
noted in his diary also went to church, exploited the situation. His father's pamphlet on the subject and the fact that the family were well-
known as slave owners provided his enemies with ready made ammuni-
tion.

He wrote to his father of the Wesleyan Methodists who concentrated their attack on the slavery question. They had hesitated to
give him their support but, he observed, they behave as "voters ought—
as men who had a duty to perform, and commands of conscience to follow." They had heard no accounts but those of the Anti-slavery Society, but they "were candid and fair beyond anything and not one of them
left . . . without leaving us his promise."[17] But not all Wesleyans in
Newark were sympathetic to Gladstone's position. A poster appeared
over the names of two Wesleyan ministers "Slavery is as inconsistent
with the spirit of Christianity, as it is opposed to the happiness of mankind. It is a most criminal violation of that law which the Deity has established among his intelligent creatures." The poster declared that the
only candidate who would be supported was one who would work for
"the immediate extinction of Colonial Slavery."[18] A little later Gladstone wrote to Helen "The Blues have very foolishly been circulating
placards about slavery against me."

Even his own supporters needed to be convinced about his position; F. Eggleston, a member of the Red Club had written to Mr. Godfrey about it. Gladstone replied that "we professing Christianity as a nation, and having embodied it both in our legislation and our laws, did
for a long time continue to bring these poor people into bondage and
hold them in it." Present selfishness and lawful caution on the subject
took on the disguise of political and religious ends. Yet, wrote Gladstone, even "at this late hour if only we address ourselves to the work in
good earnest, we may have still remarkable facilities for raising the negroes to the condition of an enlightened Christian population."
Throughout Gladstone emphasised the responsibility of providing a
true Christian education to slaves, which he believed to be a divinely

given responsibility placed upon slave owners. In a letter to his father on the day before his departure from Newark he referred to two men who opposed him on conscientious grounds "because I do not go far enough about slavery."[19]

He delivered his "election address" on Monday 8 October "at a great Red Club meeting, of perhaps 200—a longer speech than usual."[20] The address was published in "poster form" the following day. Reference is made to the Reform Bill that, "undiscriminating desire for change" which disturbs our peace, destroys confidence and strikes at the root of prosperity. The removal of all this will be through the "restoration of sounder general principles," especially that principle on which alone "the incorporation of religion with the state, in our constitution can be defended: that the duties of governors are strictly and peculiarly religious." Special attention should be given to the poor and the receipt of fair wages. Exactly half the address is allotted to the "momentous question of slavery"; while found in scripture "we are agreed, that both the physical and the moral bondage of slaves are to be abolished." The Christian instruction and religious improvement of negroes should be set up with sovereign authority. On the question of emancipation "Let *fitness* be made the condition . . . and let us strive to bring him to that fitness, by the shortest possible course." He ends "if promises be an adequate foundation . . . our victory is sure." On that confident note he left Newark for a short visit to his patron, the Duke of Newcastle. Reference to the visit in the diary is brief, but Gladstone produced two other documents relating to the event.[21] Long conversations with the Duke occupied much of the time; Gladstone's written account of these suggests that politics and the church were their two main topics.[22]

Wisdom, diplomacy and protocol restricted some of the answers to the Duke's observations on a number of religious topics such as "Let a man keep God in his mind as much as he pleases—and let him remember his God in every action of his life—but it does not therefore follow that he is to be always talking about him." To which William replied "It seems to me, my Lord, that there is a kind of indelicacy in the religious feelings of the present day." Discussion took place on evangelical preaching, Calvinism, church patronage, the clergy, enthusiasm and the downfall of the papacy. The Duke had written a number of short, strong, protestant pamphlets; one on Roman Catholic claims was read by Gladstone in the coach on 11 October as he travelled to Wakefield where he stayed with his friend Gaskell.

Conversations with Gaskell, writing up his "journal from Torquay" and his "visit to Newark" and some verses, reading, mainly theological, billiards, riding, whist, learning poetry by heart, and numerous social meetings and calls filled in most of his time, with the addition of some letter writing. A "personally most gratifying" letter from home prompted him to pray "may the Almighty Father enable us to reap fruit herefrom." That day he wrote to his father[23] "I know of no higher sanction than a parent's and of no livelier enjoyment than that which a parent's praise confers." Recent events at Newark, Clumber and Wakefield must all have contributed towards the concern he expressed to his father "notwithstanding apparent prosperity" there are many difficulties and dangers in my path, the difficulty of maintaining the equipoise of the mind amidst strong surrounding excitement from without and the danger of substituting popular procession for honest practice."

At the time he was still writing up his "visit to Newark," towards the end of which he states "It was impossible not to foresee, that political life must in its infinite varieties include an immense mass both of temptations and advantages. It is full of the knowledge of good and evil . . . may I throw myself on Him from whom all light and strength proceed." That day he met, once again, the sister of F. D. Maurice who, on hearing of "my altered destination" said, "I am sorry to hear it." Her remark is recorded in his diary with the comment "I should be sincerely thankful for this honest opinion." A week later, despite the request for a return visit to Newark "which I am most anxious to avoid," he left for Leamington to rejoin his family. While the election campaign continued, and his future destiny hung in the balance, he managed to remain with his family for just over a month.

Tuesday, 27 November marked the completion of his document "A Visit to Newark." That day he committed to paper his political philosophy, in which he tried to work out what it would mean to be a Christian politician called by divine providence to serve both church and state and in so doing to work for the redemption of mankind: "I have recorded . . . the sincere feelings of my *soul,* and the *especially guiding* principles of my present conduct." As so often with Gladstone the meaning of what he wrote is not easy to understand, but here he covers himself by stating that what he had written was "without art, perhaps without discretion." At that stage he felt he could not go further in trying to comprehend the outworking of this great call. "I have striven to express a secret of my heart, as it shall be developed in that great day, when the secrets of *all* hearts shall be made known. I have scarce ever been able to get farther into the subject than I have here." What Gladstone wrote on this occasion was intended only for the eye of the one to whom "the secrets of all hearts shall be made known."

The will of God for the Christian politician is, he wrote, "to maintain the principles of Church and State." He must strive to "show how high are the moral responsibilities of governments, as well as to teach the religious duty of submission on the part of subjects." More particularly he must show "how infinitely extended are the means of good which Providence has put into the hands of the rulers of this nation, and under God and with his blessing, to struggle for their effectual use." "To restrict the sphere of politics to earth" is to make it "a secondary science." For him politics must be firmly established in the will of God, for men "admit the duty of governors to maintain the laws of Him by whom they govern—admit that the intellectual and the spiritual nature of man are legitimate objects of their solicitude, and then if you can estimate the moral dignity of him who is taught of God and enabled to apply the most powerful engines and the most extended resources of which our worldly condition admits, to the promotion of the benevolent and lofty purposes of God in the redemption of mankind."

His place as a member of Parliament was far from certain, for the battle at Newark continued and so he wrote "The prospect is distant: it may be visionary. Notwithstanding, is it worth the trial?" His answer was in the affirmative, and moreover this he now seemed to feel, perhaps quite apart from his father's wishes and the question of parental authority, that the way of the Christian politician was God's will for his life, and so he wrote "So long as my conscience replies in the affirmative, and hope lives and burns within, I need not repent that I have cast my humble lot into the lap—that I have committed myself, my hopes, my desires, my destinies, to the rude and tumultuous ocean."

On Thursday 29 November William wrote to Mr. Tallents, his election agent at Newark, and heard from him that night. Convinced of the way forward in the service of God and man, in what he had now worked out and believed to be a high calling from God, he was consumed with a burning zeal, the conviction that he had a divine mission to fulfil. The next day he felt that he "should proceed to Newark forthwith." He arrived there late in the evening of Saturday 1 December 1832. On Sunday he went to church and received the Sacrament. The next day parliament was formally dissolved and the final stage of the election campaign began.

Slavery was still the major issue in the days running up to the election. He carefully re-read his father's pamphlet *Facts Relating to Slavery*, "in consequence of a placard assailing it and turning it against me—and wrote an Address embracing that and other matters at some length."[24] A long letter was written to his father on the subject[25] on Tuesday 11 December, the day the nominations were made. At the meeting that day Serjeant Wilde spoke for an inordinate length of time, mainly on slavery, and yells and groans were directed towards Gladstone. He records how he "stood between six and seven hours, with some pressure, on the hustings, questioned for two or three of them." Just after four o'clock he was allowed to speak for about fifteen minutes; as the room darkened candles were brought in. The meeting ended and a "Show of hands carried against us."

That night a letter was written to Tom, telling him of the problems he was facing and how everything depended upon the events of the next few days.[26] A letter was dispatched to Helen "The crisis is aweful—my heart sinks within me to think how much is suspended upon it—not as connected with this contest, but looking ahead . . . May God, who alone can, rule all for the best."[27] Three days later on Friday 14 December the radical change which had taken place at Newark was made public: Gladstone was elected with 887 votes; he recorded the triumphant moment in his diary "I am now member for Newark. May the Almighty give me strength to perform the duties of this solemn office."

Among the letters received after his success was one from Martin Farquhar Tupper whom he had known at Oxford, "You are called upon by the Providence of God to do what you can towards being a witness for the one Truth that it is a national as well as an individual duty to acknowledge God in all our ways and have Him in all our thoughts."[28] The Archdeacon of Liverpool wrote to him "I hope and pray that it may please your heavenly Father to keep you still steadfast in your purpose to serve him . . . it is impossible to say how much good a single righteous man may do in that assembly."[29]

CHAPTER ELEVEN

CONCLUSION

The aim of this volume has been to examine systematically all the relevant Gladstone manuscript material now available and also recent studies including Checkland's outstanding book and the contributions of scholars like Foot, Matthew, Butler and Shannon, and from these sources to establish an accurate and objective analysis and exploration in depth of the personal religious life and development of William Ewart Gladstone during his formative years.

His often tortuous pilgrimage from a wealthy, secure and evangelical background at Liverpool, through Eton and Oxford to his election to Parliament shows how he sought both "godliness and good learning." It has been established that it is impossible to understand the young Gladstone, and by implication the later seasoned man in politics, outside the context of his Christian faith. There were a number of landmarks in his spiritual formation and growth during the period examined, as well as a number of influences which were to have a lasting effect upon him. Here we see how various threads are inseparably interwoven, the spiritual, the emotional and the intellectual. A number of issues recorded in his "autobiographical memoranda" serve to illustrate that Gladstone, in his later years, is not always exact concerning his own spiritual development or theological position. A clear and more accurate picture can sometimes only be achieved by a careful examination of what was actually written at the time.

In the past most writers on Mr. Gladstone's early years, and indeed on his later life, when commenting upon his Christian faith have sometimes failed to understand the theological implications of his position, or make brief statements about his religious life, but do not enlarge upon them. We are told that he "said his prayers," "read his bible," had "an acute sense of sin," "moved away from his evangelical position," "believed himself called to ordination." In this work deeper insight is offered into the richness of his religious life and development.

We have shown how his family and family life helped to fashion his spirituality and that to understand Gladstone one must be fully aware of his spiritual inheritance. Among the manuscripts and contemporary evidence now available are those housed at St. Deiniol's Library, to which previously unknown manuscripts have recently been added. This material throws further light on at least four people who influenced Gladstone: his father, mother and his two sisters. His ambitious, shrewd, domineering, autocratic father, who exercised a "worldly spirituality," had great ambitions for his talented youngest son, over whom he exercised considerable influence, especially on the subject of his profession. An acute awareness of divine providence, which pervaded William's life possibly came to him from his grandfather, Thomas, via his own father, but also from other sources. The practice of sermon reading as a devotional exercise, and the need for careful records of income and expenditure, the stewardship of money, were undoubtedly influenced by his father.

Previous knowledge of Mrs. Anne Gladstone is augmented and throws further light on her part in William's spiritual formation. Prayer and bible reading were essential to her daily life, while to know and do the will of God were paramount. Her regular self-examination and her sense of utter unworthiness and sinfulness help us to understand William's own feeling of sin and unworthiness before God. Probably she introduced him to the practice of keeping a diary in which to record his "spiritual pilgrimage." Both Mrs Gladstone and her husband recognised and practiced a wide range of charitable work and giving which William began to emulate at an early age.

His sister Anne emerges as an intense and deeply religious young woman who followed the pattern of her mother's spiritual discipline. Although of evangelical persuasion, she was not averse to looking beyond the tenets of that school in order to attain a fuller understanding of her faith. This openness to new ideas influenced William's thinking and approach in his theological studies. He idolised his "sainted sister," who became a "soul friend," fashioning and encouraging his spiritual development. In some areas she was obviously the link through which their mother's influence reached him. Following Anne's death Helen came to play an increasingly important part in his life and he a prominent part in hers. At her request he became her spiritual "mentor," which helps to explain William's actions and attitudes towards her in later life.

This account of his family background shows how William inherited all the essential elements of the spiritual life from his family. In William these fundamental constituents of evangelical spirituality were systematized and intensified as he passed through Eton and Oxford. Prayer and bible reading, practiced both morning and evening, became fundamental to his daily life as he strove for a deeper union with God through Christ. The bible was read both devotionally and academically, and was recognised as the foundation of his life, and the supreme authority in matters of faith and Christian practice, and the means through which God speaks to His children. Even by evangelical standards his self-examination and his sense of utter unworthiness were excessive and were undoubtedly influenced by his inner turmoil and feelings of guilt, caused by his adolescent sexuality. The Eucharist, as a means of grace, came to play a central part in his spirituality. Religious observance touched every part of life: his stewardship of time, his use of money, his charitable activities, his reading, his leisure pursuits, sabbath observance, Sunday worship and sermon reading. Only the highest and the best were good enough for the young Gladstone who strove for perfection, and when he failed to achieve it, was naturally frustrated. What he preached to others he did not apply to himself, that God accepts the penitent sinner "in Christ" and offers forgiveness and assurance.

His move away from this evangelical inheritance was almost imperceptible and is perhaps the reason why he himself, and his later biographers, have been unable to determine the "moment" of his move. For the first time we have a detailed account, which traces his "evolution as a churchman," and his move away from his imbibed evangelicalism to a "Catholic-Evangelical" position. This study in depth helps to establish more accurately than ever before the time of that shift. It is based upon a wide range of evidence, including an examination of the actual books belonging to Gladstone which fashioned his thinking during its evolution.

The fundamental change in his churchmanship began when he accepted the doctrine of baptismal regeneration on the ground that both scripture and the church are "teachers" of the faith. His sole authority in matters of faith had been the bible; now he recognised how tradition, the teaching of the early Fathers and "eminent English divines," i.e. the church, could offer new insight into both the meaning of the scriptures and the Christian faith. In accepting the church as a "teacher," in addition to scripture, he moved away from traditional evangelicalism. With this recognition of an additional source of doctrine the flood-gates were opened. Wide reading undoubtedly influenced his thinking and spiritual development. The "theological themes" written while at Oxford record how he worked out his position on a number of crucial theological issues. Later he wrote of the need for a synthesis within the Church of England, the drawing together of the best elements of the evangelical school and of the "catholic tradition." In later life he seems to have failed to recognise that this had happened in his own spiritual pilgrimage as he came gradually to accept those four aspects of the faith, neglected by the evangelical school but acknowledged as central in a catholic understanding of the Christian faith. They are: the necessity of baptism as a means of grace and of entering the church, coupled with a recognition of baptismal regeneration; the centrality of the eucharist in the Christian life, accepted as an essential means of grace in the process of sanctification; a recognition of the visible and corporate nature of the church, seen as God's instrument on earth in his redemptive work; and the place of the threefold ministry as a mark of the church linking both the church and ministry, through the New Testament, with Christ himself. Before leaving Oxford all these doctrines had been accepted, although not yet in a fully developed form, but this was to come.

Theological investigation, in an attempt to establish his position, was closely linked with another search, that of determining God's will for his life. Ever since his miraculous escape from death in childhood he had believed that God had a definite purpose for his life. His task was to discover God's will and to respond accordingly, and this concept of divine providence came to dominate his life. Two issues, the church and politics, both of which seemed to offer viable areas of service, had occupied his mind as far back as Eton. He was inclined towards the church and ordination, but his father's expectations were towards law and politics. His extensive theological reading and his intensive spirituality suggested that God was calling him to the ordained ministry. While the ordinal sees the average age for ordination to the diaconate as twenty-three, Gladstone pleaded "youth" and "inadequacy" as arguments against accepting such a call. The Anglican Church today has a well-established system of testing those who feel that they have a vocation to the priesthood. Present-day experience and knowledge relating to the selection process would suggest that up to the

end of 1831, when Gladstone was twenty-two, he had a genuine call to
the ordained ministry. Moreover, Gladstone's diaries and letters suggest
that he believed ordination was God's will for his life. If he had such a
call then why did he fail to respond?

The complexity of the subject is such that even recent writers
on Gladstone including Matthew and Shannon have stated that he had
no such call, and so entered politics. This book rejects such a conclusion. His father wanted him to be a politician and he was no easy person to oppose. It could be argued that William himself had been strongly drawn to the possibility of a career in politics for many years. He
was undoubtedly highly ambitious and wanted to achieve both success
and recognition, and politics would offer opportunities for both. And
yet the main reason for not seeking ordination could partly have been
the result of his own spirituality. He felt himself incapable of reaching
the high standard of life which he believed God required of him. Likewise his highly exalted view of the priestly life, coupled with his own
sense of utter unworthiness, and possibly his sexual problems, made
him feel that he could never achieve what God required of his priests.
Such idealism might have caused him to doubt seriously that God could
call him to such a high vocation and so once again Gladstone failed to
apply to himself the doctrine that God accepts the sinner as he is "in
Christ."

Together these things seem to have overshadowed a call from
God to the ordained ministry. William found the situation unbearable;
while he saw everything pointing towards ordination, in the end he
could not accept this. Was ultimate certainty of God's call denied him
because he could not take the decisive step of faith, or because he
lacked "assurance," or because the attractions of ambition, worldly success and politics were too strong? Then there was his father! Unable to
accept God's will, or to be sure what God was saying to him, he shifted
the responsibility for the ultimate decision from himself to his father.
He established the theory that his father was God's earthly instrument,
through whom He spoke to make His will and purpose known. If his father exercised such divine authority over him, surely he must obey an
authority which was next to that of God. If his father wanted him to enter politics, then this was God's will for his life. Even if he had made a
mistake he could not later abandon the idea of a divine destiny and began to work on the premise that God had, after all, given him a call
equal to that of a priest, to serve Him and His people in both state and

church. But if Gladstone had made a mistake and later believed that he had denied God's call to ordination, then what are the implications? Because there is much which Gladstone did not reveal about himself and his inner feelings one can only speculate. Could it have been that for the rest of his life as a "man in politics," in the family, in the church and in society, he sought to justify himself before God?

While this conclusion has attempted to define the pivotal issues, to establish where further insights have been achieved and to answer questions raised, it also raises issues which cannot be dealt with in the period ending December 1832. Some of these issues were worked out by Gladstone during the later stages of his life, and must be left to further extensive research in the years to come and will be examined in the second volume of this "spiritual biography." They include Gladstone's ultimate churchmanship, his final position on the various parts of his spirituality, for example prayer, bible reading, fasting, self-examination, confession, the eucharist and many other central issues. There is also his understanding of the visible church, corporate worship and the threefold ministry. The many implications of being the head of a Christian household, the working out of his Christian stewardship and the need for a "reasoned faith," especially in the field of politics, all became important issues to which he gave his attention. Attempts to deal with some of these eventually led to a variety of publications, including *The State in its Relations with the Church (1838), Church Principles Considered in their Results (1840), The Impregnable Rock of Holy Scripture (1890) and a Manual of Prayers from the Liturgy, arranged for family use.*

As the year 1832 drew to its close, and he waited to enter Parliament, William Ewart Gladstone wrote in his journal "On this day I have completed my twenty-third year . . . The future is as full of interest, as the past of shame. May my aim be, to cut off *every* merely selfish appetite and indulgence, and to live with my best energies uniformly and permanently bent towards the great objects for which even I, mean as I am, am appointed to live—the promotion, O Holy Father, of thy glory, and the establishment of thy Kingdom upon earth."

NOTES

CHAPTER 1. A CHRISTIAN HERITAGE

1. G-G Thos. G. to J.G., 12 June 1800

2. *See* S. G. Checkland, *The Gladstones: A Family Biography. 1764-1851* (1971), p. 4

3. G-G Thos. G. to J.G., 31 March 1787 *see also* Thos G. to J.G., 31 May and 26 August 1793

4. Ibid., 17 July 1787

5. Ibid., 12 August 1787

6. Ibid., 21 November 1787

7. Ibid., 6 August 1787

8. Ibid., 24 December 1788

9. Ibid., 11 July 1789

10. Ibid., 4 September 1789

11. Ibid., 31 December 1788, *see also* 29 August 1788, 23 June 1789, 27 April, 5 May 1800

12. G-G E. Corrie to J.G., 29 November 1789 *see also* Thos. G. to J.G. 24 October 1789

13. G-G Thos. G. to J.G., 27 November 1789

14. Ibid., 2 January 1790

15. Ibid., 1 February 1790, *also* 2 April 1790

16. Checkland, *The Gladstones*, pp. 24-5

17. G-G Thos. G. to J.G., 29 August 1788, 24 December 1788, 23 June 1789

18. Ibid., 12 June, 14 July 1800

19. Ibid., 15 January 1803

20. Ibid., 21 September 1807

21. *See* Checkland, *The Gladstones,* p. 18., where he wrongly attributed this appeal of the 27 August 1788 to J. Gladstone's birthday, but John was born on 11 December 1764

CHAPTER 2. THE FORMATIVE YEARS

1. BL Add. MS 44790, f. 157, *see Autobiographica*, p.149

2. BL Add. MS 44790, ff. 5-25, *see Autobiographica*, pp.13-22

3. *Autobiographica*, pp. 58-9

4. G-G Hannah More to Mrs G., 19 January 1813 *See* M.G. Jones, *Hannah More* (1952)

5. G-G Hannah More to Mrs G., 16 February [1813]

6. Ibid., 19 January 1813

7. Ibid., 16 February [1813]

8. Ibid., 22 March 1814

9. BL Add. MS 44790, f. 12, *Autobiographica,* p. 15

10. G-G Hannah More to Mrs G., 13 October 1815

11. Ibid., 29 November [1817] *see* Jones, Hannah More, especially pp.125-205

12. Ibid., 23 August 1817

13. G-G Divie Bethune to Mrs G., 24 April 1816

14. Ibid., 15 December 1817

15. G-G Mrs G. to J.G., 2 February 1820

16. G-G Mrs G. to A.M.G., no date, 1815

17. G-G T.G. to J. G., 1 October 1820

18. G-G Miss E. Whitmore to Mrs G., 30 November 1815

19. G-G MS 1286 (1812-1817)

20. BL Add. MS 44724, ff. 164-75

21. *See* W. Wilberforce to J.G., G-G MS 321

22. G-G J.G. to Mrs G., 9 June 1818

23. Ibid., 26 June 1818

24. Ibid.

25. *See* Checkland, *The Gladstones,* pp. 185-200, 263 - 77

26. Ibid., p. 195

27. *See* James Walvin, *England. Slaves and Freedom* 1776-1838 (1986), p.139

28. Checkland, *The Gladstones*, p. 198

29. Ibid., pp. 193-4, 197

30. *See* Ibid., pp. 199-200

31. *See* G-G J.G. to the Rt. Hon. Robert Peel 7 April 1831 -MSS 2868-9

32. A Collection of correspondence between John Gladstone and William Huskisson on the Demerara Slave rising and emancipation is preserved in the G-G Collection. G-G MS 353

33. G-G Mrs G. to T.G., 12 May 1817

34. See William Hill Tucker, *Eton of Old:1811-22* (1892), pp. 121, 125

35. G-G J.G. to T.G., 21 April 1820, compare W.E.G's letter to one of his sons; see John Morley, *The Life of William Ewart Gladstone*, 3 vols (1903) Vol/ i, pp. 205-6

36. Ibid.

37. Ibid.

38. Ibid.

39. G-G un-named and undated newspaper cutting in the St Deiniol's MS Collection (May 1824) *see also* press cutting dated 14 May 1824, G-G MS 1249 and MS 1250

40. Although William Ewart Gladstone's son Willy, when a child, expressed great appreciation of his grandfather's letters and counsel *see* G-G William Henry Gladstone to J.G., 6 March 1849. *See also* Morley, *Gladstone*, Vol. i, pp. 205-6

41. BL Add. MS 44790, f.159 *Autobiographica,* p.149

42. D.C. Lathbury, *Mr Gladstone* (1907), p. 3

43. *See* George W. E. Russell, *Mr Gladstone's Religious Development: A paper read in Christ Church May 5, 1899* (1899) p. 3

44. BL Add. MS 44790, f. 156, *Autobiographica,* pp. 148-9. *See* H.C.G. Matthew, *Gladstone, 1809-1874* (1986) pp. 28-9

45. *See* Peter Toon, *Evangelical Theology 1833-1856: A Response to Tractarianism* (1979), p. 5

46. *See* D.C. Lathbury, *Correspondence on Church and Religion of William Ewart Gladstone*, 2 vols (1910), Vol.ii., p. 333, W.E.G. to Revd D. Fairburn. It would be difficult to sustain this statement. The Church Missionary Society was founded in 1799 with full evangelical support and intended to replace the treasures brought by the slaves by "the offer of spiritual peace and Christian freedom." *See* Michael Hennell, *John Venn and the Clapham Sect* (1958), p. 284

47. BL Add. MS 44791, f.1., *see Autobiographica,* p. 140

48. Checkland, *The Gladstones*, p. 384

49. G-G T.G to J.G., 23 January 1820

50. Ibid., 27 May 1821

51. G-G R. Ainslie to Mrs G., 11 February 1818

52. G-G correspondence between Miss Margaret Buchan and Mrs G., 16 September 1823 to 20 March 1829

53. G-G Printed details of "Liverpool Dorcas Society," G-G MS 1287

54. G-G Printed "Rules of the Indigent Clothing Society," G-G MS 1287

55. G-G printed "Directions to be Observed by the Parents of those

children who are admitted into the Liverpool Female School of Industry," G-G MS 1287

56. T. Chalmers, *On the Christian and Economics Policy of a Nation, more especially with reference to its large Towns. See* Checkland, *The Gladstones,* pp. 127-8

57. See G-G Revd Dr David Johnson to J.G., 22 February 1805, 16 Feb 1819, 27 Feb 1819

58. G-G Zachary Macauley to J.G., 2 May 1818

59. Ibid., 27 March 1819

60. *See* Checkland, *The Gladstones*, p. 126

61. John Gladstone's Account Books *see* G-G MS 1133 Ledger 1807-14, MS 1134 Ledger 1814-29, MS 1135 Cash Book 1803-20

62. G-G Janet MacDonald to Mrs G., 21 April 1821

63. G-G Revd. William Patterson to Mrs G., 12 October 1815

64. G-G MS 2430 A list of houses and property in Liverpool and Seaforth J.G. 1846 (1 vol)

65. *See* Checkland, *The Gladstones,* pp. 414-15

66. G-G Revd. Charles Simeon to Revd P. Charrier 27 September 1814

67. G-G Letters to George Henry Law, Bishop of Chester (1812-1824) to J.G., 4 July 1814, 9 September 1815, 29 Sept 1815, 6 November 1815

68. BL Add. MS 44790 ff. 9-10, *see also* ff. 22-3, *see Autobiographica,* pp. 14-15, 20-1

69. G-G J.G. to Mrs G., 22 October 1815

70. G-G Thomas Chalmers to J.G., 6 August 1817

71. Ibid., 13 February 1818

72. G-G Hannah More to Mrs. G., 22 March [1814-15]. For a fuller account of her critical attitude towards the Methodists *see* Jones, *Hannah More*, pp.78-80, 86-7

73. *See* Checkland, *The Gladstones,* p. 79

74. G-G Revd. William Rawson to J.G., 6 September 1821

75. G-G J.G. to William Rawson 7 September 1821

76. G-G William Rawson to J.G., 23 October 1821

77. G-G J.G. to Revd R. P. Buddicom 9 November 1821

78. G-G W.E.G. to Aunt Johanna Robertson 29 July 1829

CHAPTER 3   THE SIBLINGS

1. *See* G-G MS 441, 568, 599, 646-7, 660, 674-5

2. BL Add. MS 44790, ff. 23-4, *see Autobiographica,* p. 21

3. G-G T.G. to W.E.G., 22 May 1829
4. Ibid., 27 December 1829
5. Ibid., 21 July 1831
6. Ibid., 27 October 1831
7. G-G W.E.G. to J.G., 29 October 1831

      Eschatology at this period was very much bound up with millennialism. Growth of pre-millennialism was prompted by a number of causes, social, political, ecclesiastical and theological, which were so interwoven that it is difficult to point to the primary cause. The French Revolution made Christians of all denominations reconsider their ideas about society and religion. Missionary attempts to convert the Jews, the Repeal of the Test and Corporation Acts 1828, Catholic Emancipation 1829, growing political radicalism in the 1830s, the cholera epidemic in 1831 and the Reform Bill in 1832, all contributed towards the new interest in eschatology. Gladstone's reference to the Second Coming of Christ in his diary 22 October 1831, "Surely the actual signs of the times are such as should make us ready for the coming of our Lord," reflect the feelings of many Christians at that time. The Church Missionary Society and men like Wilberforce, Simeon and Venn embraced the expectation that when the gospel had reached the ends of the world all men living would be saved and Christ would return to reign. Such an optimistic eschatology and evangelism was very anti-Calvinist. With the growth of pre-millennialism came the expectation of the personal return of Christ to establish his kingdom on earth. Such millenarians believed that the world was so corrupt that only the return of Christ could solve the problems which were now so widespread. The Apocryphal controversy gave millenarians reason to attack what they believed was the unsound view of scripture held by evangelicals. They were equally critical of the progress of the evangelical revival and the view that the work of the missionary societies in preaching the gospel to the ends of the earth would soon bear fruit on a grand scale. But their opposition did not deter the great missionary crusade of the optimistic evangelicals. Available evidence does not suggest that Gladstone had a consistent or a great interest in eschatology and its associated issues; nevertheless, it did concern him and was an issue to which he gave much thought. *See* D. H. Hempton, "Evangelism and Eschatology," in *Journal of Ecclesiastical History,* Vol. 31, No. 2, April 1980, pp. 179-94, *also* D. Newsome, *The Parting of Friends: A Study of the Wilberforces and Henry Manning* (1966), pp. 10-12

      8. G-G W.E.G. to J.N.G., 8 June 1823
      9. Richard Shannon, *Gladstone, Vol.1. 1809-1865* (1982), p. 28
      10. BL. Add. MS 44790, f.11, *see Autobiographica,* p.16
      11. 1894 *see* BL. Add. MS 44391, ff. 1-19, *see Autobiographica, pp.*
140-8

12. BL. Add. MS 44790, f. 159, *see Autobiographica,* p. 150

13. Correspondence and other manuscript material relating to Ann MacKenzie Gladstone was transferred from the Gladstone Estate at Fasque to the Glynne-Gladstone Manuscript Collection at St Deiniol's Library, Hawarden in 1982

14. G-G A.M.G. to W.E.G., 29 November 1821

15. Ibid., 6 December 1828

16. Ibid., 28 April 1825

17. G-G Mrs G. to W.E.G., [Autumn 1823]

18. G-G A.M.G. to W.E.G., 16 and 18 October 1828

19. Ibid. 29 March 1824

20. Ibid., 21 July 1824

21. G-G A.M.G. to W.E.G., 23 February 1827

22. *The Record* was the first Anglican weekly newspaper, begun in 1828 its proprietor, Alexander Haldane was nephew of Robert Haldane a rabid Scottish Calvinist and fundamentalist, the sort of Calvinism and fundamentalism expressed by Bulteel. This paper emphasised an aggressive Calvinistic Evangelicalism. The monthly *Christian Observer,* organ of the Clapham Sect, and edited by Zachary Macaulay, steered a middle course between Calvinism and Arminianism and was an active supporter of both the Church Missionary Society (CMS) and the British and Foreign Bible Society, *see* Toon, *Evangelical Theology,* pp. 6-7 and *passim* and Michael Hennell, *Sons of the Prophets: Evangelical Leaders of the Victorian Church* (1979) , pp. 4, 8, 12-14 and *passim*

23. G -G A.M.G. to W.E.G., 31 October 1828

24. Ibid.

25. G-G A.M.G. to W.E.G., 15 August 1827 *see* Michael Hennell , *Evangelicalism and Worldliness 1770-1870* in *Studies in Church History.* Vol. 8 (1972), p. 233

26. G-G A.M.G. to W.E.G., 25 and 27 April 1823

27. Ibid., 25 September 1827

28. G-G Mrs G. to W.E.G., 19 February 1830

29. Ibid., 4 June 1830

30. G-G W.E.G. to Mrs G., 19 February 1830

31. *Diary,* 17 April 1831

Gladstone's comments here and elsewhere suggest that he lacked the experience of "Assurance," i.e. that the believer, in spite of his imperfections, is not under the condemnation of his conscience and has no sense of sinful alienation from God. Evangelicals believe that the New Testament both teaches and promises this experience to every believing Christian. Such "assurance" gives the Christian confidence about his present standing before God and also his "eternal inheritance." While Gladstone had such assurance concerning his sister Anne's eternal inheritance, he had no confidence about his own present or future state. This was a contradiction to the faith he professed. For this assurance is based upon the Cross of Christ and the sufficiency of Christ's sacrifice for the sin of the whole world, a belief which he accepted without reserve. The granting of this assurance is connected with the inward witness of the Holy Spirit; and all the Christian has to do is to accept it, which Gladstone seems to have been unable to do. *See* W.M.F. Scott "Assurance," pp. 59-67 in *Evangelicals Affirm : In the year of the Lambeth Conference* (1948); Matthew, *Gladstone*, p. 7

Anne's death, and his annual recalling of that event, raises the issue of his understanding of the "Communion of Saints." He seems to have both believed in this doctrine and also enjoyed the experience. Henry Venn felt that his union with his wife was not broken by her early death and therefore he was unable to remarry, *see* Hennell, *Sons of the Prophets*, p. 73, *also* T. E. Yates, *Venn and Victorian Bishops Abroad* (1978)

32. G-G W.E.G. to H.J.G., 15 September 1822
33. Ibid., 30 October 1825
34. G-G H.J.G. to W.E.G., 1 November 1825
35. *See* BL Add. MS 44803, B and also 44719, ff. 126-86
36. See Glynne-Gladstone Collection MS 386
37. G-G W.E.G. to H.J.G., 24 August 1828
38. G-G H.J. G. to W.E.G., 7 February 1829
39. G-G W.E.G. to H.J. G., 19 February 1829
40. G-G H.J.G. to W.E.G., 7 March 1829
41. G-G W.E.G. to H.J.G., 3 June 1829
42. G-G H.J.G. to W.E.G., 2 July 1829
43. G-G W.E.G. to H.J.G., 11 October 1829
44. Shannon, *Gladstone*, p. 25
45. G-G H.J.G. to W.E.G., 18 October 1829
46. Ibid., 27 December 1829
47. G-G W.E.G. to H.J.G., 8 January 1830
48. Ibid., 28 June 1834
49. G-G H.J.G. to W.E.G., 29 June 1830
50. G-G W.E.G. to H.J.G., 23 October 1831
51. G-G H.J.G., 21 March 1832
52. G-G W.E.G. to H.J.G., 7 December 1832

CHAPTER 4.   ETON: 1821-1827

1. G-G Mrs G. to T.G., 23 May 1817

2. *See* Robert Isaac Wilberforce, *The Life of William Wilberforce* (1839) 5 vols. vol. 3., p. 348, and Charles Smyth, *Simeon & Church Order: A study of the origin of the Evangelical Revival in Cambridge in the 18th Century* (1940), p. 52, Jones, *Hannah More,* p. 220

3. W.E.Gladstone, *Gleanings of Past Years,* 7 vols (1879), vol. vii, pp. 138 and 214

4. G-G W.E.G. to Mrs G., 29 September 1821

5. *Diary,* 2 December 1827. Colin Matthew's conclusion that Gladstone privately practiced his religion at Eton and did not try to convert his friends needs qualifying, *see* Matthew, *Gladstone* pp. 9, 15-16

6. BL Add. M.S. 44832, and G-G MS 1737

7. G-G W.E.G. to Mrs G., 23 October 1825

8. G-G W.E.G. to J.G., 18 September 1825

9. G-G W.E.G. to Mrs G., 2 October 1825

10. BL Add.M. 44790, f. 157, *see, Autobiographica,* p. 149 *see also* Matthew, *Gladstone,* pp. 15-16

11. *See* Peter Toon, *Evangelical Theology,* pp. 189, 192, also Peter J. Jagger *Clouded Witness: Initiation in the Church of England in the Mid-Victorian Period 1850-1875* (1982), p. 10

12. *See Diary,* 1, 4, April, 6, 20, 27 May, 3 June, 22, 29 July, 21, 28 October 1827

13. *See* Philip Magnus, *Gladstone: A Biography* (1954), p. 7., Checkland, *The Gladstones,* p. 204

14. *Diary,* 19 March 1871

15. G-G W.E.G. to Mrs G., 29 September 1821

16. The "Theme" referred to his weekly Latin Essay. Almost all his themes for 1825-27 have been preserved *see BL* Add. MS 44717-8, for list of subjects *see* 44717, ff. 263-4

17. J. B. Sumner, between 1815-29, published a number of theological works reflecting evangalical views. The book here referred to was probably *Evidence of Christianity derived from its Nature and Reception* (1824). When Sumner was made Bishop of Chester in 1828 Gladstone wrote in his diary "for wh we shd I think be thankfull," *see* 1 August 1828, he was appointed Archbishop of Canterbury by Lord John Russell in 1848

18. Edward Young, *Night Thoughts,* (1742-5). Young was born in June 1683. The morality arising out of *Night Thoughts* forms the bulk of the Poem and covers a wide range of topics including, On Life, Death and Immortality, on Time, Death, and Friendship, the Christian Triumph: containing our only cure for the fear of death; and proper sentiments of heart on that inestima-

ble blessing, the Infidel Reclaimed. The last two sections are Virtue's Apology: or, The Man of the World Answered; in which are considered, the love of this life; the ambition and pleasure, with the wit and wisdom, of the world; The Consolation: containing, among other things, (1).A moral survey of the nocturnal heavens. (2). A night address to the deity. This book must have been rather heavy going for a 15 year old, even for Gladstone, who was to write his own religious/moral poetry from time to time

    19. John Septimus Grover was a fellow from 1814 and vice-provost 1835-51

    20. James Montgomery, *Greenland and other Poems* (1819). A number of Montgomery's better hymns were to find a place in *Hymns Ancient and Modern*, some of which are still popular and sung regularly in the Anglican Church

    21; Walter Kerr Hamilton, 1808-69, Bishop of Salisbury 1845, a regular correspondent with Gladstone *see* Add. MS 44183

    22. Table of Authors *see* Add. MS 44718, ff. 195-6

    23. "Sock" an Eton term for "Tuck"

    24. G-G W.E.G. to A.M.G., 7 July 1822

    25. G-G W.E.G. to J. G., 20 March 1827

    26. G-G W.E.G. to Mrs G., 3 December 1824

    27. G-G W.E.G. to Mrs G., 3 December 1824

    28. G-G W.E.G. to J.G., 20 March 1827

    29. G-G T.G. to W.E.G., 20 February 1821

    30. G-G W.E.G. to J.G., 21 November 1822

    31. BL Add. MS 44715, f.123 |April 1823]

    32. BL Add. MS 44801, ff.16-18 marked "Private" May 1825, Eton.

    33, G-G W.E.G. to J.G., 6 March 1825 *see also* Charles Milnes Gaskell, *An Eton Boy: Being the Letters of James Milnes Gaskell from Eton and Oxford 1820-1830* (1939), pp. 49-55

    34. Arthur Hallam to W.E.G., BL Add. MS 44352, ff. 29-30, 6 August 1827

    35. *See* Morley, *Gladstone,* , Vol., i, p. 34

    36. *See Diary*, Sunday 7 October 1827 "Wrote a thing on Canning's death purporting to be in Westminster Abbey—remiss somewhat." See *Eton Miscellany*, Vol., ii, pp. 79-81

    37. BL Add. MS 44790, f. 20 *see Autobiographica*, p.19

    38. BL Add. MS 44790, f. 12, *see Autobiographica*, p. 15 *see also* Jones, *Hannah More, passim* whose wide range of Christian literature had a profound effect upon many in her day

    39. *See Diary*, 29 October 1825, *see also* 20 July, 1 August 1826

    40. BL Add. MS 44715, f. 127

    41. BL Add. MS 44801, f. 8-12

42. BL Add. MS 44717, this volume also contains many religious verses

43. BL Add. MS 44717, f. 236

44. G-G MS 1453

45. G-G W.E.G. to J.G., 25 June 1826

46. G-G W.E.G. to J.G., 20 March 1827 *See* Matthew, *Gladstone*, pp. 13-14

47. W.E.G. to William W. Farr, 31 October 1826 and 22 November 1826 reproduced in *Autobiographica*, pp.181-6

48. See *Diary*, 9 May 1827, *Edinburgh Review*, xiv., 423 and 513 (March 1827)

49. G-G W. E.G. to J.G., 10 July 1823

50. Jagger, *Clouded Witness*, pp. 126-33

51. G-G T.G to W.E.G., 2 February 1821

52. G-G W.E.G. to Mrs G., 27 June 1826

53. G-G W.E. G to J.G., 7 July 1826

54. A. C. Benson, *Fasti Etonenses* (1899), p. 500, *see also*, p. 297

55. *See* G-G W.E.G. to J.G., 8 February 1827, *see also Diary* 8, 9 February 1827

56. G-G A.M.G. to W.E.G., 7 February 1827

57. Jagger, *Clouded Witness*, pp. 112-19

58. G-G W.E.G. to Mrs G., 4 March 1827

59. BL Add. MS 44802, "F"

60. *See* Edward Bickersteth, *Treatise on the Lord's Supper* (1822), published in an abridged edition under the title *A Companion to the Holy Communion*, which by 1848 had gone into its eighteenth edition. His work on the Lord's Supper was the most useful and widely circulated of his books. There is no indication that Gladstone read either of these works at this period, although he would have found the *Companion* useful with its aim to "lead the devotions of the Communicant." The *Companion* contains preparatory meditiations, meditations, for use during the communion and numerous other meditations some linked to the festivals of the Christian Year. Prayers for self-examination are also included. In his formative work *Treatise on the Lord's Supper*, Bickersteth, as a leading evangelical theologian and successor to Simeon, puts forward a "high view" of the Holy Communion. He tells his readers that by neglecting their obligation to take the Holy Communion they are undervaluing their baptism. A right conception of Communion by the believer gives an assured hope that the blessings of redemption belong to him, as well as to increase his faith and advance his sanctification

His teaching on the Lord's Supper continued to influence later evangelicals and is extensively quoted in Max Warren, *Strange Victory: A study of the Holy Communion Service* (1946). A full account of Bickersteth's life as a leading evangelical is given in T. R. Birks, *Memoir of Rev Edward Bickersteth*, 2 vols, (1851). *See also* Hennell, *Sons of the Prophets*, pp. 29-49

61. G-G A.M.G. to W.E.G., 15 August 1827

62. G-G A.M.G. to W.E.G., 24 October 1827

63. G-G W.E.G. to T.G., 25 September 1825

64. G-G W.E.G. to J.G., 8 February 1824

65. *See* Hennell, *John Venn*, pp. 157-9, George W.E. Russell, *A Short History of the Evangelical Movement* (1915), pp. 133-5, Hennell, *Evangelicalism and Worldliness*, pp. 229-36

66. *See* Morley, *Gladstone*, vol. i., pp. 34-88, George W.E. Russell, *The Right Honourable William Ewart Gladstone* (1891), pp. 9-14, Matthew, *Gladstone*, pp. 10-13

67. *See* Russell, *Gladstone*, p. 8., Robert Ornsby, *Memoirs of James Robert Hope-Scott of Abbotsford, D.C.L., Q.C., Late Fellow of Merton College, Oxford with Selections from his Correspondence*, 2 vols (1884), there is no mention of Gladstone in Hope's Eton period

68. *See Autobiographica*, Appendix i., pp. 179-219, W. E. Gladstone's letters to William Windham Farr, 1826-32

69. *See Eton Miscellany*, 2 vols. June-November 1827, vol. ii., October-November, 1827, pp. 79-81

70. Russell, *Gladstone*, p. 7

71, *See* Gaskell, *An Eton Boy,* pp. 14-44

72. Ibid., pp 18-19, 23-9, 32-4

73. G-G W.E.G. to J.G., 7 July 1826, *see* Matthew, *Gladstone*, p. 11

74. *See* Charles Milnes Gaskell ed., *Records of an Eton Schoolboy* (1883) letter from James Milnes Gaskell to his mother 16 July, 1827, pp. 84-6

75. Gaskell, *An Eton Boy,* letter to his mother 27 July 1827, pp. 106-9

76. BL Add. MS 44790, ff. 84-8, *See Autobiographica*, p. 29

77. See article by William Ewart Gladstone in *The Youth's Companion,* 6 January, 1898, vol. 72, No 1., published in Boston, Mass. USA, and reprinted as a pamphlet under the same title, *Arthur Henry Hallam. See also* article in the *Daily Telegraph,* 5 January 1898; and Matthew, *Gladstone*, pp. 11-12

78. Letters Arthur H.Hallam to W.W. Farr, *The John Rylands Bulletin*, vol. 18, 1934, pp.224-8, *see also* pp.197-205. *See also* W. E. Gladstone, *Arthur Henry Hallam*, p. 9; on the Eton Society, *see* Matthew, *Gladstone*, pp.10-13

79. Shannon, *Gladstone*, pp. 17-18, see also, Matthew, *Gladstone*, p.11

80. Shannon, *Gladstone*, p. 17

81. BL Add. MS 44790, f. 87, *see Autobiographica*, p. 29

82. Perry Butler, *Gladstone: Church, State and Tractarianism. A*

study of his religious ideas and attitudes, 1809-1859 (1982), p.18

83. BL Add. MS 44790, ff. 26-35, see Autobiographica, pp. 35-6

84. Butler, Gladstone, p. 18

85. Gaskell, An Eton Boy, pp. 19-23

86. BL Add. MS 44790, ff. 107-8, see Autobiographica, p. 38

87. Letter A.H.Hallam to W.W. Farr 24 September 1826, in Bulletin of the John Rylands Library, vol. 18, pp. 220-4

88. See Joachim Jeremias, Infant Baptism in the First Four Centuries (1960), The Origins of Infant Baptism (1963), see Kurt Aland, Did the Early Church Baptise Infants? (1963)

89. See Diary, 13 July 1826

90. Letter A.H. Hallam to W.W. Farr, John Rylands Bulletin, vol. 18, p. 245. For the association of Methodists with Evangelicals see J. S. Reynolds, The Evangelicals at Oxford. 1735-1871: A record of an unchronicled movement (1953), p. 2

Evidence suggests that Hallam's comment was intended to be humorous. He wrote to Gladstone on {7} January 1827 from Wimpole Street expressing his admiration of Gladstone academically and as a person, stating that (underlining four times) you are a no party man, BL Add. MS 44352, ff. 16-17. In his religious conviction William always sought to be "a no party man." Later that year Hallam wrote to Gladstone "received your superb Burke yesterday: and hope to find it a memorial of a past and a pledge to a future friendship." A.H. Hallam to W.E.G. 27 July (1827) Add. MS 44352, f.28. Hallam reciprocated by sending him a copy of his father's book

91.BL Add. MS 44790, ff. 66-7 see Autobiographica, p. 23

92. W.E.G., pamphlet Arthur Henry Hallam, pp. 11-12

93. Diary, 4 August 1825

94. A.H. Hallam to W.W. Farr, postmark 1 February 1827, John Rylands Bulletin, vol. 8, pp. 231-4

95. Checkland, The Gladstones, p. 203

96. See for example, Morley, Gladstone, Vol. i., pp. 81-4; Magnus, Gladstone, pp. 9-10, 232, but see p. 9; Checkland, The Gladstones, pp. 246-7; Shannon, Gladstone, pp. 28-30, 34-5; Butler, Gladstone, pp. 30-31, 34

97. See Ornsby, Memories of James Robert Hope-Scott vol i., pp., 66-86, 95

98. G-G W.E.G. to J.G., 3 November 1824

99. BL Add. MS 44801, ff. 6-7 see also Diary, 29 January, 26 February 1826

100. Diary 21 January 1826

101. Ibid., 2 December 1827

102. BL Add. MS 44719, f..235 [1828-29] No date or watermark; see Diary, 20 December 1828

CHAPTER 5: A PERIOD OF PREPARATION AND SEARCHING

1. BL Add. MS 44791, f.19, 26 July 1894, *see Autobiographica*, p. 148, BL Add. MS 44791, ff.1-19 incorporates additions and alterations made 7 February 1897, *see also Autobiographica*, p. 148

2. The Editor of the Gladstone *Diary* made a mistake when stating, in a footnote to the *Diary* entry 25 January 1828, that Gladstone's companion was Atherton Legh Powys. This mistake leads to a possible further mistake in the footnote to 27 February 1828. See W.E. Gladstone's letter to his Eton friend W.W.Farr, 11 March 1828 in the *John Rylands Library*, also *Autobiographica*, pp. 201-2 and Russell, *Gladstone*, pp. 15-16. These sources make it clear that it was Horatio Powys who was at Wilmslow; in view of the fact that at that time Gladstone was searching for his true vocation the implications of his close contact with a young man anticipating and preparing for ordination a few months later are far more important than contact with Horatio Powy's younger brother.

3. BL Add. MS 44804, "A" 1826-June 1830, which records his personal expenditure

4. Reynolds, *The Evangelicals at Oxford*, pp. 44-6, 57-64 and *passim*

5. Butler, *Gladstone*, pp. 20-21, Shannon, *Gladstone*, pp. 20-21, Matthew, *Gladstone*, p. 251

6. Butler, *Gladstone*, p. 21

7. BL Add. MS 44791, f.10, *see Autobiographica*, p. 144

8. Butler, *Gladstone,* p. 22

9. The four pamphlets published in this controversy between Dr James Walker and Edward Craig, which belonged to Gladstone, are all bound together and preserved in the St Deiniol's Gladstone Pamphlet Collection.

10. BL Add. MS 44719, f.235 [circa 1828-29] no date or water mark

11. BL Add. MS 44791, f.1-2, *see Autobiographica*, p. 140

12. BL Add. MS 44790, f.159, *see Autobiographica*, p. 150

13. BL Add. MS 44803, "B", "Opinions of Eminent Writers and Confessions of Faith" W.E.Gladstone June 1828. While on the subject of Baptism and Fasting only two pages are given to fasting and thirty-one pages to baptism. Quotations on baptism are given from Waterland, Cranmer, Jewel, Andrews, Latimer, Taylor, Hall, Ridley, Tindal, Hooker, Justin Martyr, Chrysostom, Ambrose and many others. A masterly collection and survey of the subject, it provides an example of the way in which Gladstone gathered facts together on many other subjects in the future in order to be fully informed before making a decision or to substantiate a position held

14. BL Add. MS 44719, f. 125, 20 October 1864, a note fixed to his note book

15. BL Add. MS 44352, ff. 70-1, W. Rawson to W.E.G. [July 1828]

16. *See* Shannon, *Gladstone*, pp. 21-3 and *Diary*, vol. 1., pp.xxix-xxx
17. G-G W E G. to J.G., 19 September 1828
18. G-G W.E.G. to A.M.G., 18 August 1828
19. G-G W.E.G. to A.M.G., 9 September 1828

CHAPTER 6. THE EVOLUTION OF A CHURCHMAN

1. G-G MS 1381 Paper by W.E.G. "The State of Religion in Oxford," 27 March, 1829, *See* Matthew, *Gladstone*, p. 27
2. Shannon, *Gladstone*, p. 28
3. *Diary* 1 March 1831
4. BL Add. MS 44791, f.4., *see Autobiographica*, p. 141
5. *See* BL Add. MS 44791, f. 15., BL Add. MS 44790, f.158, ff. 164- 65, *see Autobiographica*, pp. 146-7, 149-50,152
6. *See* James Milnes Gaskell to his mother 23 March 1830 in Gaskell, *Record of an Eton School Boy*, p. 155
7. *See* Gaskell, *An Eton Boy*, pp. 170-1
8. See Toon, *Evangelical Theology*, p. 5
9. BL Add. MS 44719, ff.237-40
10. BL Add. MS 44801, ff.33-4, *see Diary*, 20 June 1830
11. BL Add. MS 44719, ff. 216-22
12. *See* G.W.E. Russell, *Mr Gladstone's Religious Development: A Paper read in Christ Church May 5. 1899* (2nd edt 1899), p. 7. *See* Butler, *Gladstone*, p. 12
13. *See* BL Add. MS 44719, ff.218-19, 221-2
14. *See* St John's Gospel 19.v.34 and O. Cullmann, *Early Christian Worship* (1962)
15. BL Add. MS 44719, f. 203
16 *Diary,* 17 July 1830
17. Gladstone, *Gleanings,* vol. vii., pp.201-41. Gladstone obviously had some "blind spots" on this subject, see Reynolds, *Evangelicals at Oxford, passim,* eg. John Hill Vice-Principal at St Edmund Hall, 1812-1851.
18. *Autobiographica*, pp. 35-6
19. *Lathbury,* vol.ii, p. 333
20. BL Add. MS 44790, ff.107-10, *see Autobiographica*, pp. 38-9
21. BL Add. MS 44791, ff.45-8, *see* Autobigaraphica, pp. 250-3, cf. p. 141
22. *Lathbury*, vol. i., p. 7
23. *See* Reynolds, *The Evangelicals at Oxford*, p. 95
24. *See* Ornsby, *Memoirs of James Robert Hope-Scott*, vol.i, pp. 31-3, 60, 71-86, 95, 99-104, *passim*

25. BL Add. MS 44809

26. G-G W.E.G., to R.G., 4 February 1830

27. Gaskell, *An Eton Boy*, letter to his mother 22 November 1829, pp. 170-1

28. Reynolds, *Evangelicals at Oxford*, pp. 97-8

29. Ibid., pp. 98-9

30. BL Add. MS 44791, ff.4-5, *see Autobiographica*, p. 142

31. BL Add. MS 44352, f.184, Letter William Rawson to W.E.G. 1 March 1831

32. *See* article "Present Aspects of the Church 1843" first published 1843, reproduced in Gladstone, *Gleanings*, vol. v., pp. 1-80. Gladstone's reactions against a debased evangelicalism were shared by many of his Oxford contemporaries as shown by D. Newsome in *Parting of Friends*.

33. BL Add. MS 44790, ff.89-90, *see Autobiographica*, pp. 158, 146

34. *See Lathbury*, vol. i., p.2 and Checkland, *The Gladstones*, p. 218

35. BL Add. MS 44719, ff.126-34

36. *See* BL Add. MS 44720, ff.86-90

37. *Lathbury,* vol. i., p. 2

38. *See* Michael Hennell article "Evangelical Spirituality" in *A Dictionary of Christian Spirituality* (1983), pp.138-40; Toon, *Evangelical Theology*, makes no reference to the place or use of the Holy Communion as a fundamental part of Evangelical theology or spirituality. *See also* Michael Hennell's contribution "The Evangelical Revival in the Church of England,"in *The Study of Spirituality* (1986), ed C.Jones and others, pp. 459-63

39. *See* Jagger, *Clouded Witness*, p. 18

40. *See Lathbury*, vol. i., pp. 421-7

41. Ibid., p. 212

42. BL Add. MS 44815, "C"

43. Jagger, *Clouded Witness*, pp. 112-17

44. BL Add. MS 44790, f.156, *see Autobiographica*, pp. 148-9

45. BL Add. MS 44790, ff. 107-8, *see Autobiographica*, pp. 38-9

46. BL Add. MS 44720, f.44, 4 April 1830

47. BL Add. MS 44790, ff.107-8, see Autobiographica, pp. 38-9

48. BL Add. MS 44791, ff.2-3, *see Autobiographica*, pp. 140-1

49 Joseph Butler, *The Analogy of Religion, Natural and Revealed to The Constitution and Course of Nature*, (2nd edt 1736), pp. 303-4

50. BL Add. MS 44790, f.159, *see Autobiographica*, p. 150.

51. *See* Gladstone, *Gleanings* vol. v., pp.11, and 12-14

52. BL Add. MS 44719, f.198

53. BL Add. MS 44791, f.7, *see Autobiographica*, pp. 142-3, *see* also pp. 150-1, *see* Morley, *Gladstone*, vol. i., pp. 88-9

54. BL Add. MS 44790, f.161, *see Autobiographica*, p. 151

55. BL Add. MS 44791, ff.7,162, see *Autobiographica*, pp. 143, 151

56. BL Add. MS 44791, f.164, see *Autobiographica*, p. 152

57. BL Add. MS 44204, ff.11-12, Benjamin Harrison to W.E.G., 10 November 1832

58. BL Add. MS 44790, f.160, see *Autobiographica*, pp. 150-1

59. *See* Gladstone, *Gleanings*, vol. v., p. 8

CHAPTER 7.   AN ANALYSIS OF GLADSTONE'S RELIGIOUS LIFE AT OXFORD: 1828-1831

1. G-G W.E.G. to H.J.G., 11 October 1829

2.*See Diary*, 4, 5, 8, 20 February and 29 May 1831, *see also* BL Add. MS 44150, ff.22-3

3. G-G W.E.G. to J.G., 11 December 1831

4. G-G J.G. to W.E.G., 13 December 1831

5. G-G J.G. to W.E.G., 12 July 1831

6. *See* for example BL Add. MS 44801, f.69 June 1830

7. G-G W.E.G. to J.G., 17 February 1831

8. BL Add. MS 44807

9. G-G W.E.G. to Elizabeth Robertson 18 January [1829]

10. BL Add. MS 44722, ff.328-42

11. BL Add. MS 44801, f.64

12. Ibid., f. 51

13. G-G Mrs G. to W.E.G., 29 November 1829, *see also* Morley, *Gladstone*, vol. i., p. 640

14. G-G J.G. to W.E.G., 23 February 1831

15. *See Diary*, 24, 26, March, 24 April, 3-8 October, 1831

16. G-G W.E.G. to Mrs G., 27 June 1831

17. G-G W.E.G. to T.G., 31 August 1831

18. BL Add. MS 44352, ff. 141-2, Edward Craig to W.E.G., 15 December 1829

19. G-G W.E.G. to Mrs G., 22 October 1831

20. G-G W.E.G. to Editor of *Liverpool Mercury* 22 December 1828

21. *See* BL Add. MS 44801, f. 26

22. BL Add. MS 44150, ff.15-16 F.H. Doyle to W.E.G., 29 November 1829

23. BL Add. MS 44801, f. 26

24. BL Add. MS 44803 "F"

25. BL Add. MS 44720, Part 1. ff.61-2 October 1830, Part 2. ff.63-8
1830

26. BL Add. MS 44816, "B" 1831

Against the optimistic eschatology of CMS and its followers Edward Irving preached a pessimistic pre-millennial gospel. He maintained that the world was in such an awful state since the French Revolution that Christ must return very soon. At times in 1831-2 Gladstone shared such pessimistic millenarian feelings, *See Diary* 22 October 1831. In spite of such interests he does not seem to have either read or heard Irving until 27 January 1833, "went . . . to Mr Irving's evening service a scene pregnant with melancholy instruction." Nothing of Irving's was read until June 1860, when he read, *For the Oracles of God, Four Orations, for Judgement to come, an argument in nine parts* (1823). *See* article "Millennium, Views of the," pp. 714-718 in Walter E. Elwelyed, *Evangelical Dictionary of Theology* (1985), and Hennell, *Sons of the Prophets*, pp. 9-11,44, Matthew *Gladstone*, p. 25

27. BL Add. MS 44833

28. BL Add. MS 44719, f.237

29. BL Add. MS 44719, f. 230

30. BL Add. MS 44801, ff. 71-2, 9 May 1830

31. *See* BL Add. MS 44722, ff. 322-7

32. G-G W.E.G. to R.G., 3 April 1830

33. BL Add. MS 44801, f. 26 [1829]

34. SL Add. MS 44821, "C" f.16

35. BL Add. MS 44801, f.64, June 1830

36. BL Add. MS 44801, f.75, 28 November 1830

37. BL Add. MS 44801, ff.73-4

38. BL Add. MS 44801, f.77, 21 March 1830

39. G-G W.E.G. to R.G., 20 May 1831

40. Butler, *Gladstone*, pp. 33-4

41. *See* BL Add. MS 44719, ff.125-6

42. Ibid., f.233

43. Ibid., f.125

44. G-G W.E.G. to H.J.G., 1 February 1829

45. BL Add. MS 44815 "C"; *see also* Add. MS 44834 (nd)

46. Lambeth Palace Library, Gladstone Papers, MS 2758, ff.86-8, 102, *See* also Peter J. Jagger ed., *Gladstone. Politics & Religion*, pp. xii-xiii

47. G-G W.E.G. to H.J.G., 7 February 1829

48. G-G T.G. to W.E.G., 22 March 1830 and W.E.G. to J.G., 29 October, 11 December 1831

49. *See* Hennell, *Evangelicalism and Worldliness*, pp. 234-5

50. G-G W.E.G. to A.M.G., 17 November 1828

51. G-G W.E.G. to Mrs G., 19 February 1830

52. The drafts of these letters are in the G-G MS 699

53. G-G W.E.G. to J.G., 27 October 1830

54. *See* for example *Diary,* 5 November 1828, 6, 8, 15 February, 14 August, 29 September, 1831, W.E.G's sixteen paged letter to his "Beloved Mother" G-G on 20 February 1831 contains two pages on Bulteel's preaching.

55. BL Add. MS 44801, f. 42

56. *See* Diary, 14 November 1831

57. G-G W.E.G. to T.G., 31 August 1831

58. G-G W.E.G. to T.G., 7 December 1829

59. G-G W.E.G. to R.G., 13 November 1829

60. G-G W.E.G. to R.G., 2 February 1830

61. G-G J.G. to W.E.G., 8 December 1829

62. *See* BL Add. MS 44815, "A" ff. 2-7

63. BL Add. MS 44204, f.13, Benjamin Harrison to W.E.G., 26 November, 1832

64. *See* Diary, 17, 18, September 1830 *also* Morley, *Gladstone*, vol. i., pp. 6, 8, 9

65. G-G W.E.G. to R.G., 26 February 1831

66. BL Add. MS 44161, f.38, J. Milnes Gaskell to W.E.G., 31 August 1831

67. *See* G-G W.E.G. to Mrs G., 4 May [1831]

68. *See Diary,* vol. i., pp.xxix-xxx, p. 265 and footnote

69. *See Diary,* 23 April 1830, 10 September 1831

70. BL Add. MS 44803, "E" May l830

71. *See* BL Add. MS 44807 August 1829

72. BL Add. MS 44801, f.41 [1829]

73. BL Add. MS 44807

74. BL Add. MS 44720, ff.235-9

75. BL Add. MS 44649, f.29

76. *See* BL Add. MS 44815, "A" f.68

77. G-G T.G. to W.E.G., 2 November 1829 *see also Diary* 5, 11 May 1829

78. G-G W.E.G. to J.G., 7 November 1829

79. G-G W.E.G. to J.G., 25, July 1830

80. G-G W.E.G. to T.G., 21 July 1830

81. G-G J.G. to W.E.G., 22 December 1829

82. G-G T.G. to W.E.G., 2 February 1830

83. G-G J.G. to W.E.G., 28 January 1831

84. G-G W.E.G. to R.G., 17 March 1831

CHAPTER 8. GOD'S WILL: CHURCH OR POLITICS?

1. BL Add. MS 44715, f. 2

2. G-G W.E.G. to J.G., 16 March 1831

3. BL Add. MS 44791, f. 51

4. G-G A list produced by T.G. for A.M.G. containing biblical texts on "Obedience to Parents" MS 1742

5. G-G W.E.G. to J.G., 15 October 1832

6. *See Diary,* 15 April 1840

7. BL Add. MS 44352, ff. 220-1, Charles Childers to W.E.G., 19 January 1832

8. BL Add. MS 44815, "F", f.3

9. BL Add. MS 44815, "A", ff.12-14,"Christ Church 1831"

10. G-G *see* J. G. to W.E.G., 23 February 1831

11. M.R.D. Foot "Morley's Gladstone: A Reappraisal," *Bulletin of the John Rylands Library*, vol., 51, 1968-9, p. 376

12. Shannon, *Gladstone*, pp. 34-5

13. Magnus, *Gladstone,* p. 11

14. BL Add. MS 44791, f.1, *see Autobiographica,* p.140

15. G-G W.E.G. to T.G., 22 November 1828

16. G-G T.G. to W.E.G., 25 November 1828

17. G-G T.G. to W.E.G., 3 December 1828

18. G-G H.J.G. to W.E.G., 7 February 1829

19. G-G W.E.G. to T.G., 3 April 1829

20. G-G W.E.G. to T.G., 20 May 1829

21. *See* Checkland, *The Gladstones*, p. 246, where he wrongly ascribes a letter to Robertson Gladstone, to 6 November 1830, the letter is dated 6 September 1830.

22. G-G W.E.G. to J.G., 4 August 1830, *see* Morley, *Gladstone*, vol.i., pp. 635-40

23. G-G W.E.G. to T.G., 9 August 1830

24. G-G J.G. to W.E.G., 10 August 1830, *see* Morley, *Gladstone*, vol. i., pp. 640-1

25. G-G W.E.G. to J.G., 12 August 1830

26. G-G T.G. to W.E.G., 13 August 1830

27. G-G Mrs G. and J. G. to W.E.G., 18 August 1830

28. G-G W.E.G. to R.G., 14 August 1830

29. G-G W.E.G. to T.G., 15 August 1830

30. G-G T.G. to W.E.G., 23 August 1830

31. G-G W.E.G. to T.G., 1 September 1830

32. G-G R.G. to W.E.G., 31 August 1830

33. G-G W.E.G. to R.G., 6 September 1830

34. G-G T.G. to W.E.G., 11 September 1830
35. G-G J.G. to W.E.G., 10 August 1830
36. G-G W.E.G. to J.G., 2 November 1830
37. G-G W.E.G. to T.G., 2 November 1830
38. G-G J.G. to W.E.G., 8 November 1830
39. W.E.G. to J.N.G. 29 August 1830, *see Lathbury*, vol.ii., pp. 223-6
Lathbury, wrongly attributes this letter to Gladstone's father it was in fact to his
brother.
40. G-G W.E.G. to J.N.G. 30 December 1830. *Lathbury*, vol.ii., pp.
226-8
41. *See* Butler, *Gladstone*, p. 31 and footnote
42. G-G W.E.G. to Mrs G., 20 February 1831
43. G-G J.N.G. to W.E.G., 14 March 1831
44. George W.E. Russell, *The Right Hon. W.E.Gladstone*, p. 21
45. Ibid.
46. Butler, *Gladstone*, p. 34
47. G-G H.J.G. to Mrs G., Friday 1831
48. G-G J.G. to W.E.G., 12 July 1831, *see* Checkland, *The Gladstones*, p. 250 for John Gladstone's attitude to the Reform Bill.
49. G-G W.E.G. to T.G., 17 July 1831
50. *See* Shannon, *Gladstone*, p. 29
51. G-G W.E.G. to J.G., [7 January] 1832
52. G-G T.G. to W.E.G., 24 January [1832] 1832 as post mark, not
1831 as Tom's date, which was a natural error at the beginning of a New Year!
53. Shannon, *Gladstone*, p. 29
54. Paper on his position re Caroline Farquhar G-G MS 1383 August
1835, See *Diary*, 22 August 1835.

CHAPTER 9. THE CONTINENTAL JOURNEY: 1832

1. G-G W.E.G. to Mrs G., 3 April 1832
2. *See Diary*, 15 February 1832
3. G-G W.E.G. to T.G., 26 May 1832
4. *See Diary*, 16 June 1832 *see also* 31 May, 4 June 1832
5. G-G W.E.G. to J.G., 25 June 1832
6. *See Diary*, 4 March 1832
7, *See* letter quoted in Virginia Surtees, *A Beckford Inheritance: The
Lady Lincoln Scandal* (1977), p. 15
8. G-G *See* copy of letter from Duke of Newcastle to Mr John Gladstone 21 June 1832

9. G-G J.G. to Duke of Newcastle, 26 June 1832
10. G-G J.G. to W.E.G., 26 June 1832
11. G-G W.E.G. to J.G., 6 July 1832
12. G-G copy W.E.G. to Mrs G., 7 July 1832
13. G-G W.E.G. to J.G., 7 July 1832
14. G-G copy W.E.G. to Lord Lincoln , 7 July 1832
15. G-G W.E.G. to J.G., 9 July 1832
16. G-G copy W.E.G. to Duke of Newcastle, 9 July 1832
17. G-G copy W.E.G. to Lord Lincoln, 9 July 1832
18. BL Add. MS 44161, f.74., James Milnes Gaskell to W.E.G., 30
June 1832

CHAPTER 10. THE CHRISTIAN POLITICIAN

1. BL Add 44791, f.12, *see Autobiographica,* p. 145
2. BL Add.MS 44777, f.1, *see Autobiographical Memoranda,* p.3.
Many quotations in this chapter are from "A Visit to Newark" Add.MS 44791,
ff.1-12, *see Autobiographical Memoranda,* pp.3-20 The importance of sabbath
observance for the Christian politician was both practised and commended by
William Wilberforce, *see,* R. Coupland, *Wilberforce: A Narrative* (1923), pp.
232-4. In 1838 Gladstone read the five volume life of William Wilberforce
written by his sons Robert Isaac and Samuel.
3. BL Add. MS 44722, ff.57-8
4. BL Add. MS 44820, ff.31-2
5. BL Add. MS 44777, ff.1-12, see *Autobiographical Memoranda,*
pp. 3-20
6. G-G W.E.G. to J.G., 27 September 1832
7. G-G W.E.G. to J.G., 4 October 1832
8. G-G W.E.G. to J.G., 8 October 1832
9. G-G W.E.G. to H.J.G., 7 December 1832
10. BL Add. MS 44353, ff.151-4
11. Ibid., ff.158, 189-90
12. BL Add. MS 44204, ff.9-10, Benjamin Harrison to W.E.G. 1
November 1832
13. BL Add. MS 44204, ff.13-14, Benjamin Harrison to W.E.G., 26
November 1832
14. BL Add. MS 44352, ff.274-5, Charles Childers to W.E.G., 28
September 1832
15. G-G W.E.G. to J.G., 9 September 1832

16. G-G W.E.G. to J.G., 15 October 1832
17. G-G W.E.G. to J.G., 27 September 1832
18. BL Add. MS 44353, f.15
19. G-G W.E. G., to J.G., 8 October 1832
20. BL Add. MS 44722, ff.59-64, 8 October 1832 these cover the two drafts and final Address. A copy of the poster "To the Worthy and Independent Electors of the Borough of Newark," Clinton Arms, Newark, Tuesday, October 9, 1832, has been preserved in the G-G.
21. BL Add. MS 44777, ff.13-14,15-22
22. BL Add. MS 44777, ff.15-22
23. G-G W.E.G. to J.G., 15 October 1832
24. Draft in BL Add. MS 44722, f.87
25. G-G W.E.G. to J.G., 11 December 1832
26. G-G W.E.G. to T.G., 11 December 1832
27. G-G W.E.G. to H.J.G., 11 December 1832
28. BL Add. MS 44336, ff.5-6, M.F. Tupper to W.E.G., 12 January 1833
29. BL Add. MS 44353, f.87, Archdeacon of Liverpool, John Jones to W.E.G., 28 February 1833

LIST OF SOURCES AND BIBLIOGRAPHY

SOURCES

A.   Primary Sources (manuscript)

B.   Primary Sources (printed)

C.   Secondary Sources.

    i. General

    ii. Articles.

NOTES

i. The British Library and Lambeth Palace Library, Gladstone Collections: every item in these Collections up to 1833 has been consulted.

ii. Glynne-Gladstone Manuscripts, Hawarden, contain in the region of two-hundred and fifty thousand manuscripts. Every letter to or from William Ewart Gladstone has been read, as have all manuscripts produced by W.E. Gladstone; or relative to him, up to 1833. Correspondence between other members of the family has been consulted as have all the other documents in this Collection up to 1833.

iii. Published Works: The place of publication is London except where otherwise stated.

A. PRIMARY SOURCES (MANUSCRIPT)

The British Library Gladstone Papers: Additional Manuscripts 44086-44835

From this Collection every folio up to 1833 has been consulted in the following volumes of manuscripts: 44092, 44117, 44137, 44150, 44161, 44183, 44204, 44210, 44261, 44262, 44276, 44299, 44336, 44346, 44350, 44352, 44353, 44649, 44681, 44715-44722, 44745, 44777, 44790-44796, 44800-44809, 44811-44822, 44831-44834.

The subjects covered in the thousands of folios contained in these volumos include the following. A wide range of personal and "official" correspondence dating from the Eton period to the Newark Election. Miscellaneous papers and note books belonging to his time at Eton cover school work and life and touch upon many topics including religion. Account books tell of his personal expenditure from 1826 and provide a record of his charitable giving. Drafts of "speeches" are preserved from Eton, Oxford and Newark. The Oxford material is wide ranging embracing memoranda of studies, a varied collection of notebooks containing classical, literary and religious subjects; which in turn include "prose selections," religious "themes," theological studies, abstracts and summaries of books read and miscellaneous papers, dated and undated, on many topics. Commonplace and other books contain devotional writings, prayers, meditations, religious verses, psalms, biblical studies and works, the Communion Service and "Secreta Eucharistica." There is an account of his mother's death and journals covering his continental tour. The Newark Election Campaign is well documented with correspondence, speeches and other related issues, while the extensive autobiographical memoranda produced by Gladstona in later life offer an interesting and important collection of material.

The Lambeth Palace Library: The Gladstone Papers

All the Gladstone correspondence available in this Collection has been consulted, MS 2758 is of particular interest. The original copies of The Gladstone Diaries are all deposited at Lambeth Palace Library.

St Deiniol's Library. Hawarden: The Glynne-Gladstone Manuscripts.

Mrs Anne Gladstone (Mother)

Correspondence:

Letters from: Anne Mackenzie Gladstone, Helen Jane Gladstone, John Gladstone, John Neilson Gladstone, Robertson Gladstone, Thomas Gladstone, William Ewart Gladstone.
Miss Margaret S. Buchan, Divie Bethune, George Canning, Miss Maria Hope, Hannah More, Charles Simeon and various minor correspondents.

Papers:

Various manuscripts on her charitable work and charitable giving and institutions, Sunday School and missionary work, devotional writings including verses, prayers, self-examinations, and her "private diary." Miscellaneous papers. Account of her death and correspondence following.

Anne Mackenzie Gladstone (Sister)

Correspondence:

Letters from: Mrs Anne Gladstone, Helen Jane Gladstone, John Gladstone, John Neilson Gladstone, Robertson Gladstone, Thomas Gladstone, William Ewart Gladstone. Character sketches of her brothers and sisters.

Papers:

Miscellaneous devotional writings including prayers, verses and other items.

Helen Jane Gladstone (Sister)

Correspondence:

Letters from: Mrs Anne Gladstone, Anne Mackenzie Gladstone, John Gladstone, John Neilson Gladstone, Robertson Gladstone, Thomas Gladstone, William Ewart Gladstone. Miss Johanna Robertson, and others.

Papers:

Miscellaneous papers and devotional writings.

John Gladstone (Father)

Correspondence:

Letters from Mrs Anne Gladstone, Anne Mackenzie Gladstone, John Neilson Gladstone, Robertson Gladstone, brother Robert Gladstone, Thomas Gladstone, William Ewart Gladstone, and various grandchildren, Thomas Gladstones, his father.

Correspondents on various subjects including James Buchanan, George Canning, Dr Thomas Chalmers, Edgar Corrie, Kirkman Finlay, William Huskisson, Revd John Jones and others, George H. Law, the Bishop of Chester, Zachary Macaulay, the Duke of Newcastle, Sir Robert Peel, Revd William Rawson and others, William Wilberforce and various others. John Gladstone's Letter Books sometimes contain copies of letters sent to the above and many others.

Papers:

Account books, cash book, ledgers, pamphlets written by John Gladstone, Lancaster election handbill, charitable work and institutions, list of houses and property owned, various press-cuttings including many relating to John Gladstone, marriage settlement with Ann Robertson, 1800, miscellaneous papers, various business papers, details of Rodney Street, Seaforth House, servants etc., Church building, various correspondence and details in connection with West Indian plantations.

John Neilson Gladstone (Brother)

Correspondence;

Letters from: Mrs Anne Gladstone, Anne Mackenzie Gladstone, John Gladstone, Robertson Gladstone, Thomas Gladstone, William Ewart Gladstone.

Robertson Gladstone (Brother)

Correspondence:

Letters from: Mrs Anne Gladstone, Anne Mackenzie Gladstone, Helen Jane Gladstone, John Gladstone, John Neilson Gladstone, Thomas Gladstone, William Ewart Gladstone.

Thomas Gladstone (Brother)

Correspondence:

Letters from: Mrs Anne Gladstone, Anne Mackenzie Gladstone, Helen Jane Gladstone, John Gladstone, John Neilson Gladstone, William Ewart Gladstone.

Papers:

Pocket Diary of Thomas Gladstone, Memorandum on the death of Anne Mackenzie Gladstone.

William Ewart Gladstone

Correspondence:

Letters from: Mrs Anne Gladstone, Anne Mackenzie Gladstone, Helen Jane Gladstone, John Gladstone, John Neilson Gladstone, Robertson Gladstone, Thomas Gladstone.

Correspondence to and from Aunts Johanna Robertson and Elizabeth Robertson.

A wide range of varied correspondence with relatives, friends and others and twelve files of type-script copies of letters and papers of W.E. Gladstone made in connection with Morley's *Life of Gladstone*. Letters to the *Liverpool Mercury*.

Papers:

Among the extensive range of manuscripts preserved and used are, various devotional writings including poems at Eton and an account of a miraculous escape, various remains of Psalters and Prayer Books, a Memorandum on the State of Religion at Oxford, bank books, rough book including accounts, personal account books including income, expenditure etc., Secret Account Book.

Newark Election Accounts, Press-cuttings etc.

Miscellaneous Family Papers

Gladstone Family Papers 1532-1758, Robertson Family Papers, Dingwall, 1748-1806, Miscellaneous papers of Andrew Robertson, provost of Dingwall. Correspondence and papers concerning churches 1814-79.

B. *PRIMARY SOURCES (PRINTED)*

Brooke, John and Sorensen, Mary, eds., *The Prime Ministers' Papers: W.E. Gladstone: 1971-72.*

    i. Autobiographica

    ii. *Autobiographical Memoranda*

Eton Miscellany. The., Vols. 1 & 2. June-November, 1827, Eton, 1827.
Foot, M.R.D. & Matthew, H.C.G., eds. *The Gladstone Diaries. Vols. 1-4, 1825-1854,* Oxford, 1968-1974.
Gladstone, William Ewart, *Arthur Henry Hallam,* published in *The Youth Companion,* January 6, 1898, Boston, U.S.A., 1898.
Gladstone, W.E., *Gleanings of Past Years,* 1843-1878, 7 vols., 1879.
Lathbury, D.C. *Correspondence on Church and Religion of William Ewart Gladstone,* 2 vols., 1910.
Matthew, H.C.G., ed., *The Gladstone Diaries, vols. 5-9, 1855-1880,* Oxford, 1978-1986.

C. SECONDARY SOURCES

(i) GENERAL

Aland, Kurt, *Did the Early Church Baptise Infants*? 1963.

Anonymous (By a Layman), An Earnest Exhortation to A Frequent Reception of the Holy Sacrament of the Lord's Supper. Particularly addressed to Young Persons, 9th edn., 1815.

     "   A Friendly Call to the Holy Communion: Wherein is shown to the meanest Capacity: The Nature and End of the Sacrament of the Lord's Supper: The Obligation to Frequent it: The Insufficiency of the Excuses usually brought for absenting from it: The proper Dispositions for receiving it: And the Advantages of a worthy Reception: With a particular Address to Servants. 12th edn., 1815.

     "   Letter to the Roman Catholics of the City of Worcester from the late Chaplain of that Society stating the Motives which induced him to Relinquish their Communion and become a Member of the Protestant Church. 3rd edn. 1826.

Ashwell, A.R. & Wilberforce, R.G. *Life of the Right Reverend Samuel Wilberforce. D.D. Lord Bishop of Oxford and afterwards of Winchester, with selections from his diaries and correspondence,* 3 vols., 1880.

Balleine, G.R., *A History of the Evangelical Party in the Church of England,* 1951.

Barrow, Isaac, D.D., the late master of Trinity College in Cambridge., *A Brief Exposition of the Lord's Prayer and the Decalogue. To which is added The Doctrine of the Sacraments,* 1681.

Battiscombe, Georgina, *John Keble: A Study in Limitation.,* 1963.

Baxter, Eric G., *Dr Jephson of Leamington Spa.* Warwickshire Local History Society, 1980.

Benson, A.C., *Fasti Etonenses,* 1899.

Bethell, Christopher, (Rt. Revd., Bp. of Bangor), *A General View of the Doctrine of Regeneration in Baptism,* 1839.

Bickersteth, Edward, *A Companion to the Holy Communion,* 18th edn., 1848

     "   *On Baptism,* 1820.

     "   *A Treatise on the Lord's Supper,* 1822.

Birks, T.R., *Memoir of the Revd. Edward Bickersteth, late Rector of Watton, Herts.,* 2 vols., 1851.

Blomfield, Charles J., *Manual of Family Prayers,* 1832.

Brigg, Asa, *The Age of Improvement, 1783-1867,* 1959.

Brilioth, Yngve. *Three Lectures on Evangelicalism and the Oxford Movement, together with a lecture on the theological aspects of the Oxford*

Movement and a sermon preached in Fairford Church on 11 July 1933, 1934.

Brose, O., *Church and Parliament: the reshaping of the Church of England, 1828-1850*, 1960.

Brown, C.K. Francis, *A History of the English Clergy, 1800-1900*, 1953.

Burnet, Gilbert. *An Exposition of The XXXIX Articles of the Church of England*, 1819.

Butler, Joseph, *The Analogy of Religion. Natural and Revealed to the Constitution and Course of Nature*. 2nd edn. 1736.

"   *A Charge delivered to the Clergy at the Primary Visitation of the Diocese of Durham, 1751.*

"   *Sermons*, Edinburgh, 1804.

Butler, Perry, *Gladstone: Church, State and Tractarianism. A study of his religious ideas and attitudes*, 1809-1859, Oxford, 1982.

Butler, Perry Andrew, *The Religious Ideas and Attitudes of William Ewart Gladstone. (1809-1859)*, Bodleian Library, Oxford, D. Phil. (Thesis), 1977.

Carpenter, S.C., *Church and People, 1789-1889. A History of the Church of England from William Wilberforce to "Lux Mundi"*, 1933.

Carus, W., *Memoirs of the Life of the Reverend Charles -Simeon*, 1847.

Chadwick, Owen, ed., *The Mind of the Oxford Movement*, 1960.

"   *The Secularization of the European Mind in the Nineteenth Century*, 1975.

"   *The Victorian Church.*, 2 vols., (vol. 1 - 1970, 2nd. edt, vol. 2 - 1970 2nd. edt.).

"   *Victorian Miniatures*, 1961.

Checkland, S.G., *The Gladstones: A Family Biography. 1764-1851*, Cambridge, 1971.

Clark, G. Kitson, *Churchmen and the Condition of England, 1832-1885, A study in the development of Social ideas and practice from the Old Regime to the Modern State*, 1973.

"   *The Making of Victorian England*, 1962.

Clarke, W.K. Lowther, *Eighteenth Century Piety*, 1944.

Coleridge, Sir J.T., *A Memoir of the Revd. John Keble, M.A., late Vicar of Hursley*, 3rd edn., 1870.

Conybeare, W.J., *Essays Ecclesiastical and Social*, 1855.

Cornish, Francis Warre, *The English Church in the Nineteenth Century*. 2 vols., 1910.

Coupland, R., *Wilberforce: A Narrative*. Oxford, 1923.

Craig, Edward, M.A. *Respectful Remonstrance. Addressed to the Revd. James Walker, M.A., senior minister of St Peter's Chapel, on the subject of*

A *Sermon preached before the Bishop and clergy of the united diocese of Edinburgh, Fife and Glasgow in St. John's Chapel, on the
22nd June, 1825*, Edinburgh, 1826.

"   *To the Revd. James Walker, M.A., Rendered necessary by his Serious Expostulation on the subject of Baptismal Regeneration,* Edinburgh, 1826.

Cross, F.L., *The Oxford Dictionary of the Christian Church,* 1963.

Cullmann, O., *Early Christian Worship,* 1962.

Cuming, G.J. & Baker O., eds. *Popular Belief and Practice.* (Studies in Church
History, vol. 8), Cambridge, 1972.

Curteis, G.H., *Bishop Selwyn of New Zealand, and of Lichfield. A sketch of his
Life and work, with some further gleanings from his Letters, Sermons
and Speeches,* 1889.

"   *In Memoriam. A sketch of the Life of The Right Reverend George Augustus Selwyn, late Bishop of Lichfield and formerly Bishop and Metropolitan of New Zealand,* Newcastle, n.d.

Darwin, Bernard, *The English Public School,* 1929.

Davison, John, *An Inquiry into the Origin and Intent of Primitive Sacrifice,*
1825.

Denison, George Anthony, *Notes on my Life, 1805-1878,* 1879.

Dictionary of National Biography, 64 vols.

"   *The Concise Dictionary,* 2 vols., 1967.

Doddridge, Philip, *The Rise and Progress of religion in the Soul . . . With a
Devout Meditation or Prayer added to each Chapter,* 1817.

Douglas, D., Gen. Ed. *The New International Dictionary of the Christian
Church,* Exeter, 1974.

Doyly, G & Mant, R., *The Holy Bible . . . with Notes, Explanatory and Practical For use of Families,* 3 vols., 1817.

Drummond, W., *Social Duties on Christian Principles,* 1831.

Edwards, David L., *Leaders of the Church of England, 1828-1944,* 1971.

Elliott-Binns, L.E., *The Early Evangelicals: A religious and social study,*
1953.

"   *Religion in the Victorian Era,* 1936.

"   *The Evangelical Movement in the English Church,* 1928.

Ewell, Walter A., ed. *The Evangelical Dictionary of Theology,* Basingstoke,
1985.

Erskine, Thomas, *The Brazen Serpent; or Life Coming through Death,* Edinburgh, 1831.

Evans, John H., *Church Militant: George Augustus Selwyn, Bishop of New
Zealand and Lichfield,* 1964.

Faber, George Stanley, *The Doctrine of Regeneration in the case of Infant Baptism. stated in reply to the Dean of Chichester's Apology Addressed to the Revd. G.S. Faber. B.D.*, 1816.

Fleetwood, W., *The Reasonable Communicant: Or, an Explanation of the Doctrine of the Sacrament of the Lord's Supper, in all its parts, from the Communion Service; In a discourse between a Minister and one of his Parishioners*, 26th edn., 1815.

Gaskell, Charles Milnes, *An Eton Boy; Being the Letters of James Milnes Gaskell from Eton and Oxford, 1820-1830*, 1939.

" ed. *Records of an Eton Schoolboy*, Privately Printed,1883.

Gilfillan, George, *Young's Night Thoughts: with life, critical dissertation and explanatory notes by the Revd. George Gilfillan*, Edinburgh, 1853.

Gray, Robert, *A Catechism in which the principal testimonies in proof of the divine authority of Christianity are briefly considered*, 1805.

Grubb, Kenneth G., ed., *Evangelicals Affirm in the Year of the Lambeth Conference*, 1948.

Haldane, Alexander, *Memoir of the Lives of Robert Haldane of Airthrey and of his brother, James Alexander Haldane*, Edinburgh, 1852.

Halevy, Elie, *England in 1815*, 1924.

Hall, Robert, *The Works of Robert Hall,. A.M.* (Published under the superintendence of Olinthus Gregory), 6 vols., 1837.

Hallam, Arthur Henry, *Remains in Verse and Prose of Arthur Henry Hallam*, 1869.

Hamilton, Sir Edward W., *Mr. Gladstone: a Monograph*, 1898.

Hammond, J. L. and Hammond, Barbara, *Lord Shaftesbury*, 1923.

Harford, George & Stevenson, Morley, eds. *The Prayer Book Dictionary*, n.d.

Hart, A.Tindal, *The Curate's Lot: The story of the unbeneficed English Clergy*, 1970.

Hart A. Tindal & Carpenter, Edward. *The Nineteenth Century Country Parson, (Circa. 1832-1900)*, Shrewsbury 1954.

Heber, Reginald, Sermons, 2 vols., 1829.

Hennell, Michael, *Evangelicalism and Worldliness: 1770-1870. In Popular Belief and Practice*: (Studies in Church History, vol. 8.) Cambridge 1972.

" *John Venn and the Clapham Sect*, 1958.

" *Sons of the Prophets: Evangelical Leaders of the Victorian Church*, 1979.

Henriques, Ursula , *Religious Toleration in England, 1787-1833*, 1961.

Herbert, George, *The Country Parson*, 1916.

Hodder, Edwin, *The Life and Work of the Seventh Earl of Shaftesbury, K.G.*, 3 vols., 1887.

Hodgson, Edwin, *Life of Beilby Porteus*, 2nd ed., 1811.

Hooker, Richard, *Laws of Ecclesiastical Politiy* (1 vol., 1676), 3 vols., 1836.

How, F.D., *Six Great Schoolmasters: Hawtrey, Moberly; Kennedy: Vaughan: Temple: Bradley*. 1904.

Jagger, Peter J., *Clouded Witness: Initiation in the Church of England in the Mid-Victorian Period. 1850-1875, Pennsylvania*, 1982.

" ed. *Gladstone, Politics and Religion: A Collection of Founder's Day Lectures delivered at St. Deiniol's Library, Hawarden, 1967-83*, 1985.

Jeremias, Joachim, *Infant Baptism in the First Four Centuries*, 1960
" *The origins of Infant Baptism*, 1963.

Jolly, Alexander, *A Friendly Address on Baptismal Regeneration*. 1st. edn., 1826; reprinted, 1842.

Jones, M.G., *Hannah More*, Cambridge, 1952.

Jones, Cheslyn, Wainwright, Geoffrey, Yarnold, Edward, eds., *The Study of Spirituality*, 1986.

Keble, John, *The Christian Year*, 1827.

Kempis, Thomas à, *Imitation of Christ*.

Kingsley, F., *Charles Kingsley: His letters and memories of his life*, 1908.

Knight, William, *Memoir of Henry Venn B.D.. Prebendary of St.Paul's and Honorary Secretary of the Church Missionary Society*, 1882.

Lathbury, D.C., *Mr Gladstone*, Oxford, 1907.

Laurence, Richard, *Lay-Baptism Invalid: An Essay to prove that such Baptism is Null and Void, when administered in opposition to the Divine Right of the Apostolical Succession*, 1710.

" *The Second Part of Lay-Baptism Invalid*, 1713.

" *A Supplement to the first and second Parts of Lay-Baptism Invalid*, 1714.

" *Dissenters and other Unauthorised Baptisms null and void*, 1712.

" *The Doctrine of the Church of England upon the Efficacy of Baptism vindicated from Misrepresentations*, Oxford, 1816.

Law, William, *A serious call to a Devout and Holy Life*. 1824.

Liddon, Henry Parry, *Life of Edward Bouverie Pusey, Doctor of Divinity, Canon of Christ Church: Regius Professor of Hebrew in the University of Oxford*, 4 vols., 4th edn. 1894-1898.

McClain, Frank Mauldin, *Maurice: man and moralist, 1805-1872*, 1972.

Mack, Edward C., *Public Schools and British Opinion 1780-1860: An exami-*

  nation of the relationship between contemporary ideas and the evol-
  ution of an English Institution, 1938.
Magnus, Philip, *Gladstone: A biography*, 1st edn. 1954.
Mant, Richard, *An appeal to the Gospel*, (Bampton Lectures) 1812.
  "   *Two tracts intended to convey correct notions of regeneration and
         conversion according to the sense of Holy Scripture, and of the
         Church of England*, 1817.
  '   *The Clergyman's Obligations Considered*, Oxford, 1830.
Mathieson, W.L., *English Church Reform 1815-1840*, 1923.
Matthew, H.C.G., *Gladstone 1809-1874*, Oxford, 1986.
Maurice, Frederick, *The Life of Frederick Denison Maurice: Chiefly told in his
         own letters; ed. by his son Frederick Maurice*, 2 vols., 1884.
Meacham, Standish, *Lord Bishop: The Life of Samuel Wilberforce 1805-1873*,
         Cambridge, Massachusetts. 1970.
Meek, Robert, *Reasons for Attachment and Conformity to the Church of Eng-
         land*, 1831.
Molesworth John, *An Answer to. . . Primitive Sacrifice*, 1826.
Moorman, John R.H., *A History of the Church in England*, 1976.
Morley, John, *The life of William Ewart Gladstone*, 3 vols., 1903.

Newman, John Henry, *Apologia pro vita sua: Being a History of his religious
         opinions*, 1890.
Newsome, David, *Godliness & good learning: Four studies on a Victorian
         ideal*, 1961.
  "   *The Parting of Friends: A study of the Wilberforces and Henry Man-
         ning*, 1966.
Norman, E.R., *Anti-Catholicism in Victorian England*, 1968.

Ollard, S. L., et al., *A Dictionary of English Church History*, 1948.
Ornsby, Robert, *Memoirs of James Robert Hope-Scott of Abbotsford, D.C.L..
         Q.C.. Late fellow of Merton College, Oxford: With Selections from
         His Correspondence*, 2 vols., 1884.
Overton, J.H. & Wordsworth, Elizabeth, *Christopher Wordsworth, Bishop of
         Lincoln (1807-1885)*, 1888.
Overton, J.H.,*The English Church in the Nineteenth Century (1800-1833)*,
         1894.

Paley William, *Natural Theology*, 1825.
Parker, Vanessa, *The English House in the Nineteenth Century*, Truro, 1970.
Paul, Herbert Woodfield, *The Life of William Ewart Gladstone*, 1901.
Pearson, John, *An Exposition of the Creed*, 2 vols., Oxford, 1820.
Perkin, Harold, *The Origins of Modern English Society, 1780-1580*, 1969.

Pollard, Arthur & Hennell Michael, eds., *Charles Simeon (1759-1836): Essays written in commemoration of his bi-centenary by members of the Evangelical Fellowship for Theological Literature*, 1964.

Porteous, Beilby, *Life of Secker*, 1797

Pott, Joseph Holden, *Observations on some controversies respecting baptism.* 1816.

Prothero, Rowland E. & Bradley G.G., T*he life and correspondence of Arthur Penrhyn Stanley, D.D. late Dean of Westminster*, 2 vols. 1893.

Reid Wemyss, ed., *The life of William Ewart Gladstone*, 1899.

Reynolds, J.S., *The Evangelicals at Oxford 1735-1871: a record of an unchronicled movement*, Oxford, 1953.

Richardson, Alan & Bowden, John, eds., *A New Dictionary of Christian Theology*, 1983.

Roberts, William, *The Portraiture of a Christian Gentleman*, 1831.

Russell, George W.E., *The household of faith: Portraits and Essays*, 1902.
"   *Mr Gladstone's Religious Development: A paper read in Christ Church May 5, 1899*, 2nd edn., 1899.
"   *The Right Honourable William Ewart Gladstone*, 1891.
"   *A short history of the Evangelical Movement*, 1915.

Scott, W.M.F. *"Assurance"*, contribution in, *Evangelicals Affirm in the year of the Lambeth Conference (1948)*,   1948.

Sealey, M., *The Later Evangelical Fathers*, 1879.

Shannon, Richard, *Gladstone. Vol. 1, 1809-1865*, 1982.

Sherwood, Mrs. *The lady of the Manor: Being a series of conversations on the subject of Confirmation, intended for the use of the middle and higher ranks of young females*, Wellington, Salop, 1823.

Smith, Alan, *The established church and Popular religion , 1750-1850*,   1971.

Smith, N.C., ed., *Letters of Sydney Smith*, 1953.

Smyth, Charles, S*imeon & Church Order: a study of the origins of the Evangelical Revival in Cambridge in the eighteenth century*, Cambridge, 1940.

Soloway, Richard Allen, *Prelates and People: Ecclesiastical Social Thought in England 1783-1852*, 1969.

Somervell, D.C., *English thought in the nineteenth century*, 1929.

Stock, Eugene, *The history of the Church Missionary Society: Its environment, its men and its women,* 6 vols., 1899-1916.

Storr, Vernon F., T*he development of English theology in the nineteenth century 1800-1860*, 1913.

Sumner, John Bird, S*ermons on the Principal Festivals of the Christian Church*

to which are added Three Sermons on Good Friday, 1828.
"   *Apostolic Preaching considered in: An examination of St Paul's Epistles,* 1826.
Sumner, G.H., *Life of Bishop C.R. Sumner,* 1876.
Surtees, Virginia, *A Beckford Inheritance: The Lady Lincoln Scandal,* Salisbury, 1977.
Symondson, Anthony, ed., T*he Victorian crisis of faiths: six lectures,* 1970

Taylor, Jeremy, T*he Rule and Exercises of Holy Living,* 1828.
Thackeray, Francis St John, *Memoir of Edward Craven Hawtrey D.D., Headmaster and afterwards Provost of Eton,* 1896.
Thompson, David M., ed., N*onconformity in the nineteenth century,* 1972
Thompson, F.M.L., *English landed society in the nineteenth century,* 1963.
Thomson, David, *England in the nineteenth century 1815-1914,* 1950.
Tomline, George, *A Refutation of Calvinism,* 1811.
"   *Elements of Christian Theology,* 2 vols., (lst edition 1799),   1843.
Toon, Peter, *Evangelical Theology, 1833-1856: a response to Tractarianism,* 1979.
Tucker, H.W., *Memoir of the life and Episcopate of George Augustus Selwyn, D.D. Bishop of New Zealand, 1841-1869, Bishop of Lichfield, 1867-1878,* 2 vols., 1879.
Tucker, William Hill,   *Eton of Old: 1812-22,*   1892.

Voll, Dieter, *Catholic Evangelicalism: The acceptance of evangelical traditions by the Oxford Movement during the second half of the nineteenth century,* 1963.

Wakefield, Gordon S. ed., *A Dictionary of Christian Spirituality,* 1983.
Waldo, Peter, *An essay on the Holy Sacrament of the Lord's Supper* 15th edn., 1812.
Walker, James, *The Gospel Commission, its import, its obligations and its influence in the Commencement and conduct of the Christian Life. Considered in a Sermon preached in St John's Episcopal Chapel . . . June 22, 1825,* Edinburgh, 1826.
"   *A Serious Expostulation with the Revd. Edward Craig, M.A., in reference to the Doctrine by him falsely attributed (in a remonstrance addressed) to the Revd. James Walker* . . . Edinburgh, 1826.
Walker, William, *The Life of the Right Reverend Alexander Jolly, D.D. Bishop of Moray,* Edinburgh, 1878.
Wall, W., *A Conference between Two Men that had doubts about infant Baptism,* 10th edn., 1812.
Walvin, James, *England, Slaves and Freedom, 1776-1838,* 1986.

Ward, A,W. & Waller A.R., eds., *The Cambridge History of English Literature*, 15 vols., Cambridge, 1907-1927.

Ward, W.R., *Victorian Oxford*, 1965.

Ward, Wilfred, *The Life of John Henry Cardinal Newnan: Based on his private journals and correspondence*, 2 vols., 1912.

Warren, Max, *Strange Victory; A study of the Holy Communion Service*, 1946.

Warton, John, D.D., ed. by his Sons, *Death-Bed scenes and Pastoral Conversations*, 2 vols., 1826-27; vol. 3. 1828.

Waterland, Daniel, *Regeneration stated and explained according to Scripture and Antiquity*, Works, vol. iv, (Works 10 vols.), Oxford, 1823.

Wilberforce, Robert Isaac & Wilberforce, Samuel, *The Life of William Wilberforce*, 5 vols., 1839.

Wilberforce, Samuel, *Life of William Wilberforce*, 1868.

Wilberforce, William, *A Practical view of the Prevailing Religious System of Professed Christians in the Higher and Middle Classes in this country contrasted with real Christianity*, 1826

Wilks, S.C., *The Right Reverend John M. Turner. D.D. late Lord Bishop of Calcutta*, 1832.

Williamson, David, *Gladstone: The Man. A Non-Political Biography*, 2nd. ed., 1898.

Wilson. Daniel, *The Divine Authority and Perpetual Obligations of the Lord's Day asserted in seven sermons*, 1831.

Wilson, (Thomas), Bishop of Sodor and Man, *A short and plain Introduction for the better understanding of the Lord's Supper, with the Necessary Preparation Required: for the Benefit of Young Communicants, and of such as have not considered this Holy Ordinance*, 1814.

Wordsworth, Charles, *Annals of my Early Life. 1806-1846*, 1891.

Yates, T.E., *Venn and Victorian Bishops Abroad: The missionary policies of Henry Venn and their repercussions upon the Anglican Episcopate of the Colonial Period, 1841-1872*, Uppsala, Sweden, 1978.

Young, Edward, *Young's Night Thoughts: with life, critical dissertation and explanatory notes by the Revd. George Gilfillan*, Edinburgh, 1853.

(ii) ARTICLES

Foot, M.R.D., "Morley's Gladstone: A Reappraisal." *Bulletin of John Rylands Library*, vol. 51, pp. 368- 80., 1968-9.

Hempton, D.N., "Evangelicalism and Eschatology", *Journal of Eccesiastical History* , vol. 31, No. 2. pp.179-94, April, 1980.

Ramm, Agatha, "Gladstone's Religion," *The Historical Journal,* 28,2 (1985), pp. 327 - 40.

Smyth, Charles, "The Evangelical Movement in Perspective," *The Cambridge Historical Journal,* vol., vii., No. 2, pp.160-74, 1942.

Zamick, M., (ed. & intro.), Unpublished Letters of Arthur Henry Hallam from Eton. Now in the John Rylands Library, *Bulletin of The John Rylands Library,* vol. 18, pp. 197-248, 1934.

NAME INDEX

Acland, A.H.D., 134

Acland, Sir Thomas, 92

Acland, Sir Thomas, 133, 134, 198

Andrewes, Lancelot, Bishop of Winchester, 177

Anstice, Professor Joseph, 129, 133, 134, 165, 194, 213-14, 216

Aristotle, 146, 147

Arnold, Dr. Thomas, 186-7, 197

Ashley-Cooper, Francis, 72

Augustine, St, 101, 116, 139, 145, 146, 147, 197

Ballantyne, J., 196

Baring, Charles Thomas, Bishop of Durham, 160-1, 162

Baron, Dr., 70

Barrow, Dr. Isaac, 112-13, 117, 144, 162, 181, 186

Belshaw, T., 196

Benson, A.C., 83

Berthomier, S., 97

Bethell, Rev . George, 65, 67

Bethune, Divie, 8

Beverley, R.M., 197

Bickersteth, Edward, Vice-Provost of Eton, 86, 142, 178

Biscoe, R., 226

Blackburn, Rev. John, 25, 26

Blackstone, Frederick, 185

Blair, Rev. Hugh, 66, 67, 74, 75

Blomfield, Charles J., Bishop of London, 163

Blunt, Rev . Henry, 241

Bowstead, Rev. T. S., 29

Bradford, Samuel, Bishop of Rochester, 117

Briggs, 67

Bristow, Amelia, 75

Buchan, Margaret, 22

Buchanan, 82

Buckley, H.W., 184

Buddicom, Rev. R. P., 28-9, 66

Bugg, George, 119

Bulteel, Rev. H.B., 50, 127, 128 129, 133, 134, 135, 163, 186

Burgess, Thomas, Bishop of Salisbury, 120

Burnet, Gilbert, Bishop of Salisbury, 128, 145-6, 147, 153

Burrows, Robert, 186

Burton, Edward, 185

Butler, Joseph, Bishop of Durham, 94, 132, 145, 146-8, 151, 187, 195, 196, 197

Butler, Rev. Dr. Perry, 33, 93, 111, 115, 118, 175, 224, 226-7, 261

Canning, Charles, 88, 90, 194

Canning, George, 16, 72-3, 78, 89, 197, 247

Carruthers, John, 98

Chalmers, Rev. Dr. Thomas, 14, 23, 24, 27, 74, 186

Champnes, Rev. T. W., 67, 84

Charrier, Rev. P., 25

Checkland, Sydney, 21, 33, 65, 99, 261

Childer, Charles, 133, 204, 254

Chrysostom, St. John, 48

Cicero, 106, 107

Clerke, Rev. Charles, 185

Close, Rev. Dr. Francis, 186

Cole, Francis, 133

210-12, 214-19, 221-3, 227-33,
235, 244, 246-7, 250, 251, 253,
254, 256, 262, 265
Gladstone, John Neilson, brother of
W.E.G., 31, 33, 67, 86, 119, 172,
184, 194, 223-4, 226, 230, 237,
243, 251
Gladstone, Robertson, brother of
W.E.G., 17, 31, 33, 39, 57, 86,
175, 191, 194, 200, 219, 221-2,
251
Gladstone, (Sir) Thomas, brother of
W.E.G., 18, 19, 21, 31-3, 40, 57,
58, 67, 71, 81, 86-7, 100-1, 106,
127, 160, 183, 191, 199-200, 204,
206, 207, 209-12, 214, 215-24,
228-29, 235, 259

Gladstone, William Ewart.

*This entry is not fully inclusive and
should be used in consultation with
other relevant entries in both the
Name and Subject Indices and also
the Bibliography and Notes.*

Academic,
ambitions, 199
success, 69-70, 175, 199-200
work, 33, 190, 199-201
Accounts,
balancing of, 193
book, 108, 193
Algebra, 117, 120
Altar, 250
Ambitions, 199, 241, 244
Anglican Divines, 48, 115, 139-
41, 177
Anne Mackenzie Gladstone, sister,
33-45
correspondence with, 34, 35, 37,

38, 39-40, 42, 105, 191, 206
death of, 40, 41, 42, 43-4, 49-50,
54, 124
discussions with, 115, 116, 118
funeral of, 40-1
godmother, his, 35
influence, on W.E.G, 21, 33, 45,
118, 141, 157
mentor, his, 36
relationship with, 47-8, 51
saint, 41, 44, 168
unworthy, W. E. G. ' s, 43
Annotations, his, 154-5, 182, 188
Apostolic Succession, 154
Articles, Thirty-nine, of Religion, 83,
96, 106, 128, 137-8, 153
Assurance, lack of, 12, 44
Autobiographica, 5, 35, 94, 111, 126,
261

Baptism, 38, 41, 48, 82, 85, 112-16,
147, 154, 176-8, 238-9, 250
adult, 141
Formularies, 141, 177
Gladstone's, 5
infant, 114
reading on, 177-8
regeneration, 39, 41, 47, 48-9, 64,
103, 112, 114-15, 116-17, 119,
127, 129-30, 132, 139-42, 176-7
salvation and, 176
writings, W. E. G.' s, on, 178, 197
Bible,
academic study of, 64-5, 82, 164
authority of, 46, 63, 117, 128, 137,
141, 222
corporate reading of, 165
daily reading of, 61, 63-4, 165
God' s word, 63-4, 164, 167
Greek Testament, 63, 107, 108,
165
high view of, 23

liturgy, 80, 186
Mass, 80, 238
Papacy, 79, 237, 239, 240, 255
Romanism, his anti-, 239, 240-1

Sabbath,
  abuse of, 250-1
  churchgoing on, 183
  observance, 39, 59, 67-8, 181-3,
    241, 250-1
  reading on, 74, 181-2
  travel on, 69, 250-1
  use of, 33, 96-8, 123
Sacramentalist, 144
Sacraments, 112, 114-115, 117, 129,
  137, 142, 176-80, see also, Baptism, Eucharist, Holy Communion
Salvation, 41, 47, 82, 101, 130-1,
  176-7, 190, 228
Sanctification, need of, 41, 44, 62-3,
  144, 159, 171, 177
Satan, 43, 250-1
Schism, 239
Scrapbooks, 67, 98-9
"Scripture Oppositions," 166
Searching, period of, 105-21
"Secreta Eucharistica," 143, 180
"Selections," 159
Self, analysis, 171
  condemnation, 69, 94, 168, 171,
    173
  deception, 233
  examination, 12, 32, 41, 42, 63,
    134, 168-76, 212
Sermons,
  God speaks through, 65
  heard, 38-9, 65, 108, 110-13, 121,
    184-6, 238, 240
  read/reading, 11, 38-9, 59, 65-6,
    109, 116, 182, 186-7
Servants, 194-5
Sex, 63, 75, 85, 93, 160, 168, 172,

173, 265
Sickness, 21
Sin, 41, 52, 61-2, 168-76, 223, 262
  Anne's influence, 172-3
  besetting, 41, 170, 172, 173, 174
  depravity, total, 42, 168, 170, 173
  fighting against, 102
  forgiveness of, 168-70, 268
  guilt, 169, 174
  obsession with, 168
  passion, 172
  reading on, 168
  repentance, 168-70
  sense of, 160, 167, 168
  sex, 168, 172
  sinfulness, his, 12, 43, 157
  sorrow for, 159
  temptation, confused with, 169
Slavery, Slaves, 75-6, 198-9, 259
  Anti-Slavery Society, 249, 255
  Christian instruction of, 256
  education of, 255-6
  Gladstone denounced, on, 249, 255
Sloth, 42, 172
Social life, 86-100
  backgammon, 86, 192
  balls, 86, 174, 243
  bathing, 86, 88, 108, 192, 194
  betting, 88, 108, 192, 194
  billiards, 86
  bowls, 86
  cards, 86, 191, 192
  chess, 86, 192
  cricket, 86, 192
  dancing, 86
  draughts, 86, 192
  fishing, 192
  gymnastics, 107
  musical concerts, 86, 117, 243
  opera, 243
  riding, 192
  shooting, 192

SUBJECT INDEX

Newspapers, 121, 242-3, 254
New York, 8
Nobility, 18
Notebooks, 13-14, 36, 84, 143,
    165-6, 171, 195
Nottingham Journal, 249
Nuneham, 121

Orders, taking, 100
Ordination, 34-5, 100-3, 105-21, 203-
    36
Oriel, 134-5
Oxford Benevolent Society, 193
Oxford Movement, 49, 68, 137, 149,
    152, 184-5
Oxford University, 40, 111, 123, 157-
    201, 216
    social advantages of, 18
    university sermon, 127

Pain, 10
Palm Sunday, 239
Papacy, 237, 255
Paris, 241
Parliament, 15, 78, 91, 133, 155, 226-
    7, 235-6, 244-7, 258-9
Peasantry, 252
Pews, 26-28, 195
Philanthropy, 17, 19-20, 21, 22, 23-4,
    27
Piano, 121
Piety, 5, 10, 15, 37
Pilgrims' Progress, 13
Poetry, 59, 68, 76, 78
Political ignorance, of people, 254
Politics, 3, 16, 18, 24, 91, 95, 107,
    175, 198, 203-236
Poor, 24, 26, 109, 252, 254
Pope, 239-40
Popery, 239-41
Pornographic literature, 173,
Portsmouth Naval College, 31

Prayer, 2-3, 6-7, 9, 10, 13-14, 19, 20,
    45, 54, 60-1, 72, 95, 113, 160,
    161-4
Preachers, 8, 9, 38-9, 66
Preaching, 8, 46, 61, 65-8,
    evangelical, 25, 131
    poor, 25
Predestination, 67, 96, 125, 127-9,
    135
Presbyterianism, 3, 15
Press, 254
Property, 16, 25
Prosperity, 2
Prostitutes, 119, 174, 195
Protestant Church, 238
Protestantism, 150
Providence, 2-3, 5, 7-8, 13-14, 18-19,
    23, 32, 71, 203-36, 254, 258-9
Psalter, 60, 167, 168-9
Psychological analysis, 34, 51
Public Houses, 253
Public life, 8, 18

Quarterly Review, 47, 75-6, 81, 106,
    116-17, 139

Record, 120, 121
Red Club, 249, 251-2, 255, 256
Redeemed, The, 8
Redeemer's Cause, 8
Reformation of Juvenile Offenders,
    22
Reform Bill, 175, 226-9, 230-1, 235,
    242-3, 246, 254-5, 256
Regeneration, *see*, Baptism
Relaxation, 19
Religious instruction, 22
Religious verse, *see*, Verse
Repentance, 39, 43, 62, 168-70
Revival, religious, 1, 9
Rheumatic fever, 39
Rivingtons, 7

MIDNIGHT
MURDERS

Katherine John

MIDNIGHT MURDERS
First published as *Six Feet Under* by Hodder
Headline 1995
This edition revised and updated by the author
Copyright © 2006 Katherine John
published by Accent Press 2006

ISBN 1905170270

The right of Katherine John to be identified
as the author of this work has been
asserted by her in accordance with the Copyright,
Designs and Patents Act 1988

Printed and bound in the UK
By Cox and Wyman Ltd, Reading, UK

Cover design by Emma Barnes

The publisher acknowledges the financial support
of the Welsh Books Council

FOR

RALPH SPENCER WATKINS

PROLOGUE

The clouds hid the moon. The only light in the garden came from the muted glow of the street lamps above and outside the high walls that enclosed the grounds. Their rays cast an eerie, pyrotechnical tinge on the tips of the Victorian iron spears that crowned the brickwork. A cool night breeze rustled the spring buds on the trees, and rattled the skeletons of the dead leaves deep in the undergrowth that had escaped the gardener's rake.

Buildings loomed, a massive Gothic silhouette surrounded by rectangular blocks of ebony; black cut-outs in a world of grey shadows. Occasionally, a pencil-thin line of light glimmered from beneath a blind and at the end of long rows of gleaming blank panes, squares of soft amber shone in kitchens, bathrooms and ward offices, testimony to those who had to work through the hours of darkness.

A phantom rippled through the garden. Softly, stealthily, it floated within the shadows that fell from the trees and the encircling wall. Occasionally it paused, but always close to a tree, or in the shelter of bushes that masked its presence. Its spine was curved into a hunchback. The shade it cast, malformed, a swollen mass crowning gangly legs. It continued to drift, bush to bush, tree to tree and when it was motionless, there was a sense of ears and senses strained to their utmost.

A clock struck, its chimes crashing raucously, disturbing the rustles of field mice and voles. A barn owl swooped low, screeching when it missed its prey. A dog barked somewhere on the suburban estate outside the wall, that sprawled on what had, until recently, been hospital land.

1

A car engine roared on the road outside the wall followed by the siren of a police car. The phantom crouched in the undergrowth, waiting for the clamour to die. Later – much later – it inched forward, faltering on the outskirts of a patch of gleaming lawn. A low hillock of soil loomed to the left. In front of it, the lip of a puddle, blacker than any ink, wavered as wind blown trees swayed above it.

Hesitation, caution, then a quick scurrying movement. The hunchback stood poised. It leaned forward, bent double, and was hunchback no longer. It stood tall and broad on the skyline. The stencil of a shovel protruded from the mound of earth. The phantom stooped, took it, and began to transfer the earth from the hill into the pit, with steady, rhythmic movements.

Silver light bathed the scene in frigid wintry beauty when the moon edged out from behind soft, grey billowing clouds. The phantom worked faster, pausing only to pass its left arm across its brow. The mound began to diminish at the right-hand edge, and still the figure worked. Ever alert, ever watchful. Pausing between each load, listening and waiting.

The bottom of the pit was dark, damp, and colder than ice.

The air stank with the mouldy reek of rot and decay. A figure bound rigidly in a sheet, resembling more giant chrysalis than human, stared relentlessly upwards. Only its eyes remained within control. It was a strain to keep them unblinking and open, gazing at the oblong of textured blue night sky, misted by clouds and punctured by the pinpricks of a million tiny stars. In the left-hand corner shone a brilliant segment of silver light. Pitted and scarred it had to be the moon. To the left Orion shone

2

down, recognised from schooldays and the one astronomy lesson that had graced the entire geography course.

Cold – and something else – paralysed. No matter how strenuously the brain willed limbs to move, they remained limp and leaden; log-like appendages to a lifeless body where only the mind roamed free, painfully and acutely alive. All strength and power that remained was focused, concentrated desperately, but in vain. The paralysis that reigned supreme denied the body even the dubious comfort of shivering.

The mind worked feverishly as the eyes stared upwards, collecting thoughts, arranging them in a logical, coherent order. The last memory was of walking from the consulting room to the gate. Feet sinking into fresh, glutinous tarmac; the smell had come too late to give warning. Newly laid, and softened by the spring sunshine, the sticky black substance had ruined brand new green leather shoes. But, as well as anger over the spoiled shoes, there had been exhilaration.

The final appointment had come and gone. The gate symbolised freedom. The walk ahead was towards liberty and independence. The depression that had resulted in incarceration, if not totally cured, could be dealt with while life was lived in the outside world.

Walking towards the gate – a shout – a cry… iron-tinged, icy darkness. Confinement by something other than paralysis and constricting cloth. Blazes of light, pinpricks that hurt overly sensitive skin, darkness… more darkness… then sky. Exquisitely beautiful, crystal-clear night sky.

A shower of earth fell, dry, dusty, powdery, rattling against the taut, drawn cloth. The sound triggered a single, devastating flash of realisation – and panic. Another shower came. There was a fierce struggle to force open

3

glued lips, to formulate a scream; but the lips, gummed tightly shut, refused to obey, and no sound was born in the throat, not even a whimper.

The frantic effort, conceived in the mind, withered and died. Terror crawled, dry, insidious, and foul-tasting. Snakes of fear slithered from the spine, saturated with the certainty of impending death.

This pit had to be *somewhere*! Perhaps people were close by. People who couldn't see the hole, but would hear a cry.

Force, concentration – skin ripping noisily, agonisingly, from raw lips. The pain diminished with the realisation that the body had finally succeeded. The mouth opened. A large damp clod fell into it, weighing heavy on the tongue. There was no more thought of sounds, only a frenzied struggle to draw breath. Tongue and teeth heaving to spit out chunks of earth. Lungs burning, bursting, with the need for air. But dirt lay crushing, choking, against the back of the throat.

Had to remain calm – had to fight – stay calm – live. Hysteria subsided as air inflated scorching lungs: air that travelled in through the dirt beginning to pack the nostrils. Another shower of fine dust was followed by yet more moisture-laden clods, they blanketed one eye, stinging, searing – filled the nose – dry – suffocating…

Someone would come. They had to. If only they would hurry. There was no air, no breath… couldn't breathe… couldn't…

Then a silhouette. Tall, wide, wielding a spade, it blocked out the light and the stars. Blackness hovered in the pit, darker than any night; its depths wavering with a rich red glow, smouldering with an intensity that scoured ineffective lungs.

4

The figure moved back. Another shower followed – and another – and another –

For the first time since that walk along the newly tarmacked path, there came warmth. Warmth and comfort. There was no more fight for air – for anything. Only a quiet drifting. Floating on a soft grey cloud of down that gently caressed and enveloped. Carrying the whole body downwards into deep, relaxing sleep.

The spade once again stood upright in the earth. The mound had lessened but not so much that a careless glance would notice, particularly the glance of a disinterested trainee. A few scuffs of the shoe, a few pats to loosen and spread the drier topsoil over what was left of the mound. One more studied glance down into the pit. There was only darkness, stillness and silence. No gleam of white betrayed the sheet that lay hidden beneath the earth.

The phantom flowed back towards the trees. A triangle of light shone briefly across the lawn, dimming when the door that had been opened closed in a room in the nearest block. Its glow had burned only for an instant, but it had been long enough to outline the figure of a woman. A woman who stood stiff and straight, hands planted on the glass pane before her, one on either side of her head. The phantom in the garden looked up, and saw.

As did the woman. And even when the light faded behind her, the white lace nightgown could still be seen by someone who knew she was there.

An unseen hand pulled down the blind. It was easy to imagine the nurse gently leading the protesting patient back to bed. A patient who had seen – how much? All? Enough to talk? Enough to – the phantom smiled as it once again retreated into the shadows. Who would believe the woman? Or any other patient who reported seeing strange happenings in the night.

Psychiatric nurses and doctors were obliged to listen to their patients. They were paid to. But sooner or later they learned to ignore the inmates. Patients who resided in Compton Castle frequently had difficulty in distinguishing between reality and fantasy.

Even if that particular woman hadn't claimed to have seen visions and apparitions before, there was always a first time. After all, she was mad. And who'd believe anything that a mad woman had to say?

CHAPTER ONE

Peter Collins thumped his horn impatiently at an old man who was dithering between the left and right turns at the entrance to the hospital visitors' car park. Hearing the horn, the elderly man panicked, pressed his foot down too hard on the clutch and stalled his car. Cursing loudly, Peter accelerated swiftly. Mounting the kerb, he drove across a neatly trimmed bank of lawn and executed a fast, furious, perfect three-point turn, which landed him in prime position to make a quick getaway once visiting was over.

Picking up two plastic carrier bags from the passenger seat of his car, he slammed the door, locked it and stormed off towards the main building, noting with grim satisfaction the queue of irate motorists building up behind the old man. Short tempered at the best of times, Peter was seething and not only because of the driver. Despite his hatred of the place, here he was visiting Compton Castle Psychiatric Hospital – yet again.

He loathed hospitals, sickness – anything that reminded him of his own mortality and potential weakness. And as he'd discovered over the past few weeks, he had a particularly strong aversion to psychiatric wards; but a nagging sense of guilt and loyalty to his long time colleague and friend, Trevor Joseph, drove him to this place whenever his free time coincided with visiting hours.

He'd been dragging himself to and from hospitals for a long time – too bloody long. He jumped over a low wall to take advantage of a short-cut across the lawns. He'd sat beside Trevor's bed while Trevor had hovered close to death during three long weeks in the intensive care ward.

He'd visited daily while Trevor had spent four and a half months on the Neuro ward in the general hospital with dedicated nurses willing and able to care for his every whim, let alone need. And despite regular visits from a *very* shapely, blonde physiotherapist, and a pretty brunette psychologist, Trevor had still failed to pull himself sufficiently together to avoid a transfer from the General to what their superior in the force, Bill Mulcahy graphically, if tactlessly, referring to as the 'The Funny Farm.'

Granted, it wasn't Trevor's fault that he'd had his head hammered to a pulp by a psychopathic serial killer, but to play the Devil's Advocate, if it had been him, not Trevor who'd faced the murderer, he was confident that he would have had the sense to handle himself differently. And fractures, even skull fractures, and infected wrist fractures, heal given time and expert medical care and Trevor'd had more than enough of both. Most injuries could be overcome if the person concerned made a determined effort to pull themselves together. Which in Peter's opinion, Trevor wasn't.

He passed the gardener and a boy who were planting a newly dug flowerbed with rose bushes. The lawn around the bed was thick with soil, and he remembered a crumbling stone cupid that had stood there when he had first visited Trevor in the Castle – was it really only three weeks ago?

He wondered where the cupid was now. It was the sort of thing he wouldn't have minded putting in his garden, if he'd had one. Home, when he went there, was a flat in a crumbling Edwardian terrace next to the sea.

'If it isn't my favourite man. Sergeant Collins, how lovely to see you.' Jean Marshall, the sister in charge of Trevor's ward, greeted Peter in the hearty voice she used to address everyone in the hospital – patient, visitor and doctor. It was a voice that reminded Peter of knots, campfires and brisk girl guiders, and it invariably set his teeth on edge.

'How is he today?' he jerked his head towards the door of the private room Trevor occupied, courtesy of his status as injured policeman rather than clinically ill patient.

'Good.' Jean nudged his ribs and he caught a heady whiff of Estee Lauder. 'He went to Spencer's art class this morning.' She left the word "therapy" out before art. 'Perhaps he'll show you what he's done.' She frowned at his plastic bags. 'Is that a clanking I hear?'

'Non-alcoholic beer and crisps. Trevor needs decent nourishment to counteract the junk you feed him.'

'Just as long as it is non-alcoholic,' she warned.

'Do you want to check?' He gave her his most winning smile.

'And if I say yes?'

'I'll owe you one if you say no.'

'I'm still waiting for you to buy me that drink in the Green Monkey, you promised me the last time I turned a blind eye.'

'One day I'll surprise you.'

'Make sure you take the empties with you,' she murmured, before running after Vanessa Hammond who was wandering down the corridor in a scarlet negligee. Peter knew from past experience that Vanessa was apt to act out the oddest bedroom fantasies.

Jean was a smart, imposing woman. She'd once mentioned a son at university, so Peter put her age at roughly forty to forty-five, but she looked younger. Tall, well built, with a majestic figure, red hair and green eyes, Peter could not deny that she was attractive. And she'd

9

made it clear that her attractions were at his disposal. Divorced and frequently lonely for female company, he rarely turned down the kind of signal that Jean was transmitting, but something about her put him off. Possibly her efficient manner coupled with the hint of hospital antiseptic that invariably overpowered her perfume. Or, the overwhelming confidence she had in her power to attract, which took away any hint of chase or conquest.

Either way, he flirted mildly with her when she made overtures in his direction, but was careful never to go near the Green Monkey, the pub opposite Compton Castle, where the staff congregated in their off-duty hours, unless he knew she was working.

Turning his back on Jean, Peter pushed open the door to Trevor's room. To his dismay Trevor was sitting in exactly the same position he'd left him after visiting two days ago. In fact, if Jean hadn't mentioned that Trevor had gone to art that morning, he could have believed that Trevor had remained slumped in the chair for two days and nights. The beard growth certainly suggested it.

Trevor was painfully, almost skeletally thin, and was wearing the crumpled pair of once black, faded grey slacks he had worn every day since he'd been told to dress. His navy sweatshirt had unravelled at the cuffs and neck, and would have been rejected as a donation to a charity shop. Peter couldn't recall Trevor ever dressing so down-at-heel, even when they'd worked undercover in the down-and-outs and junkies' habitat of Jubilee Street.

'Brought you beer.' Peter dumped the carrier bags on Trevor's lap. 'It's cold. Straight from my fridge.'

'Thanks,' Trevor murmured mechanically.

'Open the bag,' Peter badgered. 'There are crisps in there too. Smoky bacon.'

10

Trevor fumbled with the top of the carrier bag.

'Not that one.' Peter snatched the bag irritably. 'That's your clean washing. I got my woman to do it for you.'

'Thanks.' Trevor didn't look up when Peter opened the wardrobe door and threw the bag on to the floor.

Peter took two of the four cans he'd thrown on to Trevor's lap. He ripped one open, and drank. 'Can you open yours, or do you want me to do it for you?'

'I can manage.'

'Can I watch?' Peter questioned caustically.

'Can you what?'

'For pity's sake man, I've come to visit. I've brought a goody bag… '

'Thank you,' even Trevor's voice sounded distant.

'It's not your bloody thanks I want, it's your companionship.'

'I'm sorry. I'm not feeling very sociable these days.'

'I can see that,' Peter retorted, before polishing off half of his can in one thirsty gulp. 'So, don't you want to know what's happening down at the station?'

'Not really.'

'Doesn't the thought of rejoining the drug squad in a week or two excite you?'

'No.' Trevor showed the first sign of animation Peter had seen since he'd been injured. He even ripped the ring pull back on his can. Perhaps the threat of work was what was needed to get him going.

'We're doing the clubs this month. Good beer, good whisky, sex-starved divorcees throwing themselves at any and every male in sight, music that'll deafen you, and all on expenses. What more could a man want?'

'A quiet life.' Trevor's gaze flickered towards a sketch pad that lay face down on the cabinet next to his

11

bed. Peter leaned over and before Trevor could stop him, picked it up.

'Florence Nightingale out there told me that you'd been to art.'

'That doesn't mean I want you to see that,' Trevor snapped.

It was too late. Peter had already peeled back the cover. He let out a long, low whistle as he studied a sketch of a woman with large sad eyes, and long hair that tumbled around her face.

'The girl of your dreams?' He tossed the book contemptuously on to the bed. 'Isn't it time you grew up and started looking at real life women who can kiss back?'

'Always got to reduce life to the lowest common denominator, haven't you?' Trevor retorted savagely.

Peter was elated, but was careful not to show it. After months of trying, he'd elicited a response. Maybe not the one he wanted, but a response nevertheless. 'And the lowest common denominator is the pub. How about I persuade the warden out there, to let you out long enough to enjoy a quick one with me.'

'No.'

There was a firmness in Trevor's refusal Peter hadn't detected since Trevor's incarceration in hospital.

'Everyone at the station sends their regards. Bill told me to tell you that he's saving the best jobs for when you come back.'

'I might not come back,' Trevor threatened.

'Haven't you heard? There's not enough jobs to go round for well-qualified, intelligent people, let alone ex-coppers who were stupid enough to get themselves mangled in the line of duty.

'Here, drink up.' Peter emptied his can. 'So what's new around here?'

12

'Not a lot.'

'I spoke to Harry Goldman about you.'

'Why?' Trevor demanded suspiciously. His opened can remained untouched in his hand.

'Because your brother and mother are stuck in Cornwall and haven't the time to come up every weekend. And, because they asked me to keep an eye on you. Whether you like it or not, doctors do not like assuming total responsibility for their patients. They like to discuss their charges with someone. Family, friends, and, unfortunately for you, in the absence of anyone better, me.'

'What did Goldman say?' For the first time since Peter had entered the room, Trevor raised his head, and met Peter's eye.

'That you're fit enough to go out. All you need is a push in the right direction.'

'And I suppose you volunteered to do the pushing.'

'You can't hide in here forever, with,' Peter jerked his thumb at the sketch pad, 'memories of what might have been.'

'I still get headaches. I'm weak...' Trevor repeated the catalogue of excuses he'd been reciting for months, but for Peter, they'd long lost any validity.

'When was the last time you left this room?' Peter went to the window and opened the curtains, flooding the gloomy cell with bright afternoon sunlight.

'You know I went to Spencer's art class this morning,' Trevor screwed his eyes against the light.

'Big deal, you walked down two corridors,' Peter mocked. 'Come on, you and me are going out, mate.'

'No.'

'Yes.' Peter looked at Trevor's worn carpet slippers, opened the wardrobe door and lifted out a pair of canvas trainers. 'Put them on.'

'No.'

'I'm not taking you to the pub, only a turn around the grounds. There's no one out there,' he lied, eyeing a procession of patients and visitors as they walked down the lawn.

'I can't stand sunlight.'

'Borrow these.' Peter pulled a pair of dark glasses from the top pocket of his blazer, pushed them on to Trevor's nose and yanked the door open. 'Either you walk out of here, or I carry you out,' he threatened. 'And given your present state of health, I could do it with one hand tied behind my back.'

Trevor stared at him for a moment. Peter thought he'd lost yet another battle, when Trevor slowly kicked off his slippers and reached for the trainers. However, Trevor's reaction was anything but positive. Lacking the energy to fight Peter's bullying tactics, Trevor had decided to take the easy way out and capitulate. After all, the man never stayed long. And when Peter left, he'd be able to return to his room, his chair, his sketch pad, and – most important of all, his "memories of what had never been" as Peter had so scornfully put it.

'One more step and you'll actually be somewhere other than this cell.' Peter laid a hand across Trevor's shoulders and propelled him out of the room.

'I need my stick,' Trevor cried as he staggered precariously on his right leg, fractured, healed, but weak from lack of exercise.

Peter took the cane from behind the door and thrust it into Trevor's hand. Much to his annoyance, he stepped out of Trevor's room only to find he'd pushed Trevor into

14

a physical altercation between Jean and the petite, sharp featured Vanessa, whom he chiefly remembered for her constantly changing hair colour. Today it was black, but it had been auburn on his previous visit and blonde before that.

Jean was lecturing Vanessa in the firm matronly voice she tended to employ whenever one of the patients was being difficult, which if his visits were anything to go by, was more often than not.

'You can't go outside until you've changed out of that negligee, Vanessa. If you walk down the ward with me I'll help you choose something… '

Vanessa slithered out of Jean's clutches. Before Jean could stop her, she pushed open the door to a narrow, shelved storeroom where a drugs trolley was being stocked by Lyn Sullivan, a stunning, six-foot, slim student nurse whom Peter lusted after and regretfully left alone on the premise that teenagers, even those heading for their twenties, were too young for him.

'Out of there, Vanessa,' Jean commanded.

'You can't order me around, bitch,' Vanessa retorted.

'No one is ordering you around, Vanessa.' Lyn clasped Vanessa's arm. 'We're concerned for you and we don't want you to get hurt.'

'You think I'm stupid' Vanessa peered into Lyn's face. 'You think I don't know about you and my Ian. You're all the same. Bitches!' Vanessa's eyes rolled in her head as her final words pitched high, ending in a screech. She flailed her arms wildly. Catching the edge of the trolley she flung it back against a shelf, forcing Lyn into a corner. Sweeping her hands over the trolley, she picked up and threw everything she could lay her hands on. Bottles and jars flew into the air, landed on the tiled floor and

15

shattered in a crescendo of splintering glass, pills and potions.

Lyn tried to duck past Vanessa and out through the door, but she wasn't quick enough. An enormous jar filled with small white pills thumped between her shoulder blades. She fell heavily, crying out in pain when she landed on the carpet of broken glass.

Laughing crazily, Vanessa grabbed a set of cast iron scales. Long since obsolete, they'd been relegated to the back corner of the shelves, but she found them. She waved them above Lyn's head. Peter and Jean both ran towards the cupboard and, like a bad comedy sketch, jammed alongside one another in the doorway. It was left to Trevor to crawl between their legs and offer a helping hand to Lyn. She grasped his fingers, but he gripped her wrist and heaved her forward, ignoring her cries as shards of glass sliced into her flesh through her thin uniform.

When Jean stepped back to allow Lyn through the doorway, Vanessa quietened. She stood for a moment in the midst of the wreckage, surveying the havoc she'd created. Peter seized the opportunity to make a move towards her.

'I know what I saw,' Vanessa whispered, staring at him.

'I don't doubt you do.' He reached out, preparing to take the scales from her.

'Come on, Vanessa,' Jean crooned, easing her way into the doorway. 'You're tired. You'll feel better after a lie down.'

'I don't want a lie down.' Vanessa lifted the scales higher. 'She's there I tell you. In the flowerbed. Planted in the garden like a tulip bulb. All of that earth on top of her. Shovel-full after shovel-full. She won't be able to move,' she assured Peter gravely. Her eyes grew rounder, the

16

whites more pronounced. 'Do you think he wanted her to grow into a people tree?' she burst into mirthless laughter. 'She's dead,' she said finally with a sudden eerie calm. 'She would be with all that earth on top of her. Dead as mutton. She's dead and not one of you cares enough to move her to the cemetery. That's where they put dead people. I know.' She lunged towards Peter and he succeeded in sliding one hand on to the scales. 'I wanted to put my Ian there, but they... ' she glared at Jean and Lyn, who'd been helped to her feet by Trevor, '... they stopped me. If I'd put him there,' she moved closer to Peter and he took advantage and laid a second hand on the scales. 'I'd have him where I'd want him. He'd still be mine because he'd have to stay there and wait for me to visit him with flowers, wouldn't he? He wouldn't be able to do anything else.'

She heaved her hands back, intending to hurl the scales at Jean, but Peter wrenched them from her hands.

'You're in league with those bitches.' Snatching the one remaining pill bottle from the trolley she flung it in his face. Holding on to the heavy scales Peter ducked, but not low enough. The bottle hit his cheek bone, splitting the skin.

'Ian's probably still with the whore, but not the whore I found him with,' Vanessa rambled. 'She wouldn't be pretty enough for him. Not after what I did to her... '

'Vanessa!' Peter commanded. 'Look at me.' Staring into her eyes, in an effort to hold her attention, he fumbled blindly for the shelf at his side and deposited the scales on them. As soon as his hands were free, he moved like lightening. Grasping Vanessa's wrists he hauled them behind her back. 'Where do you want her?' he asked Jean.

17

'Out of that damned dispensary for a start,' Jean said hollowly, sickened by the chaos Vanessa had wrought in the secure drug cupboard.

'You should have locked it.' Peter yanked Vanessa into the corridor.

'The lock jammed three months ago. When we asked for it to be repaired they put a padlock on the outside, which is a fat lot of good when you're working inside. I've complained every day for three months and got absolutely nowhere.'

'I phoned security, they're on their way. I've also asked for a couple of porters and an extra nurse,' Lyn whispered from the open door of the ward office. Trevor had helped her into a chair and she was sitting, dabbing ineffectually at the glass-studded cuts on her arms and legs with a handkerchief.

Jean studied her with a professional eye. 'Phone for an ambulance to take you to casualty in the General.'

'I'm fine,' Lyn sipped the water that Trevor had brought her from his room.

'No arguments, telephone now. I'll check how "fine" you are as soon as I've dealt with this. Can you keep a grip on Mrs Hammond, Sergeant Collins?'

'I'll manage.' Peter tightened his grip as Vanessa tried to kick his shins. It was an ineffectual gesture given that she was wearing slippers.

'I thought everyone was in the garden.' Lyn apologised.

'It appears everyone was, except us and this lady.' Peter gave Vanessa a crocodile smile.

Jean retrieved the key to the padlock from the debris on the floor and pushed the door to the drug cupboard over the carpet of broken glass. 'Talk about bolting horses and stable doors.'

18

'I'd rather not think what could have happened if any other patients had been here, or you hadn't.' Lyn handed the glass back to Trevor.

Peter sensed Vanessa becoming restless under his grip. He saw her staring at a security guard, two porters, and a male nurse who were making their way up the corridor towards them. Jean snapped the padlock shut.

'Bring Mrs Hammond into the treatment room please, Sergeant Collins,' Jean asked.

Peter pushed Vanessa inside. The male nurse joined them.

Jean continued to speak softly while the male nurse primed a syringe behind Vanessa's back. The moment the syringe was ready, she pulled up Vanessa's sleeve. Vanessa quietened within seconds and Jean had no difficulty in leading her out of the room into a four bedded ward.

'Here we are, Vanessa, a nice clean bed. All we have to do is draw the curtains and you can take a nap,' there was more than a hint of irony in Jean's voice.

'I don't want to sleep,' Vanessa slurred. 'You bitch... you bloody bitch... ' she fell silent and Jean joined Peter in the corridor.

'Thank you, we couldn't have managed without your help.' She led him back into the treatment room.

'Any passing visitor would have done the same.'

'Most visitors wouldn't have been able to keep a hold on her. If you come in here, I'll put something on that cut on your cheek.'

'Shouldn't you see to Lyn Sullivan first?' Peter was reluctant to allow Jean near him.

'She needs more attention than I can give her here. Besides, I wouldn't dare encroach on Karl's territory.'

19

Peter looked into the office and saw the male nurse bending over Lyn while Trevor stood ineptly by, still holding the glass of water. He ran his fingers over his left cheekbone and when he withdrew them he was surprised to find them covered in blood.

'It always looks and feels worse than it is, when it's on the face,' Jean commented.

'I've discovered that the hard way.' Peter allowed her to clean up the cut and cover it with a plaster.

'Vanessa would have to choose visiting hours on a Sunday afternoon to go berserk,' Jean complained when she washed her hands. 'Weekend cover is barely half of normal, and a quarter of the few staff we have are on tea break at this time of day.'

'Sod's law.' Peter winced as the cut stung viciously back to life.

'Do me a favour?'

'I didn't see or hear anything. I wasn't even here.'

'It's not that I want to deny you a medal, but I'll never see the end of the paperwork if they find out that I allowed a visitor to manhandle a patient.'

'What visitor?' Peter wasn't slow in demanding a return favour. 'Can I come back later with a take-away for Trevor? He looks as if he hasn't eaten for months. He used to enjoy late night suppers in the station.'

'It will be a miracle if he eats it.'

'I'd like to try.'

'Be my guest.' She led the way out of the treatment room and locked it with one of the keys that hung from a belt at her waist. They passed the storeroom, where the porters were clearing the mess of broken glass and spilt drugs under the supervision of the security guard. 'As ward sister it's not my place to say this, it's Mr Goldman's. You do know there's nothing we can do for

20

Trevor. He's depressed, but not clinically so, at least no more than anyone who's been through what he has is entitled to be. And certainly no more than anyone who's capable of reading the daily papers from cover to cover. But he's become institutionalised. It's long past the time when he should have returned to the real world. Mr Goldman's been suggesting short solitary afternoon outings since the second day he was admitted. As far as the front gate would be a start. If Trevor doesn't make an effort and take his advice soon, we'll be putting the boot behind him.'

'We were on the way out when you distracted us,' Peter said.

'I appreciate you trying to help, but the effort has to be his, not yours,' Jean halted when they reached the office.

Peter looked inside where Trevor was still hovering behind Lyn's chair. 'He did drag Lyn Sullivan out of the cupboard.'

'So he did.' Jean watched Karl bandage Lyn's leg. 'It could be the first small step.'

'I'll give him the push he needs to make the second.' Peter felt better about Trevor than he had done since the day the doctor in intensive care had told him that his friend was going to live.

'Make sure you come in with that meal before I go off at eight,' Jean warned, artfully. 'The night sister isn't as accommodating as me.'

'I'm on duty myself at nine, so I'll probably make it around seven.'

Peter's reply wiped the smile from Jean's face. If he'd come at the end of her shift she had hoped to inveigle him into the Green Monkey.

It had been almost four years since her scrap metal dealer husband had left her for a beauty queen less than half her age. She'd picked her lawyer well and paid him enough to ensure that she'd come out of the divorce financially sound. Her share of her husband's assets included their luxurious four-bedroomed apartment on the marina, a five-berth yacht, and enough gilt edged securities to make work a pastime she could give up any time she chose.

But she had discovered that money was no substitute for emotional and sexual satisfaction. She was tired of singles groups, the bridge club dominated by obscenely happily married couples, and sleeping alone. Peter Collins was a hard man, but he was physically fit, more than passably good-looking in a clean cut, military way, and she had a shrewd suspicion that if she ever succeeded in enticing him into her bed she'd find his soft centre.

She didn't doubt that he had one. In her opinion, all men did. It was just a question of the right handling. All she had to do was make the initial breech through his defences.

CHAPTER TWO

'Take this wheelbarrow and shovel,' Jimmy Herne, the chief gardener at Compton Castle, thrust the implements at Dean Smith, his seventeen-year-old trainee. 'Proceed to that point beneath the willow tree, where I've marked the turf with lime,' he continued. 'You listening to me, boy?' he bellowed.

Dean shrugged his shoulders, which irritated Jimmy even more. Dean was used to being screamed at, and not only by Jimmy Herne. His parents had done so for as long as he could remember, and as soon as he was old enough to go to school, his teachers had followed suit. As a result, he was immune to any display of anger from anyone in authority.

He lived for the hours he spent shooting aliens and outwitting commandos in the gaming arcades, and ogling girls while downing pints of illicit beer with his mates in the Little Albert – the only bar in town that catered for under-age drinkers.

'I'll check on you in ten minutes,' Jimmy threatened. 'And if you haven't finished lifting the turf, and digging out a good couple of inches by then, you can look out. You hear me, boy?'

'Yes, Mr Herne.' Dean threw his spade into the barrow and trundled to the willow tree. He poked the spade half-heartedly into the grass, and gingerly lifted the turf he'd cut. If he didn't trim the edges neatly, it would set the old geezer off again, and that would mean sweeping leaves and clearing gutters for the rest of the week. He and Jason Canning, the other trainee assigned by the council's horticulture department to Compton Castle, constantly vied with one another for the dubious privilege of being the lowest common denominator in Jimmy Herne's bad books. Fortunately for him, today was Jason's turn. Jimmy had caught him chatting up Mandy Evans in the kitchen when he should have been bedding out geraniums, so it was Jason who was doing the dirty work.

Dean lifted out four square inches of turf, laid the tiny sod in the centre of the barrow, leaned on the shovel and rested before lifting out the next section. A fat, pink worm was oozing back into the darkness of the soil. It didn't ooze quickly enough. Dean chopped it in two with his spade, and watched both ends writhe.

'Here, boy.'

A prod in the back with the pointed end of an umbrella diverted Dean's attention from the worm.

'Dig over there.' The umbrella swung in the direction of the flowerbeds he'd dug out the week before.

The woman was short, with a beaky face that reminded him of a teacher who'd taught him in primary school. But she was wearing a white jacket. And that put him on his guard. Only doctors wore white jackets, and even Jimmy Herne listened to doctors.

'I dug out those beds last week, miss.' He lapsed into the jargon of his recent schooldays.

'I don't care when you dug them out. You will dig that one out now!'

The "now", coupled with her air of authority, made Dean jump to it. Throwing his spade into his barrow, he wheeled it to the flowerbed.

The woman reached the spot before him. She ground the heel of her shoe into the loose earth, and pinpointed the place where she wanted him to dig. 'Here, and put your back into it.'

Dean lifted his spade from the barrow and pushed it into the earth. It slid in easily. The soil was loose, crumbly and fairly dry.

'Don't put what you take out in the barrow, idiot. A deep hole's needed here, for a – tree. There'll never be room for everything you take out in there, and I don't want you wasting time carting it around. Pile it up on the grass.'

'It won't be easy to clean up afterwards. Mr Herne...'

'Mr Herne nothing,' she dismissed. 'All you'll need to clean it up is a stiff brush. Pile it up. I want to see a hole deep enough for a mature beech in ten minutes.'

Dean wanted to ask why the rush, when he couldn't see a tree, but he didn't dare. The woman stood over him, while he dug slowly downwards. Occasionally she looked over her shoulder, scanning the garden as though she was expecting someone. Dean presumed it was the someone with the tree. And, in between, she chivvied him as though her life depended on his progress.

'An old man of ninety could dig faster than you, boy. Put more swing into it. There's no time for that.' She clouted him on the arm with her umbrella when he rested momentarily on his shovel. He glared at her. Not even Jimmy Herne had dared hit him, but he pushed the shovel back in the hole, which in his opinion was already deep enough for any tree.

'What the hell do you think you're doing, boy?' Jimmy Herne thundered over the grass towards them, a look of fury darkening his wizened monkey face.

'He's working for me.'

Dean continued to dig, happy to delegate the explanations to the woman.

25

'A deep hole needs to be dug here, for a tree. And it needs to be dug this minute.'

'First I've heard of it, and this is my garden,' Jimmy asserted. 'This here is a flowerbed, not a tree site, and it's been dug out enough. All it needs is a barrow or two of manure and it will be right to plant out the roses.'

'Not before this hole has been dug.'

Something in her manner rang a warning bell in Jimmy's mind. 'You're one of *them*, aren't you?' He laughed and slapped his thigh. 'Boy, have you been had. Had, good and proper.' He grinned at Dean, who was staring white-faced into the hole he'd dug.

'Mr Herne, look at this.' Dean stared at Jimmy through dark, frightened eyes. The gardener stepped forward, and peered into the hole.

Locks of blonde hair had clumped and bunched around a single eye set in a segment of grey face. It stared upwards from the earth in blank, blind terror. Jimmy gripped Dean's shoulder.

'Inside, boy. Tell them to call the police. Tell them I said so.'

The woman in the white jacket was dancing and skipping around the pile of earth heaped on the grass, chanting, 'I told them so – I told them so – I told them all, but they wouldn't listen.' She clutched at Dean's shirt when he passed her. 'But you listened, didn't you, boy? You listened, and you found her.' Her face loomed close to his. He could see hairline veins of red in her eyes, deep pores that pockmarked her skin, her make-up caked into creases that lined the valleys of her wrinkles. 'You hit the jackpot, boy.'

Her cackles of laughter followed him as he ran headlong into the main building.

Spencer Jordan, the resident art therapist at Compton
Castle, was respected and liked by both patients and staff,
but everyone conceded that it took time to get to know
him. New patients were intimidated by the sheer size of
him. Six-foot-seven, with the slim, strongly muscled
frame of a basketball player, a physique he'd put to good
use during the year he'd spent after art college, studying
textiles in a Californian university. His hair was long and
neatly trimmed, as were his beard and moustache. He was
quiet, softly spoken, and dressed casually in jeans or black
slacks with sweaters – and his sweaters were the first
thing that people noticed about him.

They were wild, colourful affairs, some mirrored
abstract modern art; others illustrated with animals and
scenery. The one he'd chosen to wear that Monday
morning depicted ferocious-looking black and white
rabbits gambolling over a background of bright-red grass,
sprinkled with green and purple daisies. And the most
amazing thing about Spencer Jordan's sweaters was he
knitted them him himself, between art classes.

'Good sketch, Trevor.' Spencer glanced over
Trevor's shoulder as he stood silently rubbing pastels on
to an easel propped in the darkest corner of the room. 'I
like the background colours. I take it that's the same lady
we've seen before, long dark hair, grey eyes. Am I
allowed to know who she is?'

'A figment of my imagination.' Trevor picked up a
grey pastel to darken the clouds above her head.

'Pity. She looks like the kind of person I'd like to get
to know.' Spencer stood behind Trevor for a few
moments, inviting further conversation. When none came,
he moved on to the next easel, where his youngest male

27

patient, Michael Carpenter, was working on a chocolate-box picture of a country cottage. Straw-thatched roof, roses climbing around a peaked wooden porch, small leaded-glass windows and, sitting dead centre of the picture, an auburn-haired girl clutching a bunch of bluebells on her Laura Ashley clad lap.

Just as Trevor Joseph always sketched dark-haired women, so Michael Carpenter always painted girls with short auburn curls. Spencer knew Trevor was a police officer suffering from depression after receiving life-threatening injuries. He had no idea where the dark-haired lady fitted into his past, if indeed she did, but he knew about Michael's lady.

Michael's sole topic of conversation was Angela and Angela was the reason he was in Compton Castle. Michael had been a bank clerk with no interests other than work, his girlfriend Angela, and building his model railway. When Angela told him there was someone else in her life and she wanted out of their relationship, he couldn't take it. He began to stalk her and her new boyfriend. He took to camping out at night in her parents' garden whenever she stayed in. Threats and warnings from her family and the police, the supportive concern of his own family – none of it had any effect.

One night, an hour after the last light had been switched off in Angela's house, Michael had cut a hole in the dining room window, set fire to rolls of newspaper he had brought for the purpose, and pushed them through the hole so they'd land on the carpet close to the drapes. The room had been ablaze in a matter of minutes and, if it hadn't been for the timely intervention of a retired police officer neighbour who had seen the flames through his living room window, the family would have burned to death in their beds.

28

Michael had arrived at Compton Castle, via the courts, prison, and an order that he undergo therapy. But Spencer was beginning to doubt whether the treatment Michael was receiving offered a solution to his problem. Michael had been attending his art class for six months, and he was still drawing idyllic cottages with his ex-girlfriend sitting in the garden. Sooner or later Michael had to accept that Angela was no longer part of his life – and wouldn't be, ever again. While he continued to reject that concept, he may as well resign himself to living out the rest of his life in an institution.

'Spencer, look at my work please.' Alison Bevan, a professional mother suffering postnatal depression after the birth of her ninth child, the result of her fourteenth "serious" relationship in as many years, fluttered her sparse eyelashes at him. Spencer walked over to her easel. She'd drawn a childlike picture of children at play. No figure had arms or legs of the same proportion and all their mouths were fixed in upturned grins. In the left-hand corner were the outsized figures of a man and a woman. The woman's face bore the same determinedly bright smile as the children, but the man's face was devoid of features.

'Isn't he happy, Ali?' Spencer pointed to the matchstick-like figure.

'He wouldn't be,' Alison retorted. 'He's a man, and everyone knows men have to do the work and bring in the money.'

'So he carries all the responsibility.'

'Isn't that what it's like for you, Spencer?' she questioned artfully.

'No, Alison, it's not.' A warning note crept into Spencer's voice. 'I've only myself to consider.'

'You must get lonely then,' she persisted.

29

'Your picture's coming on.' He ignored her final comment. 'I like the touch of the flowers on the ground matching those in the children's hands.' He moved on to Lucy Craig, a plump, nervous seventeen-year-old, who had cracked under the pressure of studying for her A Levels.

'Look, Mr Jordan.' Despite Spencer's prompting, Lucy could never bring herself to use his Christian name. 'There's a police car driving on the lawn. It's churning up Mr Herne's turf. He won't be pleased.' She glanced at Spencer, but he was watching Trevor. Head down, Trevor was diligently smudging pastels, evincing no interest in what was happening outside. Spencer wondered how much truth that lay behind the maxim, "Once a policeman, always a policeman".

Constable Michelle Grady stood twenty yards from the hole Dean had dug in the flowerbed. The stubby heels of her walking shoes had sunk into the turf, and her uniform was hot, prickly and stuffy in the warm spring sunshine, but she didn't move an inch from her post. She'd heard a number of stories in Police College about rookies allowing crucial evidence to be destroyed at a crime scene, and she was determined that no one would be able to accuse her of negligence.

Her trained eye had spotted flecks of earth amongst the blades of grass, some distance from the pile of earth Dean had heaped up. She smiled at the thought of pointing this out to her superiors, then imagined Sergeant Peter Collins' voice, loud in contempt.

"Of course the hole must have been dug out more than once you stupid woman. If it hadn't, the damned body couldn't have been buried there in the first place."

She rocked back on her heels. She must be careful not to state the obvious. Sergeant Collins wasn't the only superior officer in the station with a sharp tongue.

She wrenched her heels out of the soil and stamped up and down. Waiting was the worse part of every day – waiting for her superiors – waiting for the serious crimes squad – waiting for the pathologist. Didn't *anyone* care about the poor victim lying at the bottom of the hole?

'There's no need to stamp your foot, Constable. Whoever's down there isn't going to complain about being kept waiting.' Dan Evans, an inspector in the Serious Crimes Squad, appeared behind her.

'Inspector.' She nodded. Dan Evans was a mountain of a man who'd been an international weightlifter. At six-foot-four, heavily built and twenty stone, he towered over everyone in the station. Before he'd joined the force he'd been a farmer, and she knew his family still worked land around Carmarthen, which explained his lilting Welsh accent and his exasperatingly slow speech.

'When you've dealt with as many cases as I have, you learn to take your time. Rush and you're apt to make mistakes.'

'I can't stop thinking about that poor woman… '

'How do you know there's a woman down there?' His drawl, coupled with his nitpicking, irritated her.

'Because she has long blonde hair. She's also wearing bright-blue eye-shadow.'

'Could be a gay,' Dan countered.

'It looks like a woman, and as she's been murdered… '

'Murdered,' Dan mused. 'How did you come to that conclusion?'

'Because she's buried here, in the hospital grounds. Someone wanted to hide the body from the authorities.'

31

'Or someone couldn't afford to pay for a funeral. They're getting pricier every day. Mint?' He thrust a crumpled paper bag under her nose.

'No, thank you,' she refused stiffly.

'You should learn to relax, constable… '

'Grady. Michelle Grady, sir.' She drew herself up to her full height of five-foot six-inches, but she still felt like a child next to him

He pushed his fingers through his fair, thinning hair and looked at a battered blue estate car edging its way through the gates.

'Here's the pathologist. Ever meet Patrick O'Kelly?'

'Not to talk to, sir.' She'd heard a lot of stories about Patrick O'Kelly, and all of them had been reinforced by the compulsory post mortem that she, and every rookie, had been forced to attend.

'You're in for a treat.' Dan Evans pushed another mint between his lips, before stepping forward to open O'Kelly's car door, as it drew to a halt on the lawn.

'What have you got?' O'Kelly left the driver's seat and heaved a battered wooden case from the back of the car.

'A face, partially uncovered in fresh-dug earth,' Dan replied shortly, 'although our constable here thinks it could be murder.'

'Could be someone wanting to avoid funeral costs.'

'That's what I told her.'

'Police ambulance here?'

'Not yet.'

'I'll make a start anyway.' O'Kelly glanced from the hole to the lawn around them. 'Who's been tramping over this site?' He peered suspiciously at Michelle.

'The trainee who dug the hole,' Michelle recited. 'The patient who ordered him to do it. The gardener. And myself.'

'What patient ordered the trainee to do what?' Dan asked.

Michelle pulled out her notebook and flicked through the pages. 'A Mrs Vanessa Hedley insisted she saw someone bury a body in the garden the night before last. When she told the staff on her ward, they wouldn't believe her; and when she persisted in repeating her allegations, they sedated her. According to the hospital administrator, Mr Tony Waters, given her history they were justified in ignoring her. Mrs Hedley wasn't allowed out of her room until this morning. She found and dressed in a white jacket in the hope that she would be taken for a doctor. Then she came out and ordered one of the trainees to start digging... '

'And he obeyed an inmate?' O'Kelly questioned incredulously.

'He thought she was a doctor,' Michelle reminded him.

'I'm confused,' Dan chipped in. 'Who exactly is in charge of this place?'

Patrick pushed his glasses further up his nose, and snapped on a pair of rubber gloves.

'I stepped in the footprints of Mrs Hedley and Dean Smith, the trainee,' Michelle continued. 'Since I arrived I have succeeded in keeping everyone away from the site.'

'Coming with me, Dan?' O'Kelly stepped across the lawn.

Dan followed Patrick to the lip of the hole. A few seconds later Patrick shouted for a spade and Michelle handed him the one Dean had abandoned. When she returned to her post, she stared disapprovingly at the

33

crowd of patients and domestic staff who were teetering on the edge of the lawn, and shooed them back. She enjoyed wielding the authority that came with her uniform. When she'd forced them to retreat a couple of token feet, she returned to her post and tried to listen in on Dan Evans' conversation with Patrick O'Kelly. But all she could make out was a succession of 'Steady's', 'There she goes', and 'Look at that', none of which proved enlightening.

A second police car arrived with her immediate superior, Sergeant Peter Collins. As he directed the erection of canvas screens around the site, she continued to stand her ground. Within minutes the entire area around the hole was shrouded off, much to the disappointment of the crowd of onlookers.

Peter Collins stepped back, stood in the crowd for a few moments to test the efficiency of the screens then joined Michelle.

'I hear you were first on the scene.'

'I was,' she answered.

'What's the run-down?'

'A trainee gardener uncovered part of a face in the flowerbed... '

'Just a face, or is it attached to a body?'

'I think it's attached to a body,' she ventured, suddenly unsure of the facts.

'Stupid place to put a body,' he observed, 'where a gardener's going to dig it up.'

'He wouldn't have, if a female patient hadn't ordered him to do it.'

'Have you asked the patient how she knew there was someone buried here?' he enquired.

'She claims she saw someone burying a body in the garden the night before last.'

'Saturday night.' Peter recalled Vanessa's ramblings during the rumpus on Trevor's ward. Instinctively he fingered the cut on his cheek. What had Jean Marshall called her? – Hedley – that was it. 'Vanessa Hedley,' he said aloud.

'You know about her?' Michelle was crestfallen at relinquishing her edge on the case.

Peter didn't hear her. 'Well I'll be damned,' he muttered. 'Some lunatics aren't so mad after all.'

For the first time since Spencer Jordan had taken over the art therapy classes, the patients grew restless before the end of their allotted time. They abandoned their sketch pads, pastels and easels for the greater attraction of the police cars and the mysteriously veiled area on the lawn. Only Trevor remained apparently indifferent to the drama being played out in the grounds.

Spencer allowed the group to disperse ten minutes before time. When everyone except Trevor had left, Spencer moved quietly around the room, collecting portfolios, gathering together pastels and picking up the odd pencil that had fallen to the floor. The whole of the time he was clearing up, Trevor continued to work diligently and silently in his corner. The hands on the clock crept around to one o'clock, and still Trevor remained engrossed in his sketch.

At five minutes past one, Spencer lifted down a rucksack from a peg behind the door. Picking up a chair, he carried it over to a table close to where Trevor was working.

'Sandwich?' Spencer opened a packet wrapped in greaseproof paper.

'No, thank you,' Trevor replied distantly, without looking up from his drawing.

'They're salad and goat's cheese. A friend of mine made the cheese, and I mixed the salad. Guaranteed organic, no chemical, no fertilisers – unnatural fertilisers, that is.' He pushed the packet closer to Trevor.

Trevor looked up, stared at the sandwiches for a moment, then, after dusting off his hands on his sweatshirt, took one. 'Thank you.' His voice sounded strange, rusty from disuse. He opened the sandwich and peered inside the twin slices of rye bread.

'No butter,' Spencer apologised. 'I try to eat healthy.'

Trevor closed the sandwich and took a small bite.

Spencer produced a bottle of mineral water from his rucksack, and a paper cup. He filled the cup and handed it to Trevor, forcing him to take it. 'Harry Goldman told me you're allowed out for short periods. Would you like to have a drink with me in the Green Monkey this afternoon? They do a nice line in non-alcoholic wines that don't interfere with medication.'

'No, thank you.'

Spencer took a sandwich, and bit a chunk out of it. 'You're going to have to make that first move sometime soon,' he cautioned. 'You don't realise what you're missing until you go outside. I know. It's not that long since I was sitting where you are now.'

'You were a patient?' The question was timidly phrased, but it was still a question, and Spencer understood what a profound step forward that represented for someone in Trevor's depressed state of indifference.

'Yes, I was a patient. In America first, then here.' Spencer ran his fingers over the scars that radiated from the glass eye in his right socket. 'I'll tell you about it sometime.' He hoped Trevor wouldn't press him. If he put him off, it might close the chink he'd just made in Trevor's defensive armour, and that could prove

36

disastrous to a man teetering on the brink of re-establishing communication with the rest of the world. But...

The "but" was the agony that Spencer had failed to live with for nearly three years. The present – including Trevor – faded as he remembered California. A sun-drenched sidewalk in the pedestrian-only area of Main Street. The beat of popular music echoing from the fashionable boutiques that catered for the young and well-heeled, drowning out the classical music from the art gallery behind him. He saw again the gilded window that held a selection of his originals, and glimpsed the walls inside, hung with limited and exclusive signed editions of his prints.

The smart set, the wealthy smart set – Alfredo, who owned the gallery, checked the bank balances of his clients before their titles and social standing – smiled at him as they made their way into the gallery. Spencer had returned their smiles. He'd had reason to be grateful to his patrons. His house had been Californian redwood built on stilts on a fashionable hillside that commanded a sweeping view of a breathtaking wooded bay. It had glass walls designed to frame the scenery. It had been furnished with designer Italian furniture, designer linen, designer crystal – in fact everything he owned and wore was the best that new and up-and-coming talent had to offer.

It would have been churlish and miserly of him to stint himself and his family, when the world's wealthy were queuing to buy his signed prints at five thousand dollars a time, and his originals at anything from fifty thousand dollars upwards. He had all that a man could possibly want. The sun, the lifestyle to go with it, a sweet beautiful wife, sweet, beautiful babies...

'Spencer Jordan, isn't it?'

37

Still back in California, Spencer stared blankly at the cropped hair and steel grey eyes of the man who appeared suddenly in front of him.

'Spencer Jordan?' the man repeated. 'I'm Peter Collins. Sergeant Peter Collins,' he emphasised. 'I'd like a word with Trevor.'

Spencer wrenched himself out of the past. He'd promised himself that he would never allow himself to drift back. It was too raw, too painful. And here he was again, only this time in broad daylight. He didn't even have the excuse of insomnia, loneliness and darkness. What had prompted it?

Trevor – he'd told Trevor that he'd been a patient.

'Use this room, Sergeant Collins.' He rose from his seat. 'I have things to do in the staff room.' He turned to Trevor. 'See you later?'

'Thank you for the sandwich.'

It was difficult to judge who was more astounded by Trevor's response; Peter Collins or Spencer Jordan.

CHAPTER THREE

After Spencer had retrieved his rucksack and left the room, Trevor moved from behind the easel and sat in a chair in front of the window. Peter pushed aside a mess of paint pots, jars and brushes on a table and perched on it, facing Trevor.

He studied Trevor critically, making no allowance for sentiment or friendship. Depression was etched into every inch of his sagging body, from the lank, greasy hair that straggled, badly in need of a cut, over his forehead and collar, to the limp colourless hands that lay inert and lifeless in his lap. Thin at the best of times, Trevor was gaunt. His pale sunken cheeks were covered with black stubble and he was dressed in the same faded, threadbare clothes he had worn the day before.

'I looked in on your flat,' Peter said. 'After I dropped in the take-away. Did you eat it?'

'Yes.'

'Good fish and chips?'

'It was curry.'

'Just testing. It's the same mess as usual – your flat,' Collins explained. 'No burglar has been in to tidy up. Frank was locking up the shop downstairs. He'll be glad to see you back; the local kids have been giving him hell for the last couple of months. It didn't take them long to realise no one was sleeping in the building. Frank's window has been smashed in three times since Christmas, and his cigarette and chocolate machines have been vandalised so often he's had to take them down.' Peter took a packet of cigars from his shirt pocket. 'Anyway, Frank said to tell you he'll call in to see you. Probably on a Sunday afternoon, because that's the only time he can afford to leave the shop.' He lit a cigar and puffed a cloud of smoke. A year ago Trevor would have protested mildly or strongly, depending on his mood. Now he sat passively breathing in tobacco fumes.

'Your mother phoned me. I lied and said that you were making progress, and that you'd write or phone her soon. Do you think you could manage that?'

'Yes,' Trevor answered absently.

'You noticed the rumpus outside?'

'Yes.'

'Aren't you interested in what's happening?'

'No.'

Peter rose, turned his back, and walked to the window. After witnessing Trevor's earlier animation, it was as much as he could do to curb his instinct to pick him up and shake him. Despite the doctors' explanations, he ascribed Trevor's continuing depression and monumental indifference to lack of effort.

If Trevor had ranted and raved against the injustice of a fate that had broken his arm, legs and head, he would have sympathised with him. But Trevor hadn't ranted and raved; instead he'd withdrawn into a monosyllabic melancholy that had erased the personality of the old Trevor, replacing him with a stranger he no longer knew nor liked.

Trevor's detachment hung between them, threatening to smother what little remained of their close, if fraught relationship. Peter contemplated the human wreckage hunched before him. Trevor had been a good friend; probably the only real friend he'd ever had. He couldn't sit back and allow him to drift into nothingness. For the first time since Trevor had been hospitalised, he let rip, allowing emotions he usually kept tightly reined to erupt.

'I never thought I'd say this, but work is a swine without you. That damned girl guide Bill's dumped on the squad is bloody useless. She's got a degree in anthropology. Do you mind telling me what bloody good a degree in anthropology is to the Drug Squad? A degree in fortune telling would be better. God only knows, it's difficult enough to cover your own bloody arse in this filthy business without having to watch out for a useless female as well.' He turned from the window and paced back to the table. 'So, the sooner you get off your backside and out of here, the better it will be for all of us. Then Bill can push Mary Poppins into a quiet corner where she can sit behind a desk and anthropologise – or whatever it is that females like her do. And you and I can get on with the job.' He confronted Trevor. 'What do you say to that?'

'I told you, I might not be coming back.'

There was a sharp rap at the door, and Michelle Grady stuck her head around the door. 'Sergeant Collins, Inspector Evans is asking if you'd go to the administration office, to check if there are any plans of this place.'

'I'll go in a few minutes,' Peter barked.

She shut the door.

Trevor wanted Peter to leave, so he could be left alone with his portrait, but Peter continued.

'A body is buried in the grounds of this place under your nose, and you saw bloody nothing when even the craziest female nut on your ward saw it happen. Where were you? Dead, or off the planet?' He walked away in disgust, slamming the door behind him.

Trevor continued to sit on his chair. After five minutes, he raised his eyes so he could once again look at his portrait.

*   *   *

'What's the verdict, Dan?' Superintendent Bill Mulcahy had been on site for less than five minutes, and already the constables and rookies were acting more alert, snapping to attention whenever he passed, trying to look as busy as any officer can who has nothing more to do than control a passive crowd.

'Patrick's still down there. We'll know more when he's ready to tell us what he's found.' Dan pulled a crumpled handkerchief from his pocket and wiped his hands. 'But, for the moment, I can tell you she's young. Early twenties, Patrick thinks, and she was probably buried alive.'

'Alive? Is he sure?'

'Her mouth had been glued. Probably with one those bond-in-seconds, stick-anything jobs, and her nose and her throat were jammed with earth. Patrick thinks she struggled for breath until the last minute.'

'Poor bitch.'

Dan inspected his fingernails. 'It couldn't have been pleasant for her.'

Bill suppressed his dark thoughts. 'You've begun interviewing hospital staff and inmates?'

'Yes, but I need to draft some good coppers on to my team.' Dan looked hopefully at his boss. 'Do you have any to spare?'

'Do I ever? There isn't a section that isn't pushed to the limit.' Bill stared at the sky, as though he hoped to find a solution in the heavens. 'You can have Constable Grady, she's a rookie, but she's keen. And Peter Collins has become impossible since I transferred her to the Drug Squad as a short-term replacement for Trevor Joseph.'

'Is Trevor still sick?'

'Sick and in here.' Mulcahy didn't even try to keep the contempt from his voice.

'Is he, now?' Evans rubbed his chin reflectively. 'That could prove useful.'

'Don't pin any hopes there,' Bill recalled the false premise that the murderer always returns to the scene of his crime, and studied the crowd gathered behind Michelle. 'Trevor's cracked; nutty as a fruit cake.'

'I thought he had depression.'

'It amounts to the same thing.'

Evans debated whether it was worth arguing the point, and decided against it. 'I'll take Grady, and anyone else you can spare. 'I'd like to have at least twenty men working on this by the end of the day.'

'You'll be lucky, but I'll look around and see who I can come up with. I might be able to lend you Peter Collins for a while.'

'I thought the whole idea was to separate him from Grady?'

'He needs separating from the rest of humanity. Trevor Joseph is the only one who could put up with his bloody moods.'

'I've a feeling there'll be enough legwork on this one even for the prima-donnas,' Dan returned his handkerchief to his pocket.

Peter Collins sat in the office of Tony Waters, Compton Castle's chief administrator. Dan had asked him to check the layout of the building, but a quick glance at the plans had told him everything. The place was a nightmare from a policing and a security point of view.

'As you see, Sergeant Collins,' Tony Waters waved his manicured hand over the papers on his desk; he was a tall man, six-foot-one or two, in Peter's estimation, with startlingly white-blond hair and pale-blue eyes, 'the whole place is a mishmash of bits and pieces from every building that's been erected on this site since Norman times.'

'It looks that way.' Peter noted the ruins of the outer wall of the Norman castle on the southern boundary and the sketched-in blob of masonry marked "Folly." He jabbed his finger on it, with a questioning look at Tony.

'It's down as Victorian, but the foundations are Norman, like the name of this place. It was easier for the Victorian architect to dovetail the solid Norman bits into the building than demolish them.'

'You sound as though you know what you're talking about,' Peter allowed grudgingly.

'I take an interest in my surroundings, Sergeant,' Waters smiled without warmth. 'If you look at these contours,' he ran his thumbnail over the plan, 'you'll see the remains of the old moat.'

Collins noted a steep-sided depression on the northern edge of the old hospital, before turning his attention to the main building. The mid-Victorian edifice was an example of Gothic architecture at its most ornate and, in Peter's eye, most horrendous, housing a vast network of narrow passages and steep staircases that led to communal wards the size of ballrooms and servants' attics that were mouse holes in comparison. There were cavernous storerooms, towers and turrets that seemed about as useful as the stone gargoyles that decorated the main facade of the building.

The rabbit warren of rooms extended from a vast cellar, which had been partitioned off to hold the incoming electrical supplies and central heating boiler, to the fourth floor attics originally designed as accommodation units for live-in skivvies.

44

From what Peter had seen on his way to the administrator's office, only a few cosmetic changes had been made in the old building since Queen Victoria had sat on the throne. Scratched and stained vinyl tiles lay over whatever flooring the Victorians had walked on, but the walls were still covered to shoulder height by brick-shaped dark-green tiles topped by a strip of oak dado; and if the sickly yellow paint that darkened the walls from dado to ceiling wasn't the original, it should have been.

'Are all these wards?' Peter pointed to the first, second and third-floor plans.

'No, all the wards have been moved to the ground floor. The first and part of the second-floor house the administration department of the local Health Authority.'

'And these.' Peter indicated units that had been erected behind the hospital. Units he knew were connected to the main building by tunnels of opaque Perspex.

'Therapy units,' Tony informed him. 'They're demountables that were erected as a short term temporary measure in the 1970s, and have never been replaced.' He shrugged. 'Financial constraints. You know how it is.'

Peter didn't comment. He turned back to the plans. As if the buildings weren't headache enough, the grounds were vast. Laid out in a park of lawns, wooded areas and shrubberies, they could have concealed a battalion, let alone a solitary killer carrying a single body.

'These gates?' Peter indicated four openings marked in the external wall that surrounded the grounds. 'Are they locked at night?'

'All but the main gates fronting on to the main road. We leave those open in case of emergency.'

'Are they manned?'

'They used to be, until our security budget was halved.'

'So anyone can walk in and out of here during the night?'

'The grounds are patrolled by a guard with a radio transmitter, and the entrances to the hospital blocks are manned at individual reception areas. This building is locked at night.'

'Do you have a problem with prowlers?'

'Frankly, yes,' Tony replied.

'Now that we've established any lunatic can walk in here off the street, what about the ones already here?'

'I presume you mean our patients?'

Peter sensed Tony Waters' temper rising, but that didn't deter him from pressing his point. 'Could they walk out of their wards at night and take a stroll around the grounds?'

'I told you, the reception areas in the ward blocks are manned.'

'Continuously? By more than one man?'

'Obviously not by more than one. The hospital budget... '

'Doesn't stretch to cover him when he goes for a pee, or to fix himself a cup of coffee.' Peter pushed the plans aside. 'What you have there, Mr Waters, is a bomb waiting to explode. The only wonder is it didn't go off sooner.'

Tony Waters insisted on accompanying Peter when he left the office. They walked through the long corridors and out of the back entrance, entering one of the perspex tunnels that connected the administration block with the wards. Neither spoke. Tony was preoccupied with thoughts of the paperwork the discovery of the body in the grounds would

46

generate, and Peter was too busy mentally filing his initial impressions of the place to make polite small talk.

Peter Collins was not a sensitive man. He relied on logic to take him through life, but even he felt uneasy as they entered the perspex tunnel. Its floor and walls were white. No image penetrated the opaque arched walls, only an intense, eerie light. He felt as though he had stumbled into a surrealist painting. And, almost as soon as they entered the tunnel, it curved sharply. He turned his head and looked back. All he could see behind him was the tunnel disappearing into itself. Ahead, the same thing. He was beset by the most peculiar sensation, of being disembodied in time and space.

'If you're not nuts when you come into this place, you could well be nuts by the time you leave,' he observed caustically.

'You don't like our tunnels, Sergeant Collins?' Tony asked.

'Do you?'

'They're cheap, and secure. No one can get into them from the outside, except by the exit and entry points, which have been kept to a minimum; and they provide a dry, direct route from the wards to the therapy blocks. The staff can send patients through them with confidence, knowing they will turn up safely at the other end.'

'Always supposing they aren't blinded before they get there.'

'The company that installed them are experimenting with other colours, including mottled-green.'

Peter noticed how the strong white light drained what little colour there was in Tony Waters' face and white-blond hair, and he reflected that a mottled-green face might look even more bizarre.

'Peter, and?' Bill greeted Peter as he and Tony strode over the lawn towards him.

'Tony Waters, hospital administration,' Peter introduced his companion to his superior.

Bill extended his hand. 'We need to set up a system for interviewing your staff and patients as soon as possible, particularly... ' Bill flicked through his notebook, 'Vanessa Hedley, the patient who ordered the gardener's boy to dig here.'

'I can organise a rota for you to interview the staff, but you'll have to consult Harry Goldman before you interview any of the patients. He's the chief psychiatrist. Patients' welfare is his responsibility.'

'Where can I find him?' Bill asked.

'At the moment, in court. He's giving evidence in a case involving one of our patients.'

'Then we'll begin with the staff.' Bill saw Dan and Patrick's shadows moving behind the screens. 'Peter, you and Michelle begin with the nursing staff working on Vanessa Hedley's ward. You've no objections Mr Waters?'

'None, Inspector... '

'Superintendent Mulcahy,' Bill corrected tersely.

Peter pulled his notebook from his pocket and strode across the lawn towards Michelle Grady. Dan and Patrick emerged from behind the screens. Patrick peeled a pair of rubber gloves from his hands, as he studied a sheaf of Polaroid photographs Dan held in front of him.

'We're ready to move her out, Bill.' Dan turned to one of his subordinates. 'Get this crowd shifted back, and the ambulance up.'

'Right away, sir.' The young officer ran off.

48

'Inspector Dan Evans, Patrick O'Kelly, pathologist, Tony Waters, hospital administration,' Bill made the introduction impatiently.

'Perhaps you can help us, Tony,' Dan began.

'I'd be delighted, but, as I've already explained to Superintendent Mulcahy, I can't authorise access to the patients. You'll have to wait for Mr Goldman's permission.'

Dan offered Tony a selection of the polaroids. 'I realise this is a long shot, but do you recognise her?'

Waters accepted the photographs gingerly. He held the first one and squinted at it.

'Blonde hair, blue eyes, five-foot six-inches tall, well nourished – you could say plump,' Patrick chipped in. 'No distinguishing marks as yet, but I may uncover some in the lab. Early twenties. Strike a chord?'

'We have over four hundred nurses here, between the day and night shifts, and that's without the auxiliaries, administrative and domestic staff. Not to mention the patients. But, I spend very little time out of my office. Could I make a suggestion?' Tony handed the photographs back.

'You could,' Bill agreed.

'Don't show these to the nursing staff, if there are patients around. Some of their minds are delicately balanced.'

'We can agree to that. We'll also try to arrange a better photograph back in the lab.' Dan studied the picture of the contorted face. Patrick had scraped away the earth, but the features were smudged with dirt, and the skin was grey, disfigured by livid blotches.

'We'll check her description with our missing person's files and put out an appeal to the media. Do you have any nurses or patients missing, Tony? Any who

49

haven't turned up for work during the last couple of days?' Bill asked.

'All our nurses are reliable. If they're sick for a day, they're meticulous about phoning in, because they're aware of the strain their absence will place on their colleagues. Patients,' Tony shook his head. 'The voluntary patients come and go because whatever the doctors' diagnosis, we have no authority to keep them here. In any given week, at least half a dozen discharge themselves.'

'And disappear?' Dan asked.

'As far as our records go. Some don't even bother to go through the formal procedure of discharging themselves from the wards, and that's not to mention those in the halfway houses – '

'What houses?' Dan interrupted.

'We have three halfway houses,' the administrator explained. 'Six-bedroomed units we use to accommodate and support patients the psychiatrists consider fit enough to be returned to the community. They're located just outside the walls, on the west side. Each patient has their own room, but they share kitchen and bathroom facilities. Some have been found sheltered job placements or training by their social workers.'

'Is a check kept on their movements?' Bill asked.

'There's a warden in each hostel, and staff sleep in on a rota basis, so we're aware if any patient stays out all night. They also have to keep an appointment with their own psychiatrist once a week.'

'These hostels are outside the grounds?' Dan checked.

'Yes.'

'There's no way the people living in them could enter the hospital buildings at night?'

'I suppose they could come through the main gate, if they wanted to,' Waters conceded.

Bill looked at Peter who'd seen Dan handling photographs of the victim and returned to get one.

'You haven't heard the half of it, sir,' Peter took a Polaroid from Dan, Oblivious to Waters' angry glare, he summoned Michelle Grady and they walked back towards the wards.

Peter had worked on the Drug Squad for ten out of the fifteen years he'd spent on the force. Drug Squad work was dirty, occasionally dangerous, often boring, wet and cold; but he operated in familiar territory. Usually he had a reasonable idea of what he was up against, and what he was looking for. Most of the time, interviewing people was straight-forward. His questions were centred on what, when, how, and where they'd seen, sold or handled illegal substances.

A murder enquiry was entirely different. This wasn't the first time he'd been drafted into the Serious Crimes Squad, but prior knowledge of what was required of him didn't make the task any easier. He hated interviewing people when he didn't know what he was looking for. At best, all he could hope for was a few scraps of information that might prove useful. Scraps that wouldn't even be recognised as useful until they were pieced together back at the station, along with fragments of gossip that his fellow officers had picked up.

He sat on a hard wooden chair in Jean Marshall's office, and stirred a cup of mud-coloured hot water the duty domestic had assured him was coffee. Michelle sat across the desk from him, nervously crossing and uncrossing her legs. They weren't wonderful legs. Too thin for his taste, but she was another body; and he hoped

51

her presence would protect him from Jean's more blatant overtures.

In the event he needn't have worried. When Jean arrived, she had Lyn Sullivan in tow, and both were carrying bottles of mineral water.

'You are brave.' Lyn's smile lit up her face, and Peter found himself smiling back, in spite of the frustration welling inside him.

'I didn't think it showed.'

'Not many people will drink that.' She pointed at the coffee. 'Heaven only knows what Josie puts into it. The latest theory includes powdered laxatives.'

'Now you tell me.' He changed the subject. 'Run the events of Sunday past me one more time.' he said to Jean.

'You were there.' She lit a cigarette.

'When exactly did Vanessa Hedley start talking about bodies buried in the garden?'

'She told me about the body when I came on duty at eight on Sunday morning,' Lyn volunteered.

Peter glanced at the expanse of thigh displayed beneath Lyn's short skirt. He hadn't seen a pair of legs as good as hers in a long time.

'Didn't you think to question the night staff about her story?' Michelle looked daggers at Peter.

'None of the staff would consider a patient's ramblings worth discussing.' Jean blew smoke in Michelle's face. 'This is a psychiatric hospital. Most of our patients, including Vanessa, have difficulty differentiating between reality and fantasy.'

'Has she said anything since?' Michelle persevered.

'Only as many variations as she can think of along the lines of "I told you so",' Jean answered.

'Do you think she really did see something?' Michelle asked.

'It's bloody obvious she did,' Peter snarled. 'She must have done, to be able to pinpoint the exact spot where the body was found.'

An uneasy silence fell over the room.

'Sorry we can't be more help.' Jean poured water into a glass, 'but you know what this place is like. Or you should do after the time you've spent visiting here. Trevor's a simple depressive, which is understandable considering the physical injuries he's had to cope with, but most of the other cases on his ward are more complicated. It's difficult for laymen to understand that paranoid delusions and fantasies are as real as these four walls to some of our inmates.'

'I hear what you're saying.' Michelle's jargon irritated Peter. 'Any one else reported odd happenings in the night lately?'

'Lyn's the one who works two weeks on, two weeks off, on night shift. I'm days, regular.' Jean stubbed her cigarette out in the ashtray. 'If there's nothing more, I have to get back to the ward. You know where to find me if you want me.'

'Patients are always imagining they've seen something at night. Only last week we had to physically restrain and sedate Vanessa to keep her from running outside,' Lyn Sullivan recalled. 'She was convinced her lover was waiting for her in the grounds.'

'Has she ever managed to get out?' Peter asked.

'Not since I've been here. To be honest, at night she's usually too heavily sedated to move one foot in front of the other.'

'We try to keep the more difficult ones under control,' Jean rose from her chair.

Michelle raised her eyebrows. 'By knocking them out with a chemical cosh?'

53

'By tranquillising them so they can't leave the safety of the ward and harm themselves,' Lyn corrected.

'Was she tranquillised on Saturday night?' Peter pushed his coffee away in disgust.

'I assume so. There's nothing in her notes to suggest the contrary.'

'Then how do you explain her being up and awake in the small hours?'

'Patients develop immunity to most drugs after they've been using them for a while,' Jean lectured.

'Then you need to increase the dosage to gain the desired effect?' Peter asked.

'Yes.'

'And Vanessa hasn't had her dosage increased lately?'

'Not according to her record card,' Jean said flatly.

'We halved Mrs Hedley's medication last Saturday,' Lyn admitted in embarrassment. 'The pharmacy was closed, and we'd run out of the sleeping pills she's written up for.'

'Lucky for us that you did.' Peter had his first piece of concrete evidence; the reason for Vanessa's wakeful night. It wasn't much, but it was a beginning. And all investigations had to start somewhere.

CHAPTER FOUR

'I'm Harry Goldman. Inspector Evans, isn't it?'

Dan shook hands with the diminutive man. Dr Harry Goldman was the caricaturist's dream of a psychiatrist: just under five-feet tall, with a mop of unruly brown hair, weak eyes half hidden behind gold-rimmed glasses, he had a scrawny inadequate body that looked too fragile to support his oversized head.

'I'm sorry I wasn't here this morning,' Goldman apologised. He looked across the gardens to the screened-off area of lawn. 'I was in court. One of our patients has applied for access to his children.'

'We need to question all of your patients and one in particular, as soon as possible,' Dan left no room for refusal.

'Tony Waters met me in the car park. I have no objection to you questioning Vanessa Hedley, or any of our patients, as long as either I or one of my senior colleagues is present. But I must caution you to treat any information you gather circumspectly. Because of the nature of their illnesses, some of our patients will be unreliable witnesses.'

'There're as many disturbed people wandering around outside this hospital as there are inside, Mr Goldman, and a fair proportion seem to find their way down to the station. Our officers are trained to interpret the information we glean. But we'd be grateful for assistance that you are prepared to give us.'

Goldman looked towards the screened-off area of the lawn. 'Given the upset this has generated, and not only among the patients, we'll be happy to help in any way we can.'

'The sooner we make a start, the better,' Dan said briskly.

'Tony Waters also mentioned that you've requested a tour of the hospital. I'll take you round myself. I'd like to show you the areas you can have free access to, as opposed to the wards where the patients' welfare is paramount. There are also sections that you'll need to gain the permission of the staff before entering and others which are out-of-bounds for good reason. If you need to search them, it will have to be done under the staff's supervision.'

'I appreciate your co-operation, Mr Goldman,' Dan replied blandly.

The doctor looked for sarcasm in Dan's voice and found none.

'Shall we start by interviewing Vanessa?' Dan headed for the building, leaving Harry no choice but to follow.

They made a detour to pick up Peter from the room where he was interviewing staff with Michelle. Aware of Peter's reputation, both as a competent detective and one who didn't pay lip service to the rules, Dan asked him to sit in on his session with Vanessa as an observer. In the absence of any other senior officer, he had no choice but to use Peter as a deputy, but Dan wanted to make it clear from the outset that he was leading the investigation.

Rightly or wrongly, more than one officer at the station blamed Peter Collins for Trevor Joseph's injuries, and Dan was determined to ensure any notions Peter entertained of schoolboy heroics remained off his beat.

They went to Harry Goldman's office, a large, square room decorated in warm shades of yellow, its sofa and chairs upholstered in a restful shade of pale-green. Typical psychologist's decor, Dan reflected when Harry offered him the use of his desk and chair. Peter sat in the most unobtrusive corner of the room, behind the door. Harry picked up a stacking chair and sat down alongside Peter.

Vanessa Hedley was brought to the door in a wheelchair. She was escorted by Lyn and Harry's assistant Dotty Clyne, a large, fair-haired, masculine woman with a ginger moustache. Lyn helped Vanessa out of the chair and she tottered into the office leaning on Lyn's arm. She was dazed, disorientated, obviously heavily sedated and dressed in a blue floral outfit that would have looked more at home at a Buckingham Palace garden party.

'Vanessa, you remember Peter Collins, don't you?' Lyn asked.

'I do,' Vanessa snapped with surprising vehemence, considering her heavy eyes.

'And here's Mr Goldman.' The young nurse guided her away from Peter towards the psychiatrist.

'I'm Inspector Dan Evans.' Dan held out his hand in an attempt to break the ice, an attempt that backfired when he rose from his chair.

Vanessa shrank back and screamed. 'It's him! The man I saw in the garden.'

'This isn't the man you saw, Vanessa. This is a police officer,' Lyn contradicted.

'Did he look like me, Vanessa?' Dan asked. 'Was he my size?'

'You're him.' Vanessa fought Lyn as the girl tried to prevent her leaving the room. 'I know you're him.'

'How do you know, Vanessa?' Dan asked, less urgently this time, in response to a warning look from Harry.

'Because I know – because I do – '

One of the joys of being a copper in a smallish town is knowing the history of most of the characters the town had to offer. Dan had been in the station the night they'd arrested Vanessa. It had been eight or nine years ago, but he had known of her before then. Her husband had owned the biggest, plushest and most popular hotel on the seafront, and Vanessa had been the right person to help build up trade, with her attractive face, trim five-foot-two figure, designer clothes, and memory like a seasoned CID officer for guests' names, faces, likes and dislikes.

Suspecting that her husband was having an affair with one of the barmaids at the hotel, one night, Vanessa had followed him when he drove the staff home at the end of their shift. She'd tailed the hotel minibus in her Porsche, at a discreet distance, not that her husband had been looking for her. He'd been too busy dropping off all his staff – but one.

Vanessa had followed him and his remaining passenger to a car park on the cliff top, and waited; when her husband and the barmaid had finished and were about to turn back, Vanessa revved her engine and crashed her car into the minibus at full speed.

The first coppers on the scene almost cried. Some talked about nothing else for days. The spectacle of a two-month-old Porsche turned into a lump of written-off scrap metal was more than most grown men could bear. Miraculously, Vanessa walked away from the wreckage without a scratch. Her husband and his lover weren't so lucky. Neither had bothered to fasten their seatbelts, and the barmaid, who was fixing her lipstick at the time, in order to allay any suspicions her new husband might have about her late return, had been thrown through the windscreen of the minibus. To quote the duty sergeant who'd interviewed her in casualty, "her face had looked like a jigsawed Picasso". When Dan saw her a couple of months later in court, her scars hadn't healed well.

Vanessa's husband still ran the hotel – from a wheelchair. And it hadn't been just his legs that had gone. Vanessa had laughed so much when the court had been told the full extent of his injuries, she'd had to be tranquillised.

'You're him!' Vanessa's screech brought Dan Evans sharply back into the present. She looked from Dan to Lyn to the two men sitting behind the door. Realising she had an audience, she played the scene for all it was worth. 'You didn't believe me,' she screamed at Peter. 'You patronised me.' She tossed her head. 'Not one of you,' her gaze lingered on Lyn, 'has ever been interested in anything I had to say. And it was all true.' Her voice dropped. 'Every word, and now you know it's true, you want to talk to me. Well I don't want to talk to you. Not after the way you treated me.'

'I can understand that, Vanessa.' Peter's tone was muted, apologetic.

Dan stared at him, dumbfounded. He'd never heard Peter speak softly before.

'I know what I saw.' Vanessa repeated. 'You buried her. You – ' she pointed at Dan.

'Not Inspector Evans, Vanessa, but someone who looked like him,' Peter broke in. 'And we know about it because, thanks to you, we found her. You were right, and we were wrong. But she's found now, and we'd like you to tell us what you saw. Will you, please?'

'He buried her right there. Right in the middle… ' she began to repeat what she'd said before, then, without warning, she said something that galvanised Peter and Dan's attention. 'It wasn't like last time.'

'What last time?' They asked the question in unison.

59

'The last time he buried one.'

'Where, Vanessa? Where did he bury another one?' Peter asked.

'Not telling you.' She clammed her lips shut, and turned her back on him.

Harry shook his head in warning when Dan moved to rise from his chair.

'Vanessa?' Peter left his chair and offered it to her. 'Won't you sit down?'

'No.'

'Please, take my chair.'

She hesitated for what seemed like hours, before finally sitting down. Harry eased himself out of his seat. Peter took it and faced Vanessa.

'Vanessa, you told me that I didn't care enough to give the body in the garden a decent burial. I promise you, I do care. And I care about the other one as well. Won't you tell us where we can find it, so we can bury that one too?'

'It's in the garden.'

'It's a big garden, Vanessa.'

She whirled around and pointed at Dan. 'He knows. He buried them. Ask him.'

Peter reined in his irritation. 'Vanessa, that's Inspector Evans. He's a police officer.'

'He did it. And I'm not going to tell you any more.' Vanessa turned her face to the wall.

Harry touched Peter's shoulder and shook his head.

Peter left his chair. 'I'm going now, Vanessa.' He stood in front of her, but she refused to look at him. 'I'll come back and see you later.'

'Sergeant Collins is going now, Vanessa, but you can stay and have a chat with me, if you like,' Harry suggested. 'Shall I send for tea and biscuits?'

60

'I'm tired.' She closed her eyes.

'Later perhaps?'

'I want to go to bed.'

Lyn nodded to the porter, who wheeled the chair forward.

Dan followed Peter out of the door. 'Ring the Station and tell them to call out the helicopter and heat-seeking cameras. I want every inch of the grounds photographed,' Dan ordered as soon as they were out of earshot of Harry's office. He fell silent as the porter pushed Vanessa's wheelchair up the corridor.

Harry joined them. 'You can't believe what Vanessa said about a second body being buried in the garden. She's had so much attention lavished on her since this morning I suspect she's simply seeking more. You wouldn't be doing her any favours by paying credence to anything she said.'

'The problem is, Mr Goldman,' Dan turned to Harry, 'after what we uncovered following her last bout of attention seeking, we dare not ignore any information she volunteers. I'm afraid the risk of not "doing her any favours" is one we have to take.'

Trevor stood poised in the doorway that separated the familiar, secure world of his ward from the frightening, unknown world of the outside. He closed his eyes, took a deep breath, and put one foot on the doorstep. Leaning on his stick he dragged his other foot forward. Stepping down on to the path, he opened his eyes again.

He swayed, overwhelmed by the noise and people rushing around. He shrank back, afraid they were on a collision course with him, although the nearest person was over ten yards away. Fighting nausea, he struggled to take another step, sideways this time, so he could remain close to the building. An officer ran past from behind, so close, Trevor could smell the sweat from his serge uniform. A group of patients walked towards him, heading for the screened-off area on the lawn. Panic stricken, he froze.

He felt as though he were surrounded by uniformed police and people in white coats – although there were less than a dozen within sight. He heard a screech and turned. Alison Bevan was leaning out of a window in the therapy block, laughing at a porter who'd dropped a sandwich into a flowerbed.

He took another breath, and turned away from the police activity to the rest of the garden. But the normally tranquil grounds were full of lines of officers, beating the bushes and combing the lawns. The drive was strewn with police cars, ambulances, and the overflow from the car parks which were jam-packed with television journalists' and reporters' cars.

Reaching blindly, he groped for the door-handle behind him; as soon as his hand closed over it, he turned on his heel, swung his stick, and in his eagerness to return to the cocooned security of the ward, slammed the length of his body painfully against the edge of the door.

Bile rose into his mouth as he fought to push the door open. But all he succeeded in doing was thumping the full weight of the metal-framed UVPC door in his face; hitting the bridge of his nose, and almost knocking himself out. He reeled backwards, dropping his stick and falling to his knees, but still retaining his grip on the door-handle.

'Trying to get in, Trevor? Let me help you.' Spencer Jordan's strong hands closed over his elbows. Easing Trevor to his feet, he opened the door, and helped him in. 'Your stick.' Spencer retrieved it and handed it to him. 'First time is always a bitch,' he lapsed into American jargon. 'I remember it well.'

Trevor only just made it to his room in time to vomit the goat's cheese sandwich into the toilet bowl of his private bathroom. Spencer held his head and sponged his face with cold water. Used to nurses ministering to his needs, Trevor saw nothing odd in Spencer's actions. When he finished retching, Spencer helped him back into his room and steered him into a chair.

'As I was saying, the first time out is a bitch.' Spencer smiled. 'But you did it. And on your own.'

'I turned and ran,' Trevor muttered, shame-faced.

'You wouldn't have if there had been fewer people around.' Spencer pulled a packet of cigarettes from his pocket. 'Smoke?'

'I don't.'

'Neither do I.' Spencer returned them to his pocket. 'I keep them for patients who do.' He fingered the packet. 'Sometimes I wish I did. It gives you something to do with your hands.'

Trevor managed a small smile.

'Feel better?'

'Yes thanks,' Trevor said diffidently. 'I don't want to keep you if you've a class.'

Spencer walked to the window, moved the curtains, and looked outside. 'I haven't a class for another hour and a half, but if you'd rather be left alone, I'll go.'

'I don't want to be a bore and monopolise your time, when you have something better to do.'

'You're not a bore and I've nothing better to do,' Spencer answered easily.

'Just one more job in your crowded day,' Trevor said dryly.

'You're not a job.' Spencer looked him in the eye. 'You remind me of myself, of where I was a few months ago. In fact, until you came along, I was beginning to wonder if I'd made any progress at all.' A ghost of a smile hovered at the corners of his mouth. 'Then, when I saw you, I realised I had moved on.'

'So, I'm good as a progress indicator, if nothing else.'

'You're different from the others. Your depression stems from your physical injuries and sometimes doctors are too ready to dismiss the havoc that severe physical damage can do to the mind, as well as the body. It's all very well for them to tell you that you're fit enough to start again where you left off, as though nothing had happened. You and I know it's not that easy. First, you're weak as a kitten because you've done nothing except lie around hospitals for months. Second, while you've been gone, the world has become larger, noisier and more threatening. Even simple everyday things like getting up in the morning, washing, dressing, talking, walking out through one door and in through another, take more effort than they did before; and that's without taking crippling pain into account.'

'You really have been through it, haven't you?'

'Yes.' Spencer went to the door. 'But today you took your first and biggest step. You went outside of your own accord.'

'But I panicked... '

'And next time you'll pick a better time, when there are fewer people around. You'll walk two or three steps more than you did today before you turn back. The day after, it'll be further. One day you'll reach the gate. And sometime after that you'll get on a bus.'

'You really think it will be that easy?'

'It won't be easy because every step and every move will take enormous effort. But as I said, you took the biggest and most painful step today. Nothing will ever take as much effort again. Keep reminding yourself of that, not the panic that drove you back. But that's enough of me lecturing. Want to come down to my room, and finish the drawing of the mysterious lady with the dark hair?'

'No, thank you.'

Spencer didn't try to persuade him. 'Perhaps later. I'll be there all afternoon.'

'Perhaps,' Trevor echoed before Spencer closed the door.

You took the biggest and most painful step today. Nothing will ever take as much effort again.

Trevor wanted to believe Spencer, but at that moment all he wanted to do was crawl into his bed, pull the sheet over his head, curl up, and never emerge again.

'There are six modern single-story ward blocks. Corridors straight down the centre linking with rooms on either side; toilets, bathrooms and sluice rooms, at the far end. Kitchens, linen cupboards and day rooms at this end; patients' double, single and four-bedded rooms in the centre. The single rooms tend to be reserved for difficult patients.'

Peter listened to Harry, recalled Trevor's single room, and suppressed an urge to thump the diminutive psychiatrist.

'This particular block is for people suffering from Alzheimer's... ' the roar of a helicopter hovering overhead drowned out Harry.

Dan looked at Peter. 'Headquarters hasn't wasted any time.'

'... They are very confused... ' Harry continued.

Peter peered through the glass wall of the day room. Twenty elderly men and women were sitting in a circle.

The room was neat, clean, and sterile, the furniture upholstered in green vinyl, the walls decorated in the same shade of yellow as Goldman's office, and hung with a series of pastel landscapes. Two nurses were trying to evoke the patients' interest in books of old photographs.

'I hope they shoot me before I get to that stage,' Peter muttered to Dan.

'Something I can help you with, Sergeant Collins?' Harry enquired.

'I hope not,' he replied.

'As I was saying, each block accommodates patients with various symptoms, some severe, some mild – although we try to treat most of the mild cases as outpatients. We do, however, try to group like with like. It simplifies the arrangements for therapy. The ward that your friend Trevor Joseph is on, for instance, principally houses patients who have been admitted for observation, alongside those who are clinically depressed. The block across the way,' Harry pointed to a parallel block, 'is where we place the majority of our phobia cases. The one directly in front of us caters for manias. The block behind us is the drug and alcohol dependency unit. We also have a block for women suffering from postnatal depression. It is slightly larger than the rest, as it has a nursery for the children.'

'If you group like with like, how come Vanessa Hedley is on Joseph's ward?' Peter asked.

'I said that we try to organise things that way, Sergeant Collins. Unfortunately, we don't always succeed. Because we try to treat as many patients as possible as outpatients, especially those with depression, your friend's ward tends to be the one with the least pressure on its resources. Vanessa is being evaluated at present, and as there was a bed available on that particular ward… '

'How long has she been here?' Dan interrupted.

'On the ward or in the hospital?' Goldman replied.

'Both.'

'I'd have to check the records. But if my memory serves me correctly, I'd say she's been on the ward about two months.'

'And in the hospital?'

'Longer.'

'Did she come here directly from prison?'

'I really shouldn't be discussing… '

'It doesn't matter.' Dan knew he could find out all he needed from the records. He glanced at the plan he was carrying. 'All six blocks are connected to the main block by perspex tunnels?'

'They are,' Harry concurred.

'But not with one another?'

'Not directly. You'd have to walk to the main block then retrace your steps down one of the other tunnels to reach a separate block.'

'And all the therapy units lie in this area here.' Evans jabbed his index finger over a large space set behind the old hospital building, in front of the modern blocks. It was dotted with the outlines of demountables.

'Not any longer. We're in the process of relocating the therapy units in the old hospital alongside the administration offices. Those blocks were purpose-built in the seventies. And, like most buildings of that era, they're sadly lacking. Their roofs are flat and leaking, there are damp patches on the walls, the windows are metal-framed and draughty… '

'In short, they are cold and wet with rotting fabric. There isn't much you can tell us about buildings built in the seventies,' Dan interrupted. 'Our station is one of them.'

67

'We all have our crosses to bear, Inspector Evans. All the blocks, apart from the postnatal depression ward, are identical, and our staff man them round the clock. If anything untoward happens in any of them, we know about it immediately. There's little point in you looking over all of them. It would gain you nothing, and the patients would be upset at the intrusion. If you have to enter any of them I would appreciate it if you and your men were accompanied either by me or Dorothy Clyne.'

'And where would we find you in an emergency?'

'The switchboard can always reach us.'

'We will have to visit them, if only to interview the patients, but I'll bear your directive in mind, Dr Goldman. We are here to conduct a murder investigation,' Dan reminded him.

'Where do you want to go next?' Harry asked.

'The therapy units, then the old hospital.'

'The therapy units, like the wards, are the province of the patients. I would appreciate it if you entered them only with a staff escort.'

'You mentioned there were some areas of the hospital to which we could have free access,' Dan said. 'Perhaps now would be a good time to tell us where they are.'

'The floors of the old hospital that have been taken over by the Health Authority's administration unit, but it might still be as well if you cleared your movements with our administrator, Tony Waters.' Harry looked at his watch. 'If you'll excuse me, I have an appointment with a patient. If you wait here, I'll ask a porter to take you to Tony's office.'

He left them in the corridor and disappeared into the ward office. Through the open door Peter saw a male nurse talking to an attractive blonde sister.

'That sod doesn't trust us,' Peter informed Dan.

'He has a hospital to run.'

'Or something to hide.'

'That's what I like to see, Peter, coppers assuming everyone guilty until proven innocent.'

Harry Goldman returned with the blonde. 'Sister Ashford has volunteered to give up a few minutes of her free time to take you to Mr Waters' office. If you'll excuse me gentlemen.' Goldman wandered off down the corridor, then turned back. 'You will keep me up-to-date with your progress, Inspector?'

'If we make any you'll be the first to know,' Evans assured him.

CHAPTER FIVE

'Dirt's clogging the sink again.' Patrick O'Kelly shouted to his assistant as he peered through the magnifying glass he was moving slowly, centimetre by centimetre, along the thighs of the body laid out on the slab.

'I thought I'd got rid of it all,' his assistant grumbled as he left the earth he was sifting, from one side of a body-bag to the other, through a fine mesh.

Patrick inched the glass upwards on to the torso. 'Superintendent,' he acknowledged Bill who walked through the double doors.

'Anything for us yet?' Bill surveyed the body stretched out on the slab and the body-bag opened out on the slab next to it.

'I haven't finished examining the body,' the pathologist retorted irritably.

'Sorry to press you, but at the moment we know absolutely nothing. A few basic facts might kick off our investigation.'

'Like?' Patrick asked, although he already had an idea what Bill was looking for.

'Like who she was, and how and why she died?'

'The "who" I can't help you with. The "how" I told you on site.' Patrick straightened his back, discarded his magnifying glass, and walked to the head of the corpse. Pushing back the eyelids with his thumb and forefinger, he prodded at the burst blood vessels that had flooded the whites with scarlet. He indicated the evidence of several smaller haemorrhages on the forehead. And those are just the ones you can see. I found more in the internal organs. Asphyxiation.'

'She was buried alive?'

'Even without the haemorrhages the build-up of dirt in the nostrils and lungs confirms it.' Patrick pushed aside the bone-cutter he'd used to open the ribcage, and removed the square of tissue he'd used to cover the slit in the skin, not out of any finer feelings for the corpse, but from the need to keep contamination of the other body parts to a minimum. 'Judging from the amount of earth and debris in the bronchial tubes,' he palpated a tube he'd slit open, and crumbs of black dirt fell into his hand, 'she struggled for breath until the last.'

'How long would that have taken?' Bill flinched at the thought of the young girl stretched out dead and naked before him, fighting for air, while being smothered by shovel-full after shovel-full of earth.

'Impossible to fix an accurate time. A lot depends on whether he worked quickly or slowly. And, then again, he might have dumped her at the bottom of the pit some time before he buried her.'

'How long would it have taken from the first breath that was more dirt than air, to the last?' Bill pressed, refusing to allow Patrick to fob him off.

'Going by what I've dug out of her tubes and lungs, I'd say somewhere between five and ten minutes; but she wouldn't have been fully conscious towards the end.' Patrick retrieved his magnifying glass and resumed his minute study of her skin. 'I was right about the lips. They had been super-glued together. She managed to tear them apart, but not that long before she died, judging by the bleeding. Bingo!' he shouted gleefully. 'Puncture marks, upper right arm. A whole beautiful series of them. Some bruised and old, some fresher, and one very fresh.' He spoke into the voice-activated dictaphone that hung above the slab before marking the sites with blue ink. 'I've taken blood samples, if it's detectable, we'll soon know about it.'

'How long has she been dead?'

'You know I hate that question.'

'And you know I have to ask it,' Bill replied.

'Body temperature was that of the surroundings when I examined her in the pit, so that puts death at least eighteen to twenty-four hours before, taking into account that asphyxiation causes body temperature to rise, not fall, immediately after death. No rigor mortis, little deterioration – that means your guess would be as good as mine.'

'I hate it when you say that.'

Patrick tore off his rubber gloves and threw them in the bin at the head of the table. He switched off the water that was rippling around the corpse, folded his arms, and leaned against the tiled wall. 'But there is something that might interest you. The stomach was completely empty, and the body dehydrated.'

'Which means?'

'She'd been starved before death. No food or water.'

'For how long?'

'After examining the small intestines, I'd say at least forty-eight hours – possibly longer.'

'Then she could have been taken and kept somewhere.'

'That's for you to find out.' Patrick looked at her face. 'Pretty girl.'

Bill looked at the corpse, really looked at it, for the first time. O'Kelly's assistant had combed the shoulder-length curls away from the face and brushed off the dirt. He had to agree, whoever she was, she had been a pretty girl.

'Have you taken new photographs?' Bill asked.

'Digital print outs are in the office.'

'Anything on her?'

'No identification. Rings, one gold, set with a red onyx stone, one silver in the shape of a wishbone, a gold chain, crucifix and Saint Nicholas, all nine-carat, and a lot of good they did her. The patron saint of travellers must have been on tea break when she was being buried.' Patrick nodded towards two piles; a small one of jewellery and a larger one of clothes heaped on a side table. 'We found a key ring with two Yale keys in the pocket of her skirt. Everything has been dusted for prints, so they're safe to handle.'

Bill picked up the key ring and fingered the tab, a miniature rubber troll with his thumbs in his ears and fingers extended.

'The clothes have chain store labels, no name tags, no markings, and nothing except the keys in the pockets,' Patrick continued, 'I've taken dental X-rays. There are fourteen fillings, so she should be on someone's records. No foreign fibres on the skin or clothes. The dirt, as you see, is still being sifted.'

'Sexual assault?'

'No signs of it. Clothes are soiled but appear undisturbed. Vaginal swabs tested negative for semen. There's a tattoo.' He took a small rubber sheet, wrapped it around the right leg and rolled the corpse on to its side. The back, thighs and calves were dark with stagnant blood. 'Butterfly high on right thigh. Nice work.'

'Age?'

'Early twenties. Blue eyes, dyed blonde hair; the rest you can see for yourself. I've told you just about everything, but if you want to listen to the tape in my office you're welcome. Word processing facilities being

73

what they are in this place, it won't be in print until tomorrow.'

'I can wait.'

'Coffee?'

'No, thanks,' Bill refused, as Patrick's assistant left the office with three specimen jars filled with murky beige liquid.

'Bring the chocolate biscuits, Alan,' Patrick called out.

Alan dumped the jars on an empty slab, opened one of the refrigerated body drawers, and removed a packet of chocolate wafers.

Bill had met O'Kelly the man after hearing about O'Kelly the legend. The first time he'd visited the mortuary he had walked in on Patrick, his assistant, and the senior surgeon from the staff of the General, sitting in a row on one of the slabs, facing an opened corpse while eating pasties and drinking cans of lager.

Patrick called it a "working lunch". They were trying to determine cause of death, but they were, as Patrick had delighted in telling him, spoilt for choice. The man had lung cancer, heart disease and liver failure. At first he'd thought that Patrick had set out to deliberately shock him, or any copper who dared to trespass unannounced on his domain. Ten years on, he knew better. The pathologist had lived with corpses for so long, he simply treated them as inanimate objects to be examined and studied with the same unemotional regard he bestowed on his instruments or the laboratory furniture.

'I'll let you know if we find anything in the dirt,' Patrick jumped up and sat on a spare slab.

'I'd appreciate it.'

'We'll carry on as soon as we've finished this.' Patrick held up his coffee.

Bill knew Patrick was dismissing him, but he lingered in the formaldehyde-ridden atmosphere. 'Lot of work on at the moment?' He glanced around the mortuary. There were no other bodies in sight, and apart from the slabs the body bag and victim were laid on, they were all clean and scrubbed, but Bill noticed that three-quarters of the mortuary drawers were tagged. And that either meant there'd been a rush for the pathologist's services, or one was about to start.

'The usual.' O'Kelly peeled the silver paper from his biscuit. 'Why?'

'We took aerial shots of the grounds of Compton Castle an hour ago.'

'Heat-seeking cameras?' Patrick looked warily at Bill.

'We can't be sure of anything yet.'

'How many sites have you earmarked to dig?'

'Three. But they could be buried compost rotting and generating heat.'

'Close to the kitchens?'

'No.'

Patrick looked to his assistant. 'Clean and repack my site kit as soon as we've finished break.'

'It's probably nothing,' Bill was afraid he'd said too much and made a fool of himself.

'I'm no detective, but even I noticed the compost bin outside the kitchen door.'

'The spots are in the flowerbeds.'

'Concentrated spots? Not a thin spread?'

Bill nodded. Patrick pushed the remainder of his wafer between his lips and finished his coffee.

'Get moving, Alan, we've work to do,' he mumbled through a full mouth.

                          *   *   *

'As you see Sergeant, Constable,' Tony Waters smiled at
Michelle, who'd been foisted on Peter yet again, much to
the sergeant's disgust, 'these attics haven't been used in
years.'

Tony halted on a landing above a steep, narrow
staircase, and opened identical opposing doors, on to long,
low-ceilinged galleries. Both were strewn with dust balls
and decorated with spiders' webs. Peter walked into the
right-hand gallery and opened the door at the far end. Box
upon cardboard box, all covered with layers of grey dust,
were piled up in a long narrow room lit by a small, narrow
window.

'Old records?' Peter asked

'I presume so. I've only opened one box. They were
here when my department moved into this building,' Tony
followed Peter into the attic.

'It seems bizarre to build new blocks out in the
grounds with all this space going begging,' Peter
commented.

'The stairs are steep. The banisters have dry rot, and
compliance with the county's disabled access policy
would mean ripping the fabric of the building apart to put
in lifts. Even if we found the money, it would be wasted.
Compton Castle was put on the list for demolition in the
1980s. We've been trying to run it down for the past ten
years. If it hadn't been for the cutbacks that held up the
building of new psychiatric wards in the General, it would
have been a pile of rubble years ago.'

Peter turned his back on Michelle and Tony and
walked down the gallery until he reached another steeper
and narrower staircase than the one they'd ascended.

'There are three staircases on this floor,' Waters informed him. 'The central one we came up by, another like this that serves the left-hand side of the building and an outside metal fire escape at the back.'

'Does each floor have access to the fire escape?' Peter noticed that Michelle was writing down everything that the administrator was telling them in her notebook.

'Yes, there's an outside landing on every floor except the ground-floor.'

'You do realise this is only a quick once-over,' Peter informed him, 'before we bring in teams to conduct a thorough search.'

'As far as this building is concerned, you can search all you like. But we'd rather that you searched the ground-floor therapy units either late at night or early in the morning when they're not being used by patients.'

'We'll bear your request in mind,' Peter replied.

'The only thing you're likely to find on this floor is spiders.' Tony hit a web.

'And mice,' Peter observed a pile of mouse droppings by the cardboard boxes.

Tony led the way back down a narrow staircase. 'Built for the maids,' Tony reached out to support Michelle's arm when she caught her heel in a stair-tread.

'Miniature maids,' Peter grumbled, as his shoulders brushed both the left and right-hand walls.

When they reached the floor below, Waters opened a door directly in front of them, and led them through a series of high-ceilinged, wooden-floored old wards packed with computers, printers and office desks.

'This looks strange,' Michelle commented.

'What?' Peter asked.

'Modern office furniture and technology in these surroundings.'

'The furniture was bought for the new County Hall offices. We had to move out last year because of pressure on accommodation.'

'God bless civil servants and the local authorities,' Peter remarked irreverently. 'You can always count on them to expand to fill every available inch of space.'

'General office,' Waters ignored his barbed comment, as he headed towards the centre of the building. He nodded to the clerks, mostly middle-aged women, with a sprinkling of young girls and boys. 'Most of the assistant administrators are on the floor below; reception and my own office are, as you know, on the ground-floor.'

They walked through the administrators' offices below the general office. They were housed in what had been one single vast ward. But the area had been subdivided by plasterboard and glass partitions to provide separate cubicles.

When they reached a door that opened on to a landing, Tony produced a key. 'These rooms are kept locked. Our cleaning bill for this place is astronomical without opening up the disused areas.' He unlocked the door and stood back to allow Peter to look in. 'Old kitchens,' he explained as Peter looked at a series of small rooms that still contained stone sinks and zinc-covered cupboards and tables. 'And pantries and storerooms.'

'These rooms lie empty, while the attics are full of boxes? Didn't anyone think to tell the removal men they could have stopped off halfway?' Peter noted the thick layer of dust that blanketed the floorboards.

'Those records were put into storage in the fifties, when this was still being used. The papers in the box I opened dated back to the turn of the century.'

'They could be worth a fortune.'

'I doubt it – but I've notified the town archivist. When he has time, he'll examine them. Shall we go down to the ground-floor?'

At the foot of the stairs Peter noticed a narrow passage behind the staircase. It led to a locked door that faced the rear of the building. He tapped on the door.

'That leads to the old padded cells. They were ripped out twenty years ago, but they hadn't been used for years.'

'Can I take a look?'

'There isn't much to see.' Irritated, Waters tried four keys in the lock before he hit on the right one. They entered a long dark passage lit by widely-spaced weak light bulbs. After twenty yards the corridor began to slope steeply downwards. Waters switched on another string of lights and halted before a row of six identical concrete cells.

'No doors,' Peter stared into the eight-foot-square, grey concrete boxes.

'They were taken off when the padding was ripped out.'

'And this door?' Peter pointed to a steel door at the far end of the corridor.

'Leads to the old laundry and mortuary. You can also enter them from the main corridor, but as we're here, we may as well go this way. He fumbled with the keys again. After a couple of minutes of trial and error, the rusty lock gave way. He switched on the lights.

'Are we at ground-floor level or basement?' Peter asked. There had been no windows in the padded cell area, but the corridor ahead also loomed dark and forbidding, devoid of natural light.

'Somewhere between the two,' Tony flicked on another light. 'It's a half-level floor, built into a low mound at the back. You can see it on the plan.'

Michelle unfolded the drawing she was carrying.

'This is probably the first time in years anyone's walked through this area from the cells. We use the old laundry for storing rubbish before it's burned in the incinerator.'

Peter looked at neat rows of bulging bright-pink plastic bags, boldly imprinted DANGER MEDICAL WASTE.

Tony selected another key and opened a wooden door. 'This is the male mortuary.'

'The what?' Michelle repeated.

'The male mortuary. The female mortuary is down there.' Tony pointed down the corridor.

'You separate male and female dead?' Peter laughed. 'What's the problem? You afraid they'll get up to something they shouldn't?'

'The Victorians built this place, not me.' Tony opened the door to a surprisingly large, light and airy room, although all the illumination came from bubbled glass panes set close to the ceiling. Fully tiled in white wall tiles and black floor tiles, it contained two zinc-covered tables, the most enormous stone sink Peter had ever seen and, facing them, a bank of twelve body-size steel drawers.

'Tin-lined.' Tony pulled one drawer out after another. They moved stiffly, their runners warped.

'I take it you don't use this place any more, either?'

'Yes, we do. But only for routine deaths that don't require a post mortem. If there's a problem with diagnosis or death certificates, we send the body to the mortuary in the General.'

'And Patrick O'Kelly?'

'Who?' Waters stared blankly at Peter.

'Patrick O'Kelly, the pathologist in the General. I thought as you worked for the Health Authority, you might have heard of him.'

'No, I haven't.'

Peter looked into a drawer. 'So these are still used?'

'Particularly when someone dies on the geriatric ward.'

'Do you have a mortuary attendant?'

'Not since we made the last one redundant two years ago.'

'Who lays out the bodies?'

'Usually a nurse. One or two of the porters can do it at a push.'

'Can we see the female mortuary?' Michelle asked.

'Want to find out if they're going to lay you out behind flowered curtains?' Peter enquired.

Ignoring Peter, Michelle followed Tony into a room, identical in every respect to the male mortuary.

'The laundry.' When they emerged from the half-level Tony pointed out a hall dotted with sinks and enormous round boilers.

'Disused?' Peter asked.

'Laundry was put out to tender years ago. Kitchens,' Tony opened another door, this time on an area bustling with noisy activity.

'Not put out to tender.' Peter gazed at the white-overalled staff who were flitting between modern cookers and stainless-steel work surfaces.

They walked down the back staircase to the cellars and a boiler room that was fed on gas, the sub-station that housed the cables for the incoming electricity supplies and the generator back-up. Remembering another case he'd worked on, Peter lifted the iron plates that covered the incoming supply, but he uncovered only thick black cables.

'The incinerator was installed only last year.' Waters pushed back a heavy sliding door and said hello to a man who was fiddling with rows of dials. Peter looked at the mass of pipes, cables, and small tunnels leading off into darkened spaces.

'We've seen the whole of the old building?'

'Yes.'

'It's a paradise for someone who wants to conceal a body,' Peter mused. 'And bloody murder for a policeman looking for clues. Absolute bloody murder.'

CHAPTER SIX

'Anything interesting?' Dan asked when Peter and Michelle walked into the administrator's office.

'Nothing obvious,' Peter replied. 'Only a nightmare of a building to search. Who's organising it?'

Dan studied his fingernails and said nothing.

'You can't do this to me.' Peter protested.

'Drug Squad officers organise the most thorough searches,' Dan flattered.

Tony spoke to his secretary in the outer office before joining them. His face creased in annoyance when he saw Dan sitting behind his desk, a notepad covered with scribbles in front of him, the telephone conveniently placed at his elbow. 'Can I get you anything, Inspector?'

'No thank you,' Dan replied. 'Your secretary has provided me with everything I need.' He moved an empty coffee mug to the edge of the desk before rising from the chair. 'And I won't be inconveniencing you long. We're moving a mobile HQ into the grounds.'

'A demountable building?' Tony asked warily.

'More of a caravan,' Dan looked through the window. 'Perhaps you can advise us on a suitable site.'

'If it's space you're looking for, there are rooms the size of football pitches going begging in this building,' Tony said.

'Our mobile HQ contains all we need, and we won't get under anyone's feet,' Dan countered. 'Where do you suggest we put it, Mr Waters?'

'I'll think about it,' Tony put off the decision.

'It'll be here in an hour,' Dan said shortly.

'How about close to the main gate, so we can keep police traffic in and out of the hospital to a minimum.'

'That's too public,' Dan stroked his double chin. 'It will attract sightseers. I thought somewhere at the back of this building. Behind the tunnels?'

'As you wish,' Tony agreed, wondering why Dan had bothered to ask his advice when he'd already decided on the location.

'I'm also expecting two teams of police,' Dan warned.

'To search the building?'

'Later, first I want them to do some digging. The heat-seeking cameras came up with a few spots. They're probably nothing, but to be on the safe side we're going to excavate your flowerbeds.'

'May I ask how long this digging is likely to take?' Tony was beginning to wonder if his day was ever going to end.

'There are two hours of daylight left. We'll start as soon as they get here, which with luck,' Evans glanced at his watch, 'will be in the next ten minutes. But if we find anything unusual, we may work through the night.'

'In the dark?'

'We'll bring up floodlights.'

'I must protest. Lights would definitely disturb the patients.'

'We may have no choice. One more thing before I go,' Dan pulled a sheet of typed paper from his pad, and a photograph. 'These came up from the station half an hour ago. Description and new photograph of the victim for you to circulate among your staff.'

Tony took the photograph, and blanched.

'You knew her, Mr Waters?' Dan asked.

'It looks like – Rosie Tywford.' Tony gripped the edge of his desk. 'The hair's right,' he faltered, 'but the face is all wrong. The skin's too dark.'

'It would be, Mr Waters. She was asphyxiated,' Dan explained. 'There's a description; five-foot-six, dyed blonde hair, blue eyes, no distinguishing marks other than a butterfly tattooed on her buttock.'

'I wouldn't know about the butterfly, Inspector.' Tony dropped the photograph on the desk. 'But everything else fits.'

'Who was she?' Peter asked as Tony sank down in his chair.

'She worked in this department as a clerk, before she had a breakdown. Then she became a patient.'

'When was the last time you saw her?' Dan demanded.

'I can't remember.'

'Think!' Peter ordered.

'Sometime last week. Harry told me that he was discharging her as an outpatient. She'd been discharged from the ward weeks ago. He said she was thinking of visiting her parents in Devon before returning to work here.'

'Where did she live?' Peter pressed.

'How should I know?' Tony replied irritably. 'A rented room or flat I suppose. I only spoke to the girl once or twice. If you want to find out more, I suggest you ask Harry or Human Resources.'

'We'll do that,' Dan said. 'Thank you for your assistance, Mr Waters. No doubt we'll be in touch again soon.'

'Where to now?' Peter asked Dan as they left the administrator's office.

'Human Resources then Harry Goldman. Here.' Dan handed Michelle the photograph and sheet of paper detailing the victim's description.

85

'You want me to do it, sir?' she bristled with pride at the trust he was placing in her.

'Be quick. I've a feeling these offices shut early, and it's four now.' Dan watched as she hurried down the corridor, her long-legged stride hampered by her narrow skirt. 'Were any of us ever that keen, Peter?'

'I can't remember.'

Dan headed into a perspex tunnel. 'What do you think of the administrator?'

'He's a stuffed shirt who might know more about that girl than he let on.'

'We can't build walls until we have foundations to lay them on,' Dan mused. 'I want you to oversee the staff interviews.'

'Must I?'

'I said oversee. That doesn't mean you have to do them all yourself.'

'But it means I have to co-ordinate the resulting information.'

'As well as supervise the search of these buildings, but I'll see to it that you have help. Bill's bringing in a couple of teams... '

'Shouldn't we check if they've arrived?' Peter prompted, before Dan could think of something else to unload on to him.

'They can start without us. You do know that apart from the sites picked up by the heat-seeking cameras we're going to have to scour every inch of garden that can be seen from Vanessa Hedley's window?'

'With probes?' Peter suggested.

'In every centimetre of ground,' Dan warned.

'Garden that size could take weeks.'

'It could.' Dan turned the corner, and once more he and Peter were locked in the strange, disembodied white tunnel world. 'But now I intend doing something I've been trying to find time for all day. I'm going to visit Trevor Joseph, and as I didn't know him that well, I'd like you to re-introduce me.'

'He's a hopeless case.' Peter hated himself for declaring it.

'I'd like to see how hopeless for myself,' Dan walked towards the wards. 'You do know where to find him, don't you?'

As usual, Trevor was slumped in the chair in his room, but to Peter's surprise he had a book on his lap, and as it was the right way up, Peter had no reason to suspect that he hadn't been reading it.

'You remember Inspector Evans?' Peter walked in and sat on Trevor's bed.

'Dan Evans.' Dan held out his hand and Trevor shook it, but he refused to meet Dan's steady gaze, and continued to stare down at his book.

'Can we talk?' Dan asked.

'I suppose so.' Trevor moved his legs so Dan could sit alongside Peter on the bed.

'You heard we found a body buried in the grounds here?'

'Yes.'

'You don't seem very interested?'

'I'm not.'

'It's murder. A young girl, early twenties, buried alive,' Evans informed him. 'I was hoping that you could help us.'

'I'm on sick leave.'

'You're also in this place.'

'As a patient,' Trevor reminded.

'You're a trained detective,' Dan persisted.

Trevor left his chair, walked to the window and looked into the garden. It was the first time Peter had seen him glance at the outside world since he'd been injured, but he suspected that Trevor was only doing so to avoid looking at Dan.

'That last case of yours...' Dan paused. 'It could have happened to any one of us.'

'But it happened to me.'

Peter had to strain his ears to catch what Trevor was saying.

'I know what you must be feeling,' Dan sympathised.

'You can have no possible idea what I'm feeling.'

'You're right, Trevor,' Dan braved the silence that followed Trevor's outburst. 'That was presumptuous of me. I can't begin to imagine what you've been through.'

'Or what I'm still going through,' Trevor added.

'I wouldn't have come to you if there was anyone else with your qualifications and inside knowledge of this place. We need your help.'

'I'm not fit enough to work.'

'All I want is for you to tell us about some of the people here. You've a trained eye; you know what we're looking for.'

'These people have been taking care of me,' Trevor protested. 'I haven't been watching them with a detective's eye.'

'But you know them?' Dan persevered.

'Not as well as they know me, and not well enough to know if one of them is a murderer.'

'Won't you at least talk to me?'

'I wouldn't be any help.'

'You must know something, this Vanessa Hedley, for instance.'

'She's disturbed. She rarely sleeps. She's always wandering around the place creating problems.'

'And Sister Marshall – Jean Marshall?' Trevor hadn't said anything that wasn't common knowledge, but Dan felt elated. Trevor was talking and who knew what else he might say?

'She's capable,' Trevor said succinctly.

'Nurse Lyn Sullivan?'

Peter thought he saw a flicker of interest in Trevor's eyes.

'She's young, pretty, too vulnerable for a place like this.'

'Spencer Jordan?'

'He's a good therapist. I'm not stupid. I know what you're doing, but I'm not in a position to help you.'

As silence reigned in the room once more, Trevor watched squads of men in white overalls move into the grounds. A police dog-handler's van pulled up in the "Doctors Only" parking bay. Bill Mulcahy in the centre of the lawn, alternately consulting the plan he was holding and an officer who hovered at his elbow.

'How many more are buried in the grounds?' Trevor asked.

'Who said there were more?' Dan replied.

'It doesn't take a detective to fathom what's happening out there.' Trevor continued to stare out of the window.

'Time you and I went to work, Peter.' Dan rose from the bed. 'All right if we call in and see you tomorrow, Trevor?'

'I can't stop you.' Trevor didn't turn around as they left.

*   *   *

'Is he always like that?' Dan asked Peter as they headed for the main door.

'You caught him on a good day. Today he answered your questions.'

'Have you thought it might be him?'

'Trevor?' Peter questioned incredulously.

'He's in here. He had the opportunity.'

'And what bloody motive?'

'He's depressed, disturbed – he's here… '

'As the result of being almost beaten to death,' Peter broke in defensively.

'I heard he became obsessed with one of the witnesses on his last case. A woman with long dark hair.' Dan looked at Peter. 'I saw that drawing on his bedside cabinet.'

'They knew one another before the case – he – they – Bloody hell, this is Trevor Joseph you're talking about!' Peter exploded.

'I shouldn't have to remind you of the first rule of detection; keep an open mind.'

'Even where one of our own is concerned?'

'Especially where one of our own is concerned,' Dan said firmly.

'We've pinpointed the sites with markers, and surrounded them with screens,' Bill announced as Dan and Peter joined him.

'Patrick?' Dan asked.

'Standing by. He can be here in ten minutes if we need him. Peter, you work with the group closest to the building. Dan, take this one.'

Peter walked across the turf towards the group Bill had entrusted to his care. It was a beautiful early spring evening. For the first time in months he took time to listen to birdsong. The sun hung, a blazing golden ball, low on the horizon; the air was redolent with the smell of magnolia and cherry blossom.

'I joined this force to catch criminals, not to pass out parking tickets and shovel bloody shit!'

Peter recognised the lament of the rookie. He stepped behind the canvas screen. 'What's your name, boy?'

'Chris Brooke, sir,' the rookie snapped smartly to attention.

'Shovelling shit is all you're likely to do while you continue to moan.' Peter thrust a spade into his hands, and stood watching while Chris Brooke pushed it into six inches of manured soil. 'You,' he shouted to a female constable standing on the public side of the canvas, 'take the plants he digs up and lay them next to that tree.'

'I haven't worked in this garden, man and boy for forty years, to have a lot of flatfoot coppers wreck it in one night.' Jimmy Herne strode across and grabbed the rose-bush Brooke was lifting over the canvas. 'These were only planted last week. You're disturbing the roots. One hard surface frost and they'll be... '

'How deep did you dig down?' Peter interrupted.

'The right depth for rose-bushes,' the old man barged behind the low canvas screen and thrust his face aggressively close to Peter.

'One foot? Two?'

'Three foot. Always three foot.' Herne snarled. 'And then lace the digging with well-rotted manure. Any fool will tell you that.'

'Thank you for that lecture,' Peter replied.

'It's hard to keep this garden going when all you have is your own two hands and two stupid boys no one else will give house-room to, and now... '

'Sorry, Grandpa,' Peter apologised, 'but it can't be helped. We'll put everything back the way we found it.'

'As if you'd be able to,' Jimmy mocked. 'I've yet to meet anyone these days who can tell a daffodil bulb from a bloody onion. Look at her,' he turned on the hapless female constable. 'Just look at her, setting that rose down. You stupid woman, you haven't a bloody clue… '

'See that man over there?' Peter pointed to Bill. 'He's in charge.'

Jimmy Herne stormed off towards Bill. Soon, his indignant screeches could be heard all over the garden.

Peter looked at the rookie. The mound of earth had grown, but the lad's pace was slackening. 'Change over,' he ordered.

'Thanks, sir.' Chris climbed out of the hole, and passed a grubby hand over his forehead.

'You were slowing up. I've no intention of spending the night here,' Peter commented.

Chris passed the shovel to Andrew Murphy. Murphy was a rarity on the force; a constable close to retiring age. He had joined the force before Peter and Trevor, and had neither sought nor received promotion, preferring the responsibility-free life of an ordinary constable to the hassle of command. Hanging his jacket on one of the posts supporting the canvas screen, he stepped into the hole. Peter crouched on his heels, watching while Murphy dug steadily downwards.

'Anything?' Peter asked when Andrew stopped.

'A bloody awful stench.' Murphy had taught not only Peter, but also Dan the ropes, and he didn't hold rank in the same awe as the rookies.

'Proceed carefully.'

'Too royal,' Murphy muttered. 'Damn!'

Peter saw a seething whirl of maggots shoot off the edge of Murphy's spade. He reeled back as the stench hit him; the foul, sickly-sweet, unmistakable reek of death.

'I've sliced the leg off a dog.' Murphy jumped out of the pit. 'A great big bloody hairy dog. And there's… '

'What?' Peter demanded as Murphy retched.

'A suitcase. A bloody suitcase. It's filthy, the top's cracked, but it's still a bloody suitcase.'

Head high, apparently oblivious to the admiring glances of the police officers who had nothing better to do than eye the nurses walking up and down the drive, Carol Ashford headed for the staff car park. She opened the door of her green, open-topped sports car, tossed her handbag inside, started the engine and drove slowly down the drive to join the flow of traffic wending along the main thoroughfare through the suburbs. She turned right at the foot of the hill, left the mainstream that was heading out from the town centre and raced out along the coast road.

It had been a long hard shift, and occasionally, like now, she regretted specialising in geriatric nursing. There were some rewards, like early promotion; but today had brought more problems than usual, probably because the patients had been unsettled by the police activity. Her oldest female patient had whined repeatedly that she wanted to go home; not the one she had shared with her husband for fifty years, but her childhood home that had been bombed during the war. Mr Greenway was so fascinated by events in the garden he hadn't made any effort to recognise his son and daughter-in-law when they visited. And Mrs Adams had managed to escape from the ward four times in as many hours.

Not for the first time, Carol wondered what she, or any of her staff were accomplishing by keeping the old dears warm and fed, when most of them barely realised they were alive.

She turned off the road into the lane that led to the farmhouse she and her husband had bought and refurbished with money inherited from her parents-in-law. Slowing the car to a crawl, she listened to the birds and smelled the blossom on the trees. She turned a sharp corner behind a high wall and drove into a farmyard. An old barn, its grey stone walls cleaned and repointed, one wall replaced by glass, housed their indoor swimming pool. Behind the house they'd had a tennis court built within the walls of the old kitchen garden; and in front of her was the house itself, its arched windows handcrafted in hardwood, framing her William Morris print curtains.

The house was something she and her husband had dreamed of, never believing they'd be able to afford anything like it until they were into their fifties. But here she was, not yet thirty, the proud possessor of everything she'd ever wanted – including, and especially, her man.

She parked next to the kitchen door. There was no sign of her husband's car, but she was used to being the first home. Although she would never have admitted it, she didn't like walking into the empty house because it was so isolated. If anything happened she could scream until her lungs burst, but no one would hear. Even the burglar alarms and the two guard dogs offered little comfort. Burglar alarms could be cut, and dogs poisoned. It happened; she read about it in the newspapers.

She walked through the back door into the porch they'd built to hold their boots, walking and working coats, and the dogs, before unlocking the kitchen door. The dogs greeted her enthusiastically and she let them into the main house. Warm air belched out into the fresh spring atmosphere. No matter what the weather, the kitchen was always warm, sometimes oppressively so. The Aga saw to that. There was a welcoming smell of food. She lifted the lid of the pot on the slow-burner. The chicken casserole she had prepared the night before was cooked to perfection. She opened the oven door and pushed the pot inside.

She whistled to the dogs and let them outside as soon as they had checked the house. It was the help's day for cleaning the brasses and oak cupboards. She could smell the polish. Dropping her handbag on to one of the cushioned bentwood rockers, she kicked off her shoes and padded barefoot around the ground floor, checking every room. The sitting room, more elegant than cosy with its hand-woven Brussels tapestries decorating the grey stone walls and its upholstered Parker Knoll chairs and sofas, was exquisite and untouched. The study, with its desks and book-lined walls, was dusty. It wouldn't be cleaned until Wednesday.

The dining room, cool and elegant with a massive period sideboard, striped upholstery, burnished silverware and a polished mahogany table that could seat twelve, yawned vacantly back at her. The den, with its media paraphernalia and pool table, was tidier than they'd left it. The litter of newspapers and circulars had been gathered up by the daily and returned to the magazine rack. And finally the morning room – the room she had claimed as her own, and furnished with pine bookcases, dressers, pretty chintz-covered sofas, and round occasional tables.

She stopped to pet her two Siamese cats, who divided their time between this room, the conservatory and the garden, before calling the dogs back in. Leaving them lying on the Persian rug in the galleried hall, she climbed the oak staircase her husband had bought from a builder who'd salvaged it from a mansion that had been demolished to make way for the marina.

She looked into the four spare bedrooms, each with its own en-suite. All were furnished in Victorian antiques. Their floorboards were polished, the rugs that covered them handmade Turkish. Although she could see into the bathrooms from the bedroom doors, she made a point of checking each unit before stepping into the master bedroom.

She sank down on the chaise-longue. The four-poster bed, handmade to her husband's specifications, was hung with lace curtains, and covered with a matching bedspread. In the corner opposite it was an antique roll-top desk and captain's chair. This one room alone had cost a fortune, but it had been worth every penny, she reflected as she opened the door to her dressing room.

She stripped off her uniform and underclothes and threw them, together with her stockings, into the linen bin that was emptied by their cleaner. Naked, she returned to the bedroom, and studied herself in the cheval mirror. Was that a pad of fat forming over her hips? She turned her back and twisted her head. She resolved to eat less and exercise more. Her husband abhorred anything less than perfect.

She touched her toes with the flat of her hands ten times, before walking into her bathroom. Her husband had his own mahogany-lined dressing room and bathroom, leading off the other side of the room. She turned on the taps of the huge Victorian bath, another product of her husband's expeditions to the salvage yard, and tossed a handful of bath salts into the water.

Humming a tuneless ditty, she pulled the pins from her long blonde hair. It swung to her waist, before she caught and rolled it up, pinning it securely on top of her head with a stick. Testing the water with her hand, she found it exactly as she liked it; stinging hot. Stepping in, she held her breath as the water burned her skin and turned it rosy pink. She submerged her body slowly, then, closing her eyes, she emptied her mind of thoughts, lay back and surrendered to the pleasure of the moment.

Without warning, the bathroom door flew open.

'Tony?' She called out, fighting the terror that rose in her throat.

'Were you expecting someone else?'

Her heartbeat quietened, she turned and smiled when she saw him standing in the doorway, his blue eyes and white-blond hair misted by steam.

'I brought you a martini. I'd hand it to you if I could find you.'

'Follow my voice.'

He handed her an ice-cold champagne glass filled to the brim and decorated with an olive and stroked one of her exposed breasts teasing the nipple to a peak.

She sipped her martini and looked at him over the rim of her glass.

'How about you get out of the bath?'

She rose from the water and he handed her a towel. She wrapped herself in it before stepping out. He took her martini and placed it together with his own on the windowsill.

'The bed or the floor?' he asked.

'The floor's wet.'

'So are you.' He stripped the towel away and flung it aside, before pushing her down on to her back.

Carol was used to Tony's lovemaking. It was abrasive, devoid of gentleness and tenderness. When they made love during daylight hours, as they often did, he rarely even undressed. He never considered her or her

97

enjoyment, only his own needs. But as she lay back, the knowledge that he took pleasure in her body was enough for her.

She loved Tony passionately, with every fibre of her being, although she was careful never to allow the depth of her obsession to show, lest he regard it as smothering. Sometimes she felt as though she existed only as an extension of his being. But, she had to be so much to him; wife, lover, friend – and child. For when the tests following her failure to conceive had revealed Tony's negative sperm count, he had been devastated. She knew how much it had hurt his fragile masculine ego. He had built everything, the house, his career, even their friends, around the life he had wanted to provide for his children. And she also knew that if she had proved infertile, he would have left her. She knew it, because he had told her so, bitterly and frequently, during that first uneasy year when they had struggled to come to terms with their misfortune.

He left her abruptly, and rose to his feet. He zipped his fly, picked up his martini and drained it. Trembling, her breasts, thighs and buttocks stinging with pain, she returned to the bath and began to soap herself.

'As soon as I finish, we can eat. It's chicken casserole,' she ventured. Tony was often aggressive and always unpredictable after they'd had sex.

'I'll eat right away.' He wasn't asking her permission, and she knew it. 'I have to get back to the hospital.'

'Must you?' She failed to keep the disappointment from her voice. Mondays were special; the one night of the week they kept for themselves, when neither of them attended any of the committee meetings or clubs they

98

belonged to, or visited or entertained their wide circle of colleagues and friends.

'The police are digging. They're searching for more bodies.'

'More?' she echoed.

'Let's hope they don't find any. One has brought me more trouble then I want to cope with. I may be late. Don't wait up.'

Every time he said those words, she had visions of a flat, a mistress – someone young and beautiful like Lyn Sullivan; but she knew better than to allow her suspicions to surface. Their inability to have children had driven enough of a wedge between them, without her voicing the insecurities that had begun to plague her since she had first detected another woman's perfume on his clothes.

Instead she forced herself to be charming, attractive, compliant and obliging. She knew that was the only way to hold Tony; to make him want her enough to return to her, no matter what escapades he indulged in.

She loved him enough to allow him free rein to hurt her. And she would continue to do so, no matter what it cost her, simply because life without him was unthinkable.

'I'll be down as soon as I'm dressed, darling,' she called out. 'Perhaps we can have coffee together?'

He didn't hear her. He had already left the house.

CHAPTER SEVEN

Peter Collins supervised the lifting of the liquid remains of the dog, which unfortunately for his team had, as Murphy'd observed, been a large and hairy one, from the pit and into a body shell. As soon as the dog was disposed of, Peter returned to the hole, where Murphy was digging out the suitcase, which had been buried beneath the dog.

It was twenty minutes before Murphy managed to scoop the case on to a canvas stretcher, and even then Peter wasn't satisfied the hole had been properly excavated. He checked out the crater himself, crumbling the earth between his fingers, before switching Chris Brooke and Andrew Murphy again, ordering Chris to dig down another three foot.

He heaved himself out of the pit, and stood on the lawn, brushing clumps of mud from his trousers and breathing in the clean, sweet-smelling evening air. There was intense activity around the other sites. As soon as the light had begun to fade, Bill had ordered portable lamps to be brought up, and they were dotted around the lawns, shining spotlights into the shadowy puddles shrouded behind the canvas screens and casting silver shadows over the lawns.

'Anything?' Peter asked Dan as he walked towards him.

'Other than loose earth no, and we've gone down five foot.'

'The Super?'

'Same as here; the deeper they dig, the softer the earth.'

A whistle blew. Dan and Peter ran towards the site, as Bill's bald head emerged from behind a screen.

'Phone Patrick,' Bill shouted.

Dan pulled out his mobile.

'Another body?' Peter asked.

'Call off the late meeting and reschedule it for tomorrow. Supervise Dan's site as well as your own for the moment.' Bill disappeared back behind the screen. Peter heard him shout at the hapless constable who was still in the hole.

'Out, before you do any more damage. Leave it for the pathologist, boy.'

Peter recalled the times that he and Trevor had taken Bill's flak. Before he had time to take a second step, another whistle blew. He whirled to the right and saw a young constable surface from behind the canvas screens that shrouded Dan's site, green-faced and retching. Once again the ghostly twilight and perfume of the tree blossoms were overwhelmed by the pervasive, sickly-sweet stench of death.

'Patrick's on his way.' Dan returned his mobile to his pocket.

'I hope he brings a nightcap with him. Something tells me we're going to see in the dawn on this one.' Peter pulled two cigars from his pocket and offered Dan one.

Spencer Jordan saw the lights and the commotion in the hospital grounds from the kitchen window of his self-contained flat as he was preparing his evening meal. The flat was on the third-floor of a halfway house, and had been nicknamed "the penthouse" by the patients who lived in bed-sits on the floors below.

Pronounced fit to return to the community, after two years as an in-patient in psychiatric wards in America and Britain, and six months in a halfway house attached to Compton Castle, the thought of returning to "normality" had terrified Spencer. Harry Goldman had suggested he apply for the post of art therapist at Compton Castle, and when he had been given the job Spencer had volunteered to take over his predecessor's role as warden of one of the halfway units. Wary of his recent illness, the Trust had turned him down citing as a reason his workload as an art therapist.

Harry Goldman had intervened again, and the Trust compromised. Spencer was given the post of assistant warden, which carried a rent-free flat, in return for two nights "sleep in" duty when he was required to supervise the residents and ensure that none of them stayed out later than midnight. Not that any of them ever tried. Recovering from phobias and depressions, their problem was being persuaded to relinquish the security of their unit for more than ten minutes, not getting them to return to it afterwards.

Although officially on duty only two nights a week, staff shortages frequently stretched the two nights to four and sometimes even six. Spencer didn't mind; he, like the residents he supervised, rarely went out in the evenings. He knew no one in the town other than the staff and patients, and there was nowhere he wanted to go. Art exhibitions, the theatre, and even the cinema conjured up painful memories he preferred to keep submerged.

Spencer's family and social life had ended in America; not even Harry Goldman could persuade him otherwise. Most evenings he returned to the soulless utility-furnished flat, to sit in an uncomfortable, institution armchair, and stare at his bare walls. The hospital authority had provided him with prints, but he had taken them down. He doubted he'd ever produce his own art again, but he remained enough of an artist to reject bad art when he saw it.

He made himself a salad, and broke a few ounces of the same goat's cheese he had used in his sandwiches into the lettuce, cucumber, grapes, peppers and tomatoes. Taking it and a bottle of mineral water, he went into the living room and switched on the television. He watched the news that catalogued the current series of global human disasters. The starving in Africa, abused orphans in the Balkans, finally ending with a series of photographs of the victims of a shoot-out between gangs in an American city; the mention of America, and the film of a city street with its familiar shop signs, hit too close to home. He changed channels and ate his salad to the accompaniment of a forty-year-old Hollywood musical.

Spencer had finished his meal and cleared up by six-thirty. The evening stretched ahead of him, an empty void to be filled – with what? He flicked through the evening paper he bought for its television page, and studied the available options. A documentary on the Dead Sea Scrolls, the third episode of a detective series he'd never seen, an American sit com, a film he'd enjoyed the first time around – and hated the fifth. He switched off the television and went to the window. Night had fallen, dusky, velvet-hued, but lights shone blindingly in the hospital grounds, casting eerie shadows over the white-clad figures scurrying between the lawns and the police cars.

An ambulance had driven on the lawn and parked next to one of the canvas screens. Two men walked around to its back doors, and began to unload body-bags and shells. Spencer drew his curtains and paced uneasily from the small living room to the tiny kitchen, the box-sized bedroom, the bathroom, and back.

He stared at the cheap, veneered sideboard and fought the urge to open its doors. He knew he wasn't strong enough to look at its contents – not yet. If he opened them, he'd suffer, a few moments – moments of what? Not happiness, that was too a strong word, and afterwards there'd be so much pain…

The temptation proved too strong. He wrenched open the door, and removed a box of photograph albums. Fingering the scars that radiated from his glass eye, he sat at the table and gently took the top album into his hands. He opened it and stared at the first page. A wedding group outside a registry office in London. Himself, smiling broadly, wearing an outrageous scarlet silk suit, navy-blue shirt, and red and purple tie; his arm wrapped around Danielle, four months pregnant, in bright-green and blue cotton voile.

The reception… friends… he could taste the wine and strawberries, hear the toast; *LONG LIFE AND HAPPINESS!*

The house in California – a naked, fat, pink gurgling baby in his arms – then in Danielle's. More friends, gallery openings, another baby – and another – he slammed the album shut. Blinded by unshed tears, he stumbled to the sideboard and returned it to the shelf.

He sat with his back to the sideboard, but after a moment's hesitation, opened the drinks compartment. He wasn't on duty. It didn't matter what state he got himself into. He took out a full whisky bottle, unscrewed the top and filled a tumbler. He drank half of it without bothering to go into the kitchen to fetch ice. Holding the glass in one hand and the bottle by the neck in the other, he returned to his chair and switched on the television again. He'd watch the film for the sixth time. It was easier to cope with what he knew – than to face the past – the future – or worse of all – the present.

Bill, Dan and Peter were leaning against the bonnet of a police car, talking, when Patrick surfaced from the last pit, and walked wearily towards them. Peter had the inevitable cigar in hand, Dan was chewing peppermints and Bill was amusing himself by shouting at any rookie foolhardy enough to stray within his sight.

'I've done what I can here. They're all in body bags and shells. I'll continue in the lab in the morning.' O'Kelly tore off his rubber gloves.

'It is morning,' Peter said.

Patrick glared at him. 'Not until after I've slept.'

'Appreciate you coming out, Patrick.' Bill helped himself to one of the cigars that protruded from Peter's pocket.

'I'll tell you what I can be sure of; but keep the questions until after the PMs.'

'You've got it.' Dan yawned as the hospital clock struck four.

'They're both female and young; one in an advanced stage of decomposition, the other skeletal, with a few rags of organs attached. Both have soil in the mouths, nose and as far as I can make out, air passages.'

'Buried alive?' Bill asked.

'I should be able to answer that tomorrow. Both were brunette, one had long hair, the other short.'

'We found a suitcase and two handbags buried beneath the dog,' Peter said. 'They're bagged, and in the ambulance.'

'Will you take a look at the dog, as well?' Bill asked. 'As a favour.'

'As a favour, I'll take a quick look before I send it on with the suitcase to the police lab. But don't make a habit of it,' Patrick moved towards his car. 'See you in a couple of hours.'

'Let's clear this place,' Bill ordered.

Peter looked over to the blocks housing the patients. Apart from the ward office and the bathroom windows, the building was in darkness. He imagined Trevor curled up warm and comfortable in his bed. 'Lucky sod!' he swore as he stared at the battlefield of trenches and mounds that had been lawns and flowerbeds.

Peter didn't reach the flat he called home until dawn had lightened the sky from deep rich navy to cold steel grey. He locked his car and walked up a short, red-tiled path to the front door of a five-storey Edwardian building. Originally a middle-class home for family and servants, it now housed six flats and four bed-sits. The flat he'd chosen for its view and its proximity to the town centre, was on the third-floor.

He turned the key and stepped into the original hall. Its spaciousness was the only thing that hadn't changed. Unconcerned with period authenticity the landlord had replaced the mahogany panelled staircase and ornate, mouldering plasterwork with functional modern substitutes.

Peter took the stairs two at a time and opened the door to his flat. He walked straight into a well-proportioned, high-ceilinged living room. The bedroom and bathroom were minute. The kitchen was built into what had once been a fairly large airing cupboard, and it had an air-vent instead of a window. But he forgave the flat its failings for the one handsome room.

He walked across the brown Berber carpet to the window, opened it and stepped on to a fire-escape that overlooked the beach. He left the window open went into the kitchen, ground a handful of coffee beans, and made himself a pot of coffee. His stomach told him he was hungry. There was half a loaf of mouldy wholemeal bread in his breadbin. He opened his fridge. A six-pack of beer, a tub of low-fat spread, a carton of long-life milk, two eggs and a stale corner of cheese. The freezer compartment held a lasagne ready meal for one, a pizza, half a pack of sausages, but no bread. He had more luck in the cupboard where he discovered a packet of Melba toasts of uncertain age.

He scrambled the eggs and layered low-fat spread on the toasts. When the meal was ready, he filled a tray and carried it, and a cushion from an easy chair on to the fire-escape. He leaned on the safety railings, dangling his legs in space while he ate, staring at the sun rising over the sea and listening to the waves and the cries of the gulls scavenging along the shoreline.

The chill in the air carried an antiseptic property that cleansed away the cloying stench of death that had fouled the night. He tried not to think of what had to be done; the identification of the victims, the tracking down of a murderer – and Trevor Joseph to wrench back into the world of the living. A perfect spring day was about to begin, and all he wanted was his bed.

He finished his meal without tasting it, threw the cushion back on to the chair, carried the tray into the kitchen, dumped the dirty dishes in the sink for his daily, and went into his bedroom. His clothes were caked with mud. He stripped them off, flung them into the linen basket and crawled beneath the duvet in his underpants. He looked at his alarm, debated whether to set it or not, and decided against making the effort. Bill or Dan would want him soon enough. Two minutes later all that could be heard was his rhythmic breathing as he slept the heavy dreamless sleep of the truly exhausted.

'Trevor.' Lyn Sullivan knocked on his door before opening it. 'It's your turn to lay the table.' She took a cup of tea from the auxiliary and set it on his bedside table, before moving on down the corridor.

Trevor leaned on his elbow and sipped the tea. His head ached from the sleeping pills he had taken. When the cup was empty he stumbled out of bed and into the bathroom, took off his pyjamas and climbed into the shower. The morning-after of drugs was deadlier than alcohol, he decided, as he held his head under the cool jet for two full minutes. On impulse he washed his hair. He discovered that it was longer than he'd ever worn it. Could he do what Spencer had suggested; take another step outside today? How long before he'd make it as far as the front gate? And how long before he went into town to have his hair cut?

He rinsed the lather from his body and hair, wrapped a towel around his waist, and stepped back into his bedroom. He looked at the threadbare tracksuit top that lay on the chair where he had dumped his clothes the night before. He thrust it and his faded trousers into his dirty linen bag. He opened the wardrobe door and flicked through the clothes Peter had brought from his flat. Two pairs of jeans, as faded as the trousers, but even more threadbare. A hand-knitted woollen jumper his mother had sent him last Christmas which had gone drastically out of shape after he'd taken it to the launderette. An anorak that stubbornly remained grubby no matter how often he flung it into a washing-machine, and a couple of white shirts. He settled on a white shirt and a pair of jeans. The jeans sagged three inches too large for his waist. He looked for a belt, and found one in a bag of underclothes and socks Peter had brought that he'd never bothered to open.

He pushed the belt through the loops at the waist of his jeans, but even when the prong was hooked into the last hole, the belt hung slack. He pulled it tighter, marked the spot where another hole was needed, and looked around for something to make one with.

Lyn Sullivan knocked the door again. He opened it.

'Good, you're up. Breakfast will be ready in ten minutes, and you haven't laid the table, but I can see why. You look smart.'

'Smart?' he repeated, suspecting she was teasing him. 'These are just a pair of old jeans.'

'Old jeans and white shirts are the latest fashion. What's the problem? Belt needs another hole?'

'I was looking for something to make one with.'

'Give it to me. I'll use scissors.' She grabbed the buckle and pulled the belt loose. 'I'll bring it back in a moment.'

Trevor brushed his damp hair away from his face with his fingers and stared at himself in the full-length mirror fixed to the wall beside the wardrobe. His clothes might be clean but they were worn, and he looked thin, tired and old. Just as his father had done just before he'd died. Was that where he was headed? An early grave? But his father had died of cancer, and he'd only been mangled in the line of duty.

It was probably as Peter constantly told him; lack of effort on his part. Sitting around all day doing nothing. He'd put action off long enough. It was time to take a step forward. He opened a drawer in the bedside table and took out his wallet. It held fifty pounds cash, and his credit cards. He was receiving sick pay so he had no money worries, and Peter had checked that the couple renting the flat he owned, but hadn't lived in for years, were paying their rent into his bank account.

Today he would aim for the gate. Once at the gate it would only be a small step to board a bus into town. He could have his hair cut, and buy some clothes. Possibly even take another bus out to see his flat. Check on both his flat and his car. It would be a beginning; and after he made a beginning he could decide on the rest of his life.

He felt sick to the pit of his stomach at the prospect of leaving the hospital, but he also felt a sense of exhilaration. For the first time since he'd been injured, he was going to take responsibility for himself.

The phone rang in Peter's bedroom what seemed like less than five minutes after he fell asleep. He stretched out his arm and picked up the receiver.

'Mortuary, ten minutes.' The line went dead, but not before he recognised Bill Mulcahy's voice. He lay back and closed his eyes, recognising even as he succumbed to temptation that it was a deadly thing to do. If he didn't move right away, he wouldn't wake for another eight hours, and not even eight hours of blissful sleep was worth incurring Bill's wrath for.

He jerked himself out of bed and headed for the shower. Five minutes later, damp but dressed, he walked out to his car. He glanced at his watch; it was just after ten. Patrick must have worked through for there to be sufficient information to justify calling a meeting. He was still hungry. The eggs and Melba toast hadn't filled much of a hole, but he knew better than to eat anything before he visited the mortuary.

*   *   *

'We're doing more tests. Early indications are it's a cocktail of several drugs. We've identified an anti-depressant, a tranquilliser, and a muscle-relaxant, effective to the point of paralysis when administered in large doses. I found curare in the bloodstream, but the effects were probably wearing off at the time of death, because she managed to tear her glued mouth open. We know that from the damage done to the skin on her lips,' Patrick dropped his scalpel on to the slab where his assistant had laid out Rosie Twyford again.

'But she was paralysed when placed in the hole?' Dan asked.

'Peter, how nice of you to visit,' Mulcahy called out sarcastically when he walked in.

Peter closed the doors behind him, fighting the smell of putrefaction that not even the stench of formaldehyde could kill.

'The degree of paralysis would relate to the amount of drug ingested,' Patrick said thoughtfully in response to Dan's question. 'There was a significant amount of curare in her bloodstream, but the torn lips, open eyes and amount of soil in her air passages suggest that she fought for her life as no unconscious person would have done. If she had been administered a high enough dose to cause paralysis, it was wearing off at the time of death. She was either conscious or regained consciousness, shortly after she was buried.'

'We're talking about the first victim,' Dan explained to Peter.

'Then this villain, whoever he is, likes to see his victims' reaction as he shovels dirt on top of them?' Bill suggested.

'You could argue that, although I've come up with no evidence to support it other than she was alive when she

111

was buried, and both her eyes were open when she was uncovered,' Patrick said carefully.

'Michelle came up trumps. We think the first victim is one Rosie Twyford,' Dan said in his slow, Welsh lilt. 'She was discharged from Compton Castle six months ago, but she returned for twice-weekly outpatient sessions with Dorothy Clyne. I rang Tony Waters early this morning, got him out of bed, and had him check her file. Her last appointment was a week yesterday and she was discharged as an outpatient.'

'Grady also checked Rosie Twyford's bed-sit last night,' Mulcahy chipped in. 'The keys we found on the corpse fit the front door, and Rosie's door. Grady spoke to the boy in the next room. The last time he saw her was the morning she left for her hospital visit. When she didn't return, he assumed she'd been kept in again. He did say that she appeared unusually nervous.'

'He didn't think to ring the hospital and check?' Peter asked.

'Apparently they didn't have that kind of relationship. They never got past "good morning, nice weather, good evening".'

'If she's the same girl Tony Waters was talking about yesterday, she has a family in Devon. Weren't they in touch with her?' Peter walked over to the tiled wall and leaned against it. The combination of the smell and the sight of the corpse was proving nauseating.

'Devon police interviewed them this morning. There's a mother, stepfather and two stepbrothers. Sometimes she wouldn't get in touch with them for weeks.'

'Then if she went missing a week ago – ' Peter began.

112

'Someone kept her alive until last Saturday night, when Vanessa Hedley saw her being buried.'

'Vanessa Hedley's story fits in with the facts.' Patrick took one of the beakers of strong black coffee that his assistant had prepared. Peter and Dan balked at the coffee, but Bill took one.

'If I don't sit down soon I'm going to fall down.' Patrick went into his office and sat behind his desk.

Bill dumped his coffee on the desk, flicked back the pages of a notebook until he found a clean sheet, pulled a pen from his pocket and started to scribble.

'Victim one, Rosie Twyford keeps appointment in Compton Castle last Monday then disappears. Nothing is heard or seen of her until Vanessa goes into the garden on Monday morning. On Saturday night Vanessa Hedley saw a bulky shadow burying a body in the grounds, and no one,' he glanced at Peter, 'took any notice of her story until Monday morning, when she bullied the trainee into digging up the flowerbed. Then we find a corpse that we can now be certain is Rosie Twyford.'

'Saturday/Sunday fits in with my calculations,' Patrick interrupted. 'I'd say she died twelve hours either side of midnight Saturday.'

'No closer?' Mulcahy pressed.

'Can't make it any closer, sorry.' Patrick didn't sound in the least apologetic.

'Which means that Rosie Twyford was kept alive somewhere around Compton Castle from Monday afternoon to midnight on Saturday,' Dan said.

'Not necessarily,' Peter played Devil's Advocate. 'She could have gone to stay with someone – a boyfriend perhaps.'

'An abduction would fit in with her physical state; the dehydration, the starvation,' Patrick closed his eyes.

'Waters took us around the whole of the old building.' Peter offered his pack of cigars.

'Was there anywhere that could be used to hide a body?' Bill asked.

Peter recalled the rambling corridors, the attics blanketed with years of dust, the cellar walls lined with pipes. 'If you knew the building, you could come up with a thousand and one places. There are corners of that place that haven't seen people or daylight in years.'

'There were twenty-five needle marks in Rosie's arm,' Patrick reminded. 'You need comparative privacy to inject twenty-five doses of muscle-relaxant, tranquilliser and anti-depressant over a period of days if you don't want to be noticed.'

'Which indicates that she'd been held captive before she was buried,' Bill commented.

'Unless she was a junkie,' Peter perched on the edge of the desk.

'Nothing on her record card, according to Tony Waters,' Dan said.

'Or in her bloodstream,' Patrick added.

'If she was held captive and tranquillised, what's the motive? Sexual?' Peter asked.

'No physical signs of a struggle,' Patrick said, 'but there wouldn't have been if she'd been tranquillised. And there were no signs of forced rape, no tearing of tissues, no traces of semen, but I can't rule out sexual intercourse. Just no signs, no stray hairs, no fibres, no nothing.'

'The other two victims?' Bill checked.

'No semen in either of the vaginas, but the soft tissue has decayed in both bodies. One had been buried for approximately six to eight weeks, the other for about four months. But those are rough calculations based on condition and depth of the burials. I may have something

114

more exact for you later.' Patrick looked grey, drained and exhausted.

'You haven't slept?' Dan asked

'I snatched an hour on a slab between PMs.'

'I managed three,' Peter said unthinkingly.

'Then you're set up for the next twenty-hour shift, Peter,' Mulcahy smiled

'You get anything from the suitcase or handbags, Patrick?' Dan asked.

'After a cursory glance I sent them and the dog to the police laboratory for further tests.'

'Right, Peter, that's your next stop, Mulcahy ordered. 'Afterwards liaise with Michelle and see what she's come up with on Rosie Twyford's last movements. I want you to be there when she interviews everyone in Rosie Twyford's house.'

Patrick rose from his chair and pulled off his lab coat. 'I'm for home and bed.'

'One more question,' Dan said hesitantly. 'Supposing we're right and the killer does pick his victims a week ahead, drugs them and keeps them somewhere in the hospital before burying them. What can you tell us about such a man?'

'That's one for the police psychiatrist. I'm a scientist who deals in facts, not a shrink.'

'But you've seen dozens if not hundreds of murder victims. Surely you're interested in the outcome. You must have an opinion?' Dan persisted.

'Off the top of my head, he could be an impotent male dominated by a female, possibly a mother, wife, sister. Someone who wants to be in control, but isn't. But that is pure speculation.'

'But it does give us one more thing to consider and work on,' Mulcahy said shortly. 'And that's where we're all going now, gentlemen. To work.'

CHAPTER EIGHT

'I *saw* him.' Vanessa Hedley glanced over her shoulder and around the room before moving her head close to Alison Bevan's and lowering her voice. Trevor, who was sitting across the breakfast table from them, found himself straining his ears to catch what Vanessa was saying.

'It was dark,' Ali Bevan pointed out, 'so how could you see anything?'

'There was a moon,' Vanessa bit back. 'I saw his features clearly. He was huge – massive. I knew he was evil. The eyes and the mouth are a dead giveaway and he had a cruel, vicious mouth.'

'If you saw that much of him, and he saw you, aren't you terrified?' Ali asked.

'Of what?'

'That he'll come after you.'

'She's right.' Roland Williams, a not so recovering alcoholic, leered. 'The murderer could be here, in this room, listening to every word you're saying.' He glanced around the dining room, which was crowded with patients, domestic staff and nurses. 'You're the only one who can identify him. He could be watching you, waiting his chance to grab you, rape you – '

'That's enough, Roland,' Carol caught the tail end of his conversation as she passed their table.

'Sorry,' Roland apologised insincerely eying her breasts beneath her thin dress.

'Rape?' Ali hissed as soon as Carol disappeared through the door. 'I didn't know the victims had been raped.'

'Of course, he raped his victims,' Roland was enjoying himself. 'Why else would he kill them, and try to

117

hide the bodies. He probably stripped them, played with them – then – '

'The murderer isn't here.' Vanessa cut him short. The one topic of conversation guaranteed to excite Roland, and keep him pontificating for hours, was perverted sexual activity – usually as practised by primitive tribes only he had heard of. And she wanted to keep everyone's attention fixed on her and her story.

'I'm only trying to warn you, ladies.' Roland slurped his tea. His double chin wobbled as he licked drops from his fat, wet lips. 'I'd hate to think of anyone kidnapping one of you, tying you up, stripping you – ' He bent his head close to Ali's. 'Stroking your breasts, putting his fingers in – '

Trevor dipped his spoon into his uneaten porridge and stirred it, mixing the crust of sugar into the glutinous mass of oats. Once a detective, always a detective, he reflected. He hadn't wanted to get involved with this case, but he hadn't been able to stop himself from listening to Vanessa, or forming the conclusion that, for all her boasting, she didn't have a clue what the killer looked like. Shadows in moonlit gardens were easily distorted. They merged with bushes and trees, wavered with the wind, contorting figures, making them appear larger and wider, or taller and wispier than they were. Vanessa's "massive killer" could have been a small man wearing a padded anorak. And he doubted that the killer had come close enough to the window for Vanessa to see his eyes.

He'd looked out of his ground-floor bedroom window that morning and watched an officer point out one of the burial sites to a colleague. He hadn't been able to discern the constables' features beneath their helmets in daylight. So what chance had Vanessa of seeing the murderer's features as he'd shovelled earth on top of his

118

victim? But if the killer heard Vanessa's prattling, would he realise that?

Trevor glanced around the room. Apart from Lucy Craig, Roland Williams and Alison Bevan, who were listening, enthralled, to Vanessa, everyone appeared to be minding their own business. He recalled a few of the stories forced on him by his fellow patients, when he hadn't wanted to listen.

If a quarter of Roland's stories were true, he had done some very peculiar things with men and women, singly and in groups, and not only under the influence of drink. Last week he had caught sight of Roland retreating into a sluice room with a brown paper bag under his arm. He had assumed the bag contained alcohol, which was banned in Compton Castle. Had it contained something more sinister?

Michael Carpenter's sole topic of conversation was his ex-girlfriend, Angela, who had jilted him. It was common knowledge that he was incarcerated in Compton Castle because he'd set fire to her house, and almost succeeded in burning her entire family to death. Had Michael decided that the only way to hold on to a girl of his own was to kill and bury her in a grave known to no one except himself? That didn't seem far-fetched when he recalled Vanessa's railings against those who had prevented her from putting her husband in a grave where she would have had absolute control over him.

'Go on, Vanessa,' Lucy pestered. 'Tell us what he *really* looked like?'

'I've told you. Huge – with thick black hair, and a mouthful of white teeth. Enormous muscled arms like the wrestlers on television. He picked up the spade as though it was a toy, and brandished it above his head – '

'Not hungry, Trevor?' Lyn, in a polo-neck red sweater, black jeans, and smelling of magnolias, took the empty chair beside him, making him suddenly and painfully aware of the shabbiness of his own clothes.

'Not for porridge.'

'Do you want some toast? Fresh toast,' she coaxed. 'Not those cold rubbery slices made ten minutes before anyone gets to eat them.'

'Sounds good,' he admitted.

'I'll help you make some in the ward kitchen. You know where it is?'

'Yes.' If Lyn had brought him the toast, he would have eaten it, but he hated going into the ward kitchen. It was always full of people, staff as well as patients.

'Come on, then.' She left her chair and waited for him.

'Lyn,' he asked as he followed her into the corridor. 'Can you get hold of Peter Collins for me?'

'I could try. But with everything that's going on he'll be busy. But you could walk down the tunnel to the main hospital. The police have set up their mobile headquarters outside the back door.' She allowed Trevor to go into the kitchen ahead of her.

If Trevor wanted to see Peter Collins, he'd have to make an effort to leave the ward, and that was the moment she'd been waiting for.

'I didn't expect to see you at work for a few days. Have your cuts healed?' Carol asked when Lyn entered the kitchen.

'They weren't as bad as they looked.' Lyn glanced at the scars on her palms that weren't covered by plasters. She turned to Trevor. 'There's the toaster. Bread's in the enamel bin next to it. Be an angel and pop a piece in for

120

me.' She took the electric kettle from the work surface behind Carol, and filled it, effectively blocking Trevor's exit from the galley.

'Ladies.' The male nurse, Karl Lane joined them. 'Any tea going?' he smiled at Lyn. Trevor saw the smile and was stung by a pang of jealousy. Not jealousy because Karl Lane was looking at Lyn, but because the glances they'd exchanged had reminded him that there were people who had fulfilling private relationships away from the public eye. Something he hadn't experienced in years. He felt angry and empty because his own private life consisted only of his mother, married brother, sister-in-law, nieces and nephews – and Peter Collins. And fond as he was of all of them, not one of them could act as a substitute for a loving girlfriend – or wife. If only –

He pushed the thought from his mind. There were too many "if onlys" in his life.

'Toast's burning,' Carol called out. She finished her tea. 'It's time I was back on my ward to check that none of my little darlings have gone a wandering.'

'What do you make of all this, Carol?' Karl asked.

'All what?'

'All these bodies.'

'Oh, yes, they've found more haven't they? What do you want me to make of them?' She turned the question back on him.

'What does Tony think?'

'The last time I saw Tony,' she recalled her husband's pale face as he'd stumbled into their bed as she was getting out of it that morning, 'he was too tired to think.'

'Do you think the killer's a patient or a member of staff?'

'It has to be a patient,' Lyn said. The other two turned and stared at her. 'Well it does, doesn't it? It's obvious. This is a psychiatric hospital.'

'So they tell me.' Karl took the tea she handed him.

'In my opinion we should stop playing guessing games and leave it to the police,' Carol went to the door. 'I've enough on my plate running my ward and my house. I can't cope with a murder hunt as well. See you later.'

Trevor's hand trembled as he offered Lyn a plate of toast he'd buttered and cut into triangles.

'Thank you,' she smiled. 'You know Karl, don't you, Trevor?'

'We met last Sunday.' Karl held out his hand to Trevor. 'But we weren't introduced. You're a police officer, aren't you?'

'I was,' Trevor corrected.

'There's nothing preventing you from being one again if you want to rejoin the force.' Lyn bit into her piece of toast.

'I'm not sure what I want any more.' Trevor picked up his own toast, which was singed and black around the edges. He'd kept the burnt pieces for himself, and made fresh for Lyn.

'I can understand that.' Karl stole a piece of Lyn's toast. 'Police duty must be almost as bad as working here; no let up, all the hours God sends, and – '

'Dealing with the dregs of society,' Trevor supplied, intuitively.

'Present company excepted. But forgive me; I don't work on this ward. I'm on manias, and they're different to assessment and depressions. More loopy. See you, Lyn.'

'He didn't mean that. It's just that this job can get to you,' Lyn apologised.

'I can imagine.' He dropped the barely nibbled toast back on to his plate.

'It's one of the terraced houses on the hill leading up to the heights,' Michelle explained to Peter. 'From the outside they look small, door in the middle, bay windows either side, and three windows above, but they're surprisingly large inside. There are six bed-sits in there, and they share two bathrooms and two kitchens.'

'I don't think that recommendation is sufficient for me to want to uproot myself.' He was tired of listening to Michelle's chatter.

The police laboratory was attached to the forensic science unit of the university in the neighbouring town, forty miles away. Normally he would have enjoyed the drive as he regarded driving time as thinking time. But he found it impossible to enjoy anything in Michelle's company.

'I only spoke to the man who lives in the bed-sit next door to Rosie Twyford's,' Michelle confessed. 'He said the walls are thin, so if she'd returned after last Monday he would have heard her.'

'Did you ask him if she had any friends she might have been staying with?'

'No. He said Rosie had only moved in three months ago, I checked the date, and it ties in with her discharge from Compton Castle.'

'And in all of three months she never once stayed out all night?'

'I didn't think to ask him.'

'You wouldn't.'

She fell silent. Peter saw her bottom lip quivering as he turned a corner, but he felt no remorse for giving her a hard time. If she wanted to be a copper, she had to get used to everything her superior officers were likely to throw at her. If she couldn't cut it, she'd have to find another career; one more suited to a girl who needed nannying.

He slowed down, signalled and took a slip-road off the motorway, turning into the network of narrow suburban streets that surrounded the town centre. Mindful that she may be asked to visit this place alone sometime, Michelle tried to follow his route, but Peter took turning after turning, delving deeper and deeper into a mixture of 1930s and 1950s housing, until she began to wonder if he was deliberately following an unnecessarily complicated route to confuse her.

Eventually he pulled up in a car park that fronted a huge red-brick, flat-fronted block set with steel casement windows. A sign outside declared it to be UNIVERSITY ANNEX B.

'We're here,' Peter announced.

Michelle jumped out so quickly she jarred her ankle, but she would have sooner died than admit to feeling pain in front of Peter. She allowed him to lead the way through the double doors into the lobby. As she'd expected he made no concessions to her presence, not even checking to see if she was behind him when he pressed the lift button.

The police laboratory was on the top floor and, as in the mortuary, the smell of rotting flesh was overwhelming. They noticed it the moment the lift doors opened. Peter made no comment as he pressed the bell for attention, but he took grim pleasure in the sight of Michelle fumbling in her handbag for a tissue. When the door to the laboratory opened, the stench intensified – choking and breath-taking.

124

The first thing Peter noticed when they walked in was the dog laid out in all its putrefying glory on a steel-topped table, strategically placed beneath a window. The suitcase and the handbags were laid out on two other tables. All the hard surfaces were covered with a grey film of fingerprint powder.

'Sergeant Collins, isn't it?' A white-coated, grey-haired man nodded to Peter. 'Recognise you from that last drugs haul. Thomas, Phil Thomas.'

'I remember you.' Peter looked at Phil's hand before shaking it.

'How's life on the Drug Squad?'

'Wish I knew,' Peter moaned. 'Been seconded to Serious Crimes.'

'Dan Evans's lot?'

'That's the one.'

'And this is?' Phil smiled at Michelle.

'Michelle Grady,' she held out her hand and wondered how long she could last in this atmosphere. She was certain the moment she took a deep breath, she'd throw up.

'New?' Phil asked her.

'Does it show?'

'Only the eagerness. Old hands like Sergeant Collins here are never eager about anything, even their days off.'

'Seen it all before.' Peter wished Phil would spare a thought for those who hadn't grown accustomed to the foul atmosphere.

Phil walked to the tables holding the bags. 'We've been through this lot with a fine toothcomb; got all the prints we could find. Only two sets, one matches one case and handbag, the other matches the second set, so the chances are they belong to the victims. Here's a list of contents found in both sets of cases and handbags.

125

Nothing a girl wouldn't take with her on holiday. Selection of clothes – hairdrier, cosmetics, shoes. There's a nurse's uniform, belt with silver buckle, and a couple of nurses' textbooks in one of the cases. There's a driving licence in the better of the two handbags for an Elizabeth Moore, twenty-four years of age. A couple of certificates rolled into a tube at the bottom of the bag identify her as a state registered nurse. Prescription in the second handbag for tranquillisers made out to a C. Moon. No address, but there's a Compton Castle stamp. If she was an inmate, you should be able to track her down through hospital records.'

'I'll get to work on it.' Peter felt as though another minute in the fetid atmosphere would suffocate him.

'Feel free to take whatever you want. I'll get one of the lads to help you with the suitcases. And here – ' He handed Peter a sheet of paper.

'What's this?' Peter squinted at the illegible scribble that covered the page.

'Report on the dog. Sorry, our assistant's sick and we don't rate a replacement. I thought you could get someone to process it in the station. Nostrils, upper part of the lungs and air passages filled with dirt. Traces of curare in the bloodstream. I'd say it had been drugged and buried alive.'

Peter paused on his way to the door. 'You sure about that?'

'You questioning my professionalism?'

'No, it's just that – '

'What, Sergeant Collins?' Phil Thomas asked.

'I wonder why someone would go to the trouble of killing a dog in exactly the same way they've murdered three women.'

126

'That's for you to find out,' Thomas said with a glimmer of a smile. 'I've done my bit. Now it's your turn.'

Trevor hesitated at the entrance to the perspex tunnel that connected his ward to the main hospital building. He paced up and down, debating whether to turn around and go into the garden. The grounds might have been a pleasant option if there weren't so many people there he knew; rookies and older colleagues he'd worked with –

He turned on his heel and retreated to the security of his own room. He gasped for breath as he fumbled with the door-handle, seeking an excuse to explain his cowardice. His wallet – that was it. If he was going as far as the old hospital, he might as well keep going. Walk to the main gate, and wait for a bus. Go into town, get his hair cut. And if he took his wallet and his credit cards, maybe even buy some clothes.

He found his wallet, opened his wardrobe door and lifted out his grubby anorak. Slipping it on over his shirt, he stuffed the wallet into his inside pocket. He stood before the door. All he had to do was open it, walk down the tunnel and he'd be in the main building, close to the police HQ.

He jerked the door open, hitting his thumb painfully as the handle sprang back. Looking neither left nor right, he walked straight ahead, to the end of the corridor and, like a diver plunging into a deep pool, set foot in the tunnel. He took one step, then another, then another – walking on blindly and mechanically.

When the white walls and floor closed around him, he fought off a panic attack. Wiping clammy hands down the sides of his jeans, he let the air slowly out of his lungs and forced another breath. Provided he kept going, one step at a time, it wouldn't take him long. Patients and nurses walked this way every day, without thinking anything of it. Closing his eyes against the blinding white glare, he drove himself forwards. He heard footsteps echoing behind him, and jumped to the side of the tunnel.

'Hi, Trevor.' Karl Lane passed him, a bundle of files tucked beneath his arm.

'Hi,' Trevor managed to whisper after Karl had moved on. He stood pressed against the side of the tunnel, his eyes closed, until he could no longer hear Karl's footsteps. Only then did he move hesitantly into the centre of the tunnel again. One step, then another, then another. Repeated again and again and again –

'Sergeant Joseph,' Sarah Merchant, a constable who usually worked in the computer room at the station, greeted him as he emerged into the hall of the main building.

Trevor wiped sticky hands over his jeans again and looked at her.

'It's good to see you up and about, sir.' She was clearly stunned by his sickly, emaciated appearance.

'Thank you, Constable Merchant,' Trevor concealed his panic behind a brusque, businesslike facade. 'Is Sergeant Collins around?'

'I haven't seen him this morning, sir, but Inspector Evans and Superintendent Mulcahy are in the mobile HQ. Would you like me to fetch them?'

Before she had a chance to walk over and knock at the door of the makeshift unit, Dan jumped down from the van and called out to Trevor.

'You've saved us a trip. We were on our way to see you. Come in.' He opened the door wide and ushered Trevor inside the mobile unit. Trevor recognised the surroundings. The overflowing ashtrays, the scattering of dirty coffee mugs, the bins crammed full of take-away food wrappings; typewritten papers and reports strewn from one end of the van to the other, and piles of tabloid newspapers badly folded and stacked in the corner, all with page-three girls uppermost.

'Coffee?' Dan thrust a mug at him, and Trevor took it, not because he wanted a drink, but because it gave him something to do with his hands.

'You look better today,' Bill commented tactlessly.

It was on the tip of Trevor's tongue to say he didn't feel any better, but he knew his whining would irritate Bill when everyone on the force was working flat-out to solve a difficult case. Instead he said the first thing that came into his head.

'Thought I'd go into town and get my hair cut.' He could have kicked himself. Now he was committed to going into the town, when it had taken all the courage he possessed to get this far.

'Good idea. You look like a stray sheepdog,' Bill agreed.

'I overheard Vanessa talking at breakfast this morning.' Trevor looked at the others, but they were waiting for him to continue. 'She's been telling the other patients that she managed to get a good look at the killer.'

'Has she now?' Mulcahy stroked his stubbly chin.

'And I thought – ' Trevor stammered, succumbing to yet another panic attack. He was back where he had been before his accident; working on a murder investigation he wanted no part of. He could get hurt again – killed even, this time.

'Being a detective, you thought that if the killer was within earshot, Vanessa Hedley's not going to live much longer,' Dan finished for him.

'That's about the size of it.' Trevor was grateful that he didn't have to say more.

'What exactly did she say?'

'She gave no useful description,' Trevor said. 'She said he was huge, enormous, with black hair – '

'Which could have been a hood or even a balaclava if he'd been wearing a coat,' Dan broke in.

'And evil eyes.'

'Evil eyes?' Dan exchanged glances with Bill.

'I watched two officers from the window of my room this morning as they walked around the flowerbed where the first body was found. I couldn't even make out their features, let alone see their eyes.'

'Are you saying that she didn't see anything?'

'No.' Trevor gripped the edge of the padded bench. He was finding it a tremendous strain to talk to Dan and Bill. He'd forgotten how cynical police officers were by nature. And he was left with the uncomfortable feeling that neither believed a single word he was saying. 'She must have seen something; the finding of the body confirms that. All I'm saying is that I doubt she could have seen his features from that distance.'

'Unless he walked up to her window?' Bill suggested.

'Or she already knew who he was,' Dan suggested.

CHAPTER NINE

Vanessa Hedley's attentive audience did not desert her that morning. Roland, Michael, Lucy and Alison dogged her from breakfast, into therapy classes, and in the garden during the coffee break. Spencer watched from his room as they followed Vanessa around the flowerbeds that were being painstakingly reinstated to their former glory by an angry, noisy Jimmy Herne, who was commanding his trainees as though he were directing army battalions in military manoeuvres.

'I know Harry's always on to us to get our charges interested in something, dear boy,' Adam Hayter lisped when he visited Spencer, 'but I think he'd draw the line at gruesome murder, don't you?'

'Probably.' Spencer was nursing a foul hangover, and had already promised himself that he would never allow alcohol in any shape or form to pass his lips again.

'I must say though,' Adam chattered, 'it's made the little darlings easier to deal with. They're too busy gossiping to think of going bonzo bananas. I even found the time to make a nice lamb stew for Dotty and me in my first class this morning. And that, darling, simply isn't normal.'

'What isn't normal?' Lyn asked, as she joined them.

'For our sweeties to be so quiet,' Adam purred. 'Look at the little angels hanging on to Vanessa's every gory word. What is it about murder that excites everyone?'

'I'm damned if I know!' Spencer exploded savagely, turning his back to the window. 'Is there anything I can do for you, Adam?'

'I came to borrow the tinsiest, tiniest choccy biccy,' Adam smirked, his diffident smile carefully calculated to bring out his dimples.

'You know where I keep them.'

Adam went to Spencer's desk. 'Thank you, darling. You won't tell Dotty, will you?' Adam helped himself to three of the biscuits, and skipped out of the door.

'It isn't often the wind blows you down here, Lyn. Can I do something for you?' Spencer asked.

'I came to beg a favour,' she began warily. Spencer was more even-tempered than most of the staff in Compton Castle, including Harry Goldman, who saw it as his duty to remain calm through everything fate, the authorities and the patients threw at him. She'd never seen Spencer snap at anyone before, even Adam, who was unfailingly irritating. 'They've finally fitted a bolt to the inside of the drug cupboard, but in the process they stripped most of the paint from the outside of the door, and it draws attention to the one place we'd like to keep low-profile. I wondered if you had any white paint to spare. It doesn't have to be gloss. Anything will do to patch it in, until maintenance gets around to re-painting it. You know how long they take.'

'I do,' he commented. 'I'll take a look at it for you at lunch time.'

'I'm on split shift today, but if I'm not there, Jean will be around.'

'Fine.' He picked up his coffee and returned to the window.

Lyn walked back to her ward. She saw that Spencer wasn't the only one watching the patients in the hospital grounds. Dotty Clyne and Harry Goldman were also studying the group gathered around Vanessa, from Harry's office window. And she saw Tony glance their

132

way as he talked to a police officer in the drive. She only hoped that the attention wouldn't send Vanessa over the edge again.

Vanessa finished her tour of the garden, and returned to the therapy block. Basking in the glow of attention, she even began to flirt mildly with Roland. As she continued to wander through the corridors and rooms of Compton Castle, she was unaware of all but the most obvious glances and comments that came her way.

But among those watching, was someone who did not seek to coax more information from her. Someone who walked discreetly down the corridors, someone who stood outside the open door of the therapy rooms as Vanessa continued to excite her audience with gripping stories of the live burial in the grounds.

It didn't matter that Vanessa's story owed more to memories of horror films than reality. Submerged in her ramblings lay the kernels of truths. But nothing could be done immediately. It was daylight – people – far too many people were around. Later, when darkness fell, there would be fewer staff on duty and Vanessa would be sleepy from the increased dose of tranquillisers she'd proudly announced were to be administered to her to help her recover from her traumatic experience. Later – no one would notice anyone slipping from one quiet room to another – later – but not too late to prevent Vanessa from spending yet another day saying too much.

Trevor stood outside the mobile police HQ. He leaned on his stick and shivered, as the fresh spring breeze penetrated the thin denim of his worn jeans and shabby anorak. He wanted to rush back up the drive as fast as his shaky legs would carry him, to the safe, familiar confines of his room. But Dan was standing next to him.

'I'll walk with you to the gate,' Dan offered.

'That's not necessary,' Trevor replied.

'I want to see the officer on gate duty, to check the names of everyone who visited this morning. We're trying to establish a pattern for the hospital. To find out exactly who – '

'Comes in, and who goes out, at certain times of the day. In other words, the people we can expect to find within these walls at any given time,' Trevor finished for him.

'That's about the size of it,' Dan said good-temperedly. 'I'd forgotten you'd worked with Serious Crimes before.'

'Not often,' Trevor conceded.

'You didn't enjoy the experience?'

'I was used to the Drug Squad.'

It was close to the staff lunchtime, and the first shift of nurses, doctors and therapists were walking through the gardens towards the staff dining room in the old hospital.

'That's interesting.' Dan monitored the groups as they walked through the side door of the main building.

'What?'

'The staff are all walking through the grounds. Every one I've spoken to, doctors, nurses, Tony Waters, they all say how useful those tunnels are, yet not one of them appears to use them.'

'Can you blame them?' Trevor asked.

'No. I don't know about you, but those shiny white corridors give me the creeps. It's like a poor man's film version of the road to heaven.'

*   *   *

134

'Inspector!' The constable manning the gate jumped stiffly to attention.

'You've met Sergeant Joseph?' Evans introduced Trevor.

'Haven't had the pleasure, sir.' The rookie nodded to Trevor.

'I'll be on my way, Dan,' Trevor moved on. If Dan hadn't been behind him, he would have turned around. But as he limped past the barrier and through the main gates, he sensed Dan's eyes boring into the back of his head.

The bus stop was just outside the gates, and when he reached it, he rested on his stick and looked around. The eyes had existed only in his imagination. Dan was standing with his back to him, talking to the constable and neither was watching him.

He stared ahead at the grey expanse of road and pavement, the trees fringing the small park across from the hospital, their delicate new leaves wavering in the wind. An old man walked towards him, leading a tired old spaniel. The man touched his hat and nodded to Trevor; his manners a relic from another, politer age.

He'd made it! He was outside the gates. The enormity of his achievement suddenly hit him. Spencer had warned him it might take days, if not weeks, before he got this far. Yet here he was at the bus stop, only one day away from the shivering panic attack that had driven him back into his room from the door leading out of his block.

He glanced at his watch; it was nearly two o'clock. Cars were streaming past, but no buses. How long had it been since he'd last sat on a bus? Ten years? He hadn't even thought to ask how often they stopped outside the hospital, and there wasn't a timetable in sight. Perhaps he should walk back? At least as far as the porter on gate duty.

A small, bright-red car drove out of the gates and pulled up in front of him. Lyn reached over and opened the passenger door.

'Going into town?'

'I was thinking of it,' he admitted.

'Hop in. I'll give you a lift.'

'There's no need – '

'The buses only run every half hour, and you've just missed one. Can't you tell? You're the only one waiting here.'

Trevor hobbled hesitantly forward. Pushing his stick into the back seat of the car, he held on to the door and climbed clumsily into the passenger seat.

'I'm working a split shift today,' she explained. 'And I hate split shifts. So I thought I'd go into town and spend some money to cheer myself up.' She slammed the car into gear and pulled off sharply, cutting in behind a fast-moving Mercedes.

'Won the pools?' he asked, after racking his brains for something to say. Had he always found making conversation this difficult? He tried to remember the people he'd talked to before his accident and what he'd said to them.

'No. Just celebrated my twenty-first birthday.'

'Congratulations.'

'You're late; it was last week. And my parents, not knowing what else to give me, sent me a cheque. I intend to buy a whole new wardrobe. An utterly extravagant and up-to-the-minute wardrobe. It hasn't been much fun trying to live on a student nurse's money for the last three years.'

'It couldn't have been,' he agreed.

136

'But hopefully all that struggling will soon be over with.'

'You've sat your finals?'

'Three weeks ago.' She held up her hand, fingers crossed.

'You'll pass.'

'I wish I had your confidence. Where are you off to? To buy a new wardrobe as well?'

'I was thinking of getting my hair cut, but you're right, I do need a new wardrobe. From the state of what I'm wearing, desperately.'

'I didn't mean it that way,' she blushed. 'I must have sounded patronising. I'm sorry.'

'Forget it.' It was most peculiar, but her embarrassment only served to put him at his ease. 'After searching through the clothes Peter brought from my flat, I've come to the conclusion that either he rummaged through my rag bag, or all my clothes should be relegated to one.'

'He probably didn't want to bring your best clothes into hospital.'

'I've never had best clothes,' he admitted. 'Undercover work for the Drug Squad called for the charity shop rejects.'

'I can't imagine someone not taking any interest in their clothes.'

He stared out of the car window, and checked off the familiar landmarks. They were travelling through the east side of town, towards the suburb where he had bought his flat. Was it really only eight years ago? Somehow it seemed as though he'd done it in another lifetime. He and his one-time girlfriend, Mags, had bought it together, although he had paid for it. She had always balked at anything that wasn't frivolous; entertainments, clothes, relationships – especially relationships. But, he and Mags had been over and done with for a long time.

Strange, he'd been devastated when she'd left him to move in with a married man who'd deserted his wife. Now he could barely remember what she looked like. Yet they'd been together for six years; longer than some marriages, and long enough for him to come to hate the flat, the decor, the furniture, the fitted kitchen and even the fancy Persian cat, all chosen by Mags and abandoned by her when she'd moved on.

He'd been lucky to rent out the place, furniture, fittings, cat and all, to another copper. He could see it now; set high on the hill that towered above the town. That had been its major attraction; the view over the town, and the bay.

Trevor thought of the scruffy, poky collection of small rooms over Frank's mini-market in the old, neglected Victorian dock area that he'd moved to afterwards. The unfashionable end the town planners hadn't even considered when they'd designed and built the new marina.

'Where do you want to be dropped off?'

Lost in thought, he'd forgotten Lyn was driving him. 'Sorry, I was miles away. Did you say something?'

'I was asking where you wanted to be dropped off.'

'Anywhere. It doesn't matter.'

'Of course it does. If you want to get your hair cut, the only possible place is the unisex salon on the Marina.'

'Your family own it?'

'No,' she laughed. 'But I approve of the results that walk out of there. And, my brother swears by Lucien who works there. And he needs to look good, he's an accountant. Like my father.'

'You have your hair cut there?'

'There's no point. Mine's so long, I trim the ends once a month with nail scissors.'

'As I have nowhere else in mind, I'll take you up on that suggestion.'

'If it's clothes you're after, you should go to one of the menswear shops in the main arcade.'

'I should?'

'Shopping is something of a passion with me.'

'I'm beginning to find that out.'

'I must sound shallow.'

'No.' He smiled at her, and she smiled back. Seeing her outside the hospital for the first time, she looked younger than her twenty-one years. Perhaps it was the change of scene. Driving into town, and chatting casually, had put their relationship on a different footing to that of nurse and patient. Somehow, somewhere on the journey she had lost whatever authority she held over him.

'My mother's a shopaholic,' she explained. 'As a child she taught me that daddies make the money and the women in the family spend it. I'm afraid she ingrained some bad habits into me from an early age, but now I curb my shopping expeditions to splurges at birthdays and Christmas. And I always buy my father and brother clothes in those small shops in the arcade. The cut on their trousers and jeans is superb, and the sweaters, especially the hand-knitted ones, are very good. Here I go rabbiting on again.'

'I don't mind. At the moment I find it easier to listen than make the effort to talk.'

'That will change. If you are intent on shopping, why don't I show you where those shops are? I don't want to be pushy, but – '

'I look like a scarecrow.'

'I didn't say that.'

'I did,' he said easily. 'And if you show me where the shops are, I'll know where to look.'

She parked her car in the multi-storey car park on the fringes of the pedestrian area, and waited while he lugged his stick, then himself out of the car. She slowed her pace to his as they walked towards the town centre.

'Here's the arcade.' She paused outside its entrance, sandwiched between two large department stores. 'The shop with the purple sign is the best. But whatever you do,' she lowered her voice to a whisper, 'don't go to the hairdresser here. It has to be the one on the marina.'

'I'll remember.'

'See you.'

She disappeared into the nearest boutique. It had a window display of feminine lingerie that drove him away as soon as he looked at it. He could almost hear Peter's jeering laugh, the one he reserved for pathetic old men reduced to ogling women's underclothes in shop windows.

He glanced up and down the arcade. One of the better things about a midweek afternoon was a half empty town. Taking Lyn's advice, he steeled himself and passed through the doorway of the shop she'd recommended.

Inside he was faced with a bewildering array of racks crammed with clothing. That closest to him held jeans, above it hung sweaters, and beyond were rows of trousers and shirts.

'Can I be of any assistance, sir?' The boy was young and anxious to please, an employee working on commission.

'I'm just looking.'

'If there's anything I can do to help, please ask.' The boy retreated behind a counter.

140

Trevor flicked through the jeans rack. They were cut differently to the ones he remembered. He held up a pair, chosen at random, realising he didn't even know what size he was.

'They won't fit you, sir. Those are a thirty-six waist. I'd say you were a thirty or thirty-two,' the boy hazarded. Trevor replaced them on the rack. He'd been a thirty-six inch waist before he'd been injured. He realised he'd lost weight; but that much?

'If you'd like to try these, sir? They're the same style, but more your size.'

Buying a new wardrobe was simpler than Trevor had expected. He was the only customer, so he had the undivided attention of the assistant, who managed to be helpful without being pushy. Trevor tried on the jeans, when he saw they fitted, he picked up a second pair. He flicked through the sweaters and found two he liked. He wandered over to the racks of trousers, and bought two pairs, a couple of casual shirts, a new jacket to replace the worn-out grubby antique he was wearing. An hour and a half later, the dust had been blown off one of his credit cards, he had a bundle of carrier bags, and the clothes he had worn into the shop were stuffed in a bin at the back of the arcade.

Outside the shop, he paused and looked down at his fabric trainers. Two doors up, he spotted a shoe shop. He picked up two pairs of designer trainers, and two pairs of leather shoes. Unable to decide between their various merits, he bought all four pairs, and discarding the shoes he was wearing, left the shop wearing new trainers.

Exhausted, he recalled that he wasn't far from the taxi rank. He took a short-cut through one of the stores and recalled chasing a drug dealer through the crowded aisles one Saturday afternoon. He doubted he was capable of chasing a tortoise the way he felt now.

The department store, like the arcade, was half empty. But as he staggered along, he inadvertently bumped into an old woman who scuttled away. He suddenly realised that he wasn't alone in feeling afraid. There were others who felt terrified every time they set about the simple everyday tasks of life; shopping, walking down the street, even opening the door to the milkman. Perhaps he wasn't so different from the rest of humanity after all.

He stopped at the menswear counter and looked at some boxer shorts and socks. Juggling with his bags and stick, he tried to pick up a pair of shorts, but only succeeded in dropping everything. An assistant came to his rescue. She picked up his stick, returned his carrier bags to his numbed fingers, and packed the underclothes he chose. He almost fell into the cab when he reached the taxi rank.

The hairdresser Lyn had recommended proved easy to find. He left his parcels at the desk and asked for an appointment. Lucien was busy but George was free. George was tattooed, camp, and chatty. Trevor relinquished himself into George's care, closed his eyes and listened to an on-going diatribe against the town councillors, who apparently had an unjustified prejudice against bikers.

According to George, his hair was out of shape, out of condition, and would disgrace a shaggy sheepdog. If nothing else, George certainly knew how to take his time over cutting and shaping. A gopher brought Trevor coffee, strong and black, the way he used to drink it before hospitals had regulated his life.

'There you are, sir.'

Trevor opened his eyes and scarcely recognised the face that stared back at him from the mirror. He was seeing himself in an entirely new light. One that he wasn't too sure he liked.

'I've left it a bit longer here,' George pulled on a few strands above Trevor's left ear, 'to hide the scars. They look rather nasty. Accident?'

'Yes,' Trevor lied. It wasn't just the sight of the scars that wound their way up as far as his left temple that had shocked him; it was the bloodless lips, the thin face and the sunken cheeks.

'Will there be anything else, sir? We do a nice range of toiletries and aftershave.'

'I'll take a look.' Trevor was beginning to understand Lyn's passion for shopping. There was something comforting about spending money; as if the new image he was buying would change his entire life.

He added a carrier bag of cologne and toiletries to his collection, and limped outside. The clock on the bell-tower of the marina struck five. A pub loomed before him; a blackboard outside bore the slogan;

HOME COOKED PUB FOOD AVAILABLE ALL DAY.

He realised he hadn't eaten anything since the toast he'd shared with Lyn that morning. He stumbled across the cobblestones and went inside. It was empty apart from a couple of middle-aged women.

He ordered a pint of beer, and a large steak with chips and salad. It had been a long time since he'd tasted steak. And Spencer was right; the first step was the hardest to take. Now he'd actually made it, he felt capable of tackling almost anything.

His mouth watered at the prospect of the steak. He downed his pint and ordered another. Life wasn't so bad after all. Why had he waited this long to pick up the threads?

'Does the name Elizabeth Moore mean anything to you?' Dan sat in the one comfortable chair Tony's office offered apart from the administrator's own.

'She used to be a staff nurse here.'

Dan thought he saw the same flicker of interest in Waters' eyes that he had noticed when Rosie Twyford's name was first mentioned. 'When and why did she leave?'

'She left about three months ago, but I'd have to check the records for the precise date. She accepted a nursing post in America. We were sorry to see her go, but that's life in British hospitals. Pay and conditions for psychiatric nurses are far better in the States than here.' He blanched. 'Don't tell me that one of the bodies you dug up last night was Elizabeth?'

'It appears to be likely.'

'No!'

Dan thought the cry carried more than shock. There was something deeper in it, something personal. 'We also have reason to believe that the other victim we found last night was Claire Moon, an ex-patient.'

'Excuse me.' Tony's PA, Angela Morgan, walked into the room and laid a tray of coffee, milk and sugar on his desk.

'We also found the corpse of a dog,' Dan continued to watch Tony reactions. 'Large, hairy, breed unknown. Grey dog with white at the tips of its fur.'

The secretary jerked her hand as she spooned sugar into Tony's cup, knocking it over. 'I'm sorry.' She rushed into the outer office in search of paper towels. 'But that sounds like Honey Boy, doesn't it, Mr Waters?'

There was a pained expression on Tony's face, but it was difficult to determine whether it had been prompted by the spilled coffee, the news of two more girls found buried in the grounds, or the dog.

'Who owned Honey Boy?' Dan asked.

'He was a stray. You must remember Honey Boy, Mr Waters.'

'Of course I do,' Tony answered irritably.

'He practically lived in this office last Winter Inspector Evans,' Angela prattled. 'He turned up in the grounds starving, without a collar. We rang the pound, but they said if they took him in and he wasn't claimed within a few days, they'd put him down. Well, it isn't as if this is a proper hospital that needs to be kept sterile or anything, so we kept him. We all chipped in with food, and… ' she dissolved into tears.

'Just when I decided to take him home with me he disappeared,' Tony said shortly. 'I already own two dogs, so another one wouldn't have made that much difference.'

Tears trickled down Angela's cheeks. 'We searched everywhere, then assumed that he'd gone back to wherever he came from. It was a shame, because Mr Waters would have given him such a good home. I tried to persuade my husband to take him in, but we live in a flat on the marina. It's not very big, and Honey Boy was a large dog and we have two cats… '

'Angela, go to personnel and pull Elizabeth Moore's file, and give patients' records a ring and ask them to send up the file of a Claire Moon.'

'Yes, sir.' She dabbed her eyes with a tissue, and left the room.

'Efficient secretary but over-emotional,' Waters declared.

'You must have hundreds of patients passing through here in a year,' Dan commented.

'Around five thousand, which is average for a town of this size,' Tony lifted out the coffee-stained papers from his in-tray and shook them over his bin.

'Do you remember Claire Moon?'

'Yes.'

'Do you have much contact with your patients, Mr Waters?'

'Not usually. But a Sunday paper did a feature on her while she was here, and I monitored the interviews at the request of the Trust.'

'Worried about adverse publicity?'

'Concerned about misrepresentation. Claire's father is Arnold Moon.'

'The businessman?'

'If you can call a multi-millionaire a businessman. She came to this town to go to university and went off the rails. She was in here for drug and alcohol addiction, and made a good recovery.'

'Where did she go when she left?'

'Spain. Her parents divorced and her mother remarried a Spanish hotelier.'

'No one contacted you to say that she never arrived there?'

'I'd have to check with Angela. We frequently receive letters from the families of ex-patients who are trying to get in touch with them. It's common for voluntary psychiatric patients to discharge themselves and go missing. You should know that, Inspector. Some of them must end up on police missing-persons files.'

'Was Claire Moon a voluntary patient?' Dan kept the questioning firmly on track.

147

'Again, I'd have to check. The chances are, with drug addiction she would have been.'

Dan left his chair. 'When the files arrive, would you send copies to our mobile HQ? And I'd be grateful if you'd keep the identities of the victims to yourself for the moment. Rosie Twyford's mother is coming up this afternoon to identify the corpse. We're trying to contact Elizabeth Moore and Claire Moon's families now.'

Bill stood in front of a clear board fixed to the rear wall of the mobile headquarters. He glanced around at the twenty or so men and women crammed around him.

'Everyone here? Right, we'll start with the victims. Constable Grady?' He relinquished his spot to Michelle, who stood stiffly to attention in her immaculate uniform. She consulted her notes.

'First victim we found, and the last in chronological order of death, was Rosie Twyford.' She pointed to a blown-up photograph of Rosie they'd found in the hospital files. 'Blonde hair, blue eyes, five-foot six-inches, heavily built, twelve stone, twenty-five years old. She suffered from clinical depression. She worked in administration in the old hospital until she was admitted as an in-patient. Rosie was discharged from the ward six weeks ago, but continued to attend outpatient clinic. Her psychiatrist was Dorothy Clyne who discharged Rosie from the clinic last Monday, as yet we haven't found anyone who saw her after she left Ms Clyne's office on Monday afternoon until she was dug out of the flowerbed on Monday morning.'

'You and Peter are returning to her bed-sit to interview her neighbours?' Bill asked.

'This evening, sir,' Michelle replied. 'We think that the second victim was murdered approximately two months ago. She hasn't yet been formally identified, but we have reason to believe she was Elizabeth Moore who worked here as a staff nurse. We're waiting for hospital administration to send us her file.' She glanced at Dan who gave her an encouraging smile. 'We think the last victim found, and the killer's first, was a patient, Claire Moon, but as her body hasn't been formally identified either, we can't be certain of her identity.'

'Thank you, Constable Grady,' Bill took over again as she sat down. 'I called this meeting because I want to save time on individual briefings. A psychologist is working on the killer's profile – ' Peter groaned. 'Sergeant Collins,' Bill turned towards him. 'Would you like to share your thoughts with us?'

'Psychologists are often proved wrong – '

'And on occasions are proved right,' Bill countered. 'Have you any better suggestions on how to catch this killer?'

'Police work.'

'This is police work, Sergeant. Twenty-first Century style. At this moment the psychologist is feeding all the information we have into a computer that holds data on all known serial killers. And that's what we have here. A serial killer who could strike again at any moment. We don't know whether he picks his victims at random. All we do know is that they all had connections with this hospital and our killer appears to have a knowledge of the hospital layout. We probably wouldn't have found any of his victims if a patient hadn't spotted him burying one in the garden. Our killer also knows how to pick his time. All the victims were either on the point of leaving the hospital, or they were voluntary patients whose absence wouldn't be missed. Because as far as we have yet ascertained, none were reported missing.' Bill pointed to notes scribbled on the far right of the board. 'The pathologist has confirmed that all the victims were drugged before death. It's also possible they were kept alive for days before burial, because Rosie Twyford and one of the other victims had needle marks in their upper arms. In Twyford's case, twenty-five separate syringe punctures. In the other victim the pathologist found twelve. The reason why he can't be more specific is because one of the victims has very little skin left. What he can confirm, however, is traces of drugs in the organs of all three victims, including tranquillisers and curare, which has a paralysing effect on all the muscles in the body. However, in Twyford's case the effect was wearing off at the time of burial.'

Bill stared at the assembled officers. 'From the time scale of Twyford's disappearance, we can assume that our killer abducts his victims and conceals them, probably within the hospital or the grounds, and keeps them drugged until such time as he can bury them in the garden – alive. All three corpses had earth in their air passages.'

'He must have a knowledge of drugs and how to administer them,' Peter diagnosed.

Bill handed a marker pen to Dan, who noted Peter's observations under the heading of KILLER PROFILE.

'Anyone think of anything else?' Bill asked.

'The killer has to be either a doctor or a nurse,' a young constable chipped in.

'What's your name, son?' Mulcahy demanded.

'Constable Pike, sir.'

'Why does the killer have to be a doctor or nurse, Pike?' Bill enquired.

'Because he knows how to administer injections, and, he has access to drugs.'

'There are patients here who can gain access to drugs, as well as the pharmacists, and porters who ferry them from ward to ward. As for administering an injection, any diabetic or first-aid course will give you the rudimentary knowledge.'

'Yes, sir.' Pike shrank back into his chair.

'Anyone else?'

'What about the dog, sir?'

'As you know more about that than me, tell them, Peter,' Bill ordered.

'Like the victims, the dog was drugged with curare and buried alive. From the lab report, approximately three to four months ago.'

'Could it have been a practice run?'

'Nice try, Michelle,' Dan complimented. 'But timing places it between the first victim and the last two.'

'Until further notice we'll have debriefing sessions every night at eleven-thirty sharp either here or at the station. I don't care how much overtime you put in, or what it costs you, your family or your social life. I want this killer caught before he has the chance to turn another young woman into fertiliser. Right, gentlemen and ladies. We all have work to do. Go out there and do it,' Bill dismissed.

Trevor felt at home in the pub on the marina. The chairs were thickly upholstered, and a log fire blazed in the hearth. He watched the flames, and ate his meal slowly, but he barely managed half the salad and steak, and less than a quarter of the chips.

'There isn't anything wrong with your meal, is there, sir?' the waitress asked, when she cleared his plate.

'Nothing,' Trevor replied apologetically. 'The food was fine. Just more than I've been used to eating lately.'

'Would you like to see the dessert menu, sir?'

'No, but thank you for asking.' He felt as though he was learning to live again. Simple conversation wasn't that difficult after all. He bought a third pint and continued to sit in front of the fire, watching the bar fill with office workers who'd stopped for a quick one on their way home. His three pints became four, and he was beginning to feel fuzzy when he heard a familiar voice.

'Trevor, you're the last person I expected to see in here.' Jean Marshall stood in front of his table, a double gin in one hand and a bottle of tonic water in the other.

'Sister Marshall.'

'For pity's sake, don't call me that outside. It makes me sound like a militant nun. It's Jean. May I join you?'

'Of course,' he moved his chair closer to the fire, to make room for her.

'I didn't recognise you at first.' She sat in the chair opposite his. 'I like the haircut, and the clothes. They're an improvement,' she complimented, as he moved his assortment of carrier bags from under her feet.

'I've lost so much weight, nothing I own fits me.'

'I wish I could say the same, but my clothes don't fit me for a different reason.' She poured half of the tonic water into her glass. 'I haven't been home yet. Thought I'd treat myself to a pick-me-up first.'

'Hard day?'

'No more than usual.' She kicked off her shoes and toasted her toes before the fire. 'It's good to see you out and about. You look – different.'

'How?'

'Not just the clothes and the hair but something else. Something I can't put a name to.'

'I feel different,' he smiled.

'See what I mean? You're smiling.'

152

'I don't know why I put off going outside for so long.' He coughed, glanced over his shoulder and saw a girl blowing cigarette smoke in his direction, 'then again, perhaps I do.'

'You don't like cigarette smoke?'

'Can't stand it.'

'Then how come you're in one of the few pubs left on the marina that allow it? And how come you worked with Peter Collins? Every time I see him he has a cigar in his mouth.'

'I used to complain non-stop. And I'd open windows wide in the office and the car, even in the middle of Winter. It's a wonder we didn't drive each other mad.' He finished his pint and looked at Jean's empty glass. 'Same again?'

'I'd love to, but if I drink on an empty stomach I'm going to get plastered. I need to eat.'

'It's probably time I was going anyway,' Trevor took her refusal as a rebuff.

'I was going to ask if you fancied a meal and a drink at my place.' She slipped her shoes back on. 'It's just around the corner.'

'I've just eaten.'

'How about cheese and biscuits and a beer? I've some first-class Dutch lager in the fridge that a friend brought back from Holland.'

'Are you sure I won't be imposing?' Trevor asked.

'Quite sure. I live alone because I like it that way, but that's not to say I don't enjoy company from time to time. Besides,' she grinned wickedly, 'there's nothing on the TV tonight. I checked the paper.' Jean led the way out of the pub and over a bridge that spanned the yacht berths. 'I live on the far side.' She pointed to one of the most expensive blocks, fronting the open sea on one side and the marina on the other.

'Nice view.'

'You'll see just how nice in a moment.' She waved to the porter as they walked through the foyer. She went into the lift and pressed the button for the top floor.

'The penthouse?'

'What else?' The lift halted. There was only one door in the lobby. Jean scrabbled in her handbag for her keys, and opened it.

Trevor stepped in behind her and found himself in a large, square, windowless hall with mahogany panelling, carpeted with a blue and red Persian rug, and hung with what turned out to be, on close inspection, very suggestive Persian prints.

'I like the Orient.' She opened one of the panels to reveal a cupboard. 'Can I take your jacket?'

Trevor handed it over as he looked for somewhere to drop his bags.

'Drop those in the corner.'

He followed her into a living room that could have swallowed his flat four times over. Two walls were glass, one overlooked the sea, the other the marina, and he felt as though he had wandered into a people-sized fish tank.

'This view is spectacular. I love the sea and can just about see the dirty corner next to the sewage works from my kitchen window.'

The other two walls were painted in shades of blue. The ceiling was pale grey, the floor carpeted in navy-blue Wilton. Even the sofas were upholstered in deep blue leather; the only soft touch was the Persian tapestry cushions on the sofas, and the hand woven Persian silk hangings on the walls.

'Orient again?' He raised his eyebrows.

Jean brushed her hand across one of the hangings, which was almost but not quite as suggestive as the pictures in the hall. The colours were perfect for the room; predominantly blue and grey, with a few touches of white and burgundy.

'You certainly know how to put a home together,' Trevor complimented, looking at the grey-washed, lime-oak glass fronted cupboards that held a selection of blue Turkish glass and Chinese porcelain.

'Thank you. Take a seat, and I'll mix us a salad and fetch the drinks.'

'I'd rather help.' He followed her into another inner hallway.

'Cloakroom,' she pointed to a door ahead of them. 'Bedrooms, bathrooms, kitchen, dining room and study,' she indicated the doors. 'It's not vast, but it's comfortable. Take a look around.'

'I wouldn't dream of it.'

'Don't be so polite. People are always curious about other people's living space. Adam Hayter asked me if I had gold-plated baths and loos when he found out where I lived. The publicity campaign the builder ran when he marketed this place backfired. People expected rock musicians and film stars to move in, not the local scrap merchant.'

'Scrap merchant?' Trevor looked at her quizzically.

'My husband,' Jean explained. 'The one who ran off with an eighteen-year-old tart.'

'I'm sorry.'

'There's no need to be. He did me an enormous favour. I was getting tired of hearing him crow about his face-lifts and lipo suction. And it was alarming to wake up next to him after the last face-lift. Something went wrong and he couldn't close his eyes. I hope his tart doesn't mind sleeping next to a wide-open stare. And I most certainly am "All right Jack", thank you very much. My share of our divorce settlement gave me this apartment, the first boat you see in the row if you look out the study window, and enough money to tempt all the toy boys I want into my bed when the mood takes me.'

She moved into the kitchen and, unable to resist his curiosity, Trevor walked into the study and looked out of its huge picture window. A large ocean-going cruiser was berthed in front of a line of yachts.

'That's your boat?' he called into the kitchen.

'The *Turkish Queen*.' she called back. 'It's five-berth. My husband had it built, and christened it after we holidayed in Turkey. At the time I thought he named it after me; now I'm not so sure. I'd like to rename it, but that's supposed to be unlucky.'

He looked at the rest of the study. Books lined the floor to ceiling oak shelves, all Everyman editions in mint condition that looked as though they'd never been opened. A bleached oak desk held a computer and nothing else. For all its expensive fitments the room looked strangely empty and characterless, like a display in a museum or a furniture shop.

He went into the cloakroom and washed his hands and face in a Victorian-style sink. The tiles on the wall were Minton, the thick fluffy towels American. Resisting the temptation to open the bedroom doors, he went into the kitchen where he found Jean mixing salad in between sips of gin.

'This room's too big for someone like me, who never cooks,' she waved her hand around the expanse of ultra-modern black and grey granite units. 'I've never switched on one of the fridge-freezers, or used the large oven in the cooker, but I'm too idle to move house, and it's better to

have too much space and too many gadgets than too few.'
She handed him a tray with the salad and a can of lager on
it. 'I'll bring in the chicken pie and cheese. Sure you
won't have some salad, too?'

'Perhaps just a little.' Trevor's appetite was
sharpened by all the beer he'd drunk.

She loaded pie, cheese, biscuits and fruit on to
another tray, and returned to the living room. To Trevor's
amazement, she opened the window.

'We'll freeze.'

'Not in a centrally-heated conservatory. It's cleverly
designed; you have to look hard to see where the glass
ends and the balcony begins. The balcony was so large,
and the winters so long, it seemed a waste of space until I
had the idea of glassing half of it in.' She set the tray
down on a cane table. Returning to the living room she
picked up two glass plates, cutlery, and a silver box of
paper napkins. 'Sorry about these disposable napkins, but
I hate washing. In fact I hate all housework.'

'This is marvellous.' Trevor sat facing both the open
sea and the marina. 'I'd forgotten life could be this good.'
He resolved to do something about his shabby little flat
the first chance he got.

Life was short, very short. It had taken a close brush
with death for him to realise just how quickly the flame of
existence could be snuffed out; and now he'd learned that
no one, least of all himself, was immortal, perhaps it
might be as well if he continued to remember his mortality
for whatever time was left to him.

Jean was showing him a glimpse of the good and
beautiful life, and it could be his if he made the effort.
He'd seen too much ugliness. It was time he looked for
something better that offered, if not the certainty of
happiness, at least the chance.

They ate and drank, quietly, companionably. Dusk fell and one by one the harbour lights flickered on. First in the pubs and restaurants, then the lamps that sent silvery sparkles dancing on the waves along the water's edge and finally the red mast lights of the boats berthed in lines along the marina.

'You don't need gold-plated baths,' Trevor said. 'This view is worth every penny you paid for it.'

'I didn't pay for it. I earned it as a reward for twenty years of marriage to a boorish lout who couldn't spell his own name. But,' she chuckled throatily, 'I think the compensation was worth every second of the sentence. Don't you?'

CHAPTER ELEVEN

'Vanessa Hedley's missing.'

'What?' Karl Lane looked up from the pile of forms he was filling in and stared in disbelief at Lyn who was standing in the doorway of his ward office.

'Vanessa's missing. I can't find her anywhere…'

'Calm down,' he ordered, exercising his authority as senior nursing officer on duty. 'You've checked the ward thoroughly?'

'Yes.'

'The therapy units?'

'All the therapists left two hours ago.'

'Spencer sometimes runs an evening class.'

'Not tonight. I checked his room.'

'Have you telephoned security?'

'Yes. I asked them to search the grounds.'

'Have you informed Tony?'

'It's nine o'clock. I assumed he'd have gone home by now.'

'He rarely leaves his office before eight on a normal evening and what's happening around here at the moment is anything but normal. I'll try him.' He picked up the receiver and dialled. 'You'd better get back to your ward. Vanessa probably just wandered off through the gates when the porter wasn't looking. You know what she's like. But wherever she is, she can't have come to any harm given the number of police officers crawling around the grounds. How long has she been gone?'

'I saw her at dinner. She left with Roland – '

'Roland?' he interrupted.

'They only went to the day room,' Lyn replied, knowing what he was thinking. 'According to Lucy,

Vanessa went to the toilet shortly afterwards and didn't return. Everyone assumed she'd gone to bed early.'

'Did you ask Lucy if Roland followed Vanessa?'

'No, but he's in his own room now. I saw him there ten minutes ago.'

'They could have gone out together earlier, and Roland returned without her. He spends half his life skulking in the gardens. I think he has a bar hidden in the bushes. We'd better get security to trawl the shrubberies. Roland's probably got Vanessa plastered and she's still searching for her knickers in the dark.'

'Karl, this is no joke.' Lyn was irritated by his flippant attitude.

'Who says I'm joking?' He dropped the receiver. 'Tony isn't in his office.'

'I think we should tell the police.'

'Why?'

'She's missing,' she repeated in exasperation. 'And she's the only person who's seen the killer.'

'Vanessa Hedley's a psychiatric patient. Psychiatric patients go missing all the time. If we rang the police every time one decided to go walkabout, we'd be the laughing stock of the Trust.'

'I think in this case we should make an exception.'

'I'm senior nursing duty officer and any decision to contact the police has to be made by the senior admin officer. It's Tony's problem, not ours. Can you imagine what the local press will make of this, if it leaks out? Compton Castle staff, ask serious crime squad to find crazy lady they misplaced. They'll have a field-day, when they find out who she is. Someone's bound to recognise the name and they'll dig up the headlines from when she tried to kill her husband and his mistress. Then there'll be a hue and cry from the people who bought luxury executive homes outside the hospital walls, and who don't want a potential murderer living in the same square mile as their offspring.'

'I can imagine the headlines this will make if she has been snatched by the killer,' Lyn said. 'Vanessa Hedley murdered by serial killer while hospital trust stays mum.'

'Return to your ward, Nurse Sullivan,' Karl said. 'You've reported Vanessa Hedley's absence to your senior. I'll take it from here.'

'Karl – '

He remembered the last night they'd spent together. She was beautiful, even with her long dark hair gathered into a knot at the nape of neck. Probably the most beautiful girlfriend he'd ever had, and the best bed mate he'd found in a long time. He laid his hands on her shoulders. 'It will be all right. No one's going to blame you. Everyone's aware that two trained staff and two auxiliaries can't supervise twenty-four patients every single minute of their day and night.'

A number of things about Karl had begun to annoy Lyn lately, not least his arrogant, patronising attitude.

'I'm not concerned with being hauled over the coals by the authorities; you stupid man, but with what might have happened to Vanessa. She's a witness... '

'Back to your ward, Nurse Sullivan.'

'Damn you, Karl. I just hope you're right and nothing has happened to her.'

'Been out, mate?' Peter slowed his car in the drive of Compton Castle, and wound down his window.

'To town,' Trevor stopped and leaned heavily on his stick. 'Give me a lift up to my ward. I'm whacked.'

'Bill received a directive from Tony Waters that all police vehicles were to keep to the first hundred yards of the main drive, well away from all wards, but you know me and rules. Jump in.' Peter opened both back and front doors, and Trevor off-loaded his bags into the back and flung his stick on top of them, before clambering into the passenger seat.

'Been shopping until now?'

'I stopped for a meal.'

'You what?' Peter stared at Trevor in amazement. Even in the darkness he could sense a change, a subtle increase in confidence and a rebirth of humour.

'Steak and chips.'

'And beer, by the smell of you.' Peter waved a hand in front of his face. 'Lots of beer.'

'Four or five,' Trevor admitted with a grin.

'And you're obviously feeling proud of yourself, even if you're on the road to alcoholism. Welcome back to the land of the living.' Peter tried and failed to mask the emotion he felt. 'It's about bloody time, even if I am jealous as hell at the thought of you munching steak and chips, when I'm confined to a diet of take-away grease eaten at ungodly hours in the mobile HQ.'

'I thought I could smell something.'

'Something getting cold.' Peter halted outside the ward block. 'Here you are. Home. Does mother know you've been out?'

Trevor pulled a pass from his jacket pocket. 'Allowed out until nine-thirty.'

'You've one minute to spare. Here, I'll give you a hand with your bags. Bloody hell!' Peter exclaimed, as he picked up the one containing the shoes. 'What have you been buying?'

'A new image,' Trevor retrieved his stick, and limped towards the front door.

162

'Good Lord, so you have.' Peter noticed Trevor's clothes as he stood beneath the light and rang the bell. 'And you've had your hair cut. Well, that settles it.'

'Settles what?'

'You'll be kicked out of the Drug Squad. You're too damned clean and neat even for Serious Crimes.'

The door opened and Trevor walked inside. When Peter returned to his car, he almost tripped over a security guard who was shining a torch beneath it.

'What are you are doing here at this time of night?' the man demanded officiously.

Peter looked him up and down. Ex-forces by his build and carriage, young, and probably working for minimum wage, he decided cynically. He brought out his wallet and flashed his badge.

'Hospital Trust has declared this area out of bounds to the police, sir,' the guard pointed out in a marginally politer tone.

'Returning an injured suspect.' Peter stepped into the driving seat. The smell of fish and chips reminded him that his supper wouldn't be getting any warmer. There was nothing worse than cold fish and chips. They reverted to blocks of solid, tasteless grease. But as he drove away from the wards towards the mobile HQ, he couldn't help feeling uneasy. Something was wrong; he could feel it in his bones. He just couldn't put his finger on whatever that something was.

'Anything new on Rosie Twyford?' Dan asked when Peter walked in.

'Absolutely bloody nothing.' Peter handed over one of the two paper-wrapped bundles. 'Thought you might be hungry,' he replied to Dan's enquiring look.

'That's kind of you.' The more Dan saw and worked with Peter, the more he was amazed by his generosity, which often came directly after a bout of particularly belligerent behaviour.

'I came back because I'd rather sit out the night here, than listen to Mary Poppins regurgitate the blanks we drew in Rosie Twyford's bed-sit.'

'It was that bad?' Dan picked up a handful of chips and squashed them into his mouth.

'The only one who admitted to knowing her was the guy in the next bed-sit, and he claimed he had only met her twice in the hallway. But as four of the other residents have been hauled in for pushing, and three for soliciting, it's not the kind of cosy household you invite your neighbour in to for a cup of tea and a chat.'

'It's the kind of household the social workers look for when they want to off-load their difficult charges.'

'You got it in one,' Peter mumbled, his mouth full.

'I'm not going to object to extra help. After we've eaten, you can give me a hand with this.'

'What is it?' Peter stared at the enormous, grey cardboard box on Dan's desk.'

'The staff files of current hospital personnel.'

'Official files never tell you anything. Friend of mine works in a press cutting agency. I gave him a staff list yesterday and he came up trumps.' Peter cornered the last of his soggy chips in the blind end of the greaseproof paper bag, then crammed them into his mouth. Screwing the greasy paper into a ball, he flicked it into the bin. 'Let's see what he found, shall we?' He walked out of the door and went to his car.

'The personnel files are a collection of CVs, medical histories, and job descriptions. If I hadn't been assured

164

otherwise by Tony Waters, I'd say they'd been sanitised for our benefit,' Dan complained an hour later, as he pushed the fourth file aside and reached for the coffee pot. 'Want one?' he held the pot in front of Peter.

'May as well.' Peter separated the national press cuttings from the mass of local paper's wedding photographs and details of charity cheque handovers. 'My friend is nothing if not thorough.' He spread out a photocopied double sheet, taken from a Sunday arts supplement.

'*Darling of the art set makes his first million,*' he read. '*Spencer Jordan has added to his phenomenal success by selling his entire current Californian exhibition to the Metropolitan Museum of Modern Art...*'

'You sure that's the same Spencer Jordan?' Dan asked.

'Take a look at the picture.' Peter passed it over. 'He's younger, better dressed and hairier, but it's the same man. What have you got on his CV?'

Dan rummaged through his files. 'Successful commercial artist. Exhibitions, lots of exhibitions, art college here, then in America... given the post of art therapist at Compton Castle two years ago. A note on his medical file says he had an eye removed, and he's made a good recovery from severe clinical depression. Isn't that what Trevor Joseph has?'

'Yes,' Peter whistled. 'Look at this,' he pushed a paper across the table. Lurid headlines blazed above a gruesome photograph that covered the front page of a tabloid.

'Has to be American press,' Dan commented. 'Not even a hardened jackal of the British press corps would sink this low.

Four bodies had been laid out on a lawn. The faces inadequately covered with tiny squares of cloth that barely obscured their features. The hair and ears were in plain view. Two were small, one a tiny baby. All the corpses were bloodied, clothes and skin slashed to shreds.

'*Artist's family slain by sect in ritual killing,*' Dan read. He turned the page. '*Spencer Jordan, the well-known British artist returned to his Californian home after hosting an exhibition in New York, to find his entire family slain and their murderers occupying his house.*'

There was another photograph on the second page of Spencer being led out of the house by a paramedic. His cheeks were bloody and a gauze bandage covered his eyes.

'*One of the sect attacked Spencer Jordan, tearing out his eye, but despite his horrific injuries Mr Jordan managed to fight his way to the front door and raise the alarm.*'

'Which explains why he suffered from depression,' Peter observed.

'The eldest child was four, the youngest two months,' Dan whispered. 'Poor bastard. No wonder he started his career here as an inmate.'

'Is his medical history in his personal record?' Peter asked.

'Nothing other than what I read out, Waters' secretary let slip that Harry Goldman fought the Trust to give Spencer the post of therapist here.'

'It's probably worth buying her a drink or two in the Green Monkey.'

'Where do you think she told me that?' Dan replied. 'I took her there earlier this evening. Find the local gossip, ply her with drink, pump her, and you'll save yourself a lot of leg work.'

'Unwritten police college motto?' Peter agreed.

'Pays every time. What do you think? The man obviously suffered.'

'But did he suffer enough to lose his marbles and turn into a killer? When did he first take up his post here?'

'Two years ago. When did this happen?' Dan rammed his finger on the newspaper.

'Four years ago. Two years missing.' Peter pushed a smaller article covering the trial towards Dan. 'There's a footnote here, Spencer Jordan could not be called to give evidence because he was incarcerated in a state mental institution. The killers were convicted on forensic evidence, and sentenced to life.'

'What's life in California?' Dan asked.

'Probably the same as here,' Peter replied. 'Ten years remission for every six months of good behaviour, a pat on the head and a directive never to be a naughty boy again when released.'

'That man's been through a lot.' Dan folded the newspaper so he didn't have to look at the photographs.

'He could be our man,' Peter suggested. 'He obviously went bananas, to end up in a state mental institution and then this place.'

'I'd end up here, if I saw my family butchered.'

'The question is, did he go sufficiently bananas to feel compelled to bury innocent people alive?' Peter sat back in his chair, 'and then again, the killer could be Vanessa Hedley.'

Dan laughed.

'Look at the facts. She tried to kill her old man and his mistress, and damn near succeeded. She spent six years in Broadmoor before coming here. The world and his friend has heard her fantasy of wanting to bury her old man so she could keep an eye on him. She's been a patient

167

long enough to learn how to give injections. Security in this place is a joke, so if she really wanted to, she could gain access to drugs. And with only one guard on at night, it's easy enough to dodge your way around the hospital grounds.'

'Your theory's fine until you take into account Vanessa's size,' Dan said. 'She's tiny, five-foot-two, and what – seven stone?'

'About that,' Peter agreed. 'But that's not to say she isn't strong.'

'Can you see her carrying a twelve-stone woman out of this place, dumping her in a hole and burying her?'

'Vanessa was the only one who knew where the body was buried,' Peter persisted.

'Then why did she ask the gardener to dig it up?'

'Because she's nuts, and nutty people do nutty things.'

'OK, where's the dirt on her clothes?' Dan asked. 'I asked Michelle to check out her wardrobe. We found nothing. What else have you got?'

'Adam Hayter.'

'The therapist?'

'Needlework and cookery.'

'It takes all sorts. What about him?'

'Soliciting with intent in a men's toilet and indecent exposure. Nabbed last Christmas,' Peter pushed the half-inch of column across the table.

'Found guilty, and fined. So what?'

'He's a pervert.'

'Only in some people's eyes. You know who he's shacked up with?'

'Enlighten me.' Peter finished his coffee and made a face, but he reached for the jug again. He needed something to keep him awake. The hours between two and three in the morning were always the worst.

'Dotty Clyne.'

'Our female impersonator. Have you seen her moustache?'

'Yes, but she's a female all right. Says so on her medical record.'

'I don't believe it.'

'Anything on Harry Goldman?' Dan rubbed his hands through his thinning hair until it stood on end.

Peter put aside the cutting he was looking at and shuffled through the remaining ones. 'Possessing and distributing pornographic material.'

'A psychiatrist? And he's still in work?'

'Says here it was for his PHD thesis on sexual deviants.'

'He should know about those, with all the examples floating around this place.' Dan stamped his feet to bring back the circulation. 'Anything else?'

'Only wedding photographs, charity photographs, that sort of thing.'

'Nothing on Tony Waters?' Dan asked.

'A photograph of him taken on his appointment. A photograph of him and his wife outside the church when they married. Good Lord, he's married to that nurse – what's-her-name?'

'Carol Ashford.'

'You knew?'

'His secretary told me. Why so surprised? Hospital staff marry one another all the time. Doctors, nurses. Administrators, nurses.'

'It's just – the name.'

'A lot of women keep their maiden names after marriage.'

'I know, but she's fanciable, and he's weird.'

'You can't charge a woman because you fancy her, or a man because he's a cold fish.'

'Pity. We'd solve this case in five minutes if we could.'

'I suggest we open a file on every member of staff and get one of the minions to enter their details in the computer. As soon as we get the killer profile from the psychologist, we'll do a cross check.'

Peter rested his head on his arms and stared at the papers littering the desk. 'You know what the problem is here, don't you?'

'I've a feeling you're going to tell me,' Dan said unenthusiastically.

. 'We've half a dozen suspects on the staff, and we haven't even started on the patients.'

'We'll start on their files tomorrow,' Dan said cheerfully. 'And then the fish and chips will be on me.'

'What's the matter?' Lyn Sullivan snapped, when Trevor left his room at three.

'Sorry, I didn't mean to startle you.' He pushed his hands into the pockets of his shabby paisley polyester dressing gown and shivered.

'Did you want to get yourself a drink?'

'No, a book. I can't sleep and I've finished the one I borrowed from the hospital library.'

'There are plenty of magazines in the office.' Her anger dissipated. Trevor looked exposed and vulnerable in his shabby nightwear. And his fashionable new haircut contrasted strongly with his pale, thin, sickly-white face. 'I was going to make myself a cup of tea. Do you want one?'

'Please.' He followed her into the ward kitchen. 'No one else around?'

'They had trouble on geriatric, so we sent our auxiliaries to help, and the other nurse is on meal break.'

'You mean you're superintending this ward alone?'

'Locked in with all you crazy people?' Lyn smiled. 'I'm used to it. It happens quite often at night, and once you realise that the reality of life on the wards isn't at all like the advert in the colour supplement that enticed me into becoming a psychiatric nurse, it's not that bad. Beats nine-till-five word-processing.' She switched the kettle on. 'Toast?'

'No, thank you.'

'Too much alcohol?' she asked intuitively.

'How did you guess?'

'It happens to everyone, first time out.' The phone rang, and she was out of the room and down the ward before Trevor realised what was happening. He took over making the tea, and had a plate of toast made and buttered before she returned.

'Anything important?'

'Geriatric asking if they could keep our auxiliaries for another hour.'

'You expecting more trouble?'

'Not really.'

'You sure?'

She eyed him over the rim of her cup. 'You really have come a long way. Now you're over the worst, you want to take up amateur psychiatry?'

'Sorry.'

'You seem to have switched from depression to… '

'Elation!'

'Not elation. If that was the case, you'd be in real trouble. Try normality.'

171

'Whatever that might mean.'

'If Goldman sees you behaving like this, he'll throw you out of the hospital.'

'I hope so.' Trevor smiled. 'I really hope so. I've begun to make plans...'

'Such as?' she interrupted.

'To change the way I live,' he didn't want to say too much in case he sounded ridiculous or naïve. He watched her pick half-heartedly at her toast. But instead of trying to make conversation with him, she constantly glanced over his shoulder and out of the window.

'Something's wrong, isn't it?'

'Yes. But I've been ordered by my superior to keep my mouth shut.'

'Tell me?'

'No.'

'Tell me off the record,' Trevor suggested. 'If I discover anything, I promise not to implicate you.'

She stared at him.

'I promise,' he repeated, sensing her hesitation.

'Vanessa Hedley's disappeared. And we can't find her anywhere.'

CHAPTER TWELVE

'What are you going to do?' Lyn Sullivan asked warily.

'Inform the police so they can organise a search,' Trevor set his cup down.

'You organise a search and I'll lose my job.' She bit her lip. 'When I told Karl… '

'Karl Lane?' Trevor recalled the good-looking male nurse who had tended Lyn's cuts after Vanessa went berserk.

'He's senior duty officer tonight. When I told him Vanessa was missing, he warned me not to tell anyone until he contacted Tony Waters.'

'Did he now?' Trevor said thoughtfully. 'That's interesting.'

'Not in the way you think. Karl's no murderer; he's just obsessed with saying and doing the right thing, lest it affect his promotion prospects. He doesn't want anyone berating him for kicking up a fuss that could lead to press headlines telling the world what a load of incompetents run this hospital.' She fell silent for a moment. 'Damn! This is one situation where I can't win no matter what.'

'I wouldn't say that,' Trevor smiled. 'You mentioned your junior nurse was on meal break. Have you had yours yet?'

'No.'

'When do you go?'

'When she gets back, which should be,' she glanced up at the clock on the wall. 'In twenty minutes. Why?'

He held a finger to his lips. 'He who asks no questions need tell no lies afterwards. Good tea, this,' he added innocently.

'What the hell was that?' Dan jumped up from the table where he'd been dozing over the last of the files.

'Fire alarm by the sound of it.' Peter ran into the outer office, where two female constables were trying to peer through a tiny window. He pushed past them and opened the door. The cool night air came as an invigorating shock after the smoke-laden stuffiness inside the van.

A security guard came running out of the main building and headed towards the wards. Peter darted after him.

'Isn't that the ward Trevor Joseph is on?' Dan caught up with Peter, and pointed to a group of patients standing in front of the building in their nightclothes.

Peter ran the last hundred yards. He was overtaken by Karl Lane who began shouting orders at the patients who were stumbling sleepily, in drugged and tranquillised confusion. A junior nurse close to panic was calling names off a list. A cloud of black smoke billowed from an open window at the far end of the same block.

A security guard pushed his way past the patients and into the porch of the building, ignoring several bewildered nurses who'd left their own wards to see if they could help.

'Very clever. I've never seen a guard without breathing apparatus or protective clothing run into a burning building before. What training school did he go to?' Dan said.

'Pyromaniac's been at it again,' Peter looked around for Trevor.

'First I've heard of a pyromaniac,' Dan said. 'Tell me more.'

'Remember a Michael Carpenter being brought into the station?'

'Set a fire, and tried to kill his girlfriend and her family.'

Peter nodded. 'The sooner we start examining the patients' files the better.'

Karl Lane continued to scream commands at the dazed patients who refused to stay still. A nurse ran after Alison Bevan who was charging down the drive in panic.

'I was in the staff dining room on break.' Lyn ran up breathlessly and grabbed Karl. 'Are they all out?'

'How in hell should I know?' he snarled. 'Your junior is bloody useless.'

Lyn took the list from the girl's shaking fingers. 'Everyone over here,' she called out coolly. 'Over here, or you won't be allowed back into your beds.' The threat did the trick. The dressing gowned and slippered figures shuffled slowly towards her.

'Alison Bevan?'

'Here.'

'John Carter?'

'Present, miss.'

Everyone laughed except Karl Lane, and some of the tension dissipated. Peter scanned the ranks of patients, then shrugged his arms out of his coat sleeves.

'What do you think you're doing?' Dan asked, as Peter moved towards the building.

'I can't see Trevor. Stupid fool's probably trying to play the hero.'

The security guard stopped Peter in the porch. 'You can't go in there.'

'Says who?' Peter squared up to him.

A fire engine raced up the drive, siren blaring, its wheels scattering gravel over the flowerbeds. Before it drew to a halt, Trevor stumbled, hunched and coughing, out through the inner doorway of the building.

'You bloody fool!' Peter threw his jacket over Trevor's dressing gown. 'Where the hell have you been?'

'Checking to see no one was left behind,' he whispered hoarsely. 'It's not as bad as it looks,' he informed the first fireman to leap from the engine. 'Just some magazines, cotton wool and a blanket bundled into the sink and set alight. I turned the tap on them.'

'Trying to roast us in our beds again, darling?' Ali Bevan glared at Michael Carpenter, who sat shivering on a bench, a sleep-numbed expression on his face.

'I didn't – I didn't – I didn't – ' he chattered like a monkey.

'Is anyone missing?' A fireman asked Lyn, seeing the list in her hand.

'Yes,' she answered, giving Karl Lane a defiant look. 'Vanessa Hedley, female, 52 years of age, five-foot-two,' she hesitated, trying to remember what colour Vanessa's hair had been that morning.

'She's a blonde today, darling,' Roland chipped in from the crowd that had gathered outside the drug and alcohol dependency unit. 'But there's no use looking for her,' he said blandly to the fireman. 'She's been missing for hours.'

'She's been missing for hours and you didn't think to inform us?' Peter turned furiously on Lyn.

'I reported her disappearance to the senior nursing officer on duty at eight o'clock this evening,' she replied defensively.

'And what pen-pushing moron… '

'Karl Lane, meet Sergeant Collins and Inspector Evans,' Lyn effected the introductions.

'A material witness in a murder case disappears, and you didn't think to inform us?' Dan turned angrily on Karl.

'She's gone missing before,' he offered lamely.

'For God's sake man... ' Peter began.

Dan interrupted, 'Has she ever gone missing all night before?'

'Not that I can remember.' Karl squirmed and looked around for Lyn. This had to be her fault, and tomorrow morning he'd see that she and not him was hauled over the coals.

'I want to see whoever's in charge of this apology for a hospital – and I don't mean you,' Dan raged at Karl. 'If they're not in our HQ in ten minutes, I'm going to the press. And not *just* the press either; television, radio – the works.'

'It's three o'clock in the morning,' Karl protested feebly.

'I couldn't give a single sweet damn what time it is,' Dan's voice dropped ominously low.

'I'll telephone Mr Waters.'

'In our HQ in ten minutes,' Dan repeated. 'And in the meantime I'm instigating a full search of the whole hospital and all the grounds.'

'You can't do that. Not without authority... '

'I have all the authority I need. Peter, ring the station. Get as many coppers here as you can. Now!'

Trevor turned back to the ward, intending to get dressed.

'You can't go in there.' The security guard tried to stop him.

'Those the only words you learnt in school?' Peter asked before making his way back to HQ.

177

Leaving her patients in the care of a staff nurse, Lyn sought out Karl. 'It's freezing out here. Where do you want me to put my patients?'

'Wherever you like.'

She stared furiously after his retreating figure. 'Right, everyone into the main hall,' she shouted. Turning to the nurses standing by she called out, 'I have twenty-four patients who need temporary housing overnight. See how many spare beds you can find in each block, make a note of the bed number and the ward, and report back to me as quickly as you can in the hall.'

'That's what I call initiative,' Dan commented to Trevor as he re-emerged, dressed in the clothes he'd worn back from town.

'I need to talk to you, in private,' Trevor croaked.

'Tell your keeper,' Dan indicated Lyn, 'where you'll be and follow me back to HQ. Perhaps you'd like to help out. We're going to need every man we can lay our hands on. Even sick ones.'

Dan poured out three cups of coffee and handed them around. 'You look fitter than the last time I saw you, Trevor.'

'That doesn't mean I'm in a hurry to get back to work. In fact I'd like to take some time off... '

'What's going on?' Bill stormed into the office, knocking over the overflowing waste-paper basket, sending greasy chip papers and empty cans shooting across the floor. 'I was woken up by some idiot gabbling on about Vanessa Hedley – '

'She's missing,' Dan interrupted.

'That's all we need.' Bill shook a cigarette from a packet he kept in the top pocket of his suit jacket. 'Can't you just hear the screams upstairs when they find out that we didn't give her round-the-clock protection? She was our only witness.'

'Who was incarcerated in what was supposed to be a secure ward in a mental institution.' Peter lit one of his cigars.

'Seems to me those wards are anything but secure.' Bill looked at Trevor. 'If they were, he wouldn't be here.'

'We wouldn't know she was missing if it wasn't for him,' Peter rounded on Bill. 'He only found out by chance, from… '

'Someone who told me that Vanessa was missed early this evening but the hospital authorities decided to keep her disappearance quiet,' Trevor interrupted, with a cautionary glance at Peter.

'She went missing early this evening and they told no one?'

'The senior duty nurse tried to hush it up.'

'Why would he do that?' Bill demanded.

'Bureaucracy. He wouldn't do anything without the admin officer's say-so, and Tony Waters wasn't available,' Trevor divulged.

'How did you find out?'

'When fire broke out in the ward block the headcount was one short.'

'What fire?' Bill looked suspiciously from Dan to Peter, to Trevor, and back.

'I wouldn't bother to investigate that one if I were you,' Dan warned.

'One of you set a fire?'

'There's a pyromaniac on the ward,' Peter puffed on his cigar.

'I still haven't worked out what you're doing here, Trevor.'

'Assisting us with our enquiries,' Dan said. 'If we're going to search this place thoroughly, we'll need all the help we can get.'

'Not from the mentally ill.'

'I was hoping to be discharged tomorrow.'

Bill looked at him through narrowed eyes. 'You're recovered?'

'I believe so.'

'If you're as fit as you say you are, you could be more use to us inside than out.'

'What do you mean?' Trevor already had his suspicions.

'If we had someone on the inside – a good detective, which you used to be, Trevor, we might make some headway with this case.'

'You're asking me to stay in the hospital so you can have another pair of eyes on the case?'

'A pair of inmate's eyes,' Bill qualified. 'Who will see a lot more than a copper who comes in to interview witnesses. What do you say? A few more days might make all the difference. I'll see that you're put back on full pay immediately.'

'I'm happy with sick pay.'

'If this Hedley woman has been abducted by the killer, the chances are she's somewhere around the hospital and still alive. You could be her only chance.'

'I thought you were planning to search the place.'

'We will, but even if we find her, there's no guarantee we'll get to her in time.'

'Mr Waters is here, Superintendent.' A constable knocked on the door and put his head round.

'I'm off to bed,' Trevor rose from his seat.

180

'Lucky, lucky you,' Peter grumbled.

'You'll think about what I said, Trevor?' Bill pressed.

'I'll think about it, but I'm promising nothing.' Trevor stepped outside and shivered. All the lights were on in his ward block. He entered the perspex tunnel. There was nothing inside, ahead or behind him. He knew because he stopped several times and looked around. But he was still left with an uneasy feeling that he was being followed. Quickening his pace, he hurried on, hammering on the locked door of his block as soon as he reached it. Lyn opened the door. She was holding a carton of scouring powder in rubber-gloved hands.

'You've been with the police all this time?'

'Gossiping.'

'They started searching yet?'

'Just getting started.' He stepped inside and bolted the door behind him. 'Want some tea?'

'Is that your way of asking me to make you a cup?'

'No. I've just drunk more coffee in an hour than I've drunk in the last month. But tea would be a way of getting you to sit down for five minutes. You look all in.'

'I am,' she admitted.

The ward was eerily silent without its patients. The rumpled beds and hastily thrown back sheets and blankets adding to the air of ghostly desertion. Their footsteps echoed disconcertingly across the tiled floor as they entered the kitchen.

'The patients have been split up between the five other wards. When the fire service finished here, I thought I may as well come back and clean up, so everyone could move back first thing.' She sank down in a chair. Trevor filled the electric kettle and switched it on. There was a strong smell of cleaning fluid and bleach, and every surface shone, free from grime and smuts.

'I'm sorry.'

'For what?' she asked.

'Causing the mess you had to clean up.'

'I'd rather clean a mess than be haunted by something I didn't do, and should have.'

'And I'm also sorry for making trouble between you and Karl Lane,' Trevor added.

'You can hardly hold yourself responsible for that.'

'I hope it doesn't affect you two,' he dropped a tea bag into a cup.

'There was something between us. And "was" is where it will stay after tonight,' she said emphatically.

He poured boiling water on top of the bag. 'How do you like your tea?'

'Milk, no sugar.'

'If you were going to hide a body in this hospital, where would you put it?' he asked.

'A hundred and one places spring to mind.'

'Try naming ten.'

'There are all sorts of odd corners in the original old building. Last Christmas some bright spark at the staff party came up with the idea of playing hide-and-seek. We found staircases, towers, and lots of little rooms. Most were locked, but not all. It's a regular rabbit warren.' She smiled.

'Something funny?'

'Karl, me and the staff nurse from manias, caught out Mr Waters. If he'd found out who we were he'd have sacked the lot of us.'

'What do you mean "caught out"?'

'Karl barged into a room at the top of the building, God only knows where. I doubt any of us could find it again. There was a mattress in the corner, and a half-naked couple going hammer-and-tongs on top of it. We stayed just long enough to register what they were doing, then beat a hasty retreat.

'You sure it was Tony Waters?'

'No other man around here has that colour hair. I'm sure the woman saw us. But if she recognised us, she couldn't have said anything. If she had, he'd have followed it up. He can be a vindictive bastard.'

'What makes you say that?'

'Nothing he's done to me. Just what I've heard from some of the other nurses; written warnings when they've booked in two minutes late for a shift, when the traffic in the town's ground to a standstill. Like last month, when there was that mammoth pile-up. Remember it?'

'I don't remember anything that happened last month – or the three before that.'

'Sorry, that was stupid of me.'

'You're not stupid. Has Waters a reputation for womanising?' He handed her the tea he'd made.

'According to his secretary, Angela. She says that strange women are always phoning him. I'd feel sorry for his wife but... '

'Carol Ashford?'

'She's a first-class nurse, but she's also a cold fish. Always gives the impression that she couldn't give a damn about anything except herself. But that comes with the job; concealing your feelings, I mean. You get hard-bitten doing work like this, whether you intend to or not. And, then again, Karl told me that he's occasionally seen her about town with some fellow – but this is nothing more than hospital gossip. You're not interrogating me, are you?'

'Absolutely not.' He handed her a box of biscuits. 'I'm sick – unfit for duty.'

'But you spend hours talking to your colleagues.'

'Policing is a funny job. You can go months without seeing a civilian outside of the villains that get booked – and when a big case needs cracking, like now, you eat sleep and drink nothing but the case. You live with coppers, eat with coppers, but you can't even socialise with coppers because there's no time for social life for the duration.'

'So I take it you don't sleep with coppers?'

'I've had to share a room with Peter and twelve down-and-outs, when we went undercover in Jubilee Street.'

'That must have been fun.'

'Police work can be funny, but not for coppers' girlfriends, family or wives. It takes a toll. None of us are married. Peter's divorce is being finalised later this year. The super's wife walked out on him during our last big case, the one I got mangled on. And Dan Evans is a widower.'

'And you?'

'I was never married,' he said shortly.

'But there was someone?'

'I lived with a girl for a while. She got tired of spending nights on her own, and found someone else.'

'And she had long dark hair.'

'Short blonde actually. Why do you ask?'

'The girl you keep sketching.'

Trevor took the biscuits from her.

'I'm sorry. I didn't mean to pry.'

'You're not. I'd probably find it easier to talk about her if something had happened between us. But it didn't.'

'You wanted it to?'

184

'Yes. But whenever we met, it was always the wrong time and the wrong place.'

'And now?'

'She's abroad. I couldn't get hold of her, even if I wanted to. Which I don't. Dreams are best left where they are.' He wondered if he meant what he'd said. He'd carried a torch for Daisy Sherringham for so long, he couldn't imagine what life would be like if he relinquished it. He'd have nothing left – nothing except bleak reality. All the time he'd lain in intensive care, he'd dreamt of her returning to him. Visiting his bedside with a smile on her beautiful curved mouth.

'*I've come back Trevor…*'

He couldn't even be sure, really sure, what he'd feel for Daisy if she did return. So much of his life – and hers – had been destroyed.

He jerked himself out of his imaginings, and returned to Lyn and their conversation.

'So, if you wanted to hide someone's body you'd go into the old hospital?'

'And hope I didn't stumble across Tony Waters indulging in extra-marital activities. Or I'd look to the grounds. There are supposed to be passages in the cellars that come up outside in the bushes. But I've never seen them, only heard the older staff like Jimmy Herne talk about them.'

'Does Jimmy Herne know where they are?' Trevor realised that if a passage did exist, it might provide an ideal route out of the building for the killer.

'According to Tony, who knows more than anyone about this place, they were all blocked up years ago. Jimmy did show me the entrance to one once, down by the folly, but the earth had caved in.' She paused for an instant. 'But knowing about the way this place is run, there'd be no need to hide a body.'

'What do you mean?'

'One extra drugged zombie wouldn't be noticed, or even counted on most wards from one week to the next. Especially geriatric.'

CHAPTER THIRTEEN

Vanessa was cold. Freezing but not shivering. There was no feeling in her body other than cold. Nothing – no sensation at all. Not the slightest tingle, the slightest pain – only numbness, as though her mind was floating, disembodied in an icy, black void. She strained her eyes and stared intently into the darkness. She knew her eyes were open because she could hear the whisper of her eyelashes. The single, alarming sound in a vacuum of silence. All around was frosty, enveloping darkness unpunctuated by the slightest glimmer of grey shadow. She wondered if the air itself had changed colour.

She tried to move, but there seemed to be no physical form for her brain to command. Her mind sent messages to nerves that no longer existed. She had no limbs, no body, only eyelashes. She heard her eyelashes again, and concentrated on her facial muscles. She screamed, but the screech resounded only in her imagination. Her lips refused to open, and the only sound born in the back of her throat was a grunt that conveyed terror and panic. She forced herself to think – to remember!

A scene from a horror film flooded her mind. A brain in a jar? No, she had to be more than a brain in jar. A head – but a head without a body. Or was she already dead? Was this what death was like? Cold, black, wakeful, aware, nothingness.

She concentrated on her immediate past. She had been – where? The day room. Roland, disgusting, fat, lecherous Roland, who put his damp sweaty hands on her knees and tried to move them higher every chance he got. She saw the small half-moon slivers of skin she'd gouged out of the back of his hand with her fingernails when he'd tried to touch her thighs.

Lucy, sweet naïve Lucy, her eyes wide open, agog with a mixture of wonder, terror, and morbid curiosity as she'd related the embroidered version of the phantom burying the body. The phantom! The phantom who buried live woman, after – if Roland was to be believed – gross violation of their bodies. Was she in the earth? Was that why she couldn't feel anything?

No. She could hear her own breath. Soft, quiet, but there; in – out – in – out. If she was buried, she wouldn't be breathing. She would be suffocated. Dead! Was this hell? No, she was cold, and hell was hot; devils hammering red hot spears of metal. She listened for the blacksmith sounds, her eardrums straining to breaking point. But the only noise was a droning that came from inside her fevered brain. Then faintly in the background the tired jingle of an old pop song. 'Bop, bop, bop, de bop' – as incessant and irritating as a dripping tap. Was that also a product of her imagination? She could no longer tell what was real and what was not.

Panic again. Hysteria when she remembered the woman at the bottom of the pit. Was she planted? Dead? A people tree? she had said something about a people tree. But there was no such thing as a people tree! Dead people didn't grow into anything. They rotted. Decayed and rotted. And Ian wouldn't know where she was. But he wouldn't have wanted to visit her. He hadn't visited her once. Not in any of the other places they'd put her in. It wasn't fair. If he'd tried to kill her, she would have visited him.

She pictured her husband as he had been when they had first met. When he'd loved her. Slowly, tenderly she recreated every detail she could recall of his features. The lock of hair that fell over his right eyebrow. His smile, lopsided, cynical. His eyes, deep dark-brown, mirroring yet concealing so many thoughts in their depths. The feel of the skin on his back, smooth, silky beneath her fingers when they'd made love in their king-sized bed in the bridal suite in their hotel. No point in stinting themselves when life was good. If the guests lived in luxury, why shouldn't they?

And afterwards, when she was alone and Ian was no longer part of her life. Horrid little cells with nasty iron bedsteads covered by ugly, grey, itchy blankets and cold cotton sheets, not the silk or satin she'd slept on with Ian. Odious little cells with chamber pots in the corners. Ugly, foul-smelling, not even clean. But then neither had she been clean when she'd been allowed only one shower a week.

A noise came from outside her head. The sharp rasp of metal scraping against metal. A light, intense, blinding, shone into her eyes, forcing her to close them. She tried to speak, but again managed only grunts. Something came towards and over her, blanketing, smothering. It touched her face, fell over her nose, but she still breathed, then it went away. The light grew dim. There was a quick, sharp pain in her arm. Despite the hurt she marvelled that she felt it. She still had a body after all.

Warmth came. A pleasant glow that enveloped her. A radiation that rapidly became an agony of scorching pain. She tried to cry out, but all she heard was a succession of the same, small, bestial whimpers as before. Metal on metal. Darkness. No light. Only agony, she could only feel pain. Total, consuming, absolute. She was pain. Absolute pain. Burning, searing, raging – nothing else existed. Nothing at all!

'All of you to the attic. Station one man at the top of every staircase, radios at the ready. The rest of you, comb the building. I want everything up there moved and searched; boxes, files, rubbish sacks, furniture. I don't care how thick the dust is, or how small the space. I want every door unlocked, every room scrutinised, every cupboard emptied, all the walls tapped. Anything that rings hollow, rip apart. This place is condemned. If we have to, we'll raze it to the ground and worry about the inconvenience later. When you've finished the top floor, leave a man on every staircase and check all the routes down to the next floor. Then repeat the procedure, until you've worked your way to the cellar. I want men left on every floor. The second you see anything suspicious, you shout down your radios. Check for gaps between ceilings and floorboards and remember to use the floor plans and measuring tapes you've been given.' Peter knew he was labouring the point, but weariness had set in, making him unwilling to trust anyone's work but his own.

'Sergeant Collins,' Michelle was at his elbow, bright-eyed, sharp as a button. Didn't the damned woman ever get tired like the rest of them? 'Superintendent Mulcahy and Inspector Evans would like to see you in the mobile HQ as soon as possible, sir.'

'Tell them I'll join them when I can.'

'There's a man from the Home Office with them, sir.'

'I'll be there, Constable.' He turned away from her and faced the teams lined up in the shabby hallway of the old hospital. 'Right, go to it. I'll be with you as soon as I can. Note everything that's remotely out of the ordinary, and call me the minute you find anything suspicious.

190

Constable Grady will go with you. She knows where we disturbed the dust the last time we took a look around.'

Reluctantly turning his back on the search parties, Peter walked through the back door to the mobile HQ. He passed through the outer office, and acknowledged Sarah Merchant, who was operating the computer, before opening the door into the inner sanctum Dan and Bill had claimed as their territory.

Harry Goldman and a burly, red-headed man he'd never seen before were sitting sweltering in the atmosphere that reeked of stale coffee, cigarettes and greasy food.

'Peter,' Bill said wearily. 'This is Professor Crabbe.'

'John Crabbe, Home Office,' the red-headed man extended a square and hairy hand to Peter. 'I've come down here with a psychological profile of your chap.'

'I thought we should run through it with Professor Crabbe, before informing the team,' Bill lit a cigarette.

Peter pulled a chair up to the table and sat alongside Dan. Bill banged on the door and shouted in a voice calculated to carry through the thin wall. 'Coffee for five.'

'Yes, sir,' came a reply from a constable. Peter sensed resentment in his voice.

Peter could detect the strain in Bill. Vanessa's disappearance had brought a new and keener edge to the investigation. Yet here they were, the three most senior and experienced officers on the case, sitting idly on their arses listening to two shrinks, instead of getting out there and on with catching the killer who had already claimed three innocent lives and was probably in the process of claiming a fourth.

'We've taken your data and fed it into a computer that holds everything we know about serial killers who've been convicted during the past thirty years, both here and in America – '

'Why America?' Peter asked John Crabbe.

'You know the saying,' John smiled. 'What America does today, we'll be doing in twenty years. When it comes to crime, that maxim appears to be true; the Americans seem to have cornered the market on serial killers.'

Peter remembered Spencer Jordan and his American connections, but remained silent. That was something to bring up later, when Harry Goldman and this Home Office chap were elsewhere.

John Crabbe lifted his steel-coated briefcase on to the desk and opened the combination lock. He extracted a thick file, bulging with loose papers. 'We're looking for a man, the computer says anything between twenty-five and forty, but I'd be inclined to lower the upper limit to thirty-five. He's a loner, finds it difficult to form relationships with either men or women, but the lack of women in his life upsets him more than the lack of male friends. He's impotent... '

'How do you know?' Dan broke in.

'No sperm,' Crabbe declared.

'I thought there was no evidence of rape?' Dan said slowly.

'Without sperm, or physical signs such as tissue tearing, it's not always possible to determine if entry has been forced. But whether the victims were raped or not is immaterial to this profile.' The Professor sat forward in his chair.

'Immaterial?' Peter asked with a feigned air of innocence.

'Psychologists have determined that rape is not a sexual crime.'

'Try telling that to some of the women I've interviewed after the event,' Peter challenged.

'Rape is a crime of violence. It's all about power. Our man takes a woman, holds her prisoner, and whether he attempts rape or not – and I'm inclined to the latter opinion – he's unable to engage in a meaningful relationship with his victim, physical or otherwise. He's a loner who needs to assert power over his victim.' The professor opened his file. 'He's from a small family, probably an only child. Unused to living with or relating to others. He lives alone or with a single domineering female relative – mother, grandmother, aunt or older sister. He has no friends. He finds it difficult to form any kind of "normal" relationships. He almost definitely comes from the lower socio-economic group. Blue collar worker or unemployed, and he's a low achiever.'

'Except in the case of murder,' Peter commented. 'Are we looking at a patient or member of staff?'

'Difficult to say,' the professor hedged. 'Could be either. As a rough guideline I'd say your man will fit at least fifty per cent of this profile, possibly more. But on occasions, we have been proved wrong. This is not an exact science.'

'We're aware of the possibility of error.' The irony of Bill's reply wasn't lost on Crabbe.

'If the killer has a police record, it will only be for minor, unrelated offences.' John Crabbe continued. 'We have discounted the kidnapping-for-profit theory. I am right in saying there have been no ransom demands?'

'You are,' Bill agreed. 'Apart from Claire Moon, the victims have not been wealthy.'

'Have you considered that this man may be a collector?' Harry Goldman made his first contribution to the proceedings.

Dan turned to the psychiatrist. 'Please explain, "collector".'

'A collector is someone who accumulates a number of related, generally useless, objects purely for his own personal gratification and the pleasure of ownership.'

'Like the people who fill books with out of date stamps?' Peter suggested.

'Precisely,' Harry concurred. 'Or butterflies, or china frogs, or photographs, and memorabilia connected with a film or sports star.'

Bill set his hands on the table. 'Are you saying our man could be a collector of marbles who's moved on to collecting women?'

'Could be,' Professor Crabbe said thoughtfully. 'Have your people noticed anything significant in where you found the bodies, or the way they were laid out?'

'What do you mean?' Dan asked.

'Were the bodies buried in a pattern? Were their feet pointing north? Is he planting them at the four corners of the hospital grounds, or in the shape of something recognisable; a star perhaps?'

Peter left his chair and walked over to the wall behind the desk. He retracted a roller blind that covered the back wall. Stuck to the glass board was an aerial photograph of the hospital grounds, marked with the burial sites of the victims and a series of photographs taken after the corpses had been uncovered, but before they had been removed.

'Take a look for yourself.' Peter pointed to the board. 'All four – that's including the dog – were buried in flowerbeds, all in holes that had been dug out by the gardeners and left unattended overnight. The last victim was laid north to south, the second north-west to south-west, and the third east to west. Personally I think the positioning has more to do with where the flowerbeds were than Voodoo circles.'

'I just wondered if you had considered all the options,' the Professor said shortly.

'I'm inclined to think that the killer simply doesn't want to do any more digging than necessary,' Peter returned to his chair.

'Never underestimate your opponent,' John Crabbe reprimanded.

'Shall we recap?' Dan went to a flip-chart and turned the pages until he hit a clean one. He wrote PROFILE at the top. 'We know he's strong because our witness saw him carrying a twelve-stone body.' He scribbled *Strong* beneath the heading.

'Big as well, if Vanessa Hedley is to be believed,' Peter added.

Dan added *Big* to the list.

'Professor, you say he's a loner – does that mean he doesn't relate to men as well as women?' Dan questioned.

'Probably,' the professor answered carefully.

Dan wrote *Loner*.

'And he's impotent?' Peter failed to keep a cynical tone from his voice.

'Almost certainly, but I wouldn't like to hazard whether his sexual impotence is physical or psychological in origin.'

'Either way, the results would be the same.' Peter watched Dan add *Impotent* to the list.

'He probably lives alone,' the Professor continued enthusiastically, pleased that Dan was taking him seriously. 'Or with a domineering female relative.'

'One – or more than one?' Bill asked.

'I'd be inclined to stick my neck out and say one, although I suppose there is a possibility that there could be a mother and an older sister,' Crabbe said.

'What about a…' Peter hesitated.

'What about a what?' Bill demanded.

Peter glanced at Harry Goldman. The psychiatrist had contributed so little to the conversation he'd forgotten that Harry was in the room, and he could hardly accuse the live-in companion of his most senior assistant of being the murderer. 'A relationship where a man and a woman live together on a platonic basis to pool expenses,' he finished lamely.

'That implies a socio-economic relationship, which your killer would shy away from. Our man has his own space, he either lives alone or has a room he doesn't allow his relatives access to,' the Professor insisted.

Dan picked up the pen again and added *Lives alone or with domineering female relative*.

'Possibly a collector,' Harry reminded. He was proud of his contribution, and knew exactly who Peter had in mind when he mentioned platonic relationships.

Dan scribbled *Collector*.

'He chooses his victim. Keeps her hidden. Does whatever he wants with her, shows her kindness, cruelty, torture, whatever his whims dictate. Then, when he tires of the game and her, he buries her.' Harry described the scenario as graphically as he could. 'The ultimate secret trophy to be added to his collection. Uniquely his, forever.'

'He must know this hospital inside out,' Peter reminded everyone, 'to spirit Vanessa away the way he did.'

'That's if he has her.' Bill lifted his feet from the desk. 'Where's the damned coffee?'

196

'He buried the others when there were security guards around.' Peter reached for his cigars. 'We know he starved the last one. He couldn't have brought her into the hospital on a number 10 bus without someone noticing something out of the ordinary.'

'As they were paralysed he could have kept them in the boot of his car,' John Crabbe suggested.

'Not since we've been searching every car that goes in and out of here.' Dan unscrewed the cap of his pen.

'Knowledge of, and access to drugs,' Peter prompted.

'He would have suffered mood swings about the time of each disappearance and murder. You've nothing more accurate to give us on dates of the first two murders?' John Crabbe asked.

'We've had to rely on the pathologist, and the only thing we can be certain of is that the last victim was buried on a cloudy night when there was an intermittent full moon.'

'You've forgotten to list his low socio-economic grouping,' Harry left his seat. 'I'm sorry, gentlemen, but I have an appointment with a patient. Trevor Joseph in fact.'

'If you sign him out fit for duty, let me be the first to know,' Bill said. 'I need every man I can get.'

A knock at the door interrupted them. Harry Goldman opened it.

'Coffee, sir,' the constable held up a tray.

'Bit bloody late,' Bill barked.

Peter took the tray from the constable. She was an attractive blonde. He winked at her and she kicked him sharply and painfully on the shin.

'So sorry, Sergeant Collins,' she apologised insincerely. 'My foot slipped.'

Harry left. Peters shut the door with his back. He dumped the tray on top of the papers on the table, to the disgust of John Crabbe, who made a great show of extracting his file from beneath it. The four men stared at the flip-chart while they helped themselves to coffee.

Strong, Loner, Impotent, No friends or visible woman in life apart from domineering mother or older sister. Possible collector. Knowledge of hospital layout, drugs, and has access to drugs. From the lower socio-economic grouping, had noticeable mood swings at times of victims disappearance and murder.

'Anything else, Professor?' Bill was anxious to be rid of the man and it showed.

'Twenty-five to thirty-five years old – possibly forty at the outside.'

Dan amended the list, and remained, pen poised next to the chart.

'He's also neat, tidy and careful,' Dan said thoughtfully.

'What makes you say that?' the Professor asked.

'Absence of hairs and fibres. The pathologist found nothing on the victims that didn't belong to them.'

Peter sipped his coffee. 'Are we any further forward?'

'Suppose we try to match our suspects to this profile,' Bill suggested.

'The staff.' Peter was still smarting from the realisation that Bill and Dan regarded Trevor as a potential suspect.

'The gardener, Jimmy Herne is too old. The administrative officer, Tony Waters is married... ' Dan began.

'To a woman so cold I wonder if she's flesh or ice,' Peter observed.

'She could be a volcano in private,' Bill smiled.

'I seriously doubt it.'

'What's the matter? Didn't she fancy you, Peter?' Bill was so tired he forgot the presence of Crabbe. All he wanted was his bed.

'If you're going to do this properly,' Crabbe interrupted, 'you should consider everyone.'

'Harry Goldman?' Peter winked at Bill.

'Single. Lives alone,' Bill pointed out.

'Wrong socio-economic group.' Dan placed his empty cup on the tray.

'Look at all the variables and mark the ones with the highest percentages,' Crabbe lectured.

'Right on knowledge of drugs, and hospital, wrong on size.' Peter crushed the remains of his cigar in an ashtray. 'He weighs what? Seven stone and two of those are his spectacles. Can you see him trotting across the lawn with a twelve-stone woman slung across his shoulders?'

'Jimmy Herne the gardener? He didn't like us digging,' Dan reminded.

'Too old, at sixty. And he's married with six children,' Bill revealed.

'Spencer Jordan?' Dan flicked through his notebook.

'Now there's a name to conjure with.' Peter reached for another cigar. 'Right age bracket at thirty-eight, tall, strong, loner, no visible women, or friends, knowledge of hospital both as a patient and staff member, I dare say he could organise access to drugs, and after three years spent in psychiatric hospitals he should know how to use them.'

'Collector?' Crabbe asked.

'He has pictures on the walls of his room,' Peter answered.

199

'It is an art therapy room,' Dan chipped in. 'And he's the wrong socio group; he's not a low achiever.'

'That depends where you're starting from. A few years ago he was a mile higher than he is now,' Peter struck a match. 'He lives alone in a hospital flat. I'd say, after visiting his work room, he's neat, tidy, careful, and he has a past that could have turned his psyche upside-down.'

'Put him down as number one on an interview list.' Bill tapped a cigarette out of a new packet. 'Next.'

'Adam Hayter,' Peter lit his cigar.

'Big, but not strong,' Dan opened the window to let the smoke out. 'He's flabby.'

'Coming from you, that's rich.' Peter joked. 'And flabby or not, he could manage a twelve-stone woman. After all, he must manage Dotty Clyne.'

'What about no visible woman in his life?' Dan asked.

'You call Dotty a woman?' Peter raised his eyebrows.

'Other criteria,' Bill looked at the list.

'Collector?' Dan read.

'I don't know about collector, but have you been in his kitchen?' Peter looked from Dan to Bill. 'Talk about everything in its place, and spotless. He's neat, tidy and careful, right age at twenty-nine, I'd go along with impotent, and as for loner, every time I see him I'm trampled by the rush of people desperate to avoid him.'

'Lower socio-economic group?' Crabbe reminded.

'Cooks are notoriously ill-paid, he has knowledge of both hospital and drugs, and he lives with Dotty who's a domineering woman.'

200

'Add his name to the list to be interviewed, then we'll move on to the patients,' Bill left his chair and paced across the room to keep awake.

'What about Dotty?' Peter suggested.

'We're looking for a man,' Bill said impatiently.

'A dyke?' Peter glanced at Crabbe. 'What do you think?'

'Rare, but they do exist. Female serial killers account for only 8% of all American serial killers, but 76% of all female serial killers worldwide,' Crabbe clearly loved statistics.

'I didn't ask for a lecture,' Peter admonished. 'Only an opinion as to whether or not it's worth considering in this case.'

'It could be, as long as you realise that statistically it's a long shot. But you said that Dotty was living with a therapist – this Adam Hayter.'

'She is,' Peter confirmed.

'In my experience, lesbians rarely live with men.'

'Precisely. She's living with Hayter.'

'Let's move on,' Dan said evenly. 'She's big, strong,'

'Impotent,' Peter interrupted.

'And a psychiatrist, which puts her out of the socio-economic group,' Bill said.

'But that's the only variable,' Peter said enthusiastically. 'She has a knowledge of the hospital, and drugs. She's the right age at thirty-six. She's impotent in male sexual terms. She has to be worth thinking about.'

'Add her to your list,' Bill ordered Dan.

'If we're going to look at one woman, we'd better look at them all. Jean Marshall, Lyn Sullivan, Carol Ashford...'

'Carol Ashford's married,' Dan ran his finger down a list of staff in his notebook.

'Happily?' Bill asked.

'She's married to Tony Waters. They live on a farm.'

'Then it's a safe bet it's neither of them,' Crabbe pronounced decisively.

'Jean Marshall's divorced, but outgoing and friendly.'

'Peter, you've known her longer than any of us.' Bill leaned against the door.

'I'd say she's more the "serial one night stand" than serial killer.'

'Lyn Sullivan's twenty-one, and has a boyfriend; the nurse, Karl Lane,' Dan commented.

'I think it's safe to leave the women,' Bill ordered. 'Let's start on the patients.'

'Roland Williams is too old,' Dan said.

'He's lecherous,' Peter observed. 'And not impotent, from what I've heard and from what I've seen, he likes to touch up females every chance he gets.'

Bill looked at the professor. 'Our man?'

'Is neither a toucher nor a lecher. In fact he's probably a prude. Wouldn't stand for public mention of sex. Outwardly he probably sees sex as something dirty. Remember the domineering woman.'

'Roland out,' Peter moved on. 'Michael Carpenter?'

'Pyromaniac – not impotent from what his girlfriend said at his trial. In fact whatever the opposite is, that's him,' Dan had done his homework.

'On to the women.'

'Vanessa's disappeared. Lucy is too scared to say boo to a goose. She's young and believes herself married to Jason Donovan,' Peter explained to Crabbe.

'An unlikely candidate,' Crabbe said decisively.

'Ali Bevan is fixated on men.' Peter flicked the ash from his cigar. 'Which means we're left with Spencer

Jordan, Adam Hayter, Dotty Clyne, or any one of the fifty-two porters split between day and night shifts. Not to mention the nurses, male and female, and the security guards...'

'Maintenance men, gardeners – ' Dan added.

'And Uncle Tom Cobley and all,' Peter sighed. 'God help us. For all of this,' he waved his hand at the flip-chart, 'it could be just one stray nut. And, as I've said before, what chance do we have of finding one nut in a bloody orchard ripe for harvesting. Now, if you gentlemen can possibly spare me from this interesting exercise, I'll see if my team has turned up something we can work on. Superintending a search isn't an intellectual exercise, but it will help me cling to the illusion that I'm doing something constructive towards finding Vanessa Hedley.'

CHAPTER FOURTEEN

Harry Goldman looked up from his desk as Trevor Joseph entered his office. 'I heard you went out yesterday.'

'Can't keep anything secret in this place, can you?'

'Sit down. Tell me, how did you find the world after your absence?' Harry waited for Trevor's response.

'It hadn't suffered unduly,' Trevor replied. Harry Goldman suddenly seemed incredibly condescending.

Goldman rested his chin on the tips of his fingers. Trevor felt that he was frantically searching his mind for something to say. 'Do you consider yourself ready to leave your ward?' he asked eventually.

'Yes, you were right. I was fit to leave weeks ago.'

'And, you think you're ready to leave right away? Today?'

'Yes.' Trevor left his chair and went the window. 'It's just that... '

'Everyone has doubts before taking such a monumental step. This place has been your second womb... '

'I don't have any doubts,' Trevor cut through Harry's jargon. 'But thank you for taking care of me when I did.' He didn't want to sound ungrateful. 'I'm going to visit my flat and sort out a few things. But there's also work.'

Goldman stared at him in amazement. 'I strongly advise against a return to such a stressful job. Aside from your physical injuries, there's the pressure. After an experience like yours, it will be difficult enough for you to cope with day-to-day living. You may believe you're ready to face more, but the balance of your mind is delicate. The slightest upset could cause a relapse. You should rest, relax, see friends, take a holiday. It would be most unwise to contemplate returning to work for at least six months.'

Trevor smiled; it was his turn to patronise. 'You don't know the police force, Mr Goldman.'

'I am beginning to find out a little about it.'

'Superintendent Mulcahy suggested that I stay here, on the inside, for a few more days, to see if I could help with their enquiries.'

'Into the murders?'

'Yes.'

'That would be most unwise. As I said, the slightest stress or strain could... '

'They're pushed. They need all the help they can get.'

'It's laudable to see such dedication in a public servant, but you have to realise that my – and your – first duty is to Trevor Joseph the patient, not Trevor Joseph the police officer.'

'They are the same man,' Trevor said shortly. 'I'm grateful to you for everything you have done to aid my recovery. Could I impose on you a little longer? Would you write me a pass that would enable me to continue living here, but to come and go as I please during the day?'

'It would be unorthodox.'

'I might be able to help clear this case up and get the police off the premises.' Trevor saw Harry wavering. 'It should only be for a week or so.'

Goldman picked up his pen. 'I'll give you a pass, on two conditions. First, you see me here every morning at eight-thirty for half an hour, so I can check your progress. And second, you limit your working time to no more than two hours a day.'

'I agree.' Trevor knew that most police work meant talking to people, so it would be difficult for anyone to determine whether he was, or wasn't, working.

'And you will have to be back in your ward every night by ten o'clock.'

'I intend to be.' Trevor recalled the timing of the last burial.

'This is still most unorthodox,' Goldman protested, finally signing the pass.

Trevor left the psychiatrist's office and walked down the corridor of the old Victorian block. There was evidence of police activity everywhere. In the fleet of cars and vans abandoned around the building, the teams of rookies combing the lawns, flowerbeds and shrubberies inch by inch on hands and knees; the crackle of voices bouncing back and forth on the radios of the officers searching the floors above him. Shuffling along, relying on his stick, he made his way purposefully towards Spencer's room.

It was break-time, and Spencer was sitting alone on a stool pulled up to one of the clay-covered work tables, a couple of slices of carrot cake and cup of decaffeinated coffee laid out on a sheet of newspaper in front of him.

'Coffee?' Spencer offered.

'Thanks.' Trevor poured himself one, without bothering to reheat the water.

'You look better today,' Spencer complimented.

'It's just the clothes and the haircut.'

'And something else. You look… ' Spencer studied Trevor, 'quietly confident.' He pushed a piece of cake towards Trevor.

'Thanks to you.' Trevor took the cake and bit into it. 'I went to town yesterday, as you can see.' He smoothed the back of his shorn neck. 'Today I'm going to my flat.'

'Leaving us?'

'For the day.'

'Harry breaking you in gently?'

'Something like that.' Trevor was grateful to Spencer, liked him even, but breaking the glass on the fire alarm last night had been a watershed. It was something he wouldn't have thought twice about doing before he'd been injured, and the action had reminded him what it felt like to be a police officer. As a rookie, he'd been warned that police officers couldn't afford the luxury of too many friends outside the force. And how well did one person ever really get to know another?

At any moment Spencer could become a suspect. And, as Bill constantly drummed into the officers on his team, "Friendship clouds judgement." There were plenty of coppers who'd made mistakes on that score, and some had ended up in the slammer.

Spencer stood looking out of the window at the officers combing the grounds. 'Are you part of the team?'

'I'm on the sick.'

'My grandfather used to say "Once a copper, always a copper".'

'Yesterday I was hoping to prove that maxim wrong.'

'And today?'

Trevor finished his coffee. 'I need to do some more thinking on the subject. That's why I want to go back to my flat.'

'Scared?'

'Frankly, yes. I haven't seen it in four months, and after recalling a few aspects of my life that I didn't like, I've begun to wonder where I go from here.'

'You don't want to carry on where you left off?'

'Before I was injured, I never had time to think about my life or where I was headed. I'd roll out of bed dog-tired in the morning, wake myself up by standing under a jet of cold water, work ten – twelve, on occasions twenty hour shifts, eating lousy lukewarm take-away in the station as and when I could. There was no time to spend on anything important, like creating a home or a relationship.'

'And now you want both?'

'You've probably heard it all before. But if there's one thing I've learned during the past four months, it's that once you're dead, that's it. You stay dead for one hell of a long time. No one's going to come round to the crematorium, pat you on the head, and say, "Well, you were a nice hard working, conscientious fellow, so we'll give you another crack of the whip". So now,' Trevor rinsed his cup under the tap in the paint-spattered sink, 'I'm determined to do as much as I can, in whatever time I have left.'

'I wish you luck.'

'In fact, I'm probably in danger of turning into a right selfish swine. I intend to make time, not only to put together a real home, but to build a relationship. Are you married?'

'I was.' Spencer crumpled the newspaper that had been under the cake and threw it into the bin.

'I'm sorry,' Trevor sympathised. 'Breaking up with someone is always hard.'

'It is,' Spencer replied.

Trevor made his way back to his ward and opened his wardrobe door, intending to dig out his new coat. He paused for a moment, staring at the clothes Peter had hung up for him when he'd been admitted. The only reasonable item was the jacket he'd bought the day before. The rest of his new clothes were still in the carrier bags he hadn't yet unpacked. He lifted them on to the bed and tossed his new jacket on top. Taking one of the black bags Peter had brought in for his laundry, he removed everything from the hangars and threw the lot into a sack. He tied the top into a knot.

'Spring cleaning?' Jean stopped outside the open door.

'Tidying up before I leave. Harry Goldman's given me a free pass for a week. After that I'll be out of here, and on my own.'

'You going out now?'

'To take a look at my flat. Thought I'd see if it's still standing.'

'How would you like to have dinner with me tonight?'

'The answer is yes if I'm allowed to buy it.' His pulse raced at the thought of taking the first step towards establishing a relationship with a woman. 'How about that pub on the marina?'

'Eat in the same restaurant two nights running and you're in danger of falling into a rut. Have you tried the Greek restaurant in Argyle Street?'

'There's nothing down there except offices.'

'It opened three months ago.'

'Turn my back for a couple of months and the whole town changes. Shall I meet you there?'

'Seven o'clock,' she whispered as approaching footsteps echoed down the corridor. 'That'll give us time for a drink afterwards.'

Trevor slipped on his jacket and tested himself by walking down the tunnel to the old block. Both his legs were aching, a nagging toothache type pain that had its origins in the unaccustomed exertions of the day before.

Ordinary, everyday sounds fell strangely around him, transformed and muted by the perspex. The roar of car engines became the cries of animals in pain. The crashing of pots of pans in the kitchen were a swordfight, the rattle of a trolley travelling over hard floors, the staccato report of machine gunfire.

He pulled himself together. The other thing a policeman couldn't afford, along with close civilian friends, was an over-active imagination. He walked through the main hall to the mobile HQ and knocked once before entering.

'Sergeant Joseph.' Sarah Merchant beamed at him, as he climbed awkwardly up the short flight of steps. 'You look in good shape.'

'I feel in good shape.' He smiled at her and the other two girls manning the telephones. 'Busy?'

'Wish we were busier,' one of the girls grumbled. 'If we were, it might mean that all this sitting around, waiting for something to happen, would be over and done with.'

'Rookies always get given the worst jobs,' he commiserated. 'But it won't last forever. There'll be another batch of recruits coming in soon, and when they do, you'll be kicked upstairs to more interesting things, and then you'll wish yourselves back here. Is the super in?'

'The super and Inspector Evans.'

'They on their own?'

Sarah nodded, and he went to the door. After he'd disappeared into the inner sanctum, one of the other girls turned to Sarah. 'Who is that?'

'Sergeant Joseph. He was on the Drug Squad.'

'The one who almost got killed?'

'Almost.' Sarah stared intently at her computer screen. Trevor Joseph had almost got himself killed on his

210

last case, but her boyfriend hadn't been so lucky. Murdered during the investigation, they hadn't found enough of him to fill a small box, let alone a coffin.

'He treats us as though we're human beings,' the girl said. 'Like we're police officers first and women second.'

'Hasn't he heard about the men in the force's official attitude to women recruits?' the other demanded.

'Perhaps it was the bang on the head,' the first one giggled.

'Perhaps a similar thump could do the same for the super and Sergeant Collins.'

'Sergeant Joseph has always been the same,' Sarah said. 'He's a nice guy, but don't let his appearance deceive you. He used to be a good policeman who knew how to get tough when he had to.'

Bill eyed Trevor as he entered the office. 'How are you?'

'Fine.' Trevor propped his stick in a corner and sat down without waiting to be asked. 'Dr Goldman's just told me I'm fit enough to leave the hospital.'

'And you came here to tell us?' Bill said sourly.

'I've decided to take you up on your offer. Goldman knows about it and he's given me a pass for the next week. I'll be sleeping here, but I'll be able to move freely during the day so you can brief me on what exactly you want me to do.'

Bill gave Trevor a rare smile. 'Mix with the natives. Pick up the vibrations. You know how it helps to have someone on the inside.'

'This is hardly undercover,' Trevor warned. 'In this place I'm known as a copper.'

'Then you do intend to rejoin the force?' Bill asked.

'You agreed to reinstate me.'

'From the day you return to work. Is today soon enough?'

'One day too soon.' Trevor rose clumsily from his chair. 'Make it tomorrow. I'd like to look at my flat today and there's not much I can do with the search going on. I'll be back tonight.'

'Want a ride into town?' Dan asked.

Bill glared at him. 'You're supposed to be running a murder investigation, not playing chauffeur.'

'Patrick rang. He has the test results on the victims' blood samples.'

'Keep me posted, I'll be at the station.' Bill picked up the telephone, dialled and began shouting at the hapless individual on the other end of the line.

'Things aren't going too well at the moment,' Dan explained to Trevor as they left. 'It's good to have you on board.'

'I'm not sure I'll be able to contribute much. And I'm not relishing the idea of staying on in this place when I don't need to.'

'The car's around the corner,' Dan remarked, seeing Trevor limp. 'Would you like me to bring it to the door?'

'No thanks. Sorry if I'm slowing you up.'

'You're not. Sometimes I think that's what's the matter with all investigations. Everyone rushing around like a load of crazed ants gathering sugar to take back to the nest, no one taking a second to stop and think, and everyone overlooking the obvious when it's right in front of them.'

'What's the obvious in this case?'

'I wish to God I knew.' Dan gazed at all the police activity. 'But it's there somewhere, waiting for us to spot it.'

Lyn tossed restlessly on her bed in the nurses' hostel. She had never slept well when she'd been on night shift. Her body-clock simply refused to adjust to hospital requirements. She turned over, and pulled the pillow over her head.

She listened to a minute tick by on the clock, then another. She lifted her pillow and stared at the electronic alarm clock. Ten-fifteen. She was due back on duty at seven-thirty, only eight hours away, and she'd promised to meet her friend Miriam for tea at five. Miriam had been in school with her, and had recently taken the post of junior mortgage advisor to the largest bank in town. Being Miriam, she hated it. But then Miriam hated everything – her job, the town, the people she worked with. And Lyn was beginning to wonder if Miriam's sole joy in life was moaning about her lot over tea and cream cakes in the most expensive patisserie the town had to offer.

Lyn closed her eyes again and cursed the daylight filtering into the room despite the thick curtains. All she could hope for was six hours sleep, and she hadn't slept for twenty-four hours as it was.

Thoughts raced through her mind. Vanessa Hedley? Where was she now? She was fond of Vanessa, despite all the upset she caused. She was a character and, unlike one or two of the other patients, not an unpleasant one. What was it her father said? "A product of circumstances." That was it; Vanessa was a product of circumstances. If her husband hadn't fooled around and if she hadn't decided to follow him that night, her whole life would have turned out very differently. She'd probably still be queening it in the hotel on the front.

Lyn heard the engines of the staff's cars as they queued at the gates. How much longer before Vanessa would be found? And when she was, would it be at the bottom of a pit like the others? Suffocated by a ton or more of earth shovelled on top of her.

The buzz of a police helicopter hovering overhead reminded her of the heat-seeking cameras used to find the others. Was Vanessa already out there in the earth? Decay raising the temperature of her cold flesh? Lyn turned on to her stomach and pulled the pillow over her ears. It was useless. What would help? A warm shower? She'd had one an hour ago. Hot chocolate? Cocoa? She'd drunk two cups that morning; any more and she'd spend half the day going back and forth to the bathroom at the end of the corridor.

The radio? A book? A boring – boring book. Had to be a nursing textbook. She left the bed and went to her book-shelf. She was poised, holding the book, when she heard a noise outside her door. A cleaner pushing a polishing mop over the floor? She stood stock still. The noise was overlaid by the quiet hiss of breathing. Was she listening to her own intake of air? She held her breath to be sure.

A thud sent her scurrying back to the safety of her bed.

The key, which had been nesting securely in the lock of the door, had fallen, pushed out on to the doormat. She stared at it for a split second. Then she screamed.

Nerves ragged with fear, she recalled the details of the murders rumoured around the hospital, and she continued to scream as she grabbed her green and purple silk dressing gown from the foot of her bed. She tried to pull it over her shoulders, only to get it hopelessly tangled. 'Lyn! Are you all right?' Above the hammering on her door she heard the voice of Alan, one of the charge nurses who had a room down the hall.

'Someone was at my door. The key… ' she finally managed to get her gown on properly and tied the belt, Hands shaking, she picked the key up from the mat. Keeping the chain fixed across the door, she tentatively opened it. Three nurses were standing outside, all in dressing gowns.

'What happened?' Alan asked. 'You're shaking like a leaf.'

She unfastened the chain and he walked in.

'I was lying in bed and I heard a noise. When I looked up the key was being pushed out of the lock. Someone was at the door… '

'Richard, go downstairs and dial 999,' Alan ordered their colleague.

'With all the police hanging around the building, it would be quicker to walk to the main block and find one.' Without stopping to pick up shoes or slippers, Richard ran down the stairs. A door banged outside, somewhere above them.

'The fire escape.' Alan rushed out through the door.

'For God's sake be careful,' Mary, a second-year student nurse, called after him.

'Wait for Richard to fetch the police,' Lyn shouted.

Both pleas fell on deaf ears.

Mary looked nervously at Lyn. 'Do you really think someone was there?' she whispered.

Lyn went to her window and opened her curtains.

Arms outstretched like a crucifixion, face squashed and distorted against the glass, the thin figure of a man stared back at her, dark eyes gleaming. He reminded Lyn of a spider, a black venomous spider. His fingers clawed at the eaves above him, his toes retained a tenuous grip on

215

the window ledge. His open mouth leered, its breath fogging his features as he pitched alarmingly close to Lyn.

Mary screamed. The figure hovered for what seemed like an eternity, then swayed. His face jerked backwards. He fell.

A cry echoed, lingering in the sweet spring air as he landed with a dull thud on the flowerbed three floors below.

CHAPTER FIFTEEN

The woman in the wheelchair was hunched forward, her face practically resting in her lap, her features half hidden by the blanket that had been draped over her head and drooped shoulders.

'Aren't they just the lucky ones? What I wouldn't give for a kip right now,' Mark Manners, a brash young porter, shouted to his fellow porter as he wheeled past a chair that contained another comatose geriatric.

He received only a curt nod from the white-coated, baseball-capped figure that wheeled the other chair. Someone new, Mark thought. Given the meagre wages porters received there was a constant and rapid turnover of staff. He no sooner got to know someone than they moved on; but hopefully one day he'd be doing the same.

'Soon be there, love,' he murmured reassuringly to the elderly patient in the chair when she stirred restlessly.

'I want to go home. Want to go home – now!'

'I am taking you home, love,' he promised rashly. As he was dumping the old dear off on Dotty Clyne, her problems would soon no longer be his. Five minutes more and he could take a break, steal a cup of tea, and chat up Mandy in the kitchen. He wondered how much longer it would be before he could talk Mandy into letting him take her out, and, what was more to the point, into dropping her knickers. One week? Two? Or would his lucky star make tonight the night?

The figure in the baseball cap pushed the wheelchair into Observation and Depression. The ward was usually deserted during the day. The patients were bundled off to therapy or clinic after breakfast; or if they were astute enough to know, and demand, their rights, the garden for an unsupervised walk.

Laughter rang in the ward kitchen. The clock pointed to ten forty-five. Coffee break had just begun. Head down, the figure pushed the wheelchair swiftly on down the corridor. At the end of the passage, close to the fire-escape, was a single room. Traditionally the last bed allocated for use on every ward, the staff kept it for emergencies or those privileged enough to warrant a private room.

The figure pushed the wheelchair into the room and closed the door softly. It was broad daylight, closed blinds would attract attention, but the chance of being seen through the window was minimal at this time of day. People were too busy to stand and stare, and there was no glow of artificial light to highlight untoward movement.

Easy – take it easy, slowly, calmly. No noise. No haste, lest mistakes be made. Steady, deliberate, determined action. A moment to wheel the chair next to the bed. Another to pull back the pristine sheet, single blanket and beige cotton bedcover. Ease the limbs forward. Hands locked around a slim, cold waistline, warm breathing face next to chill, leaden one. A lift, a push – tuck the small stiffening figure between the sheets. On its side lest the knees remain upright with the onset of rigor. Raise the blonde head on to the pillow. Brush the ruffled hair forward, to hide the face.

A shudder, as a lifeless arm rolled out and dangled, the fingers inches above the floor. Pick it up. Push it beneath the sheets and between the knees to hold it fast.

The chair! Fold it. Place it next to the bed. A quick glance in the mirror. Pull the baseball cap lower. Listen at the door. The voices were still chattering in the kitchen. A few seconds was all it took to slip out through the fire door, muffling the bar with a rubber-gloved hand lest its click be heard. Head down and then into the garden, fresh air. Pass one block, then another, and another. Easy – so easy. And done!

'Do you know him?'

Lyn nodded and sank her teeth into her lower lip in an effort to stop herself from crying. Peter saw shock registering on her face, and accorded her grudging respect. Shaken, upset by her ordeal, her slender and – he noticed lustfully – shapely body trembling beneath her thin robe, she hadn't protested when he'd asked her to follow him outside to identify the body. But she was a nurse, and all nurses had seen corpses, even psychiatric nurses – although possibly not those of people they had known in life.

'Lyn, I've just heard. Are you all right?' Karl Lane, dark hair combed away from his face, jumped the fence and strode towards her and Peter through the flowerbeds.

'Perfectly,' she replied too forcefully.

'Sergeant, do you think you should be questioning Nurse Sullivan so soon after her ordeal?' Karl stared at the body stretched out on its back about six feet away.

'The best time to question a witness is when events are still fresh in the mind, Mr – '

'Lane,' Karl said abruptly. 'Senior Nurse Lane.'

'Karl, you're not helping matters. Please go away.' Lyn directed the anger she felt at the waste of Michael's life at Karl, because he was there when she didn't want him near her. She turned her back to him. 'That is Michael Carpenter, Sergeant Collins. He is – was – a patient in the ward I work on.'

Peter spoke to a constable who was hovering at his elbow. 'Have you sent for the pathologist?'

'Yes, sir.'

'Keep everyone at bay until he arrives. And make sure no one else puts their big flat feet on those flowerbeds. There are a couple of prints there that should be cast.'

'Yes, sir.'

'You,' Peter called to another constable nearby. 'Alert Inspector Evans and the super.'

The constable pulled out his mobile phone.

Peter turned to Lyn. 'I'm sorry, but I have to ask you a few more questions. Shall we talk inside?'

Michelle Grady arrived breathlessly at the front door as Lyn and Peter were entering the hostel.

'I came as quickly as I could, Sergeant Collins. I thought you might need a woman.'

'You offering?' he enquired snidely.

'Only in one sense,' she responded tartly.

He looked at her with a new respect.

Lyn showed them into a communal lounge as bleak and soulless as the day rooms in the hospital. A blank television screen stared, a sightless eye, from the corner of the room. The carpet was a vivid, clashing combination of orange and purple swirls on which islands of hard, upright gold-vinyl upholstered chairs stood uninvitingly.

After draping her dressing gown around her bare legs, Lyn sat with her back to the television opposite Peter and Michelle. Karl, who had insisted on joining them, perched on the windowsill. Peter wondered if Karl had been sent as Tony Waters' deputy until he could get away from whatever meeting was claiming his attention.

'I'm Constable Grady.' Michelle introduced herself to Lyn and Karl, knowing she could wait forever before it occurred to Peter to carry out the common courtesy.

'Lyn Sullivan,' Lyn responded.

'Karl Lane,' Karl added.

Peter eyed Lyn as he held his pencil poised over his notebook. 'I've already heard part of the story from the first officers at the scene. He glanced out of the window to the two constables who were standing guard over Michael's body. 'You were trying to sleep in your room and you heard a noise. You opened your curtains and screamed, your fellow nurses came running... '

'Mary, Richard and Alan,' she interrupted.

Peter checked his notes again. 'And that would have been about a quarter past ten?'

'About that, yes.' She plucked nervously at the hem of her dressing gown. 'I couldn't sleep, and I was looking at the clock every few minutes... '

'Watching the clock is no good,' Michelle interrupted. 'The only thing to do when you can't sleep is to go for a brisk jog.'

'I thought we were interviewing witnesses, not running Auntie Michelle's advice column,' Peter cut in.

Lyn gave the policewoman a sympathetic glance. 'Thank you for your advice. I'll try that next time.'

'Works wonders with me,' Michelle said in defiance of Peter's mounting exasperation.

'You couldn't sleep,' Peter reminded Lyn.

'I heard a noise at my door,' Lyn continued.

'What kind of a noise?'

'A scuffling. At first I thought it was one of the cleaners with a polishing mop. Then I heard breathing... '

'Heavy breathing?' Peter interrupted.

'Yes. When I turned around, I saw the key fall out of the lock on to the carpet.'

'Do you always leave your key in the door?'

'Yes.'

'I take it the door was locked?'

'I always lock my door and leave the key in it when I'm sleeping. Day or night. I know it's not wise, when you consider what could happen if fire broke out, but I feel safer. There've been prowlers around.'

'First I've heard of it.' Peter stopped writing.

'There are always prowlers around nurses' hostels. You of all people should know that, Sergeant Collins.' Tony Waters strode into the room. 'Sorry I couldn't get away earlier, but I had to attend a meeting.'

'Have you reported these prowlers to the local police?' Peter asked Tony.

Tony sat in a chair next to Michelle and ran his hand through his thick, white-blond hair. 'Not recently. The last incident was about a year ago, but I'd have to check to make sure. The man was caught and charged with disturbing the peace.'

'Convicted?' Peter checked.

'I assume so. I can't remember the details.'

'And when was the last reported sighting of a prowler around the hostel?'

'I really couldn't tell you off the top of my head. Karl?' He turned to the charge nurse. 'Do you know where the incident book is kept in this hostel?'

'I do. I'll get it.'

'Nurse Sullivan identified the corpse of this particular peeping tom as Michael Carpenter, a patient in this hospital. Can you explain how he could have gained access to this building?' Peter asked Tony.

'Not before checking with Michael Carpenter's ward sister, Sergeant Collins. The emphasis of modern psychiatric treatment is on rehabilitation within the community. The old notions of incarcerating the mentally ill in secure wards out of sight of the general public are no longer in vogue. If this young man was one of our patients, it could be that he was here voluntarily, in which case he would have been at liberty to come and go as he pleased, and not only within the hospital and its grounds.'

'This particular "young man" has been convicted of arson, attempted murder and threatening behaviour towards his ex-girlfriend and her new boyfriend,' Peter tried to recall details of the two year old case. 'In short, Mr Waters, Michael Carpenter has been convicted of crimes which marked him as a danger to the public.'

'His doctors could have since considered him cured and of no further risk... '

'He died prowling round a nurses' hostel. God alone knows what damage he would have done, if he hadn't been seen.'

'Nothing is proved.'

'The bastard is lying out there with his neck broken after falling from a windowsill!' Peter exclaimed. 'If he is our killer, I'd say he was close to securing victim number five.'

'We can't be sure there's a fourth victim yet.'

'Our only witness to a murder disappears, and you're not sure she's a victim?' Peter left his chair. 'You,' he jabbed his finger at Tony, 'and all the bloody, do-gooding clowns like you disgust me. What the hell is the point of the likes of me working around the clock to catch the rapists, killers and villains of this world if all you do is give them the benefit of the doubt, until there's another dead victim dumped in front of you? And even then, all you give their killers as punishment is a couple of years' holiday in a camp like this, under the name of rehabilitation. Before patting them on the head and sending them out of the door to carry on in their own sweet way again.'

'Sergeant, may I remind you just who you're speaking to,' Tony countered.

'I know exactly who you are.' Peter pulled a cigar from his pocket. 'That's why I'm so bloody angry. Fools like you shouldn't be given the authority to clean a latrine. And if I were in your shoes, I'd be doing a headcount of your nurses right now.'

'He didn't get inside the hostel,' Karl observed in Tony's defence.

Peter glanced at Lyn. 'Someone eased Lyn's door key out of the lock.'

'You can't say for certain whether or not it was Michael Carpenter,' Tony insisted.

'No, I can't, but as he wasn't wearing any gloves, we'll find out. And if it wasn't Michael Carpenter then there were two prowlers creeping around this hostel this morning. Which option would you prefer, Mr Waters?' Peter snatched the incident book from Karl and left the room.

'Lyn?' Karl followed her up the stairs. 'If you're nervous about being on your own, I can stay with you until your next shift starts.'

'No thank you, Karl. I'm going to shower and dress.'

'I've watched you dress before,' he reminded.

'Cling to your memories, Karl. It's not something you're likely to see again.' She ran up the stairs away from him.

'I caught a bus last night for the first time in years, but it wasn't a wonderful experience,' Trevor commented as Dan drove him out of the suburbs and into the town.

'Is that why you're going to take a look at your car?' Dan asked.

'Peter found a garage in the alleyway at the back of Frank's place. When I saw the rent he'd signed up for on my account, I wondered if the car was worth it.'

'With all the back pay you've accumulated over the past few months, you can afford to treat yourself to a new car.'

'I could,' Trevor agreed.

'So what happens when this case is wrapped up? Back to the Drug Squad?'

'Or wherever else Bill wants to put me.'

'Are you returning to the force because you can't think of anything else to do?'

'I like the company,' Trevor said dryly. 'And the pension is good.'

'You have a sense of humour. That explains a lot.'

'What in particular?'

'How you've put up with working with Peter Collins all these years. But, I admit I found the man better than his reputation,' Dan slowed at traffic lights.

'Peter's all right.' When Trevor thought of everything that Peter had done for him since he'd been injured, he felt that "all right" was miserly. 'He's a good friend, and a good copper. He just needs someone to keep his temper in check now and again.'

'I'll try to remember that.' Dan stopped his car outside a mini-market with boarded-up windows in the run-down dock area of the town. 'This where you live?'

'It is.' Trevor reached for his stick.

'Place looks derelict.'

'Only way to stop the locals vandalising it even more.'

'I hope today goes well for you.'

'Thank you.' Trevor left the car. Supporting himself on his stick, he pulled his keys from his jacket pocket and went to the side door, but Frank spotted him from inside the shop, and came rushing out.

'You're back. You look great.' He shook Trevor's hand vigorously. 'Peter said you might be in hospital for months.'

'I'm only back for the day, Frank. I have to return to the hospital tonight.'

'But you'll soon be out for good.'

'I hope so.' Trevor limped towards the door set in the side wall beyond the shop.

'I can't leave the shop,' Frank said tactfully, sensing Trevor's need to be alone. 'You'll call down and see me before you go?'

'Yes.' Trevor waited until Frank disappeared before inserting his key in the lock. He pushed open the door and, after placing a steadying hand on the wall, negotiated the narrow flight of stairs that led to the first floor. He unlocked the single door facing him at the top, and walked into the living room of his flat. The room was lighter and larger than he remembered, and not so cluttered. The three-piece gold dralon suite, stained and shiny with wear, had been moved closer to the small, double-bar electric fire in the fake mahogany fireplace. The bent-wire magazine rack, which usually overflowed with old newspapers that he always meant to clear out, was empty. He ran his finger over the surface of the imitation teak sideboard. It was thick with grey dust. No one had cleaned the place in weeks, if not months, and yet it was tidy.

Propping his stick against the sofa, he sat down and stared at the scarred surface of the coffee table, bare except for the telephone and directories. Then he recalled that his mother and brother had stayed here during the first traumatic weeks after he'd been injured when he had hovered somewhere between life and death on the intensive care unit of the General. He pictured his mother, small, grey-haired, duster in hand, tut-tutting as she cleaned the battered second-hand sticks of furniture.

Leaving the sofa he limped into the kitchen. It was peculiar; everything was familiar, yet all the time he had been away he hadn't given the place a single thought. The Formica-topped kitchen table stood in the centre of the room. The same strip of ugly, torn wallpaper dangled over the skirting board in the corner, as it had done since the day he'd moved in. Blue tiles, chipped, cracked but clean, framed the sink top. His mother had given the place a through going-over in his absence. He looked out of the window at the moss-covered brick wall that hemmed in the back yard. He'd seen better views out of a prison cell.

He walked into the bathroom, which was as worn and depressing as the kitchen; saw the clean folded towels hanging over the bath in the absence of a rail. The new bar of soap laid on the cracked washbasin, the black patches gleaming dully in the cast-iron bath where the enamel had worn thin. He went into his bedroom. His bed had been made up with clean sheets, blankets and an orange candlewick bedspread.

He recalled the luxurious decor of Jean Marshall's apartment. This flat was past the kind of redecorating he was prepared to do in a place that wasn't, and would never be his own. The rooms were a stop-gap, the sort that students and young people who lived more out than in could put up with for a while. It was no home for a man of his age. He had to do something with himself – with his life. Spencer had been right; what had been enough wasn't any longer. And to think that his mother had actually expended time and effort cleaning this place. His mother! He suddenly realised he hadn't spoken to her in weeks. He walked into the living room, picked up the telephone and dialled her number.

'Do you think Michael Carpenter could be our man?' Dan asked Patrick as they watched the body shell containing what was left of Michael Carpenter being loaded into the back of an ambulance.

'Difficult to say.' Patrick pulled off his rubber gloves and threw them into a plastic bin. 'If you'd asked me, I'd have said that our man wasn't the kind to go scaling three stories of a nurses' hostel in broad daylight. But there's no accounting for people's actions, especially where the insane are concerned. He could have started off when it was dark and become over confident until he believed himself invisible.

'What I can't understand,' Peter mused, 'is why a killer should turn peeping tom.'

'The two aren't usually synonymous,' Patrick agreed.

'And even supposing he had wanted to kidnap Lyn, he could never have spirited her out of the hostel in daylight. There are too many people around. He couldn't have done it unseen. Not down all those corridors and stairs, and in daylight. And even if he had by some miracle managed it – where would he have hidden her?'

Bill studied the hostel and its surroundings. 'One of the joys of hospitals is the way they landscape their grounds. Half the poor buggers inside can't raise themselves high enough in their beds to see out of the windows, but they still spend an enormous amount of money on trees and shrubs.' He pointed to a screen of thick, high greenery that fringed the back of the hostel. 'You could hide the whole nursing staff in there. Supposing he did get her out, he could… ' Bill followed the path and contemplated the side of the building facing the shrubbery '... have gone out through that fire door. There's only a narrow gap between there and the bushes.'

'We've fought our way through every bloody inch of that shrubbery,' Peter pointed out. 'And we found absolutely bloody nothing. So now what?'

'We go back to HQ and sift through files,' Bill started walking.

'Wouldn't it be easier to arrest everyone here, put the whole bloody lot in the cells and watch to see who turns killer?' Peter suggested.

'We haven't enough cells. And we have to face the possibility that our villain could be an outsider.'

'But the knowledge of the hospital... ' Peter broke in.

'A lot of people have inside knowledge of this hospital. Over four hundred staff have been made redundant in the last five years. Nursing – office – catering – cleaning,' Bill's smile tightened. 'And you're going to rake through every single one of their files with a fine toothcomb for me. Aren't you, Peter?'

CHAPTER SIXTEEN

'That was a good meal.'

'A very good meal.' Trevor screwed his paper napkin into a ball and threw it on to his plate. 'Dessert?'

'After all I've eaten, you must be joking,' Jean Marshall smiled.

He picked up the bottle of wine they'd shared and poured the last of it into her glass. 'More wine?'

'No,' she drained her glass. 'But I do know what would go down a treat. Coffee and brandy.'

Trevor raised his finger to the waiter.

'The bill, please,' Jean said, before Trevor spoke. 'We'll indulge ourselves in my flat. That way I can drink as much as I like without worrying about driving home.'

'If you're sure.' Trevor had been looking forward to returning to Jean's flat, but now the prospect was about to become reality, he wondered what he, in his present battered and worthless state, had to offer a mature, attractive and confident woman like Jean.

'I'm sure.' She left her chair. 'I'll get my coat.'

Trevor handed his credit card to the waiter and flicked through his wallet looking for a tip. He fumbled and dropped it. The waiter picked it up for him. Trevor signed the chit and laid the tip on the waiter's tray. He reached for the stick he'd propped against an empty chair, and waited for Jean. It was ridiculous; here he was, a grown man of over thirty, nervous as a schoolboy because a woman had invited him to her place for a drink. But it had been a long time since he'd been on anything resembling "a date" and the last time hadn't been successful. He could almost hear the brush-off again,

"Thank you, Sergeant Joseph, but I've more man in my life than I can cope with right now… " Always another man, never him.

Even with Mags. "Not tonight, Trevor. I'm not feeling up to the mark." One woman in six years, and none at all for the last two, only a pathetic hopeless crush that hadn't, and never could have, led anywhere.

'Ready?' Jean tapped his arm. Using his stick he followed her out through the door to her car.

Lyn Sullivan didn't return from town until six-thirty. She'd deliberately left herself barely enough time to take a shower, change into her uniform and walk to the ward. And none to brood on the traumatic events of earlier in the day. She needed to keep busy, keep working and get on with her job. But her limbs ached and her eyes were strained from lack of sleep.

She took care to lock the shower room door securely. Even that wasn't enough; she jammed her slippers beneath it, and hung her wash-bag on the door-handle, so she would hear the rattle of her soap dish if someone attempted to force the lock. She showered quickly, glancing from the translucent shower door to the patterned glass in the window. Nerves at breaking point, she turned off the water and dried herself in the cubicle. When she dusted herself with talcum powder, her hand trembled so much she shook most of it over the floor.

She knew she was being absurd. Michael Carpenter was dead – and the dead couldn't walk. There was no reason for her to be nervous. But Michael had been young and, apart from his obsessive behaviour over his ex-girlfriend, naïve, childlike and trusting. Could he really have been a murderer? Had he taken those women and planted them in a hole in the ground, watched while they

231

slowly – ever so slowly – suffocated, fighting for each and every breath, as the blood vessels burst in their eyes?

She expelled the graphic images of lingering death from her mind, and concentrated on cleaning the powder from the floor. Tying her dressing gown cord securely around her waist, she threw back the bolt on the door and stepped into the corridor.

'All right now, Lyn?'

She jumped as though scalded, dropping her wash-bag.

'Sorry, didn't mean to scare you,' Richard apologised as he left the adjoining bathroom.

'I'm a bit edgy,' she confessed as she bent to retrieve her bag.

'You on night shift?'

'Yes.'

'So am I. I'll walk up the drive with you, if you like.'

'There's no need. I'll be fine.' She recalled what Sergeant Peter Collins had said that morning. If Michael Carpenter hadn't been the murderer, then it could be anyone in the hospital. She looked at Richard's brown hair, his pleasant nondescript features, his brown eyes – could it even be him?

'Don't be silly. I'd welcome the company – and protection,' he added not entirely ironically. 'See you downstairs in ten minutes. Mary will be walking up with us. Alan isn't working tonight, and the poor girl is set for a nervous breakdown.'

'See you downstairs,' she agreed, feeling ridiculous. How could she suspect Richard, of all people?

She returned to her room, hung her dressing gown in her wardrobe, and put everything in its allotted place. If someone entered her room during the night and disturbed anything, she wanted to know about it.

Mary and Richard were waiting for her in the foyer. It was picking with rain, so she pulled the hood of her anorak over her head before following them on to the drive. They walked quickly and in silence, all three glancing uneasily into the twilight shadows that had gathered between the bushes and trees.

'Sit down, I'll get us a drink.' Jean left Trevor in her living room and went to the kitchen to fetch ice. He walked over to the window and looked out over the marina, watching the pale, soft glow of early evening dim as lights flickered on across the bay.

'Everyone who comes here makes the right noises about the view, but you really do like it, don't you?' Jean returned with glasses of brandy and ice and handed him one.

'It's magnificent. There's something hypnotic about the sea.' He held up his glass. 'Is this wise after half a bottle of wine?'

'You only drank a quarter of the bottle, and we've been cutting down your drugs for the last three weeks. A brandy isn't going to do you any harm. But, as I warned you earlier, I won't be able to drive you back after this.'

'I wouldn't expect you to.' He took a tentative sip of the brandy – his first in months. 'I'll call a taxi. I'm not up to facing a bus. After months of hot-house hospital temperatures, night winds whistling through open bus shelters are likely to bring on pneumonia.'

'I can give you the number of a reliable firm. My car had to be serviced last week. It was easy enough getting a taxi from here to the hospital, but hopeless trying to arrange one the other way.'

'They probably thought you were a patient playing a practical joke.' He sipped his brandy and contemplated

233

the mix of Victorian, Edwardian and modern housing that fringed the shoreline below. 'I hope I'm not offending you by asking, but what do these apartments fetch?'

'Less than they did when my husband was talked into buying one. As you've probably noticed, half this block is up for sale.'

'That's why I asked.'

'Are you thinking of moving here?'

'Not especially. Just somewhere better than where I live at the moment.'

'The apartments here are cheap for a reason. This penthouse isn't bad because there's no one living above or to the side of me, but the walls are paper thin in the apartments below. Do you see that terrace?' She pointed to a dozen Victorian bay-windowed houses that faced the sea. The entire row was painted white, with Grecian columns set either side of the front doors, supporting a strip of balconies that ran the length of the terrace.

'It looks like it's been sympathetically renovated.' He noticed their new roofs, and the long gardens that ran from the fronts of the houses down to the beach.

'It has. I wanted one, but my ex-husband insisted on buying this because it was "prestigious" whatever that means, and we would have had to wait a year for the renovations on the terrace to be completed.' She fetched the brandy bottle and topped up their glasses. 'I have a superb view, but little privacy. If I sit in my conservatory, or even in here, with my curtains open I'm on view to the entire marina.' She moved to the sofa and sat down. 'You can't see past the stained, etched and frosted glass into those houses.'

'The garden walls are low,' he commented.

'You can always grow vines on a trellis.'

'At least four are for sale,' he observed.

'Eight actually, and you may be able to pick one up below asking price.'

'Why?' he enquired suspiciously.

'The builder who renovated the terrace is on the verge of bankruptcy. He bought high, before the last slump, did a no-expense-spared conversion, waited so long for buyers to pay above the going rate, he lost innumerable sales and if he doesn't succeed in off-loading them before the end of the month the bank has threatened to foreclose. And yes, I've put in an offer for two. They'll be a good investment.'

'How do you know all this?'

'I have a friendly – very friendly bank manager.' She saw Trevor pull a receipt out of his wallet and pat his pockets in search of a pen.

'Here,' she handed him a pen and notepad. 'I take it you want the estate agent's name and number.'

'Thank you.' He took them from her.

'It would be nice to have a police officer close by. I'd feel safe knowing that you could look up here any time and check on me.'

'You make me sound like a peeping tom.'

She shuddered. 'That isn't funny after what happened in the nurses' hostel this morning.'

'What happened?'

'You don't know?'

'I've been in town all day.'

'Michael Carpenter climbed up the outside wall of the nurses' hostel, this morning. Lyn heard him, opened her curtains, and saw him trying to look through her window.'

'Poor kid,' Trevor said. 'She must have been frightened out of her wits.'

'Not as frightened as Michael. He lost his hold, fell and broke his neck.'

'Dead?'

'Very,' Jean assured him. 'And rumour has it that your lot have stopped hunting for the killer.'

Trevor tried to think through what Jean had just told him, but the brandy on top of the wine blurred his thoughts. 'Michael was a nice enough kid, just mixed up. I wouldn't finger him as a killer.'

'You can never tell with obsessives,' Jean the professional said. 'They can get peculiar notions unconnected with their original fixations.'

'You nursed him. Do you think he could be the killer?' Trevor asked.

'I've been looking at everyone sideways since they dug up the first body. Including the gardener, who's sixty if he's a day. I can't tell you if Michael was a murderer, but I'll still be carrying this.' Jean reached for her handbag and tipped its contents on to the cushion. She picked up a can of cheap body-spray. 'Better than mace and it's not classed an offensive weapon. I also have this.' She rummaged through the mess and pulled out a rape alarm.

'Just make sure you don't go anywhere alone,' Trevor warned. 'And that includes the hospital corridors.'

'No one's going to have a go at me. I've read up on the psychology of victims. Most announce their vulnerability in the way they walk, the way they… '

'Don't you believe it,' Trevor broke in. 'One of the victims was a nurse. And everyone remembers her as being a very efficient, together sort of person.'

'Including me. That's if the rumours flying round the wards are true. You have found Elizabeth Moore?'

'No formal identifications had been made when I left the hospital this morning.' Trevor drank the remaining brandy in his glass. 'Do you mind if I call a taxi now?'

'Yes.' Jean looked at him and saw the edge of excitement in his eyes. 'You're working, aren't you? Undercover, in the hospital.'

'No,' Trevor shook his head.

'Yes, you are,' she contradicted.

'Do you think I got myself into this mess,' he looked down at his battered legs, 'just to go undercover inside the hospital? Besides, I was there before they found the first body.'

'Harry Goldman wanted to release you a week ago.'

'A week ago there was no murder hunt, and I wasn't ready to be released.'

'You've made a rapid recovery.'

'That's down to a kind nurse who befriended me in a pub, and reminded me that some people have a social life,' he glanced around the room. 'And live graciously in comfort, luxury and beauty.'

She moved closer to him. 'It's kind of you to say so.' Wrapping her arms around his neck, she pulled his face down to hers and kissed him.

His senses reeled. He was engulfed in the warm, moist, sensual feel of her mouth caressing his. He closed his eyes, and attempted to kiss her back, fighting to make the embrace an equal effort, trying to give her something of himself, before he became totally lost, overwhelmed by her rich musky perfume, the urgency and blatant sexuality of her caresses.

She pulled back, away from him for a moment. Seconds later, her naked arm brushed against his cheek as her hands closed once more around his neck. He looked down and saw that she had shed the silk blouse she'd been

237

wearing. He stared at the half globes of her tanned breasts, the nipples hardening as she thrust herself against him.

'We could go into the bedroom,' she nuzzled his ear.

'Jean, I... ' he faltered, embarrassed by the injuries that had drained his strength. For the first time since Mags had left him, a woman had undressed for him, yet he felt no more than a flicker of lust that could have been roused by a quick glance at one of the soft porn magazines that littered the station.

Jean leaned past him to press a button on the coffee table. The lights dimmed and the drapes swished together. Before she embraced him again, she sloughed off the remainder of her clothes. She unbuttoned his shirt and flies, and he allowed her to undress him, feeling as though he was back on the ward at the General. The nurses there had dressed and undressed him because he'd been too weak to do so himself, but when Jean's hand slipped down between his naked thighs he realised that he was well and truly out of hospital. That she had succeeded in arousing passions within him that he had almost believed dead.

He pressed her down on to the sofa beneath him, but even as she lay on her back and opened her legs to receive him, he felt as though it was not he who was making love to Jean, but Jean who was swallowing him whole. He felt cannibalised, consumed by her greed and hunger, a hunger he realised – as he rose to meet her thrusts with his own – that could have been satisfied by almost any man – and probably better than him in his present state.

'It's too bloody neat for my liking.' Peter walked over to the chart Dan had drawn up. 'How many murderers fall three storeys and break their necks just before we close in on them? Besides, he doesn't fit our profile.'

'I thought you didn't pay any credence to profiles,' Bill said.

'That was this morning,' Peter replied irritably. 'The age is wrong for a start. Michael was nineteen, not twenty-five to thirty-five. His father's a bank manager, his mother a solicitor, so that leaves out the working-class, blue-collar hypothesis… '

'What did he do?' Dan interrupted.

'Bank clerk,' Peter answered. 'But he wasn't showing anywhere near the same promise Daddy did at his age. In fact he probably wouldn't have got into the bank at all if it hadn't been for his father's influence. Far from living alone with a domineering female relative, he lived with both parents and three brothers before he was admitted here.'

'But he did try to burn down his girlfriend's house while her entire family was asleep inside,' Bill said.

'Only when she went off with another fellow. There's a world of difference between desperately trying to hang on to one particular girl and picking up anyone who comes along and burying them alive.'

'Where are we on dates?' Bill asked.

Dan consulted his notebook. 'He was held on remand in the hospital wing of the local prison for four months. After sentencing he was transferred here and that was a year ago.'

'He was admitted before the murders, he had the opportunity, the personality, and he was caught red-handed. I say we've got our man.' Bill was eager to wrap up the case. If the profile didn't fit the suspect, then that was the fault of the psychiatrists who'd drawn it up. They'd got it wrong before.

239

'Until two months ago, Michael Carpenter was locked in a secure ward for twenty-four hours a day,' Dan remarked, still studying his notes.

'Secure secure – or secure Compton Castle style?' Bill queried.

'Your guess is as good as mine.'

'Stop guessing and find out the facts!' Bill exploded.

'As we've never been allowed into that hallowed unit, it's a fair assumption the inmates would find as many difficulties getting out as we've had trying to get in,' Peter propped his feet on the edge of Bill's desk.

The telephone buzzed.

'I said no interruptions,' Bill barked, knowing his voice would carry through the thin partition wall.

'It's Mr O'Kelly, sir. You did say that you wanted us to put him through,' the constable's tone was so subservient it bordered on insolence.

Bill snatched up the receiver. 'Patrick?'

'Just finished Michael Carpenter. He died instantly. A clean break at the top of his spinal column which severed his spinal cord. I've opened the cranium and sliced a few frozen brain sections, but so far there's nothing. Not a single abnormality. Some barbiturate and tranquillisers in the bloodstream, but no more than you'd expect to find in a patient in a psychiatric hospital… '

'I need to know if Michael Carpenter is our man.'

'He didn't have murderer tattooed on his forehead. If you want to know any more, you can look at the results when you come down here this evening. The relatives are coming to identify three of the bodies, remember?'

'I remember,' Bill repeated.

'You're creating a corpse jam down here,' Patrick hung up.

'Anything?' Dan dared.

240

'Bloody nothing.' Bill crumpling the inevitable polystyrene take-away container in his hands.

'Looks like we're back to square one,' Peter rose to his feet. 'Carpenter might or might not be our man and after utilising our entire manpower on this morning's search, we still don't know where Vanessa Hedley is. In fact, we know sod all.'

Trevor had always felt faintly embarrassed after sex, and more so with Jean than he had with Mags. As Jean eased herself out from under him and they both reached for their clothes, physically close, but mentally estranged, each engrossed in their own thoughts, he wondered if it was that way with everyone. It had been easier while he was living with Mags; at least their lovemaking had taken place under sheets, in the dark. And usually both of them had been so worn out at the end of it there was no time or energy to do anything other than roll over and fall asleep.

'I'll call that taxi for you.' Jean finished dressing and picked up the telephone.

He buckled his belt and pulled his pullover over his head. He limped towards her and kissed her gently on the cheek. 'Thank you.'

'For calling a taxi?'

'No. For being there when I needed someone, and being understanding when I needed sympathy, and... ' he glanced at the sofa they had just vacated.

'All part of the nursing service,' she smiled. 'Count it as an NHS extra.'

Ten minutes after Trevor left Jean's flat, the telephone rang. She picked up the receiver.

'Can I come over?'

She knew the voice. She didn't have to ask the name. 'I thought you wouldn't be able to get away this evening.'

'I can get away now.' The voice was curt, impatient.

'When will you be here?' She was grateful that Trevor had gone, for her lover, who was so offhand and neglectful most of the time, could be uncontrollably jealous when the mood struck.

'Twenty minutes.'

She remembered the champagne she'd put in the fridge, the sheets she'd changed that morning in the hope of enticing Trevor to stay the night. Strange that ten minutes of intense physical grappling on the sofa had killed all urge for conversation between them, and stifled her desire to keep Trevor with her longer. 'I'll tell the porter to expect you. You can use your key.'

'Want me to check inside for you, miss?' One of the constables on duty in the grounds joined Carol Ashford as she unlocked her car. 'I have a torch.' He switched on his powerful, police-issue torch.

'Thank you,' she said gratefully. 'All the staff are on edge.'

'Not surprising, when you consider what's been happening.' The constable opened the driver's door, shone his torch inside and looked at the passenger and back seats. 'No bodies, alive or dead, lurking inside,' he joked tastelessly. 'I'll check the boot for you as well.'

'Please,' she said quickly, and the constable noticed that she was trembling. He swung the torch high as he closed the boot and noticed that she was beautiful. Cool shining bob of smooth blonde hair, mesmerising deep blue eyes, full luscious lips...

'Thank you, Officer.'

'Glad to be of assistance, Nurse.' He realised he was still staring at her. She sat in the car and he closed the door on her, watching as she locked herself in. He wondered if she was married, but before he could summon the courage to ask her out, four other nurses and Adam Hayter walked into the car park, and as they'd seen him do a check of Nurse Ashford's car, they all demanded the same service.

'Everything quiet, Tom?'

The officer looked up from the interior of Hayter's car, and pushed aside Adam who was hovering too close for comfort. 'Yes, Sergeant Joseph.' He automatically addressed Trevor by his rank. Old habits died hard.

'Anyone in HQ?'

'Inspector Evans, Sergeant Collins and the super have gone down to the mortuary.'

'Have a quiet shift.' Trevor walked on down the drive.

He had walked a couple of hundred yards when he heard a muffled scream in the bushes on his right. He stopped and peered into the darkness, wondering if it was a cat or a fox. Squeezed out by the suburbs encroaching on their old habitat, packs of them had taken to living in and around the town, scrounging out of bins and raising their litters in burrows on waste ground. And the hospital gardens, though smaller than they had once been, were still vast by the tablecloth standards of the "executive homes" outside the walls. Trevor saw a bush move, heard a rustle of leaves.

He swung his stick forward on to the lawn. It sank into the soft earth. He saw a flash of white cloth, a pair of gleaming white naked legs stretching out from beneath a bush. He took another step – a burst of crimson exploded in his head, darkening the grey shadows into unrelieved

243

black, and bringing in its wake a sickening tide of nausea, pain and afterwards blissful, numbing unconsciousness.

CHAPTER SEVENTEEN

Jean stretched out in the bed, searching for a cool patch of satin sheet. Her companion's slow, rhythmic breathing rose and fell in the still air of the bedroom. She envied her lover and wished that she too was sunk in blissful rest. But sexually aroused and frustrated she would have waken him – if he hadn't had an uncertain temper.

She couldn't recall feeling like this when she had been younger. Was disappointment a feature of maturity? Maturity or old age? she debated, her forty-six years weighing heavily on her mind. It was unfair. Her companion was obviously fulfilled; why not her? Had she become more demanding, or had her appetite increased with her years to the point where it could no longer be alleviated?

She slid her hand over the smooth skin of his abdomen. She moved downwards, her fingers brushed his pubic hair with feather-light strokes she hoped would provoke a response; but the caresses only intensified the fire that burned within her. She elicited no reaction, the same steady sounds of breathing continued to fill the room.

She turned over and stared at the face that lay on the pillows alongside her own. The blond hair shone like cold moonlight in the darkness, highlighting chiselled features. The firm lines of the mouth, softened by sleep, curved into a full-lipped smile.

There had been a time, and not that long ago, when she would have given almost anything for a night of passion with the love of her life; but three years of secrecy, of keeping her feelings hidden in public, of long lonely nights and holiday weekends, continually aware of and jealous of her lover's other life, had worn the gilding from the flush of love.

Three years ago she wouldn't have gone out with Trevor, let alone taken him, if not into her bed, on to her sofa. But she'd used Trevor as she'd used so many others during the past year; as a stopgap, someone to help her while away empty hours. He wasn't the first man she'd slept with since she'd taken her lover, nor was he likely to be the last, but he had been the least successful.

Her sexual appetite made no allowances for weakness – and prolonged sickness had made Trevor weak. If anyone needed tenderness, gentleness and understanding, it was Trevor. She should have left him alone. If she had succeeded with Peter Collins – she pictured his hard, firm-muscled body, his grim set mouth, eyes that never betrayed his inner thoughts – and smiled.

The man lying next to her moved. She was in bed with the man she had professed to love while thinking of another. Perhaps she was no longer in love? What was "love" anyway? As a schoolgirl she would have answered the question with certainty. Love was the all-consuming, wonderful emotion that incited men and women to heroic, unselfish deeds, and inspired poets like Byron to pen immortal lines. After her marriage she would have defined love as a transitory madness that caused women to fling aside every ounce of pride and independence. And now – now she knew that its passion, pleasure and fleeting happiness, also gave rise to the uglier more selfish emotions of envy and rage.

Perhaps it was time to make a clean break, to lift herself above the second-class status of "mistress". To say no when the telephone rang, to re-build a life outside of a relationship that existed only in snatched, borrowed moments. But – she looked at the face next to her own, and knew that once those eyes opened she would not be capable of thinking of anyone or anything else.

A whistle blew, blasting Trevor into agonising consciousness. The explosion in his head had left a residue of pain that intensified the moment he tried to move. He tried to speak, but his mouth was filled with something damp, and foul-tasting. He choked, coughed, and spat out a clump of soil. He was lying on something soft and yielding like –

'Sergeant Joseph?'

He heard shock and dismay in the voice.

'Andrew?' He pushed himself up on his hands, and slumped, one arm sinking into cold damp earth, the other into – he suddenly realised what he was leaning on.

'Here, sir. I'll give you a hand.'

His first thought was that Andrew was being ludicrously formal considering they had been constables together. He couldn't remember Andrew calling anyone, not even Bill "sir" before. The ground beneath him reverberated as he was helped up.

'Oh, my God!' The voice was young. A rookie's?

'What the hell – '

Trevor heard a stream of curses that sounded like Dan's voice being played at the wrong speed. He opened his eyes.

'Prop him against the tree.' Dan's voice again, shocked as Andrew's had been, but more urgent. Trevor looked up. He was surrounded by a ring of torches and Dan was peering down at him, while shouting orders over his shoulder.

'Call an ambulance.'

'Sir.'

'Fetch the super.'

Men ran off towards the brilliantly lit windows of the main building.

Trevor lifted his hand to the back of his head. When he withdrew it, his fingers were sticky with dark clotted blood. Dan was staring at the body on the ground.

'What happened?' he asked Trevor.

'I was walking down the drive and I heard a noise,' Trevor looked over to the tarmac shining in the moonlight twenty yards to his left. Had he walked that far across the lawn? He struggled to focus his mind and eyes. The shapes he saw lying beneath a bush, and on a flowerbed merged. He ran his hands down his jacket and realised that the blood wasn't just on his head. His clothes were soaked in it.

'What happened?' Dan reiterated.

'I was walking down the drive – ' Trevor repeated.

'Where had you been until this time of night?'

Trevor didn't need to look into Dan's face to know what he was thinking. 'Town.'

'Until now? It's nine-thirty.'

'I had dinner with a friend. Jean Marshal,' Trevor revealed testily. His head hurt, he was in pain, and he was angry that his condition didn't appear to concern anyone else. 'We went to a restaurant.' Trevor was seeing three of everything, including Dan. He turned his head and skinned his ear on the trunk of the tree he was leaning against. Bile rose into his mouth, and he barely had time to turn before he vomited.

'Sergeant Joseph came in by taxi.' Chris Brooke volunteered the information.

'How long ago was that?' Dan looked from Trevor, bloodstained, vomiting and dazed, to the mutilated body on the flowerbed behind him.

'No more than ten minutes or quarter of an hour ago, sir.'

'Which was it, constable? Ten minutes or quarter of an hour?' Dan demanded.

'I – I'm not sure,' Brooke stammered.

'Who is it?' Trevor's voice was quiet, detached and remote, but it cut across the night air like a whiplash. Everyone fell silent. 'Who is it?' Trevor reiterated.

'I don't know. It could be one of the patients,' Dan replied. 'There's something familiar about her. I think I saw her on the geriatric ward.'

'Is she… '

'She's dead,' Dan answered.

'How?'

'Cut up, possibly with a broken bottle. There are shards of brown glass protruding from her windpipe and jugular.'

'Has she been dead long?' Even in his dazed and disorientated state, Trevor knew that he had to clear himself of suspicion.

'Difficult to say. She feels cold, but there's very little blood on the body.'

'It's all over me,' Trevor said ruefully.

Dan shone the torch over him and took a closer look. 'Glass is embedded in your chest. Whatever you do, don't move.'

'It's my head that's hurting,' Trevor complained.

'I don't know what happened,' Dan bent his head close to Trevor's. 'But,' he glanced over his shoulder at the officers around them, 'it's vital you tell me everything you remember before the ambulance arrives.'

Trevor turned and vomited the last of Jean's brandy and the Greek meal on to the grass.

Peter Collins hated accompanying relatives into the mortuary for two reasons. The first was that the moment they entered, the mortuary lost its impersonal, laboratory feel, and took on an atmosphere that was half chapel of rest, half graveyard; the second was that the murder victims were no longer evidence in an inquiry. Weeping mothers, fathers, sisters, brothers, boyfriends, husbands, transformed them into people, lovable or otherwise, who had breathed, loved, laughed, fought, argued, worked and played, and not that long ago.

Like hospitals and cemeteries, relatives visiting mortuaries reminded him of his own mortality; and he hated any reminder of his own frailty. He arrived in the car park in time to see a red-eyed Michelle Grady lead a wild-eyed, fair-haired, middle-aged woman out of the mortuary. Her resemblance to the photograph of the first victim they'd discovered was striking, and he knew he was looking at Rosie Twyford's mother. A man with a beer paunch walked slowly behind them, misery etched into every line of his bloated face.

'Mr and Mrs Moore and Mr and Mrs Moon are still waiting,' Michelle Grady whispered as she walked past. Peter nodded and pushed open the door to the bleak, comfortless waiting room.

'Sergeant Collins, this is Mr and Mrs Moon.'

Peter nodded to the couple Bill had introduced. Mr Moon looked every inch the successful businessman in his hand-tailored suit. Mrs Moon was attractive, suntanned and also well-dressed, but behind their fine clothes he saw a look of nervous misery and expectancy that he recognised. They still hoped. Despite the overwhelming evidence of the suitcase, and the dental records the lab boys had slaved over, they still hoped that their daughter was alive.

'I'm taking Mr and Mrs Moore in,' Bill opened the inner door. 'Patrick will send for you when he's ready.'

Given the choice, Peter wasn't sure whether he'd prefer to supervise the identification of the badly decomposed body or the skeleton. Perhaps it was just as well that Patrick had made the decision for him. He sat across the room from Mr and Mrs Moon.

'If you'd like a cup of coffee, I could rustle up something,' he offered, uneasy with their despair. The metre that separated the Moons' chairs stood testimony to their mental estrangement. They'd borne a child together, yet both were facing the loss alone, without even the dubious comfort of one another's touch. Peter had never had a child, or felt the desire for one, but even he grasped that to lose a son or daughter before your own death must be one of the greatest hells on earth for a parent.

'Thank you, Sergeant Collins, but I'd prefer not,' Mr Moon said stiffly. Mrs Moon shook her head. A painful silence fell over the room.

'I'd like to extend my sympathies and those of everyone on the police force.'

'Thank you, Sergeant Collins,' Mr Moon replied mechanically.

'What I can't understand – ' Mrs Moon pulled out a handkerchief and held it to her nose, 'is why she wrote to us and said that she was going away with a friend. That last letter was so – so – ' Sobs choked her speech. '– so happy,' she finished at last. 'It was full of plans for the future. I thought – ' she looked at her husband and there was such a wealth of bitterness in his return glance Peter was taken aback.

251

'Where did you think she was, Mrs Moon?' he prompted gently.

'On a round-the-world trip. She asked her father for money for the ticket, and we – I,' she corrected herself, 'sent her some spending money. She knew if she ran out, she could always have more – ' She dabbed her eyes with her handkerchief again.

'Do you have that letter?' Peter asked hopefully.

'With me.' She opened her handbag and pulled out a tattered and creased envelope. She offered it to him with a shaking hand.

'You don't mind me reading it?' he took it.

'We don't mind, Sergeant Collins.' Mr Moon left his seat and walked to the window. He looked out through the slats of the Venetian blinds at the car park and box-like facade of the General Hospital. 'But I don't think you'll find it helpful. I must have read it a hundred times since we discovered Claire was missing.'

'When was that?' Peter asked.

'About two months after she left here. Belinda, – ' he acknowledged his ex-wife's presence for the first time since Peter had entered the room, '– contacted me, and asked if I'd heard from her. It was then that I realised the last contact either of us had with her was regarding the money for her trip, so I reported Claire missing. Not that anyone in authority took me seriously,' he added curtly. 'I was told that youngsters go missing every day, and sooner or later the majority turn up again, none the worse for wear. Of course, we all know different now, don't we, Sergeant Collins?'

'I am sorry, sir.' The words sounded inadequate, but Peter didn't know what else to say. He looked down at the envelope and removed the letter. It was written in bright blue ink, fountain pen or felt, not biro, and the letters were

252

large, rounded, those of a child. Another factor that removed the living Claire from the bundle of mildewed bones and sorry remnants of tissue and hair that he had seen laid out on Patrick's slab. He unfolded the single sheet of paper, and began to read.

Dear Mummy,

I know you don't like using the computer so this is just a short note to thank you for the money, and to let you know that I am getting better all the time. The doctor was right; now that I am out of the hospital for part of every day I am getting stronger in every way.

I went into town today and bought some cool summery things. We have decided to stop off at Hong Kong and Sri Lanka on our way to Australia, from there it is anyone's guess as to where we'll go, so you mustn't worry if you don't hear from me for a while, I'm sure that the postal service in those out of the way backwaters must be dreadfull. I will e-mail Daddy though if I find an internet café.

As well as being fit I am also very happy. That's Happy with a capital H. You were right Mummy when you said that there is someone special for everyone. When I come home I will introduce you to him. But for now I want to keep him to myself. Hug him close to me and keep him secret. But it feels good, knowing there's someone special who cares for me every bit as much as I care for him.

Take care of yourself, Mummy darling. Love to everyone in Spain, especially Sebastian. I'll write again when I'm settled for a while.

Love and Kisses
your Claire

Peter refolded the letter and replaced it in the envelope. 'Would you mind if we took a copy of this?' he asked Mrs Moon.

'Not if it would help.'

'Sergeant Collins?' Patrick's assistant was in the doorway. 'Mr O'Kelly is ready for you now.'

As Peter rose to his feet, he saw Bill talking to Mr Moore in the car park. Mrs Moore was as hysterical as Rosie Twyford's mother had been. He glanced at Claire Moon's mother, and felt that he hadn't drawn the short straw. He might be landed with the skeleton, but he was also landed with a mother who seemed made of sterner stuff than the common breed.

Peter's mobile rang as Patrick was showing the Moons the contents of their daughter's suitcase and, more poignantly, the personal jewellery and remnants of clothing that had been retrieved from her corpse. Deciding that whoever it was could wait, Peter switched off his phone. Mrs Moon kept her mouth and nose covered with her handkerchief as she looked at the artefacts. All she could do was nod. Mr Moon was more forthcoming.

'That's the Rolex I gave Claire last Christmas.'

'I'm sorry to have to show you your daughter's remains, Mr Moon, Mrs Moon,' Patrick apologised, 'but, as Sergeant Collins will tell you, the formalities have to be observed.'

'Will it suffice for just one of us to identify the remains?' Mr Moon asked Peter.

'Yes.' Peter opened the door for Mrs Moon to leave. She hesitated at the head of the slab, fingering a ring. A cheap silver ring decorated with an enamelled masked head. Peter looked to Patrick who nodded. 'You can take that with you if you like, Mrs Moon.'

'Thank you, Sergeant.' She lifted her head, and Peter thought that he had never seen such anguish in another human being's eyes.

'The rest of Claire's things will be given to you later.' Peter looked around for Michelle Grady, but she was nowhere in sight. Patrick led Mr Moon down the long narrow mortuary towards three shrouded slabs at the far end. Peter had to witness the identification, but he could hardly leave Mrs Moon unattended. He signalled to Patrick's assistant, but by the time he had seen Mrs Moon escorted back into the waiting room the remains had been uncovered.

Patrick kept most of the skeleton covered, revealing just the skull. The hair, long, luxuriant and golden brown, clung to the cranium, held in place by a cap of dried skin. The sightless eyes stared blankly at the ceiling, the nose cartilage had crumbled. Threads of gum clung to the yellowed, earth stained teeth.

'It's Claire's hair.' Mr Moon's voice sounded strained, inhuman.

'Thank you, sir,' Patrick draped the sheet back over the skull.

'I want – I demand to know how it happened,' Mr Moon shouted angrily. 'How – how did she die?'

Patrick looked to Peter.

'We think she suffocated,' Peter said, twisting the truth.

'You don't know?'

'The corpse we found buried close to Claire's bore signs of suffocation,' Patrick intervened. 'And from the facts that I have been able to glean from examining your daughter's body, I assume – '

'Assume!'

255

'Clive?' Moon's ex-wife was standing in the doorway, flanked by Patrick's assistant and Michelle. 'We have arrangements to make.'

Her calm restored his senses. 'Thank you, gentlemen.' He might have been thanking a shopkeeper for his assistance.

Peter watched the Moons walk out of the door, followed by Michelle. After the door swung shut on them, Patrick opened one of the refrigerated drawers and removed two frosted glasses filled with chilled amber liquid.

'Drink?' Patrick handed a glass to Peter.

Peter tossed the contents back. 'Good whisky.'

'The best. I left yours in the drawer, I didn't know how long you'd be,' Patrick said to his assistant when he returned. The telephone rang in the office and Patrick went in to answer it. As soon as he hung up he called for his emergency kit.

'Not another one?' Peter whispered hoarsely.

'Yes, and at Compton Castle,' Patrick answered.

'Vanessa Hedley?'

'Your guess is as good as mine. You coming?'

Peter remembered the phone call earlier. 'I'll take my own car.' He followed Patrick out of the door.

CHAPTER EIGHTEEN

Peter drove through the gates of Compton Castle and, following a constable's directions, over the lawns to the area where floodlights had been set up. Patrick followed, climbed into his overalls, gathered his kit from the back of his car and headed for the taped-off area. Peter looked around for Dan or Bill. He didn't have to look far; they came running towards him as soon as they spotted his car.

'Another burial?' Peter asked when they reached him.

'No,' Bill snapped. 'We got to this one before our man had a chance to start digging.'

'Vanessa Hedley?'

'No. Elderly woman, stabbed with a broken bottle, and it looks like rape.'

Patrick called them over and they donned paper overshoes and walked towards him.

'You can stop there,' Patrick ordered. 'No doubt about rape this time.' He dropped a swab into a test tube and closed it. 'Semen's fresh, not dried, but death occurred days rather than hours ago. First impressions – I'd say she's a victim of necrophilia.'

'And we've caught the bastard red-handed,' Bill growled. 'Lying on top of the corpse, blood all over him.'

Something in the tone of Bill's voice struck Peter as ominous. He looked from the super to Dan. 'Who?' he asked.

'Trevor Joseph. He had a stick – '

'A walking stick, his legs have been broken,' Peter interrupted.

'He was unconscious – '

Peter leaned over the corpse, and ignoring Bill and Patrick, who was busy taking more samples, stared at the victim's face. The features were contorted, slashed to ribbons, the nose and ears hanging by threads of skin. But the first thing that struck him was the age of the woman. The wrinkled skin was parchment yellow in the strong glare of the floodlights.

'She was a sweet old lady from the geriatric ward?'

Peter saw Bill standing at his elbow. 'You can't believe Trevor did this? Not after all the years you've known him.'

'The man's nuts.'

'You didn't think so this morning when you asked him to start work again.'

'No sane man would agree to go undercover in this place.'

'No sane man would bloody well want to work with you, but we do,' Peter retorted. 'Look at the marks on her. Those blows were inflicted with a hell of a lot of strength. Trevor's been sick, he's weak – '

'We found him lying on her covered in blood, with a lump of glass stuck in his chest. Maybe the poor old biddy fought back.'

'A two day old corpse fought back!' Peter sneered.

'We can't be sure of the time of death until we get the pathologist's full report.' Bill wanted to postpone thinking about this scenario until after he'd slept.

'Where is Trevor?' Peter asked.

'The General,' Dan answered. 'He had glass embedded in his chest and a cut on his head.'

'Is anyone with him?'

'A couple of constables.'

'Is he under arrest?'

258

'As soon as the doctors have finished we'll start questioning him,' Bill snapped.

Peter turned to Dan. 'You can't possibly think Trevor did this?'

Dan looked at Bill. His boss was swaying on his feet, his face grey with fatigue. He knew that if he expressed an opinion either way, he'd only succeed in provoking a head-on confrontation. 'As soon as Patrick's given us the basics we'll talk to Trevor,' he hedged, 'then – ' He was speaking to thin air. Peter was running back to his car.

Ignoring Dan's shouts, Peter dived into the driving seat and hit the accelerator. And he didn't slow down until he was outside A and E at the General.

Peter strode down the restricted area that housed the cubicles. 'Trevor Joseph – police officer?' he demanded of a nurse.

'The public aren't allowed back here,' he replied authoritatively.

'Police – not public.' Peter pulled out his I.D and waved it at him. 'I need to see him immediately.' He pushed past the nurse and saw Chris Brooke standing guard at the end of the corridor.

'This way, sir,' Chris called, assuming that Peter had been sent to interview Trevor.

Andrew Murphy was standing in a corner of the cubicle. Trevor was sitting on the examination couch. A doctor was washing her hands in the sink, and a nurse was swabbing Trevor's head with cotton wool and antiseptic.

'The stitches will need to come out in a couple of days. Don't worry, we've shaved off very little of your hair, Trevor. But it's so thick it hardly shows,' the nurse reassured.

'If you experience any of these symptoms,' the doctor handed Trevor the standard "signs of concussion" card, 'or if you're concerned in any way, come back immediately.'

Trevor winced as the antiseptic being dabbed on his wound touched raw flesh.

'The cut on your chest is deep, but the wound's clean and your X-rays are clear – who are you?' The doctor asked when Peter walked in.

Peter waved his I.D card. 'Police. I need to talk this man. Alone.'

'I'll be finished in a few moments, but he should return to Compton Castle to rest.'

'That's all right, doctor.' Trevor looked around for his stick. 'I want to talk to him.'

Peter offered Trevor his arm. 'Bill has your stick. No doubt he thinks it's evidence,' he added cynically.

'Don't forget to come back in four days, so we can take out those stitches,' the nurse reminded. 'You can make an appointment in reception.'

'Fine.' Trevor made a mental note to ask Jean to look at them. The last thing he wanted to do was return here to waste another hour sitting around waiting to be treated.

'I'm taking Trevor back to Compton Castle,' Peter announced to Chris and Andrew as he helped Trevor limp into the corridor.

'But, Superintendent Mulcahy...'

Andrew Murphy elbowed the rookie out of the way and winked at Peter. 'We'll see you back there, sergeants.'

'What the hell happened?' Peter asked Trevor as soon as they were in his car.

'I wish I knew.' Trevor sank his head in his hands. 'I'd been out, I returned by taxi. While I was walking up

260

the drive, I saw a pair of legs lying on the grass. I walked towards them and that's the last I remember.'

'You think someone hit you?' Peter could smell alcohol on Trevor's breath. And Trevor never had been able to handle spirits. 'Or did you fall and hit your head?'

Trevor put a hand to his head and winced as his fingers touched the stitches. 'I think that's unlikely given that the cut is on the crown of my head, unless I did a head dive. And I've no memory of attempting one.'

Peter inspected the wound. There was an enormous, split lump on Trevor's crown, blood clots matting the thick black hair around the area that had been stitched.

'Given that you were found on a body in a flowerbed of soft earth, I agree.' Peter started the car.

'Surely Dan and Bill don't think I attacked that woman?' Trevor had felt pleasantly merry as he'd walked up the drive, but he was now stone-cold sober. A combination of cold night air, vomiting, and pain had cleared his stomach, if not his breath, of alcohol, and the expression on Peter's face was enough to penetrate the fog of concussion. 'For God's sake… '

'Save your breath. It's not me you've got to convince, mate,' Peter interrupted as they hit the main road to Compton Castle.

'Well?' Bill asked Patrick as he rose stiffly to his feet.

'I'm not sure how she died, but she's been dead for at least two days, and that's official. All the injuries you can see, including the rape, were inflicted after death.'

'You sure?'

'No localised bleeding. Those cuts were definitely made after death.'

'But the blood… '

261

'I've taken swabs. It looks a lot, but it's spread thinly. Head wounds bleed. I'd say it was all Joseph's.'

'And you're sure she was raped?' Dan checked.

'The corpse was interfered with. Yes.'

'You'll type the blood and the semen?'

'Don't I always?' Patrick dropped the samples he'd taken into his case.

'Trevor Joseph… '

'If you're going to caution me, Bill, take it as done,' Trevor sat back in the passenger seat of Peter's car.

'No one's accusing you of anything,' Bill leaned on the open door.

'Yet,' Peter qualified. 'Patrick,' he called out to the pathologist. As you're here, take a look at the cut on Trevor's head.'

Patrick pushed in past Bill. 'Nasty,' he said, probing the stitches with his finger.

'I hope you washed your hands after you played with corpses,' Trevor reprimanded. He closed his eyes. Peter had asked endless questions on the journey from the General. His head was throbbing, and Bill hadn't helped by demanding his bloodstained anorak and sweater as soon as Peter had stopped his car. He felt hot and sticky and desperately in need of a bath and sleep. His mouth was dry, foul with the aftertaste of spicy food, too much beer, brandy and vomit.

'You should be in bed.' Patrick folded Trevor's sweater and anorak into a plastic bag.

'He can rest as soon as we've cleared a few things up.' Irrational with fatigue, Bill was too stubborn to walk away for the night.

'I've already talked to Trevor,' Peter removed the keys from the ignition of his car and stepped out, 'we've established the timing and it will be easy enough to check as Trevor arrived back here by taxi, and taxi drivers keep logs.'

'Not all of them,' Bill said. 'And certainly not the ones who moonlight.'

'I'll find the guy,' Peter broke in. 'And even without him, Trevor said he spoke to a constable in the car park. That at least can be verified.'

Bill and Dan watched Trevor stumble from the car and slide slowly to the ground.

'Now can he go to bed?' Peter questioned acidly.

'So, you've found Vanessa Hedley, Inspector?' Tony Waters joined Dan on the drive as the police ambulance drove away.

'No, Mr Waters.'

'Not more problems?' Tony frowned.

'You turning up like this is fortuitous. It saves me having to send for you,' Dan observed.

'It's not fortuitous,' Tony countered. 'The DMO sent for me when she saw the activity in the grounds.'

'DMO?'

'Duty medical officer. In this case Dotty Clyne. She telephoned to see if I knew what was happening. We were hoping you'd found Vanessa Hedley.'

'No such luck, but we have found another body. And we have reason to believe that it's another of your patients.'

'Who?' Tony asked quickly.

'The body hasn't been identified.' Dan waved to Bill who was driving towards the gates. 'May I ask where you've been all evening?'

'In my office until eight-thirty. Then at home. Why do you want to know?'

'Just building a picture of everyone's movements.'

'Was the patient murdered?'

'We'll know in due course, Mr Waters, and when we do I'll let you know.' Dan thrust a paper bag in front of him. 'Peppermint?'

'Taxi driver confirms the time he dropped Trevor off as nine-thirty.' Peter slumped in a chair next to Dan in the mobile HQ.

'You did well to get it verified so quickly.'

'Connections,' Peter said.

'Where's Trevor?'

'I left him with Lyn Sullivan on his ward. Chris Brooke is outside his door.'

'Brooke called me on his radio at nine-forty-five,' Dan poured out coffee for both of them.

Peter picked up the cup. 'It takes, what, ten minutes to walk from the front gate to where Trevor was found?'

'Five,' Dan corrected.

'Ten in his present state,' Peter argued. 'Which leaves Trevor with five minutes to discover, mutilate and rape a corpse – I don't buy that it was simply lying there. And just mutilating that corpse would be a tall order for someone in Trevor's condition. And where do you find a corpse anyway?'

'In a mortuary,' Dan replied automatically.

'Of course. The mortuary here.'

'Where are you going?' Dan called after him. The door banged behind Peter as he left the room. Dan picked up the telephone and dialled the number for Compton Castle's administration.

Peter saw the lights on in the mortuary in the General as he parked outside and he blessed Patrick's conscientiousness. He'd guessed that Patrick wouldn't leave this PM until the morning but he had to bang the door three times before Patrick's assistant, tired and bleary eyed, opened the door and let him in.

Patrick was working down at the far end of the room.

'Peter, what a pleasant, unexpected surprise. How is Trevor?' Patrick tossed a ball of cotton wool into a bin at the top of the slab.

'Sleeping I hope.'

'Tell him what he's come here to hear.' Patrick said to his assistant, who was fiddling with a row of test-tubes on a side bench.

'We found only one blood group. Sergeant Joseph's.'

'His blood was on his sweater, the anorak, and the sheet that covered the victim.'

'She wasn't dressed?'

'Just wrapped in a sheet and a shroud. As I said, she'd been dead for at least two days. And Trevor's blood group doesn't match the semen I found in the corpse's vagina,' he added. 'I've sent the sample for DNA analysis to see if there is a match on file. Whoever our necrophilia dabbler is, it isn't Joseph.'

Lyn Sullivan felt uneasy. She spent most of the night checking and double checking her patients, pausing first at Vanessa's empty bed, then Michael Carpenter's, and finally outside Trevor Joseph's door, which was still guarded by a policeman. Mercifully, her other patients slept peacefully, unperturbed by the two empty beds in their ward.

She wondered what had happened. The police had told her nothing but it was rumoured that another corpse had been found. The officer in the ward refused to confirm that it was another murder, but if it was, that

265

would mean Michael Carpenter wasn't the killer. And there were Trevor's injuries. Sergeant Collins had been angry when she'd asked about them, but, she reflected, Sergeant Collins was always angry.

The trainee made coffee at four-thirty, and Lyn took hers into the office. She didn't bother to switch on the light. Instead she opened the blinds and stood in darkness looking out over the hospital grounds. The police were patrolling the area, shining lights, presumably watching and waiting for – what? Michael Carpenter's ghost to appear? Or someone else? Someone who still prowled free.

If Michael wasn't the killer, was the murderer here in the hospital, now, tonight? Were the police hoping that he would run the gauntlet of guards in an attempt to bury Vanessa the same way he'd buried the others?

Lyn pictured Michael, his shy diffident grin, and instinctively knew that he hadn't killed the women buried in the grounds. He had been a sly peeping tom, not a cold blooded murderer who shovelled earth on top of living, breathing beings. But if it wasn't Michael, then who?

She gazed out again at the floodlit lawns, shrubberies and high walls that hemmed in the grounds. Above the brickwork she could see the top storey of one of the halfway houses. Its curtains were open, the lights on, and the tall, dark silhouette of Spencer Jordan paced back and forth between two rooms. She wondered what was keeping him awake. Indigestion, or something more sinister?

She looked to the left, towards the old hospital. There were lights on in the administration block, and she wondered if Tony Waters was working. Was something more than pressure of work keeping him awake? A guilty conscience perhaps? Shuddering, she finished her coffee.

She was being foolish. Seeing bogeymen under every bed, as she had never done even as a child. Was there anyone she didn't suspect in the hospital? Tony? Spencer? Karl? Adam Hayter? –

'Why stand in the dark?'

The lights clicked on behind her, and she closed her eyes against the sudden brightness. Karl moved over to join her at the window.

'I wanted peace and quiet.'

'And I want to apologise for last night.' Hauled over the coals early that morning for not reporting Vanessa's absence as soon as Lyn had alerted him, he felt low and miserable. Particularly at Tony's threat to demote him. But then he'd remembered Lyn, how angry she'd been, and how his life, and not only his sex life, had improved since she'd been around, so he'd decided to make an effort to reinstate their relationship. 'I'm sorry. You were right and I was wrong.' Confident his apology would be accepted as soon as it was made, he slid his arm around her waist.

The feel of Karl's warm fingers clamped against her cool flesh irked Lyn. She moved away.

'Didn't you hear? I said I'm sorry.'

'I heard you.'

'Lyn, we've all been under a terrible strain for the past few days. All this upset with police, and bodies, and two patients on your ward involved… '

'And now another one,' she said coldly.

He looked at her blankly.

'Haven't you heard? Another corpse was found in the grounds tonight.'

'I didn't know. How… who… ?'

'The police won't elaborate. They only said they'd found another corpse. Apparently Trevor Joseph arrived at the scene before anyone else. He was hurt… '

'I haven't heard any of this. I've been working on Drugs and Alcohol. Roland went wild tonight. It took four of us to get him to bed, even with a tranquilliser.'

She continued to stare out of the window, although all she could see with the lights on was their reflection in the glass.

'I thought we had something good going between us… '

'So did I,' she interrupted.

'Don't let a stupid row end something as special as us. I was hoping that we… '

'What, Karl?'

'Move in together,' he suggested. 'I… '

'That "I" is the reason I'll never move in with you, Karl. There will only ever be one "I" in any relationship you're involved in.'

'That's unfair.'

'Is it?' Her grey eyes blazed. 'What about yesterday? You think an apology is enough for the way you put me down?'

'Lyn, I'm the senior nursing office. I have to make decisions. I can't let personal considerations interfere with the running of this hospital.'

'Personal considerations? All I asked you to do was report a patient missing from my ward.'

'And she was reported missing.'

'Not until a fire broke out.'

'A fire that someone deliberately set.'

'I was on break.'

'Very convenient… '

'I don't have to listen to this.' She tried to pass him, but he grabbed her arm.

'Lyn, please, let's not quarrel.'

'Let me go!'

'You're hysterical.'

'I'm not.'

'Just listen to yourself. Lyn, it's all right. I understand. You're safe with me. No one's going to hurt you.' He wrapped an arm around her shoulders, and she cried out. The door burst open and Dan barged in.

'I'm sorry.' Embarrassed at breaking in on what he took to be a lover's tiff, he said, 'I wanted to check on Trevor.'

'I was just about to do that, Inspector Evans.' Lyn brushed past him on her way through the door.

'This murder business is stretching everyone's nerves to breaking point,' Karl complained.

'So I see,' Dan agreed softly.

CHAPTER NINETEEN

Edith Jenkins hummed the latest coffee advert ditty to herself as she whirled the electric polisher across the vinyl floor in the corridor.

'You're happy today, Edith.' Jean called out as she pushed the drugs trolley down the ward.

'Got to make the effort, haven't you?' the cleaner shouted above the noise of the machine.

'Could you give the four-bedded ward at the end of the corridor a going over and the single room as well, please,' Jean asked. 'Both are empty.'

'The four-bed is empty?' Edith checked in surprise.

'We had a reshuffle; moved everyone out of there and into the other wards.' Jean didn't want to talk about what had happened to Vanessa or Michael although she didn't doubt that the cleaner knew and had hoped to coax more information out of her.

Edith pushed her polisher to the end of the corridor and entered the four-bed ward. With no patients underfoot, she finished the floor in a quarter of an hour. She changed from the coffee jingle to a few bars of a chocolate advert's background music. She was ahead of herself this morning. The corridor and one room done, and it wasn't half past eight. She wouldn't be able to press ahead with the rest of the rooms for another ten minutes until everyone was at breakfast and out of her way. But there was still that empty room at the end. She hadn't been in there for over a week and it was bound to be dusty. Wheeling the polisher in front of her, she passed Sister Marshall who was dishing out painkillers to the nice young policeman in the first room. Putting her back against the door, she depressed the handle and swung around to enter.

The smell sent her reeling back into the corridor, a rotting stink that reminded her of the time a mouse had died behind the skirting boards of her flat and her husband had to rip the place apart to find it. She scanned the floor. Whatever and wherever it was, maintenance could deal with it. Her job description was cleaner, and cleaners cleaned; they didn't look for dead animals or carry them out of rooms.

Coughing and spluttering she went to the window and opened it wide. Edith didn't look at the bed until she turned around. Then she screamed.

Andrew Murphy, who'd been told to stay with Trevor until Bill could interview him, reached the room the same time as Jean. Trevor hobbled behind them, leaning on a stick Jean had found for him.

Overpowered by the stench, Murphy caught the hysterical cleaner in his arms, and stepped back.

'A body?' Trevor already knew the answer. One of the first things he had come to recognise after joining the force had been the smell of death.

'A ripe one.' Murphy's reply brought on a fresh fit of hysterics from Edith.

'It looks like – ' Jean clasped her hand over her mouth.

'Vanessa?' Trevor suggested.

She nodded.

'Phone HQ and tell them to get over here.' Trevor automatically assuming command, despite his battered state. 'I'll keep everyone away until Patrick arrives.' He looked into the room from the doorway. Lead trailing, the polisher stood at the foot of the bed. The curtains and window were wide open. Careful not to step any further than Murphy had done, he leaned forward. All he could see was a section of black, bloated face beneath a mop of blonde hair. 'Have you a tissue?' he asked Jean.

She took a pack from her pocket and handed him one. Wrapping it around his fingers, he gingerly pulled the door closed.

The cleaner began to wail again.

Jean gazed mutely at Trevor.

'We can't do anything until the pathologist arrives.' Trevor stood in front of the door. 'When was this room last used?'

'I gave that room a good going over only last week,' Edith whispered as soon as she'd recovered enough to speak. 'It's not used often.'

Jean helped the ashen-faced cleaner across the corridor and into the sluice. Edith sank on a chair. Trevor had left his bed so quickly his legs were beginning to give way beneath him. Jean looked at him and pressed a buzzer to summon help.

'Bring a chair down here,' Jean shouted to the auxiliary who'd answered her call. 'Quickly, before Trevor keels over.'

The young woman ran off into the day room and dragged out an unwieldy armchair. Jean pushed it in front of the door leading into the single room, and helped Trevor into it.

'Look at those drag marks you've made on my nice clean floor,' Edith cried. 'Just look – '

'It doesn't matter.' Jean handed the auxiliary her keys. 'Fetch a brandy for Edith. The bottle's in the medicine cupboard in my office.'

'Brandy?' Edith perked up.

'You've had a nasty shock,' Jean said wryly. She turned to Trevor. 'Do you want a drink?'

'It wouldn't go well with my thumping headache.'

'The painkillers I gave you should start working soon.'

'That's good to know.' He looked impatiently down the corridor. 'Where the hell has Murphy got to?'

'He's probably outside. Mobile signal is lousy in the ward.'

The auxiliary returned with the brandy. Jean left Edith in her care and went to Trevor.

Peter strode in, Andrew at his heels. 'I presume it's Vanessa Hedley?'

'Looks like it,' Trevor answered.

'He's made us look a right load of Charlies this time. While we were all creeping around the grounds and searching the old hospital, he calmly walks in here to dispose of his latest victim.'

The staff canteen was full to bursting. Every chair was taken except the five ranged at a table on a dais at the far end of the room. The heat was overpowering, as was the din of conversation.

Tony Waters stood in the doorway. 'I didn't expect to see the night-shift here. I assumed they'd come to this evening's meeting.'

'They're scared and they're hoping to find out something that will make them less scared,' Peter pushed his way through to join Bill, Dan and the police officers at the back of the hall.

'Safety in numbers,' Harry Goldman joined them. 'One of their neighbours might be a murderer, but the chances are it won't be more than one.'

'We should start,' Bill went to the table and motioned Dan, Peter, Harry and Tony forward.

'I did tell everyone ten-thirty,' Tony reminded.

'The room is full to bursting now.' Bill took the centre seat, Dan and Peter sat on his right, leaving Tony and Harry Goldman the other two chairs.

'Would you like to begin?' Bill asked Tony.

Tony rose and tapped the microphone that had been set up. A hollow boom echoed around the packed room. 'This meeting... ' he had to repeat himself three times before the noise subsided and he could make himself heard. 'This meeting has been called to put an end to the wild rumours that are sweeping this hospital. I don't need to remind you how unsettling the present atmosphere is for our patients. It negates everything we are trying to accomplish here. There is no need for panic, but we should all take some simple precautions to ensure our personal safety and the safety of our patients; and we should also assist the police in every way we can,' he acknowledged Bill and Dan, 'so they can resolve this unpleasant situation quickly. Inspector Evans?' He poured a glass of water from the carafe and took a sip before sitting down.

It was Bill not Dan who took the microphone.

Peter muttered 'If he calls murder unpleasant, what would he call a massacre?'

'Offensive,' Dan suggested.

'The man's a total prat,' Peter continued. 'Four dead bodies, five if you count the dog, and the man tells his staff not to panic. How many more does this idiot want?'

'Ssh,' Dan hissed, conscious of heads turning in their direction.

Bill pulled the microphone towards him. Unlike Tony he didn't enjoy public speaking, and he elected to

274

remain seated. 'I will give you as many of the facts of this case as I can without jeopardising our investigation. Four women have been murdered, and the corpse of a patient was found in the grounds last night. However, it has been proved beyond doubt that she died of natural causes two days ago. Her body was removed from the mortuary here and if any of you can shed any light on this macabre theft, Mr Waters would be glad to hear from you.'

Dan left his seat and pulled a sheet of paper from a board that stood beside the table, uncovering a photograph of one of the victims. He pointed to it while Bill spoke.

'Rosie Twyford, the first victim to be discovered buried in the grounds, but not the first to be murdered. We believe she was abducted last week. The last sighting we have of her was when she kept her last appointment at the outpatient clinic of this hospital on Monday afternoon. We think that she was kept hidden – possibly in the hospital – until Saturday night when she was murdered.'

Silence reigned thickly in the atmosphere.

'She was buried alive,' Bill said flatly, 'after being drugged with tranquillisers and barbiturates. After we disinterred the body of Rosie Twyford, a thorough search of the hospital grounds yielded two more victims. Inspector Evans.'

Dan revealed a second photograph.

'This is the girl we believe to be the first murder victim. She was killed four or five months ago, again, she was an ex in and outpatient, Claire Moon.'

Everyone in the room focused on the smiling image of the pretty young girl with soft grey eyes and long dark hair.

'Approximately two months after Claire Moon was murdered, the killer buried an Elizabeth Moore.'

A gasp tore through the assembly when Dan unveiled another photograph. Compton Castle wasn't so large that the name or face went unrecognised, even three months after Elizabeth Moore had left.

'Claire Moon and Rosie Twyford were both patients,' Bill continued. 'Both suffered from depression, and both had attempted suicide. Elizabeth Moore was a nurse. One of the most alarming aspects about the disappearance of all three victims is that none of them were missed immediately and no connection was made between their disappearance and this hospital. Claire Moon was the only one of the three to be reported missing, and her parents believed that she'd disappeared some time after leaving Compton Castle. Rosie Twyford's parents would undoubtedly have reported her missing in due course, but probably they, like Claire Moon's parents, would have assumed that she had disappeared after leaving the hospital. Elizabeth Moore was divorced, her friends and family believed she was in America and too busy to contact them. I believe that we are dealing with a calculating, cold-blooded killer who chooses his victims with care,' Bill said flatly. 'An hour ago we found the body of the only witness to Rosie Twyford's burial, Vanessa Hedley.'

Everyone's attention again turned to the board as Dan uncovered Vanessa's photograph.

'You knew she was a witness, why didn't you protect her?' a porter demanded.

'We tried,' Bill's excuse sounded lame even to his own ears.

'You obviously didn't try hard enough,' an angry voice shouted.

Bill ignored the interruption. 'She disappeared from her ward during the late afternoon, when the day room was full of patients, and the ward was staffed with the half-hour overlap of shift change. I'd like every one of you to think just where she could have been held captive for the past week. If it was outside the hospital, I'd like to know exactly how she was spirited in and out of the grounds through the security barriers… '

'Which weren't erected until twelve hours after she disappeared,' Peter glared at Tony Waters.

'If she was held somewhere within Compton Castle I find it difficult to believe that a fully-grown woman could be concealed here without someone in this room knowing about it. I want all of you,' Bill hit the table with his fist, 'to go over your movements during the last week. Did any of you see Vanessa, on one of the other wards? Did you pass her in a corridor? Was she being pushed on a trolley or in a wheelchair by someone you didn't recognise? Or by someone you did? Someone who knows the hospital and has free access to the wards and buildings took her, hid her, possibly killed her – we're awaiting the results of the PM – and placed her in the room where she was discovered. We are doing all we can to trace that person or persons.'

'You think more than one person could be involved?' Tony Waters asked.

'We're keeping an open mind,' Bill answered. 'Any of you who has something to report, please go to one of the tables at the side of the room, where officers are waiting to take your statements. And please remember, no matter how small and insignificant you think your contribution; it might just be the vital piece of evidence we need to bring this case to a conclusion.'

'Shouldn't we close the hospital?' one of the domestic staff asked. 'None of us are safe with this murderer on the loose.'

'Inspector Evans will reassure you on that point.' Taking the coward's way out, Bill handed over to Dan.

Soon Dan's slow Welsh drawl could be heard in every corner of the room. Unlike Bill and Tony he didn't use the microphone.

'It would be pointless to close the hospital, because we'd have to find alternative accommodation for everyone here, and if the killer is a patient or member of staff, we'd only be transferring our problem, not solving it.'

'That makes sense,' a voice drifted up from the front row.

'You are all aware of the strong police presence in the hospital,' Dan said. 'We have stationed officers alongside the security guards at the gates and in the car park. Please co-operate with the routine searches of all vehicles entering and leaving these premises. I apologise for any delays, and would like to thank all of you for your co-operation and patience. A few words of advice, walk to and from your wards in threes and fours if you can, not pairs. If you must drive to the hospital, arrange a car pool so you arrive in a full car. Threes are good, fours are better. If you have to drive into the car park alone, do not walk to your ward alone, no matter what the time of day. Wait until the duty police officer assigns you to a group. While working on your ward, stay in constant touch with the other staff... '

'What happens if there's only one member of staff on a ward at night?' Jean asked.

'We have a minimum of four staff members working on a ward at any given time,' Tony insisted.

'Only in theory,' Alan contradicted. 'Even during the day we can drop to one if two staff take a meal break and another has to take a patient to therapy. And at night, if someone's sick we're often down to one.'

'If there are problems get on the phone to me, and I'll get an agency nurse over,' Tony replied.

'At night?' Alan persisted.

'I'll look at the staffing ratios after this meeting. If there's a shortage I'll book extra agency nurses.'

'Halleluiah!' Jean said loudly.

'There'll be a police presence close to every nurses' hostel, every ward, throughout the grounds, and in the old hospital building,' Dan said. 'And the Trust is issuing every member of staff, male and female, with personal alarms. If you should see something suspicious, use it. I'd rather see a red-faced person who's tripped up and accidentally set it off than another corpse.'

'What about the patients?' Alan asked.

'Mr Waters is arranging for headcounts to be carried out every two hours.'

A series of groans greeted his words.

'I know it'll be a bind.' Dan held his hands up for silence. 'But Mr Goldman convinced us that it isn't practical to issue the patients with alarms.' A burst of laughter rocked the room. 'If you could all make your way to one of the tables, where you will be issued with your alarm, and be able to make a statement to one of the officers... '

'And a good time was had by all.' Peter watched the queues form.

One woman, alarm in hand, hesitated for a moment in front of the door. Trevor, who had stood at the side of the hall with the constables, noticed her hanging back.

'Can I help you?' he asked.

'You're Sergeant Joseph, aren't you? I'm Angela Morgan, Tony Waters' secretary.' She glanced over her shoulder to check that her boss was still engrossed in his discussion with Bill. 'Could you give Inspector Evans a message for me?' she continued nervously. 'Tell him I'll meet him after work today – but not in the Green Monkey, in – in the – '

'Where do you live?' Trevor interrupted.

'The marina.'

'How about the pump house on the marina at six?'

'It may be nothing but… '

'The Inspector will be there.'

'Thank you.' Clutching her personal alarm she hurried out of the door.

Dan took Peter to the pub with him. They walked in at a quarter to six and Peter picked up the menu.

'We're working,' Dan rebuked.

'And I'm starving. There's no rule that says a copper can't eat during an interview.'

'All right,' Dan capitulated. 'If they do sandwiches, I'll have one too.'

'Leave it to me.' Peter went to the bar and ordered two twelve-ounce steaks, with chips and peas, and two pints of beer, while Dan sat at a secluded corner table.

'What's the cutlery for?' Dan asked suspiciously when Peter returned.

'Open sandwiches.' Peter lied.

They'd almost finished their beers when Angela Morgan turned up at ten minutes past six, with her husband.

'Sorry I'm late, Sergeant… '

'Peter,' he corrected, recognising a press reporter at the bar. He rose to his feet. 'What are you drinking?'

'I hope you don't mind me bringing my husband,' she gabbled nervously. 'It's just that – '

'Not at all,' Collins interrupted, wishing the woman would shut up before she attracted any more attention. 'What are you drinking?' he repeated.

'I'll have a...' she gazed blankly at the rows of bottles behind the bar.

'A sweet white wine and a beer,' her husband volunteered for both of them.

Peter heard her piercing voice, as he ordered the drinks.

'I hope you don't mind me bringing my husband, Inspector Evans. I brought him along for moral support – and I wasn't sure what I should tell you. It's not as if I have any actual proof. It's just that – well I don't know what you'd make of it.'

'What exactly is it that you want to tell us, Mrs Morgan?' Dan Evans pressed.

'Well, it's all those girls, isn't it?' she whispered in response to a gesture from Dan.

'The victims?' Dan guessed.

'He knew them all.' She lowered her voice again so Dan and Peter, who'd returned with the drinks, had to bend their heads to catch what she was saying. 'They were all special to him in one way or another. Every one of them. And if you want my opinion,' her voice was now so low that they found it a strain to listen to her, 'he was having affairs with all three of them. At different times, that is.'

CHAPTER TWENTY

Angela fell silent as the waitress set two large oval plates overflowing with steak and chips on to the table.

'Sauce, vinegar, salt?' the girl enquired pleasantly.

'Nothing, thank you.' Dan was annoyed at the interruption and Peter's interpretation of "sandwich". But Peter's attention was riveted on the first decent meal he'd seen in days.

'I'll have vinegar, salt and English mustard if you've got it, love.' He winked at the waitress. 'Would you like something?' Peter asked the Morgans, the food in front of him making him uncharacteristically generous.

'I put a casserole in the oven,' Angela said distractedly.

'I presume that you were telling us about Mr Waters,' Dan prompted.

'Mr Waters has a roving eye. And it's a pity – for the girls who get involved with him, I mean.' Angela wrapped her fingers around the glass of wine that Peter had bought her. 'It's not as if there's only the one, or that he cared, really cared, for any of them. He couldn't, could he?'

'Why not?' Peter asked, in between mouthfuls of steak.

'Being married. But they all telephoned him… '

'Did you ever listen in on their conversations?' Dan interrupted.

'No, that wouldn't be right!' she exclaimed, affronted by the suggestion.

'Never inadvertently overheard anything?' Peter offered her a legitimate excuse.

'No.'

'Yet you're sure he was having affairs with all three women?' Dan pushed three fat chips on to his fork.

'There was the staff party last Christmas, when some of the nurses caught him and… '

'And who?' Peter asked when she fell silent.

'No one would say, but everyone had their suspicions. He was caught en flagrante as it were – stark naked in one of the rooms at the top of the old building – and – ' She turned crimson.

'And?' Peter pumped mercilessly.

'Who saw them?' Dan asked when she didn't reply.

'I can't remember all of them, but one was that pretty nurse who works on the ward your friend's on.'

'Jean?' Dan suggested.

'No, the young one.'

'Lyn Sullivan?' Peter supplied.

'That's her.'

Dan took out his notebook and wrote down the name.

'Sounds like damning evidence of adultery to me,' Peter stopped long enough to down the remainder of his beer.

'It's his wife I feel sorry for.' Angela shook her head. 'She's so pretty. And they've got everything. Beautiful house – you wouldn't believe how beautiful. Not that I've been inside, but I've seen pictures, and heard what other people say about it.'

'You've told us about what might have been a one night stand. What makes you think Tony Waters had affairs with all three victims?' Dan asked.

'The first one, Rosie Twyford, he used to take her home. I was sick for four months. I had a hysterectomy. I was ever so poorly… '

'And Rosie?' Dan steered the conversation back on course.

'Rosie Twyford was personal assistant to Mr Chalmers, and he was made redundant the same time I had my operation. So, she was sent down to cover for me. The girls who came to visit me in hospital used to joke that I wouldn't have a job to come back to because Rosie and Mr Waters were getting very friendly. He used to take her home after they both worked late.'

'Do you often work late?' Peter intervened.

'Not now,' Angela informed him. 'Not with all the cutbacks, but we did then. It was just after we – the department that is – moved out of County Hall. I think that's why I had to have the hysterectomy. It was lifting all those heavy boxes… '

'And Rosie Twyford used to work late along with Mr Waters?' Dan cut her short again.

'She told the girls they were straightening the office. But when I came back to work and she had to return to the general office she had a nervous breakdown. Rumour had it because he'd lost interest in her. But when she was ill, he sent her flowers… '

'Wouldn't any boss do that?' Dan asked.

'I suppose so,' she agreed grudgingly.

'Did he send you flowers when you were ill?' Peter lifted the last piece of steak to his mouth.

'Yes,' she admitted. 'But, it's not just Rosie Twyford. There's Claire Moon. Her father was important, and when that Sunday newspaper came to do a feature about her, Mr Waters took a great deal of interest in it.'

'Wouldn't that be because he was wary about what the papers would print about the hospital?' Dan sprinkled salt on to his chips.

'That's what I said.' Mr Morgan spoke for the first time since he and his wife had sat down.

'But he used to walk around the grounds with her every chance he got,' Angela protested. 'And a lot of people said that Elizabeth Moore was the nurse he was seen with at the staff party.'

'I thought you said no one knew who it was?' Dan reminded her.

'Not for certain,' Angela conceded. 'But whoever she was, she had auburn hair and when I saw all three photographs up there, side by side this afternoon, I knew I had to talk to you. And Carol Ashford…'

'Is she the jealous sort?' Peter stared at his empty plate.

'I wouldn't say that,' Angela sipped her wine.

'Does she often visit your offices to see Mr Waters?' Dan asked.

'Hardly ever. If she does, it's only because of work.'

'Do you think she knows about her husband's philandering?' Peter pushed his plate aside.

'She must do, mustn't she?' Angela added as if she had only just considered the idea. 'After all, it's common gossip around the hospital.'

'Would you tell her?' Dan asked.

Angela looked at him vacantly.

'Not many people would be prepared to tell a wife when her husband strays,' Peter explained.

'I suppose they wouldn't,' she conceded.

'Is there anything else you can think of? Anything you've seen, or heard?' Dan was still hoping for some hard facts.

'You promise what I say will be treated in confidence?'

'Yes,' Dan assured her.

'Well, there is one other thing,' she glanced at her husband. He turned away. 'When Mrs Hedley first went missing, Mr Waters wouldn't let anyone go into the electricity sub station in the cellar. I heard him have a real set-to with the engineer from the electricity people about it. But he still wouldn't let him in.'

'What do you think?' Dan asked Peter after Angela Morgan and her husband had gone home for their casserole and a night of television. The two officers were sitting back nursing fresh pints of beer.

'I think she's genuinely concerned,' Peter handed Dan one of his cigars.

'Concerned and agitated enough to put two and two together and make eight.'

'Probably. But if I were in charge of this investigation I'd get the forensic team to check the sub station all the same.'

'I wouldn't ask if we weren't stretched, Trevor. And I'll get one of our men patrolling the grounds to call in every hour and check you're all right.'

'I'll do it.' Trevor was amused to think that Bill, who last night had been prepared to believe he was a rapist and murderer, was now asking him to sit up all night to keep an eye on the ward.

'Upstairs is demanding results.' Mulcahy justified his request, although Trevor had neither asked for, nor expected an explanation. 'It might be helpful if you came to the briefing. Nine-thirty, in the mobile HQ.'

'What about the ward when I'm at the briefing?'

'I've two extra bodies assigned to every shift. I'll see that one of them is here.' Bill left Trevor's room and headed down the tunnel towards the old part of the hospital.

'So you are working?'

Trevor turned to see Lyn in the corridor outside his room. 'What makes you say that?'

'Senior policemen in the middle of murder investigations don't have time to make social calls to the sick.'

'If it was anything other than a case on the doorstep I wouldn't have been drafted in. But after what happened to Vanessa, it's all hands to the pumps.'

'In case he strikes again?'

Trevor didn't answer.

'You think he will strike again?'

'Your guess is as good as mine.'

'It's horrible to think that someone could be out there watching us.' She looked past him and stared out of the window.

'You have every right to be terrified.'

'I'm not usually jumpy. It's just that since Michael climbed up on to my window – and that meeting when I realised – '

'When you realised that all four victims spent some on this ward?' he guessed.

'The corpse in the garden last night didn't help.'

'It didn't help anyone,' he instinctively put a hand to his head.

'Was that the murderer?'

'We don't know,' he said honestly. 'No one saw anything except me, and I only spotted the body after it had been laid on the ground. But from now on you will have me and my trusty weapon to protect you.' He lifted the walking-stick Bill had returned to him. 'And I give you my most solemn promise, Nurse Sullivan, that I won't allow anything to happen to you. Is that a good enough guarantee?'

'As no one has offered me anything better, I'll accept it, Sergeant Joseph.' She walked across his room and closed the blinds against the twilight. 'How about I make both of us a cup of coffee?'

'It might work,' Bill said cautiously.

'It's the most harebrained suggestion I've heard of,' Peter snorted. He and Dan had been in the mobile HQ for ten minutes, and already two of the girls in the outer office had gone off to take an early tea break, out of earshot of Peter and Bill's argument.

Bill folded his arms across his chest. 'Let's see you come up with something better, Peter.'

'When has a killer ever been caught by a ruse as basic as that outside of a TV show?' Peter derided. 'The only way we're going to nail this villain is with police work. Dull, boring, routine police work.'

'Our psychiatrist says… '

'I might have known that one of your bloody Home Office shrinks dreamed up this one. Has he ever left his snug office and taken a short holiday in the real world?'

'Shut up and listen for once in your life,' Bill roared. 'We've been talking… '

'Who's we?' Peter demanded. 'Dan and I weren't consulted in any of this.'

'The "we" being your superiors,' Bill informed him icily. 'This case has developed a press profile almost as large as your bloody ego. We have to be seen to be doing something.'

'By the press?' Peter sneered. 'That's bloody marvellous. You put someone in undercover in the hope of flushing out a killer, then you call a press conference?'

'Not the press,' Bill bellowed. 'By the men upstairs and the Trust… '

'Great. They sit on their backsides in an upholstered office, while we send some poor sod out as bait to catch a killer. Just remember Harries while you update those suits on our progress or lack of it. He proved great bloody bait, didn't he? We didn't even find enough of him to bury.' Peter referred to the last high profile case that had almost cost Trevor his life and had cost another officer his.

'That was unfortunate…'

'Unfortunate?' Collins reiterated. 'You're talking to the officer who had to scrape what was left of Harries off his shoes.' He took a cigar from his top pocket, and pushed it between his lips. 'I know I'm talking to the mentally deficient…'

'One day you'll go too far, Peter, even for me.'

Peter softened his voice, but the anger remained etched in his eyes. 'Who's won the lucky draw this time?'

'We decided on more than one. We thought we'd try a member of the hospital staff as well as a patient.' Bill looked at Peter, expecting another outburst. When none came, he continued in a quieter vein. 'We went through all the staff profiles looking for someone we could eliminate completely from our suspects.'

'And?'

'It wasn't easy. But Jean Marshall was with Trevor in the Greek Restaurant at the time of Vanessa Hedley's disappearance.'

'Pity you didn't remember that last night,' Peter said frostily. 'If you had, you might have saved Trevor some trouble.'

'We called her in earlier,' Bill ignored Peter's barbs. 'We explained what we're trying to do, then asked if she'd hand in her resignation, to take effect from a week today.'

289

'Does anyone in the hospital have a clue as to what you're up to?' Peter asked.

'No one besides Jean Marshall and these four walls.'

'Not Harry Goldman or Tony Waters?'

'No one,' Bill repeated. 'The story is that she's decided to go to Canada, to spend a year with her married sister who lives out there.'

'Does she have a married sister in Canada?'

'Yes.'

'And you expect everyone to swallow that?'

'Everyone already has.'

'Who's shadowing her?'

'Michelle Grady.'

'She's not even out of kindergarten. The girl's worse than useless. She thinks in terms of brownie badges.'

'There'll be other back-up.'

'Of the same kind Harries had?'

It was one crack too many. 'If I were you I'd be looking to my stripes, Sergeant.' Bill's voice and temper rose precariously.

'You said there was going to be more?'

'Yes,' Bill replied shortly. 'We're putting someone else in the same ward as Joseph.'

'Who?'

'Sarah Merchant. She volunteered,' Bill added, in an attempt to pre-empt Peter's objections.

'You do know she was Harries' girlfriend?'

'I didn't,' Bill admitted.

'She could have volunteered because she's feeling suicidal – have you thought of that?'

'She passed the psychological test.'

'A bloody child of two could run rings around our psychologists. The test questions are so damned obvious,

290

they're farcical. Isn't it enough that her boyfriend died last year, without you trying to kill her too?'

'No one is going to die.' Bill leaned across the table. 'We've three people inside the ward; Jean, Sarah, and Trevor who's a trained detective… '

'A sick, physically frail and unfit detective, who was your number-one suspect yesterday,' Peter reminded.

'We have men everywhere, ready to provide back-up at a split second's notice. In the grounds, in the old hospital, outside the ward.'

'For how long?'

'Two weeks,' Bill admitted reluctantly. 'If nothing happens by then, we have orders to run down the manpower working on this case.'

Peter propped his feet on a metal waste-bin. 'So if our villain gets frightened off by this activity, all he has to do is go to ground for a fortnight. Afterwards he can go back to burying the remaining complement of patients and staff whenever he feels like it. I've another theory for you. He – whoever he is – could be an undercover agent for the Trust. His mission being to save them a fortune in redundancy pay for the staff, and relocation expenses for the patients. They'll probably pay him a bonus and still be quids in when he buries the last inmate of this nut house. Then all the Trust needs do is warn the re-developer not to dig down deeper than six foot when they build the upmarket housing estate that'll replace this place. And bingo, the new residents on this site will get an added bonus of well fertilised gardens.'

'You're sick, Peter. Sick and twisted. When this case is over, I'm putting you up for transfer,' Bill threatened.

'Promises,' Peter glared at Bill. 'Bloody promises, that's all I ever get.'

'One day you're going to argue yourself out of a job,' Dan cautioned Peter after Bill had left the HQ.

Peter struck a match to light his cigar. 'Ten years of trying, and I still haven't pushed Bill far enough to get near commonsense. Have you phoned forensics about that sub-station?'

Dan shook his head and reached for the telephone. Mulcahy had been right about Peter. He was good, but he was also hell to work with.

'Your people have searched every inch of this cellar three times this week.' Arnold Massey, head of a maintenance staff that had shrunk from fifteen to two over the past five years, complained.

'Between you and me, we've had a tip-off,' Peter said. 'And if we don't act on tip-offs, everyone starts breathing down our necks. Press, politicians, higher ups, Joe public, and all.'

'I can imagine,' the man agreed, slightly mollified by the confidence.

Dan, who was following Peter with the technician from forensics, wondered why Peter never bothered to soft-soap the brass the way he did the public. A tenth of the patience he'd expended on Arnold would have transformed his relationship with Bill. But he'd discovered that Peter was a Jekyll and Hyde personality, and, as his temporary partner, he was grateful for the times when Jekyll surfaced – like now.

'This cellar goes on forever,' the forensic expert shifted his heavy case from one hand to the other.

'Over half a mile from end to end,' Arnold informed him. 'And two miles of passages in total.' He ducked his head beneath a bridge of grimy central-heating pipes. 'This is your sub-station.'

They halted in front of a securely locked iron door set in a solid brick wall. 'By rights I suppose I should have called the electricity people... '

'There's no need,' Peter tested the door. 'The fewer people involved, the less the risk of contamination. You do know enough to tell us what's safe or unsafe for us to touch?' he checked.

'Ay, I know that much. And most of the dangerous stuff is labelled.' Arnold pulled an enormous bunch of keys from his pocket and unlocked one of several locks on the door. It took him five minutes to find the keys needed to unfasten the second and third locks. He opened the door, slipped his hand inside and switched on the light. 'It's all yours.'

The lighting was brighter inside the sub-station than it was in the corridor. Peter and Dan stared at an array of dials, switches, and gleaming black paraphernalia that meant nothing to them.

'It's all right to go inside,' Arnold assured them. 'Just be careful with anything that's labelled in red. And don't pull any switches, or you'll black out the wards.'

'Floor's not dusty,' the technician observed.

'As I said, your people have been in and out of this place like yo-yos this week,' Arnold reminded.

Peter stepped gingerly inside and looked around. 'Who else has keys to this place?' he asked Arnold.

'Electricity people, but they don't have keys to the building so they can't come down here without one of us knowing about it.'

'One of "us" being maintenance?' Dan asked.

'Or administration. Mr Waters has master keys in his office.'

'Including this sub-station?'

'Of course. He'd need them, wouldn't he, in case of emergency.'

'I suppose so,' Dan said slowly, beginning to think that all the clues on this case seemed to lead back to Tony Waters.

'Where do you want to start?' the technician called to Dan, from inside the sub-station.

'You're the one with experience, wherever you like,' Dan replied.

'Floor up, or ceiling down? Front to back, or back to front?'

'How about ceiling down, back to front,' Peter walked to the end wall and looked back.

Nothing larger than a shoe box could have been hidden above ground level, but when they examined the floor, Dan saw distinct possibilities. It was covered with heavy metal plates, each a foot wide and three feet long. It took the combined strength of Peter and the technician to move them and underneath was a gap more than a foot deep.

'You could hide a corpse in there,' Dan said.

'A thin one,' Peter agreed. He looked to the forensics expert. 'What do you think?'

'I'll get out my kit.'

Dan and Peter removed the rest of the plates, carried them out into the corridor and propped them against the cellar wall, while the technician set to work. He opened bottles, arranged test tubes to hold any specimens he might find, donned rubber gloves, slipped rubber socks over his shoes, and stepped out on to the narrow cement band surrounding the newly opened floor. Crouching on hands and knees he began to check the area, centimetre by centimetre, with his magnifying glass.

'Cigar?' Collins pulled a packet from the top pocket of his shirt and offered them to Arnold and Dan.

'Don't mind if I do.' Arnold took one, and held it in his mouth as Peter lit it. 'Do you think you'll strike lucky?'

'We can hope,' Dan leaned against the wall.

'If I were you I'd take a closer look at the therapists,' Arnold suggested.

'Why?' Peter asked.

'I'd want to know why that big man – the one who's lost an eye… '

'Spencer Jordan?' Peter asked.

'I'd want to know why he's taken to carrying women's clothes around with him.'

'Are you sure?' Dan glanced into the sub-station to check the technician's progress.

'Saw him plain as I see you. Sitting in his room at lunchtime, playing with a woman's pink scarf and a blouse. Crying like a baby, he was. Sobbing his heart out.'

Peter looked over at Dan, and Dan nodded. The same thought went through both their minds. They didn't want any more clues. They were both beginning to feel as though they were caught on an endless treadmill leading nowhere.

CHAPTER TWENTY-ONE

'Trevor, can I have a word?' Bill asked as the officers who'd attended the briefing filed out of his room in the mobile HQ.

'I should get back to my ward.'

'I told Andrew Murphy to look after things until you return.' Bill waited until only he, Dan, Peter and Trevor were left in the room then kicked the door shut. 'I won't keep you long. We've a long night ahead. But I think we should pool our knowledge in the light of new evidence.'

'Can we eat while we talk?' Peter went to the door.

'Make mine fish and chips,' Dan said.

'Twice,' Bill added.

'Trevor?' Peter asked.

'Nothing, thanks. I ate earlier.'

'Hospital food,' Peter scorned. He opened the door and shouted to the girl manning the reception desk. 'Phone down to the gate, love, and order four cod and chips from up the road for us, please.'

'Now can we start?' Bill asked testily.

'Anytime that suits you,' Peter reached for the tower of plastic cups and poured out four coffees.

'As I mentioned during the briefing, I've had all the interview reports in.' Bill lifted a pile of blue-jacketed files from the shelf behind him, and dumped them on to the table. 'What I didn't say, Peter, was that Harry Goldman criticised your interviewing techniques.'

'You win some, you lose some.' Peter shrugged.

'Tread carefully in future,' Bill snarled. 'I'm tired of apologising for you.'

'So, we here to pool ideas, or what?' Peter asked.

'Yes,' Bill looked around. Trevor looked exhausted, Peter was being belligerent again – 'Dan, you start.'

'As I said in the briefing, Angela Morgan's convinced that Tony Waters is the killer, but forensics went over that sub-station with a toothcomb and found nothing that shouldn't have been there. Not as much as a fibre or a stray hair.'

'Only traces of mud,' Peter said. 'Probably carried in on people's shoes. But they're going to sift it, and test it to see if it's surface or subsoil.'

'If it is subsoil, it could have been carried there by the killer – or anyone who walked through the flowerbeds, so that would prove nothing.' Bill said. 'Dan, do you think there's anything in Arnold Massey, the maintenance man's story about Spencer Jordan crying over women's pink clothing?'

'When did he see this?' Trevor asked.

'He claims every lunch-hour for the past week,' Dan revealed. 'The storeroom where he eats his sandwiches overlooks Jordan's room.'

Let's look at Spencer as a potential suspect,' Bill sat down. 'He cracked up. He's odd, he knits – '

'You're accusing a man of multiple murders, because he knits?' Trevor said incredulously.

Bill went to the flip-chart and flicked the sheets over until he came to a clean page. He wrote *Spencer Jordan* at the top. 'He's been here long enough to commit all the murders. He's familiar with the place, both as a patient and a member of staff. He probably knows enough to administer drugs, he's intelligent, and he had a breakdown after he saw his wife and three children carved up by a group of maniacs.'

'He what?' Trevor demanded.

297

'Sorry. I must give you the files so you can get up to speed.'

'I'm ahead of you.' Peter reached for the files stored behind the table, and extracted the one containing the press cuttings he'd brought in. He handed it to Trevor.

'What about keeping the victims hidden?' Dan asked Bill.

'He lives in a halfway house just outside the wall,' Peter answered for Bill. 'And he works in the old building, so he must have a reasonable knowledge of the layout.'

'But where did he keep them?' Bill demanded short-temperedly.

'For my money, somewhere in the old hospital. The newer buildings and the wards have too many people around. He'd run a greater risk of discovery there. Besides, there are no nooks and crannies, only straight corridors, square rooms… '

'Where the killer chose to hide Vanessa, in plain sight,' Bill reminded.

'Lyn Sullivan said – said – ' Trevor lost the thread of what he was trying to convey as he stared at the photographs and headlines detailing the murder of Spencer Jordan's family. Sickened, he slammed the file shut.

'Said what?' Dan prompted.

'Said that if she wanted to hide someone in this place, she'd drug them, wrap a blanket around their shoulders and put them on one of the wards, preferably geriatric.'

'The lady has got a point,' Peter nodded. 'Do they hold regular headcounts here?'

'Not often, judging by the number of people they seem to lose,' Bill commented.

'We were talking about Spencer Jordan,' Dan reminded. 'We're all agreed that he has the knowledge of this place, and the means – '

'Where's his motive?' Trevor asked.

'He's nuts,' Peter stated.

'*Was* nuts, and in your opinion so was I,' Trevor reminded acidly.

'You're one of us so we make allowances for your nuttiness.' Peter saw a pulse throb at Trevor's temple, an indication that Trevor was about to lose his temper. He backed down. 'OK, so Jordan's now sane and he didn't have a motive, but you tell me, what motive could anyone have for kidnapping women, drugging them, and burying them alive?'

'None that's obvious that I can see,' Dan said.

'The psychiatrist suggested power.' Bill finished his coffee and crumpled his cup.

Trevor set aside the file on Jordan. 'Have you considered that those women might not have been chosen at random? They were all leaving or had just left the hospital. Has anyone found out why?'

'Twyford and Moon were patients who'd just been discharged.' Bill reined in his irritation when he recalled Trevor was a newcomer to the investigation.

'Why weren't they reported missing?'

Peter finished his coffee. 'Claire Moon told her mother that she planned to travel with a friend. We found her passport, foreign money – '

'So whoever he is, he isn't a thief.' Trevor pushed his cold coffee aside.

'Rosie Twyford told her mother she was going on holiday. And Elizabeth Moore was leaving for a job in America.'

'Why America?' Bill asked.

'Tony Waters said higher wages and better working conditions. She'd recently divorced.'

'And there's a rumour going around that she was having an affair,' Peter interrupted.

'Do we know who with?' Bill asked.

'According to Angela Morgan, Tony. But in her opinion he was having affairs with virtually every female in the hospital.'

'Why didn't you mention this at the briefing?' Bill demanded.

'Hearsay,' Dan said baldly.

'All sour grapes and no facts,' Peter supported Dan. 'Nothing you can get your teeth into; only a middle aged woman who's probably griping because her boss has made a pass at everyone working here except her.'

'And Vanessa Hedley?' Bill asked.

'She's the wild card in the pack.' Peter reached in his pocket for a cigar but found it empty. 'She saw him doing away with the others, and got done because she could identify him.'

'But she couldn't,' Trevor remonstrated. 'That's just the point.'

'Murderer obviously thought so.'

'Even if Tony Waters did have affairs with all three women,' Trevor continued, 'that wouldn't explain why he'd want to kill them.'

'You live like them, you grow like them. He works in a madhouse, doesn't he?' Peter saw pain flash across Trevor's face and regretted his poor joke.

'I've interviewed Tony Waters and his wife,' Dan said slowly. 'It's easy to see who wears the trousers in that household, and Tony's secretary agrees he's the dominant partner.'

'Suspect number two.' Mulcahy turned the page, and wrote *Tony Waters* on the top of the next sheet. 'Like Spencer, he's been here long enough to have carried out all four murders. And he has knowledge of the hospital.'

'He knows this place better than anyone.' Peter paced to the window.

'What about medical knowledge?' Bill asked.

'He was a medical student for two years before he switched to a business studies course.'

'I didn't know that.' Peter answered a knock at the door. Chris Brooke was outside with four bundles wrapped in white paper. Peter put his hand in his pocket and handed him a twenty pound note. 'Thanks, mate, I owe you one.' He shut the door before the constable could hand him his change. He tossed the parcels across the table, and Trevor had a sense of being caught in a time warp. He'd been in a room with Peter, Bill and fish and chips before, and it had led to – he pulled himself up sharply, reminding himself that this time it was different. It was a new year and Dan was working with them.

'Did Spencer Jordan know Vanessa Hedley?' Bill asked Trevor.

'She attended his art therapy classes.'

'So, he could have overheard her bragging about seeing the murderer?'

'Along with all the other staff and patients,' Trevor lifted the corner of the paper wrapped around his fish and chips. Dan and Peter were already breaking off large lumps of battered cod.

'What about the other victims?' Bill ferried a clump of greasy chips to his mouth.

'Claire Moon and Rosie Twyford also attended his classes.' A piece of cod fell back on to the paper, leaving Peter snapping at thin air.

301

'And Elizabeth Moore worked on Spencer's ward when he was a patient,' Dan continued.

'So Spencer Jordan knew all of the victims.' Having finished his chips, Mulcahy wrapped his cod in the greaseproof bag and bit into it. 'Any other ideas?'

'Adam Hayter,' Peter offered.

'Why?' Bill demanded.

'Because he's an obvious pervert, because I don't like him, because he's been here for two years, and because he has the relevant knowledge.'

'Not medical knowledge? He teaches needlework and cookery,' Bill demurred.

'All the therapists are competent first-aiders,' Dan pushed the last piece of fish into his mouth, and crumpled his papers into a ball. 'It was part of a cost-cutting package brought in by Tony Waters. They were all issued with tranquillisers to be used in emergencies, taught how to administer them, and in return all nursing cover was withdrawn from therapy groups.'

'So Spencer Jordan and Adam Hayter have medical knowledge as well as knowledge of the hospital,' Bill conceded.

'Look at Adam Hayter's profile,' Collins threw his chip papers into the bin. 'Obsessively neat, lives with a domineering woman, impotent – '

'I thought you didn't like profiles,' Bill reminded.

'I don't think it's Hayter,' Dan said.

'Why?' Peter pressed.

'I can't give you a reason. I just feel it in my bones.'

'He's got enough pluses to go on the list of suspects. Let's keep going. Anyone else?' Bill asked.

'Harry Goldman fits all the criteria on the profile. Separated from his wife after six months of marriage. Divorced after two years. Lives alone. Collects trains – '

'Collects what?' Trevor asked.

'Trains,' Peter rummaged through the file until he came up with one marked *Goldman*, he passed it to Trevor. 'Toy trains.'

'Is there anyone we shouldn't be watching?' Bill asked caustically.

'No one's mentioned the patients.' Trevor pushed aside the chips and cod he'd barely touched.

'Michael Carpenter is dead. Patrick's checking Vanessa's body for time of death. But he doesn't fit the profile.'

'What about Roland?' Trevor suggested.

'Lechers aren't impotent. Psychiatrist threw him out,' Bill replied.

'For my money he's a more likely candidate than Spencer Jordan.'

'Trevor, just because you like the guy – ' Peter began.

'He's no killer,' Trevor said firmly.

'On what basis?'

'He's too sensitive.' Trevor handed back the file on Spencer Jordan.

'Now you're saying killers can't be sensitive? What about all those concentration camp guards who used to weep when they heard Beethoven and Mozart?'

'Sensitive to music isn't sensitive to people. Psychopaths are often charming, cultured, but cold and dispassionate.'

'Now you've decided our villain is a psychopath.'

'Not necessarily.' Trevor fell silent. He sensed the others looking at him and he knew he was on probation.

'In conclusion we have good reason to watch half the men in this hospital, but not enough evidence to hand one of them a parking ticket,' Bill concluded wearily.

*   *   *

Peter slowed his pace to match Trevor's as they crossed the lawn and headed for the ward blocks.

'You think it's Spencer Jordan, don't you?' Trevor asked.

'I don't know. What I do know is that my head hurts from thinking about it. You know what it's like on the Drug Squad. A junkie goes down, we pick up a cache, and we start looking. And we always know where to look, given that there are only four major dealers in this town. Your usual murder coughs up one or two obvious suspects, but this one – ' Peter stopped and stared into the shadows that surrounded the buildings ahead of them. 'This one has to have – how many staff did you say worked here?'

'I didn't.'

'One week on this case and I feel as though I've been thinking about nothing else for years. I'd give a week's leave for a night off. I'd have a couple of jars down the pub – '

'I still think there has to be a connection between the victims,' Trevor cut in.

'They're not all women. There's also the dog,' Peter reminded.

'I forgot about the dog.'

'How could you. The dog Angela Morgan wept over, when it disappeared.'

'I thought it was a stray.'

'It was.'

'Could it have attacked the killer as he was burying one of the victims?'

'We'll probably never know,' Peter walked on.

304

They paused outside the ward block. Trevor looked up into the clear, star-studded night sky.

'You coming back to join us, then?' Peter asked.

'I am back,' Trevor corrected.

'So you are,' Peter smiled. 'How long before you're back to normal?'

'What's normal?'

'You snapping at me like now,' Peter grinned. 'I suppose if nothing more happens here in the next two weeks, you can pack and go back to your flat.'

Trevor recalled the empty, grubby, dismal rooms, the lonely workaholic life he'd led before he'd been injured. And he knew that he didn't want his life to continue like that. Not any more. He had a mental image of Jean Marshall's apartment, and he suddenly knew that he didn't want that either. Then he remembered a woman with long dark hair and sad eyes –

'Trevor!' Peter shook his head. 'You can't even stay awake when someone's talking to you.'

'Sorry, just thinking about something.'

'Save it until the morning, you need to be on the ball tonight.'

Tony Waters was in the ward office with Lyn and an auxiliary nurse. Trevor could see them through the glass window between the office and the corridor. Lyn's dark head was bent close to Tony's fair one, as they studied a sheaf of papers.

'The hospital has come up with new security arrangements for the wards,' Andrew Murphy waylaid Trevor and handed him a file.

'Any good?' Trevor asked.

'How should a mere constable know?'

'I suppose any measure has to be an improvement,' Trevor said hopefully.

'Especially on the ward that live women are spirited out of and dead ones spirited back in.'

'Sergeant Joseph, I take it you're back on duty?' Tony walked out of the office.

'No,' Trevor opened the door to his room. 'I'm just being used as an extra pair of eyes.'

'I've arranged for one extra nurse to work on this ward. Day and night.'

'That's good,' Trevor glanced at Lyn through the glass.

'The Trust held a meeting this afternoon. They passed a resolution ordering that outside doors will be kept locked at night and all qualified nurses to hold keys, in case of emergency. Also a headcount of patients will be carried out every two hours.'

A woman's high-pitched screaming pierced the air.

'Lucy Craig again,' Lyn left the office and ran down the corridor.

'It's a problem keeping the security low-key, so it doesn't upset our patients,' Tony watched Lyn enter Lucy's room.

'Better an upset patient than a dead one, like Vanessa Hedley.' It was the sort of cheap remark Peter would have tossed off without a second thought, but the hostile glare Tony sent his way lingered afterwards in Trevor's mind.

'This is ridiculous,' Jean Marshall poured herself a brandy after handing Michelle a cup of coffee.

'What's ridiculous?' Overawed by the opulence of Jean's apartment, Michelle was perched on the edge of her chair.

'You being here.' Jean had begun to realise just how much this female bodyguard was going cramp her style. 'There's a porter on duty downstairs, electronically-activated doors and safety devices, so there's no way anyone could get up here without my permission or the doorman knowing.' She conveniently omitted to mention the fire escape. While Michelle Grady was dogging her movements, there was no way she'd find the privacy to telephone, let alone see her lover.

'Just remember what happened to Vanessa Hedley and the others.'

'They were taken from the hospital.'

'Vanessa certainly, but we can't be sure of the others.'

'I suppose you can't,' Jean agreed. 'Well, take your pick of the spare bedrooms. There's clean towels and soap in all the bathrooms, help yourself to whatever you need. I'll go to bed with this,' she lifted the brandy bottle.

'You have your personal alarm to hand?' Michelle asked.

'Never go anywhere without it.' Jean lifted her arm and Michelle saw it dangling from her wrist.

'The first all-night shift I worked, I thought it would stay dark forever,' Lyn walked into the ward kitchen to see Trevor standing next to the kettle.

'The first night I worked,' Trevor smiled, 'I learned that a new day always dawns, no matter what happens during the night.' He held up a jar of instant coffee.

'Please. It's a way of killing another ten minutes. I've checked everyone, extra staff as well as patients, and all's quiet. God, I hate nights. Roll on tomorrow.'

'Back on days?'

'Not for two whole weeks.'

307

'Holiday?'

'My parents have a house in Brittany.'

'Lucky you.'

'It's not luxurious, just a cottage on the beach, but we had some super times there when I was a kid. Beachcombing, finding mussels, crabs and winkles for tea, learning to speak French – and how to drink wine.' She took the coffee he handed her. 'When I get back you'll have left, won't you?'

'Probably. I don't suppose I'll be able to spin out my stay longer, although I may still be on this case. With all this activity, our people in the grounds and the corridors, extra staff drafted on to the wards, our killer is likely to lie low for a time.'

'But you think he'll strike again?'

'If he conforms to serial killer pattern, but we'll get him in the end,' Trevor said, with more confidence than he felt. But all he could think of as he looked into her eyes was; before or after another murder?

CHAPTER TWENTY-TWO

'You were right, Sergeant Joseph. The dawn did come after all.' Lyn set a cup of coffee on the desk in front of Trevor.

He opened his eyes, blinked and tried to focus, but remained disorientated.

'Don't worry, I won't tell anyone you slept,' she whispered as he rubbed his hands through his hair.

'Oh God, I'm – '

'In the ward office and everyone is safe. I've just counted them; staff and patients.' She put her own coffee next to his, sat in the chair behind the desk and snapped open the blind. The cold clear light of a new day was stealing through the ragged border of trees that fringed the lawns.

'Did anyone come round to check after half-past four?' his voice was thick with sleep. Half-past four was the last thing he remembered, and it was now – he glanced at his watch – seven o'clock.

'Only Constable Murphy and I told him you were interviewing the night staff.'

'Bless you,' he said gratefully. 'Just as well it wasn't Bill; if he'd seen me he would have put me back on the sick.'

'Where you should be, considering the state of your head and legs. And who's Bill?' she asked.

'The super who thought I was fit enough to sit up all night.' Trevor wrapped his fingers around his coffee cup. 'I don't think I'm going to be much use to the force for a while.' He smiled. 'I'm too accustomed to getting my eight hours every night.'

'And two hours in the afternoon?' she teased.

'And two hours in the afternoon,' he echoed. 'Thanks for the coffee.' He rose from his chair, walked to the window and stretched his arms.

'I don't envy you trying to sleep today.' She picked up both their cups. 'Not with all the extra activity on the ward.'

'If it's noisy I'll go – ' he faltered. He'd almost said "home". His flat wasn't home. 'To my place,' he amended. 'I'll get the car out of the garage. It might come in useful now I'm working again.'

'If you bring it up here, leave it in the staff not the visitors' car park,' she warned. 'Neither is safe, but you're more likely to find your car jacked up on bricks in the visitors' car park.'

'Thanks for the tip, but no car thief would want to take mine, and even the joy riders would give it a wide berth.'

'You haven't seen some of the cars that have disappeared from here.'

'No, I haven't.' He smiled at her. 'Right, I'm for a shower and then, if you've finished your shift I'll walk you to your hostel.'

'Is that really necessary, with half the town's police force lining the garden?'

'Call it a thank you for not snitching on me last night.'

'What's snitching?'

'A word that was probably in vogue before you were born.'

'You sound like my grandfather.'

'At the moment,' he picked up his stick and hobbled to the door, 'I feel like him.'

*   *   *

310

'Nothing, bloody nothing,' Peter swung his feet down from the bench seat and reached for the coffee pot.

'Did you really expect something to happen last night?' Dan dropped two plastic cups in front of him.

'I believed in Santa Claus until I was ten.' Peter raised his eyebrows as a scuffling sound resounded outside the door of the inner office, but neither of them felt energetic enough to move out of their seats to investigate.

Trevor walked in.

'You look like I feel.' Peter moved along the bench so Trevor could sit down. Trevor parked his stick in the corner of the room and dropped down next to him.

'Nothing?' Trevor looked from Peter to Dan.

'Sweet nothing,' Dan repeated. 'And, as the day-shift is about to take over, I'm for home and bath.'

'Be careful,' Trevor warned. 'You look tired enough to fall asleep and drown.'

'There might be baths big enough, but I don't possess one. I can either soak my legs or my back. It's not big enough for both.'

'Have you ever thought it's not the bath that's the wrong size?' Peter pushed a cup towards Trevor. 'Coffee?'

'No ,thanks. I came to see if I could beg a lift back to my place. I've decided to bring my car back here.'

'Tell a man he can crawl, and he tries to run a marathon. Sure you're up to driving with that leg of yours? Peter asked.

'I can but try. How about it?'

'You're on,' Peter agreed. 'But only if you buy me breakfast in that transport cafe on the docks.'

311

'All you ever think about is your stomach,' Trevor complained. He reached for his stick and followed Peter out of HQ.

With Peter's help, Trevor managed to push his car from the lock-up Peter had rented. He left the battery on charge in the back room of Frank's shop and went upstairs and lay on his bed, intending to catnap for an hour or two. Nothing was going to happen in daylight, not with every inch of the hospital grounds under surveillance by the largest force Bill had assembled to work on a single case.

He took off his jacket and stretched out, but was too restless to sleep. A line of suspects kept intruding into his mind's eye. Spencer Jordan – Tony Waters – Harry Goldman – Adam Hayter – he visualised them, and tried to match them to Vanessa's description of a big man with evil eyes. But no matter how he tried, he couldn't make any of them fit the profile of a serial killer who buried his victims alive.

He pictured the girls lying conscious and helpless in a pit while someone slowly, infinitely slowly, shovelled earth over them, covering every visible inch; heard the dry patter of dried earth and the dull thuds of damp, sticky clods as they fell. Saw a small rectangle of night sky as they must have seen it. The face of the moon shining behind the silhouette of their killer.

Did he take time to study his victims' features as he covered them? Had they known who he was before they died?

Trevor closed his eyes, but the images refused to disappear. He saw Jean Marshall, her auburn hair spread out like a halo behind her head just as it had been on the cushion of the sofa the night he'd made love to her. Her

312

eyes round, terrified, the irises crimson with bursting blood vessels as earth fell…

He woke in a sweat, and realised he'd slept. He went into the bathroom and splashed cold water over his head. The battery should be charged by now. He'd get Frank to help him lift it back into his car, and then talk to him. He looked around his flat before he locked the door. It was a talk that was long overdue.

'I was wondering where you'd got to,' Jean greeted Trevor when he returned to the ward at midday. 'You couldn't cope with the food outside so you've come back for a delicious hospital lunch?'

'I bought sandwiches.' Trevor tossed a plastic carrier bag on to his bed.

'Everything's quiet, and I'm well protected. Constable Grady is in the kitchen making coffee.'

Trevor walked over to the door and closed it behind her.

'Why, Sergeant Joseph.' She batted her eyelashes theatrically.

'Do you have any idea of the risk you're running?' he asked, on edge after his nightmare.

'Someone had to do something. Besides, what can happen to me? I've a round-the-clock female dogging my every step, which is more of a bind than I thought it would be. And a man outside the door of every building I'm in, whether it's here, the canteen, or my flat. A mouse couldn't creep near me without being flattened, but thank you for your concern,' she said sincerely. 'It's nice to know that someone cares about me.'

'I'm worried about the whole hospital.'

'You really are concerned, aren't you?'

'There's a killer on the loose, and you ask if I'm concerned?'

With the memory of their evening's lovemaking lying between them, he couldn't meet the searching look in her eyes. He picked up the carrier bag, and took out the sandwiches he'd scrounged off Frank. He heard laughter and he looked outside. A group of policemen were standing in front of his window smoking, and drinking coffee from disposable cups.

He didn't have to say any more. Jean was sensitive enough to read embarrassment in his sudden preoccupation with his sandwiches.

'About the other night,' she said briskly. 'It was a one-off – you do know that, don't you?'

'I'd still like to thank you for it. You showed me that there was life outside these four walls.'

'Call it part of the recovery process.' She managed to keep the bitterness from her voice.

'You leaving us, Lyn?' Dressed in his bathrobe, and clutching his toilet bag, Alan peered through the open door of her room on his way from the bathroom.

'Holiday. I booked these two weeks last Christmas. My brother and I are going to join our parents in the cottage in Brittany.'

'Lucky you. Want a hand to carry your case downstairs?'

'It's not as heavy as it looks, but thanks anyway.' She lifted her case into the corridor, picked up her handbag, and locked the door behind her. 'It's mainly washing; I still keep most of my things at home.'

'It must be nice to have a real home in the same town you work in.'

'As opposed to travelling all of fifty miles away,' she joked.

'Unlike yours, my mother doesn't do my washing. Have a good time, and don't go drinking too much wine.'

She gave him a sideways look.

'Stupid thing to say. Do drink too much wine.'

'There won't be anything else to do. I'll send you a postcard if I can find one rude enough.'

'Rotten sod,' he grinned as he went into his own room.

Lyn heard Mary's high-pitched giggle from behind Alan's closed door, and she smiled. It was good to know that someone was still in love and happy in Compton Castle.

After Jean left Trevor, he rummaged in the bottom of his wardrobe for the cans of beer Peter had given him. He found half a dozen, all lukewarm. He opened one and picked up a book from his locker to read as he ate his sandwiches. The hands on the bedside clock pointed to two-thirty. The usual hum of hospital noises, interspersed with voices he recalled from the force buzzed around him. Strange how little he'd thought of work all the time he'd been ill, yet how easily he'd slipped back into the routine of take-aways, long shifts, and caustic exchanges with his colleagues.

He woke at five, the sandwiches still in their packet on his lap, the book unopened. Then he heard it again, the crashing thud that had woken him. He was out of the chair in seconds. He wrenched open the door and looked into the corridor. White-faced, Michelle was outside the ward office, watching Jean grapple with dark-suited figure behind the glass window.

'He's locked the door.'

'Phone for help!' He picked up a lightweight stacking chair from the corridor and threw it at the glass window. It bounced back, the legs falling away from the moulded plastic seat. While Michelle spoke urgently into her phone, he picked up the chair legs. Hitting the window hard on its corner, he succeeded in cracking the glass, but not shattering it.

Andrew Murphy dashed through the door, followed by Chris Brooke. They sized up the situation and put the full weight of their shoulders to the office door. There was a snapping, splintering sound and the lock gave way.

Jean was pinned against the wall, her face red, her eyes bulging. Roland was in front of her, one hand around her throat, the other wielding a syringe perilously close to her eyes. Andrew nodded to Chris. They took Roland's arms and dragged him out of the office. When he was in the corridor, Andrew kneed him in the back, and pinned him to the floor.

'Cuffs!' he held out his hand. Chris gave him his.

The door at the end of the corridor flew open. Dan, Peter and Tony Waters burst in.

'Who is it?' Peter shouted, as Trevor fought his way past Roland, Chris and Andrew and went into the office.

Jean gasped as Trevor helped her on to a chair. 'Roland, I was working in here when he came in, slammed the door and pulled out a syringe.'

'Where did he get that from?' Tony demanded from the corridor.

'You tell me.' Jean leaned against the back of the chair.

'They've taken Roland to the secure ward,' Peter announced as he walked into Trevor's room ten minutes

316

later. Trevor and Dan were sitting drinking warm beer straight from the can. 'That's my beer.'

'You gave it to me.' Trevor tossed him a can.

'For you to drink, not hoard.'

'We're drinking it now.'

'Is Roland our killer?' Dan voiced the question uppermost in all of their minds.

'I checked his record with Bill,' Peter opened his can. 'He's an alcoholic; he's been here six months – '

'Long enough to have carried out all four murders.'

'And he's a private patient. His family, his doting aged parents that is, have money enough to pay his bills here. If they didn't, he would have been out of this place long ago.'

'That explains why the staff are prepared to put up with his drinking and letching.' Trevor sat on the edge of his seat. 'But I didn't realise there were private patients here.'

'Your room is paid for by medical insurance,' Peter said pointedly.

'Is it?' Trevor asked in surprise.

'Tell that man what time of day it is, Dan.' Peter wiped the beer froth from his mouth, and sat on the bed next to Dan.

'So he had the time, the knowledge – ' Dan began to mull it over.

'What was in the syringe?' Trevor asked.

'Initial diagnosis is probably water, but they're checking that now, along with all the medical stores, for signs of theft or tampering. I managed to talk to Roland briefly before Tony Waters took over. Damned man sent for a lawyer, and won't let us question Roland until he comes.'

'Accused's legal right,' Dan reminded.

'Tony Waters is covering his backside against the flak that's beginning to fly.' Peter finished his can and held out his hand for another.

The room in the secure unit was unpleasantly warm. There were thick iron bars on the windows, and as if they weren't enough, they were fronted by wire mesh screens that blocked out most of the light. Roland was sitting across a narrow table from Dan, flanked by the solicitor. Both table and chairs were chained to the floor. Karl Lane, Carol Ashford and Dotty Clyne sat in a row at the far end of the room. Peter hovered in the corner.

'Come on, Roland,' Dan pleaded. 'Tell us where you found the syringe.'

Roland lifted his bloated face from his arms, and stared at Dan.

'Why did you attack Sister Marshall?' Dan tried another tack.

'We have yet to establish that an attack took place, Inspector Evans,' the solicitor reprimanded.

'There are four witnesses,' Peter interrupted. 'All police officers.'

'But can they identify Mr Williams?'

'Yes,' Peter replied flatly.

'Why did you attack Sister Marshall?' Dan reiterated.

Roland remained obdurately silent.

'All right, Roland, let's move on. You were holding a syringe. Where did you get it?'

'Rubbish.'

The single word was enough to galvanise Dan's attention. 'What rubbish, where?'

'In the sacks.'

'Where are the sacks kept, Roland?' Dan persisted.

'In the corridor.'

'Which corridor?' Dan was beginning to feel as though he was caught up in that irritating children's nursery verse, "In a dark dark wood, there's a dark dark place, and in the dark dark place there's a dark dark house…"

'The corridor where the rubbish sacks are kept,' Roland closed his eyes.

'They're kept in a room in the cellar of the old hospital,' Peter chipped in.

'Did you go into the old hospital, Roland?' Dan pressed.

Roland sank his head on his arms again, and closed his eyes.

'You're not going to get anything else out of him Inspector.' Carol Ashford rose from her chair in the corner. 'He was so agitated we had to tranquillise him.'

'You could try again later, Inspector.' Karl suggested, above Roland's snores.

'How much did you give him?' Peter asked.

'The standard dose,' Carol replied. 'It had to be done.'

'He was violent,' Karl brought in a wheelchair and parked it next to Roland.

'We'll let you know when he wakes, Inspector,' Carol helped Karl lift Roland into the chair and walked beside it as Karl pushed it out of the room.

'Roland's profile and records don't match those of a potential murderer,' Harry Goldman assured Peter and Dan. 'But I've asked Dotty Clyne to call in as soon as she's free. Roland's one of her patients.'

'What is the profile of a murderer?' Bill enquired.

'There'd be evidence of psychopathic or sociopath tendencies,' Goldman answered. 'You asked for my opinion, Superintendent Mulcahy, and I'm giving it to you. I don't believe that Roland is your man.'

'But you can't say for sure?' Bill left his chair. 'No matter, we have enough to book him.'

'Only if Sister Marshall presses charges,' Tony Waters interposed.

'It was aggravated assault, grievous bodily harm, and he tried to attack two police officers.' Bill stared Tony in the eye.

'If you move Roland, there's a risk of him regressing and losing the headway he's made under Dotty's supervision during the past six months.'

'Given the nature of Roland's crime, and this case, that's a risk I'm prepared to take. We'll charge him as soon as he wakes then transfer him to the station.'

'I protest. You'll destroy my staff's hard work… '

'Hard work?' Bill sneered. 'Have you any idea how much your recovering alcoholic drinks?'

'Have you any evidence?'

'Every time I've spoken to the man he's been stinking of booze.' Bill went to the door. 'We give him two hours to sleep it off. After that, Sergeant Collins will charge him. Then we'll hold him in our cells. They appear to be more secure than yours.'

'Anything on Spencer Jordan?' Bill stormed into the back room of the mobile HQ.

'Nothing,' Dan sensed Bill's mood and trod warily.

'The pink silk thing?'

'Sarah… Constable Merchant saw it. She joined his therapy class today. She's moving into the ward tonight.'

'What exactly did she see?'

'A woman's headscarf.'

'Judging by his taste in knitwear, his own,' Peter broke in.

'Anything else to report on Jordan?'

'He left the lights burning in the bedroom and living room of his flat for most of the night.'

'Guilty conscience?' Bill raised the idea.

'Could be indigestion.' Peter reached for the coffee pot and a box of biscuits. 'When he woke up he cooked himself breakfast, then left for his therapy room, and that's where he's been all day.'

'Playing with the silk scarf,' Bill snapped.

'And working with his art groups.'

'Does he ever leave the hospital?'

'Not that we've seen.'

'Keep him under surveillance, and put someone on Harry Goldman,' Bill barked.

'And Adam Hayter?' Peter suggested.

'If we've a spare man.'

'Then you don't think it is Roland?' Dan asked.

'I don't bloody well know,' Bill cursed. 'A full week into this case and no one has come up with any hard evidence implicating a particular suspect. What am I leading here?' he demanded. 'A police investigation or a game of bloody Cluedo?'

'We'd stand a better chance with a game of Cluedo,' Peter stepped out of the door. 'Fewer suspects.'

'What's the problem?' At the beginning of the second leg of a split shift, Andrew Murphy was tired, irritable, and ready to bite the head off the security guard on gate duty, who was arguing with a young, slim, dark-haired man.

'He wants to see someone in the nurses' hostel,' the guard explained. 'I've had orders to ring through the name of every visitor, and the girl he's asked for left this morning to go on holiday.'

'Give him the date she gets back,' Andrew said impatiently.

'That's just it, Officer.' The young man pushed his way into the booth. 'It's my sister and we were supposed to travel together to my parents' house in Brittany. We arranged to meet at home, but she didn't turn up.'

'You probably missed her on the road,' Andrew looked at the queue of traffic building up on the road outside the gates. 'It is the rush hour.'

'You don't understand.' The young man's voice pitched high in temper and something else. Something Andrew recognised as fear. 'It's nearly six o'clock, and she was supposed to meet me at ten this morning.'

CHAPTER TWENTY-THREE

A sick, empty feeling rose from the pit of Trevor's stomach as he stepped into the mobile HQ. 'What did you say?'

'We think Lyn Sullivan is missing,' Dan repeated slowly.

'Are you sure? She was going on holiday to Brittany… ' His voice faded as he recalled the stench in the ward where they had found Vanessa.

'Peter's with her brother in the hostel. They've emptied the place by ringing the fire alarm, and they're checking with everyone to pinpoint the last sighting of her.'

'How long has she been missing?'

'We'll know more when Peter's finished.'

Trevor sank down on a chair. All the time he'd been having nightmares about Jean, the killer had been stalking Lyn. He imagined her fresh young face, pale in terror, her eyes staring upwards, as she lay at the bottom of a pit. Earth shovelled spade-full by spade-full, covering her arms, her legs – and finally her face…

'This bastard is always one step ahead of us,' Andrew Murphy stepped inside the van and handed one of the girls a sheet of paper.

'Found her car?' Dan Evans asked.

'It's still in the car park. Lab boys are springing the locks on it now.'

'Ever get the impression that someone is goading you, laughing in your face?' Dan asked no one in particular.

'We sew this place up tighter than a monkey's bum and he still gets himself another girl.' Andrew helped himself to a cigarette from a packet lying on top of the computer. For once, none of the girls manning the desk objected.

'You all right?' Dan turned to Trevor.

'I will be in a moment.' Trevor lifted his head out of his hands.

'We will find her.'

'Like we found Vanessa?' Trevor asked. No one dared answer him.

'I want the hospital sealed off now – this minute,' Bill's voice reverberated through the thin walls of the van. 'From this moment on, not so much as a moth flies in or out of the gate without being searched and giving us its name and address.'

'We sealed off the place when Vanessa Hedley was taken,' Trevor said when Bill stepped inside the van.

'And we'll do it again,' Bill reiterated. 'We'll go over every inch of the buildings and the grounds. Once a room or an area is evacuated, it's toothcombed, sealed, and a man is put on surveillance until we've finished the whole complex.'

'And the personnel?' Dan asked.

'Those working the wards can go back to them, but the administrative staff will be searched and eliminated from our enquiries before they will be allowed out. If they're driving cars, we'll strip them back to the chassis.'

'You want me to tell Tony Waters that we're closing down the admin offices?'

'Until further notice,' Bill concurred.

'And the grounds?' Dan checked.

'Same principle; searched, tagged, wrapped in tape, and men covering the area at intervals. Every bloody inch!' Bill had reached the end of his patience. 'Dog handlers are already in the girl's room, being primed with her bed linen.'

'I know we've been here before.' Peter climbed the last few steps to the top of the old building. He stopped on the small landing and looked down at the twenty men following him. 'But we start again, room by room; ransack every cupboard, every nook, every cranny, every box and every file. Tap every wall, every stair, every ceiling, seal off everything as you go. Take it slowly, floor by floor. Five of you start that end,' he pointed to his left, 'and five this end,' he indicated right. He looked at Trevor. 'We'll do this quicker if you take ten men and start in the cellar. We'll meet in the middle.'

'It will save time,' Trevor agreed.

'When we meet we'll compare notes and double-check to make sure we've covered everything.'

Trevor leaned heavily on the banister, and looked at Chris Brooke. They walked silently down the stairs until they reached the cellar. They began by checking the incinerators, the dog-handler working ahead of them. They checked every sack of rubbish, every crack in the solid cement floor, every inlet and outlet of heating pipes, and the ceiling. And even after the whole area had been thoroughly sniffed over a second time by the dogs, and Trevor had seen everything through his own eyes, he still wondered if they could have missed something.

It was a tedious job that progressed even more slowly when Tony Waters appeared and insisted on dogging their footsteps. He had grudgingly given Trevor a full set of keys, and Trevor, who'd heard about the sub-station from Peter, supervised the lifting of every iron plate from the floor again.

'Nothing, sir,' Chris Brooke said flatly.

'Nothing, sir,' the dog-handler repeated.

They checked, searched and double-checked. Knocked every wall, shone torches over every inch of the floor, every inch of wall, every inch of cellar.

'If there's a bloody mouse that we haven't tagged down here, I'd like to know about it,' Andrew Murphy complained bitterly at the end of two hours of futile effort.

'Stairs and corridor to next floor,' Trevor ordered abruptly.

'Half floor,' Tony Waters corrected.

Trevor considered Tony too cool and collected for an administrator who had just lost another nurse, possibly to the same killer who had already murdered a nurse and three patients. He looked back into the empty cellar as he posted a seal on the door. 'You,' he called out to the last man. 'Stand here. And you,' he shouted to another officer. 'Guard the far entrance in front of the locked door. Use your radios. Every ten minutes to main control, and every five to each other.'

Trevor couldn't resist the temptation to look back as he walked away. Were there secret passages beneath the floor, dating back to the days when a Norman Castle had occupied the site? Was Lyn hidden down there, half dead, if not dead already? Was she conscious and suffering? Hoping for a rescue that might never come?

'My wife will accompany you when you search this floor.'

It was the first time Trevor had heard Tony refer to Carol as his wife. Tony folded the note Carol had brought him into his pocket.

'I'm sorry to have to leave you, Sergeant Joseph, but I have to attend an emergency meeting.'

326

'I'm sure Sister Ashford will look after us,' Trevor said. As Tony walked away and Carol drew closer the dogs went wild, pulling at their leashes.

'I'm sorry,' the handler apologised.

'It's all right.' Carol patted the dog. 'I keep two Dobermans.'

'You also use the same perfume as Nurse Sullivan and half the other females in this hospital.' The handler addressed Trevor. 'Dogs have gone berserk over seven nurses already, sir.'

'I'm afraid Laura has a lot of customers.' Carol explained.

'The staff here shop together?' Trevor asked.

'No time for shopping, so we grab what we can. Laura Stafford, the staff nurse in Alcohol and Drug Abuse, is married to a pharmacist. We give her our orders, she gives us discount, and this perfume was last month's special.'

'All of which makes our job bloody impossible – begging your pardon, sister,' the handler apologised.

Carol smiled absently at him. 'You know this floor is scarcely used now, Sergeant Joseph?'

Trevor referred to the notes Peter had thrust into his hand as they'd separated. 'According to this, except for the rooms opposite the old padded cells. The hospital stores rubbish in them that's destined for the incinerator.'

They climbed up the stairs, one dog and its handler preceding them, another bringing up the rear. The men regularly tapped the walls, but there was no point in testing the concrete steps. The stairwell beneath them was an empty void.

'Note that we haven't looked at the outside steps,' Trevor said sharply, studying a plan of the building to make sure there were no oversights. He walked down a grey corridor, floored and walled in concrete. A row of bare light bulbs hung overhead casting pools of weak light, but the officers still swept their powerful torchbeams over dusty corners. While Trevor tagged off the areas they had searched and locked partition doors, they moved on to the room where the rubbish was stored. The handlers allowed the dogs to sniff each bag before they were slit open. Foul-smelling waste tumbled out, carpeting the concrete. The officers spread it thinly, poking, prodding, and turning it over with long canes the team that had preceded them had left. They searched through used syringes, stained balls of cotton wool, and clumps of damp, dirty paper towels.

'Does this job come with a free Aids test?' Andrew Murphy asked.

'Move on to the end of the corridor.' Trevor ignored him, as he watched the last of the rubbish being scraped off the floor into fresh bags by Murphy and Brooke who were both wearing thick rubber gloves.

'Do you want to search the mortuaries?' Carol asked as they approached the male mortuary.

'Yes.' Trevor pulled the ring of keys out of his jeans pocket. 'Do you keep them locked?'

'Always, when there are bodies in them. That's why we can't understand how the body of Mrs Hope appeared out in the grounds.'

'Mrs Hope was the corpse I landed on?' Trevor opened the door.

'She was,' Carol acknowledged. 'We've had two more deaths on geriatric earlier today. One senile dementia, ninety-two, and one heart attack, eighty-four.'

Trevor opened the door and allowed the dogs in first, but they still persisted in showing more interest in Carol's perfume.

'There's no need to stay. We'll check out the body drawers,' Trevor said to the handlers.

Trevor walked in with Andrew Murphy and looked around the large square room. Two sinks had been fixed to the back wall, large, stone and open, without cupboards beneath them. Three plain wooden tables covered by sheets of zinc stood in the centre and a large bank of a dozen body drawers, four wide and three high, ran the full width. Andrew jerked out the top left-hand drawer, and he jumped back, as a pair of greyish white feet twitched towards him, the gnarled and yellow toenails pointing upwards.

'The 92-year-old senile dementia,' Carol joined him and heaved the drawer out further. She folded back the sheet that was wrapped around the slight, emaciated body, and uncovered the face of an elderly man Trevor had last seen sitting and trembling on one of the benches in the garden.

'Will you transfer him to the General?' Trevor asked.

'No. We only transfer the ones who need a post mortem, Sergeant Joseph.'

'We've seen all we need to, Sister.' Andrew looked away from the corpse.

Carol covered the body again and closed the drawer. Trevor pulled out one empty drawer after another.

'Careful!' Carol shouted, as the whole bank leaned forward. Chris Brooke ran towards them and threw his weight alongside Andrew's, while Trevor and Carol closed one rusty drawer after another. By the time they'd succeeded in setting the unit on an even keel again, they were all exhausted.

'At least we know there's nothing behind those drawers,' Andrew took out his handkerchief and covered his nose.

'Check the floor under the sink,' Trevor ordered Chris Brooke, as he walked to the window and examined the mesh covering it.

'Nothing, sir.'

Trevor was beginning to hate that word more than any other in the English language;

'Nothing,' Andrew echoed, as he managed to force the last drawer home.

'Tag it and we'll move on to the female mortuary.' Trevor waited until everyone had moved on before sealing the door. He followed and watched while Chris Brooke and Andrew Murphy fought with another set of rusted body drawers. But this time they were careful not to open more than two at a time.

Clenching and unclenching his fists, Trevor stared at the joins between walls and ceiling. There had to be a body sized gap somewhere! People simply didn't vanish into thin air.

Dogs and men sniffed round the huge tubs, sinks and old dry linen cupboards of the laundry.

'Nothing,' Chris Brooke repeated dully.

The word echoed from the floor above where Peter's team was already working. He imagined Lyn's face, so beautiful in life, frozen in death.

'Shall we move on to the kitchen, sir?' Chris had to repeat himself before Trevor heard.

The staff moved into the dining area while Trevor's team opened stoves and refrigerators, emptied freezers, pantries, even the microwaves and food processors.

'Nothing – nothing – nothing – ' Trevor felt as though he would go mad if he heard that word one more time.

Peter appeared at his side.

'Where to now?' Trevor asked him.

'Interview Roland. I've just had word he's awake and Bill wants us to give him the third degree.'

Peter dumped a stack of files on the table before he sat down and faced Roland. Trevor closed the door and took the only vacant chair, next to Dotty Clyne.

'Did you see Nurse Sullivan this morning, Roland?' Peter launched straight into the important questions.

Roland shook his head so vigorously his fat cheeks and chin wobbled.

'Did you see Nurse Lyn Sullivan at any time this morning?' Peter repeated.

'No.' Roland's voice was so low Trevor had to strain his ears to catch what he was saying.

'Where were you this morning?'

'Therapy.'

'Which therapy?' Trevor asked.

'Art,' Roland was so terrified he was almost gibbering.

Trevor left his chair, opened the door and beckoned to Michelle Grady who was standing in the corridor. He pointed to his chair, and indicated she should take his place.

'Why did you attack Sister Marshall?'

Trevor heard Peter's question, but not Roland's answer, as he made his way down the corridor to the therapy rooms. It was only when he reached the other end that he remembered the old block had been evacuated for the search. He nodded to the officer stationed at the door and went into the garden.

Bill was standing in the drive, directing the outdoor search operation and talking to Tony. Trevor approached them.

'Do either of you know where I can find Spencer Jordan?' he asked.

'We moved his class into the day room of the drug and alcohol abuse ward,' Tony replied.

Trevor moved on and saw Spencer through the ward window. He was leaning over Lucy Craig's chair, studying her sketchbook.

'Come to join our class, Sergeant?' Spencer asked when he saw him in the doorway. It was the first time Spencer had addressed him by his title, and Trevor detected a condemnatory note.

'Not at the moment,' Trevor said quietly. 'But could I have a private word with you?'

Spencer joined him in the corridor and closed the door on his class.

'I'm sorry to interrupt… '

'I bet you are,' Spencer said bitterly.

'We're all having a hard time… ' Trevor was taken aback by his vehemence.

'Some harder than most. Have you any idea what it's like being interrogated by that man?' Spencer demanded.

'Who?' Trevor asked.

'Your bloody superintendent.'

'Bill? Oh yes.' Trevor lifted his eyes to meet Spencer's. 'I know. And I also know what happened to your family. I'm sorry.'

'You're sorry?' Spencer repeated caustically.

'If we rode roughshod over you, I apologise, but we're trying to save Lyn Sullivan's life. And we don't believe we have much time. You, more than anyone here, know what it's like to lose someone to senseless violence. Her brother is frantic. Her parents are travelling back from France… '

'I'll help in any way I can,' Spencer replied. 'Just tell me how.'

'Was Roland in your therapy class this morning?'

'Yes. Surely to God you don't think it's Roland now?' he demanded wearily.

'We don't know. He attacked Jean Marshall.'

'I heard about that. But attacking Jean Marshall isn't the same thing as kidnapping and burying women alive.'

'We're fumbling in the dark, and hoping our fumbling doesn't cost Lyn her life,' Trevor replied honestly.

Spencer thought for a moment. 'Roland came in this morning at half past nine, along with everyone else. I remembered him tripping over Alison Bevan's easel.'

'And afterwards?'

'He stayed with me all morning, even through break. They all did. Lucy Craig and Alison were upset. They wanted to sit and talk.'

'Did Roland join in the conversation?'

'Oh, yes. I don't have to tell you what he's like.'

'When did he leave?'

'He went with the others at lunchtime.'

'It was just after lunch he attacked Jean,' Trevor reflected. 'Did he leave the therapy room at any time?'

'He might have gone to the toilet. I don't clock people in and out, you know that.'

'But he could have left the room?'

'If he did, and I'm not saying he did, I doubt that it was for longer than five or ten minutes. He and Alison were making papier-mâché models at the sink in front of the window, and I seem to remember non-stop conversation in that area. You could check with Alison Bevan and Lucy Craig.'

'I will. And thanks.'

*   *   *

Trevor spoke to Lucy and Alison then went to HQ to find out which constable had been posted closest to the therapy room. The officer corroborated Spencer's story. No one had walked in or out of the door he'd manned all morning.

The last sighting of Lyn had been by Alan in the hostel at ten. And, as she was already carrying her suitcase out of her room, the chances were she'd been waylaid shortly afterwards. Otherwise her car wouldn't have been left in the car park – someone had called her back into the hospital.

Trevor returned to the secure unit to find Roland slumped in a torpor, and Peter fending off a verbal attack from Dotty Clyne.

'You cannot intimidate patients in this fashion, Sergeant. You have no idea of the long-term damage you could cause… '

'I do have a fair idea of the damage he has already caused,' Peter retorted.

'Sergeant, as a patient in this institution, Mr Williams is entitled to certain rights… '

Peter turned and saw Trevor standing in front of the door.

'Roland?' Trevor spoke softly, pitching his voice below Dotty's in an effort to gain Roland's attention. 'Where were you all morning?'

'Therapy,' Roland answered.

'And afterwards?'

'Went to eat lunch.'

'And after that?'

'In the office with… '

Trevor turned to Peter and shook his head.

'Confirmed?' Peter asked.

334

'By staff, patients and police.'

'You see, Sergeant Collins,' Dotty crowed triumphantly.

'There's still the matter of the assault charge.' Peter gathered his papers together.

'Sister Marshall won't press charges,' she announced.

'Do I take that to mean that she won't have a job here if she does?' Peter enquired before he and Trevor left the room.

CHAPTER TWENTY-FOUR

Bill was too calm, Trevor thought as he stepped into the crowded back room of HQ. Experience had taught him that whenever Bill was this composed, it was the still before gale-force ten struck.

'We start interviewing,' Bill began, before the last of the team entering the HQ had time to find a seat. 'There'll be four teams. Sarah Merchant is looking at the staff who are still on the premises. Dan, you take one team; Peter, another; Trevor a third. I'll lead the fourth myself. The priority is to establish everyone's movements and whereabouts between the hours of nine-thirty and twelve this morning.'

'And if it's an outsider, like the milkman or the laundryman?' Peter checked.

'We've searched every vehicle that has entered the gates since Vanessa Hedley's disappearance.' A frown creased Bill's forehead as he glared at the hospital security chief and the officer he'd put in charge of traffic flowing in and out of the hospital. 'There's been no let up in security since then?'

'None,' the security chief assured him. 'Nurse Sullivan couldn't have been taken out of this place this morning, without us knowing about it. I'm willing to stake my reputation on it.'

'You just did,' Peter opened the door.

Trevor watched the dietician as she left the dining room where he was conducting his interviews alongside Sarah Merchant. In the opposite corner Peter was working in uneasy tandem with Michelle Grady. He waited while

Sarah keyed the essential information from their last interview on to her laptop.

'Name – age – position held in Compton Castle?'

'Herne, Jimmy Herne. Fifty-eight. Head gardener.'

'Where were you this morning between ten and twelve?' Trevor was bored with the tedium of repeating the same questions. He wanted to do something more constructive towards finding Lyn.

'Let me see now… ' Herne scratched his bald head thoughtfully, trying Trevor's frayed patience. 'I cut the lawn first thing. I never trust the boys to make the early cuts, when the grass is still tender… '

'What time did you finish cutting the grass?' Trevor interrupted, thinking of the fifty-two other people waiting to be interviewed.

'About ten, I think.'

'And what did you do then?'

'Had second breakfast with the maintenance men, like I always do.'

'What time did you finish this second breakfast?'

'Half past ten, same as always.'

'And afterwards?'

'I worked on the flowerbeds with those damned useless boys who can't tell a… '

'Until when?' Trevor cut him short again.

'Dinner time.'

'Which is?'

'Half past one.'

'Those boys you were with – did they eat second breakfast with you?' Trevor wished he could rid himself of the feeling that all of this was a waste of time. That the people – the computers – the interviews – wouldn't bring them any closer to solving the mystery of Lyn's disappearance. He glanced at his watch. Nearly six o'clock. Lyn had been missing for eight hours.

'Is there any truth in the stories you told Jean Marshall and Lyn Sullivan about tunnels in the grounds leading from the cellars to the folly?'

'Yes,' Jimmy snapped, piqued at the implication that he'd lied.

'Could you lead me to them?' Trevor asked.

'Well, I could… then again I couldn't… not exactly.'

'Explain.' Trevor ordered.

'They were all blocked off years ago,' Jimmy admitted. 'When the therapy blocks were built.'

'How long ago was that?' Trevor pressed.

'Let me see… it must have been sometime in the sixties. Builders went round the grounds and the old block, plugging all the tunnel entrances.'

'With temporary shuttering?' Trevor asked hopefully.

'Nothing temporary about what they did. They had cement mixers and they concreted the holes. Tons of cement and rubble they poured in. Tons and tons,' Jimmy emphasised.

'Could you show me where they poured it?'

'Now, let me, see… I think I could find the spot, if you wanted me to.'

'Take the rest of Mr Herne's statement.' Trevor said to Sarah. 'I'll be back after I've found a plan of this place.'

'There has to be someone who can take over from me,' Trevor begged Bill.

'These interviews might be our only chance of finding Lyn Sullivan alive.' Bill looked at Trevor and saw that he remained unconvinced. 'How often have you said,

338

the only way to catch villains is through routine police work?'

'Never!'

'Then it must have been Peter.' Bill was nonplussed.

'While we're standing here talking, she could be suffocating… '

'All right,' Bill conceded. 'Get Andrew to take over from you and check out the bloody tunnels if you're convinced they exist. And while you're about it, find out if those rookies have come up from the police college and if they have, deploy them in the grounds.

'I'll do that.' Trevor walked away. Even if the tunnels had been sealed off as solidly as Jimmy Herne had said, there was always a possibility that a gap might have been left. A loose side brick – a plug that had worked loose and fallen out – possibilities wormed through his mind. A small gap, that's all he needed. One just big enough to take a crawling man, dragging an inert, drugged, lifeless body behind him.

'Sealed off, just like I told you.' Jimmy Herne pulled back a hydrangea that had spread its branches within the decaying walls of the folly. He exposed a concrete plinth set below the original floor level. Balancing on his stick, Trevor leaned over and inspected the concrete. He ran his hands around the edges and picked up a fistful of wood chip.

'We use that to keep down the weeds,' Jimmy informed him.

Trevor signalled to the recruit behind him. The girl hadn't even finished her six weeks training, but with experienced officers thin on the ground, he hadn't felt justified in taking anyone else on what could turn out to be a wild-goose chase.

'See if you can find any gaps around that concrete,' he ordered.

The girl dived forward and ran her hands around the edge of the plug.

'It's set in solid Georgian brickwork, that,' Jimmy declared. 'I watched them fix it. Six men worked for two days just on this plug. The tunnel was open both ends before then. That was the problem; people kept trying to walk through. Student nurses out for a lark, you know the sort of thing.'

'I can imagine,' Trevor said.

'One of the nurses got caught in a fall of earth. Halloween it was. Lucky they pulled her out before she snuffed it. After that the Authorities ordered the tunnel sealed.'

'Where was the other end?'

'The cellar.'

'It seems solid enough, sir,' the rookie ventured tentatively.

'Let's go.' Trevor used his stick to propel himself swiftly forward.

'Where?' Herne protested. 'I can't hang about with you lot all day. I've a garden to run, and this is the busiest time…'

'Your work can wait,' Trevor countered. 'I need you down the cellar.'

The constable who was still standing on the cellar steps, in exactly the same position Trevor had left him, nodded, 'All quiet, sir.'

Trevor handed Herne and the rookie torches from the pile heaped at the foot of the stone steps. He took two for himself. 'Where was this entrance?' he asked Jimmy.

'Bearing in mind that I only walked down the tunnel once and that was when I first started here... Did it for a bet,' he wandered off on yet another digression. 'The older lads were always egging us youngsters on. Well, there was a lot more of us in those days. Twenty experienced gardeners and fifteen boys... '

'Can you find the tunnel end?' Trevor stepped forward and flicked a switch. A single row of dim-wattage light bulbs flickered on overheard, shedding a leprous glow over the grimy concrete floors and dusty pipes that snaked around the walls.

Jimmy made his way uncertainly through the cellar until he came to the electricity sub-station. 'I seem to remember it was here. Yes, this is it,' he patted a large cement patch on the wall that hadn't gone unnoticed by the search teams. But, after tapping it to ensure that it was solid, they had ignored it, not realising that there had once been anything behind it.

Trevor knocked at it. It looked solid, but what if there was something they'd missed? A side-tunnel perhaps, that opened out somewhere else.

'Constable?' Trevor shouted back to the man on duty.

'Sir?' The boy leapt forward, bright-eyed and eager.

'Go upstairs and fetch a pickaxe. And – ' Trevor looked at the fragile, blonde, petite rookie who stood next to him , 'another man. A dog-handler if you can find one.'

Fortunately, both the constable and the dog-handler he'd commandeered were in better physical shape than Trevor. They took it in turns to wield the pickaxe, and within twenty minutes of hard, banging graft that shook the cellar, they broke through the thick covering skin of concrete to reveal a gap plugged with rubble.

341

The first hole was barely two inches wide, but it was a start. With Trevor's chivvying, both men managed to enlarge the hole to a rough three-foot square in a matter of minutes.

'That's the beginning of the tunnel you remember?' Trevor turned to Jimmy Herne.

'Yes, but you can't be thinking of going in there. It was sealed up because of earth falls. No one's been down there in more years than I care to remember. It's dangerous. You could get killed ...'

'Did you ever hear of any side-tunnels? Anything leading off from this end or the other?' Trevor persisted.

'Plenty,' Jimmy said flatly. 'The usual sort of buried treasure nonsense. These tunnels were supposed to have been built as secret passages leading out from the dungeons of the old castle. There are stories that a Medieval king stashed his gold here. An Edward or perhaps it was a William. I can't remember the details... '

'But there were rumours of side-tunnels?' Trevor repeated.

'Legends, yes. But nothing that I ever saw.'

'Give me a hand to get in here.' Trevor beckoned to the constable and propped his stick against the wall.

'Sir?' The constable looked at Trevor's leg as he stood awkwardly in front of the hole. 'You can't be thinking of going in there?'

'Why not?' Trevor asked.

'It's not my place to be saying this, sir,' the lad ventured diffidently, 'but... '

'You're quite right,' Trevor stripped off his jacket. 'It's not your place. You're out of order.'

The tunnel was damp, icy-cold, and crumbling. After the constable had helped him in, Trevor inched forward, propelling himself on his elbows. He pushed the two torches in front of him, one lit, the other held in reserve. Every time he slithered forward, clods of wet earth fell on his back, soaking his thin shirt. After ten feet of painstakingly slow crawling, the tunnel widened. He pushed himself forward and fell, in a clatter of torches and shower of earth and rubble on to a stone floor. The torch went out and he fumbled blindly in total, terrifying darkness for five panic-stricken minutes before his fingers closed around it again and he found the switch. He pressed it downwards, and a blessed warm glow of light dispersed the gloom.

'You all right, sir?' the constable's voice echoed down the tunnel. Trevor shone his torch back into the hole.

'Fine,' he rubbed his legs. 'I've broken through into an area high enough to stand in.'

'Do you want me to follow you, sir?'

'Not much point until I've had a look around,' Trevor shone his torch upwards and his heart missed a beat. A bulge of earth, held precariously in place by a network of tree roots loomed barely inch above his head. He tried to ignore it and looked for a continuation of the tunnel. A few large stones were set at the foot of the walls, presumably put there at some time to contain the earth falls that had covered the outer edges of the stone floor with a layer of mud. Dark, crumbling walls of earth met his torch beam at every turn. Starting at the point at which he'd entered, he walked slowly around the open area.

He'd almost worked his way around the chamber when he thrust his hand against the wall, lost his balance and plunged headlong into a hole. He tried to cry out, but dirt clogged his eyes, his nose and his mouth as he fell downwards, unable to save himself. Again, he tried to shout, but he couldn't breathe, let alone speak.

He'd been careful to keep a tight grip on his torch but there was too much earth between his hands and his face for him to lift it into view. Choking, coughing, spluttering, he remembered the victims who had been buried alive, and wondered if that was going to be his fate as well.

He summoned every ounce of energy he possessed and fought to propel himself upwards, out of the dirt. Pushing up with his hands, he finally managed to create a little space around his face. It gave him the impetus and air, he needed to fight his way back to the chamber. After what seemed like eternity, he collapsed on the stone floor, in inches of freezing, sticky mud. He was filthy, soaked to the skin, icy-cold. But he was alive. And as his scalded lungs heaved in more damp, stale air, he was grateful for that much.

A fat worm slithered across his legs. Then he realised, the air was chill only because of the layers of insulating soil above and around him. He could feel no fresh draughts. The earth he'd tumbled into had obviously fallen and blocked the tunnel. If there were any side shafts, or networks of secret passages, he could see no sign of them. He rose slowly and with great difficulty to his feet.

'I'm coming back.' He turned to where he thought the tunnel should be and saw only a blank dirt wall. He spun the beam of his torch around. All he could see was walls of earth. He breathed in and forced himself to remain calm. If he took it slowly, inch by inch, he was bound to find his entrance point. It had to be there. Even if it was covered, that covering wouldn't be very deep. It couldn't be…

He crawled around the walls and began to study every clump, every pile of earth…

'Sergeant Joseph what?' Peter bellowed down the radio.

'He went into the tunnel fifteen minutes ago, sir, and we can't see or reach him. We can't even see a light. The tunnel is in darkness.'

'Where are you?'

'Cellar, sir. Close to the sub station.'

'Stay there. Don't move. Don't do anything. I'm on my way.' Peter left his seat and broke into a run.

'Where's he going?' Bill bellowed as he watched Peter disappear out through the door.

'Over here, sir,' the constable called, as Peter charged down the cellar steps.

'What happened?' Peter demanded.

'Sergeant Joseph ordered us to break through the cement plug into an old tunnel… '

'He went in there and you didn't try to stop him?' Peter stared at the square that they had hacked in the concrete plug.

'We did try, sir,' the dog-handler protested.

Peter squinted at the girl wearing a rookie's uniform. 'But he wouldn't listen, would he? The stupid bloody hero,' he muttered under his breath.

'Sir?' she questioned.

'Nothing.' He took off his jacket and thrust his radio into his shirt pocket. Was he getting old, or was the force picking up recruits from junior comprehensives these days? The girl looked about fifteen years old. 'Right, I'm going in.'

'You'll get caught in a fall, too,' Jimmy said. 'I'm warning you.'

'Get some rope,' Peter ordered the dog-handler. 'I'll tie it around my waist. If there's a problem, I'll shout out and you can pull me back.'

Unlike Trevor, Peter didn't need any help to climb into the tunnel. He pushed himself forward, stretched out full-length with a torch carefully poised in front of him, dug his toes into the soft earth and propelled his body into the inky blackness ahead. It took him only ten minutes of hard, and despite the temperature, sweating work to reach the earth wall at the end of the tunnel. He prodded it gingerly and a shower of earth fell over him. He sheltered his face in his arms as it continued to fall. Even after he dared to raise his eyes, he could still hear the soft thud of damp clods falling too close for comfort.

He shone his torch around the top and sides of the tunnel looking for an exit that he might have missed. Seeing nothing, he yelled at the top of his voice.

He held his breath, and waited a few moments. Had he heard an answering cry – or was it only wishful thinking? He called out again and shielding his head with his arms, dug his toes in and charged.

Trevor sat on the stone floor, thinking what a complete and utter fool he'd been to rush in and play Sir Galahad. It went against all his training. How often had it been drummed into him that simple, boring, routine legwork caught villains – not heroics – or climbing blindly into underground passages.

A black mass hurtled out of the wall, and fell on top of him. Thick clouds of dirt filled the air.

'Trevor, you bloody idiot, are you there?'

Too shocked to be grateful, it was as much as Trevor could do to whisper; 'Yes.'

'If you can see me, grab hold. I'll rope us together, so they can heave us out of this mess.'

'See anything?' Peter demanded as he and Trevor were dragged head-first out into the cellar.

Trevor shook his head. He coughed violently to clear his lungs.

'Nothing?' Peter pressed.

'No one's been down there in years,' Trevor croaked.

'I told you so,' Jimmy chanted.

'Haven't you gardening to do, Jimmy?' Peter bent down to help Trevor to his feet.

Jimmy moved towards the door. Peter looked ruefully at his torn, filthy shirt and muddy trousers 'Right bloody predicament you got us into this time, Trevor.'

'Thought I was on to something,' He groped for his stick.

'You.' Peter turned to the rookie. 'Report to the duty officer on the gate. They need every body they can lay their hands on. Even ones as small as yours.'

Too intimidated by Peter's air of authority to quote equal opportunities act, she disappeared up the cellar steps.

'If you can manage without me, sir, I'll show her the way,' the dog-handler suggested.

'Always got to play the cowboy in the white hat, haven't you?' Peter complained as soon as he and Trevor were alone. 'And now I suppose you expect me to help you back to your room?'

'Thanks,' Trevor limped forward, glanced at Peter and for one blissful moment they forgot the urgency of the search and burst out laughing.

*   *   *

Despite Peter's pleadings, Trevor refused to stay in his room a minute longer than it took him to strip off his filthy clothes, shower and change. Peter followed Trevor into the shower and borrowed a clean shirt and sweater but as his waist was considerably larger than Trevor's he had to content himself with wiping off his muddy trousers.

They went to the mobile HQ and found Sarah Merchant sitting alone in the outer office loading discs into a computer.

'The wanderers return,' Bill looked at Peter. 'Been for a mud bath?'

'Something like that.'

'Tell me.' Bill pressed.

'We didn't find anything in the cellar.' Trevor stumbled towards a chair. He felt weak, impotent and exhausted. And there was no prospect of rest in the near future. Not until Lyn had been found – one way or another. 'We found the tunnels. But they hadn't been used in years.'

'So your little trip was a complete waste of police time.'

'No,' Peter broke in. 'Now we know that the tunnels exist, and there's nothing in them, we can forget about them.'

'Something coming up on screen, sir,' Sarah Merchant interrupted, as the VDU began to flash.

'What are you doing?' Bill barked.

'Cross-checking and cross-referencing the alibis. Any that don't match will come up.'

'What time-scan have you programmed?'

'Ten to twelve o'clock this morning, sir.'

'There's bound to be some discrepancies,' Bill commented. 'If only in the way people remember things.'

'You do realise there are no patients on this list?' Peter reminded.

'Obviously not, since we haven't interviewed any,' Bill retorted.

'For my money, our villain has to be a patient.'

'One thing at a time, Peter.'

The first name flashed up on to the screen.

'Angela Morgan?' Dan read.

Sarah pressed the return key on the computer, and Angela Morgan's statement flashed on screen.

'Worked alone in her office between ten and eleven and then went for break eleven to eleven-twenty in canteen. Returned to office, where worked alone until twelve,' Dan read.

'You can't think our killer's Angela Morgan!' Peter exclaimed.

'No,' Bill said flatly.

'But if she was alone, where was Tony Waters?' Dan asked.

'Check Tony Waters' alibi,' Bill ordered Sarah.

Sarah keyed in Tony Waters' name. The information appeared on screen.

Slept alone at home until twelve. Entered hospital at twelve-forty-five. Saw no one. Alibi unsubstantiated.

Bill left his chair and tapped Dan on the shoulder. 'Bring him in.'

Before Dan had time to respond, Michelle knocked and opened the outer door.

'Mr Waters to see you, sir.'

'Superintendent, I've only just discovered that your officers have knocked a hole in the wall of the cellar. I'm surprised that I have to remind you of our previous conversations regarding the age and condition of this building. They could have undermined the foundations...'

350

Bill opened the door to the inner office. 'Shall we discuss this in private? Inspector Evans, please join us.'

Dan followed Bill and Tony into the room, and closed the door behind him.

'Is there an intercom in here?' Peter asked.

'They'd hear if I switched it on,' Sarah replied.

'Got a glass?'

'If there's anything we'll find out about it soon enough. How about you carry on running that programme.' Trevor pulled up a chair alongside Sarah's.

'You weren't in the hospital this morning?' Bill asked Tony.

'No, but I've come here to… '

'Complain? We'll get around to that later. Right now we'd like to verify your movements this morning.'

'As I said to Constable Grady,' Tony continued testily. 'I was at home asleep until twelve o'clock.'

'Because you worked late last night?' Bill asked.

'Because I've worked late several nights. What is this?'

'This is one of several interviews of hospital staff who cannot account for their movements during the time Lyn Sullivan disappeared.'

'That's ridiculous. You can't suspect me… '

'We suspect everyone, Mr Waters,' Bill said formally. 'What time did you get home last night? What time did you go to bed? Would any of your neighbours have seen your car…? '

Trevor and Peter were staring intently at the screen, watching the computer cross-match alibis, when Dan walked into the outer office.

'Can't break his story.'

'Try booking him?' Peter suggested.

'On what charge?'

'Make one up.'

'This isn't a dropout that we've picked up with a pocketful of hash. He's educated, he has connections, we haven't enough to pin a parking ticket on him. And, unfortunately, he knows it. He's already shouting for his solicitor.'

'Does any part of his alibi check out?'

'No one to check it with. When he got home last night his wife was asleep. She left before he woke this morning. He has an alarm clock, not a wake-up call. No one telephoned him. He has no neighbours near enough to see his car coming or going. This morning he saw no milkman, no postman – no one. Even his daily cleaner called in sick last night so she didn't work this morning.'

'So where do we go from here?' Trevor said, impatience making him angry.

'I was wondering if it's worth tackling this from a different angle,' Bill suggested. 'You two could have a chat with Tony Waters' wife. Chances are, if there is any funny business, Carol Ashford would know about it.'

'You know what they say about wives.' Peter left his chair and looked around at the mud smears left by his trousers. 'They're always the last to know when the husband goes a wandering.'

'We'd like to talk to Sister Ashford,' Trevor said to the trainee nurse who walked out into the ward corridor to meet them.

The girl looked at her watch. 'She's just about to finish her shift.'

'This won't take a moment.' Peter stepped past the nurse, and Trevor followed.

352

'I'll get her, if you'd like to wait.' The girl opened the office door.

Peter walked in and looked through the glass window that overlooked the corridor. He pulled down a roller-blind, screening the room from the rest of the ward. The click of high heels on vinyl tiles echoed down the corridor. The door opened.

'Sergeant Collins, Sergeant Joseph.' Carol Ashford entered the office. 'Staff said you wished to speak to me?'

'We do,' Peter answered.

'Then you won't mind if I sit down. I've been on my feet all day.' She sat behind the desk, and waited for them to speak.

'We'd like to ask you a few questions about your husband,' Peter began.

'Tony? If you think it will help.' If she was surprised she showed no sign of it.

'Could you tell us what time you left your house this morning?' Peter began.

'Six forty-five, the same as usual.'

'And your husband?'

'He was in bed asleep.'

'What time did he come home last night?'

'Some time after I fell asleep. Could you give me some indication as to what this is about, Sergeant Collins?'

'We're trying to establish his movements over the past two days.'

'Are you saying that Tony is a suspect?'

'What do you think?' Peter asked. When she didn't reply, he continued. 'He's the only member of staff who can't account for his movements between the hours of ten and twelve this morning.'

353

'The time when Nurse Sullivan disappeared?' She sank her face into her hands. 'Where did he say he was?'

'Sister Ashford, is there anything you want to tell us about your husband?' Peter probed.

When she didn't answer, Trevor pressed. 'If you know anything, anything at all, about Lyn Sullivan's disappearance, please tell us. Otherwise we'll almost certainly have another corpse on our hands. Please, you knew Lyn… '

She dropped her hands. 'I'll tell you everything I know, Sergeant Joseph. I only hope that it will be enough.'

Patients on geriatric wards are routinely bedded down earlier than those on other wards. In the intervals when Carol Ashford wasn't speaking, the silence was filled with small, soft noises; the quiet whirr of the electric clock on the office wall, the last tentative notes of evening birdsong in the garden, the voice of the officer stationed in the foyer making radio contact with headquarters.

Carol was speaking to Peter, but she looked at Trevor. 'My husband was charming when I met him. I believed that he possessed every quality I'd ever looked for and wanted in a man. He was handsome, courteous, considerate; he had a marvellous sense of humour. His parents adored me, and they were wealthy on a scale I'd only dreamed about. They'd given Tony everything; the best schools, the best university, the confidence to talk to people – important people that is. He had influential and glamorous friends, he took me to the right places – you can have no idea how overwhelming that can be to someone like myself who was brought up on a slum of a council estate. When I first met Tony… '

'In this hospital?' Peter interrupted her.

'No, Greenways in Kent. He seemed so sophisticated, so wonderful, I couldn't believe my luck. That he'd actually chosen me to be his girlfriend.' She lowered her long, thick eyelashes. 'The first time I went out with him, I was swept off my feet. Literally. He knows how to treat a woman. Flowers, chocolates, cards, presents. I married him eight months after I met him, and by then we were both working here, in Compton Castle. He comes from this area. We moved down soon after his mother was diagnosed with cancer. A week after her death, his father shot himself. It was – ' Tears filled her beautiful navy-blue eyes, but they didn't affect the clarity of her voice. 'It was then that I think he became unhinged. He adored his parents. He was an only child. Or perhaps he'd been unhinged all along, and I'd simply chosen to ignore his mental state because I didn't want to confront his problems, or see any flaws in my Prince Charming.'

'Exactly what are his problems?' Peter asked.

'His cruelty,' she admitted. 'He has a sadistic streak. It started when I didn't get pregnant straight after our wedding. Our sex life changed,' she whispered. 'He started to beat me.' She rolled up the sleeve of her sweater and revealed black and purple bruises that encircled her upper and lower arms. Pulling down the roll-neck collar, she showed them multicoloured contusions on her neck. 'And his demands increased with his brutality. Nothing I did was good enough for him. In the kitchen, our home, in bed, in work – you must have seen what a perfectionist he is. I have never managed to keep a domestic help for more than three months, although I pay double the going rate. He'd begin to criticise their work, and then they'd leave…'

'Do you know of any links between your husband and the missing girls?' Peter pulled out his notebook.

355

'With all the girls that were found dead, except Vanessa Hedley.'

'Go on,' Peter ordered abruptly.

'I have no proof except a couple of letters and intercepted telephone calls. But I know, Sergeant Collins,' she looked Peter in the eye. 'I know that he had affairs with all three of them, and when Lyn disappeared this morning I feared the worst.'

'Why?' Trevor interrupted.

'Because I saw him talking to her yesterday afternoon in the ward office and saw the way that he was looking at her.'

Trevor had a sudden flash of memory. Tony Waters' chair pulled close to Lyn's. White-blond and black hair touching as their two heads bent over the notebook in her lap.

'I'm afraid for Lyn and I think he took her. You know Lyn, Sergeant Joseph,' she appealed to Trevor. 'I can't imagine her agreeing to go anywhere with Tony, not so soon after she broke up with Karl Lane. And if Tony asked, and she refused… ' tears poured down her cheeks. 'I believe that he could have abducted her.'

'Where do you think he's hidden her?' Trevor asked.

'If I knew, I'd tell you. There have been nights, so many nights, when he hasn't come home at all. And there's one more thing; he's impotent.'

'You mean he can't make love?' Peter asked bluntly.

'He's capable of performing the physical act, after a fashion, if that's what you call "making love". But he can't have children. And since he found out, he's resorted to… ' She burst into a paroxysm of weeping that made further questioning impossible.

Peter smiled at Trevor. 'Got the bastard.'

'But not Lyn,' Trevor said bleakly. 'We're still no nearer to finding her.'

Peter put a call out for a woman police constable to take care of Carol Ashford.

'I would like to go home,' Carol pleaded, through her tears. 'I'd like to shower, change my clothes.'

'We may need you again,' Peter said. 'And I'm reluctant to let you go until we've finished questioning your husband. There may be something else you know… ' The telephone rang and he picked it up. 'That was Michelle,' he turned to Trevor. 'Bill's suggesting Sister Ashford could join Jean Marshall and Michelle in a hospital flat. Spencer Jordan has volunteered his.'

'How long do you intend to keep me, Sergeant?' Carol Ashford demanded.

'Just as long as it takes to get your husband to tell us where he's hidden Lyn Sullivan,' Trevor answered.

Tony Waters was stunned. 'Superintendent, the whole idea is bizarre, the fabrications of an insane mind. You simply can't believe… '

'The mind is your wife's,' Bill broke in. 'You had the means, the opportunity. On your own admission, you know this place inside out.'

'Where have you hidden Lyn Sullivan?' Peter stopped pacing around the room and loomed threateningly over the table where Tony was sitting.

'Nowhere! I haven't even seen the girl. I want to call my solicitor – now.'

Bill picked up the telephone, and slammed it down in front of Tony. 'But I warn you; make that call and we're charging you.'

'With what?'

'Four counts of murder and five of kidnapping.'

'That's absurd. You have no proof. If you did, you'd have taken me to the police station.'

'To all intents and purposes this is a police station. And the reason we haven't moved you is a six-foot, slim, attractive black-haired nurse you've hidden somewhere on these premises. Is she still alive?'

'I wish I could help you, Superintendent. But I know nothing.'

Peter produced the statement Carol had signed before Michelle had taken her to Spencer's apartment. 'Do you deny having affairs with Claire Moon, Elizabeth Moore, and Rosie Twyford – and receiving phone calls from them at your home?'

'I might have received one or two calls from them, but... '

'Go on' Bill pressed.

'Receiving phone calls is not a crime. And even if they did call me, the chances are that those calls were connected with business.'

'Like the affairs you had with them?'

'Affairs, like phone calls, are not crimes,' Tony countered.

'And the bruises you inflicted on your wife?'

'Carol enjoys rough lovemaking.'

'Lovemaking?' Peter sneered. 'From a man who fires blanks.'

'What the devil do you mean?' Waters turned crimson and Peter knew he'd hit a raw nerve.

'You can't have children.'

'Whether I can father children or not is none of your damned business!' Tony Waters turned purple with rage.

'Where is Lyn Sullivan?' Peter thrust his face close to Tony's.

358

'I swear, I haven't seen her since yesterday.'

'You didn't take her?' Bill asked sceptically. 'You didn't grab her from the hostel?'

'No.'

'That's not what your wife told us.'

'Carol? But she knows – she – '

'Knows what?' Peter asked.

Tony remained silent.

'Your wife has made a statement.' Peter waved it in front of Tony. 'She confirmed that you had affairs with all three women.'

'That doesn't make me a murderer.'

'No, but it doesn't mean you're able to engage in normal lovemaking either.' Peter stabbed at Tony's Achilles heel.

'For pity's sake, I'm normal. Just ask Jean Marshall.'

An eerie silence fell over the room. Trevor rose from his chair and slammed the door on his way out.

CHAPTER TWENTY-SIX

Trevor stumbled as he flung himself down the steps. Peter, who was running close on his heels, reached out and steadied him.

'You're going to see Jean Marshall?'

'You thinking what I'm thinking?' Trevor asked.

'Either our esteemed administrator or his wife is lying,' Peter replied. 'The question is which one. Taxi?' he shouted to the driver of a police car, who was standing nearby, chatting to the constable on duty. 'To the halfway houses, and step on it.' He dived into the back of the car.

'You've been on duty since Constable Grady escorted the two women inside?'

'Yes, sir.'

'Our little bird is still cooped up,' Peter gave Trevor a grim smile.

'If this little bird proves to be the one I think it is, I won't be buying any birdseed until I see her for myself.' Trevor led the way into the building.

The Trust had tried and failed to turn the communal area on the ground floor of the halfway house into something resembling a private home. Still life prints of fruits and dead pheasants that no one would willingly chose to hang on their walls were the only ornaments in the beige-carpeted and magnolia-painted rooms. The coat rack in the hall was bare, as though no one dared to use it. All the adjoining doors were open, including one to the cupboard under the stairs, which held a neat display of cleaning tools; vacuum cleaner, brushes and mops. The kitchen

360

surfaces were bare, and the spotless stove had a disused air.

Peter and Trevor saw Spencer sitting on the edge of an uncomfortable upright chair in the lounge, playing chess with a slim young man Trevor recognised as a past inmate of his ward.

'You're here to see Jean and Carol,' Spencer guessed. 'I'll take you up.'

'Don't disturb yourself.' Peter went to the foot of the stairs. 'Just point us in the right direction.'

'Top floor, it's the door facing you at the top of the stairs.'

'Thanks.' With Trevor lagging behind, Peter climbed the first flight of stairs. Five closed doors greeted him, all fitted with Yale locks. As he began on the next flight of stairs, a man rose to his feet from the top step.

'Slacking on the job, Andrew?' Peter asked.

'Resting my feet before you dump the next load on me,' Andrew replied.

'Anyone gone in or out?'

'No. And apart from some classical music, it's been as quiet as the grave.' Andrew pushed a coffee cup into the corner behind him.

'When did they give you coffee?' Trevor winced in pain as he tried to put his right foot on the floor.

Andrew glanced at his watch. 'About an hour and a half ago.'

As there was no bell, Peter banged on the door. There was no response. 'Constable Grady, it's Peter Collins. Open up.'

The silence that fell after his frenzied banging hung heavy with foreboding.

'Got a key for this door?' Peter asked Murphy.

'No.'

'Run downstairs and get Spencer's,' Trevor suggested.

'No time.' Peter put his shoulder to the door and heaved. The wood splintered and the door swung inwards, its lock hanging free. He barged through the tiny hall into the living room, tripping over Michelle Grady, who lay on the floor, still holding a coffee cup in her right hand. The dregs had spilled over the beige carpet, staining the area around her head. Jean Marshall was lying on the sofa.

Peter knelt between them. 'They're both breathing, hopefully just tranquillised. Call an ambulance.'

Spencer superintended the evacuation of the hostel before the paramedics dashed upstairs.

'What I can't understand,' Murphy said, 'is how she got out. I was in touch with our man at the back and our man downstairs every ten minutes and neither reported any unusual sightings.'

Peter opened the window and leaned out. 'There's barely four foot between this building and the next. If she climbed up instead of down, she could have… '

'Jumped across?' Trevor suggested.

'I don't know if you noticed, but she's an athletic-looking girl.'

'I noticed,' Trevor rested on the arm of an easy chair.

'Can I come in?' Spencer hovered in front of the splintered wood that had once been his front door.

'The bird's flown the coop, so there's no need to ask,' Peter replied.

'One of the girls in the house next door saw the commotion and came round. She says she hung her Mac on the rack by the door, but now it's gone.'

'What colour was it?' Trevor asked.

'Green. She'd only just bought it… '

Trevor didn't wait for the rest of the sentence. He turned to Peter. 'Car park?'

'I'm ahead of you'

An officer had been on duty in the car park since six o'clock. He insisted nothing out of the ordinary had occurred; only the usual staff had come and gone.

'Sister Ashford?' Peter asked.

The man gazed at him vacantly.

'Tall, slim, blonde, blue-eyed, beautiful,' Trevor elaborated.

'The one married to the chief administrator?'

'That's her,' Peter confirmed.

'She took her husband's BMW. She said her Peugeot was giving her trouble, so he'd offered to take it to the garage.'

'Take us to mobile HQ,' Collins ordered the police driver he'd commandeered.

'Why not follow her?' Trevor demanded urgently.

'Because she could be anywhere.' Peter snapped. 'And because, if we're going to find Lyn Sullivan before it's too late, we'll need all the help we can get. And in my opinion we should begin with the person who knows the killer best. Tony Waters.'

Tony Waters was still sitting at the conference table at HQ. Dan was thumbing through computer printouts of the interview reports and Bill was bawling down the phone at the officer who'd been manning the gate when Carol Ashford had driven out of the hospital.

'Don't tell me that you didn't know she was a suspect – every person in this hospital is a suspect... '

'Mr Waters?' Trevor pulled out a chair alongside Waters. 'Have you any idea where you wife could have gone?'

He stared at Trevor through hollow eyes. 'I don't know. She didn't keep in contact with anyone from her past, and she didn't have many friends. Lots of acquaintances; people she met through clubs, charity committees – that sort of thing. But no real friends.'

'The house. You think she might have gone back there?' Trevor pressed.

'I don't know.'

'Do you keep money and your passports in the house?' Peter took the chair opposite Trevor's.

'There's money in the safe. Our passports too.'

'She has the key to the safe?' Peter asked.

'It's a combination lock, she knows the number.'

'There's no point in both of us going.' Peter said when Trevor rose stiffly to his feet. 'You'd slow me down. As Lyn wasn't in the car Carol drove out, carry on looking for her here. I'll keep in touch. Mr Waters, you'd better come with me. We may need you. Dan?'

'I'm with you.'

'All cars leaving the hospital have been searched thoroughly for days. Lyn Sullivan *must* be hidden somewhere in this hospital,' Trevor stressed to Tony. 'Please. You know this building better than anyone. Do you have any idea where Lyn could be hidden?'

'Do you think I didn't think of that when Vanessa Hedley disappeared?' Tony retorted acidly. 'Everywhere, absolutely everywhere has been thoroughly searched by your people and mine.' He followed Peter and Dan out of the door.

*　　　　*　　　　*

Tony gave the police driver precise directions to his farm, but the driver twice missed turnings in the winding country lanes, and they lost frantic minutes while he manoeuvred turns in impossibly narrow spaces.

When they finally reached the farmyard, it was floodlit, with two large Dobermans barking and circling crazily by the front door.

Tony climbed out of the car and called to the dogs. They stopped barking and ran over to him. He pulled out his keys and shut them in the conservatory. Peter walked to the front door. He held out his hand.

'Keys,' he said to Tony.

'I'll open it.' Tony seemed strangely reluctant to hand them over.

'Stand back,' Peter ordered. 'I can smell gas.'

'Then shouldn't I... '

Tony didn't have the chance to say another word. Dan lifted him off his feet, and yanked him back while Peter inserted the key gingerly into the lock. He pushed the door open tentatively with his fingertips.

'You on mains or Calor gas?' Dan asked Tony. But he never heard the reply to his question.

A deafening explosion ripped through the house, blasting the front door off its hinges. It caught Peter's shoulder as it hurtled back, carrying him to the centre of the yard in a hurricane of shattering glass and shooting flames that blew the windows, roof and walls outwards. For five full minutes all Dan could do was lie flat on the ground, his nose buried in the dirt, as he watched flames lick out of the building into a strange, red unnaturally silent world. He saw Peter was lying, eyes wide open, as he lay half buried beneath a heap of smouldering debris.

Covered in shards of glass, their driver had managed to stagger back to the car. Dan saw his mouth move as he

365

yelled down the radio phone for the fire brigade, back-up units, and ambulances.

Tony had been partly shielded by Dan's massive figure when the full force of the blast had struck, so he wasn't as badly hurt as the other three men. Dan could only watch as Tony scrambled to his feet and ran towards the house. A blackened, shrivelled scarecrow, skin blistering and bubbling was crawling through where the front wall had stood only minutes before.

Tony took off his coat and flung it over the scarecrow's baked flesh.

'I couldn't bear it.' Words left the lipless mouth.

'Bear what, darling?' Tony cradled what was left of Carol in his arms.

'I thought you'd leave me for one of those girls. That's why I took them from you. I didn't want to kill them – just keep them away from you. But I couldn't hide them forever, and I couldn't hurt them, so I buried them. It was easier that way – even the dog. It was always in your office...'

'Where's Lyn?' Dan crawled over the debris in the yard towards them.

'Vanessa saw me. I injected her with air. It's a quick way to go – I couldn't – '

'Where's Lyn?' Dan reiterated.

Peter stumbled towards them cradling his left arm. 'She was in the hall; she lit a match as I opened the door...'

'She was expecting me.' Tony looked down at what was left of his wife. She was quite still, her sightless eyes staring up into his.

Peter sank to the ground. 'Damn her for dying. She can't tell us where Lyn Sullivan is now.'

Dan put his hand on Peter's shoulder. He turned his back on Tony who continued to cradle the mutilated body of his wife. He could find no words of comfort to offer the man, but he could and did offer privacy – of a kind. 'You're going to hospital, Peter,' he said as the first siren sounded in the distance.

'Peter's in hospital but he's not badly hurt,' Dan reassured Trevor before turning to Bill and Harry Goldman who was visiting the mobile HQ. 'Carol Ashford turned on all the gas appliances in the house and lit a match when Peter opened the door. Peter was blown back by the blast; his back and arms are scorched, and his collarbone broken, but after a couple of days in hospital and a few weeks' rest at home, he'll be back to normal.'

'And you?' Bill asked.

'Slightly deaf… '

'Slightly pitted,' Bill commented looking at the burn marks on Dan's face.

'They treated the driver for superficial cuts and burns. Tony Waters is in shock. They're keeping him in overnight.'

'Damn Carol Ashford,' Trevor cursed. 'We haven't a clue where she hid Lyn Sullivan… '

'I've a feeling if we don't find her soon; we may as well stop looking.' Bill paced across the room. 'We have to be missing something. All of you, think!' Bill went to the table and thumbed through the search reports before looking at the team leaders sitting around his desk. 'Close your eyes and think back to our last search. Relive it in your mind. Crawl through it, step by step… '

Step by step – Trevor mentally inched his way around the cellar. He recalled the tunnel – the flagstone floor – Tony Waters and Jimmy Herne relating stories

367

about the place – the bare, once padded cells that didn't offer enough shelter to conceal a fly – the room where the rubbish was kept – the mortuary – Carol Ashford in the mortuary – the dogs going wild over her perfume – the geriatric corpse with the yellowed skin and thick horny toenails – the corpse in the garden – the corpse that had been stolen because the mortuary had been left unlocked. Why had it been unlocked? Because someone had thoughtlessly left the door open. Someone who had removed a body. A body that shouldn't have been there – a body that had to be hidden in a room rarely used – Vanessa's body.

White-faced, he left his chair.

'Where you off to?' Bill demanded.

'The mortuary.'

Harry and Dan stared at him.

Trevor picked up his stick and hobbled as fast as he could through the door, down the outside steps, towards the rear of the building. Once he reached the corridor he raced along, Dan and Harry Goldman lapping at his heels. Switching on lights as he went, he rushed to the male mortuary, and heaved at the door.

'Damn, it's locked.'

'Of course it is.' Harry was close behind him.

'Do you have the key?'

'A master key, I'm not sure it fits these old locks.'

The two minutes it took Harry Goldman to open the door dragged an eternity. As soon as it was open, Trevor burst in. He paused and stared at the bank of drawers. Which one? The top left-hand?

He heaved on the handle. It grated sluggishly. He tugged at it again. The same corpse was still inside. He recognised the feet that looked as though they'd been wrapped in yellow parchment. The face was covered by a sheet. Peeling it back he uncovered the body of the old man. Thrusting his hands beneath the surprisingly light corpse, he lifted it out and laid it on one of the zinc-covered tables. Beneath it was another sheet; thick, lumpy. Scarcely daring to breathe, Trevor drew it aside.

The white face of Lyn Sullivan stared up at him, eyes open, muscles immobile. He could hear Dan calling down his radio for a doctor. Trevor laid his hand on her sweater and felt her heart beat. Slow, but definite.

'She's alive.' He leaned against the table. The hand of the corpse rolled aside and hit his back. 'She's alive,' he repeated, only just beginning to believe it.

'Thanks, Trevor. That was a good film and a good meal.'

'The film was good,' Trevor agreed. 'I have my doubts about the fish and chips.'

'Perhaps it was the company.' Spencer pushed his bicycle clips on to his trouser legs and opened the front door of Trevor's new home.

'Shall we do the same next week?' Trevor suggested.

Spencer managed a tight smile. 'Yes, I'd like that.'

Trevor stood on the step watching Spencer ride past Peter who, arm in sling, was walking up the path.

'Came to see if you'd like to go out for a drink after all the hassle of moving.'

'Some other time.' Trevor led Peter past the lounge and dining room, both carpeted in plain green Wilton but devoid of furniture, and into the kitchen. 'There's still one or two things I need to do.'

'One drink?'

The telephone interrupted them. Trevor picked up the receiver. Peter leaned against the fridge, and listened to the one-sided conversation.

'Yes… yes… fine… yes… see you a week Monday, then. Yes… look forward to working with you. Goodbye.'

'You took it, then?' Peter watched him replace the receiver.

'What?' Trevor asked.

'The job Dan offered.'

'You knew about it?'

'There's been talk of nothing else down the station. Special Crimes Sergeant. You won't forget us poor sloggers in the Drug Squad when you're lording it in your new office, bored out of your mind, waiting for a murder to happen, will you?'

'Would you let me?'

Peter saw a pile of dirty dishes in the sink. 'Want me to tackle those?'

'With one arm?' Trevor smiled. 'I was just about to load the dish washer.'

Peter studied the shining antiseptic surfaces of the gleaming blue and white kitchen. 'You've done well for yourself here, but do you think you'll survive uncluttered cleanliness?'

'I can but try.'

'Must have cost a bomb.'

'A small one,' Trevor agreed. 'I couldn't have done it if the sitting tenants hadn't bought my old flat.'

'I don't suppose you could,' Peter said wistfully remembering the house he had handed over fully furnished to his undeserving ex-wife. 'Come on, just one quick one.'

'Tomorrow evening,' Trevor compromised.

'I know you and your tomorrows.'

'I'm busy,' Trevor said impatiently. 'Tomorrow night or nothing.'

'You'll slide back into a depression if you're not careful. Staying indoors, moping around… what did you do in Cornwall?'

'Eat, sleep, play with my brother's kids.'

'My point exactly. You may have bought a great house, but what's the point in hanging another millstone around your neck if all you're going to do is spend every spare minute thinking about furniture and fittings, instead of having a good time? It's what you do, not what you own that's important.'

'I'm grateful for your advice,' Trevor said. 'But I'm tired. I'll go for a drink with you tomorrow.' He ushered Peter back down the passage towards the front door. 'Right now all I want is a bath and an early night.'

'I can take a hint.' Peter dumped a bottle of wine he'd been carrying on the floor next to the door. 'We'll drink that tomorrow – after the pub.'

'See you around nine?'

'I'll be here.' Peter turned back as he stepped on to the garden path. 'They're not prosecuting Roland for mishandling that corpse.'

'That's not surprising. There isn't much you can do to a man who steals a corpse from a mortuary, carries it out to a garden and attacks it, except lock him up in an institution. And as he's already there, there seems little point in wasting taxpayers' money on a trial.'

'He's locked up now,' Peter said. 'But what will happen to him when he's released?'

'The same thing that will happen to all the others,' Trevor said philosophically. 'He'll be out in the community again.'

'Think we should apply for doubling of manpower?'

'Either that or a new prison. See you.'

After he closed and locked the door, Trevor checked that all the downstairs windows were locked. He loaded the dishwasher, tidied round, switched off the lights and looked into the empty lounge and dining room. Tomorrow he'd choose some furniture – perhaps start off in the antique shops. If he couldn't find anything there, he'd visit one or two of the better class furniture shops. There was no hurry. He was going to be in this house a long time, so he could afford to take a few months to find the right pieces. He'd already furnished the master bedroom; it was large enough to take the television, video and chaise-longue he'd bought, as well as a king-size bed. The builder had turned the fourth bedroom into a walk-in dressing room and wardrobe. That had made all the difference to the upstairs and still left two guest rooms. Enough for any visitors.

He opened the fridge, stowed away the wine Peter had brought and removed a bottle that had been cooling all day. He walked slowly up the stairs, concentrating on putting one foot in front of the other. It wasn't easy without his stick, but he was getting there. Another two to three months, the physiotherapist said, and then he'd be walking properly again.

Switching on the small lamps at either side of the bed, he opened the French doors to the balcony that ran the full width of the second floor of his house. Sitting here, he could only be overlooked from the beach, and at this time of night it was deserted.

He set the bottle and two glasses on the wrought-iron pub table he had bought in a second-hand shop in Cornwall, and sat on one of the matching chairs. He took his time over opening the wine, drinking in the beauty of the glistening path painted by the moon on the shimmering surface of the sea while listening to the quiet hiss of the waves as they broke on the pebble-strewn shore.

'I might have known I'd find you out here.' Lyn moved behind him, her hair wrapped in a towel, another wrapped around her slim inviting body.

'Wine?'

'If I didn't know you better, I'd think you were trying to get me drunk.'

He poured her a glass and handed it to her.

'If we're going to sit out here, I suppose I'd better put on something more substantial than this.' She stepped back into the bedroom, and he followed her. Reaching out he held her close for a moment, revelling in the warm, sensual feel of her and the rhythm of her heart beating against his. As she raised her face, he kissed her slowly and deeply.

'You're not sorry I moved in with you?' she teased.

'Someone has to make sure that you stay in one piece, and if you carry on working the way you did today, you'll save me a fortune in cleaning bills.'

'I won't cramp your style, then?' She wrapped her arms around his neck allowing the towel she was wearing to fall to the floor.

'I'm not sure I had a style before I met you.' He kissed the hollow above her collarbone.

'The wine's going to get warm,' she warned.

'There's a cool breeze.'

'That's all right then.' She pulled him back on to the bed.

'Lyn?' He looked into her eyes as she unfastened the buttons on his shirt.

'Yes?'

He smiled at her. 'Nothing.' He kissed her again, and there was no need for more words between them for a long time.

Lyn was a miracle that had transformed his life. And, experience had taught him that miracles shouldn't be analysed or questioned. For once he'd struck lucky, but it wouldn't last – it never did, and in this case it couldn't. There were thirteen years between them; a wealth of bitter experience on his side, and youth and beauty on hers. But for now at least, she was his. He had learned a hard lesson in Compton Castle, but he had learned it well.

Now was all anyone ever had. And this now was more than he deserved.

Katherine John

Katherine John is the daughter of a Prussian refugee and a Welsh father. Born in Pontypridd, she studied English and Sociology at Swansea College, then lived in America and Europe before returning to Wales and a variety of jobs, while indulging her love of writing.

She lives with her family on the Gower Peninsula, near Swansea.

Also by Katherine John….

BY ANY NAME

A bloodstained man runs half naked down a motorway at night dodging high-speed traffic - and worse. Cornered by police, admitted to a psychiatric ward suffering from trauma-induced amnesia, all he can recall is a detailed knowledge of sophisticated weaponry and military techniques that indicates a background in terrorism.

When two armed soldiers guarding his room are murdered and Dr Elizabeth Santer, the psychiatrist assigned to his case, is abducted at gunpoint a desperate hunt begins for a dangerous killer.

Terrorist - murderer - kidnapper - thief whatever he is, he remembers a town in Wales and it is to Brecon he drags Elizabeth Santer with the security forces in all-out pursuit. There, a violent and bloody confrontation exposes a horrifying story of treachery and political cover-up.
Is Elizabeth in the hands of a homicidal terrorist or an innocent pawn? Her life depends on the right answer.

ISBN 1905170254
Price £6.99

WITHOUT TRACE

In the chilly half-light of the dawn a bizarre Pierrot figure waits in the shadows of a deserted stretch of motorway. The costumed hitch-hiker's victim is a passing motorist. The murder, cold-blooded, brutal, without motive.

Tim and Daisy Sherringham, doctors at the local hospital, are blissfully happy. The perfect couple. When an emergency cal rouses Tim early one morning, he vanishes on the way from their flat to the hospital.

Daisy is plunged into a nightmare of terror and doubt...

ISBN 1905170262
Price £6.99

MURDER OF A DEAD MAN

Jubilee Street –the haunt of addicts and vagrants – is a part of town to be avoided at all costs, especially when it becomes the stalking ground of a brutal and ruthless murderer.

A drunken down-and –out is the first casualty, mutilated and burnt alive. But his grisly death raises even more problems for the investigating officers, Sergeants Trevor Joseph and Peter Collins, when they discover that their victim died two years earlier. So who is the dead man? And what was the motive for the bizarre crime?

While they seek a killer in the dark urban underworld, the tally of corpses grows and the only certainty is that they can trust no man's face as his own.

ISBN 1905170289
Price £6.99